American-Vietnamese Relations
in the Wake of War

American-Vietnamese Relations in the Wake of War

Diplomacy After the Capture of Saigon, 1975–1979

CÉCILE MENÉTREY-MONCHAU

McFarland & Company, Inc., Publishers
Jefferson, North Carolina, and London

LIBRARY OF CONGRESS CATALOGUING-IN-PUBLICATION DATA

Menétrey-Monchau, Cécile, 1978–
American-Vietnamese relations in the wake of war : diplomacy after the capture of Saigon, 1975–1979 / Cécile Menétrey-Monchau.
p.   cm.
Includes bibliographical references and index.

ISBN-13: 978-0-7864-2398-9
ISBN-10: 0-7864-2398-6 (softcover : 50# alkaline paper)

1. United States—Foreign relations—Vietnam.
2. Vietnam—Foreign relations—United States.
3. United States—Foreign relations—1974–1977.
4. United States—Foreign relations—1977–1981.
I. Title
E183.8.V5M46   2006
327.730597009'047—dc22   2006004317

British Library cataloguing data are available

©2006 Cécile Menétrey-Monchau. All rights reserved

No part of this book may be reproduced or transmitted in any form or by any means, electronic or mechanical, including photocopying or recording, or by any information storage and retrieval system, without permission in writing from the publisher.

On the cover: POW flag ©2006 Photodisc; handshake ©2006 Clipart; American flag ©2006 PhotoSpin

Manufactured in the United States of America

*McFarland & Company, Inc., Publishers
Box 611, Jefferson, North Carolina 28640
www.mcfarlandpub.com*

To my mother and father,
Annie and Daniel

ACKNOWLEDGMENTS

I would like to express my gratitude to several people who made this work possible, especially the professors and historians of the Faculty of History of the University of Cambridge. First and foremost I would like to thank Mike Sewell for his support and guidance. Without him this work would not have been possible. Very special thanks go to John Thompson, Tony Badger, John Dumbrell, Donna Jackson, Mary King, and Peter Bourne for their advice and suggestions in bringing this work to publication. I also owe a special debt to Christopher Goscha and Larry Berman, who helped me access French sources in Paris.

I am also grateful to the staffs of the Jimmy Carter Presidential Library, the Gerald Ford Presidential Library, the National Archives, the Center on Southeast Asian Studies and Indochina of the University of Berkeley for their invaluable advice and guidance and for their having patiently supervised my long hours of tedious xeroxing. Special thanks also go to the Arts and Humanities Research Board for its generous support of my research over three years, and to the Gerald R. Ford Research Fund, the Faculty of History of the University of Cambridge, and Fitzwilliam College for financial support to help meet the expenses of my various research trips.

I am deeply indebted to David Aaron, Elizabeth Becker, Peter Bourne, Zbigniew Brzezinski, Bui Tin, Hodding Carter, former president Jimmy Carter, Dr. S.R. Ekovich, Dr. Michel Fournié, William H. Gleysteen, Jean Lacouture, Pr. Ngo Vinh Long, John McAuliff, Congressman Gillepsie V. "Sonny" Montgomery, General William Odom, Ken Quinn, Sophie Quinn-Judge, Holli Rotondi, Alain Ruscio, Jan Scruggs, Frank Sieverts, Judith Stowe, and Mr. Vu Anh Quang, who kindly took the time to answer my letters. They helped color grey and dusty archives with the lively touch of their own personal memories.

This book, of course, could not have been written without the support and kindness of my family and friends. Thank you for your patience over my long hours of work, my doubts, and my absence.

Contents

Acknowledgments	vi
Preface	1
Abbreviations	5
Important Names and Offices	7
Introduction	11

I : Ford and Vietnam's Peace

• A New Start for Vietnam and a First Opening to Washington	21
• Hanoi and Saigon's Application for Membership to the United Nations	32
• Adapting to a New Environment: Vietnamese Policies and Ford's Election Campaign	51

II : The Advent of the Carter Years

• The Fourth Party Congress	77
• The New Socialist Man, the New American Man and the New China	83
• The Woodcock Mission	91

III : Talks Turn Cold

• The Paris Negotiations (January–May 1977)	108
• The Nixon Letter	115
• Background to the Nixon Letter	121
• The Paris Negotiations (June and December 1977)	130
• The Spying Affair	144

IV : COLD WAR CLASH

- Brotherhood Turns Sour — 148
- Vietnam Changes Its Mind — 151
- The Hoa Crisis — 154
- Vietnam's Dual Opening to Moscow and Washington — 161
- Brzezinski's Growing Influence and His Visit to China — 165
- Consequences of the Brzezinski trip to China on the NSC Perception of the Sino-Cambodian-Vietnamese Conflicts — 173

V : REVERSAL IN U.S. FOREIGN POLICY

- Vietnam's American Card — 176
- The Thach Delegation to New York — 192
- The Drawing of Lines — 203
- Normalization with Peking — 210

VI : WINNING THE THIRD VIETNAM WAR

- Vietnam Invades Cambodia — 217
- Deng's Visit to the United States — 221
- China's Lesson on Vietnam — 227

Conclusion — 235

Appendix 1: Message from the President of the United States to the Prime Minister of the Democratic Republic of Vietnam, February 1, 1973 — 243

Appendix 2: Message of the Prime Minister of the Democratic Republic of Viet Nam to the President of the United States of America (February 23, 1973) — 245

Appendix 3: U.S.-Vietnamese Exchange of Six Diplomatic Notes, 1976 — 247

Appendix 4: Letter from President Jimmy Carter to Chinese Vice Premier Deng Xiaoping (January 30, 1979) — 252

Chapter Notes — 255

Bibliography — 291

Index — 301

PREFACE

This book describes postwar negotiations between Washington and Hanoi during the late Ford and early Carter years, from the end of the American war in Vietnam to the third Indochina conflict of late 1978 and early 1979. It focuses on the U.S.-Vietnamese attempt and failure to achieve recognition and normalization, and highlights how the issue of normalization—interwoven with Hanoi's relations with the USSR, China, and Cambodia—came to affect the growing tensions within the Indochina peninsula. This work describes the changing diplomatic strategies of two administrations, and attempts to shed light on the various mechanisms that led each to either reject or encourage the establishment of bilateral contacts, depending on domestic political agendas and foreign policy ambitions. Bilateral contacts went through three distinct stages: the U.S. bitterness under Ford in the immediate postwar era; renewed initiatives of the early months of the Carter administration; and the reversal of U.S. priorities in early to mid–1978, when attention turned away from Hanoi and towards Peking.

During the Ford years diplomatic contacts remained tense and fruitless. The administration, which harbored bitter and rancorous feelings for the Indochinese after the fall of Saigon, responded to Hanoi's first requests for diplomatic rapprochement in 1975 with great distrust. Only a few congressional initiatives, including those of Congressmen Gillespie "Sonny" Montgomery, head of the House Select Committee on Missing Persons in Southeast Asia; Representative Jonathan Bingham; and senators George McGovern and Edward Kennedy attempted to bridge the gap between the two countries, and with only limited success. But after first rejecting dialogue and promoting blame and accusations at Hanoi, Ford's candidacy for reelection in 1976 brought about the need to adopt a two-fold policy aimed at gaining maximum domestic leverage by seemingly responding to Vietnamese overtures and publicizing efforts to account for U.S. servicemen missing in Indochina (MIAs), while at the same time rejecting all offers to negotiate with the newly reunified Vietnam. The issue of MIAs, first emphasized under Nixon, was now used by his successor to justify postwar hostility and promote his own chances for reelection. This tactic failed. Upon entering the White House, Carter strove to de-emphasize the issue and remove this obstacle from negotiations with Hanoi. However, the issue remained at the forefront of bilateral relations under Carter, as did Vietnamese requests for U.S. reconstruction aid promised in a secret letter from Nixon to North Vietnamese Premier Pham Van Dong in 1973.

The Carter administration departed from Ford's policies as it shifted towards a softer stand. The administration first initiated contacts with Hanoi, through the Leonard Woodcock mission, testing the Vietnamese privately before launching official, publicized talks. Mutual misunderstandings led each side to declare the mission successful and to believe in rapid reconciliation. A series of bilateral talks in Paris followed in 1977. These brought to light numerous misperceptions still separating the two countries. Carter's genuine wish to extricate U.S. relations with Vietnam from a bipolar East-West framework might have led to normalization had not other factors (inner–VCP rivalries, increasing Vietnamese radicalism, mutual misperceptions, Carter's inexperience in dealing with communist Third World nations, U.S. legislative prohibitions and pressure, military-like Vietnamese diplomatic tactics and reversals of stance, and simply bad luck) intervened and led these initiatives to a diplomatic dead end. The talks soon came into conflict with Hanoi's impatience to obtain U.S. economic aid. The Vietnamese then released the Nixon letter. As an angry Congress renounced this pledge—partly reviving the mutual bitterness encountered in the Ford years—bilateral relations stalled and new political priorities emerged in each country. The Carter administration failed to achieve Carter's initial goal of rapid normalization, while the emergence of a Vietnamese spying affair in the U.S. confirmed the impossibility of normalization in early 1978.

That year saw a reemergence of globalist priorities in Washington and a second phase in the administration's positioning of Vietnam on its foreign policy agenda. As Hanoi's disputes with Cambodia and China escalated, Hanoi shifted to a more moderate stance, secretly aiming to secure normalization before Vietnam's invasion of Cambodia made it impossible. At the same time, Hanoi was cozying up to Moscow in preparation for the invasion, much to China's displeasure. The Carter administration, perceiving Soviet interference in conflicts in such regions as the Horn of Africa, was shifting to a globalist foreign policy. This was influenced by the anti–Soviet National Security Adviser Zbigniew Brzezinski, at the expense of the State Department regionalist approach. Despite Secretary of State Cyrus Vance's calls for caution in handling Sino-Soviet rivalry, Brzezinski saw China as a geopolitical card to be played against Moscow. Normalization with Hanoi, now an official Soviet ally, had become unthinkable to the National Security Council (NSC). But this theme alone cannot account for the bogging down of normalization efforts, as the failure of rapprochement under Ford demonstrated. Intra-administration competition, U.S. skepticism as to true Vietnamese intentions regarding Cambodia, the refugee exodus, Soviet-Vietnamese "friendship" and the fear of jeopardizing Democratic chances during the 1978 congressional elections delayed American response to Vietnamese overtures. Despite further talks in the fall and some calls for normalization from liberal Democrats in Congress, Washington established relations with China in December. The U.S. postponed normalization with Hanoi indefinitely after Vietnam's attack on Cambodia that same month, and covertly supported China's punitive military intervention against Vietnam in February 1979. After opting for a regionalist approach to foreign relations, the administration had returned to viewing foreign policy within a Cold War framework entailing a globalist approach, in which normalizing with Peking and allowing an attack on a "Soviet proxy" were intended to create a Sino-American axis to contain Soviet expansionist ambitions. Contrary to most studies, this last section rejects theories that suggest Hanoi had been pushed into the Soviet camp by a wavering American diplomacy and seeks to explain the 1978 American shift in bilateral diplomatic relations with Vietnam within the framework of U.S. perceptions of the East-West conflict.

ABBREVIATIONS

ASEAN	Association of Southeast Asian Nations (Singapore, Philippines, Indonesia, Thailand, Malaysia)
CCP	Communist Party of China
COMECON (also CMEA)	Council for Mutual Economic Assistance
CPK	Communist Party of Kampuchea
DK	Democratic Kampuchea
DRV	Democratic Republic of Vietnam
IMF	International Monetary Fund
JEC	Joint Economic Commission
KNUFNS	Kampuchean National United Front for National Salvation
KPRCG	Kampuchean People's Revolutionary Coalition Government
LPRP	Lao People's Revolutionary Party
NLF	Vietnam's National Liberation Front (which becomes the PRG after the fall of Saigon)
NSC	National Security Council (U.S.)
PRG	Provisionary Revolutionary Government of Vietnam
SALT	Strategic Arms Limitations Talks (and subsequently Treaty)
SEATO	Southeast Asia Treaty Organization (dissolved in 1977)
SRV	Socialist Republic of Vietnam
UN	United Nations
USUN	U.S. Mission to the United Nations
USSR	Union of Soviet Socialist Republics
VCP	Vietnamese Communist Party (formerly VWP)
VWP	Vietnam Workers' Party (renamed VCP in December 1976)

Important Names and Offices

United States of America

Henry Kissinger: secretary of state and national security adviser to president Gerald Ford
Daniel Moynihan: U.S. ambassador to the United Nations (1975)
William Scranton: U.S. ambassador to the United Nations (1976)
Zbigniew Brzezinski: national security adviser to president Jimmy Carter
Michael Oksenberg: National Security Council China specialist
Cyrus Vance: secretary of state to president Jimmy Carter
Richard Holbrooke: U.S. assistant secretary of state for East Asian and Pacific affairs
Leonard Woodcock: president of the United Autoworkers Union (UAW) and U.S. ambassador to China (March 1979)
Senator Gillespie "Sonny" Montgomery: chairman of the House of Representatives Select Committee on Missing Persons in Southeast Asia
Frank Sieverts: State Department official in charge of MIAs
Robert Oakley: Richard Holbrooke's deputy for Southeast Asia

Socialist Republic of Vietnam

Pham Van Dong: Vietnamese prime minister
Nguyen Duy Trinh: Vietnamese deputy prime minister and minister of foreign affairs
Le Duan: secretary-general of the VCP
Le Duc Tho: organizational secretary of the VCP
Nguyen Co Thach: Vietnamese foreign minister

Phan Hien: Vietnamese vice-foreign minister
Nguyen Thi Binh: South Vietnamese PRG foreign minister
Tran Quang Co: Head of the North American section of the Vietnamese Foreign Ministry
Van Tien Dung: chief of the general staff of the North Vietnamese Army
Vo Nguyen Giap: Vietnamese defense minister
Vo Van Sung: North Vietnamese ambassador to France
Nguyen Van Luu: North Vietnamese ambassador to the United Nations
Dinh Ba Thi: South Vietnamese ambassador to the United Nations, then ambassador to the UN for the reunified Vietnam (until early 1978)
Do Thanh: liaison officer between the Vietnamese and the U.S. embassies in Paris
Hoang Tung: editor of *Nhan Dan* (VCP daily)
Xuan Thuy: secretary of the VCP
Ha Van Lau: Vietnamese ambassador to Cuba, then Vietnamese ambassador to the United Nations as of 1978

Cambodia (and Democratic Kampuchea)

Pol Pot (Saloth Sar): secretary of the CPK
Ieng Sary: vice-premier and foreign minister of Democratic Kampuchea
Khieu Samphan: prime minister of Democratic Kampuchea
Heng Samrin: president of the People's Republic of Kampuchea

People's Republic of China

Zhou Enlai: Chinese premier
Deng Xiaoping: vice-chairman of the CCP
Hua Guofeng: chairman of the CCP
Li Hsien-nien: Chinese vice-premier
Huang Hua: Chinese foreign minister
Teng Ying-Chao: Zhou Enlai's widow

Soviet Union

Leonid Brezhnev: Soviet Communist Party leader
Aleksey Kosygin: Soviet premier
Nikolai Podgorny: Soviet president
Andrei Grechko: Soviet defense minister
Anatoly Dobrynin: Soviet ambassador to the United States

Notes on Spelling in Direct Quotations

All direct quotations are quoted using the original spelling. Misspelled words and names are spelled as they appeared in the original source.

Vietnamese names within the main text and in the footnotes are quoted in full (and are non-hyphenated) to avoid confusion, although names of recurrent characters were shortened (examples: Phan Hien is shortened to "Hien," Pham Van Dong to "Dong," Le Duc Tho to "Tho," Nguyen Co Thach to "Thach," Nguyen Duy Trinh to "Trinh," Nguyen Thi Binh to "Mrs. Binh," and Dinh Ba Thi to "Thi").

Introduction

In November 2000, U.S. president Bill Clinton's visit to Vietnam confirmed the thawing of a quarter of a century of icy relations between Washington and Hanoi. The cooling of Sino-American relations, the Vietnamese withdrawal from Cambodia in 1989, Pol Pot's death in 1998 and the melting of global superpower contentions opened new options for the development of stable bilateral relations. The forty-second U.S. president, whose past opposition to the Vietnam War had produced some controversy, now acted as the link to bring the two countries together. Memories of the war still lingered, however, and Clinton safely chose to delay his visit until the end of his second term, after the presidential election, when what might have been a sensitive visit no longer represented a risk for his party.

Prior to his departure, Clinton, like his predecessors, made clear that he would not apologize to the Vietnamese about either the war or the ensuing peace.[1] Nor did American public opinion consider it a self-redemptive move for the nation or an acknowledgment of past military or diplomatic mistakes. Throughout the visit each side kept to its own perception of history, remembering not only the war but also the ensuing diplomatic quicksand, the repeatedly aborted reconciliations, and the geopolitical squabble of the third Indochina conflict, with its own images and vocabulary. As Peter Peterson—former prisoner of war and new U.S. ambassador to Vietnam as of 1997, following American-Vietnamese normalization in 1995—pointed out to the American press, Clinton's visit represented the extension of an olive branch "that opens a lot of minds here [in Vietnam], toward talking about what we can do together." But Hanoi's press still labeled the Americans "imperialists."[2]

Something had stopped the healing of past pains and forbidden the bridging of this historical gap. Twenty-five years of peace had neither drained decades of mutual bitterness from contemporary political exchanges, nor halted the diplomatic hostility that replaced direct firearm fighting after 1973. Intrigued, a senior administration official reflected: "[The Vietnamese] know they won the war, but they are wondering what went wrong with the peace."[3]

♦ ♦ ♦

The sudden ending of the Second Indochina War in April 1975 brought about the need to redefine Washington's role, both as a world leader and in its relationship with Vietnam. As Saigon, renamed Ho Chi Minh City,[4] was steadily integrated into a new Vietnamese political entity, the time had come for Washington to decide whether to recognize the new Vietnamese communist authorities and to normalize relations with a former foe—an issue left pending since Ho Chi Minh's initial offer in 1945.[5] Through this diplomatic process the two countries would mutually acknowledge the other government's existence and sovereignty over its own nation, engage in bilateral trade, and exchange ambassadors to enable *normal* diplomatic contact.

The question of normalization had hovered around American-Vietnamese relations for several years. In January 1973, shortly before announcing the signing of the Paris Peace Accords, Nixon declared: "It is our firm intention in our relationship to the Democratic Republic of Vietnam to move from hostility to normalization, and from normalization to conciliation and cooperation."[6] The Paris Agreement, claimed a U.S. report, would "usher in an era of reconciliation with the DRV as with all the peoples of Indochina."[7] But while Article 22 called for "a new, equal and mutually beneficial relationship between the United States and the Democratic Republic of Vietnam" leading to normalization and cooperation, the Nixon administration's stated intention to begin an era of peace was largely disingenuous.[8] In Washington, the peace document represented more than an unclear and indirect pledge for cooperation. For the United States, which had spent more than $134.8 billion dollars—representing $7,000 for each member of a South Vietnamese population of 22 million[9]—and had lost more than 57,000 men until the signing of the Agreement on 27 January 1973, the accords had brought "Peace with Honor," through the safe withdrawal of U.S. troops from the military quagmire of Indochina.

Following the signing of the Agreement, Kissinger and his North Vietnamese counterpart Le Duc Tho were nominated for the Nobel Peace Prize, but while Kissinger accepted his prize, Tho refused his on the grounds that the Paris Peace Accords had brought anything but peace to his country.[10] Kissinger carefully deleted Tho's refusal of the prize from his latest memoirs, simply noting that "Le Duc Tho answered my note of congratulations with an insolent message regarding American violations."[11] Tho's appraisal that peace had not been achieved proved correct. Despite the signing of the Peace Accords, war raged on for another twenty-seven months.

On April 30, 1975, North Vietnamese troops marched into Saigon, and Washington rescued its last U.S. Marines in utter chaos from the embassy rooftop.[12] All other embassies—with the exception of those of Belgium, France, India, Japan and Switzerland—had already been evacuated. The Americans had been the last and most reluctant to leave.[13] Following the fall of Saigon to the communist forces, and that of Phnom Penh two weeks earlier, Laos, the last Indochinese state, also succumbed to the communist offensive of the Vietcong-backed Pathet Lao in December.[14] The United States, like the French twenty-two years earlier, had lost Indochina.

As "peace" settled in Vietnam for the first time in forty years, American-Vietnamese normalization became an issue.[15] But as the continuation of the war had demonstrated the impossibility of peace as provided for in the Paris Peace Agreement, the ensuing peace highlighted the inadequacies of its postwar provisions.

Pointing at the damages it had suffered from the war, Hanoi adopted a strong line against the U.S. and called on Washington to implement Article 21 of the Agreement:

> In pursuance of its traditional policy, the U.S. will contribute to healing the wounds of war and to postwar reconstruction of the DRV and throughout Indochina.[16]

In exchange, Hanoi would implement Article 8b:

> The parties shall help each other to get information about those military personnel and foreign civilians of the parties missing in action [MIA], to determine the location and take care of the graves of the dead so as to facilitate the exhumation and repatriation of remains, and to take any such measures as may be required to get information about those still considered as missing in action.[17]

However, as early as spring 1975, immediately after the end of the war, Washington began to argue that the Accords were "void" due to Hanoi's violations of the ceasefire and that, while Washington was no longer obliged to offer Hanoi any economic or "reconstruction" aid, Hanoi was still to account for missing American soldiers and to help repatriate their remains to America. Understanding that the labeling of the Paris Agreement as void also meant that Washington was renouncing Article 8b, the U.S. stressed that accounting for MIAs was not part of the Agreement and represented a normal "humanitarian" obligation. Meanwhile, Hanoi urged Washington to fulfill its share of "obligations" through the granting of aid, prodding successive administrations with threats to publish a secret letter from Nixon to North Vietnamese Premier Pham Van Dong, in which he had promised Hanoi $4.75 billion in postwar reconstruction aid. Washington attempted to counter Hanoi's claims through various diplomatic maneuvers whose scope and aggressiveness echoed trends in public opinion, fluctuations of congressional interest and shifts in international politics.

This book discusses the negotiations on the normalization of relations between Washington and Hanoi, the diplomatic goals and achievements of each country, and the ensuing repercussions affecting domestic and international politics during the Ford and Carter administrations, from the fall of Saigon in April 1975 to the Chinese invasion of Vietnam in February-March 1979. By picking up where most narratives finish, it breaks with the traditional view of postwar diplomacy as an end chapter to the war, and presents it instead as a series of events in a new era in American-Vietnamese relations, emphasizing the conflicting priorities and political goals, both at home and abroad, of these two countries.

Few publications have tackled this issue; also, some archival material has not yet been declassified. This book is therefore based, as much as possible, on recently declassified documents from the Ford and Carter presidential libraries, and from the National and Congressional Archives in Washington. Further material was found at the University of Berkeley Indochina Archives, which holds a private collection of U.S. policy documents regarding Vietnam. This collection, never screened by the U.S. government archival censoring services and seldom analyzed by historians, was donated in 1997 by Vietnam expert and former U.S. official Douglas Pike. After completing his studies in journalism and international communications, Pike joined the State Department's

Foreign Service in 1960 and was sent to Saigon as an expert on the Vietnamese communist army. In the mid-1960s he ran a psychological operations program in Vietnam, then was assigned to various posts in the Far East (Hong Kong, Taipei, Tokyo) before returning to Vietnam in 1973–1974. Pike retired from the Foreign Service in 1982 and worked for the Congressional Research Service and the Department of Defense. He also began the *Indochina Chronology* series and became the director of Indochina Studies at the University of California, Berkeley (1982–1996). In 1997 he moved to Texas Tech University. To this day Douglas Pike remains one of the main U.S. observers of Indochina. He compiled his archives while working, mostly in Saigon, for the State Department Foreign Service between 1960 and 1982, in addition to conducting independent research throughout his career. Comprising a variety of intelligence reports, personal notes to the State Department, newspaper cuttings, inter-agency memoranda, and policy analyses, allowing formidable insight into U.S. decision-making, these were never screened by U.S. authorities and thus remain uncensored and therefore invaluable. This collection, separate from other Pike papers now available on the internet via Texas Tech University, is kept in the offices of the *Asian Survey*. It remained unused by scholars until Pike's death in May 2002.

Further research for this book was conducted in Paris in the collections of the French Ministry of Foreign Affairs, which had maintained an onlooker status on Vietnam since the Geneva Accords of 1954. Although French legislation forbids the opening of archives before a thirty-year lapse, the organization of an international conference, held in honor of the thirtieth anniversary of the Paris Accords in January 2003, encouraged the Foreign Ministry to open some of its files to researchers under special authorization. These collections, partly declassified in December 2002 and the Jean Sainteny papers at the Archives of Contemporary History, provided formidable insight into the diplomatic mechanisms surrounding the creation of the Peace Agreement.

A wide selection of media press sources were used—American, British, Vietnamese, Soviet, Chinese and French—offering a fascinating range of opinions that allows us to place American-Vietnamese relations within the broader context of a globalist appraisal of superpower contentions and their regional repercussions. French scholarly works and journalistic sources, published for the 250,000 members of the Vietnamese community in France, also offer interesting and occasionally critical views of American-Vietnamese interactions that have seldom been studied.

In addition, a closely knit network of French scholars and Vietnamese informers enabled interviews of Vietnamese immigrants, such as former *Nhan Dan* assistant editor and Vietnam Communist Party (VCP) member Bui Tin. Other interviewees include BBC Vietnam expert Judith Stowe, U.S. politicians such as Zbigniew Brzezinski and Congressman Gillespie Montgomery, and historians. Memoirs and existing oral evidence were relied upon when personal interviews were refused or impossible. Thus, personal insights unavailable in written histories were obtained, such as on the issue of inner-Party factionalism and political priorities, on which documented evidence is still classified.[18] However, given the scarcity of Vietnamese material available—and the language barrier—this research is based primarily on American perspectives despite efforts to balance both viewpoints.

While the events covered in this book may seem relatively recent, many of the political actors have died—Congressman William Ashbrook (1982), Le Duan (1986),

Le Duc Tho (1990), Nguyen Co Thach (1991), Philip Habib (1992), Pham Van Dong (2000), Michael Oksenberg (2001), Leonard Woodcock (2001), Senator Mike Mansfield (2001), Cyrus Vance (2002), General Van Tien Dung (2002), and Douglas Pike (2002). Others, such as Jimmy Carter, Gerald Ford, Henry Kissinger, and Richard Holbrooke, either politely declined to be interviewed or did not respond. Deputy Director of the NSC David Aaron was more straightforward in stressing that "of all the subjects that I tried to stay away from, Vietnam was at the top of the list," and that he intended it to remain this way.[19] Another striking response came from NSC military adviser General William Odom, whom my interest in this topic greatly surprised since "nothing" had happened between Washington and Hanoi following the fall of Saigon. The analysis of post-war diplomatic relations, he claimed, would "fit on one side of a page."[20] This illustrates the difficulty with which "Vietnam" is invoked even today and the extent to which postwar bilateral interactions were directed by only a small group of individuals within the State Department.

This book takes a chronological approach to postwar relations between the U.S. and Vietnam. During the four years between the Second and Third Indochina Wars, Washington's dialogue with Hanoi went through three distinct stages, of which this book attempts to highlight the recurring themes and patterns, the elements of opposition and the sudden diplomatic shifts. Chapter I of this analysis focuses on the Ford years, from May 1975 to December 1976. Besides one extremely brief and incomplete reference to bilateral relations during the Ford administration in Steven Hurst's *The Carter Administration and Vietnam*, this period has been neglected in secondary sources, and this book is therefore the very first to offer a detailed insight into bilateral relations in 1975 and 1976. Beyond its filling of a bibliographical gap, the study of this period provides the basis for understanding later exchanges between the two countries, and its omission from the existing literature highlights the incomplete and distorted aspects of contemporary secondary sources. Indeed, several themes—such as mutual bitterness, Hanoi's constant exultation in Vietnamese victory, the U.S. denial of responsibility, the division between executive branch policies and congressional pressures, the weight of public opinion and the gap between executive branch public declarations and behind-the-scene acts, the emergence of new friendships and feuds between communist powers, and each side's use and distortion of the MIA issue to support its own diplomatic and domestic interests—emerged from this period and gave birth to diplomatic patterns that remained well into the Carter years and beyond. Without a close study of these themes during the Ford administration, bilateral relations under Carter cannot be satisfactorily explained.

The first chapter of this book depicts how, in the midst of this crisis of confidence, the Ford administration responded with great distrust to Hanoi's first requests for diplomatic rapprochement; repeatedly vetoed Vietnamese applications for admission to the United Nations for fear of its entailing further international humiliation; and finally, during Ford's candidacy for presidential reelection, adopted a two-fold policy aimed at gaining maximum domestic political leverage by seeming to respond to Vietnamese overtures on MIAs while simultaneously rejecting all offers to negotiate with the newly reunified Vietnam. The episode highlights contradictions in executive branch public statements and private intentions, a recurring theme of this book. Secondary sources, such as Nayan Chanda's *Brother Enemy* and Gaddis Smith's *Morality, Reason and Power*, fail to expand on the Ford administration's dialogue with Vietnam, preferring to focus immediately on the Carter era. Such a gap in the historical narrative distorts perceptions of events and fails to explain how mutual bitterness, nurtured during the Ford years, came to affect bilateral relations under Carter. Similarly, Washington set out to show its allies and enemies that its military power and national resolve had not been affected by the Indochina debacle and that the U.S. would reshuffle its alliances and adapt to the changing world order—a theme, muted during Carter's first year of office, that re-emerged in 1978.

The second section of this book, chapters II and III, focuses on the first year of the Carter presidency. While some of the main themes of the Ford years remained under Carter—such as the need to counter public pressure, the weight of Congress on executive policies, congressional divisions over the issue of normalization and aid, the gap between official policies and unpublicized declarations—this section describes the disappearance of the executive's bitterness towards Vietnam, encouraging friendlier, although hardly more fruitful, contacts. The Carter years present a shift from the Ford administration, which alternated between publicized confrontation and deliberate ignoring of the Vietnamese as suited U.S. domestic policies, as Carter developed a regionalist approach to foreign policy and a genuine wish for reconciliation. These themes governing diplomatic relations remained only temporary—a parenthesis between Ford's hostility in 1975–76, and Carter's shift to a stronger stance on Vietnam in 1978. However, as the contrast between the Ford and Carter administrations' handling of the issue of Vietnam demonstrates, the failure of normalization cannot be solely attributed to an American shift from regionalist to globalist policies, as Hurst implies. This book shows that postwar relations cannot be summarized so simplistically. Chapters II and III explain how relations were plagued by a series of misperceptions, misunderstandings, ill-timed openings and aggressiveness, which survived into the Carter years. This period also witnessed the emergence of inter-government rivalries both in Washington and Hanoi, which, as they developed in 1977–1978, came to impact strongly on bilateral relations in 1978 during the second part of the Carter presidency.

Chapter II depicts the beginning of the Carter administration, coinciding with the reorganization of the VCP in December 1976. This book agrees with Hurst's assertion that Carter departed from his predecessor's policies in shifting to a softer stance regarding Hanoi. In his first attempt at negotiations, he sent a non-diplomatic delegation, headed by United Auto-Workers president Leonard Woodcock, to test the Vietnamese, with the concealed aim of de-emphasizing the MIA issue at home to ease tensions surrounding bilateral dialogue. This continued to highlight the gap between official declarations and unofficial intentions, although the aims were friendlier than under Ford. Chapter III analyzes how the apparent success of this visit—despite mutual misperceptions and misunderstandings—fathered a series of bilateral talks in Paris in 1977. Such initiatives soon crossed paths with mutual misunderstandings and Vietnamese impatience to obtain reconstruction aid as promised in Nixon's secret letter, whose publication in May 1977 triggered congressional wrath and closed the door on any possibility of obtaining economic aid. Despite some mutually friendly overtures during the summer of 1977, and Vietnam's admission to the United Nations, bilateral relations stalled following allegations of Vietnamese spying in the U.S.

The third section of this book, which includes chapters IV, V and VI, begins with the year 1978 and focuses on the many diplomatic and ideological shifts that affected bilateral relations. The impact of Sino-Soviet rivalries on Vietnam's foreign policies and on U.S. perceptions of its former enemy, while muted in the first year of the Carter presidency, re-emerged in full force in 1978, as did the need for each country to reposition itself in a new world order. Although both Washington and Hanoi's domestic interests had governed bilateral relations since 1975, as illustrated in the first three chapters, the driving force of negotiations switched to exterior and international ideological concerns in the second year of the Carter administration. Picking up on Raymond Garthoff's analysis of Washington's interplay between "Détente and Confrontation" in its relations with the Soviet Union, this third section of the book highlights a parallel pattern in Washington's dealings with Hanoi, shifting from a hope for *détente* with Moscow and reconciliation with Hanoi to an era of diplomatic confrontation with both countries starting in 1978. Consequently, this last section can be regarded within the broader framework of existing Cold War literature as a case study of U.S. dealings with a Third World communist nation—an issue further complicated by the remnants of a history of war and mutual animosity.

While agreeing with Garthoff's appraisal of the U.S. ideological shift toward a stronger stance vis-à-vis Moscow, this expands on his brief mention of Vietnam as an example of diplomatic casualties with Third World countries in Soviet-American relations.[21] The particularity of U.S. relations with Hanoi, however, confirms Odd Arne Westad's and John Ehrman's arguments that Carter did not adopt a "standard" foreign policy orthodoxy in dealing with Third World countries, and his administration's relations with Vietnam cannot be seen as a textbook example of U.S. relations with developing countries.[22] Rather, this work builds upon historian Dana Allin's observation that U.S. perceptions and foreign policy formulation were plagued with "Cold War illusions" and a disproportionate fear of communism, transposing Allin's remarks from European powers to the complex arena of Southeast Asia. Add to this the continued impossibility of the two countries bridging their mutual misunderstandings and each grasping the other's mindset—an ongoing theme in both administrations—it was little surprise that normalization efforts failed. Therefore, while the case of U.S. relations with Vietnam is in no way typical of U.S. diplomatic behavior, and underwent some fundamental changes over the years, some patterns remain similar.

Chapter V depicts Vietnam's increasing diplomatic difficulties with Peking and Pol Pot's new Cambodian regime, which reached a peak in late 1978. At the same time, international events had led to the growth of National Security Adviser Zbigniew Brzezinski's influence on Carter at the expense of Secretary of State Cyrus Vance's softer policies, which were aimed at simultaneous recognition of Peking and Hanoi, while Brzezinski redirected Washington's foreign policies towards China, as depicted in Chapter IV. Contrary to some observers, such as Jerel Rosati and John Dumbrell who date Carter's tilt from a regionalist to a globalist and anti–Soviet appraisal of foreign policies to 1979, this book sides with Steven Hurst, Odd Arne Westad and Donna Jackson who claim that the shift began in the first half of 1978, following the Soviet-backed border wars in the Horn of Africa.[23] It supports the view, expressed in Chanda's *Brother Enemy* and Elizabeth Becker's *When the War Was Over: Cambodia and the Khmer Rouge Revolution*, that Brzezinski's visit to Peking in May 1978 played a pivotal role in closing the Carter administration's dialogue with Hanoi—albeit with the added impact of Washington's doubts as to Vietnamese intentions in Indochina and American concerns for the swelling refugee exodus.[24] It disagrees, however, with Hurst's view that the NSC and the State Department "concurred" on shelving normalization, and stresses instead the clash of opposing diplomatic programs between the two institutions.[25]

Too late, the Vietnamese attempted to recapture American attention, with obvious efforts to woo Washington during the summer of 1978, by informing several visiting humanitarian and congressional delegations that Hanoi had dropped its aid request, meanwhile strengthening its alliance with Moscow to secure political and military backing for its upcoming invasion of Cambodia. As described in Chapter V, following fruitless bilateral meetings in New York in September, Hanoi signed a friendship treaty with China's diplomatic enemy Moscow, while Washington finalized Sino-American normalization. Chapter VI retraces the Vietnamese invasion of Cambodia, the overthrow of the Pol Pot regime and the subsequent Chinese "lesson" on Vietnam, which, indirectly supported by Washington, was aimed as much at punishing Hanoi for its attack on Phnom Penh as at punishing Moscow for its attempted interference in Asian affairs.

This book investigates both nations' diplomatic behavior and seeks to explain the true purpose of their often seemingly bizarre or counterproductive stances. Given recent archival and oral revelations, it rejects theories such as those presented by Gaddis Smith in *Morality, Reason and Power*, or G. Evans and K. Rowley in *Red Brotherhood at War*, that the failure of normalization was a casualty of U.S. diplomatic clumsiness. Smith's book could be criticized for being overly critical of Washington in its dealings with Vietnam, perhaps due to the early date of its writing and to the lack of material available in the 1980s. Nayan Chanda's *Brother Enemy*, first published in the same year and based on oral evidence and on the author's personal experience as a journalist, is perhaps the least outdated of secondary sources of the 1980s. Although he refrains from portraying Washington as a diplomatic bully, as was common in such writings in the 1980s, and offers one of the first explanations of the regional and global context in which American-Vietnamese bilateral exchanges evolved, Chanda's analysis is rather incomplete and is occasionally misled by his interviewees.

This book seeks to analyze each side's political ambitions and responsibilities in the light of recently released archival material. It highlights each country's attempts at opening up to a former enemy, the difficulties Washington encountered in coming to terms with its past conduct in Indochina, and Vietnam's nagging insistence on obtaining "compensation" for the war—more as a symbol of victory than as a true economic requirement. It explains how domestic concerns and bilateral bickerings—mainly the swelling of the MIA issue in the U.S., and that of reconstruction aid in Vietnam—combined with the regional Cambodian-Vietnamese and Sino-Vietnamese conflicts account for the failure of normalization. Whereas secondary sources claim that the turning point in American-Vietnamese relations in 1978 was due to Hanoi's external difficulties and to international factors, the causes for such a reversal were also rooted in the Vietnamese domestic arena dating back to 1976, if not earlier. Thanks to a number of interviews with Vietnamese and foreign observers, this analysis sheds light on these nebulous tensions, and evaluates the impact of VCP first secretary Le Duan and organizational secretary Le Duc Tho's ideologies and of their swelling authority within the Politburo up to the Vietnamese invasion of Cambodia in late 1978.

Chanda is the only author who tackles Vietnamese inner-Party rivalries—if only briefly, perhaps because of lack of materials on the issue, although one may suggest another interpretation. Chanda was one of the few foreign journalists Hanoi viewed favorably. He was, for example, among a handful invited to visit the Vietnamese-Cambodian border after the invasion of 1978. Therefore, it is possible that he may well have preferred to maintain a low-key analysis of Vietnamese policies so as not to lose Hanoi's trust in him—especially as his book was published in 1986 when both Le Duan and Le Duc Tho were still alive. One therefore has to rely on Vietnamese exiles such as Bui Tin in *Following Ho Chi Minh: Memoirs of a North Vietnamese Colonel* and Hoang Van Hoan in *A Drop in the Ocean: Hoang Van Hoan's Revolutionary Reminiscences* for greater insight—although their memoirs are stained with profound bitterness. These authors' claims can then be compared with the authorized Vietnamese version of this period of history, as presented in VCP member Luu Van Loi's *Fifty Years of Vietnamese Diplomacy, 1945–1995*.

This work assesses the impact of the failure of American-Vietnamese normalization in all arenas—local, regional and global. It analyzes how this failed attempt to obtain peace affected Vietnam's decision to align itself with Moscow and to reconsider its position within Indochina, and confirmed the reshuffling of alliances between the three superpowers. Again, it disagrees with most theories that Washington's refusal to normalize pushed Vietnam towards the Soviet camp. Instead, it sides with recent writings, such as Stephen Morris' *Why Vietnam Invaded Cambodia*, which does not deny U.S. responsibility for the reshuffling of world powers and its regional consequences, and offers greater insight into Vietnamese aims within the Sino-Cambodian-American-Vietnamese squabble. Morris presents an interesting alternative view through the use of recently declassified material from Soviet archives. However, Morris' lack of attention to American-Vietnamese relations in the emergence of Sino-Vietnamese rivalry often undermines his claims, as well as hinting at his hard-line position on the issue of the Vietnamese-Cambodian conflict.[26]

This book argues that factionalism within both the American and Vietnamese governments bogged down the last chance for diplomatic rapprochement until individual ambitions sacrificed bilateral relations on the altar of superpower rivalry. By building on recent reappraisals of American-Vietnamese relations, this study observes how, in the longterm, the failure of normalization led both countries to become enmeshed in a third Indochina conflict, and how this local clash became "globalized" into a proxy confrontation between Peking, Washington and Moscow.[27]

While offering new insights on American-Vietnamese relations, this book seeks to clarify the following points still obscure in secondary writings: what were the reasons for and means of achieving normalization? How did political leaders reconcile the postwar quest for cooperation and reconciliation with a history of nearly two decades of hostility? How genuine were these attempts? How did the motivations and ideologies of individuals within the governments affect the ongoing dialogue? To what extent did each country's geostrategic ambitions sidetrack bilateral relations? How did the general

Cold War context, superpower rivalry and Sino-American perceptions of Soviet ambitions play upon the shift from a regionalist to a globalist framework in U.S. policy-making and its effect on American-Vietnamese relations? How did this result in diplomatic failure and an awkward military and political squabble?

I

FORD AND VIETNAM'S PEACE

A New Start for Vietnam and a First Opening to Washington

Following the collapse of President Nguyen Van Thieu's regime in South Vietnam, the National Liberation Front (NLF), reincarnated as the Provisional Revolutionary Government (PRG), embarked on a slow process of reconstruction and socialist transformation. The Senate Subcommittee on Refugees evaluated the weight of bombs dropped on Indochina at 7.8 million tons—more than twice the tonnage of U.S. bombs dropped during World War II—with an added 5.5 million tons of ammunition.[1] In the words of Nayan Chanda, one of the leading experts on Indochina, the North had been "bombed back into the Stone Age."[2] With more than 2.2 million dead, 5.1 million wounded, 1 million widows and as many orphans, a total of 16.5 percent of the population had been either killed or maimed.[3] By 1974, a further 57 percent of the population had been made homeless, swelling towns and cities throughout the country and bringing the population of Saigon from 300,000 to 3 million by the end of the war. After decades of fighting Japan, France and the United States, the time had come for the Vietnamese to turn to rebuilding the country and healing its war wounds. The Vietnamese were in urgent need of social, economic and agricultural reconstruction.

Among the numerous plans of action designed to reshape the two Vietnamese states into one united and competitive nation, the new communist authorities ordered South Vietnamese soldiers to register at reeducation centers "to study and transform themselves" and wash away their "sense of guilt" by becoming full members of this new society.[4] Should these individuals "repent," the new authorities would pardon "even those who in the past had committed crimes."[5] But reality was less appealing.

After a year of peace an estimated 200,000 former South Vietnamese officials were undergoing re-education, assigned to various tasks such as filling in bomb craters, clearing minefields and repairing roads, while also being taught the basics of socialist revolutionary theory.[6] The number rose to more than a million by the end of 1975.[7] Popular meetings were similarly organized, such as the Le Van Duyet Stadium meeting in Saigon in the summer of 1975, urging some 4,000 people to denounce war criminals who were later sent to re-education centers.[8] Amnesty International reported that among the thousands of former Southern officials registered for re-education, about 40,000 were sent to camps, including, to quote the Vietnamese government, "29,000 puppet military personnel, 7,000 civilian officials, 3,000 policemen and security officials, and 900 members of reactionary parties and organizations." By December 1979, officially, 26,000 people were still undergoing re-education.[9] Many would remain in re-education camps for many more years.

Similarly, an attempt was made to counter the disastrous effects on the Southern rural economy of mass displacement of the population. New Economic Zones (NEZ) were established in the countryside where volunteers were supposedly encouraged to start a new life.[10] According to Hanoi, far from being prisoners, the young able men who joined NEZs were volunteers who would cultivate land and contribute to feeding the country. The West and South Vietnamese refugees declared that NEZs amounted "to the same thing" as being sent to "a concentration camp," and were often labeled "gulags" by Western observers to hint at Soviet influence on Vietnam.[11] The pro–Vietnamese Western press responded that Washington, disappointed that the predicted communist bloodbath had not occurred, had shifted its accusations to NEZs, referring to both NEZ residents and re-educated Vietnamese as "deported," reporting the existence of 800,000 political prisoners.[12]

Vietnam was in urgent need of reconstruction, by whatever means. Despite humanitarian controversies surrounding NEZs, it is undeniable that these new zones motivated rapid expansion of the labor force and productivity with restricted economic expenditure. This new network of economic zones also contributed to the repopulation of the countryside through a partial relocation of the millions of people uprooted during the war, the resettlement of some of the three million unemployed South Vietnamese, and the rehabilitation and cleansing of the 47 percent of arable land burned by 72 million liters of herbicides and Agent Orange.[13] "As long as we still have to ask for food assistance from outside," Ho Chi Minh had warned, "we cannot say that we have complete independence and freedom."[14] NEZs were therefore rapidly set to meeting both North and South Vietnam's need for rice, the cornerstone of economic independence that would then allow the government to focus its efforts on socialist transformation.

By the summer of 1975 all foreign journalists had been expelled from Indochina and had to rely mostly on refugee stories and secondary accounts to keep track of the changes in the three new communist countries.[15] To counter Western accusations, the Hanoi-controlled Saigonese "liberation" radio *Giai-Phong* hailed the patriotism of tens of thousands of South Vietnamese "eagerly and willingly volunteering" to join NEZs to promote the agricultural and economic development of the country.[16] At the same time, *Saigon Radio* began broadcasting South Vietnam's national anthem, indirectly signaling that South Vietnam would not be crushed by northern political domination.[17] Symbolically, on May 13, the postal link between North and South Vietnam was reopened after a twenty-one year interruption, as a first step toward reuniting the two states.[18] The next day, the PRG appealed to South Vietnamese refugees to return to their homeland, now that they had been assured that no bloodbath would occur, and sent a formal note to neighbor countries that had accepted South Vietnamese refugees and to the United Nations High Commissioner for Refugees to assist on this issue. This gesture, however, was rapidly interpreted as international propaganda rather than genuine humanitarian concern for fellow Vietnamese nationals when Hanoi delayed the repatriation of several hundred refugees over the following years as a diplomatic lever on the United States.[19] But meanwhile, the gesture signaled that Hanoi intended to clear its image in the international arena to attract foreign friendships now that the Second Indochina War had come to an end.

Vietnam was slowly embarking on a long march towards reconstruction. The war had exhausted the economy and Hanoi realized, even before the communist victory, that reconstruction, reunification, and socialist transformation were nothing more than empty words if sought without financial support. Only Washington had the economic capability to meet the needs for the rebuilding of Vietnam.[20] Hanoi certainly remembered the figure of $12 billion with which the United States had artificially kept the South Vietnamese economy afloat during the war years.[21] Applying to the world's first economic power for financial help had long been on Hanoi's agenda, but the pursuit of "cooperation," after twenty years of war, ended with Vietnamese victorious boasting and American wounded pride. A long quest for normalization began.

Only three weeks before the fall of Saigon, a strange message to the United States was read by Frank Sinatra, Bob Hope, Bert Schneider and Peter Davis during the American Academy Awards ceremony as scenes from the movie *Hearts and Minds*, about the Vietnam War, were shown. The message was a greeting of friendship from Vietcong officials, an olive branch to the representatives of American popular culture and, through them, to the American people at large.[22] Much as it had successfully used the anti-war movement to undermine world opinion against the U.S. during the war, Hanoi was once again appealing to the people rather than to the U.S. government for friendship and cooperation. Indirect openings to Washington followed two weeks later, when Frances Fitzgerald, Pulitzer Prize winner for her work on Vietnam, reported that Hanoi would welcome American investments in the country after the war. Hanoi officials, she added, would welcome "a fairly dense network of economic relations within the non–Communist world [Washington]" as provided for in the Paris Peace Agreement.[23]

A few days later Kissinger responded to the declaration by cautiously stating that Washington would "see what the conduct of this government [Hanoi] is internationally and partially domestically."[24] At this early stage in post–Vietnam War diplomatic relations between the two countries, Washington was not looking forward to bilateral contacts and, as Kissinger was formulating, opted instead for a "wait-and-see" policy.

As Saigon fell into Vietnamese communist hands on April 30, 1975, and communist popular propaganda cheered at the American defeat, Hanoi refrained from openly nagging the United States for the loss of its South Vietnamese position, in the hope that restraint would foster chances for reconciliation. The final attack on Saigon had even been delayed to allow the United States time to evacuate the remaining Marines from the southern capital. After the capture of Saigon, the American embassy building was not forced to fly a National Liberation Front (NLF) flag as a nagging reminder of American defeat. Instead, it was cleaned and locked, and the $110 million worth of U.S. property was removed for storage to prevent robbery.[25] Editor of the Vietnamese Workers' Party (VWP)'s daily *Nhan Dan*, Hoang Tung, announced that documents and tapes seized in the U.S. Embassy and known as the Saigon papers, would not be published so as not to "rub salt in the American wounds."[26]

Hanoi, demonstrating that the Vietnamese now enjoyed sovereignty on their territory, declared that the building would be handed over to the government of Algeria, one of the first countries to present its credentials to the new regime.[27] The declaration, one of the first examples of Hanoi's awkward and double-edged diplomacy, was not aimed at taunting Washington but rather at stimulating the United States to engage in bilateral diplomatic rapprochement with its former foe. As embassies are not the property of the host country's government, but of the country holding the building, the Vietnamese threat to hand the building over to a third party was hardly plausible, and Hanoi's declaration was merely an attempt to encourage foreign governments to recognize the new government in Saigon.[28] However, it demonstrated Hanoi's wish to remain firm in dealing with Washington while simultaneously extending an olive branch to Americans and calling for "friendship and cooperation." This dual and contradictory stance, inspired by long years of opposition and traditional harsh communist rhetoric, would become typical of Vietnamese policies towards Washington in the postwar period. Eventually, the embassy building became the headquarters of the National Oil and Gas Commission.

But Washington was in a less conciliatory mood. As Kissinger stepped up to announce the fall of Saigon at a press conference in Washington, he added that he would personally oppose any granting of U.S. aid to Hanoi for postwar reconstruction. "[T]he premises of the Paris accords," he explained, "in terms of aid, of the possibility of aid, and in terms of other factors, tended to disintegrate [as the war continued]. I see no purpose now in reviewing that particular history."[29]

Kissinger's announcement was one of a series of executive decisions aimed at isolating the Vietnamese regimes. That same day, the Treasury Department froze all South Vietnamese assets in the U.S., including real estate, private and non-bank assets, for a total value of $70 million.[30] Only the property of Vietnamese diplomats, former officials and refugees remained untouched by the Treasury Department. The U.S. Trading with the Enemy Act was also invoked, prohibiting any trade relations with Vietnam.[31] Interestingly, the Vietnamese kept comments on the American move low-key so as not to needlessly irritate Washington.[32] The fact that the Vietnamese were simultaneously seizing American assets in South Vietnam may also account for mild criticism of the American move in the Vietnamese media. Thus, *Quan Doi Nhan Dan*, the North Vietnamese army newspaper, labeled the U.S. move only an "outmoded policy."[33] Two weeks later, on May 16, a trade embargo on both Vietnamese states and Cambodia, again imposed without consulting Congress, closed the last U.S. economic links with Indochina, shunning the three countries for nearly two decades.[34]

Chairing a hearing of the House of Representatives Subcommittee on International Trade and Commerce on June 4, Jonathan Bingham (Democrat, New York) openly blamed Kissinger for the decision and harshly criticized the new policy on Vietnamese assets:

> Policy responsibility for these actions rests with the Department of State. The Subcommittee on Trade and Commerce considers the decision to embargo these nations to have serious foreign policy implications. It has been my hope, and that of many Members of Congress, that our peacetime policies toward Indochina would not be mere extensions of our wartime sanctions—that the end of the fighting in Vietnam and the end of U.S. military

involvement there would make possible a gradual normalization of relations with the peoples and governments of Indochina. Imposition of an embargo, even before the policies and new governments of South Vietnam and Cambodia have been tested, does not bode well for such a gradual normalization. Embargoes—as our experience with Cuba well illustrates—have little effect other than to prolong hostility.[35]

These measures were but the first in a series of the U.S. executive branch's hostile diplomatic actions against Vietnam that triggered congressional criticism. The legislature, which had wished to end the war despite opposition from the executive branch, now urged reconciliation with the Vietnamese. But such congressional initiatives were of little avail to the White House.

When the United Nations debated its $100 million assistance program in early May, Washington refused all cooperation with North Vietnam. In an effort to temper any potential congressional frustration over this decision, Clarence C. Ferguson, the American representative, announced that Washington would, however, consider South Vietnamese requests "with great care and compassion."[36] A month later, the program had received less than 15 percent of the planned funding, with no participation from Washington, and the other Western countries, not wishing to irk the United States, refused to openly support the program.[37]

In the following weeks, the Treasury Department unilaterally took a series of similar measures preventing the shipment of technical material, medical support and agricultural equipment to Vietnam. Even mail and written public communication between refugees and their families in Indochina was prohibited. The American government prevented all economic aid, even private, from being sent to Indochina and probably believed that preventing letters and parcels from reaching Vietnam would stop refugees from sending their savings to their families. "We felt it was only prudent and orderly to impose these controls," explained Deputy Assistant Secretary of State Robert Miller, on June 4, "so that we could monitor the situation as it evolved with the takeover of these new regimes."[38] The intent was hardly genuine, as future events eventually proved that hostility had become a constant reaction in Ford policies towards Vietnam, aimed at rejecting bilateral contacts rather than "monitoring" them.

In Congress, mainly liberal Democrats stood up against the wave of anti–Vietnam national sentiment. In a report delivered on June 9, Senator Edward Kennedy (Democrat, Massachusetts) called for a continuation of low-level diplomatic contacts with the three Indochinese capitals, Hanoi, Vientiane and Phnom Penh to allow the negotiation of "such humanitarian issues as the reunification of families, the free exchange of communications and parcels between refugees and their families and the gathering of information on missing American servicemen." The Senator also urged American adherence to the United Nations Indochina Assistance Program.[39] Although Congress, during the Ford years, demonstrated Democratic majorities potentially sympathetic to reconciliation with Vietnam, most former anti-war liberals had experienced hostility in their constituencies and would not risk endorsing such pacifist views in the middle of a congressional election year.[40] Beyond the grumbling of the Subcommittee on International Trade and Commerce and independent congressmen, Congress remained silent, indirectly allowing the executive branch relative freedom in its actions.

In July, the American Friends Service Committee and the Mennonite Central

Committee reported that they had been denied authorization to ship fishing equipment to North and South Vietnam on the grounds that it was "considered to be more economic ... than humanitarian aid."[41] Similarly, a Church World Service application to ship aid, filed in June, remained unanswered for several months after being accidentally "mislaid" by the Department of Commerce—but was recovered after AID intervened on the issue.[42] Although the Treasury Department admitted that it had approved similar licenses in the past, American post-war bitterness had led to a severe reversal in U.S. policy.[43]

After recalling that the State Department had assured the subcommittee in June that "charitable humanitarian exports" would be allowed, Representative Jonathan Bingham declared that executive branch policy toward Vietnam "is one based far more on past realities than present possibilities. It is in a very real sense a policy of retribution and recrimination, rather than one looking toward reconciliation." Again, the executive branch's move had been unilateral, without prior consultation with Congress. Reportedly, too, it had been urged by Ford, despite Kissinger's opposition.[44]

In hindsight, Bingham's appraisal appears the most accurate as the analysis of future events during the Ford administration would indeed show. This theme of U.S. executive branch rejection of reconciliation would govern bilateral relations under Ford until the promotion of softer policies by the Carter administration starting in early 1977. Meanwhile, *status quo* on humanitarian exports to Vietnam was maintained until mid-November, when the State Department, under growing congressional pressure, eventually authorized the shipment of limited private humanitarian aid to Vietnam.

In September, the administration further tightened its grasp on U.S. citizens and institutions wishing to remain in contact with Indochina. The State Department added both its former allies—South Vietnam and Cambodia—to the list of nations where American passports would be invalid if not otherwise specified by the secretary of state. This decision, with the existing ban on use of American passports in North Vietnam, made the presence of U.S. residents in Vietnam and Cambodia—and indirectly of American humanitarian institutions—either illegal or closely regulated by the State Department.[45]

On September 10, furthering his efforts to ease relations between the two countries, Representative Jonathan Bingham proposed an amendment to the Trading With the Enemy Act to lift the trade embargo on North and South Vietnam:

> Notwithstanding any provision of this or any other Act, no embargo on trade with North or South Vietnam shall be authorized or implemented except with respect to war and other materials defined by the Mutual Defense Assistance Control Act of 1951 as amended (22 USC 1611–13) and regulations pursuant thereto.[46]

Again, the amendment, voted by Congress, was vetoed by President Ford.[47]

While this episode may seem trivial, its long-term implications played a larger role in the unfolding of American-Vietnamese relations. Although the Vietnamese had benefited from the support of strong left-wing lobby groups during the war, U.S. withdrawal from Indochina in 1973 and the end of the war in 1975 had triggered the dwindling of U.S. popular support for and interest in Vietnam. The American public and Congress, except for a minority of congressional "post-war doves," were no longer willing to lend a friendly ear to Vietnamese claims. Hanoi could now rely only on a relatively weak lobby of religious groups such as the Quakers or Mennonites, non-profit organizations such as the American Friends Service Committee, and independent intellectuals. This lobby, which generally supported normalization, enjoyed little political leverage and focused mainly on providing humanitarian aid to Vietnam.[48] Over the next four years, Hanoi was slow to understand that it no longer enjoyed American domestic support and needed to adapt its dialogue to its new political environment.

While Washington was recovering from the loss of its former South Vietnamese ally through national recrimination, Hanoi had apparently opted for a shift from wartime confrontation to a desire for diplomatic cooperation and peace. On May 7, North Vietnamese Premier Pham Van Dong sent a message to Washington via Sweden reiterating Ford's view that "a chapter ha[d] been closed" and that Hanoi looked forward to enjoying "good relations with the U.S."[49] All impending questions must be "settled as soon as possible," declared Foreign Minister Nguyen Duy Trinh during a National Assembly speech, and he asserted that Hanoi was ready to open discussions.[50] Should Washington agree to "bind up the wounds of war" through economic aid, privately hinted Hanoi, "this would constitute the beginnings of normal relations."[51] Hanoi would even welcome a small U.S. mission in Saigon under the new South Vietnamese government.[52]

Interestingly, while the request for aid would become a redundant argument in Hanoi's dealings with Washington, it was portrayed by the Vietnamese as a legitimate continuation of U.S. responsibilities towards Vietnam, and was a theme that also appeared in Hanoi's negotiations for normalization with other countries, betraying Vietnam's anxiety to rebuild its country and economy. In normalizing relations with Formosa in 1973, Hanoi had requested $150 million in "war reparations" and later compromised for $50 million in "non-reimbursable aid."[53] Similarly, a request was made on normalizing with Japan the same year but the exchange of ambassadors was postponed over Hanoi's failure to endorse responsibility for the former South Vietnamese regime's debts, and Tokyo's refusal to grant reparations. In September 1975, Tokyo provided Hanoi with non-reimbursable aid and compromised regarding the debt problem in 1978.[54] Normalization with the Federal Republic of Germany in 1975 met with the same difficulties.[55] In dealing with Washington, Hanoi would cling to the aid issue, insisting that it should be linked to the normalization process, undermining its own position and credibility in ongoing diplomatic dialogue with both administrations and beyond.

The U.S. remained silent about the Vietnamese opening. On May 22, Pham Van Dong received a letter signed by twenty-seven U.S. representatives requesting that information on Vietnam War MIAs be given to Washington.[56] A week later, the State Department called on Hanoi to bear responsibility for MIAs.[57] The Pentagon listed as many as 965 missing in action (MIA) servicemen who had never returned from Vietnam and remained unaccounted for, while another 1,100 had legally been declared dead—killed in action (KIA)—but their bodies had never been recovered. The Joint Casualty Resolution Center, a military unit established after the signing of the Paris Accords to account for missing servicemen of both sides, had been greatly handicapped by the war, and operations had stalled after the murder of an American representative in 1973.[58] The end of the war, though, had brought renewed hope to attempts in the United States to account for its missing servicemen.

Compared to other wars of the twentieth century, American MIAs remain relatively few. For instance, an estimated 80,000 American soldiers who took part in World War II are still missing today and a further 8,000 U.S. servicemen are still unaccounted for from the Korean War, representing approximately 15 percent of the KIA in this conflict. France still numbers 20,000 MIAs from the French Indochinese conflict; and in the year 2000, Vietnam still numbered 300,000 Vietnamese as missing in action after the war with the United States—that is, more than 150 times more than Washington's initial total of MIAs and KIAs put together.[59] However, for no other war had the United States so firmly insisted on recovering its missing soldiers. The swelling of the Vietnam War–related MIA issue over the three decades that followed the end of the war may therefore appear puzzling.

Although accounting for MIAs was always an important issue for Washington during the war, it grew to surprising proportions in the aftermath of the fall of Saigon. Accounting for MIAs seemed to become an unconscious, redemptive and reconciliatory move towards reuniting a divided nation and healing its wounds after the first defeat in American history.

Pressure also came from the National League of Families of Prisoners and Missing in Southeast Asia, a lobby group supported by the Pentagon, but which, although strong during the Ford and Carter presidencies, only developed into a full-scale collaborator of the administration in the 1980s. By 1983, under Reagan, the League had become part of the decision-making process of the executive branch. Reagan promised the League's president, Ann Mills Griffith, that any decision regarding U.S. policies towards Vietnam and Cambodia would be made after complete clearance by the League and that the League would benefit from direct briefings from the NSC, the State Department and the Department of Defense.[60]

While American insistence on an accounting had always been an issue, especially since Nixon's emphasis on MIAs in May 1969 through his "go public" campaign, to justify the continuation of the war in the light of Hanoi's "inhumane" treatment of POWs and the MIA issue, the League increased its pressure on the administration after the war.[61] In turn, the Ford administration picked up on the issue, urged by both Congress and powerful lobbies, as a convenient pretext to counter Vietnamese calls for economic aid, to justify hostility towards Vietnam and to publicize the administration's concern for MIAs at election time. This issue, the most important theme in postwar bilateral relations, grew in importance during the Ford and Carter eras.

On June 3, during a National Assembly speech, Pham Van Dong reminded his audience of the American "criminal war of aggression," and repeated his offer to normalize relations with Washington in a rather moderate manner.[62] The tone of the appeal and the delay between the fall of Saigon and this first direct initiative hinted that the rapidity with which Hanoi had conquered the South had not allowed the drafting of the new regime's policies and that Hanoi preferred to reevaluate its position before opening up to Washington.[63] Dong nevertheless attached a precondition to normalization—that Washington "seriously implement" Article 21 of the Peace Agreement, which pledged postwar economic aid to North Vietnam. "On this basis and on the principle of equality and mutual advantage," he explained, "the Government of the Democratic Republic of Vietnam will normalize its relations with the United States ... and will settle other pending questions with them."[64] The next day, Nguyen Duy Trinh again stated that

Washington "must" fulfill its obligations, but also proposed talks to resolve "all the sequels of war concerning Vietnam and the United States."[65]

The State Department, at first refusing any immediate comment on Dong's declaration, angrily labeled the proposition as "ironic" since, in Washington's view, it was the Vietcong who had violated the Agreement in continuing the war.[66] This position, as Steven Hurst rightly emphasized, was highly disingenuous as recent sources now revealed that Saigon, backed by Nixon, was the initial violator of the cease-fire.[67] State Department spokesman Robert Anderson repeated that Washington had no intention of granting any direct economic aid to North Vietnam, had not and would not request congressional authorization for it, and noted that Congress had already introduced several amendments to foreign aid bills barring such aid on the grounds of Hanoi's violations of the Peace Accords, mainly on the issue of MIAs. Nevertheless, he refrained from calling the agreements void—a position that Washington adopted a few months later to further repel Vietnamese calls for cooperation, especially during the presidential election year of 1976.[68] Washington's vindictiveness would increase over the months as Hanoi increasingly pressed for bilateral contacts, in turn encouraging Vietnamese animosity toward Americans.

A few days after Dong's speech of June 3, Hanoi sent Washington another message via Moscow. Understanding American refusal to address the issue of reconstruction aid, the Vietnamese refrained from mentioning the question. Instead, the message repeated Hanoi's call for "good relations with the United States based on mutual respect" and stressed that, in delaying its final attack on Saigon to allow the American evacuation, Hanoi had proven its goodwill. "[T]here is no enmity toward the United States in Vietnam," said the Vietnamese who wished to "see the same from the American side as well."[69] "The United States side bears no hostility in principle toward the DRV side," responded Washington two days later. The U.S. was willing to "proceed on this basis in any relations between the two sides and is prepared to listen to any suggestions which the DRV side may wish to put forth."[70] But the next day Press Secretary Ron Nessen reiterated that Washington considered the Paris Agreement "moot," and the American claim that Hanoi had declined to allow the search for MIAs triggered Hanoi's anger. The Vietnamese accused the United States of "shirking of its own responsibility for the implementation of the [peace] agreement"[71] which constituted a "betrayal and violation of international law."[72]

Interestingly, while opening to Washington through back channels, Hanoi was simultaneously launching an attack on U.S. responsibilities in the postwar era. On June 10, in an indirect warning to Washington, *Hanoi Radio* explained that it is "precisely because the United States lacks a serious attitude and goodwill that the location of the Americans missing in action and the remains of the Americans who died in Vietnam could not make progress recently."[73] North Vietnamese Workers' Party daily *Nhan Dan*, in an article also broadcast on *Bangkok Radio* for widespread international syndication, added that in the absence of postwar economic aid to both North and South Vietnam, the U.S. would be refused the right to search for its 2,000 MIAs in Vietnam. The broadcast also reiterated Dong's request that Washington "seriously implement the spirit" of the Peace Agreements, and recalled America's "continued crimes" and "obligation" to fulfill its commitments under the Paris Agreement.[74] The first Vietnamese indication, in mid–March, that Hanoi would release information on MIAs had been tied to the resignation of President Nguyen Van Thieu and to the halting of Washington's military aid to South Vietnam. Hanoi was adapting its claims to the changing situation.

But these declarations also clearly indicated, for the first time, that Hanoi considered the issues of aid and MIAs linked, and hinted at the emergence of these two issues as tools for political blackmail in the forthcoming bilateral dialogue. This linking of MIAs with aid, which U.S. media often attributed solely to Hanoi, would in fact be used by both sides to extract concessions from their adversary.

The search for American MIAs, like reconstruction aid to North Vietnam, had been provided for in the 1973 Agreement—in Article 8b. The Vietnamese intended to prove that Washington's consideration of Article 21 as no longer valid also meant that Article 8b, on MIAs, was in jeopardy—highlighting the inherent contradiction within the American argument. The introduction of Article 8b as a diplomatic lever, for the first time clearly linking aid to the search for MIAs, was accompanied by a boastful but ill-considered reminder of the communist victory that did little to encourage American malleability. Following the Vietnamese broadcast, State Department spokesman Robert Funseth sneered that Hanoi's numerous violations of the Peace Agreement did not allow Washington to seriously consider Hanoi's position.[75] Faced with Hanoi's hard stance and the Vietnamese decision to prohibit MIA searches, Washington angrily declared the Agreement obsolete, as the State Department now repeatedly reminded the press. *Quan Doi Nhan Dan* immediately responded that Washington's denials that the Agreement was still valid were obvious "smacks of irresponsibility" demonstrating Washington's "frivolous" attitude.[76]

The recent *Mayaguez* incident proved a strong argument to Washington's claim of Vietnamese untrustworthiness with regard to peace agreements and international law. On May 12, the U.S. merchant ship *Mayaguez* and its thirty-nine-member crew were kidnapped by Cambodian forces off the coast of Cambodia and held for four days. The vessel and its crew were accused of conducting spying operations on Cambodia. But the United States had understood the capture of the ship as a Soviet-backed communist provocation to further discredit the United States in Southeast Asia following the collapse of the U.S.-backed regimes in Indochina a few days earlier. The crew was eventually freed during a disastrously orchestrated rescue operation costing the lives of forty-one Marines and wounding fifty more.[77]

"New regimes have come to power in Asia in the past few months," explained Kissinger to the Japanese Society in New York on June 18. "They have flouted international agreements and flagrantly violated accepted international standards, and that we cannot ignore."[78] Little did it bother Washington to associate the act of an independent Cambodian militia with the broad Indochinese and particularly Vietnamese official code of conduct for foreign policy. Washington was, therefore, both irritated and amused by Hanoi's call, in June 1975, for the postwar implementation of the Paris Peace Agreements.

Washington, continued the secretary of state with a clear reference to the Chinese fear of postwar Vietnamese expansionist ambitions in Southeast Asia, would "not turn away from Asia" and would continue to oppose any country's attempt to impose its dictum by way of military strength in the region.[79] As far as Washington was concerned, it could not possibly envisage making the first step toward political reconciliation and normalization with Indochina. However, Kissinger added that Washington was "prepared ... to look to the future. Our attitude towards them will be influenced by their attitude towards us."[80] Clearly, Washington did not refuse reconciliation altogether and was requesting Vietnamese demonstration of goodwill, friendliness and democratic intentions.

Three days later *Nhan Dan* sharply criticized Kissinger's "distorted allegations" and Washington's "neocolonialist" policy regarding Asia.[81] However, the Vietnamese were unwilling to give up what they saw as their right to obtain reparations. On June 21 Pham Van Dong answered the May 22 letter from the House of Representatives calling for information on MIAs, repeating that the issues of aid and the accounting for MIAs, according to the Paris Agreements, were linked and could not be separated. The "fulfillment of [Washington's] obligation to contribute to the healing of the wounds of war and to postwar reconstruction in the two zones of Vietnam," he further claimed, was the first step in creating "the conditions for the establishment of normal relations." However, he stressed that his people, "imbued with humanitarian feelings, deeply sympathize with the anxiety of the close relatives" of MIAs—a claim that may have seemed profoundly ironic in Washington considering Dong's previous arguments. Dong again expressed his hope to normalize diplomatic relations with the United States.[82]

Representative Richard Ottinger (Democrat, New York), in releasing the texts of both letters, expressed congressional disappointment in Dong's "unconscionable" reply, which he saw as a hindrance to future dialogue with Hanoi.[83] However, the visit of leading U.S. businessmen to Vietnam, such as the week-long visit, in June, of the vice-president of Bank of America to assess Vietnamese economic needs, may have comforted Vietnam in its belief in its own importance in the eyes of Washington. The United States, declared the enthusiastic American visitor almost certainly without executive branch backing, were more amenable to an American-Vietnamese rapprochement than their public references might show.[84]

The first months of "peace" were marked by the emergence of two opposing views as to the nature of future relations between the two sides. Vietnam portrayed normalization as a side-issue towards which both governments could move only after the granting of aid. Washington clung to its request for no preconditions to normalization while imposing its own precondition that only a satisfactory accounting of MIAs and dropping of the Vietnamese request for aid could lead to a breakthrough on normalization. As Representative Bingham remarked in September 1975, U.S. policy toward Hanoi was one of recrimination. Washington rejected Hanoi's offers of reconciliation and continued wartime hostility on a diplomatic level. Although the means and tactics of the dialogue varied—refusing shipments of aid to Vietnam in spring 1975, objecting to Vietnamese admission to the United Nations in 1975 and 1976 and finally by publicizing U.S. animosity and over-emphasizing the MIA issue in 1976 to promote Ford's chances for reelection—the essence of the exchange remained widely the same during the Ford administration.[85] The continued hostility would highlight the gap between Ford-Kissinger tactics and Carter's friendlier policies of early 1977, at least until Carter adopted a stronger stance against Hanoi in 1978, albeit for geopolitical reasons rather than for the vindictiveness that characterized the Ford years.

Hanoi and Saigon's Application for Membership to the United Nations

Saigon and Hanoi not only hoped for normalization with Washington but also for international recognition and cooperation. On May 7, the North Vietnamese government's membership of the United Nations' World Meteorological Organization was approved. But Hanoi was more interested in testing the Western world's present political climate than in sharing its views on meteorology. While in Geneva, North Vietnamese officials had also been negotiating the opening of Hanoi's first UN observer office with UN Secretary General Kurt Waldheim.[86] Hanoi knew that observer status at the UN would be a first step toward both North and South Vietnam's official admission to the organization as member states. Not only would this provide them with official access to international recognition as legitimate nation-states, but it would also make them eligible for economic aid through international relief organizations.

The following month, three members of the Vietnamese delegation to a World Conference on Women in Mexico City informed Waldheim that both North and South Vietnam would soon submit their application to join the United Nations, preferably before the next General Assembly session in September.[87] The applications were submitted separately the following month, Saigon's on July 15 and Hanoi's on July 17.[88]

Since the fall of Saigon, the PRG had already applied to several UN organizations to publicize its independence from Hanoi and had indicated, through Algeria, its interest in being considered for membership in the UN.[89] After refraining from opening observer missions, for fear this might jeopardize Vietnamese chances of admission as a full member, North and South Vietnam decided, following their applications, to reverse this policy.[90]

When North Vietnamese observers Nguyen Van Luu, Pham Duong, Pham Ngac, Nguyen Van Cau and Tran Van Van arrived in New York on July 30 and reiterated to the press Hanoi's wish to normalize with Washington, the crowd at the airport greeted them with both cheers and protests.[91] On July 8, Hanoi extended a friendly hand to Washington, signaling that it was ready to resume negotiations on all issues, including aid and MIAs.[92]

In order to increase its chances for international recognition and economic cooperation, and to signal that Hanoi still enjoyed its political independence from the Soviet Union and China, North Vietnam officially applied to Algerian president Houari Boumediene, at the end of July, for admission to the Non-Aligned Movement. South Vietnam had already been welcomed as a member state since the 1973 conference in Algiers and North Vietnam certainly hoped for sympathy in applying through Algeria. The tactic proved successful as North Vietnam became a full member in August during the movement's conference in Lima.[93] On August 17, in its first speech as a member state, Hanoi called on Washington to implement its share of the Paris Accords. "For the United States," explained Pham Van Dong, "with whom we are prepared, however, to normalize relations, this is a question of conscience, responsibility and honour which it can by no means elude."[94]

But it soon appeared that Washington had chosen to retaliate for Hanoi's recent provocative and boastful appeals for American implementation of the Peace Agreements and the granting of aid. U.S. ambassador to the United Nations Daniel Patrick Moynihan wrote to Kissinger regarding the stand Washington should adopt toward the Vietnamese applications and expressed the need to reestablish "order" in the post–Vietnam War American crisis of confidence:

> According as we act, the world system the United States established after the Second World War could commence to come apart altogether. Or by acting with courage and conviction on this issue America, as the President proposed in his Tulane speech, "can regain the sense of pride that existed before Vietnam." Here at the United Nations we can begin to regain the initiative in the quest for a stable and liberal world order.[95]

The secretary of state shared many of Moynihan's views, at least during the latter's service as ambassador to the UN, despite some personal animosity between the two men that would lead to Moynihan's resignation in February 1976.[96] Kissinger sided with the ambassador's approach to the Vietnamese issue and shared an inherent bitterness towards Vietnamese communists. Kissinger and Ford refused to undergo what they perceived as further humiliation from the Vietnamese, and backed Moynihan.[97] Reflecting on the position to adopt on the issue of the Vietnamese applications, Douglas Pike jotted down the following comment in his notes with striking soundness: "major problem is gone with the wind syndrome (forgetting the Vietnam war now that it is no longer an issue) ... essential to buy time, let dust settle, prevent deep freeze situation."[98]

Moynihan, a neoconservative with strong anticommunist beliefs, viewed Vietnam with an unsympathetic eye.[99] As he explains in his memoirs:

> The war was over, and in the end [the U.S. had] been utterly humiliated. The admission of the two new regimes would symbolize and confirm that, and also the end of the period in which the United States was *the* principal actor in world affairs, responsible for everything going on and for whatever changes were taking place; required to facilitate some and to prevent others; responsible for keeping order.[100]

In Moynihan's view—and that of the executive branch—the dual admission of the Vietnamese states should be countered for both ideological and geopolitical reasons. But issuing a veto against these countries' applications was out of the question. "For us to veto the admission of the Vietnams would be a calamity," Moynihan cabled the White House:

> We would be seen to act out of bitterness, blindness, weakness and fear. We would be seen not only to have lost the habit of victory, but in the process to have acquired the most pitiable stigmata of defeat. But there would be little pity. The overwhelming response would be contempt.[101]

The solution lay in finding an excuse that would justify a veto and save face in the eyes of the international community while continuing hostility towards Vietnam through alternative means and rejecting Hanoi's call for rapprochement and normalization—an approach that broadly applies to all bilateral contacts during the Ford years. While the records of this episode are still largely classified, and secondary writings are scarce, one can draw a relatively clear picture of the ensuing events, although certain areas will be further clarified when archival collections open.

On July 29, barely two weeks after the applications, South Korea notified Waldheim that it wished to renew its previous application, dormant since having been vetoed by the Soviet Union in 1949.[102] While the roots of this decision cannot be explored, it is undeniable that its timing was perfect for Washington.

During preliminary discussions on the Vietnamese applications, Washington immediately insisted that they be linked to that of South Korea in a "package proposal"—knowing that South Korean membership was not likely to be accepted.[103] Both the Soviet Union and China rejected this proposal.[104] In fact, several sources began hinting that Washington may have requested South Korea to renew its application to counter the Vietnamese applications and, indeed, the rapidity and vehemence with which the U.S. supported the South Koreans seemed to confirm this view.[105] Little did it matter that the International Court of Justice of May 28, 1948, prohibited the linking of the admission of a country to that of another, and stipulated that no conditions other than those of Article 4 of the UN Charter should be tied to a nation's admission to the United Nations.[106]

In a telegram to Kissinger in July, Moynihan had proposed to support both North and South Korea's applications, granted that "there is probably not now a sufficient number of votes available even to get the South Korean application inscribed on the Council agenda."[107] Eventually, Moynihan's wishful thinking proved correct, and South Korea was not accepted to the UN until sixteen years later, on September 17, 1991.

But in 1975, linking the Vietnamese and South Korean applications would give Washington a face-saving pretext with which to reject the Vietnamese admission. While the means of rejecting Vietnamese admission varied in the last year of the Ford presidency—albeit keeping the face-saving gap between official declarations and private intentions—the aim remained the same.

Nguyen Van Luu and Dinh Ba Thi, representing North and South Vietnam, respectively, issued a joint statement criticizing this American ploy.[108] They added, rather unceremoniously, however, that their offer of normalization with the United States was still valid, if negotiated within the terms of the Peace Agreements, and that both North and South Vietnam were prepared to discuss "all the questions which need an early solution," including those regarding MIAs.[109] "We have made the first step in showing our goodwill," explained Dinh Ba Thi, "with regard to the re-establishment of normal relations with the U.S. and eventually the friendship between the two people. We are now waiting for a responding move from the U.S. side."[110]

The next day, a 12–1 vote in the Security Council put Vietnamese membership applications on the UN agenda, but the South Korean application was officially rejected. In fact, the Council even opposed discussing South Korea's case—as Moynihan had expected. In response, Washington immediately announced that it would veto Vietnamese admissions, citing their excuse that since Vietnam was not unified it could not be accepted as a member state.[111]

In fact Washington's fear was legitimate since not only would the Vietnamese be accepted as member states, humiliating the United States, but Hanoi would hold two votes in the UN—one for each state.[112] However, to justify the ambiguity of this position, State Department spokesman Robert Anderson added that linking Hanoi and Saigon to South Korea—a U.S. ally—should not be interpreted as a willingness to alter the American refusal to normalize with the Vietnamese.[113] "Nobody believed the American excuse," scorned an American journalist, "not even the Americans themselves."[114] On August 8, Vietnamese observers issued an angry statement against Washington's "unreasonable attitude" and warned that if "the U.S. government deliberately continues its hostile policy ... it will have to bear full responsibility."[115]

On August 9, in an attempt to soften the American stance before UN consideration of the applications, Hanoi informed the State Department that it would soon return the bodies of three U.S. Air Force pilots shot down during the war and whose names the Vietnamese had disclosed to Senator Kennedy in April.[116] The timing of this revelation suggested that the Vietnamese were attempting to buy American friendliness with the remains of Uncle Sam's lost soldiers. But Washington did not welcome this declaration as Hanoi had expected. That day, the White House repeated that it would veto both North and South Vietnam's admissions.[117] This decision, charged *Saigon Giai Phong*, showed the Americans' "hatred toward the Vietnamese."[118]

Moynihan kept his word. On August 11, after cordially greeting Nguyen Van Luu and Dinh Ba Thi who had been allowed to attend the session, Moynihan vetoed the admission of both Vietnamese states despite their unanimous approval by the fourteen other voting countries.[119] In keeping with Washington's face-saving pretext to oppose the Vietnamese admissions, he explained this first American veto on a country's membership by blaming the Security Council for refusing to consider the South Korean application, which went against UN insistence on "universal membership."[120] "We must not apply partisan political tests to UN membership," he claimed—a phrase that, although intended to depict the Security Council's handling of the South Korean application, could also have applied to Washington's opposition to the Vietnamese admissions. A leak from the State Department hinted that the American veto might indeed have been intended "in part" to keep the two Vietnamese states from joining the organization.[121] Consequently on August 13, North Vietnam went back on its promise to release the three remains, labeling the American veto a "stupid move."[122] Further exchanges in September failed to convince the Vietnamese to review their position.[123] This first example of Vietnamese withdrawal of information on MIAs and its use of the issue to punish American actions remained a recurring and key pattern under Ford, under Carter, and well into the late 1990s.

In his memoirs Moynihan records his satisfaction that none of the violent retaliation he had feared from other member states occurred, despite a few angry speeches, especially from the two Vietnamese observers. "If anything," he proudly concludes, "the United Nations seemed to have been reminded of American power."[124]

"All fair-minded people," angrily retaliated Dinh Ba Thi and Nguyen Van Luu in a joint statement, can conclude that the aim of the United States is to deliberately prevent the admission of the RSVN and the DRVN to the United Nations. The question of South Korea only serves as a pretext to justify its actions." The United States' present "discrimination" against the Vietnamese states, they warned, could in the future be directed "against all other countries which victoriously fight against the U.S. neo-colonialist aggression."[125]

At the same time, the South Vietnamese foreign ministry vehemently condemned the U.S. action as "ugly" and "erroneous," stressing that Washington had "clearly revealed that it has not abandoned its policy of opposing the legitimate right to self-determination of various nations."[126] The following day, however, in a rather moderate declaration during a press conference, Nguyen Van Luu reiterated the wish of both Vietnamese states to normalize with Washington along the lines of the Paris Agreement.[127]

The General Assembly voted to "reconsider immediately and affirmatively" the

Vietnamese applications via the Security Council in September.[128] But on September 13, Ford declared that "Vietnam is attempting to bribe the U.S. into backing Hanoi's effort to enter the UN by offering information on Americans still listed as missing in action"[129] and that Hanoi may still be holding Americans hostage—the strongest accusation to date, which immediately hardened Hanoi's position and was rejected as "brazen fabrication."[130]

In the light of the approaching election, Ford raised the issue of MIAs, which had stirred such controversy on the domestic scene, and transposed it from the bilateral to the international arena for self-serving purposes. While his concern for MIAs remained more electoral than genuine, the issue remained at the forefront of the bilateral dialogue and of the UN stage until the end of his presidency, justifying continued U.S. hostility towards Vietnam and promoting domestic support for Ford's policy. The attempt to de-emphasize the issue and shrink U.S. anger back to reasonable proportions fell on Carter in 1977, at a time when Vietnam was less willing to accept American overtures.

In turn, the PRG foreign ministry threatened that Washington's refusal to provide aid, the trade embargo and the veto had "created obstacles to the normalization of relations between Vietnam and the United States and to the implementation of some outstanding provisions of the Paris Agreement, including the problems of U.S. killed or missing in action."[131] This threat not only demonstrated that Hanoi was prepared to use the MIA issue to promote its own interests and to bargain for U.S. concessions, but also confirmed Ford's accusations on September 13 that Hanoi sought to "bribe" Washington with the issue of MIAs. Clearly, Vietnam was undermining its own interests, fuelling the hostility of both the U.S. executive branch, and American public opinion.

Meanwhile, seeing that U.S. aid would not be easily obtained, Hanoi sent a delegation headed by Deputy-Premier Le Thanh Nghi to Peking to discuss terms for an economic agreement for the reconstruction of North Vietnam—announcing the recurring pattern, under Carter, of Vietnam's counterbalancing overtures to Washington with friendly visits to the communist powers, aimed at reaping the benefits of both worlds while exploiting East-West and Sino-Soviet tensions to Vietnamese advantage.[132]

The delegation received a cool welcome from Le Thanh Nghi's Chinese counterpart Li Hsien-nien, and the Chinese press preferred to focus on the upcoming visit of a Cambodian delegation rather than on the Vietnamese guests.[133] The Chinese leadership did not agree to grant aid, claiming that Peking had also encountered economic difficulties and could offer no help at present.[134] Nor did the Chinese endorse the Vietnamese statements against Washington so as not to jeopardize chances for Sino-American rapprochement. Although the Vietnamese press described the visit in positive terms with no reference to the Chinese change of mood, Hanoi rapidly understood that no aid would be obtained.[135] The Vietnamese delegation then left Peking for Moscow where Soviet aid to Vietnam for 1976 was discussed along the lines of the USSR-DRV aid agreement of 1972.[136]

The coolness of the Chinese welcome was the latest in a series of signs of the increasingly wavering relationship between the two communist neighbors. Following the end of the Vietnam War China had failed to obtain Vietnamese friendship in return for Chinese support during the war, and Peking now found itself competing for regional influence with its former protégé. "More than the United States," writes Nayan Chanda, "it was China who lost the war."[137] With two avowedly pro–Soviet states now on its frontiers (Afghanistan and Mongolia), and two more slowly tilting towards Moscow (Vietnam and Laos), Peking was becoming increasingly nervous.

In 1940, Ho Chi Minh had proclaimed that the Vietnamese "have only two real allies in whose successes [they] can rejoice: the Soviet Red Army, and the Chinese Red Army," placing the Soviet Union and China on an equal footing regarding Vietnamese friendship.[138] During the Vietnam War, both Moscow and Peking had supported their communist friends, shipping food, ammunitions and commodities and supporting the nationalist struggle of the North Vietnamese with generous economic grants and loans. Soviet aid amounted to 80 percent of Hanoi's war expenses in the late 1960s, amounting to $500 million per annum. China's economy could not compete with Soviet generosity; Chinese aid reached only $300 million, mainly in rice and other commodities.[139] Although during the early to mid–1960s Vietnam had attempted to minimize the dispute and, failing to do so, had cleverly exploited it to obtain advantages from both sides, the Sino-Soviet split had finally opened a rift between Vietnam and its benefactors—each asking Hanoi to take sides—until, as the South fell to communist hands, the two powers impatiently urged Vietnam to make a decision.[140]

By then, Peking had redefined Moscow as its "most dangerous and most important enemy."[141] After supporting Vietnamese revolutionaries for more than fifteen years, Peking was growing uneasy over the prospect of their victory and of the new balance of power it would produce in Asia. The end of the war would mean a decrease in Chinese influence on Vietnam, which would no longer require as much military or economic support and would thrive on its own political and economic independence. In Kissinger's words, China "now has 40 million Vietnamese on its border who do not exactly suffer from lack of confidence in themselves."[142]

Although Moscow, in the early 1960s, had remained rather timid in its support of Vietnam, it had opted by 1970 for rapprochement with Vietnam and an endorsement of the Vietnamese cause, at a time of growing Sino-Vietnamese discord over the handling of the peace negotiations.[143] The Soviet Union, whose eastern territory covered most of northern Asia, considered itself entitled to play a role in Asian affairs, and despite Southeast Asian warnings against Soviet neocolonialist ambitions, certainly cherished the hope of an alliance with Hanoi, which would give it a foothold in the region.[144]

If the Vietnamese tilt towards Moscow had not yet become official, it is clear that by the mid–1960s Hanoi favored Moscow over Peking, a partiality that developed over the years until the signing of the Soviet-Vietnamese Treaty of Friendship and Cooperation in November 1978.[145] Explaining such a tilt remains a complex exercise even in the light of recent studies. In Douglas Pike's words this rapprochement was "born more of circumstance than of choice, at least, as far as the Vietnamese were concerned, and the direct product of the unanticipated traumatic condition that descended on Indochina at war's end."[146]

China and Vietnam had slowly grown apart over the last few years of the Vietnam war and, as Deng Xiaoping acknowledged in 1977, while the war had brought the two communist parties into a marriage of convenience, the peace had eroded the superficiality of their fragile friendship, bursting into a large-scale military conflict between the two countries in early 1979.[147] Among the reasons for Hanoi's shunning of Peking were historical animosities between Vietnam and China, Peking's rapprochement with Cambodia, its progressive cutting of economic aid to Vietnam and its patronizing impatience at Vietnamese "ungratefulness" for Chinese support during the Vietnam War. This global reshuffling of alliances and ambitions led to the birth of a new political order in Southeast Asia in the late 1970s whose first signs appeared in 1975.

Neither Chinese sulkiness nor American demonstration of political strength at the UN crushed the Vietnamese sense of pride. "Nothing is more important than independence and freedom" proclaimed a banner across the front of Thieu's former palace.[148] A similar banner bearing the same slogan had also been placed at the entrance of the Tan Son Nhut airport from where the Americans had organized their evacuation until the bombing of the airport by Vietcong troops on April 28.[149] "There are no more sharks in the sea, no more beasts on earth; the sky is serene," quoted a high ranking North Vietnamese official at the end of the war; a XVth century Vietnamese saying which initially celebrated the withdrawal from Vietnam of the last Ming invaders "Now is the time to build peace for ten thousand years."[150]

A "War Crimes Exhibition" opened in Saigon displaying a wide range of examples of the "U.S. war against nature"—interestingly however, not a "U.S. war against Vietnam or its people." Figures and statistics presented by the PRG referred solely to the destruction of plantations, orchards and forests, and refrained from mentioning human and material losses.[151] It seemed as though Vietnam, while showing it had suffered from the war, did not wish to launch what could be seen by Washington as provocative criticism of the "American aggression."

On September 2, while Vietnamese officials and their Laotian, Cambodian, Chinese and Soviet guests were admiring the festivities and military parade of the thirtieth anniversary of the Vietnamese declaration of independence, Pham Van Dong's anniversary speech repeated Hanoi's readiness to normalize with the United States.[152] Beyond a reiteration of the Vietnamese stance, Dong's comment reminded the Soviet and Chinese delegations that Hanoi wished to maintain the independence they had cherished for thirty years, and to seek new friends wherever these might be found—even among former enemies.[153] But neither Moscow nor Peking was willing to accept the concept of Vietnamese independence and urged Hanoi to take sides in the divorce of the two communist giants. Chinese Vice-Premier Deng's speech for Vietnamese National Day reminded Vietnam that "superpower contention for world hegemony" could jeopardize peace and security. *Moscow Radio* later sneered that Peking was again trying to sell its "notorious superpower thesis" although "the Vietnamese people clearly know the difference between friend and foe" and were aware of the Soviet Union's "invaluable and unselfish support."[154] But if relative independence was still possible in 1975, Hanoi would eventually have to take sides in the ideological divorce of the two communist giants.

On September 19, after a large campaign for the reconsideration of the Vietnamese applications for UN membership launched by Algeria, China and the Soviet Union, the General Assembly voted (123–0–8) that the applications return to the Security Council for further consideration.[155] The General Assembly, and the 65 nations that had supported the Vietnamese memberships, recommended a positive settlement of the affair. In the meantime, in the light of the intensity of the debate surrounding its own application, South Korea had notified that it would not reapply for membership during the next session, thus depriving Washington of its argument for dual admission of South Korea and the Vietnamese states.[156]

However, Washington retained the same position. The United States refrained from voting, again claiming that it would reject a UN show of "selective universality" supporting one country while "unhappily ... there are those fully qualified whose admission is being denied for political motives."[157]

In his speech to the Assembly, Dinh Ba Thi explained that although the Vietnamese would welcome diplomatic rapprochement with Washington, American hostility had never ceased. He insisted that Washington had stopped private organizations from shipping humanitarian aid to the Vietnamese states. Moynihan immediately denied these accusations and claimed that no law prohibiting private humanitarian assistance existed in American legislation.[158] The series of bans imposed by the executive branch in May and June 1975 suggested that if American legislation did not ban humanitarian aid, the executive's policies represented an indirect impediment to their shipment.

Two weeks later, during a news conference in New York, representatives of the American Friends Committee, the Church World Service, and the Bach Mai Hospital Relief Fund officially announced, in the presence of Nguyen Van Luu, the launching of operation "Friendshipment" through which one million dollars' worth of assistance and material would be sent to the Vietnamese states.[159] The announcement, certainly made in defiance of the administration after an initial application to send aid had been rejected in early summer, tested the U.S. Ambassador's word. Some American Friends Committee officials, seeing that their requests to send aid to Vietnam had been rejected, had warned two months earlier that they would defy the congressional ban on assistance to Vietnam and risk jail if need be.[160] It seemed as though Dinh Ba Thi's recent accusations at the UN had opened a loophole in the congressional ban allowing these institutions to proceed with their assistance to Indochina. By mid–November, cornered by Dinh Ba Thi's accusations and pressure from the Subcommittee on International Trade and Commerce, the administration granted licenses for these shipments.[161]

Meanwhile, VWP secretary-general Le Duan headed a new delegation to Peking—the most important Hanoi had sent abroad—where he received a relatively cold welcome.[162] Le Duan's visit, only a month after that of Le Thanh Nghi, proved that the Vietnamese were concerned about the cooling Chinese mood and felt the need to mend breaches with Peking. Two high-level Vietnamese trips to China in barely five weeks were no doubt intended to flatter the Chinese.[163]

Peking had termed the Vietnamese reluctance to follow its ideological and political lead as Vietnamese "ungratefulness" in the light of past Chinese sacrifices and support for the Vietnamese liberation struggle. Nothing short of a complete endorsement of Chinese international views could prove Vietnam's goodwill in honoring its debts to Peking.[164] "The threat from the North [from China] is the main theme [in Vietnamese declarations]," Deng Xiaoping complained to Le Duan. "We are not at ease with this," he continued, emphasizing that the "threat from the North for us is the existence of Soviet troops at our northern borders."[165] The Chinese also may have been angered by Moscow's pledge, during Soviet premier Mikhail Solomentsev's visit to Hanoi in early September, to support Vietnamese efforts toward reconstruction.[166]

However, during a banquet speech, Le Duan notified his hosts that the Vietnamese would not deviate from their desire for an independent Vietnam. Hanoi and Saigon would maintain good relations with both camps despite Peking's constant warnings against Moscow.[167] Clearly China no longer wished to compete with the Soviet Union to obtain Hanoi's friendship as it had during the war; and while Moscow continued to woo Hanoi with economic aid, China had switched to the more passive attitude of warning Hanoi that Peking would not tolerate Soviet influence on Vietnam. The two countries failed to issue a joint communiqué, possibly due to Vietnamese refusal to include an antihegemony clause and jeopardize prospects of improved relations with Moscow, and the Chinese press remained silent on the outcome of the talks.[168]

However, Vietnam was given an interest-free loan and an annual agreement was signed for a mutual supply of goods representing $200 million—remarkably little compared to Vietnam's postwar needs. However, Chinese aid no longer came as gratis economic support but as a loan—the last aid agreement signed between these two countries during the 1970s.[169] Although China would continue to implement its past pledges of support to Vietnam—even if only partially—until mid-1978, the Vietnamese had certainly expected more. "Today, you are not the poorest under heaven," Mao lectured Le Duan on September 24. "We are the poorest. We have a population of 800 million. Our leadership is now facing a crisis," and he pointed at his and Zhou Enlai's ill health for greater emphasis.[170] China had "made a tremendous effort," said the weak Zhou Enlai as Le Duan visited him at his hospital bed. "At present our aid to Vietnam still ranks first among our aid to foreign countries. You should let us have a respite and regain strength."[171]

The previous month, however, Zhou had given a Cambodian delegation a $1 billion interest-free loan with a $20 million gift to fill Phnom Penh's external trade deficit.[172] At the end of the Cambodian trip a joint communiqué had claimed both countries' opposition to "contention for world hegemony between the superpowers," in a direct attack on Moscow.[173] China's former interest in Vietnam had begun tilting toward the new Cambodian regime with which Peking shared common—mainly anti-Soviet—ideologies, but remained uncertain until the end of 1977.[174]

In contrast, the Soviet Union seemed to be quite pleased with the Sino-Vietnamese cooling of relations. The day after Le Duan's banquet speech, Soviet foreign minister Andrei Gromyko himself appeared at the UN General Assembly and urged the member states to support the Vietnamese application.[175]

Three days after Gromyko's speech, in a message to the UN Security Council, Moynihan declared that the U.S. would again veto admission of the Vietnamese states, as South Korea's application had still not been accepted. Washington, he explained, "must insist that all three applicants be treated equally":

> It is not my government's desire in any way to stand in the way of the admission of the Democratic Republic of Viet-Nam and the Republic of South Viet-Nam but my government will continue to support in every feasible way the Republic of Korea's desire to participate as a member in the United Nations.[176]

Similar to the American warning, Chinese foreign minister Chiao Kuan-hua issued an oblique attack against Hanoi's foreign policies after the war, expressing his trust that the Southeast Asian nations would know better than to "let the tiger in through the back door [the Soviet Union] while repulsing the wolf through the front gate [the American defeat in Indochina]"—clearly an open attack on Vietnam's unclear opening to the

Soviet Union.[177] While Sino-American friendship had not yet developed by the end of 1975, the two countries were beginning to share similar views on such topics as mistrust towards the Vietnamese.

On September 30, the U.S. again vetoed the Vietnamese applications during the Security Council vote on the grounds that the Council had refused to even consider South Korea's application.[178] Hanoi had no doubt that the veto had stemmed from the past American humiliation in Indochina and represented a diplomatic continuation of the war. Dinh Ba Thi expressed Hanoi's anger:

> [T]he United States is obviously continuing its hostile policy started decades ago against the Vietnamese people. It is now preventing the Vietnamese people from occupying their rightful place and making their voice heard in the United Nations, just as in the past it tried by every means to deny them their fundamental national rights and their right to self-determination. [179]

On September 30, Dinh Ba Thi and Nguyen Van Luu furthered their attack on the U.S. in a letter to the UN General Assembly stressing that the U.S. "policy of hostility is the sole cause for the deadlock on other problems outstanding between the United States and Vietnam."[180] The statement went beyond its sharp condemnation of the first veto and charged that "whenever the United States needs a pretext to oppose Vietnam's entry into the United Nations, South Korea, on U.S. orders renews its UN application."[181] The veto also stirred a wave of protests from member states that called on Washington to respect UN resolutions and to withdraw the "tyranny" of its veto.[182]

In late October, Le Duan traveled to the Soviet Union. His visit, echoing his trip to China the previous month, signaled Hanoi's wish to maintain diplomatic equilibrium over the Sino-Soviet split, spending as much time with one party as with the other, while prodding both for aid.[183] The warm and cordial welcome he received in Moscow, in contrast with China's coolness and U.S. open diplomatic hostility in the UN, certainly surprised the Vietnamese.[184]

In the final communiqué, Le Duan endorsed Soviet support for world détente, which the Chinese had long dismissed as a Soviet ploy to gain world domination, possibly to punish Peking for its cold reception in September.[185] Le Duan also expressed his support for the Helsinki Conference on European Security, which had dealt with the acceptance of existing borders, and declared that the conference had achieved "very significant" and "positive results" for Europe.[186] Le Duan's remark angered the Chinese who had sarcastically termed the Helsinki Conference "the conference on insecurity," and warned that the "'Materialization of Relaxation' Means Intensifying War Preparation."[187]

Le Duan, however, refrained from endorsing the Soviet view that the Chinese be expelled from Communist International. Likewise, Vietnam refused Moscow's invitation to join COMECON as a full member, although an observer Vietnamese delegation had attended the COMECON meeting in May. In exchange, Moscow promised to "lend money to Vietnam with the most-favored nation clause" through two aid agreements; to coordinate the two countries' development plans; and to train Vietnamese technicians in various fields of science, technology, culture and economics.[188]

According to a CIA report, the Vietnamese received "unusually warm Soviet praise."[189] During his visit Le Duan even issued a private statement saying he would remain in Moscow "for a short rest" probably to signal to Peking that the Vietnamese would not side with the constant Chinese criticism of the Soviet Union and would welcome economic and material support wherever found, even in Moscow.[190] Two months later Moscow furthered this move by signing the first postwar aid agreement, pledging to fund 60 percent of Vietnam's 1976–1980 economic plan—representing a $2.1 to $3 billion contribution.[191] However, the Vietnamese show of independence failed when, on November 7, Soviet defense minister Marshal Andrei Grechko delivered a speech at the Lenin Mausoleum, in Le Duan's presence, which caused the Chinese ambassador to walk out.[192] Chinese representatives in Hong Kong began speaking of a North Vietnamese tilt towards Moscow.[193]

By the end of 1975, Washington understood that bilateral relations could be exploited to enable the release of information on MIAs, which, if negotiated successfully, would prove an invaluable boost to Ford's electoral campaign in 1976. After the fall of Saigon, the Ford administration sought to redeem its past errors by recovering its lost soldiers and closing the haunted book of 'Nam.'

Along with tense relations with Vietnam, Ford was experiencing national discontent. He reorganized his administration at the end of October. He replaced James Schlesinger with Donald Rumsfeld, appointed George H.W. Bush to replace Colby at the head of the CIA, and removed Kissinger from the chairmanships of the NSC and the "Forty Committee" that controlled all of Washington's clandestine operations.[194] Ford was also experiencing increasing difficulties with Congress. The end of the war, he claimed, had made Capitol Hill "more rebellious, more assertive of its rights and privileges"—"more irresponsible" he added, as if an afterthought.[195]

Amongst what the President viewed as congressional acts of "irresponsibility" was the softening, starting in the fall of 1975, of congressional hostility towards Vietnam and its Indochinese neighbors. House members began calling for an easing of humanitarian and other non-strategic trade restrictions as a first step towards levering Vietnamese cooperation in accounting for MIAs. It also urged the administration to open talks on the limitation of American and Soviet presence in the Indian Ocean.[196] In 1976, the State Department eventually supported a number of congressional delegations seeking to negotiate with the Vietnamese.

Sensing that the upcoming elections and the congressional awakening might encourage diplomatic dialogue, Hanoi made an unexpected goodwill gesture to show the U.S. that it might benefit from bilateral cooperation. Softening its previous claim that aid was a precondition to any negotiations, Hanoi declared, on October 30, that a group of nine Americans captured in March 1975 would be released.[197] Furthermore, it announced that searches would be carried out for MIAs. The remains of three pilots, promised in April and August, would be returned along with information on two Marines killed during the evacuation of Saigon. Although the Vietnamese had originally mentioned these three MIAs to the U.S. on April 22, 1975, Hanoi had preferred to postpone their release until December hoping that the delay in the release of information would allow greater diplomatic leverage on Washington.[198]

Washington's response to Hanoi's volunteering of information was immediate although limited in scope. On November 14, the newly created House of Representatives Select Committee on Missing Persons in Southeast Asia, led by Congressman Gillespie "Sonny" Montgomery (Democrat, Mississippi), met with Kissinger. The secretary of state announced that Washington would allow private humanitarian aid to Vietnam. Since May, Senator Bingham, Head of the House of Representatives Subcommittee on International Trade and Commerce, had insisted that the United States not oppose humanitarian aid to Vietnam so as not to suppress the possibility of bilateral dialogue. After several months of "wait-and-see" policy and close scrutiny of Vietnamese diplomatic moves, Washington understood that its interests lay in showing signs of a thaw. "We assume this will be taken as a sign of goodwill," Kissinger confided to Montgomery's Select Committee.[199]

The State Department notified Senator Bingham that it would now allow the shipment of aid of the American Friends Service Committee, after having denied it authorization for five months. The authorization, declared the State Department, "takes into account the North Vietnamese release of nine American prisoners who had been captured during the Spring 1975 offensive" although the State Department remained concerned about the fate of fifty more Americans remaining in Saigon "many of whom ... have not yet been permitted to leave by the Vietnamese." Future applications for humanitarian shipments would be considered "on a case-by-case basis, taking into account the nature of the assistance, the current laws, regulations and policies, and the attitudes and actions of the Vietnamese towards us and towards their neighbors."[200]

The State Department, probably fearing that public opinion might view this gesture as a weakening of Washington's stance, issued a statement stressing the reciprocity of this move.[201] Vietnamese goodwill, stressed Kissinger, would signal the "commendable beginning" of American flexibility.[202] Kissinger repeated Washington's position that normalization not be tied to the "dead" Paris agreement, or aid.[203] On Christmas day, the State Department approved humanitarian programs of the Mennonite Committee and the Bach Mai Hospital Fund. Similar small-scale gestures were repeated in early 1976.[204]

Washington's shift to less hostile policies certainly came as a response to congressional pressure. Hostility encourages hostility, as Senator Bingham had repeatedly remarked and several voices in the legislative branch had risen to denounce the counterproductive strategy of U.S. hostile policies towards the Vietnamese. The creation of the House Select Committee on Missing Persons in Southeast Asia on September 11, 1975, set up by a 394–3 vote, and co-sponsored by 280 representatives, had demonstrated Congress' interest in opening a dialogue with Hanoi to account for missing servicemen from the Indochina War and to assess the executive branch's efforts on the issue of MIAs.[205] Faced with this powerful congressional pressure and skepticism as to the effectiveness of its policies, the White House shifted to softer stands, hoping to demonstrate that the executive branch shared congressional concerns for MIAs. Over the next few months, Montgomery would become the main congressional figure at the helm of U.S.-Vietnamese relations, even after the dissolution of the House Committee in the first weeks of 1977.

Congressman Montgomery's House Select Committee was appointed for fifteen months to hold an investigation on missing U.S. military personnel and civilians, and aimed at "gaining as full an accounting as possible [on MIAs] from former enemies; and *assessing the efforts of the Departments of State and Defense* with respect to the problems associated with missing Americans."[206] The wording of the Committee's goals highlighted the congressional feeling that the executive had not done its utmost to encourage the release of information on MIAs from Hanoi.

The Vietnamese welcomed the creation of the Committee but insisted that it should not represent "an instrument of the Secretary of State" if it was to be "effective" and should not confine the dialogue purely to MIAs.[207] Eventually, the creation of this Committee would counter the void left by the absence of recognition between the two countries that had left little opportunity for diplomatic dialogue. The Committee became an important lobby in the developing of U.S. diplomatic relations with the new Indochinese states.

During his meeting with the Montgomery Committee on November 14, Kissinger heard the congressmen's views on U.S. relations with Hanoi, and briefed them on new White House policies. Kissinger explained to Committee members that:

> As far as we are concerned there is no reason not to normalize but we want to do it without being blackmailed.... We have no permanent hostility to Vietnam. The logic of events will force Vietnam to normalize relations with the U.S. to balance the Soviets and the Chinese, so it is inevitable that our relations would improve.... If it weren't for the MIA issue the U.S. could wait them out ... [and] substantial normalization would come within 2–3 years.... The MIAs are a lever they have, and the more anxious we appear the more they'll turn the knife ... and dangle it as a form of blackmail. However, we are ready to reciprocate if they do anything positive ... there is now a possibility of normalization of relations.[208]

Montgomery, a former Vietnam hawk, was strikingly sympathetic to the Vietnamese.[209] He stressed that Kissinger could see "no obstacle" to the issue if normalization were not based on the Paris Peace Agreement, which he once again dismissed as "dead." "The Secretary voiced no objection to the Committee's proposed discussions with the Vietnamese," reported Montgomery. "[H]e suggested that it would be more effective to discuss the MIA issue in the context of normalization rather than in a framework of the Paris Accords, which the North Vietnamese had violated."[210] Kissinger told the Committee members:

> The North Vietnamese have no humanitarian feelings and will try to use the Committee's overtures for whatever ends they can generate for themselves ... I consider the Vietnamese the most bloody-minded bastards I ever dealt with. Of all great powers we are the least dangerous to the Vietnamese, the least threatening to them, the most disinterested party they can deal with.[211]

In avoiding discussion of the Paris Accords, Washington would indicate that North Vietnam would be given no direct aid in exchange for MIAs, which the Vietnamese repeatedly requested by linking together Articles 8 and 21 of the Agreement, and that the MIA issue was independent, strictly unrelated to any other. This approach, and the American declaration that the agreement was now "dead," meant that Hanoi no longer had any right to claim American reparations.

However, the American logic of refusing to implement its responsibilities per the Paris Peace Accords, while calling on the other side to fulfill its humanitarian obligations as listed in the same document, represented an awkward negotiation tactic, as perceived by several members of Capitol Hill. "This counterproductive position," remarked Senator McGovern a few months later, "reflects the administration's consistent and short-sighted posture of active hostility toward Vietnam."[212]

Intrigued by Vietnamese insistence on economic aid, representative Henry Gonzalez (Democrat, Texas) inquired whether "any side memorandums, any codicils, any letters or missals or writings or verbal understanding ... [existed that had] not been disclosed." Kissinger's answer, in Gonzalez' words, was "categorically no, plus the assurance that he had on his appearances before the pertinent Committees said everything"—a claim that eventually proved untrue.[213] Kissinger added:

> We were originally prepared to discuss economic aid.... But the Congress was against it at the time when it would have done us some good.... I believe it would be possible to discuss aid in its own merits—but not on the basis of the Agreement they massively violated.... I must say I gag at the thought of economic aid to Vietnam, but if that is what the Congress wants, we'd go along.[214]

By late 1975 Kissinger's involvement in the writing of a secret letter from Nixon to Pham Van Dong in February 1973 promising several billion dollars in reconstruction aid to Vietnam, behind the back of Congress, had not yet become public. The Committee members could therefore not have grasped the full disingenuousness and irony of this latter remark.

Montgomery announced that the Committee would seek to meet North Vietnamese officials in North Vietnam and Paris[215]—a move Kissinger had given his full blessing, stressing that "friendly and reciprocal gestures might be effective in creating a climate in which an accounting could take place."[216] The executive branch, adopting a softer line on Vietnam to demonstrate its concern over MIAs, assured Montgomery of its support, if only grudgingly. This Congressional impetus would breach the executive's hostility toward Vietnam and open a dialogue that Ford and Kissinger had sought to keep shut.

In response, the Vietnamese demonstrated their goodwill by accepting more than 1,600 South Vietnamese refugees who had fled Vietnam during the collapse of the Saigon regime and who now wished to return to their homeland.[217] Three weeks earlier Hanoi and Saigon had severely criticized the U.S. for planning to send these refugees back to Vietnam, but American agreement to discuss normalization had inhibited Vietnamese opposition to the return of the refugees.[218]

On November 21, during a news conference of the *Vietnam News Agency*, broadcast in Tokyo, South Vietnamese foreign minister Mrs. Nguyen Thi Binh further encouraged the recent American softening.[219] She stressed that although Hanoi would welcome normalization, the outcome depended on Washington's "giv[ing] up [of] its hostile attitude."[220]

The State Department kept to its promise of a softened stance on Vietnam. On November 24, as if in a direct reply to Mrs. Binh, Kissinger indicated in a speech, at the Economic Club in Detroit, a readiness to "reciprocate" should Hanoi respond to U.S. concerns:

> This Administration inherited the conflict in Indochina and brought our involvement to an end. That chapter in our history is now closed.... As for our relations with the new governments in that region, these will not be determined by the past; we are prepared to look to a more hopeful future ... [and will] respond to gestures of good will.

Washington did not wish "to continue the Indochina war on the diplomatic front."[221] Normalization, concluded the American press, was now a true possibility. Hanoi remained silent on Kissinger's declarations, noted the State Department.[222]

Several congressional initiatives aimed at bilateral rapprochement at a time when the executive branch was attempting to overcome the difficulties of dealing with this issue.

This congressional trend, which had started with Representative Bingham's declarations in spring 1975, continued via various congressmen, mainly Democrats.

On November 17, Senator Kennedy sent a letter to Nguyen Duy Trinh stressing his concern over the MIA issue, also stating his intention to request the sending of agricultural, medical and technical experts to Vietnam. Kennedy even openly declared his support for the granting of aid to Hanoi. "I am hopeful," he wrote, "that the United States will actively facilitate and support these efforts [international humanitarian programs], and contribute meaningfully toward healing the wounds of war."[223]

Trinh replied on December 19 by welcoming Kennedy's position on aid and stressed that he would "attend favorably" to the sending of American experts to Vietnam. He also announced that the remains of two U.S. servicemen killed during the bombing of Tan Son Nhut airport in April 1975 had been identified and would soon be handed over to the U.S. government.[224] As for Vietnamese insistence on aid, Trinh's letter—in Pike's words—"seemed to show some restraint on the issue."[225] Similarly, in responding to two letters from Montgomery, Trinh stressed on February 25, 1976, that "the United States must take similar attitude [of goodwill] if favorable conditions are to be created" for normalization, but made no mention of aid.[226]

On December 6, Montgomery and eleven congressmen, including eight members of his Committee, met North Vietnamese ambassador to France Vo Van Sung and PRG chargé d'affaires Huynh Thanh in Paris. Talks were held on the fate of the 820 American servicemen still unaccounted for and on "other matters interesting both parties," including the trade embargo and aid. Discussing normalization with a former enemy was very delicate only eleven months before U.S. elections, and *"other matters"* was a discreet term—a way of tackling the issue when under public scrutiny.[227] Congress had demonstrated its interest in these meetings by dispatching, along with the Select Committee, several congressmen from other Committees, demonstrating that it was ready to discuss issues other than that of the MIAs, as the Vietnamese had repeatedly requested.[228]

Hanoi understood that its chance for rapprochement with Washington lay with Montgomery's Committee. Vo Van Sung told the American delegation that no POWs remained in Vietnam and that, in a joint effort, both North and South Vietnam were gathering information on MIAs.[229] Montgomery asked about two Marines who had perished under rocket-fire on the last day of the war and whose bodies had been left behind in the havoc of the evacuation.

In order to prove Vietnamese trustworthiness, Sung announced that the remains of three U.S. pilots would be returned in a matter of days, insisting that they be handed to the Committee itself.[230] Montgomery reported that Hanoi "had no objections to other American members of Congress coming to Hanoi."[231] "The DRV has clearly decided ... to give the Select Committee maximum involvement in the return of the remains," noted the U.S. ambassador to Paris in his report to Kissinger—possibly to attempt a breakthrough with the legislature at a time when the executive remained unmotivated.[232] Although the Vietnamese emphasized that issues such as aid remained unsolved, they stressed that Hanoi would welcome "normal and even friendly relations" with Washington.

"[B]oth groups," reported Montgomery, "alluded to a bridge of understanding that might be built if each side reciprocated to gestures made by the other." By agreeing to the release of the remains of the three U.S. pilots, he added, the "Vietnamese [have] committed themselves to constructing the first plank of the bridge."[233]

The American delegation seemed pleased. So did Sung, who termed the meetings a "success."[234] Reporting on his exchange with the Vietnamese, Gareth Porter, a member of the Indochina Resource Center in Washington who worked with the House Select Committee on issues touching upon MIAs, remarked that they "have made great efforts and shown gestures of good will on the question of American MIAs."[235] "If only our government could communicate as well as the Ambassador and the congressmen," observed Montgomery after the meetings, "we would have some real action."[236]

Meanwhile, in early December, Ford set out to tour the Pacific. In addition to leveraging popular domestic support for his candidacy for presidential reelection the following year, the tour also aimed at reaffirming U.S. interest in the Asia-Pacific region. During a stopover in Honolulu, Ford described his "new Pacific Doctrine,"[237] pledging growing U.S. ties with the Far East and announcing that the "preservation of the sovereignty and independence of our Asian friends and allies remains a paramount objective of American policy."[238]

Ford's Pacific doctrine reassessed American objectives and announced a plan to rearrange U.S. forces in the Pacific. By late 1975, Washington was multiplying negotiations for bases in Thailand and the Philippines as well as upgrading the American military presence in Japan, which led *Hanoi Radio* to call Japan an American "assault soldier," reaching a total of 96 U.S. bases in Asia in the mid–1970s.[239] The Vietnamese saw the Pacific doctrine as a "substitute" for Nixon's doctrine in Asia and sneered that Washington was presenting an "old reactionary doctrine" for a "new weak situation."[240]

But this strategy was meant to reorganize U.S. strength in the area after the loss of the American-backed Saigon regime, to prove to the world that Washington intended to keep its promise not to back out on its commitments regarding Asia, and to secure a continuation of the American capacity to intervene via all three oceans. The "U.S. strength is the basis for safeguarding the sovereignty and independence of our friends and allies in Asia," declared the president while the Vietnamese newspaper *Quan Doi Nhan Dan* in an article, also broadcast on *Hanoi Radio*, termed Ford's doctrine "the U.S. Counter-Revolutionary Strategy in Asia after Vietnam."[241] However, the Vietnamese press remained cautious not to jeopardize chances for rapprochement with Washington and refrained from harsh criticism of Ford's new policies and this first exercise in the American quest for bipartite agreements with China and the ASEAN nations.[242]

Ford's declarations during the tour demonstrated a U.S. shift towards endorsing Chinese and ASEAN policies on the region. During his first banquet speech in Peking, Ford endorsed the Chinese view that potential Soviet dangers threatened weaker countries and reaffirmed that Peking and Washington held a "mutual interest in seeing the world not dominated by military force or pressure."[243]

On a bilateral basis, Ford stressed that "U.S. policy toward the new regime in Indochina will be determined by their conduct toward us. We are prepared to reciprocate gestures of goodwill" and pointed at the return of MIAs.[244] During the president's visit to the Philippines and Indonesia, following his trip to China, Ford announced that if the new Indochinese communist states "exhibit restraint towards their neighbors and constructive approaches to international problems, we will look to the future instead of the past."[245] This remark indicated that he had certainly been briefed on the Chinese fear of Vietnamese expansionism and on the Vietnamese's dangerous leanings towards the Soviet Union.

If Ford's trip to China was aimed at raising popular support for his presidential candidacy, this certainly signaled to the Chinese that Washington, as early as 1975, was inclined to endorse Chinese international political views regarding the Soviet Union but also Vietnam—a slow-growing alliance that materialized in 1978 at the expense of Hanoi.

Overall, however, Ford's visit remained a limited success. Ford's decision to change his plans—from a lengthy visit to China to a general tour of Southeast Asia using China as a stop-over—offended the Chinese. But Ford's decision to shorten his visit was also aimed at gaining support for his upcoming electoral campaign against Reagan from conservative Republicans, who resented a Sino-American rapprochement.[246] Withdrawing from the budding American-Vietnamese dialogue would be the next step in wooing the U.S. electorate.

In December 1975, Montgomery and three other members of the House of Representatives Select Committee on Missing Personnel in Southeast Asia—Richard Ottinger (Democrat, New York), Benjamin Gilman (Republican, New York) and Paul McCloskey (Republican, California)—became the first American congressional delegation to Hanoi since the end of the war. During the congressmen's trip to Hanoi, the House of Representatives Subcommittee on International Trade and Commerce again called on the White House to lift the trade embargo against Vietnam—in vain.[247]

Four days before Christmas, in a gesture of friendship, the Vietnamese handed the bodies of the three MIAs promised to Montgomery and further declared that other remains might soon be handed to the U.S.[248] Hanoi kept its promise and on December 30, Senator Kennedy received a letter accepting the Senator's offer to send American health and agriculture specialists to Vietnam and matter-of-factly informing him that two extra sets of remains requested by Montgomery were ready to be handed to the Americans.[249]

Following meetings with Vo Van Sung in Paris two weeks earlier, Montgomery had briefed the President on Hanoi's stance and, for his trip to Hanoi, Ford provided him a letter for the Vietnamese "setting forth his views on reciprocity, stressing that the United States looked to the future and not to the past."[250] The letter responded to the Committee's request for proof of American willingness to reciprocate Vietnamese friendly gestures.[251] Montgomery's role, as Ford requested, was now to "ascertain the list of quid pro quos desired by the Vietnamese."[252]

While the remains of the three MIAs were flown for identification to a U.S. military laboratory in Thailand before being sent back to the United States, the American delegation remained in Hanoi for further talks.[253] The Vietnamese furthered discussions on normalization and international matters and reiterated their wish to ease relations with Washington. Hanoi asked Washington to "demonstrate in clear ways that we are anxious" to resume dialogue.[254] Pham Van Dong even expressed his wish to visit the U.S. and to welcome more American visits.[255] The Committee "received the impression that they did want normal relations with us," Montgomery told Kissinger.

However, the talks had also brought to light the first hints of Vietnamese uneasiness with regard to relations with China and the Soviet Union. These would increasingly affect bilateral relations over the future months. "We detected a great concern on their part about China and the Soviets," Montgomery added in discussing his visit with Kissinger.[256] Vietnam's complex relations with its communist neighbors would become one of Hanoi's main foreign policy concerns in late 1977, developing into Hanoi's geostrategic realignment with Moscow in 1978 and to the Khmero-Vietnamese and Sino-Vietnamese conflicts of late 1978 and 1979 at the expense of Vietnamese relations with Washington.

During the talks, Dong expressed discontent with Ford's speech in Hawaii, his portrayal of Japan as "the dominant power in the Pacific" and the presence of American troops on Thai military bases.[257] However he concluded that "[t]his was a meeting starting peace and friendship between the two countries." The two sides agreed on improving relations through "acts of reciprocity."[258] However, the Americans felt that Hanoi considered aid a reward for efforts in recovering MIAs.[259] Deputy Foreign Minister Phan Hien refused cooperation with a third party to investigate crash sites, claiming that "if local people cannot find crash sites no one can."[260] His irritated reply indeed echoed Hanoi's earlier threat that MIA searches would be halted until the U.S. had agreed to provide economic aid. Instead, Phan Hien reiterated Hanoi's request for the implementation of Article 21 but stressed that Washington could make its own proposals as to the form this aid should take, adding that Hanoi did not wish "anyone to lose face—that would not be beneficial to anyone."[261]

While refusing to consider Vietnam's claims to Article 21, Montgomery "suggested that it would be more realistic to pursue movement in areas such as trade, technical assistance, health care and humanitarian assistance" and conveyed Ford's wish for a "written list of gestures the Vietnamese would consider of importance."[262] Dong then provided "a shopping list of wants" comprising a one- and a five-year plan for the economic reconstruction of North Vietnam. This list, he added, was "really the JEC [Joint Economic Commission] list," submitted to Washington three years earlier as the two countries sought a peaceful end to the war.[263] The congressmen said that the Vietnamese would "definitely welcome our assistance on humanitarian and economic problems."[264]

Committee members had also questioned the Vietnamese on the potential existence of secret U.S. commitments on aid. To their surprise, the Vietnamese disclosed the existence of a letter from Nixon to Pham Van Dong, dated February 1, 1973, barely two weeks after the signing of the Paris Peace Agreement, in which he had secretly promised up to $4.75 billion in reconstruction aid after the end of the war "without any political conditions," comprising $3.25 billion in economic aid and $1.5 billion in food and commodities.[265] Montgomery, stunned by the secret letter, replied that, in Washington, aid "appeared to be out of the question."[266]

However, the revelation of the existence of the letter opened a new dimension in the Committee's appraisal of bilateral exchanges with Hanoi, and on the hidden goals of the past administration, as Congressman Gonzalez' testimony highlights:

> My mind reverted to January 1973 on the occasion of the funeral of President Johnson, which was coincident with the news of the Paris agreements. I had access to foreign press, the Spanish language press, the French language press, the Portuguese language press, and each one of them carried a release stating categorically that one of the terms of the agreement was a binding commitment for reparations—and they used the word "reparations"—on the part of our Government. This never did appear in the American press.

So, while on the bus, on the way to Johnson City, I asked the chairman of the Appropriations Committee, and he said that he understood some figure had been mentioned of near $3 billion, and added further that he doubted Congress would ever approve any such thing.

Well, I wondered why this had never been really revealed either to the Congress or by indirection to the American people.[267]

On his return Montgomery started an investigation on the hidden letter, which would soon become a major clue in the American-Vietnamese puzzle.[268] After telephoning Nixon on February 2 following his return to the United States, he reported that "the reconstruction program, which had been under consideration for several years, was contingent upon Vietnamese compliance with the Paris Peace Agreement and congressional approval."[269]

From then on, the official executive branch stance acknowledged the existence of private correspondence between Dong and Nixon exploring the possibility of granting aid, if approved by Congress, and planning the creation of a joint economic commission to decide upon specific Vietnamese needs. But the White House stressed that the letter should in no way be regarded as an agreement or official commitment.

Fearing that publicizing the letter might entail strong reactions from Congress, behind whose back Nixon's pledge had been made, and give birth to a congressional push to implement the provisions in the letter, the Ford administration did not release its text to the Committee.[270] Hanoi made its full text public in May 1977, indeed inciting congressional wrath as Capitol Hill turned to Nixon for further explanation, but also shutting the congressional door on Hanoi and dimming hopes of reconciliation.

While North Vietnam and the two-week old communist government in Laos had welcomed the delegation and accepted files on MIAs, the Cambodian regime had refused an American visit, despite encouragement from Hanoi and Vientiane.[271] The American request illustrated Washington's belief that Hanoi controlled both Vientiane and Phnom Penh. In fact, although recent clashes between Cambodians and Vietnamese had been reported in the U.S. press, delegation members' behavior indicated that Washington was utterly unaware of the hostility developing between the Indochinese states and, in a schematic view of Indochinese policies, considered them as one cultural and political entity. This episode illustrates how such misperceptions—as Robert McNamara, discussing the war years, highlights in *Argument Without End*—continued to plague American appraisal of the situation in Indochina as it degenerated in 1977 and 1978, leading to a striking misunderstanding of forces and ideologies at play in the region and to the misreading of the Vietnamese mindset in negotiations.[272]

Meanwhile, Washington declared itself ready to maintain "an open mind" regarding Vietnam. Washington "has no interest in continuing the Viet-Nam conflict on the diplomatic front," stated an official report on December 31. "On the contrary, we envisage the eventual normalization of relations" should Vietnam rescind its aid precondition and respond positively on MIAs.[273] However, these claims seemed largely disingenuous and Ford reversed this stance four months later under electoral pressure.

In January 1976, in order to permanently deprive Hanoi of its claim to the economic provisions of the Paris Accords, the text of the agreement was dropped from the State Department's annual publication of *Treaties in Force*, indicating that the document had officially been renounced and declared void.[274] Interestingly, this point was noted more than one year later in a memorandum from Assistant Secretary to Far East and Pacific Affairs Richard Holbrooke to Secretary of State Cyrus Vance—the two main actors in the American-Vietnamese attempt for rapprochement during the Carter administration. The existence of this memorandum highlights the Carter administration's efforts to bridge relations between the two countries by de-emphasizing issues of contention and correcting the hostile policies of the Ford era, including unofficial acknowledgement of Vietnamese claims to reconstruction, as will be further discussed in the next chapter.

Adapting to a New Environment: Vietnamese Policies and Ford's Election Campaign

In the meantime, the Vietnamese had understood that in light of Hanoi's difficulties with Cambodia and China, reunification of North and South Vietnam had become a priority. Not only would it strengthen the country both economically and politically—which China had long come to fear—but it would promote contacts with foreign countries and multiply trade and diplomatic opportunities. The sense of urgency for reunification may also have stemmed from the increased Vietnamese fear of foreign ideological or political infiltration in the spheres of the Hanoi leadership, as the purge of pro–Chinese political leaders would demonstrate in December 1976. Reunification would reduce the risk of foreign interference in South Vietnam encouraging opposition with the North or renewing armed conflict between the two states, as may have pleased China, always keen to maintain Vietnam in a situation of political and economic dependence. It would also crush Washington's argument that *two* Vietnamese states could not be accepted as full members of the United Nations.[275] Complete reunification, initially planned to take a minimum of five years, was hastened as foreign hostility grew.[276]

In early June 1975, the North Vietnamese government was reorganized following a four-day session of the National Assembly.[277] All nine deputy premiers were re-elected and immediately began drafting a five-year development plan due to begin in January 1976.[278] A communiqué announced the upcoming "rapid achievement of reunification ... [leading] the entire country toward socialism according to the most earnest aspirations of the whole people."[279] The following day, the new cabinet, headed by Pham Van Dong, announced in a *Hanoi Radio* broadcast that Hanoi would be chosen as capital of the reunified Vietnam.[280] In mid–July, only a few days before Hanoi and Saigon's formal application for membership to the United Nations, *Vietnam Courier* and a North Vietnamese broadcast for international hearing announced, in the first official statement on reunification since the end of the war, that its process would be "considerably shortened."[281] In August, Hanoi proposed, on a nationwide scale, the Five-Year Plan (1976–1980) that had initially been drafted for the North. Not only did this decision officially announce the speeding up of the reunification process, it also meant reorganizing foreign policy to encourage foreign trade and investments and meet the $10 to $12 billion figure required by the plan.[282]

However, the speeding up of reunification did not become visible until the Fall—coinciding with the second American veto of the admission of the two Vietnams to the

UN, and with Le Duan's fruitless visit to Peking. As was common in Hanoi, difficulties encountered in foreign affairs became the catalyst for the speeding up of domestic policies and the emphasis on national cohesion and protection.

In September, the twenty-fourth plenum of the Party Central Committee formally agreed to proceed toward reunification.[283] In early October, in the South Vietnamese newspaper *Tin Sang*, Dong explained that although an *unofficial* reunification had already taken place in the Vietnamese mind, the official administrative one would occur shortly.[284] "The reunification of the country is already an accomplished fact," explained a Politburo member in Hanoi praising brotherly relations between North and South during the celebration of the thirtieth anniversary of Vietnamese independence. "Reunification ... is purely an internal matter for the Vietnamese people."[285]

In early November, two twenty-five member delegations from North and South Vietnam, headed by National Assembly chairman Truong Chinh and an old friend of Le Duan's Vietnam Workers Party, member Pham Hung, met in Saigon.[286] A joint communiqué announced that reunification and elections for the creation of a national assembly would take place in the first half of 1976.[287] Saigon's foreign minister Mrs. Nguyen Thi Binh announced at a press conference that Vietnamese conditions to normalization would be "very favorable" should Washington agree to heal Vietnamese wounds—by granting aid.[288] While the terms of reunification were being discussed in Saigon, a vast press campaign, launched in both Vietnamese states at the beginning of the month, aimed at preparing the Vietnamese for the establishment of a single state.[289]

Following a Party congress in December, it was announced that reunification would be completed by April 30, 1976, to mark the first anniversary of the communist takeover of South Vietnam.[290] China refrained from sending any personal greetings and Peking would certainly have preferred Vietnam to remain divided and thus relatively weak. Moscow, however, loudly applauded Hanoi's decision to hasten reunification, which would protect Hanoi from Chinese influence.[291]

The Vietnamese plans proved too hasty; formal reunification took place on July 2, 1976. Unsurprisingly, Hanoi became the official capital of the new Socialist Republic of Vietnam (SRV).[292] The former North Vietnamese flag, national emblem and national anthem were approved to represent the reunified nation.

The new Assembly, elected on April 25, 1976, met in June and voted to elect the leaders of the SRV. The VCP remained largely untouched.[293] Most former North Vietnamese leaders were elected to high-ranking ministerial posts, while former South Vietnamese leaders were named to rather low-ranking and domestic-oriented ministries.[294] In order to secure the passing on of socialist ideologies to the new government, several Communist Party Politburo members were given ministerial posts—possibly to hide the fact that the VWP was the true decision-making institution controlling the government.[295] Thus, North Vietnamese Politburo member and prime minister Pham Van Dong retained this ministerial title in the new government while his former South Vietnamese counterpart Nguyen Thi Binh was safely named education minister.[296] Similarly, Truong Chinh, chairman of the National Assembly Standing Committee, was also a high-ranking member of the eleven-member Politburo; rather pro–Chinese although he followed the main pro–Soviet trends of the Politburo; and an old rival of Le Duan's.[297] His authority grew during the reunification process, to which he had greatly contributed, but Le Duan would later gain the upper hand during the Fourth Party Congress of December 1976, leading to the emergence of the communist "southern" and pro–Soviet predominance within the leadership.[298]

While this rapid reunification points at Hanoi's haste to counter its changing alliances with China and the troublesome new regime of Democratic Kampuchea, the delay of the adoption of a new constitution, in December 1980, hints at the existence of a domestic struggle between Politburo factions and to the need to carefully weigh the new world order.

In late April or early May, the North Vietnamese Council of Ministers voted on new legislation: the Vietnamese army would, for a few years, retain the power and number of troops it had during the war. The excuse was that troops would be demobilized and set to rebuilding the country under the aegis of the Ministry of National Defense headed by General Vo Nguyen Giap. "[W]hile building itself into a highly prepared, modern people's army in defense of the fatherland," explained Giap at a meeting in Hanoi, "our army should endeavour to carry out its task of building the economy."[299] Perhaps the decision not to demobilize troops and maintain combat readiness stemmed from increasingly difficult relations with Cambodia and China, and from Hanoi's growing sense of insecurity. In addition, dispatching troops to all regions of both North and South Vietnam permitted control of the population, which, especially in the South, was not always keen on following northern orders.

China accused reunification as having been conducted "at Soviet instigation"—which the Vietnamese rapidly denied so as not to jeopardize chances of new regional and international alliances, especially among non pro–Soviet nations.[300] The Chinese reaction betrayed Peking's long-standing fear that Vietnam should emerge as a powerful state threatening Chinese power and influence in the region. It had not escaped Hanoi's notice that Peking had sought for several years to jeopardize Vietnamese chances for rapid reunification in the hope that it might delay or halt the strengthening of its southern neighbor.

In 1974, nearly a year before the end of the war, taking advantage of Vietnamese weakness, the Chinese invaded some of the Paracel and Spratly islands in the South China Sea, to which the Vietnamese had also laid claim, as had Taiwan and the Philippines.[301] The move came as a response to the North Vietnamese proposition in late 1973 to solve the dispute over territorial rights on these islands. Sensing that the war would soon come to a close, the DRV was now tackling the prospects of postwar economic reconstruction and intended to prospect for oil around the Tonkin offshore islands. While agreeing to talks, Peking had also sent its troops to occupy the islands.[302]

Peking's decision to seize the islands betrayed Chinese uneasiness as the prospects of a communist victory were becoming increasingly likely, and clearly signaled that the Chinese leadership did not look forward to the reunification of Vietnam.[303] Furthermore, China would control the sea route stretching from Tokyo to Singapore and thus cut off Vietnam from almost all maritime supplies. Although Peking explained its move by referring to past Chinese property of the largely uninhabited islands, using archeological and historical evidence dating back to 200 BC, it was quite clear that China cared only to strengthen its grasp on Indochina.[304]

Despite the seizure of the islands and Peking's publicizing of its territorial claims on the South China Sea, which copiously overlapped with those of Vietnam, the Vietnamese were too busy fighting the Americans to respond to Chinese provocations—nor would they postpone victory in the South, as Peking would have wished, to solve the island issue—and, therefore delayed action.[305] Talks between the Chinese and Vietnamese vice-foreign ministers therefore did not begin until August 1975. They did not meet with much success and were finally suspended in November.[306]

Once reunification was complete, Hanoi turned to solving the island issue with China. Shortly after reunification, the SRV issued its first new postage stamp, representing a miniature map of the two Vietnamese states now reunified as one country—clearly showing the Paracel and Spratly islands against a deep blue sea.[307] The stamp was an open act of defiance to Peking, showing the Chinese that although Hanoi had not responded at the time of the Chinese capture of the islands, it had not renounced its rights to this territory altogether.

Further disputes over sea and land borders would further arise as tensions grew between Hanoi and Peking over the following years, as shall be described in a later chapter. In 1977, the Vietnamese announced the establishment of an "economic zone," stretching 200 miles into the South China Sea, which greatly displeased Peking.[308] In early 1978, Hanoi reiterated its wish to negotiate with Peking as it had with the Philippines and which had led Hanoi to accept Filipino control over five islands in the Spratlys in return for Manila's official recognition of Vietnamese sovereignty over the three largest islands of the group. But Peking rejected Hanoi's proposition to draw a line between the Vietnamese coast and the Chinese Hainan island, referring to the verbal accords of 1954 and 1958 which had accepted Chinese sovereignty over the islands in the South China Sea and declaring the islands non-negotiable "Chinese territory since the Ancient Times."[309] Vietnam would see in the Chinese move on the islands the reemergence of "Han chauvinism" and a cause for increasing concern as to the long-term intentions of its northern neighbor.[310] As the decade would come to an end, Chinese fear of Vietnam would fuel Vietnamese fear of China.

It therefore came as no surprise that, cornered between Washington's demonstration of hostility and Chinese coolness, Hanoi had begun, immediately after reunification, to reinforce its alliances or create new ones with neighboring countries. On July 5, 1976, Nguyen Duy Trinh offered to normalize with the ASEAN nations with which Hanoi did not yet enjoy diplomatic relations.[311] Deputy Foreign Minister Phan Hien toured Malaysia, Singapore, Indonesia and the Philippines to improve relations and to demonstrate the friendliness of the newly unified Vietnam.[312] "Hanoi appears to have matured overnight," remarked a Western observer noting this change in attitude.[313] On July 12, Hanoi normalized diplomatic relations with the Philippines, then with Thailand on August 6, thus completing the establishment of diplomatic relations with all ASEAN states.[314] Furthermore, Hanoi obtained pledges of aid from Malaysia and Thailand.[315]

The new Vietnam, strengthened by the recent reunification of its two states and the birth of new regional alliances, was preparing itself for emergence as a new internationally oriented diplomatic power. The wartime stigmata of the two separate and opposed Vietnamese states had disappeared and Hanoi could publicize the hurried reconciliation between its two peoples as proof of the superiority of the Vietnamese socialist model.

Washington, absorbed in the early stages of the presidential election, remained silent on Vietnam's renewed gestures of goodwill over the summer.[316] Only a few congressional or private appeals for rapprochement marked the early months of 1976.

On December 25, 1975, Senator McGovern announced his plans to visit Hanoi with several members of the Senate Near Eastern and South Asian Subcommittee. His trip, from January 15–17, would seek to "explore Vietnamese interest in resuming relations with the U.S." and pursue congressional efforts in accounting for MIAs.[317] Pham Van Dong assured him:

> We are very much concerned with the three points you raised [MIAs, the return of American citizens and their relatives to the U.S. and the return of Vietnamese refugees to Vietnam]. There is no difficulty with the first two. The third we will have to consider, but on principle there will be no difficulty.[318]

Hanoi's reply was positive. Once again, Dong confirmed that no live POWs or MIAs remained in Vietnam and that the Vietnamese would do their utmost to account for MIAs.[319] Dong also agreed to provide Washington with a status report of the MIAs whose names would appear on a list handed to Hanoi prior to the visit.[320] However, he repeated that only the "full implementation" of Article 21 could "create favorable conditions" for normalization.[321]

Just before his departure, Mrs. Nguyen Thi Binh informed the Senator that all Americans and their relatives would soon be allowed to emigrate to the U.S. and that the remains of the two MIAs mentioned in Nguyen Duy Trinh's written exchange with Senator Kennedy would soon be returned to the U.S. government. Hanoi's press quoted McGovern as having said that it was in Washington's interest to fulfill its share of the 1973 Accords. This point, not reported in the United States, may well have been Vietnamese propaganda, or deliberately omitted in the U.S. press. The Vietnamese media welcomed the delegation as "clearsighted" and "progressive." More generally, McGovern reported that the Vietnamese were ready to look to the future and develop a friendship with Washington. Regarding rumors of Soviet diplomatic pressure on Hanoi, he reported to Washington that the Vietnamese "do not consider themselves to be aligned with any country. They want to be friends to all."[322]

A few days following McGovern's return, *Nhan Dan* published an article for the anniversary of the peace agreement presenting a less moderate position. Following the vehement exchange between the two countries, the previous summer, over Vietnamese admission to the UN, the Vietnamese shift to a softer stance appeared once again as a demonstration of Hanoi's fluctuating and double-edged policies incessantly shifting from friendly to antagonistic. The article no longer linked normalization to Article 21 but to Washington's cessation of its "hostile policies" and its showing of "goodwill."[323] A few days later, during a World Health Organization meeting in Manila, Deputy Health Minister Hoang Dinh Cau accused Washington of having reneged on its promise to heal the Vietnamese wounds of war.[324] Similarly, while in Paris for the 22nd French Communist Party congress, Mrs. Binh declared that although some clauses of the peace agreement no longer applied, Washington should contribute to Vietnamese reconstruction and urged for the lifting of the trade embargo.[325]

Impressed by the welcome he had received in Vietnam, McGovern wrote a report to Congress, upon his return to Washington in February 1976, recommending that the

United States show "the wisdom, sensitivity and compassion for which we would like to be known."[326] The report recommended lifting the trade embargo, normalization, admission to the UN, and the granting of humanitarian aid. "[T]hose steps [if not taken]," he said, "can only insult and offend the government whose cooperation we must have if we are to end the anxiety of.... American families."[327]

While in Vietnam, McGovern was repeatedly briefed on the secret Nixon letter, which had been mentioned to Montgomery. Dong had stated that: "The exact sum is not mentioned in the Paris Agreement, but it is a matter of honor, responsibility and conscience."[328] The Vietnamese press reported that McGovern, like Montgomery, was given a copy of the final economic agreement signed by the Joint Economic Commission in 1973, and stressed that no doubt remained as to the nature of American obligations.

Although McGovern's report refrained from calling for a clearance of the suggested $4.75 billion debt, it concluded that "at the outset we should indicate that we are prepared to join other countries with at least a modest program of aid." In response, the State Department promised it would initiate a "dialogue" with Hanoi—even if half-hearted, as future events would prove.

The executive branch yielded to McGovern's request, but opted for a discreet approach to the Vietnamese, especially as Ford's campaign for the upcoming presidential election was about to begin. On February 26, the U.S. Embassy in Paris delivered a message to the Vietnamese embassy, "the substance of which," Douglas Pike reported in his private notes, "is to broach the idea of an across-the-board discussion on issues in contention, and soliciting an early response." However, he noted that Kissinger's motives "appear[ed] to be mixed (and ambiguous)" and possibly based on "other domestic election year considerations."[329] Only a few weeks away from the elections, the White House was treading on thin ice in its relations with Vietnam, requiring maintenance of a difficult equilibrium—between hostility, to woo hawkish voters, and careful overtures to Hanoi, to prove its concern for an accounting of MIAs.

On March 12, meeting with the secretary of state, the Montgomery Committee unanimously urged Kissinger to resume negotiations on trade and normalization with the Vietnamese should Hanoi continue its efforts to account for missing U.S. servicemen.[330] The secretary said he would study this recommendation, and approved it a week later. The Committee had already met with the president on January 26 to decide on the "various options which the administration might consider in reciprocating the gestures already made by the Vietnamese."[331] These two meetings would initiate an exchange of six unpublicized diplomatic notes, as the administration resumed dialogue to satisfy the Committee and Congress, while simultaneously exhibiting open hostility so as not to endanger Ford's chances for reelection in November.

This dual policy of secret exchanges would allow the administration to regain the initiative in bilateral relations after Montgomery and McGovern had expressed their wish for concessions to Hanoi, while at the same time the executive branch had no desire to improve relations with Vietnam. The executive would continue this two-sided policy until the end of the Ford presidency, initiating a dialogue with Hanoi while carefully wording U.S. notes so as to prevent any diplomatic breakthrough.

In the face of this complex choice between policy options, the president turned to seek the advice of his aides. An NSC memorandum in February had recommended the resumption of talks in order to "[a]llow the Executive Branch to regain control from the Montgomery Committee of our negotiations with Hanoi [which] is moving much too fast toward making major concessions to Vietnam without exacting any real results in return." Resuming talks, continued the report, would enable the exchange of information on MIAs although it also presented the "disadvantage" of "giving Hanoi false encouragement about the prospects for U.S. economic aid."[332] Kissinger agreed, and warned the Committee that "the tactics of policy making should be reserved to us [the State Department]."[333] The Committee, however, warned Ford that Kissinger "has bitter memories" of Vietnam and that "[w]hat we want to remember is it isn't the same [today]."[334]

But this meeting also provided Montgomery an opportunity to inquire about the Nixon letter the administration still declined to produce.[335] "That letter," he said,

> articulated the agreement that a Joint Economic Commission would be formed to consider reconstruction aid to North Vietnam in the spirit of Article 21 of the Paris Peace Agreement.... According to the Secretary, neither the Joint Economic Commission proposal nor the Nixon correspondence was an agreement as such, but rather was tentative in nature and dependent on both strict adherence to the terms of the Paris Peace Agreement and on American constitutional processes. The latter, he said, translated to approval by the Congress of any proposed programs.[336]

In explaining his failure to provide a copy of the letter, Kissinger added that any congressional leader would be proud of the way he and the Nixon administration had handled the affair. Similarly, during a hearing by the Committee in July, Assistant-Secretary of State for East Asia and Pacific Affairs Philip Habib also failed to produce the text of the letter but promised to ask the president for a copy of it and gave a vague summary of its content. He denied, however, its having the value of a pledge or commitment towards Hanoi:

> There is no agreement, there was no agreement, there never was an agreement as far as I know, and I think I would know at this stage.... That letter was simply a letter primarily designed to set up a Joint Economic Commission pursuant to Article 21 of the Paris agreement. The truth of the matter is there was no agreement.

He explained that the fact that the Nixon letter had been kept secret for more than three years, away from public and congressional scrutiny, was not to exercise secret policies behind the backs of Congress but a necessity to successfully support the peace initiative in Indochina. "[I]t is quite clear that if you want to have a successful ongoing contact on matters as delicate as this you would be better off if you don't go and publicize every time you have a contact."[337]

Although these explanations satisfied the Committee, it remained doubtful that the Vietnamese, who possessed a centralized political system with unchallenged decision-making, had grasped the subtleties of the U.S. domestic political infrastructure and preconditions as set by the Nixon administration—especially regarding the condition of obtaining congressional authorization prior to the granting of any aid to Hanoi. "It must be noted," Kissinger had told the House in 1973 on the issue of potential aid to North Vietnam, "that it's not always clear to the North Vietnamese what American constitutional processes are," which had sent the chamber laughing—a strikingly ironic remark considering that at that same time, Nixon was pledging several billions to Hanoi behind the back of Congress.[338] In August 1973, American representatives handed their Vietnamese counterparts a series of documents summarizing the "key role" of Congress in all foreign aid decisions, as well as the processes of American executive and legislative bureaucracies and congressional statements on the issue of aid to North Vietnam.[339] While Nixon had intended his secret pledge to Hanoi to be altogether vague, strictly conditional on American domestic factors and, all in all, unlikely to occur, the Vietnamese had taken aid for granted.

Meanwhile the Ford administration had taken the first step in renewing dialogue, but the hard stance adopted by the White House indicated that the U.S. opening was linked to the upcoming election rather than to a genuine wish to establish a fruitful dialogue with Hanoi. On March 26, Kissinger released, through Paris, the first of an exchange of six diplomatic notes to Hanoi encouraging discussion on "outstanding issues" and calling for the holding of preliminary talks. "I believe that the interests of peace and security will benefit from placing the past behind us," explained Kissinger in the note, "and developing the basis for a new relationship between our two countries. We are prepared to open discussion with your Government in pursuit of this objective."[340]

The note called on Nguyen Duy Trinh to present his "views on such discussion and on what [he] believe[d] might be the procedure and issues involved."[341] At the same time, Kissinger declared that Washington, in principle, did not oppose normalization. However, he insisted that while all recoverable remains of MIAs should be returned to Washington, a "full accounting" for all those whose remains could not be recovered was "the *absolute minimum precondition*" to normalization.[342] After rejecting Vietnamese preconditions for nearly a year, Washington had unilaterally come back on its position and introduced its own precondition into the debate. Speaking to the Montgomery Committee, Kissinger later admitted that the introduction of this precondition had aimed at bringing Hanoi to give up its claim for aid once the Vietnamese had realized that "they need normalization more than we do."[343] In order to prove once again that Washington was not abandoning its allies and withdrawing from the Asian continent, Washington stressed the "need for assurances of Hanoi's peaceful intentions towards neighbouring countries in Southeast Asia." As for other issues, including aid, Kissinger did "not hold out much prospect for that."[344] The Vietnamese welcomed this move and Hanoi announced on March 30 that it would take "necessary measures" to recover MIAs.[345]

Three days later the Vietnamese Embassy in Paris responded by calling for a mutual implementation of the Paris Accords and stressing that Hanoi had already demonstrated its goodwill on several occasions.[346] On April 3, Vietnam agreed to release two Americans detained since U.S. personnel were evacuated the previous year and whose names had been given to McGovern during his visit to Hanoi earlier that year. But the true response to the first American letter came on April 12, in a diplomatic note delivered by Vietnamese first secretary to cultural affairs Phan Huy Thong and third secretary Ngo Nguyen Phuong to the U.S. Embassy in Paris. The note, dated April 10, replied to Kissinger's correspondence of March 26 in harsh terms. Hanoi was prepared to collaborate on all issues, including MIAs, but highlighted that "the U.S. side has so far refused to fulfil its obligation to contribute to healing the wounds of war and to post-war reconstruction in Vietnam." Only if all issues were considered simultaneously would Hanoi normalize with Washington.[347] The note stressed that:

[The United States] has gone so far as taking hostile actions against the Vietnamese people and using discourteous and slanderous terms towards the Government of the Democratic Republic of Vietnam [in a reference to Ford's remarks in March that the Vietnamese were a "bunch of international pirates"]. Should your government really desire to hold talks to normalize relations with the Democratic Republic of Vietnam, the United States would have to show the same good will and serious intent as the Democratic Republic of Vietnam.

The Government of the Democratic Republic of Vietnam is prepared to consider any concrete proposal of your government.[348]

Rather than responding to the American note, Hanoi was restating its position, refusing to drop the aid issue. The note was accompanied by an aggressive article in *Nhan Dan* recalling the "reasonable stand of the DRV government," calling on Washington to prove its goodwill and declaring that "for all its alluring words, the Ford Administration does not yet want to normalize relations with Viet-Nam."[349] An editorial in *Nhan Dan* noted that the president was most untrustworthy and that his language could range from "discourteous and tendentious" to "more honeyed phrases" depending on whether his audience was conservative or liberal.[350] Given American imperviousness to Vietnamese overtures, Hanoi stated on April 13 that it would now refrain from overt signs of friendliness until Washington had demonstrated a willingness to reciprocate.[351] On April 15, during a press conference in Paris, a DRV official repeated almost word for word the content of the Vietnamese note released on April 12.[352]

Understanding that the executive branch was more concerned with electoral affairs than with foreign policies, Hanoi once again turned to the legislative branch in the hope of friendlier contacts. On April 22, the Vietnamese embassy in Paris informed McGovern that two Americans detained in South Vietnam, and whose upcoming release had been announced on April 3, were now allowed to leave Vietnam.[353] By informing Congress rather than the executive branch, Hanoi was ignoring diplomatic protocol and demonstrating its frustration over Ford and Kissinger's policies.

Hanoi made a public show of its hostility to the Ford administration's position. On April 16, *Quan Doi Nhan Dan* criticized Washington's use of diplomatic notes "for deceitful propaganda purposes" and its "boast[ing] about the so-called 'U.S. initiative' in sending a note to our side and unilaterally publiciz[ing] the exchange of notes ... regardless of the points already agreed upon."[354] In fact, in agreeing to begin such an exchange of notes, the United States had initially rejected Hanoi's request to publicize the text of the letters but then reneged and revealed the existence of the exchange to support Ford's presidential campaign. That same day, *Nhan Dan* stressed that Ford had failed to provide "any concrete proposal" as the president was too busy with the "noisy diplomatic ploy and public campaign" of the election.[355] In the meantime, while an English-language broadcast on *Hanoi Radio* claimed that "the Ford administration ha[d] not seriously responded to the note of the DRV" and had "give[n] it a false interpretation," the Vietnamese-language version further charged that "U.S. Secretary of State Kissinger continues his slanderous allegations against the DRV and tries to shirk all responsibilities belonging to the U.S. side."[356]

"The Vietnamese domestic propaganda is slightly more vituperative than their English language broadcasts," noted an U.S. intelligence memorandum,

> perhaps reflecting the contradiction between their continued use of the United States as an "enemy figure" for internal political reasons and the need to respond to our offer. They seem

to be showing some sensitivity to being portrayed as the party blocking rapprochement with the United States.[357]

The constant contradictions and vehemence in Vietnamese rhetoric, while common for communist regimes, betrayed a gap between Hanoi's continued use of war-time language, inherited from decades of war, and the requirements of peace-time politics. But this double-edged diplomacy would become increasingly difficult to decipher in Washington as the complexity of bilateral contacts and intercommunist bickerings developed over the months and years.

On April 17, *Nhan Dan* furthered its attack by publishing excerpts of the Nixon letter and pointing at American responsibility for healing Vietnamese wounds.[358] However, the American press failed to report on the release of the letter, which went unnoticed or ignored by the American media. However, by 1977, this letter, which may have appeared as trivial propaganda, would turn into a crucial document that would negatively affect future bilateral relations between the two countries. While its existence remained unknown to the U.S. media and public opinion for another thirteen months, the Vietnamese certainly considered that the *Nhan Dan* article and the presentation of the letter, to the Montgomery Committee and to Senator McGovern, were enough to encourage Washington to reciprocate and to provide the promised aid. U.S. failure to extract this information from the Vietnamese daily and Washington's ignoring of the existence of the letter would account for much of the *status quo* between the two countries over the next eighteen months and for Hanoi's misunderstanding of the violent U.S. congressional and public reaction when the full text of the letter was publicly released in 1977.

In addition to Hanoi's unhappiness with the cool American stance, the upcoming Vietnamese elections of April 25 awakened cold diplomatic winds and strong propaganda in Hanoi, especially regarding its former enemy. Thus, until June, the Vietnamese remained rather reserved in their dealings with Washington.[359]

While the White House was secretly exchanging notes with Hanoi, it was also busy preparing Ford's campaign and sending contradictory signals to the Vietnamese, to the American public and to international audiences. The president faced a strong primary challenge from his right-wing opponent Ronald Reagan, which forced him to rearrange his priorities and to consider U.S. relations with Vietnam within the scope of the upcoming presidential campaign. Polls in January had given Ford a 46 percent disapproval rating and the time had come to improve his image in the eyes of his party.[360] In the face of Reagan's success as a *hawkish* challenger to the president, who had lost Saigon, Ford's recent overtures to the Vietnamese might appear as a weakness to the electorate. Nor were the meager Vietnamese concessions sufficient to convince this skeptical electorate of the effectiveness of such proposals.

In order to woo right-wing supporters, the administration began to harden its position on Indochina.[361] On March 20, at the beginning of the primaries, Ford confirmed Washington's policy shift by depicting the Vietnamese as "a bunch of international pirates." "[W]e must be certain," he warned, "that we do not capitulate to a government that has broken its word every time we have ever made a deal with them."[362] *Quan Doi Nhan Dan* immediately dismissed Ford's insults as a "spiteful election maneuver" while *Hanoi Radio* labeled them a "rude and odious slander."[363] More discreetly, Vietnamese liaison officer Do Thanh telephoned the U.S. embassy in Paris on the pretext that he wished to confirm Hanoi's receipt of a letter from Montgomery requesting authorization for another visit to Vietnam. Do Thanh then mentioned that Dong hoped that both sides would refrain from making hostile declarations against each other and defined Ford's statement as "not very polite."[364]

The election campaign was now gathering speed. Kissinger reminded people that although the Vietnam War—a sensitive issue for Ford—had shaken the nation, it had by no means altered the "fundamental truths" that were the foundation of America's greatness.[365] Conservatives sneered at Kissinger's statement and attacked his quest for détente, leading to Ford's decision, in March, to ban that word forever from the administration's vocabulary.[366]

On the issue of Vietnam, Ford was caught between the pressure to woo Republican conservatives away from Reagan by hardening his own positions, and the necessity to secure the confidence of the Montgomery Committee, the League of Families and, through them, public opinion at large. During a press conference on March 25, he declared that:

> I have also indicated [that] my administration will make all efforts ... to achieve as full accounting as possible for our men still missing in Southeast Asia. We therefore are prepared to meet with Vietnamese representatives at [a] mutually agreeable location to discuss the MIA question as well as future relations.[367]

Ford's contradictory statements of inviting the Vietnamese "pirates" to hold talks when each side considered it "mutually agreeable," fuelled Reagan's attacks on Ford's dealings with Hanoi. During an interview on April 22, Ford bluntly rejected Reagan's "totally fallacious allegations" that the White House was studying normalization with Vietnam, as the president had "no intention whatsoever of recognizing North Vietnam—none ... under no circumstances."[368] "I never said that we were going to normalize relations or recognize the North Vietnamese," he again confirmed the next day.[369]

Jimmy Carter, the Democratic front-runner, seized the opportunity to accuse Ford of "playing internal Republican Party politics with American foreign policy and the hopes of MIA families," and of turning "our Indochina policy over to his opponent, Mr. Reagan" in an "example of weak, vacillating national leadership." Carter pledged that, should he be elected, he would "leave open the option of normalizing relations with North Vietnam after they have assured [him] of a full accounting" of MIAs.[370] He repeated this stance a few days later, adding that he too would reject the granting of economic aid to Hanoi.[371] Carter was appearing more right-wing than he genuinely was, and his claims reflected the necessity to woo conservative public opinion more than his true views.[372] He would return to softer views within a few days of taking office.

On May 8, at the height of the primaries, Washington issued a second note to the Vietnamese. Despite the executive branch's hostile claims against Hanoi, the Department of State had concluded that although Trinh's previous message was "hardly encouraging," it was considered "sufficiently positive to warrant a second round of messages."[373] The message, wrote Pike to Kissinger in discussing how Washington should respond, is "tendentious and patronizing, but it does not shut the door to talks."[374] In this second note Washington again requested the holding of talks, but pointed out that "talks on the basis of the selective application of past agreements ... would not be fruitful." In accordance with Ford's public stance aimed at countering the Vietnamese claim to aid and at Hanoi's argument that it had been planned in Article 21 of the Paris Agreement, the letter referred to MIAs as a "humanitarian" concern rather than an article of the peace document, which would have entailed reciprocity from Washington. "The humanitarian concern of a full accounting for our missing men will be one of the primary issues of the United States in such discussions," stated the note. "Until this issue is substantially resolved, there can be no real progress between our two countries." As for Hanoi, it should feel "free to raise any issue of concern to it."[375] Over the next six months Ford's emphasis on MIAs would increase as electoral pressure grew, giving rise to doubts as to his genuine concern for the issue.

Meanwhile, on May 16, Senator Kennedy, still believed to be running for the Democratic nomination, called for normalization and the admission of Vietnam to the United Nations. After reading a recently released Senate report on Indochinese refugees, Kennedy declared that these were the only means by which the Vietnamese could be brought to the negotiating table to solve both the MIA and the refugee problems, and called on Ford to appoint a delegation to discuss these issues.[376] But the White House, wading through the dark waters of the primary season, was less than inclined to show signs of a diplomatic thaw with Hanoi. In an interview in May, Kissinger redefined the American position, claiming that the full accounting of all MIAs and the return of their remains was "the absolute precondition without which we cannot consider the normalization of relations." "The North Vietnamese believe they can blackmail us by using the remains of Americans to extort economic and other aid," he later angrily declared, "and we will not be blackmailed by American sufferings."[377]

The introduction of this new concept regarding the impossibility of normalization without a prior and total solution to the MIA issue demonstrated that Washington's priorities had changed and were a barely veiled end to the diplomatic dialogue until after the election. Kissinger's main condition, a total accounting of all MIAs, represented an impossible task to fulfill as the Vietnamese constantly reminded Washington. As early as January 1974, Deputy Assistant Secretary of Defense for International Economic Affairs Roger Shields had already explained that: "[W]e have never promised families a complete accounting in the sense that we would know what happened to every single individual. This is impossible."[378] "We understand, of course," explained Under-Secretary of State Philip Habib in 1976 with electoral tact, "that many were lost in circumstances which make it unlikely that any direct information about them will be recovered."[379]

Much like Nixon had initially used the POW/MIA issue to leverage domestic approval for the continuation of war, Ford and Reagan were using it to justify peace-time hostility toward Vietnam, to control public opinion and attract new votes. While the issue was presented to Hanoi as a humanitarian concern, at home it remained politically sensitive at election time. The issue became an object of vehement indignation in Washington in view of Hanoi's lack of interest for American concerns, but also a delicate subject on which the administration wished to appear passionate and combative so as not to later be charged with ineptness—or worse, lack of concern. Nor could the secretary of state suddenly de-emphasize the MIA issue after his decision to "donate the entire proceeds [of his Nobel Peace Prize of 1973] to a scholarship fund for children of American servicemen killed or missing in action in Indochina."[380] "No one has the guts," privately concluded Montgomery Committee member Representative McCloskey, "to tell these people there's no *rational* basis to believe that any of these men is still alive."[381]

In 1982, Murray Hiebert, a member of the Indochina Project of the Center for International Policy in Washington, reported that Kissinger explained during a private meeting with the Montgomery Committee that American insistence on accounting for *all* MIAs was merely a ploy through which the Vietnamese would be forced into dropping their request for reconstruction aid.[382] But this position also aimed at halting all progress in a rapprochement with Hanoi while appearing to continue contacts to woo MIA families and earn potential votes. Pike warned:

> This is a hard line and comes perilously close to being an ultimatum. It offers little incentive to the Vietnamese to do anything. It is not even cooperative in terms of resolution of casualties. It is highly ambiguous in that it does not fix, even in a general way, the criteria we will employ in determining our satisfaction in accounting for the MIA's.[383]

Pike's warnings remained unheard.

Beyond representing a purely diplomatic card against Hanoi, the request for a total accounting may also have represented Ford's attempt to redeem the loss of Saigon through a disproportionate show of concern for those who had perished in defending American honor and ideologies in Indochina. After winning the primaries against Reagan on June 8, a stronger emphasis on MIAs appeared to be a logical continuation of his policies towards Vietnam and a timely effort to woo the Republican right after the defeat of the long-time right-wing favorite, Reagan.[384] Ford's sudden passionate and nearly fatherly anxiousness to account for all MIAs—which he shared with other candidates also in quest of additional votes—countered the previous criticism of public opinion regarding the American debacle in Indochina. Ford's foreign policies regarding Vietnam were made to suit his domestic policy agenda.

On June 19, Hanoi issued a response—the fourth piece of correspondence—to Washington's note of May 8 that had introduced MIAs as a humanitarian issue. The Vietnamese response was swift and stinging. The note accused Washington of political fraud in calling the Paris Agreement obsolete in order to evade responsibility for contributing to the reconstruction of Vietnam while simultaneously claiming that the Vietnamese failed to implement their part of the Accords to account for MIAs. The note recalled Vietnamese efforts to account for MIAs "to relieve the anxiety of those American families," and accepted the American offer to open negotiations should Washington "adopt a goodwill and serious attitude."[385] Hanoi, stated the letter, agreed that talks would contribute to "creating favourable conditions for normalization of relations between the two countries."[386] In handing the note to the American embassy in Paris, Do Thanh, the Vietnamese Liaison officer, again requested that talks be held in a "discreet" location, away from electoral concerns and prowling cameras, so as to promote chances for a diplomatic breakthrough.[387] During a speech in Manila on July 13, Phan Hien reiterated Hanoi's readiness to open talks with Washington. The joint Filipino-Vietnamese communiqué, aimed at wooing both China and Washington and at refuting rumors of a Soviet-Vietnamese rapprochement, declared that neither nation would "allow any foreign country to use one's country as a base for direct or indirect aggression and intervention against the other country or other countries in the region."[388]

A week later, on July 19, Hanoi received a third note from Washington agreeing to hold talks and proposing that they be held at the U.S. embassy in Paris. The letter, however, restated Washington's opposition to aid. The tone indicated that Washington may have been surprised by Vietnamese eagerness to hold talks and had had to respond in the affirmative, perhaps rather unwillingly, to justify its pledge to the American people that all would be done to account for its missing.[389]

Publicly however, the administration commented only on the development of American-Vietnamese relations in terms of Washington's indignation over Vietnam's failure to account for MIAs. Interestingly, on July 21, Philip Habib stated to the Montgomery Committee that the administration would reject negotiations until Hanoi had delivered satisfactory information on American citizens still in Vietnam. He explained:

> [T]he only means that I can foresee at this point for making some progress is to convince the North Vietnamese that they must be prepared to accept the accounting as a primary responsibility, and our concern on this issue as a primary factor, before any progress can be made on these relations.[390]

Hanoi understood the message. That same day, the Vietnamese ambassador to Paris Vo Van Sung informed several U.S. congressmen that all U.S. citizens and their families still held in Vietnam, numbering a total of about fifty people, would soon be authorized to leave.[391] The Vietnamese decision, besides being a direct response to Habib's statement, also represented the extension of an olive branch to Montgomery who, in April and May, had privately communicated his disappointment to North Vietnam regarding the lack of progress in permitting U.S. citizens to leave Vietnam.[392] At a time when dialogue with the executive branch proved difficult, Hanoi was turning to Montgomery and Congress in the hope of support.

On July 23, Montgomery and several members of the House Select Committee on Missing Persons in Southeast Asia warned the National League of Families that the Committee had found "no evidence that any of the men are alive" and that the accounting for MIAs would "never be 100% complete."[393] Given these conclusions, he explained, the Committee's deadline for its investigation would not be extended beyond the original date of September 11, 1976.

The next day, speaking to a convention of the League, Ford pledged that "[w]ithout a satisfactory solution of the MIA issue no further progress in our relations [with Vietnam] is possible." Ford took up a remarkably strong stance against the Vietnamese telling the League:

> [A]s all of you know, we are dealing with a government that has demonstrated very little concern for your feelings. The Vietnamese claim to have established agencies to search for the missing, but thus far they have withheld this information, totally without justification.

He concluded that he would "not rest until the fullest possible accounting of your loved ones has been made." While Montgomery claimed that a total accounting was impossible, Ford had adapted his statement to Montgomery's conclusions by calling for a "fullest possible" accounting rather than a "total" accounting as he had previously insisted on. In doing so, he justified U.S. refusal of diplomatic reconciliation while expressing his concern for MIAs to an important electorate—the League. Carter would soften this stance in his effort to de-emphasize the issue of MIAs in 1977 by calling for a "satisfactory" accounting, relying on this vague phrasing to allow him to remove the obstacle of MIA accountings from direct bilateral negotiations.[394]

Interestingly, Ford's appearance in front of the League recalled that of Richard Nixon, on October 16, 1972, who had similarly pledged that the "most immoral thing [he] could think of" would be "to abandon our POWs and our MIAs."[395] In the closed world of U.S. politics, the issue of MIAs and POWs remained an interesting emotional catalyst encouraging votes for candidates, and becoming a political tradition that would be exploited by successive presidents or political actors until today.

In an attempt to attract a few extra votes with the emotional magnet of the MIA issue, Jimmy Carter sent telegrams pledging full support and sympathy to the families attending the convention of the League.[396] Hanoi immediately termed the sudden revival of Washington's hostility towards Vietnam an "electioneering trick" in which MIAs were being used to attract votes in Ford's crumbling scramble to win the November elections.[397] Both parties had learned to use MIAs to their own advantage.

However, the reunification of the two Vietnamese states had triggered a renewal of the Vietnamese effort to establish friendly relations with foreign nations—as Hanoi's recent normalization with some ASEAN countries had shown—including the United States. Hanoi would welcome normalization with Washington, explained Phan Hien, even if the American side had "not been entirely friendly." He repeated that the Vietnamese would accept talks without any preconditions despite American insistence that an accounting for MIAs be provided prior to the opening of negotiations on other issues. The Vietnamese position, repeated Hien, was that reconstruction aid was a "moral obligation" linking Washington to Hanoi, as the United States had already provided through such policies as the Marshall Plan.[398] Less than three weeks after Vietnamese reunification, Senators Kennedy and McGovern released a telegram from Vietnamese ambassador to Paris Vo Van Sung in which he had announced that the Vietnamese government had approved the release of all U.S. citizens who had been stranded in South Vietnam after the end of the war.[399]

On August 1, responding to Vo Van Sung's pledge that U.S. citizens in Vietnam would be released, the UN arranged for a first group of forty-nine Americans to be flown from Saigon to Thailand, bringing the alleged number of Americans still in Vietnam to only four.[400] On August 7, Richard Hughes, the head of a humanitarian children's organization in Saigon, was released, followed, a few days later, by an American volunteer worker and his family.[401] Keeping its promise, the State Department responded positively to the Vietnamese gesture, although rather coolly. It approved licenses allowing the Mennonite Central Committee, the Bach Mai Hospital Fund and the Church World Services to ship $850,000 in food and medical equipment to Vietnam, bringing to $3,000,000 the total amount of humanitarian aid sent to Vietnam through humanitarian agencies since the fall of Saigon.[402] A few days later, Washington opposed Vietnam's attending a UN conference on Food and Agriculture held in Manila on the grounds that Vietnam was not a UN member-state. This led to the outbreak of a verbal conflict between the countries.[403]

Hanoi was rather disappointed by the American indifference. During a speech at the Non-Aligned Nations conference in Colombo, Dong declared that Vietnam was looking forward to the development of economic ties with the Western capitalist world, and to the establishment of normal diplomatic relations with Washington.[404] He nevertheless reminded his audience that U.S. participation in the reconstruction of Vietnam represented "a question of conscience, responsibility and honour which [the U.S.] cannot elude."[405] The wooing of Washington clashed with Dong's trumpeting of the "historic and total victory achieved by the people of Vietnam in their struggle against aggressive U.S. imperialism."[406]

On August 20, Vietnamese permanent observer to the UN Dinh Ba Thi informed Secretary General Waldheim of Vietnam's wish to renew its application to the UN—this time as one reunified state.[407] Senator Mansfield welcomed this move and called on the executive branch not to use its veto, claiming that "relations with the nations of Indochina should be shaped to fit reality."[408]

At the same time, the former American consulate, which had functioned in Hanoi until the Geneva Accords of 1954, was being repaired as if to indicate to Washington that it might wish to recover its former offices in what was now both Vietnams' political capital. But Hanoi also emphasized its suffering from the war, hinting at a need for reparations. The Vietnamese Ministry of Culture declared both the U.S. embassy and the former presidential palace in Saigon historical monuments, recalling the "criminal U.S. aggression in Vietnam" and the "total collapse of their Vietnamese valets."[409] As previously stated, the "War Crimes Exhibition," which had opened in Saigon in 1975, was a particular example of the Vietnamese wish to present themselves both as the victims and victors of the war.[410] While showing that it had suffered extensively during the American involvement in Indochina, Vietnam deliberately restrained its accusations against the United States so as not to needlessly irritate Washington.

On August 27, Hanoi responded to Washington's third diplomatic note, which had agreed with Hanoi's request for talks. The new Vietnamese note welcomed this stance but rejected the American proposal that talks be held at the U.S. embassy in Paris. Instead, Hanoi suggested that Vietnamese and American officials meet in a neutral location in Paris.[411] In handing the note to the U.S. embassy in Paris, Do Thanh inquired which arrangements would suit the American side, including locations and staff members involved, and stressed that Counselor Tran Hoan from the Vietnamese embassy and three other officials would represent the Vietnamese side.[412] One cannot ignore that the mildness of the Vietnamese response and its issuance, barely a week after Hanoi announced its renewed application to the UN, signified that Vietnam hoped for American clemency.[413]

But the Vietnamese had misread U.S. signals. In fact, the note embarrassed rather than relieved the administration. "Do you want meetings?" Kissinger inquired of the president upon reception of the note. "We could say it was for MIA's.... Of course we could drag it out, and certainly no conclusion would come before November."[414] The executive branch was clearly using the issue of bilateral relations with Vietnam to advance Ford's chances for reelection. Accounting for MIAs was no longer a genuine concern but a pretext, and Kissinger's remark highlighted the primacy of domestic politics and individual ambitions. The memorandum leaves little doubt as to the role that Kissinger played in initiating this policy.

The White House did not respond to the note immediately, certainly preferring to reflect on new policy options in light of domestic priorities. Other international events such as the mass anti–American demonstrations in Thailand in the summer of 1976, calling for the withdrawal of U.S. presence from Thai soil, may also account for the postponement of Washington's reply.[415]

On September 1, Dinh Ba Thi requested that Washington refrain from vetoing Vietnam's admission to the UN, stressing that recent bilateral contacts had opened a new range of possibilities regarding MIAs and the issue of aid.[416] The same day, while Hanoi was celebrating the SRV's first national day and the thirty-first anniversary of Ho Chi Minh's declaration of independence, a broadcast monitored in Bangkok quoted excerpts in English of the American Declaration of Independence—an appeal for American restraint recalling both countries' pledge for equality and democracy. Beyond highlighting that Vietnamese and American declarations and love of freedom bore some similarities, Hanoi certainly intended this reading to lecture Americans into respecting Hanoi's right to participate in the international dialogue of nations when Vietnam's application would be considered at the UN.

The White House and its UN officials declined to comment on Dinh Ba Thi's declaration, but Kissinger, amused at being pressed for an answer, replied to a group of journalists on September 2: "I would not want to deprive you of the suspense that is inherent in this question prematurely. For us, the issue of the missing in action is of course a key issue, and we want to see whether any progress can be made there."[417] MIAs, he evasively declared, remained the key issue.[418]

In fact, Kissinger had decided to renew the U.S. veto of Vietnamese admission as early as July 1976. From a memorandum from Pike, Kissinger chose Option 4—the most hard-line: "Indicate in advance to Hanoi, directly or indirectly, that we could not consider permitting Vietnamese entry without prior substantial satisfaction on MIA's; abstain in the unlikely event such action is forthcoming, veto if it is not"—however reinforcing the strong position in the paper by adding in the margin: "But without advance notification."[419] Much as it had the previous year with the South Korean application, Washington sought to justify its upcoming veto with a face-saving pretext, expanding U.S. hostility onto the international arena while simultaneously justifying its unilateral rejection of normalization. MIAs had become an excuse to gain electoral leverage, rather than a true concern of the executive branch.

In hindsight, this position seems to have been leaked to the Vietnamese. On September 6, Do Thanh telephoned the U.S. embassy in Paris to arrange an urgent meeting and, upon his arrival at the embassy, delivered an oral note to Washington. The note stated Hanoi's hope that the upcoming talks in Paris would "achieve positive results in answering the interests of the two parties" and that in "this spirit" Hanoi had agreed to the release of the names of twelve yet unaccounted for American Air force pilots.[420] A few hours later, the Vietnamese embassy in Paris released the twelve names.[421] The official announcement highlighted Hanoi's hope that Washington would "show its goodwill and take concrete action to settle postwar problems between the two countries."[422] This sudden move and the release of a large number of names suggested that Hanoi was indeed using MIAs as a political lever as Washington had charged and that the U.S. strategy of linking the threat of a veto with MIAs had been fruitful. As Washington did not deviate from its hard stance, the remains were not released to the new administration until six months later.

Although Washington welcomed the release of this information, Vietnamese officials in Paris were informed that Washington still expected "as full an accounting as possible ... without further delay."[423] Kissinger instructed U.S. representatives to the UN to suggest to the Vietnamese that "[i]f the SRV does not have such necessary information on MIA's now available [a full accounting] they might then wish to seek deferral membership question until they are in a position to do so."[424] Kissinger had reversed his previous stance that Hanoi not be informed of the U.S. intent to veto the Vietnamese application until information on MIAs had been released, perhaps hoping that the release of remains or information would help Ford in his race for reelection. Washington repeated its wish for a full accounting and called on Hanoi to show that it did not "wish to trade on the misery of American families."[425]

The next day Ford reiterated his demand for a total accounting, hardening his position by calling Hanoi's release of only a few names a "callous and cruel" move designed to "exploit human suffering."[426] The release of remains, he declared, had been obtained only after he had ordered the American embassy in Paris to press the Vietnamese on MIAs. But the timing of release of the names proved that the initiative had come from Hanoi.[427] A White House spokesman later revealed that, at the time of this remark, Ford had just been told that Carter had planned a meeting with MIA families. This sudden presidential upsurge against Hanoi was, therefore, designed in the hope of regaining the initiative over Carter.[428] But Hanoi had anticipated the American show of hostility. On September 7, the American mission to the UN reported that the Vietnamese, in order to secure international backing, had been circulating a memorandum presenting a chronology of Hanoi's various "gestures of goodwill" with a selection of statements on normalization from high-ranking officials, and of U.S. responses to them.[429]

On September 9, pointing at the incomplete Vietnamese "gesture" of September 6, new U.S. ambassador to the UN William Scranton declared that the MIA question would be brought to the United Nations as bilateral contacts had failed to solve the issue.[430] American backchannel sources described the Vietnamese as dismayed by Washington's cool reaction to the release of information on the twelve MIAs.[431] The Vietnamese press condemned Ford's "insolent" attitude and accused Washington of "deliberately prolonging abnormal relations with Vietnam."[432] The Security Council, probably embarrassed by the incessant bickerings over Hanoi's application, postponed consideration of the issue to the following week.[433]

But before the Security Council could meet again, Ford, on September 13, ordered Scranton to veto the application, due to Hanoi's failure to meet the Charter's standards on humanitarian and peace-loving grounds.[434] The announcement also coincided with presidential candidate Jimmy Carter's declaration that he would meet with families of MIAs during the week.[435] However, Scranton stressed that "politics played no part in the decision," and that the U.S. veto constituted a reaction only to Vietnam's "brutal and inhumane" treatment of MIA families and its breaching of the rules of "humanitarianism" required in UN membership.[436] "[W]e have not been attempting to play politics," Scranton explained. "The United Nations is an international organization and one which we handle on a nonpartisan basis."[437] During a speech at the National Conference of Editorial Writers on October 2, Kissinger stressed that:

> we have no conflict with Vietnam now ... [and normalization] eventually will come.... On the other hand ... we believe that the behavior of the Vietnamese in not turning over to us lists which we are confident they must have is a cruel and heartless act and one for which we are not prepared to pay any price.[438]

Other than this issue, he could see no major obstacle to diplomatic rapprochement.[439]

Discrepancies arose as to the reason behind the American announcement of its upcoming veto. Senator Peter Domenici (Republican, New Mexico), for instance, who was running for congressional reelection, saw the veto as a direct continuation of the war. The U.S. position, he told *U.S. News & World Report*, was a "matter of principle:"

> [I]t would be impetuous of us to capitulate so shortly after such a huge episode and to say: "Now you can just come in" ... North Vietnam took over South Vietnam in a war. We ought not to be quick to approve that kind of thing even if they are unified in one Government. If we water down our opposition to that kind of an armed aggression and then say afterwards, "Well, it doesn't make much of a difference," we disseminate that attitude throughout the world.[440]

However, as the Security Council did not accept bilateral bickerings between countries as a legitimate excuse for a veto, Scranton explained the American decision by claiming that Vietnam had shown neither "humanitarianism" nor "peaceful intent" requested by the UN Charter. Although UN membership is open only to "peace-loving nations," no mention of "humanitarianism" is made in the Charter. However, Washington repeatedly used this concept and depicted the issue of MIAs as humanitarian, responding to Hanoi's releases of information by granting authorizations for reciprocal humanitarian aid from private American groups. Therefore Scranton's insistence on "humanitarianism" certainly had more to do with bilateral relations than it did with the UN Charter, and was largely criticized by other member states.[441]

Washington "will have nothing to do with war payments or reconstruction aid until they [the Vietnamese] give full accounting of men missing in action," declared White House Deputy Press Secretary John Carlson after Ford's September 13 announcement—interestingly blending together the bilateral issue and the UN debate.[442] On October 1, Scranton repeated the American decision to use its veto.[443]

But Washington would be deprived of its opportunity to cast this new and highly publicized veto. Sensing the pressure of the upcoming U.S. election in American declarations, the Security Council again postponed the consultation of Vietnam's application until after the election in November.[444] According to a French foreign ministry official, it was France that had made this move, with the approval of Vietnam.[445] Although the State Department denied this claim, a leak by the Libyan ambassador to the UN confirmed this information.[446] After consulting with the Vietnamese in Paris following Ford's September 13 announcement, the French decided to prolong the decision and, after a prior understanding between Kissinger and French president Valéry Giscard D'Estaing, Vietnam's consideration for membership was postponed.

The U.S. embassy stressed that this Security Council decision "should not be interpreted as involving any future commitment on our part [after the elections]."[447] This secret verbal agreement between the American secretary of state and the French president hinted that the sudden revival of American hostility in the UN might indeed merely have been an "electioneering trick," as the Vietnamese had claimed, designed to divert attention from the issues of normalization and aid and prevent diplomatic rapprochement.[448] Ford's "real concern is not for the MIAs," declared an official in Hanoi, "but on the votes in his election campaign."[449] A disgruntled Vietnamese official at the UN responded that only a reversal of the "Ford Administration's hostile policy" towards Vietnam would resolve the issue of MIAs.[450]

Hanoi's reaction went even further. Immediately after Ford's September 13 decision to veto the Vietnamese application, Hanoi released the texts of the six diplomatic notes exchanged with Washington, as well as a statement by the foreign ministry regarding this secret dialogue.[451] The Vietnamese had previously requested American authorization to disclose and comment on the nature of these notes, to which Washington had objected, but Hanoi was now using this correspondence for its own defense.[452]

Calling at the U.S. embassy in Paris a few hours before the official release of the notes, Do Thanh explained that release of the notes was a response to Scranton's declarations that the MIA issue had not been resolved through bilateral contacts and needed to be brought before the United Nations. Washington, claimed Hanoi, had distorted "the nature of the contacts which have taken place in Paris" and the notes had to be released "so that public opinion can be aware of the truth."[453] "This is a maneuver to blatantly distort the truth," claimed the official statement of the Vietnamese Ministry of Foreign Affairs accompanying release of the texts of the diplomatic notes, a "volte-face" and a gesture "contrary to reason and international law."[454] Washington, announced a radio broadcast in Hanoi, was "still deliberately pursuing an arrogant, hostile policy ... engaging in deception and misleading public opinion" and should promptly respond to the Vietnamese note of August 27 in order to settle all pending problems.[455]

The publication of these documents brought to light the backstage dialogue between the two countries during Ford's electoral campaign, placing Ford in the difficult position of having to justify the existence of secret diplomatic channels at a time when he openly rejected direct contacts with Hanoi. This correspondence showed that despite differences between the claims of both countries, both had agreed to resume the diplomatic dialogue initiated the previous year.[456] In addition, Washington's failure to respond to Vietnam's last note placed Ford in the awkward position of having refused a dialogue with Hanoi after openly declaring he would "not rest" until all MIAs had been accounted for.[457]

The publication of these documents, aimed at embarrassing Washington by bringing to public knowledge information Washington had hoped to keep secret and which could jeopardize Ford's chances for reelection, brought to light another dimension in Vietnamese thinking that would develop over the next few years. Hanoi had shown its ability to retaliate massively—and perhaps disproportionately as was common in U.S. versus communist diplomatic relations—on the diplomatic stage, for Washington's refusal to yield to Vietnamese pressure. After orchestrating the release of information on MIAs in order to woo Washington into allowing Vietnamese admission to the UN, Hanoi was severely punishing Washington for locking the UN door. Both countries' refusal to acknowledge the other's position showed that the war of arms had shifted, in the post–Vietnam war era, to a war of face and a war of words.

While attempting to achieve new friendships and diplomatic alliances with the international community, Hanoi was aware of the need to develop trade and increase foreign capital. Despite its need for foreign support and assistance, and the present complexity of its relations with the United States, Vietnam still preferred to walk the diplomatic tightrope of ideological and political independence, at least publicly.

In mid–September, while threatened by American veto in the UN, the Vietnamese were accepted as full members of the World Bank and the IMF, retaining former South Vietnam's seat in these institutions despite unsuccessful American opposition to Hanoi's membership. Reunified Vietnam also replaced South Vietnam in the Asian Development Bank.[458]

Refraining from openly expressing a tilt to one side of the ideological border separating Moscow from Peking, Hanoi took great care to spend as much time with one side as it did with the other. But when, on September 23, the Chinese canceled their October 1 reception to mourn Mao's death, the Vietnamese found themselves caught in a dilemma. The canceled meeting disrupted the careful equilibrium of the Vietnamese diplomatic timetable, which Hanoi had made a point of distributing equally, to the very minute, between time spent with Soviet officials and time spent with their Chinese counterparts. Consequently, a few days later, in order to reestablish a safe balance and not show any preference for the Soviet side, the Vietnamese ambassador snubbed his Soviet hosts at a reception given for the 59th anniversary of the October Revolution in Moscow, by walking out of the reception room to discuss his future trip to Paris with the French ambassador.[459]

That same month, Le Duan was dispatched to Peking. But although he obliquely warned against Soviet intentions in developing countries, his hosts failed to be impressed.

In Washington, the pressure of the upcoming election hit the White House with great strength, and the campaign of Ford's new opponent Jimmy Carter was gathering speed after Carter won the primaries against Hubert Humphrey for the Democratic nomination. In an interview in *Playboy* in the later half of September, Carter indirectly attacked Ford's handling of the Indochina debacle. The justification of past positions during the Vietnam war had long become a favorite theme among American thinkers, and an issue that could not be avoided during elections. On his own record regarding the war, Carter regretted his failure to have stood up against American involvement which he labeled a moment of "personal fallibility."[460] "I don't think I would ever take on the same frame of mind that Nixon or Johnson did—lying, cheating, and distorting the truth," Carter commented.[461] Ford's loss of Indochina placed him in a less immaculate position.

Indochina became one of the main axes of the Ford-Carter duel and Carter increasingly attacked the president on the need to account for MIAs.[462] On September 19, Carter pledged to the National League of Families that, should he be elected president, he would "not normalize relations with the Vietnamese Government until I am convinced they have made a complete accounting of those who are missing in action." During a meeting in Buffalo he again asserted that his administration would:

> account for the POWs and the MIAs before we reestablish any relationship with Vietnam and you can depend on that. We need a presidential delegation ... not only to go to Vietnam but also to Cambodia and Laos and that will be one of the first responsibilities that I assume that we want to get our boys either back or accounted for.[463]

During a television debate on October 6, the president reiterated his intention to veto Vietnam's admission to the UN until a full MIA accounting had been obtained. But Carter highlighted that MIAs had been a side-issue and that Ford had refrained from appointing a presidential commission to seek information on MIAs directly in Southeast Asia—which he termed an "embarrassing failure." "We need to have an active and aggressive action on the part of the president ... to seek out every possible way to get that information which has kept the MIA families in despair and doubt, and Mr. Ford has just not done it."[464]

A week later, at Harvard, responding to Carter's attack on Ford's failure to engage in direct talks with the Vietnamese over the MIA issue, Kissinger announced that talks with the Vietnamese would open in the near future.[465] In response, *Nhan Dan* condemned the American "fuss about the so-called 'forthcoming conference'" as a "noisy propaganda campaign ... aimed at deceiving the U.S. people who are discouraged, displeased and indignant with the Ford [A]dministration's domestic and foreign policies"[466]—a "crafty electioneering move" agreed another source.[467]

Unfortunately for the outgoing president, the General Accounting Office issued a report on the *Mayaguez* on the eve of the debate concluding that the rescue operation had caused useless bloodshed. The report angered the president and he retaliated that its authors were no more than "grandstand quarterbacks." However, his argument that he would have been "criticized very, very severely for sitting back and not moving" was quickly countered by his opponent. "The President," Carter declared, "has an obligation to tell the American people the truth and not wait eighteen months later for the report to be issued."[468]

Carter furthered his attack by criticizing Ford's pardon of Nixon in September 1974 and linking the two presidencies with the term "the Nixon-Ford Administration."[469] This had been a recurring theme in Carter's campaign, and as early as March 1976 Carter had accused Kissinger of "slapping in the face all those Americans who want a foreign policy that embodies our ideals, not subverts them."[470] Carter furthered his attack declaring that "our foreign policy has been conducted almost exclusively by Henry Kissinger. I don't think Mr. Ford has any interest in foreign policy."[471] Given U.S. recent history in Vietnam and Kissinger's vacillating popularity, Carter's comment was sure to please its public. A Gallup poll showed that 50 percent of the people felt Carter had won the television debate while only 27 percent supported Ford.[472]

Hanoi viewed the U.S. presidential campaign debates with great curiosity, as depicted in the numerous references and cartoons in Vietnamese journals over the Ford-Carter bickerings, and revised its policies accordingly. Hanoi too could play politics.

In an interview with the Italian *L'Europeo*, issued on October 8, Pham Van Dong astonished Washington by demonstrating a complete shift in Hanoi's policy. After declaring that the search for MIAs came as a "priority over the search for our own compatriots," the premier announced that Hanoi no longer linked MIAs, aid and normalization.

> As for the possibility of the establishment of diplomatic relations we are not adopting the intransigent stance of accelerating the establishment of relations at ambassadorial level only if the Americans respect the agreements ... we declare our own willingness [to negotiate] solely on condition that Washington ceases its anti-Vietnam propaganda and that Ford ceases to describe us as pirates! All we are asking for is an act of good will.... Only on this condition are we prepared to establish diplomatic relations with the United States.[473]

Hanoi's reference to Ford's labeling of the Vietnamese as "a bunch of international pirates" on March 20 signaled that Vietnam was seeking apologies, but the tone of the declaration was conciliatory despite the cooling of relations in the election year. Aid was no longer directly described as a precondition to normalization, although the premier made a veiled reference to the need for "an act of good will." On October 12, in response to Carter's attack on Ford's Vietnam policy, Washington proposed that talks be held on

October 28. On the same day, Hanoi rejected the date and proposed November 5 instead, three days after the election.[474] "Hanoi obviously has our election in mind in proposing this date rather than accepting our suggestion for October 28," commented a U.S. State Department observer to Kissinger, in discussing the Vietnamese proposal.

> They may think we chose the latter for possible effect in the campaign, but in any case they probably wish to know the results before entering into discussions.... The exact date of a meeting, however, does not appear to be critical, as long as we do not appear to be quibbling, stalling, or backing away from such a meeting.[475]

On October 24, in response to Carter's attack on Ford's failure to send a commission to Hanoi, Kissinger announced on *Face the Nation* that Washington had extended an invitation to Hanoi to open the first formal talks on MIAs since the end of the war, at the embassy level in Paris after the American presidential election and that dates were being discussed.[476] In the light of the approaching Security Council consideration of Vietnamese UN membership, the Vietnamese had had little choice but to accept talks. Undoubtedly, Kissinger's announcement during one of the most popular television shows of the presidential campaign pointed at the Ford administration's wish to repeat its concern for missing servicemen one last time before the presidential election. But this last-minute move failed to impress Ford's electorate.

On November 2, Jimmy Carter was elected to replace Ford in the Oval Office. The same day, Washington turned down Hanoi's offer that talks be held on November 5 and proposed November 12 instead.[477] Hanoi immediately informed the U.S. embassy in Paris that it approved this date.[478] The next day, Do Thanh and American officials met at the U.S. embassy in Paris to arrange the details of the meetings.[479]

Despite Ford's defeat, the White House remained firm in dealing with Hanoi. The Vietnamese, however, perhaps intimidated by the election of the new American president, had shifted to a softer stance, perhaps testing the new president's reactions. Before opening talks, in reply to Kissinger's earlier demand for a *full* accounting, Hanoi stated that it was "ready to carry out *fully* [its] obligations regarding the provisions of Article 8(b) ... and to undertake discussions with a view to normalization." The statement appeared as a direct response to Ford's declaration in September that Washington demanded a "full accounting." Washington, continued Hanoi, should give "proof of its goodwill ... [and] adopt a more realistic attitude."[480]

Deputy Chief Samuel Rhee Gammon of the American Embassy immediately questioned his Vietnamese counterpart Tran Hoan on MIAs, stressing that the issue was independent of the Paris Agreement, but was "based on [the] Geneva convention and [on] normal humanitarian practice." The resolving of the issue, he hinted, would be a precondition to normalization despite Vietnamese objections.[481] But the Vietnamese position, linking the question of MIAs to that of reconstruction aid, had not changed.[482] Nor, stated the Vietnamese, had Washington's linking of the MIA issue to Vietnam's admission to the UN.[483] Tran Hoan, however, answered that he would "look into" Gammon's informal request that American citizens and their dependants remaining in Vietnam be allowed to leave.[484] Following the meeting, the Vietnamese issued a communiqué reiterating their usual position that although Hanoi was ready "to discharge its obligations under Article 8(b) of the Paris agreement ... the American side must [still] assume its obligations to contribute to healing the wounds of the war and to reconstruction."[485]

Washington had ordered that no direct comments be made to the press during the bilateral meetings. The White House and the State Department would report on the talks.[486] In New York, questioned by the U.S. press on whether preliminary talks in Paris had altered Washington's position on Vietnamese admission to the UN, Scranton sneered that "[y]ou will have to test whether this was just an election gimmick"—referring to Vietnamese statements that U.S. policies towards Hanoi were aimed at wooing American voters.[487] A few hours later, State Department spokesman Robert L. Funseth announced that, given the lack of progress during the talks, Washington's intention to veto Vietnam's admission to the UN would remain unchanged.[488] As the talks ended the next day, the Vietnamese, attempting to counter another veto, issued a moderate communiqué that the French termed a promising opening to future talks with the next administration.[489]

Two days later, on November 14, Ford ordered Scranton to veto Vietnam's admission to the UN during the next day's Security Council meeting, and the next day Vietnam's request for membership was rejected on the grounds that Hanoi was using the remains of MIAs as bargaining chips, and had failed to "show satisfactory humanitarian or practical concern" in dealing with this issue.[490] Among the numerous protestations, Lao ambassador to the UN Vithaya Sourinho referred to the Vietnamese release of twelve names of MIAs in September as proof of Hanoi's goodwill regarding the MIA issue.[491] Scranton further supported the American position by charging that Vietnam was using the "deep anguish and uncertainty" of MIA families as a lever for "economic and political advantage." However, he added that Washington might shift to a softer response if Vietnam proved more concerned with the issue.[492] In July, to justify the veto, Philip Habib, talking to Montgomery's House Select Committee, indignantly noted:

> I know of no instance in which an adversary so openly treated this humanitarian problem in this way. We thus recognized from an early date what we were up against and countered by making release of prisoners and accounting for the missing a basic element of our own negotiating strategy.[493]

President-elect Carter openly approved Ford's decision to renew the U.S. veto.[494] The issue returned once more to the General Assembly.

Washington turned a deaf ear to other countries' arguments that Vietnamese admission to the UN would facilitate the release of information on MIAs, and that bilateral disputes should not affect UN decisions.[495] On November 17, Sri Lanka presented a communiqué from the Coordinating Bureau of the Non-Aligned countries requesting a favorable vote from the General Assembly over Vietnam's application.[496] On November 26, the General Assembly voted on this resolution expressing "deep regret and concern" over the American position, presenting Vietnam as a fully qualified state, and calling for a favorable reconsideration of its application—as it had in September. Only Washington voted against the resolution adopted 124–1–3.[497] Scranton again stated that by refusing to resolve the MIA issue, Vietnam had "shown itself unwilling to fulfill basic humanitarian obligations consistent with UN membership."[498] On November 26, the UN General Assembly, however, voted a resolution (124–1–3) introduced by Sri Lanka on behalf of the Non-Aligned Countries, and sponsored by 81 countries, calling for a favorable reconsideration of the Vietnamese application.[499]

Vietnamese observer to the UN Dinh Ba Thi, who had requested to attend the

General Assembly debate over Hanoi's admission to the UN, reminded Washington that Hanoi had already appointed a special committee to identify the remains of MIAs and that a list had been handed over to Washington on November 12.[500] The American veto despite the Vietnamese gesture, he declared, demonstrated that "the Ford-Kissinger policy is still one of bitterness." The Vietnamese foreign ministry broadcast severe criticism of the American position, charging that Washington was attempting to "cover up its wrong acts and mislead public opinion." MIAs and reconstruction aid, it added, were bilateral issues that could not be tied to the Vietnamese application to the UN and were presently "being examined by representatives of the two countries at meetings in Paris."[501]

The following day, *Nhan Dan* issued a far more severe attack, depicting the veto as "the rancor of the defeated pirate" through which the U.S.—"an international hoodlum"—had "only shown its stubbornness expressed by blunt contentions." Washington was again making an "abusive use of [its] power."[502] Questioning whether the issue of MIAs was not "a sheer pretext," the editorial rhetorically asked:

> If the U.S. side is really concerned with the problem of Americans reported missing-in-action as provided for in Article 8B of the Paris agreement then why does the U.S. Government deliberately evade the implementation of Article 21 concerning its obligation to contribute to the healing of the wounds of war in Vietnam?[503]

In an interview a few days later, State Department official in charge of MIAs Frank Sieverts explained that the accounting of all MIAs remained a precondition to the negotiation of normalization and had been approved as such by the Ford administration, Congress and president-elect Jimmy Carter.[504] However, some congressmen, especially Democrats, stood against American hostility towards Vietnam. During the reconsideration of Hanoi's application on November 26, for instance, Representative Bella Abzug (Democrat, New York) claimed that Vietnam's admission would encourage the release of information on MIAs.[505]

That same day, Senator McGovern issued a letter to Kissinger and Donald Rumsfeld requesting that Washington withdraw its veto from the Security Council vote if it did not wish to appear "weak and ridiculous."[506] On September 10, Senators McGovern and Mark Hatfield (Republican, Oregon) had already requested in vain that Washington refrain from using its veto against Vietnam.[507] But McGovern had also understood the need to de-emphasize the MIA issue in order to push through on rapprochement with Hanoi and to ease the release of information on MIAs, although accounting for missing or killed servicemen in Vietnam always remained one of McGovern's main priorities. "Is it not a fact," he asked, "that the Defense Department has information based on intelligence sources and interrogation of other combat personnel that these M.I.A.'s in Vietnam aerial combat were actually killed in action?"[508] While accounting for missing servicemen would indeed be cause for dispute between the two countries, accounting for dead servicemen—which most likely were—could be downgraded to a question of bilateral cooperation and not a humanitarian issue. His request that Washington withdraw its veto from the United Nations Security Council remained unheard.

On November 29, Washington proposed that a second round of talks be held on December 20.[509] Although Hanoi had initially allowed its representatives in Paris to accept a second meeting without referring to Hanoi, these instructions were modified following the new veto and Hanoi delayed its reply to Washington. The Vietnamese simply signaled to Washington that Hanoi still pondered over the date of December 20.

Similarly, Hanoi also postponed the return of the twelve sets of remains promised on September 6. The Vietnamese, reported Do Thanh in Paris, felt humiliated by the U.S. move at the UN, as they considered Vietnamese membership "to be so much more important than the MIA question."[510] To the American public, Do Thanh's clumsy statement came as a confirmation of a Vietnamese lack of concern for American MIAs.

On December 15, Hanoi officially rejected the proposal for meetings in December and suggested that talks resume instead on January 10, perhaps hoping that the delay would allow it to deal with the new Carter administration at a time when possibilities with the Ford administration had reached a dead end.[511] Five days later, Washington informed Hanoi that January 10 was inappropriate due to the upcoming change of government but refrained from suggesting any other date.[512] Vietnam was left to hope that the Carter administration would bring more fertile negotiations and a renewal of American goodwill.

The period from the fall of Saigon to the end of the Ford presidency witnessed the emergence of some themes and diplomatic patterns that remained at the forefront of American-Vietnamese relations over the years covered in this book. Among these—and the most significant under Ford—was the emergence of a deep-rooted bitterness born out of the American loss of Vietnam.

In late 1975 and 1976 this bitterness remained within the executive branch, and demonstrated a predisposition to adopt aggressive policies towards Hanoi, while liberal congressmen either turned their attention away from Indochina or called for reconciliation. Meanwhile, Hanoi trumpeted its claim for reconstruction aid in a counterproductive publicizing of U.S. responsibilities and introduced the concept of exchanging MIAs for aid—a pattern that would govern bilateral relations until the 1990s. U.S. rejections of Vietnamese openings and American opposition to Vietnamese admission to the UN stemmed from Washington's vindictiveness and fear of losing face by accepting a dialogue with its former enemy, the victors of America's longest war, and the pressure of the upcoming election. During this period a gap emerged between the executive branch's public statements pledging efforts to account for MIAs to the U.S. electorate and a sterile behind-the-scene hostility as shown through the exchange of diplomatic notes in 1976. This pattern of a dual diplomacy continued under Carter, although with the reversed aim of promoting reconciliation while avoiding negative interventions from Congress or lobby groups. Therefore, 1977 witnessed a reversal of U.S. domestic trends as the executive branch opted for reconciliation, and congressional conservatives jeopardized chances for diplomatic rapprochement. While the Ford era was characterized by the primacy of domestic politics and the impact of Kissingerian strategies on executive policies, the Carter administration shifted to a more balanced approach.

By early 1977, Ford had used up much of Vietnamese patience. Radicalism emerged in Hanoi, undermining chances for diplomatic rapprochement between the two countries, and highlighted the continuation under Carter of numerous mutual misperceptions and misunderstandings observed in 1975 and 1976. While the Ford and Carter administrations' policies towards Hanoi varied in both aims and means, some patterns remained.

II

THE ADVENT OF THE CARTER YEARS

The Fourth Party Congress

While Washington witnessed the setting up of the Carter administration, political reshufflings took place in Hanoi. While these went relatively unnoticed in the United States, they would greatly affect bilateral relations over the following years.

By late 1976 and early 1977, disputes among Vietnamese ruling circles and Hanoi's difficult relations with Peking and Washington forced Vietnam to reevaluate both its foreign and domestic policies and to reassess the organization of its leadership. In June 1976, *Quan Doi Nhan Dan* published several references hinting at the need to purge the party of foreign spies and saboteurs. The ferocious tone of these writings, believed to emanate from members of the army and security services, was the first hint of the rise of radicalist tendencies in Hanoi. On August 29, 1976, it was officially announced that the VWP would soon be reorganized.[1] This new line of thought, at least partly fathered by American impermeability to Vietnam's requests for diplomatic rapprochement and by the cooling of China's relations with Hanoi, entailed a readjustment of Vietnam's approach to its internal problems. In turn, the emergence of a new radical leadership may also have hardened Vietnamese policies towards Washington during the last months of the Ford administration and throughout the Carter years, and encouraged the cooling of relations with China and Cambodia.

From December 11–20, 1976, the VWP convened the Fourth Party Congress to decide on the paths that the reunified state should follow. This congress, the first since 1960, allowed the distribution of power among Vietnamese leadership. But the congress also brought to light the reemergence of factionalism within the party. While inner-party political factions dated back to the creation of the VWP in 1951 and had developed since the death of Ho Chi Minh, they had remained relatively dormant until December 1976.[2] In the words of former North Vietnamese officer Bui Tin, the reemergence of opposing factions within the Vietnamese leadership would account for much of the "disease of subjective arrogance" that affected Vietnam after the fall of Saigon but that climaxed during the Carter years as the Vietnamese became "lax, intoxicated and dizzy with victory."[3]

On December 20, the People's Revolutionary Party—the South Vietnamese communist party—merged with the VWP to create the Vietnamese Communist Party (VCP). While the VWP had been initially named to avoid any direct reference to the communist nature of the organization, it had now reversed this strategy and openly attached itself to Marxist-Leninist ideologies.[4] Although Vietnamese communism had been long known to the rest of the world, and the creation of the VCP merely finalized the reunification of the country by unifying its leading organizations, this merging confirmed the death of a southern administrative independence and signaled the birth of a new and more powerful ruling order led by Hanoi.

Perhaps more importantly, the congress marked the confirmation of pro–Soviet Le Duan's ascendancy to power—backed by Le Duc Tho—as he was reappointed Secretary-General of the Central Committee of the VCP, a title which he had served since 1960 and which he would keep until his death in 1986.[5] The post was the highest in the VCP, as the chairmanship of the party remained vacant in honor of Ho Chi Minh's memory.[6]

A short note should be added regarding these new leaders in the consideration of such factionalism within the VCP, since the nature of the new leaders' motivations and political priorities are of primary importance in explaining subsequent diplomatic exchanges between Vietnam and Cambodia or China, and consequently with Washington, from 1977 on. While Le Duc Tho held only the position of organizational secretary of the Party, which he had enjoyed since 1956, he was responsible for the appointment of most members of the leadership. Several of them held positions superior to his own, such as his long-time friend Le Duan, secretary-general of the VCP since 1960. Contrary to Ho Chi Minh's advice, Le Duc Tho had brought Le Duan to Hanoi in 1957 and officially appointed him secretary-general three years later to replace Truong Chinh, after the latter's dismissal following the utter failure of the Chinese-inspired agricultural reforms of the 1950s.[7] Bui Tin recalled that:

> These ... men [Le Duc Tho and Le Duan] progressively tried to neutralise Ho Chi Minh as well as the Prime Minister, Pham Van Dong. With the latter it was not difficult, since he had no wish to become involved in an internal power struggle both as a matter of principle and because of weakness of character.[8]

But Ho Chi Minh's legendary figure could not be easily overthrown. Le Duc Tho and Le Duan's influence first became visible during Ho Chi Minh's illness, starting in 1965, then more openly after Ho's death in 1969.[9] According to Vietnamese defector Hoang Van Hoan writing in *Beijing Review*, Le Duan sought to dismantle the system of collective leadership and installed a wide program of surveillance and control of party members. Le Duan's ambitions were further enhanced in 1975 when the building of peace underlined the rift between "professional revolutionaries," such as Le Duc Tho and Le Duan, and the "intellectuals," such as Vo Nguyen Giap or Nguyen Co Thach who advocated softer policies and military caution.[10] It was after the end of the war, in Hoang Van Hoan's words, that Le Duan "did ... openly betray the ... revolution" specifically starting during the Fourth Party Congress of 1976, when, "instead of trying to remold himself ... to serve the revolution, he took advantage of the revolution to raise his own position and prestige."[11]

Both Le Duan and Le Duc Tho's radical views and sense of Vietnamese superiority would rapidly become apparent in their policies—a first example of which had been Le Duc Tho's "churlish" behavior in turning down his co-nomination for the Nobel Peace Prize in 1973 alongside Kissinger.[12]

In fact, several sources focus on Le Duan's authority and imply that, in the words of historian Stein Tonneson, he "was clearly the second most powerful Vietnamese communist leader in the 20th century, after Ho Chi Minh."[13] But the line separating these two characters was not so clear-cut. Bui Tin's choice to refer to Le Duan and Le Duc Tho as "these two men" in the above quote is in itself a revealing detail and may lead one to speculate whether this "collusion"—a term often used to label their relationship—was not in fact a more clever association between a mastermind—Le Duan—and a more discreet but strategically placed "enforcer" of policies, in Judith Stowe's words, a "hard man behind the scene" and "the *éminence grise*" in the duo.[14] By the end of 1976, following national elections and reunification of the two states, the reappointment of Le Duan was confirmation of the power of these two fascinating figures that would develop further over the years.

In fact, although no archival sources yet come to confirm this point, perhaps until the Hanoi archives are made available for research, it seems that Le Duc Tho, much like Stalin in the early days of his rise, gradually came to exercise his authority from behind the scenes. While maintaining a relatively low-key position, Tho backed Le Duan's policies with appointments of pro–Le Duan Vietnamese leaders, to suit their political agenda. Other political personalities, such as Nguyen Duy Trinh and especially Pham Van Dong, were left to stand as figureheads of the official government while Le Duan and Le Duc Tho discreetly held the reins of power.[15] Writing in 1966, P.J. Honey tackled the issue of Ho's succession and concluded that Dong

> would be unlikely to become the national leader.... It is more probable that he would survive a local conflict for power and subsequently be invited by the victor to serve the new government in a senior capacity ... [being] essentially a follower rather than a leader.[16]

And indeed that seemed to be the case. Commenting on his being the oldest and longest-serving prime minister in the world, Dong once privately remarked that he could "do nothing," adding that: "[w]hen I say something, nobody listens ... I cannot even choose my own ministers."[17]

While the Fourth Party Congress called for cultural purification of Vietnam, it also promoted the reorganization of the VCP under Le Duan's supervision. Thus, while the Politburo was expanded from 13 to 17 members and the Central Committee from 71 to 133, these were also purged of their pro–Chinese members—representing about half the members of the Committee—to the benefit of new pro–Soviet leaders regarded as more sympathetic to Le Duan's policies. However, moderate pragmatists, such as Nguyen Duy Trinh and Le Thanh Nghi, who had once been labeled "pro–Chinese" for their hesitation in embracing pro–Soviet views, retained their position.[18] So, of course, did Dong.

Under the leadership of Le Duan, the Fourth Party Congress signaled drastic administrative and ideological changes within the VCP leading to the re-teaching of a different basic concept of "society" based on Marx's dictatorship of the proletariat and the advent of the "new socialist man."[19] "The important task of ideological and cultural work," explained Le Duan,

> is to combat bourgeois ideology ... and other nonproletarian ideologies; to sweep away the influence of the neo-colonialist ideology and culture in the South; ... to give absolute predominance to Marxist-Leninism in the political and spirited life of the people; ... step by step to build a new culture with a socialist content and a national and popular character, to build and foster a type of socialist man in Vietnam.[20]

"The new socialist man," he explained in a rather utopian definition,

> is the new Vietnamese whose most outstanding features are his collective mastership, labour, love for socialism and his spirit of proletarian internationalism. This man is the embodiment and development of what is best and noblest in the Vietnamese mind and character forged through four thousand years of history.[21]

Beyond the common propaganda aspect of these declarations, the open tilt towards Marxist-Leninism and the definition of the "new socialist man" betrayed the coming out of Hanoi's pro–Soviet ideology. In fact, the immediate effect of the decisions of the congress was a shift to pro–Sovietism paired with the identification of China as a growingly potential threat. The Vietnamese later revealed that a secret resolution was passed during the congress determining that China stood as a long-term threat to Vietnamese independence. This represented a sudden and decisive change from Hanoi's former position of denying its pro–Sovietism. Cambodia's recent political cozying up to Peking and both countries' mutual hostility towards Hanoi were reassessed within this perspective.[22] Also, Hanoi did not fail to note that both Phnom Penh and China had declined the Vietnamese invitation to attend the congress.[23] Peking had pointed at domestic problems to explain why the Chinese delegation no longer attended foreign meetings, but nevertheless officially saluted the opening of the Vietnamese Congress.[24]

The confirmation of the developing power of Le Duan during the Fourth Party Congress not only signaled the growing alignment with the Soviet Union, but also the reappraisal of Vietnamese priorities and ideologies both at home and abroad. It signaled the Vietnamese intention to purify the country by ridding it of all dissidents to the party and external elements that had infiltrated Vietnam. Thus, not only was China declared a potential threat, but Chinese indirect influence in Vietnam was also considered a danger and would later account for Hanoi's gradual persecution of the ethnic Chinese or Hoas in 1977 and especially 1978.[25] The Hoas, living mainly in South Vietnam, had retained a nationalistic attachment to their native land and had developed a thriving capitalist-oriented economy during the Vietnam War years, giving birth to increasing distrust on the part of the Hanoi leadership as Sino-Vietnamese relations deteriorated. Thus, the development of capitalist economic habits, usually observed in the ethnic Chinese community and dubbed "mandarinism," was stated as one of the dangers jeopardizing the success of the socialist revolution. Le Duan's attack on "bourgeois ideology" was as much aimed at pro–Chinese party members as at the Hoa community itself.

Linking word to action, the VCP launched a "political education and self-criticism and criticism campaign" which led to the expulsion from the party of "several thousands," as claimed by Le Duc Tho. The decision followed the publication in the party's theoretical review *Hoc Tap* of an article criticizing "the decline in revolutionary quality." "[O]pportunist elements," Le Duc Tho explained, had been "infiltrating the party and assuming power with a view to seeking fame and wealth," thus becoming "degenerate as far as politics, quality and ethics are concerned."[26] In an indirect attack on the Hoas, Deputy Minister of Interior and VCP Central Committee member Le Quoc Than further declared that:

> imperialism and other international reactionary forces are feverishly taking advantage of political and diplomatic activities, economic and cultural exchanges and scientific and technical cooperation to advance their schemes of intelligence, espionage and sabotage.[27]

This new line of thought triggered the dismissal, punishment and re-education of a great number of Vietnamese cadres.[28] Also, a new inspection committee was created to insure maintenance of the party's socialist unity and to fight rightist influence.[29]

But while Peking perceived ousting of the pro–Chinese faction from the party as a tilt towards Moscow, the Vietnamese still publicly continued to resist the Soviet pull. Mitchail Suslov, who headed the Soviet delegation to the Fourth Congress of the Workers' Party in Hanoi, saw his offer to Hanoi to join COMECON politely declined by his Vietnamese counterpart, despite his assurances that there were "many new and still greater possibilities to deepen further the relations of economic cooperation among socialist countries."[30]

Vietnamese resistance to Soviet wooing may perhaps have been more a show than a genuine concern for ideological independence. In fact, on the eve of the first day of the congress, the Vietnamese met with the Soviet delegation in order to—in the words of *Hanoi Radio*—study "the future development of cooperation between these two countries."[31] Suslov reminded his Vietnamese hosts that the Soviet Union offers support to Soviet allies through a demonstration of "the power of international solidarity," but the Vietnamese seemed unmoved by Soviet wooing.[32] Nor did they allow the Soviet representative, whose strong stance against the Chinese was well known, to make any mention of Peking.[33] Suslov manifested his discontent with an early withdrawal from the congress and, in the following months, Moscow began delaying shipments of oil and spare parts to Vietnam.[34]

Simultaneously, a series of hostile articles was published in the Chinese press, starting in early December 1976, indicating China's resentment of Vietnam's tilt towards Moscow. These articles further encouraged American military presence in Southeast Asia and hinted that the Soviet Union might be granted access to Cam Ranh Bay, a former U.S. military base of crucial strategic importance in which the Soviets had repeatedly manifested considerable interest despite Vietnamese opposition to a Soviet military presence on the base.[35]

Certainly Peking's announcement two months later that it was unable to renew its economic aid to Vietnam and would simply continue the programs it had started before 1977 were a reaction to Hanoi's reorganization of the VCP and its purging of pro–Chinese members.[36]

The belief in Vietnamese superiority would also lead to Hanoi's shaping of unrealistic domestic plans, based on an idealized appraisal of Vietnamese capabilities to overcome the economic hardships imposed by the war. The Fourth Party Congress decided upon a new five-year economic and agricultural plan that would stabilize the national economy and promote development of the South. Among themselves, officials termed this effort the "northmalization" of the South.[37] Now that national reunification had been achieved, Hanoi opted for speeding up economic reconstruction to become a modern nation-state and decided to launch a vast industrial and agricultural campaign aimed at turning Vietnam into a fully developed country by the year 2000.[38]

More broadly, according to Stalinist doctrine, the emphasis on the need to develop heavy industry and to promote collectivization and industrialization of agriculture was created to counter the risk of tilting toward capitalism and encourage the resurgence of *compradore bourgeoisie*, against which the congress incessantly warned.[39]

This five-year plan developed the settling of New Economic Zones, and planned the resettlement of North Vietnamese cadres in the South to coordinate production, manage businesses and collect taxes from South Vietnam which, in the eyes of Hanoi, experienced difficulties getting back to work for its own maintenance after twenty years of American economic "spoon-feeding."[40] In 1974 alone, American economic and military aid to South Vietnam had amounted to $2.9 billion, most of which was in the form of consumer goods and, during the last two years of the war, the survival of the southern regime had relied mostly on American rice imports.[41] The Fourth Party Congress was now expecting a national economic growth of 18 percent per year, mainly supported by domestic efforts and foreign investments.[42]

However, the plans soon appeared entirely unrealistic. While in 1976 the annual growth rate represented 9 percent — half the expected rate — it had dropped to 2 percent in 1977. The year 1977 witnessed the reemergence of famine in Vietnam — a phenomenon that had not been observed since 1955.[43] In 1982, Le Duan openly admitted that the Fourth Party Congress had failed to understand "the difficulties and complexities" of economic transformation.[44]

While the Vietnamese leadership had excelled in the art of war it was unprepared for peace-time disciplines such as economics and daily international diplomacy. Perhaps also, Vietnam's failure to adopt a new constitution during this congress signaled a wish to stabilize the leadership, but also betrayed the difficulty that the "professional revolutionaries" found in adapting to peace.[45] Hanoi, led by hard-liners such as Le Duan, clearly did not understand the need to shift from what historian William Duiker termed the "fortress mentality" of the war years — in which an offensive stand was appropriate — and to adapt to peace-time policies both at home and abroad.[46] What had initially been a winning military strategy became a standard but counterproductive Vietnamese diplomatic line both with the United States and in Hanoi's handling of Sino-Soviet rivalry, playing Peking, Moscow and Washington against each other as it had during the war, with apparently no understanding of Vietnam's decreased strategic importance in superpower triangular relations since the end of the war.

Consequently, as economic difficulties increased in 1977, a debate arose within the leadership over which course of action to adopt. As Steven Hurst explains, while one group opted for partial liberalization of the country's economy, the dominant faction chose to hasten the "northmalization" of the South with the economic aid it intended to receive from Washington. This strategy, he explains, found its roots in the belief that

Washington, more than Vietnam, needed normalization. Marxist-Leninist ideology led the Vietnamese leadership to believe that Washington, lured by the economic bait of Vietnamese trade, would eventually come back to the Vietnamese and seek normalization. Washington's obstinacy in fighting many years of war in Vietnam had convinced Hanoi of its own value in American eyes, and encouraged Hanoi to maintain a strong stance against Washington, including maintaining the aid precondition. This misperception would lead even the most radical elements in the leadership to await proof of American repentance that would never come.[47]

The emergence of Vietnamese radicalism accounted for the growing animosity towards Washington in 1977 and the heightened emphasis on Hanoi's claim for aid, as Hanoi handled politics the way it would a military battle. One of the long-term effects of this growing factionalism was Hanoi's open turn to Moscow in 1978, reviving Cold War tensions between the U.S., the USSR and China, and shifting the nature of Hanoi's foreign policy with Washington.

The New Socialist Man, the New American Man and the New China

By the end of 1976, American public opinion had shifted from the immediate post–Vietnam War trauma to hints of renewed optimism.[48] Carter, mocked an Indian newspaper, simply stood as "a God-fearing, deeply disturbed American, who reflected their [the Americans'] sense of guilt and shock [over the Vietnam War]."[49] The recently unknown former peanut farmer, once nicknamed "Jimmy Who?" for his lack of public notoriety, had become the thirty-ninth president of the United States.[50] His election, with a 51–48 majority in the Senate, shifted the reins of power from Republican to Democrat hands.[51] "There's a mood in America," Carter declared:

> We've been shaken by a tragic war abroad and by scandals and broken promises at home. Our people are searching for new voices and new ideas and new leaders.... And once again as brothers and sisters, our hearts will swell with pride to call ourselves American.[52]

The new president promised his electorate never to lie and to draw the executive branch closer to his people, in order to avoid any reenactment of Watergate or of Nixon's secret dealings with Vietnam and other foreign countries. "As a political candidate," he explained during his campaign, "I owe special interests nothing. I owe people everything."[53] In the early months of 1977, Carter thus began to take part in call-in radio shows from the Oval Office, and to plan family visits to several states for a direct encounter with the American people.[54] With an admitted lack knowledge in international affairs and no congressional experience, he who had been described as "a flash in the pan" by the outgoing president during his primaries had been offered the White House by an electorate only too eager to dust the Oval Office of reminders of past failures.[55]

"You have given me a great responsibility," Carter declared in his inaugural address, "to stay close to you, to be worthy of you, and to exemplify what you are. Let us create together a new national spirit of unity and trust"—in other words, a *New American Man*. His inaugural speech, remarked the American press, "was more a sermon than an agenda for the nation."⁵⁶ Interestingly, Carter's ideology of repentance and his will to restore the original luster of the nation were remarkably similar to those of the Vietnamese reform policies during the Fourth National Congress. "I am convinced that among us 200 million Americans," had stated a campaign poster, "there is a willingness—even eagerness—to restore in our country what has been lost—*if* we have understandable purposes and goals and a modicum of bold and inspired leadership."⁵⁷

On his first day in office, on January 21, 1977, Carter demonstrated his break with the bitterness of the Ford administration and the new theme of redemption of his policies, with a pardon of draft evaders of the Vietnam War.⁵⁸ This pardon replaced Ford's earlier amnesty for both draft dodgers and deserters issued on September 16, 1974.⁵⁹ Beyond this gesture of healing the wounds that Vietnam had inflicted upon his nation, this move also signaled Carter's wish to ease relations between Washington and its former enemy by reducing domestic tensions regarding the war and preparing public opinion for renewed contact with Hanoi.

Keeping within his rhetoric of repentance and forgiveness, Carter explained his choice for a pardon in the following words: "Amnesty implies what you did was right; a pardon [like Ford's] says that whether what you did was right or wrong, we forgive you for it."⁶⁰ In order to avoid popular discontent over too large a pardon, it was restricted to "those who violated Selective Service laws" by dodging the draft and occasionally to some deserters under specific conditions.⁶¹

When Carter entered the White House, both Hanoi and Peking hoped for positive changes in U.S. foreign policy. In early 1977, *Nhan Dan* commented that

> with Nixon at the helm, the U.S. ship sank further into a deep and comprehensive crisis.... Today, with Jimmy Carter as captain, many people aboard the U.S. ship do not yet clearly see where they are going. They have the feeling that they are still groping around in heavy fog.⁶²

This remark, however, seemed a projection of Vietnamese sentiment.

On the day following Carter's election, Vietnamese foreign minister Nguyen Co Thach, who strongly favored an inroad to the West, voiced his hope that Carter's policies towards Vietnam would be wiser than Ford's.⁶³ "Concerning Vietnam," noted *Nhan Dan* on November 7:

> Carter has said nothing different from the shopworn views of ... Ford and Kissinger.... Carter has made several promises. In the opinion of hundreds of millions of Americans, the problem is whether the Carter Administration will fulfill any of these promises—or if everything will go with the wind again.⁶⁴

By January, the Vietnamese press was calling the failure of Ford's policies towards Hanoi a "Lesson for Carter."⁶⁵ Now enjoying diplomatic recognition from 97 countries and holding 22 memberships in international organizations, the Vietnamese remained doubtful as to the outcome of their exchanges with the new administration.⁶⁶

Carter's initial intentions were pacific and Wilsonian in nature. Carter, like Woodrow Wilson before him, believed in the need to alleviate tensions with the Soviet Union to draw the Cold War to an end and to turn Washington away from the self-centered realpolitik that had governed previous administrations.⁶⁷ In historian Odd Arne Westad's words, Carter thought himself "capable of breaking through the ice that the

Cold War had cast over U.S. foreign policy with regard to enemies and allies alike."[68] Carter wished to free the country of its "inordinate fear of communism"[69]:

> Our national security was often defined almost exclusively in terms of military competition with the Soviet Union. This competition is still critical, because it does involve issues that could lead to war. But however important this relationship of military balance, it cannot be our sole preoccupation to the exclusion of other world issues which also concern us both.[70]

A new world order would be sought in which all nations would enjoy the right to self-determination, cooperation, free trade and mutual defense. Carter hoped that adopting a regionalist approach to foreign policy and considering Third World countries outside the framework of American-Soviet confrontation would de-emphasize the East-West conflict so as not to allow it to dominate foreign policy-making.

Upon entering the Department of State, Secretary of State Cyrus Vance followed Carter's initiative by ordering all U.S. embassies and diplomatic posts abroad to conduct foreign policies "as openly as possible ... [in accordance with] traditional American values." Carter was seduced by the idea and extended Vance's instructions to the White House staff.[71]

Only after early 1978, under the influence of National Security Adviser Zbigniew Brzezinski, did Carter shift to a more aggressive approach to foreign policy, swapping his regionalist views for a less-refined globalist view of world order in which local conflicts, such as that between Vietnam and its Chinese and Cambodian neighbors, were perceived within the larger context of superpower competition.[72]

In the early months after his election, Carter seemed ready for rapprochement with Vietnam. One of Carter's stated goals during his campaign had been the establishment of normal relations with some fourteen nations, including Vietnam, which had no official ties with Washington. Soon after taking office, Carter instructed Vance to draw up a list of these nations and to comment on the "prospects" and "advisability" of normalization.[73]

In his memoirs, the president argues that automatic recognition of all established governments, which most European nations already followed, "would give us a toehold in the unfriendly country and an opportunity to ease tensions, increase American influence, and promote peace."[74] Moreover, this concept revealed Carter's wish to view Third World countries as independent states, rather than superpower proxies, torn between the two camps and offering potential for expansion of Soviet hegemony abroad. Such an approach, in Carter's words, would create a "world-wide mosaic of global, regional and bilateral relations"—a concept of a "global community" of cooperating nations.[75]

Brzezinski, who began the Carter era by favoring a rather regionalist view of foreign policy-making in the early days of the presidency before shifting to an all-out globalist appraisal of the world in 1978, agreed with this initial approach. He described Carter's policy as an attempt to build "new relationships with friends, with adversaries, with the developing world, even with the whole world—in the hope thereby of renovating the existing international system" and of involving "the entire international community of more than 150 nation-states."[76]

Normalizing with Vietnam therefore had its place on Carter's agenda, especially in view of his pledge to restore the confidence of his nation following its recent history in Indochina. In an interview in the mid–1990s, Brzezinski explained that Carter's primary motivation [regarding Vietnam] was non-strategic, it was historical-moral. The president wanted to heal the wounds of the Vietnamese war in general, both inside America and in terms of America's external policies.[77]

In a press conference on March 24, Carter explained:

> My own natural inclination is to have normal diplomatic relationships with all countries in the world ... I don't know what the motivations of the Vietnamese might be. I think part of the motivation might be to be treated along with other nations in economic assistance from our country and in trade, and development of their fairly substantial natural resources, including oil.
> Other considerations might be political in nature. They might very well want to balance their friendship with the Soviet Union and not be completely dependent upon the Soviet Union. That is just a guess on my part. But I am willing to negotiate in good faith. But as far as describing what our economic relationship might be with Vietnam in the future after the relationships are established, I just couldn't do that now.[78]

Hanoi seemed skeptical. "Just as we did during the war," commented a senior Vietnamese official, "we have decided to wait patiently and watch until something positive has been demonstrated."[79]

Carter appointed Cyrus Vance Secretary of State on December 3, and, on December 16, Zbigniew Brzezinski, National Security Adviser.[80] The Vietnamese had perhaps sensed that Zbigniew Brzezinski would not be an ally in winning American friendship. The NSC adviser had brought from his native Poland a deep anticommunist and anti–Soviet animus, and a profound distrust of Kissinger's quest for détente which earned him the reputation of being "a theoretician of anticommunism."[81] Brzezinski, whom Carter had met in the Trilateral Commission, favored a "trilateral relationship" between Washington and its European and Japanese allies rather than collaborating with the Soviet camp through treaties such as SALT—an issue he eventually let the State Department handle as his attention increasingly turned to China.[82]

Brzezinski would probably be "Carter's Henry Kissinger—not as Secretary of State but as an inside guru at the White House," predicted American foreign policy specialist Stephen Barber, and, indeed, Brzezinski's concept of a hard-liner philosophy was close to that of Kissinger, although different in nature.[83] While criticizing Kissinger's "Lone Ranger" diplomatic approach, Brzezinski's own style did not significantly differ.[84] Brzezinski's authoritarian personality, charisma, and taste for competition and secrecy greatly resembled Kissinger's and had led some journalists to refer to Brzezinski as a "Polish Kissinger."[85] In fact, both Kissinger and Brzezinski had been lecturers at Harvard and both had been called to Washington to serve, for a short while, in the Kennedy administration. But while Kissinger had returned to Harvard and joined the Rockefeller team, Brzezinski established his own research institute on communism at Columbia University. The two men became academic rivals, each attempting to outpace the other.[86]

Although Vance and Brzezinski initially recommended each other for these posts, their conflicting views of world politics soon clashed, causing their relationship, in the words of historian Patrick Taylor, to develop into an "all-out civil war" in the administration.[87] While Vance supported regionalist policies, Brzezinski opted for a large-scale globalist approach, closer to Kissinger's.[88] Brzezinski, a "first rate thinker," as Carter recalled, offered "innovative and often provocative" ideas. Although Carter's aides had warned him that "Dr. Brzezinski might not be adequately deferential to a secretary of state," the president had already made up his mind.[89] Consequently, "while Cy Vance became [Carter's] acquaintance," Chief of the White House staff Hamilton Jordan recalls in his memoirs, "Zbig Brzezinski became his friend."[90] Vance later reported that Brzezinski "would attempt increasingly to take the role of policy spokesman."[91] Over the months, the Vance-Brzezinski rivalry would recall the diplomatic feud that had caused Kissinger to oppose Secretary of State William Rogers under Nixon.[92]

According to Kissinger, Vance was a "[d]eliberate, soft-spoken, honorable" man, the "epitome of the New York corporation lawyer, meticulously executing his assignments, wisely advising his clients."[93] Vance represented, in historian John Dumbrell's words, a "traditional elite figure" quite different from Brzezinski's Cold War aggressive persona, and embodied the post–Vietnam War passivity that Brzezinski disdained.[94] "Vance," explained *Newsweek*, "was the sort calculated to reassure Washington and the world—a well-bred, Yale polished insider described by one mostly admiring academic as 'the epitome of the eastern Establishment.'"[95] Vance's appointment, according to Carter, had been a "natural selection for Secretary of State."[96]

The president's choice of a man respectful of the established hierarchy signaled his wish to break with Kissinger's "Lone Ranger" attitude and tendency to outplay presidential authority. This was in keeping with Carter's wish to break with past administrations' obscure handling of foreign affairs.[97]

Brzezinski's appointment as head of the NSC would counterbalance Vance's softer policies, and mark a turn to a harder line against détente and the Soviets.[98] The bureaucratic slowness of the State Department and the political softness of its secretary would remain Brzezinski's main cause for irritation throughout the Carter presidency, and eventually his influence on the Oval Office defeated Vance's recommendations for a softer stance on foreign policy.

Vance's initial strategy recommended normalization with both Peking and Hanoi, a progressive de-escalation of the Cold War and the signing of a second Strategic Arms Limitation Treaty (SALT) with Moscow.[99] Since 1969, Vance had served as vice-chairman of a UN policy panel on conventional arms control whose work had culminated in 1976 with the publication of a study deploring the growth of world arms trade. SALT remained one of his priorities—an issue that Brzezinski rapidly downgraded, informing Vance only seven months into the administration that, in his view, détente would not occur before two to eight years.[100] On the contrary, Brzezinski saw no point in making concessions to the Soviets whether through SALT or any other foreign policy issues.

Keeping within the same perspective, Vance, who shared the Chinese distrust of the Soviet influence in Southeast Asia, believed that normalizing with Hanoi "could increase [American] influence with Vietnam and offer it alternatives to excessive political, economic and military dependence on the Soviet Union."[101] Vance had been greatly affected by Vietnam while serving under Johnson, and had served as delegate to the peace talks in 1968—a detail which *Nhan Dan* reported with unusual rapidity, flanked with portraits of the new secretary.[102] The Vietnamese had, however, remained prudent and refrained from making any comments.[103]

During his confirmation hearing on January 11, Vance endorsed the president's view that American intervention in Vietnam was "in the light of hindsight ... a mistake." He added:

> I think, however, that we have learned a number of lessons as a result of the Vietnam experience and hopefully I am the wiser for these ... I must say that I think the motivation in the initial involvement was not one based upon evil motives. I think it was based upon misjudgments and mistakes as we went along.[104]

Carter agreed with Vance that Vietnam wished to maintain its political independence and that normalization would pull Hanoi away from the Soviet Union. Therefore the two men initially viewed relations with Vietnam within a regionalist framework and understood the importance of normalization, not only for bilateral purposes, but to keep Soviet influence from Indochina. Vance was even ready to request aid from Congress should Hanoi offer a satisfactory accounting of MIAs.[105] Thus, in early 1977, Hanoi's chance for dialogue seemed to lie with the State Department.[106]

During the campaign, Carter had appeared more conservative than the Vietnamese had hoped, adopting Ford's stance that the United States should veto Vietnam's admission to the UN until a full accounting of MIAs had been obtained. But after the election, Carter was in a more conciliatory mood.

In October 1976, Vance had sent a memo to Carter suggesting that, were he elected, a presidential envoy should be sent to Hanoi in early 1977 to resume talks on MIAs. The Vietnamese would be told "that the U.S. would be prepared to put to the Congress a program of humanitarian assistance in such areas as housing, health and food, once there was an accounting for the MIAs."[107] It was soon time for the moralistic Carter to live up to his promises.

In December 1976, the Montgomery Committee, after fifteen months of investigation, published a report on the status of MIA searches in Indochina. It concluded that although no Americans were still being held prisoner in Vietnam, a full accounting of *all* MIAs "is not possible and should not be expected." While the report encouraged bilateral dialogue to resolve pending issues, it also opposed "any conditions even faintly resembling blackmail" from Hanoi in negotiating the MIA issue.[108] Immediately following its release, Carter had reiterated his insistence that a full accounting of all MIAs should be obtained prior to the start of any negotiations on normalization.

> I don't know about the [Montgomery] report or its accuracy. I said during the campaign and I still maintain the position that until I am personally convinced that there has been the maximum possible accounting for those who are missing in action that I would not favor normalization of relationships with Vietnam. But I have not seen the report, have no way to know the origin of it or the accuracy of it. If I'm convinced that it's accurate, that all the MIAs have been accounted for, then I would proceed to normalize relationships with Vietnam.[109]

However, some doubts arose as to Carter's stated intent during the election campaign, to obtain a full accounting, when new U.S. ambassador to the UN Andrew Young leaked to the press that both the president and Vance had informed him of their wish to normalize with Hanoi as soon as possible.[110] Carter had certainly shown himself more hawkish than he genuinely was. As one of Carter's campaign promises had been not to normalize with Hanoi before obtaining an accounting for MIAs, Young's leak embar-

II. The Advent of the Carter Years

rassed the executive branch. The administration had opted for normalization even before Hanoi had been tested on MIAs, reversing the Ford administration's stand.

This interesting contradiction between Carter's official stance and his secret wish for rapprochement with Hanoi would become visible throughout his dealings with Vietnam in the first full year of his presidency. Normalization with Vietnam, supported mainly by Young, Vance and Assistant Secretary to Far East and Pacific Affairs Richard Holbrooke, was considered part of the national healing process that he wished to conduct.[111] But it represented a delicate issue only eighteen months after the end of the American debacle and a few weeks after his access to the White House. The early establishment of normal relations would arouse vast opposition from conservative hawks who might perceive this move as a sign of weakness and a selling off of MIAs for a cheap ideology of national redemption. But far from being a purely ideological gesture, Carter understood normalization as a necessary step towards healing the wounds of his country and a most likely way of obtaining an accounting of MIAs. In late 1976 and early 1977, while publicly repeating his concern for MIAs and adopting Ford's strong stance, Carter was preparing for the resumption of talks which, presented as talks on MIAs, would also unofficially test Hanoi on normalization.

In a speech at the UN on December 27, 1976, Young departed from his predecessor's claims by explaining that the building of a "strong Vietnam" and the easing of American-Vietnamese relations would benefit the United States. Young was following Carter's lead in a regionalist approach to foreign policy. "We need a strong Vietnam," he declared. "Vietnam could develop into an independent communist nation like Yugoslavia and be a buffer against China." Young's statement was the first official American declaration, since the fall of Saigon, to oppose China's view of Vietnam as a danger to Southeast Asian security and to attribute the possibility of regional military aggression not to Hanoi but to Peking. Young further pushed the parallel with Yugoslavia in explaining that Vietnam was "a kind of Asian Yugoslavia that will not be part of, or a puppet of, China or the Soviet Union, but will be an independent nation."

The new administration's larger goal in foreign policy would be to establish a new form of international dialogue through which communist nations would "relate to the United States instead of each other," thus making Washington the new umpire of international exchanges, at the expense of Moscow. Carter certainly hoped that such a strategy would withdraw Soviet imposed political behaviors and serve as a catalyst for the democratization of the communist world. The question of normalization with Hanoi, Young added, might well represent a "first test" of Carter's foreign policy.[112]

A month later, during his confirmation hearing on January 25, Young expressed his wish that normalization take place before the opening of the next UN session, where Hanoi would certainly reiterate its request for membership.[113] Although Brzezinski claims that normalization with Vietnam was "never considered a priority," Young's statements seem to indicate that it certainly represented an important issue on the administration's agenda.[114] Young's disclosure of the new administration's normalization plans, only four days after Carter's inauguration, did not please the White House. The planning of a candlelight vigil by the National League of Families in front of the White House the next day reminded the new administration of the need for diplomatic tact on the issue of Vietnam.

Young's overly enthusiastic comments or gestures during his service as UN ambassador repeatedly threw the administration into great embarrassment, having to temper or explain his claims, leading to his resignation in 1979 after breaching a strict policy guideline by engaging in unauthorized dialogue with representatives of the Palestine Liberation Organization in 1979.[115] State Department spokesman Frederick Z. Brown attempted to correct Young's statements by explaining that although the administration had placed normalization on its agenda, a decision would depend on satisfactory resolution of key issues, including MIAs.[116] After hinting that the White House had tempered his eagerness regarding normalization plans, Young dutifully stated to a press conference the next day that the development of American-Vietnamese relations would strictly depend on Hanoi's conduct regarding the MIA issue.[117]

Nevertheless, although discreet, Washington's wish to become more receptive to Hanoi became visible. In early January the World Bank dispatched an economic "reconnaissance" mission to Vietnam and negotiated loans to the new communist nation.[118] Although the United States refrained from opposing such a mission, the State Department declared that this move should not be perceived as a softening of the American stance or progress on normalization. A few days later, the IMF loaned Hanoi $35 million to cover its export shortfalls, with the consent of Washington.[119] Congress went along with Carter's friendly initiatives in acquiescing to a $4 million contribution for "humanitarian purposes" to Hanoi through international agencies.[120] The previous tensions between the two countries seemed to ease.

The issue of normalization with China, left pending since Nixon's first efforts towards rapprochement in 1971–72, also remained on the presidential foreign policy agenda. "Eventually we are going to have to recognise the existence of the People's Republic [of China]—fully normalise relations and exchange ambassadors," declared Carter during an interview a few days before his election. However, "[w]e would continue with détente," he added, "but on a realistic basis and not as a one-way street. It must be pursued on a mutually beneficial basis through sustained and low-key discussions—not just dramatic and secret agreements among two or three national leaders."[121] Following Ford's empty visit to China the previous year, Peking seemed to welcome the new administration and its apparent inclination, through Carter and Brzezinski, towards a harder line on Soviet issues.[122]

However, the president was very critical of the Nixon-Kissingerian approach to the Chinese and warned that "we should not ass-kiss them [the Chinese] the way Nixon and Kissinger did."[123] Therefore Carter first opted for Vance's recommendation to normalize with both Peking and Hanoi. As for Brzezinski, in addition to his presenting a personal antipathy for Vietnam, his anti–Soviet ideology led him to side with Chinese criticisms of both Moscow and Hanoi.[124] He would soon perceive Vietnam as a political lever with which to exacerbate Sino-Soviet antagonisms.

On December 7, Carter received an invitation to visit China but explained that he would rather first welcome a Chinese politician to Washington.[125] The new president did not wish to repeat Ford's mistake by honoring Peking with a visit from each successive American president without receiving any return visit from the Chinese side. The new Secretary of State Cyrus Vance would nevertheless be sent to China in May 1977 to prove Washington's continued interest in easing its relations with Peking before what appeared to be a Sino-Soviet rapprochement had time to develop. Leaks from the White House hinted that normalization with Peking would eventually occur but not before the 1980 presidential election.[126] But, due to Brzezinski's influence, Sino-American normalization would take place nearly two years ahead of schedule.

The Woodcock Mission

In a time of political turmoil following Watergate and the fall of Saigon, Carter had won the presidency by portraying himself as foreign to the international political scene and its scandals.[127] But what had functioned as a political virtue during the election became a severe handicap when the time came for foreign policy formulation. Carter adopted no overall foreign policy orthodoxy, resulting in often vague or even contradictory foreign policy formulation, as his first overture to Hanoi would demonstrate.[128]

Considering recent U.S. history in Vietnam and the sensitivity of the issues at stake, Carter's sense of urgency in proceeding with normalization with Hanoi had as much to do with the practicality of securing the president's position at home and proving his skills in foreign policy as with the necessity to live up to campaign promises regarding MIAs. Quite simply, early attempts to normalize would allow sufficient time for U.S. public opinion to forgive Carter for normalizing with a former foe, should the process succeed, or to forget, should it fail, before the next presidential campaign.[129] For these reasons, Carter simultaneously tackled the sensitive issues of normalization with Cuba, and Cambodia, as well as talks with Panama over the canal treaties within the first weeks of his administration.[130]

Public opinion seemed ready for Carter's intended shift to a friendlier attitude toward Vietnam. On January 30, nineteen former anti-war activists signed an advertisement in the *New York Times*, addressed "to the American people, the Carter Administration and the Congress" and calling on the new president to fulfill seven diplomatic goals to ease relations with Vietnam.[131] These goals included the resumption of direct negotiations with Hanoi on outstanding issues, American support for Vietnam's admission to the UN, lifting of the trade embargo on American trade and travel, diplomatic recognition, granting of economic aid for postwar reconstruction, announcement of a presidential pardon for all military deserters and U.S. military with less than an honorable discharge, and the establishment of better facilities and aid to Vietnam veterans. The advertisement showed that changing public opinion allowed new possibilities that had appeared impossible in the Ford years, thus bringing hope into bilateral relations.

Carter's new initiatives began shortly following his inauguration. Breaking with the bitterness of the previous years in declaring that "the destruction [of the war] was mutual," Carter adopted more realistic negotiation positions than his predecessor.[132] Hanoi too seemed ready to mend breaches. During Carter's first days of office, Phan Hien informed the visiting American Friends Service Committee that Hanoi was prepared to receive American officials for talks.[133] Vietnam, explained the Committee's report to the president, had insisted that "one side cannot demand that its priority question be settled before the priority question of the other side can be taken up" and urged reciprocity.[134]

On January 31, Carter met with seven members of the former Montgomery Committee, and reiterated his campaign promise to send a delegation to Vietnam to resolve the MIA issue. Contrary to his hard-line statements a month earlier when the text of the Montgomery report was made public, Carter announced that he had replaced Ford's demand for a "full" accounting to a "satisfactory" report. In addition, he had ordered that the issue no longer be imposed as a precondition for the resumption of negotiations.[135] State Department spokesman Frederick Brown declared that Washington was now amenable to the shipment of private and international humanitarian aid, including the UN Development Program's provision of $44 million in development aid—a pledge Carter honored, allowing several million dollars to be sent to Vietnam through private U.S. aid initiatives, as well as $34 million via international institutions in 1977.[136]

Hanoi responded favorably. A few days later, Vo Van Sung, Hanoi's ambassador to Paris, agreed to a series of interviews in which he stated that Vietnam was ready to "discharge [its] obligations concerning the provisions of the Article 8B of the Paris Agreement and to hold discussions" should Washington assume "its obligation concerning its contribution to the healing of the wounds of the war."[137] Remarkably, although he quoted Vietnamese obligations regarding Article 8B, the ambassador failed to name Article 21 and simply mentioned "what has been agreed upon in Paris in 1973 in the joint economic commission." The State Department interpreted this delicate phrasing and the sparing of U.S. patience over the Vietnamese phrase "reparations," as proof of Vietnamese sincerity.[138] The Chinese news agency *Xinhua* echoed the Vietnamese position and also refrained from naming Article 21, hinting that China had encouraged Hanoi to reach an understanding with Washington.[139] Although Peking reversed this stance in late 1978, this declaration implied that, while China supported Hanoi's initiatives, it also hoped that American influence on Vietnam, enhanced by normalization, would reduce the security risk that its Indochinese neighbors represented.

Wooing Carter's interest in human rights, which had been one of the leading themes of his electoral campaign, the Vietnamese ambassador rejected accusations regarding Hanoi's re-education programs.[140] A few days later, the Vietnamese press publicized the interview of Wallace Collet, chairman of the board of directors of the American Friends Service Committee, in which he described his witnessing of the "humane policy of the Vietnamese Government" during his recent visit to Vietnam.[141] On February 7, during a visit to New Delhi, Phan Hien stated that Hanoi would welcome U.S. representatives for the holding of talks. Hinting at Hanoi's hope that Carter's policies would depart from those of his predecessor, Hien also had intimated that he deplored Washington's linking the issue of MIAs to that of Hanoi's admission to the United Nations.[142]

On February 11, in a meeting with officers of the League of Families, Carter reiterated his intention to break with Ford's hostile policies and rejection of bilateral talks, and announced that he intended to send a delegation to Vietnam to help resolve the MIA issue, as both the League and Congress had requested.[143]

In response, Hien repeated that Vietnam was "ready to implement its commitments ... and hand over a list of [MIAs]" should Washington fulfill its share of the agreement. He added that Hanoi would agree to receive a U.S. delegation to hold talks.[144] A few days later, the Senate adopted resolutions calling on Carter to establish a committee and demand a full accounting of MIAs, much as Ford had while in office.[145] This request was the first sign of a shift, on Capitol Hill, towards a harder line on Vietnam, perhaps due to the irritating episode of the Vietnamese application to the UN a few months earlier that had created doubts about Hanoi's willingness to help account for MIAs.

After first considering Young, and veteran envoy Averell Harriman, who had headed delegations regarding Laos under Kennedy,[146] then Vance,[147] and later Senator Mansfield,[148] as possible heads of the mission, it was announced on February 25 that Carter had opted for president of the United Autoworkers Union (UAW) Leonard Woodcock.[149] Vietnamese approval to receive the committee had been secured through contacts between the embassies in Paris, following an exchange of letters between Vance and Nguyen Duy Trinh.[150]

Leonard Woodcock seemed a rather unusual choice to head Carter's first delegation to Vietnam. Although well-known for leading the notoriously successful, longest-ever, 67-day strike against the auto giant General Motors in 1970, his line of expertise did not seem to include foreign policy. However, Woodcock embodied values that Carter sought to promote. Working in the assembly line as a machine assembler, he had climbed his way up to become one of the most famous labor leaders of his time, an embodiment of the American dream of poverty, gaining success and notoriety via the sole power of labor. Woodcock was also a member of the NAACP and American Civil Liberties Union, which fitted nicely into Carter's civil and human rights policies. On a more practical and personal level, Woodcock's appointment as head of the mission would reward his successful shifting of a majority of the labor movement in favor of Carter, during both rounds of the presidential election.[151] Overall, however, and despite his talents as a negotiator, his appointment as head of Carter's first and therefore most sensitive delegation to Vietnam showed Carter's lack of experience in understanding of foreign policy formulation. Obtaining normalization with Vietnam was certainly a more complex exercise than a labor leader's usual tasks.

Woodcock, although enjoying the support of congressional leaders and former members of the Montgomery Committee—an important ingredient to encourage congressional support on the executive's foreign policy regarding Vietnam—represented neither the administration nor Congress. His appointment suggested Carter's desire to test the Vietnamese mood with an initial, unofficial contact before risking a more open move. Also, Carter clearly wished that Congress and the League would support his initiatives and therefore considered it a point of honor to keep both institutions informed of the commission's aims. "I want to explore in an unpublicized way the attitude of the Vietnamese," Carter had explained to the League of Families on February 11.[152] Should it fail, the administration's name would not be uselessly damaged.

Woodcock's appointment was also strongly symbolic as he had been the first major labor leader in America to come out openly against the Vietnam War, and his appointment to head the mission was evidently part of Carter's strategy to signal his break with the hard-liners of the Ford administration. This mission, announced the press release, "is a further, measured step ... to put the Indochina conflict behind us"—both as a foreign policy issue and as a cause for domestic ideological division.[153] Also in the mission were former UN ambassador Charles Yost, who had also been outspoken in opposing the war; Montgomery, who, despite having supported the U.S. involvement in Vietnam, had recommended normalization in the December 1976 report; Senator Mike Mansfield

(Democrat, Montana); and Marian Wright Edelman of the Children's Defense Fund.[154] Assistant Secretary to Far East and Pacific Affairs Richard Holbrooke, who had participated in the peace negotiations alongside Vance, would be the delegation's contact in Washington.

"The composition of the Commission," Holbrooke explained a few months later, "was very carefully made up by the president personally to reflect the kind of message he wanted to convey to the Vietnamese Government."[155] It had not escaped Hanoi's notice that Carter's presidential campaign had been punctuated by references to the inhumane aspect of the war, and the Vietnamese saw the United States' reliance on such personalities as a sign that America was ready to compromise, if not to expiate its crimes—a far different meaning from Carter's intended message for peace and cooperation on an equal basis. Hanoi saw Washington's reliance on high-ranking and mainly liberal members as a signal of American readiness to compromise and of the importance that Washington now placed on normalization.

Hawkish opposition to easing diplomatic relations with Hanoi prior to a total accounting of MIAs, as well as strong pressure from the National League of Families, meant that, far from being an obstacle to negotiations, MIAs could be used as the stated aim of talks behind which normalization could be discussed privately without public or congressional interference. The mission's stated aim was therefore to open talks in order to solve the MIA issue.[156]

Although the mandate did not officially "include authorization to engage in negotiations on the substance of bilateral issues," backstage the Commission would seek common ground on the question of establishing diplomatic relations, before further official negotiations could later complete the last details of the rapprochement on a more formal basis.[157] In fact, before his departure, Woodcock had already discussed with Carter the possibility of granting aid to Vietnam on a humanitarian basis and the president, although opposed to any direct aid, seemed willing to give aid and obtain congressional approval later.[158] The idea had originated with Vance, who had suggested that Hanoi be informed of Washington's intention "to put to Congress a program of humanitarian assistance in such areas as housing, health and food," should the Vietnamese provide "an accounting for the MIA's."[159]

The mission, stated the White House on February 25, was designed to "seek information on our personnel, including the return of recoverable remains" but would also "be prepared to receive from the Vietnamese Government their views on matters affecting our mutual relations."[160] Woodcock himself later remarked:

> I don't think you can have one [accounting for MIAs] without the other [normalization]. Obviously, there has to be a solution to the one to make the other possible. It is my ... personal conclusion it is in the national interest of this country to have a stable Southeast Asia. You cannot have a stable Southeast Asia without having stability with regard to our relationship with the Socialist Republic of Vietnam.[161]

Carter, aiming at a prompt establishment of relations with Hanoi, had greater ambitions for the Commission. In December 1976, the Montgomery report had confidently claimed that all POWs and MIAs should be declared dead and reclassified as killed in action (KIA). "War destroys," explained Montgomery. "A full accounting is impossible."[162] However, five of the ten members of the Committee disagreed with some of its conclusions, which, along with popular reluctance mainly from the League and its supporters, postponed reclassification of MIAs as KIAs.[163] On July 18, 1976, Montgomery had already expressed his view that the nearly 800 American servicemen and news correspondents declared missing were presumably dead, and had later requested that the Department of Defense declare "a presumptive finding of death."[164] Four months later, in November 1976, the Pentagon had hinted that the administration might soon announce the reclassification of MIAs as KIAs.[165]

Carter understood that if Woodcock confirmed the findings of the Montgomery report, the way would be eased toward normalizing with Hanoi. If no more American servicemen were listed as missing or prisoners of war, Washington would simply be requesting the release of remains rather than live prisoners or hostages, bypassing popular and congressional opposition to rapprochement, and depriving Hanoi of a bargaining card for reconstruction aid and similar preconditions to normalization.[166] On the domestic front, the issue of the return of MIAs, now considered KIAs, could no longer be considered a case for diplomatic incident but simply an issue that bilateral contacts could resolve peacefully. The reappraisal of MIAs as KIAs would eliminate the sense of urgency that would no longer need to be resolved *before* normalization. In addition, conservatives and hawks would no longer be able to link MIAs to Vietnam's admission to the UN, Ford's tactic in 1976.

Furthermore, confirmation of the Montgomery Committee's findings would de-emphasize the issue by drawing a line between the various statuses of these servicemen as missing (MIA), killed/body not recovered (KIA/BNR), and prisoners of war (POW). In the late 1960s, the Nixon administration had grouped together these three statuses to inflate the number of potential prisoners of war held by the Vietnamese communists. In manipulating these numbers Nixon had hoped to create sufficient domestic indignation to suit his own political agenda, using U.S. casualties and missing servicemen as a pretext to justify a continuation of the war until all American servicemen had returned home. But in so doing he also gave birth to the League of Families' belief that more Americans could return home than were actually held alive in Indochina.[167] While Ford had continued this trend to justify continued U.S. postwar hostility, Carter took up the difficult task of de-emphasizing the issue without altogether abandoning it. The Carter administration now sought to bury memories of Vietnam along with its dead, opposing the rehashing of the war trauma by families of the missing men.

Over time, MIAs had been the primary factor halting establishment of diplomatic relations with Vietnam and had become more a political than humanitarian issue. In former member of the American Friends Service Committee John McAuliff's view, the reclassification of MIAs would "eliminate the political obstacle" from negotiations by getting "it off bilateral policy level" and allow progress towards reconciliation.[168] Accounting for MIAs could then be obtained through normal diplomatic processes.

Normalization, explained Vance during his confirmation hearing, was "in the interests of both countries." He stressed that the new administration would follow the recommendations of the Montgomery report, accepting the conclusion that no MIAs remained alive in Indochina but pursuing negotiations to recover their remains:

> I acknowledge the fact that there is an impediment at this point [on normalization] with respect to the question of a full accounting of the missing in action. I have noted from the

report of the Montgomery Committee that they have stated that they presume there are no Americans who are still captive. However, they did recommend that we pursue the matter with the Vietnamese, the Laotians and the Cambodians.

My personal view is that we can expect to do so. With respect to the question of aid, I also note that the Montgomery Committee recommends that consideration be given to humanitarian assistance, not reparations. We will consider this recommendation.

If bilateral contacts were fruitful, Vietnamese admission to the UN might also be envisaged.[169] Vance's testimony suggests that Carter indeed wished to use the Woodcock mission to confirm the findings of the Montgomery Committee and to provide a legitimate reason to proceed towards reclassification of MIAs and rapprochement with Hanoi. In his confirmation statement Young gave away the administration's program:

> [G]iven 60 to 90 days, I would hope that the Secretary might follow up on his intention to begin conversations confirming the reports which have already come back from the House [Montgomery] Committee, and working out any additional information that might be available in regard to our missing-in-action.... Then, I understand, if those questions are satisfied, the President says that he has no objection to moving toward certainly some kind of recognition and admission to the United Nations.[170]

In late January, while preparing for the Woodcock mission, Carter had met with seven members of the former Montgomery Committee, which led to some suspicion among the American press as did Montgomery's appointment as a member of the Woodcock delegation.[171] Montgomery had suggested that two of the five congressional members of the delegation be chosen from among his former Committee, and had offered his candidacy.[172] The administration defended its choice of members, explaining that it had simply picked people with good negotiating abilities and who had no emotional involvement in the issue, as MIA family members, for example, might have. Montgomery and Woodcock, specified the White House Congressional Liaison office, fulfilled these conditions.[173]

On February 25, the administration, announcing the mission, for the first time hinted that most MIAs were probably deceased, suggesting that Carter's policies would abide by the conclusions of the Montgomery report. Carter was, however, careful to highlight that a change of status would not affect Washington's efforts to recover those men. The press release stated:

> [W]e are concerned about all Americans lost in Southeast Asia, our servicemen and civilians, those still listed as missing as well as the *larger number* who have been presumed dead with no accounting being provided. *The fact that a man has been declared dead for legal purposes does not affect our determination to seek information about him and to arrange for the return of his remains if they can be recovered.*[174]

While Carter had angled the delegation's task so as to resolve the MIA issue and clear the way towards rapprochement with Hanoi, the League of Families and conservative public opinion would be quick in condemning the findings of the delegation.[175]

It was not until a week later, on March 3, that Hanoi announced the upcoming mission to the Vietnamese press. The announcement did not come in the usual form of radio commentary but through a foreign ministry spokesman's interview with *Vietnam News Agency*. Although this indicated the importance with which Hanoi viewed the mission, the delay in its announcement hinted that Hanoi still remembered the hostility of the past U.S. administration and would remain firm in its dealings with Washington.[176] This delay also betrayed a tinge of Vietnamese arrogance in implying that Washington, more than Hanoi, was eager to proceed towards diplomatic rapprochement. The foreign ministry spokesman reiterated that Vietnam was "prepared to consider and settle with goodwill a problem of concern for the United States." However, he warned that the White House should "disassociate itself" from the negative attitude of the Ford administration and the "U.S. Government ought to show a similar attitude regarding a problem about which the SRV is interested [reconstruction aid]."[177] He refrained from focusing on the Paris Agreement or mentioning Article 21 perhaps so as not to needlessly irritate Washington at this still early stage.

Carter misperceived the Vietnamese overtures as diplomatic concessions. On March 3, in order to thank Vietnam for its welcoming of the upcoming mission and to prove Washington's goodwill, the administration allowed the refueling, on American soil, of foreign ships and aircraft on their way to or from Vietnam, thus partially relaxing the trade embargo imposed in May 1975. On March 8, Carter furthered this gesture in lifting the ban, imposed since the American evacuation of Saigon in April 1975, on American citizens traveling to Vietnam, thus responding favorably to the request of the nineteen former war activists published in the *New York Times* at the end of January.[178] The lifting of this ban, effective as of March 18, also concerned travel restrictions on North Korea, Cambodia and Cuba.

On March 12, after two meetings with the League of Families and the American Friends Service Committee, several members of the Woodcock delegation met with Carter and Vance. Woodcock recalled that:

> The President expressed his deep concern about obtaining a satisfactory MIA accounting and his hope for future normalization of relations.... The Commission was directed not to apologize for past relations, but to emphasize the President's desire for a new beginning with these governments on the basis of equality and mutual respect.[179]

An enthusiastic Carter was waving the flag of a possible breakthrough with the Vietnamese. In the privacy of the White House, Carter's satisfaction appeared in full light. Checking the details of the mission, the president cheerfully told Holbrooke, with a mock-threatening look: "And if this doesn't succeed, Richard, it's your ass."[180] Publicly, Carter's pleasure was more restrained, especially given his hard-line position during his election campaign. Answering telephone questions on a radio show, he mildly stated that he was encouraged by Vietnam's response to American concerns.[181]

On March 14, two days before departure, delegation members were summoned for a last meeting with State Department officials. To their surprise, copies of the Nixon letter were distributed to them, then taken back after they had been given four or five minutes to read its content.[182] Beyond preparing the Commission for Vietnamese claims for aid, this gesture demonstrated Carter's wish to break with the Ford-Kissinger strategy of denying the existence of this letter. While Carter probably did not intend to honor Nixon's pledge, it betrayed his wish to begin relations on a new basis, involving honesty with Vietnam as well as with American intermediaries and political actors.

Carter had requested that journalists accompany the Commission, to ensure wide public coverage and to publicize the administration's efforts to solve the MIA issue, and

Hanoi had agreed to five.[183] After briefing Woodcock before his departure, Carter optimistically commented that the Commission's work could provide a foundation for potential normalization and would open up new possibilities for an accounting of MIAs.[184] However, Woodcock, whose long experience as a negotiator had endowed him with a more realistic appraisal of the situation than Carter, was less confident of the outcome of the mission. "There are very few negotiations that I've been in with as little leverage on our side," he commented aboard the jet.[185] "I'll tell you what we don't want to hear," he told the five journalists before his departure:

> ... and that is the continuing talk by them about the linking of issues.... They know they can use the issue [of MIAs] to gain extra concessions. But unless they break out of the sterile negotiating mold of the past, there will be a freeze on between us for a long time.[186]

The Woodcock delegation left for Hanoi on March 16, and Vietnamese vice-foreign minister Phan Hien greeted them in person at the airport, declaring that he would act as their chief host during their entire stay. The vice-minister's presence was a strong signal that Hanoi attached much importance to the delegation.[187] While still at the airport, Hien discreetly requested that an extra meeting be added to the delegation's schedule.[188] The members of the delegation became the first foreign visitors to be housed in the Government Guest House and were allowed to wander freely about Hanoi, which, as Woodcock himself noted in his report, certainly conveyed a deeper political message than might appear.[189]

Yet, Washington remained unaware of the political hierarchy in Vietnam and while Woodcock's meeting with Pham Van Dong had more to do with the polite formality of protocol, he experienced tougher diplomatic negotiations in his encounter with Hien. Woodcock explained that his visit "laid the basis, at the will of the president, for moving toward normalization of relations."[190] He further praised the Vietnamese as "courageous people" to the American press.[191] "You come here with good will," Dong greeted the Americans. "President Carter obviously wants to solve the problems between us in a new spirit. There are no problems about this. We are ready." Woodcock stressed that relations should start on a new basis of putting aside the past. "Everything stems from that fact," Dong agreed.[192] However, Woodcock warned that his delegation had no authority to hold official talks on issues other than MIAs. "We are not a diplomatic mission," he told Dong, "we are personal representatives of our new president." Dong looked puzzled. "What's the difference?" he asked.[193] The subtleties of Carter's management of American public opinion and conservative opposition seemed to take the Vietnamese aback. The concept seemed awkward to and remote from the Vietnamese domestic political pattern that consisted of a centralized government which expected unconditional support from its population, with no legal opposition groups.

Dong received a written message from Carter by Woodcock's hand, calling for friendship and cooperation, and Dong entrusted the Commission with a similar letter for the president, agreeing to bilateral talks.[194] If all talks with Vietnamese officials are conducted in the same way, commented Woodcock, "we will have a constructive report to present to President Carter."[195] But the Vietnamese premier remained doubtful. The following day, Dong told a Danish news agency that no immediate breakthrough would come out of these talks, and added that the "ball is now in the American court."[196]

After the meeting with Dong, talks with Hien proved less conciliatory. But the Americans nevertheless found pleasant changes from the earlier Vietnamese stance. Holbrooke recalled that there "was an advance from Vietnam's previous position, in that other issues—aid and normalization of relations—were no longer described as preconditions for progress on MIA's."[197] "There was a conspicuous absence of polemics or harsh rhetoric on either side," further noted Woodcock.[198] Another breakthrough lay in the fact that Hanoi, although still calling for aid, refrained from using the Nixon letter as a diplomatic lever. Aid, however, clearly remained an issue of utmost importance for Hanoi even if it was not explicitly expressed as such.

Far from being a concession, as the Americans seemed to imply, this new stance represented a cleverly disguised reformulation of Vietnam's former stand. "This is not a question of what amount of money," stated Vice-Foreign Minister Ngo Dien. "It is a question of responsibility, honor and conscience, and it does not relate to Nixon—it relates to the U.S."[199] The minister added:

> We will not bind America to that [Paris Peace] agreement, you must bind yourselves ... I am sure the American people cannot feel at ease with themselves and they cannot forget the past unless they do something constructive about it.... That the war took place is the responsibility of the United States....[200]

The aid issue had not been dropped, even if it was expressed in softer tones than during prior exchanges with the Ford administration. But the United States rejected anything that implied the existence of a debt, whether moral or economic.[201] Washington did not want to be seen as the wrongdoers granting "reparations" as a final economic trophy, allowing Hanoi to be internationally recognized as the victor of the war.

Irked by this rhetoric, Woodcock asked Hien for a private "off-the-record" interview, a move that had previously been discussed and agreed upon by the other delegation members and which, if fruitless, would be considered as having never happened.[202] "We did not come halfway around the world to engage in idle polemics," Woodcock warned Hien when they were left alone. He insisted that the peace agreement was "dead" and that their countries' respective concerns should be resolved on humanitarian grounds. "I told them," Woodcock explained, "that if they closed the door on us, then it might take 10 to 12 years before we were back."[203] He told Hien:

> You are saying in a sense that you will sell us the remains of our MIAs in return for economic aid. No American President or Congress could approve such a deal. If you are truly interested in better relations with the United States you must drop that demand or the day of normalised relations will be put off for years.... *Separate all these issues recognizing, nonetheless, that further efforts will be made to seek aid for Vietnam later, after normalisation.*[204]

"You will not be disappointed in us," answered Hien.[205] Woodcock's message to separate the two issues had been heard although misinterpreted as a pledge of aid.

During the fourth meeting, Hien tempered his stance and, in his opening statement, presented the MIA issue, American aid to Vietnam and the establishing of diplomatic relations as separate issues, as Woodcock had requested, although he added that these issues were "interrelated."[206] Hien's claim appeared as a reformulation rather than the altering of the Vietnamese position that these issues were linked. "In short we have obligations which are related to each other, so we should start from this position."[207]

> Regarding the question of normalization of relations between Vietnam and the United States, we have clearly stated to the American side that we are ready to look to the future but we cannot cut ourselves altogether from the past, as the latter has left behind a certain number of problems which, short of a satisfactory solution, will create obstacles on the path to normalization of relations between the two countries.[208]

He assured Woodcock that Vietnam would help Washington to recover the remains of MIAs because it constituted a humanitarian concern and insisted that Washington should reciprocate, adding that Hanoi was flexible as to the form the aid should take. Dong explained:

> On the question of Articles [8B] and 21 we are not being formal. If the United States wants them to be settled within the framework of the Paris Peace Agreement, that is alright. If on a legal basis, that is also alright. If on a moral basis, that is also acceptable. We regard this as a matter of honour for both sides—but it must be a two-way settlement.[209]

Should Washington prefer to call it "humanitarian aid" rather than the "reconstruction aid" of the Peace Agreement, that was merely a question of terminology to the Vietnamese. While Washington believed that Hanoi had dropped the aid precondition, Hanoi understood that Washington was prepared to pledge aid, renaming it "humanitarian" rather than the more aggressive Vietnamese catchwords of "reconstruction," "reparations" or "obligations" that Hanoi had used with Ford and which recalled American responsibility for war-time destruction in Indochina. Clearly the new Vietnamese position, while adapting its language to American requests, had not changed the substance of its demands.[210]

Hanoi had changed the terminology but not the meaning of its request. The nebulous understandings, based on mutual misperceptions and the absence of any clear timetable, meant that each side would be able to draw from these meetings the conclusions that best suited its own interests. This initial misperception would reshape bilateral relations during 1977 into an awkward dialogue of mutual misunderstandings and increasing diplomatic tension. The Woodcock mission is the best example, illustrating McNamara's comment on the war and postwar era that:

> Each side fundamentally misread the mindset of its enemy. The fact that they became and remained bitter enemies for a quarter of a century is testament to the depth of the misreading, the utter inability of leaders in Washington and Hanoi to penetrate the thoughts, perspectives, and emotions of those on the other side.[211]

However, Woodcock misperceived this new formulation as a change of policy, and noted in his report that the Vietnamese "indicated that they understand our domestic political constraints on this issue." However, he warned that although "the Vietnamese seemed prepared to de-emphasize references to U.S. aid as coming from U.S. obligations under the Paris Agreement," the aid issue "is likely to continue to be an important factor in working out new or improved relations." While "[t]he Vietnamese clearly expect a significant U.S. contribution to their postwar economic reconstruction period they indicated flexibility about the form this aid might take."[212]

The exchange between the two sides and the terminology used had been sufficiently vague to allow each side to draw its own conclusions from the dialogue, and while Washington interpreted the talks as an American diplomatic victory, the Vietnamese had perceived them as a final American acknowledgement of its past mistakes and yielding to Hanoi's demands. Former Vietnamese assistant foreign minister Luu Van Loi recently reported in his publication on official contemporary Vietnamese history that the Woodcock delegation "*thought* that Vietnam was prepared for normalization ... without conditions with the understanding that after relations were normalized the U.S. would give aid to Vietnam."[213] Indeed, the administration noted that Hanoi was no longer presenting aid as a precondition to the resumption of talks or to the providing of MIA information as they had threatened during the last weeks of the Ford administration.[214]

The Vietnamese press reported that the Americans had acknowledged that labeling the Paris Accords "dead," as the Ford administration had termed them, to avoid tackling the issue of aid also implied that Article 8(b) on MIAs had become obsolete.[215] Should it please Washington, the Vietnamese leadership would consider aid and MIAs as humanitarian issues independent of the Accords, so long as the pledge of aid remained. Back in Washington, Woodcock spoke in favor of aid but added that, for the time being, "the present channel through international agencies is the correct one."[216] In contrast, Hien continued to speak of aid as Washington's "undeniable duty."[217] On March 28 after the delegation's departure he declared on *Hanoi Radio* that: "[w]e affirm that U.S. contribution to healing the wounds of war and postwar reconstruction in Vietnam is an undeniable duty in terms of international law as well as morality and human conscience."[218]

Linking actions to words, Vietnam, "proceeding from its humane policy," handed over the remains of the twelve American pilots which had been promised in September before the U.S. veto in the UN.[219] "We did not get everything we came for," privately commented Woodcock, "but this makes up for a lot."[220] His remark suggested that he understood the Vietnamese gesture not only as a sign that Vietnam had broken with its hard stance of the Ford years, but that he also considered this move a legitimate reason to reciprocate. The gesture had met Carter's expectations.

The Vietnamese also assured Woodcock that Hanoi would consider the servicemen still listed as missing and declared its plan to return another set of remains.[221] However, Woodcock ordered the American MIA experts holding separate talks with Vietnamese officials not to submit the files they had prepared in order to preserve the fragile entente he had created on this sensitive issue, insisting that they be dispatched later from Washington so as not to create a "negative impression" of Hanoi due to a too big and sudden focus on MIAs.[222] A few days later, Woodcock confided to the House Subcommittee on Asian and Pacific Affairs: "It is our belief they had information then that they could have made available to us."[223]

As the twelve metal coffins were given the military salute before being flown to Honolulu for further identification, Woodcock judged the situation sufficiently favorable to submit a personal request to the Vietnamese. Taking Phan Hien aside, Woodcock asked if the fiancée of Colonel Paul Mather, an official of the Joint Casualty Resolution Center in Hawaii and a personal friend of Woodcock's, could be released from Vietnam. He also requested, on behalf of South Korea, the release of intelligence agents captured in 1975. Seizing the opportunity to prove Vietnamese goodwill, Hien accepted, and a few months later the young woman was flown to the United States.[224]

On the eve of departure, Woodcock made a courtesy call to Pham Van Dong; their televised interview created euphoria in the streets of Hanoi. Although the Americans interpreted this popular move as a celebration of the rebirth of bilateral relations, Nayan Chanda, well acquainted with Vietnamese mood, commented years later on the profound misunderstanding: "For the Vietnamese it was the final hour of triumph. The envoy of the defeated powerful enemy had come to seek a new relationship."[225] For the Vietnamese the Woodcock mission seemed an ironic twist in history, as they thought that Washington, repenting its past involvement in Vietnam, would finally honor Nixon's pledge of aid.

A few days later, in a news conference, Woodcock described his talks as "positive and constructive" and stated that his visit had "started a process which will improve the prospects of normalizing U.S.-Vietnamese relations"[226]—a major "bridgehead" toward normalization, commented the U.S. press.[227] Washington had clearly looked for cooperation rather than diplomatic confrontation as it had during the Ford years. Former Senator Mike Mansfield enlarged the chairman's remark with a more optimistic assertion, saying that the mission had helped to give the United States a "new beginning" in the region.[228] Woodcock even sent a copy of his report to Hien through the American embassy in Paris, as the vice-minister had requested.[229]

But, shortly after Woodcock's return, it was revealed that one of the sets of remains returned by the Vietnamese was in fact that of a fifty-year old Vietnamese male. A White House aide also reported that another body was apparently that of another American rather than the one whose name was given by the Vietnamese authorities. Hanoi immediately assured Washington that it would "undertake further efforts in these cases without delay."[230] Although some critics complained that the Vietnamese had attempted to fool Washington, Carter, in the press conference of March 23 that followed his meeting with the Commission and the release of the report, stated that he believed the Vietnamese had made an "honest mistake" in their failure to identify the remains. This "human error," confirmed Woodcock, "simply underscores the enormity of the task of recovering those missing in action."[231] The president's remarks highlighted his genuine belief in Vietnamese goodwill, and his wish to temper the remnants of wartime bitterness that still clung to American collective memory. The affair was dismissed and the remains were buried with nation-wide interest.

To show his trust in Vietnamese good intentions, Carter expressed his belief, at a press conference the next day, that the Vietnamese had acted in "good faith" in promising to make further efforts to account for MIAs. Sweeping away doubts about misidentified remains and quoting the positive conclusions of the delegation's report, Carter could claim that Washington had been given the long-awaited signal that Hanoi agreed to friendship and cooperation.

> I have always taken the position that when I am convinced that the Vietnamese have done their best to account for the service personnel who are missing in action, at that point, I would favor normalization, the admission of Vietnam into the United Nations, and the resumption of trade and other relationships with the Vietnamese. I believe the response of the Vietnamese leaders to the Woodcock Commission was very favorable.[232]

Carter agreed to Pham Van Dong's offer to reinitiate diplomatic discussions, and accepted the Vietnamese invitation to begin a new round of negotiations in Paris aiming at normalization, triumphantly reporting that "there are no preconditions requested [by Hanoi] and there will certainly be no preconditions on our part for those talks."[233]

Carter had succeeded in breaking with the Ford years and restoring optimism with regard to bilateral contacts. He was pleased by what he perceived as Hanoi's refraining from imposing any "preconditions," which he termed an "act of reticence."[234] Most importantly, the report concluded that normalization stood as "the best prospect for obtaining a further accounting of our missing personnel and recommends that the normalisation process be pursued vigorously."[235] Carter's declaration, before the Woodcock mission, that he had set as a precondition to normalization a *satisfactory* accounting for MIAs had been sufficiently vague to allow him now to declare that such an accounting had been obtained, giving a green light to the opening of talks. Furthermore, as Carter had intended, the Commission confirmed the findings of the Montgomery report that no Americans remained alive in Indochina, de-emphasizing the issue of MIAs. The president declared that Woodcock had conducted a "superb mission," performing his "assignment in an absolutely superlative way" and realizing "[e]very hope that we had for the mission."[236] A few weeks later, the White House termed the Woodcock Commission one of the "major achievements" of Carter's first hundred days of office.[237]

Carter's open enthusiasm was more than the Vietnamese response deserved. Hanoi's statements had not been less cold than during previous bilateral dialogues but the vague pledges made during the visit, paired with Carter's inexperience in dealing with a battle-hardened government and his genuine wish for reconciliation, had convinced him that a breakthrough could be achieved at a low price. Responding to the Vietnamese pledge to establish a special bureau to investigate MIAs, Carter ordered the immediate translation into Vietnamese of the American MIA records, provided relevant maps and, in a week, dispatched the information to Hanoi.[238] Washington established a telephone line between the State Department and the office of Vu Hoang at the Ministry of Foreign Affairs and an invitation was extended to the Vietnamese to send representatives to Honolulu to visit the TriService Mortuary at Travis Air Force Base and learn about the identification of human remains.[239]

Vietnamese reaction seemed encouraging. At the end of the month a U.S. intelligence report indicated that Hanoi had ordered all provinces to report any information on MIAs. This would complete a list of recovered remains established in 1976 but not yet handed over to Washington.[240] However, the report called attention to the fact that the Vietnamese seemed to have compiled this list during the months of sterile bickerings with the Ford administration and had reserved it for future dealings with the new administration. Although the intelligence report—if true—came as a confirmation that Hanoi had used MIAs to extract concessions from Washington, it also indicated Vietnamese readiness to reverse this stance and to opt instead for cooperation.

Carter was so pleased by the Vietnamese response that he gave clearance to the State Department to seek normalization without precondition in the forthcoming Paris talks, and even confided to Holbrooke his decision to drop the American objection to Vietnamese admission to the UN.[241] Later events showed him to have been too hasty in understanding the Vietnamese effort on MIAs as a durable concession.

During his press conference on March 23, Carter reiterated his view that, although Washington had no moral responsibility to contribute to the rebuilding of Vietnam, he would not rule out economic aid provided it was viewed as "normal assistance" not "reparations," and should assistance be arranged as part of successful negotiations to open normal diplomatic relations. True to his word, Carter declared that he was "willing to face the future without reference to the past.... That is what the Vietnamese leaders have proposed. If, in normalization of relationships, there evolves trade, normal aid processes, then I could respond well." However, on the issue of reconstruction aid he added: "I don't feel that we owe a debt, nor that we should be forced to pay reparations at all."[242]

Following Woodcock's return to Washington, Carter demonstrated his friendliness toward Hanoi in granting licenses for $5 million in private humanitarian aid to Vietnam despite the continuing trade embargo.[243] Given that Ford had postponed all shipments of humanitarian aid for nearly seven months after the fall of Saigon and had only granted a few licenses under pressure from the Subcommittee on International Trade and Commerce and Representative Bingham, Carter's gesture further indicated his wish to break with Ford's hostile policies.

Carter would, however, have to face the cooling of the more conservative or hawkish wings of public opinion, the media and Congress. Repeating the claims of the League of Families, a freelance journalist in a study of the history of Vietnam MIAs, argued that the Woodcock report might have been falsified to suit the administration's needs, and that Vietnamese claims that no living MIA remained in Vietnam were accepted as such and not verified, as protocol would have required.[244] While the charges seem extravagant in hindsight, it is true that the Vietnamese had been rather evasive in saying that "all Americans who had registered with them had been allowed to leave" and had refused to elaborate on what "registration" implied or on cases of Americans who might have refused to register.[245]

Some congressional conservatives, endorsing the League's view, complained bitterly about the conclusion of Woodcock's report that no MIA remained alive in Vietnam.[246] Congressman Benjamin Gilman (Republican, New York), who had been a member of the Montgomery Committee, criticized the Woodcock Commission for not having prepared properly and for having jumped too hastily to conclusions. Moreover, during the hearings on the Commission's report, he attacked Carter for having shifted from his promise to the League during his presidential campaign that normalization would occur only *after* an accounting had been obtained.[247] Gilman even dropped a hint that the Montgomery report might have been falsified, and said that the Woodcock Commission had "compounded the felony" of the Montgomery Committee.[248]

Carter attempted to reassure his audience with rhetoric strongly resembling Ford's during the election campaign. On March 24 he explained:

> [W]e are never going to rest until we pursue information about those who are missing in action to the final conclusion ... I will do the best I can. But I don't want to mislead anybody by giving hope about discovery of some additional information when I don't believe that hope is justified.[249]

The anger of the League, if misdirected at Carter and Woodcock, can be explained in both moral and economic terms. For nearly a decade the MIA issue had been manipulated to fit the domestic political agenda of two administrations since Nixon's decision to emphasize the issue, in 1969, to fit his own domestic political agenda and justify the continuation of the war in Vietnam until all POWs and MIAs had been returned to

Washington. The belief in live Americans still being held in Vietnam was too deeply enshrined in the League's thinking to be easily dismissed by a sudden reversal of policy.

Therefore, when the Pentagon announced that the status of missing servicemen would be reviewed and that it expected all MIAs to be declared dead within a year, the National League of Families and Congressman Gilman launched a severe criticism of the reclassification process. The administration insisted that this "action in no way alters the U.S. Government's intent to obtain as full an accounting as possible" from the Vietnamese, as Hanoi had immediately been warned.[250]

Furthermore, beyond the purely legal aspects of such a reclassification, the change of status, it would cause many dependants to suffer sharp financial loss as the wives— now widows—could no longer continue to draw full pay and allowances if their husbands were still alive.[251] From a strictly legal perspective, this change in status signified that Washington, if the claims of the Montgomery report were confirmed by the Woodcock team, would be saving a considerable amount of money as a KIA widow, according to the Montgomery report of December 1976, would receive only about half the income of an MIA widow.[252]

The League threatened to reject the findings of the Commission even before its return to Washington.[253] Barely a month after the announcement of the reclassification process, the families of twenty-one MIAs filed suit against Carter, his secretary of defense, and the heads of the Air Force, the Army and the Navy departments. Claiming that the Montgomery and Woodcock reports had been based on insufficient research and supported by unverified evidence, the families requested that the reclassification launched by the Pentagon be declared unconstitutional.[254]

On September 7, a judicial order temporarily barred the federal government from proceeding with the status change of some MIAs in cases where the missing servicemen had no dependents or when the beneficiaries did not oppose reclassification. This order, explained Judge Jack B. Weinstein, would protect the rights of the MIAs themselves until the court had come up with a final decision.[255] Two weeks later, however, Judge Weinstein lifted his previous order and allowed the federal government to resume its reclassification process on the basis that no proof had shown that the government had lacked either consideration or respect for the MIAs and their dependents.[256]

In fact, the administration had obtained enough information from Hanoi to be convinced that such a reclassification, after long years of investigation, was legitimate and in the normal and logical process of postwar bureaucracy. For no other war had Washington insisted on recovering *all* the remains of its missing soldiers. "The Commission," noted Woodcock, "was impressed by data showing that the number [of U.S. servicemen] unaccounted for in Indochina is about 4% of those killed in that conflict. As indicated in the [Montgomery] Report, this contrasts with the 22% unresolved cases in World War II and Korea."[257] In his December 1976 report, Montgomery had concluded that:

> 2,546 Americans did not return from the war in Southeast Asia ... [and] of these, 41 are civilians, including 25 missing or unaccounted for and 16 unrecovered dead or presumed dead ... [and] of the 2,505 servicemen, there are 1,113 killed in action whose bodies have not been recovered, 631 who have been presumed dead, 728 still listed as missing, and 33 still listed as prisoners of war ... [and] of the 33 listed as POW, at least 11 were actually POW's who have

not been accounted for by their captors, 6 were improperly classified as POW's at the time of their loss, and there is no evidence that the other 16 were actually taken prisoner.

The report further stated that deserters or defectors, some of whom had been initially listed as POWs, might remain in Vietnam. The report concluded that "no Americans are still being held alive as prisoners in Indochina, or elsewhere, as a result of the war in Indochina."

The Montgomery report therefore revealed that among the 2,505 American soldiers considered missing in Vietnam, only 728 were truly unaccounted for, representing a comparatively small number compared to the 200,000 Vietnamese soldiers still missing and the two million casualties suffered during the war.[258] The question of helping Hanoi recover its own missing soldiers was never put to the Vietnamese for fear Hanoi might exploit the issue to extract greater concessions from Washington.[259]

Perhaps on this issue, more than on any other, could the cultural and historical gap between Washington and Hanoi truly be felt. How, in the minds of the Vietnamese, could Washington be serious about the peace by insisting on an accounting of so few missing personnel? "Any country that goes to this much trouble to account for every soldier it loses," sarcastically concluded a member of the delegation during the Woodcock visit to the Joint Casualty Resolution Center in Hawaii in returning from Hanoi, "probably ought not to fight a war."[260] The issue of MIAs and the belief that American servicemen were still being held prisoner in Indochina would never cease to be one of Washington's main concerns in its dealings with Vietnam until today.

Setting aside harsh criticism of Montgomery and Woodcock, it should be reiterated that U.S. relations with Vietnam could well have stalled over the 1975–1977 period had it not been for these two men, making the Vietnamese release of information on MIAs even more complex. In Holbrooke's words, Montgomery was the link between the executive branch and Hanoi under the Ford administration. Montgomery "kept something alive during a period of maximum noncommunication. President Carter, through the Presidential Commission [Woodcock], moved it into a continuing government-to-government flow."[261]

Carter's reward for Woodcock demonstrated the president's satisfaction with the mission. At the time Woodcock was dispatched to Hanoi, he had been about to retire as president of the UAW and was expected to obtain a top job in the new administration. Although he had been short-listed for several posts, including the UN ambassadorship, Woodcock had expressed his interest in becoming Washington's ambassador to Peking.[262] His diplomatic performance in Hanoi, if successful, was expected to become a first step in his new political career.

Carter personally thanked Woodcock for his "willingness to serve [his] country in this worthy effort."[263] "You have contributed substantially to the healing of our own war wounds," he wrote. "Your compassionate yet firm negotiating abilities elicited the maximum possible response from the Vietnamese."[264] The president named Woodcock head of the U.S. liaison office in China on April 20.[265]

Perhaps this was a sign that Carter was now taking American-Vietnamese rapprochement for granted, appointing his representative to another task and leaving the details of normalization to be handled by State Department bureaucrats. But inasmuch as Carter had utterly misperceived the results of the delegation to Hanoi, his choice of Woodcock to represent Washington in Peking would prove a largely successful decision, as Sino-American normalization in late 1978 would demonstrate.

III

TALKS TURN COLD

The Paris Negotiations (January–May 1977)

The apparent smoothness with which the Woodcock talks had been carried out led Carter to think that normalization with Vietnam could be obtained relatively easily. But the misunderstandings that had arisen during the Woodcock mission to Hanoi would soon begin to affect bilateral relations throughout 1977 and 1978, as both countries began to realize that the other's position had not changed. The two sides would spend the latter half of 1977 reiterating each country's position and justifying their stands. While Vietnam grew irritated and aggressive, the U.S. executive branch remained disappointed and distraught, looking for a diplomatic compromise while simultaneously attempting to contain growing congressional wrath. If 1976 was the year of rancor and divorce, 1977 stands out as the year of missed opportunities for diplomatic rapprochement.

Washington was pleased that Vietnam had dropped its insistence on economic aid as a precondition to further development of relations, or to the releasing of information on MIAs, and had shown its interest in reciprocal cooperation. Carter appeared in a conciliatory mood. In mid–April 1977, the White House announced that high-level talks would be held in Paris on May 3, following a short delay apparently to allow for the re-election of Dong as premier.[1] Holbrooke, who had supervised the Woodcock mission from Washington, was designated to represent the administration and subsequently became a key figure in the dialogue. During the talks, Holbrooke's role, as decided by Carter, would be to work towards normalization without precondition.[2]

Holbrooke, who had been assigned to Vietnam in 1962–66 as his first foreign service posting, now wanted to be the one who, less than a year after reunification, would lead the two countries to normalization. Some of his critics maintained that he intended, in his dealings with the Vietnamese, to "over-compensate for the fact that he was something of a hawk in the early days of the Vietnam War."[3] In the late sixties however, Holbrooke had turned against American involvement in Indochina, had drafted one of the volumes of the Pentagon Papers and had participated in the Paris peace talks of 1968 along with Vance.[4] At thirty-six, Holbrooke was well acquainted with the Vietnamese language and culture and had a genuine desire to bring the two countries together.

Commenting on the upcoming Paris talks, Carter announced what he had confided to Holbrooke following the Woodcock mission:

> If we are convinced, as a result of the Paris negotiations and other actions on the part of the Vietnamese, that they are acting in good faith, that they are trying to help us account for our MIAs, then I would aggressively move to admit Vietnam to the United Nations and also to normalize relationships with them[5]

This was by far the greatest concession Washington had yet offered, a striking break with Ford's policy of opposing Vietnam's admission to the UN, signaling that Washington genuinely desired to work towards normalization and expected similar concessions from Hanoi. But the Woodcock delegation had seen the best of the Vietnamese mood, despite the numerous incoherences and mutually contradictory signals that had arisen during the mission and, in Paris, American overtures met with renewed Vietnamese coolness.

The next day, Phan Hien followed Carter's declaration by stressing that establishing relations with Washington depended on "whether [the U.S.] would give up its erroneous policies of the past... If the United States continues to block Vietnam's admission to the United Nations or links this question with others as an element of a bargain," he warned, "they will commit a gross error which could only harm the United States itself."[6] The Vietnamese behavior of returning to cooler declarations on normalization showed that Hanoi encouraged rapprochement with Washington, but still expected the United States to make the first step and provide concessions. In no way did Hanoi consider the two countries to be on the same level regarding debts and responsibilities. Meanwhile, Washington provided Hanoi with further information on MIAs and requested the Vietnamese to concentrate on several cases, which, in Holbrooke's words, would provide "the background ... of our talks in Paris."[7]

The French, who had always exhibited a great interest in playing the role of the mediator between the superpower and its former colony, welcomed the principle of hosting negotiations in Paris, as they already had in 1973. In the last months of the war U.S. ambassador to Saigon Graham Martin had ordered a door to be cut between the American and the French embassies in Saigon, which stood next door to each other, to facilitate communication and to seek French support in organizing the evacuation of the last Americans.[8] Likewise, in March 1975, as the upcoming U.S. loss of Indochina was becoming unavoidable, French prime minister Jacques Chirac sought to establish links with North Vietnam at a presidential level in an attempt to find a compromise and settle the dispute in Vietnam. But Chirac's proposition of creating a "balkanised"[9] Vietnam comprising three republics failed to impress the parties concerned and Kissinger dismissed it as being "more a reflection of nostalgia for lost colonial influence than a realistic assessment of how to conclude the Vietnam tragedy."[10] Paris now saw the spring negotiations as a self-serving step to preserve French interests in Indochina.[11]

Washington, in its eagerness to resume talks, wrongly believed that Woodcock had achieved a breakthrough in obtaining Hanoi's dropping of the aid issue. While preparing the May talks, Hanoi demonstrated its goodwill by turning down several offers from

Ethiopia, Libya, North Korea, Pakistan, Peru and Turkey, as well as from guerrilla groups in Malaysia, Thailand and the Philippines to purchase military material which the United States had left behind at the war's end.[12] This open show of restraint and pacifism, designed to woo Washington, also served the purpose of maintaining the full military strength of the Vietnamese army, as tensions with China and Cambodia were growing daily.

At the time, Hanoi seemed to be drifting away—at least temporarily—from the Soviet sphere. In April, stopping in Moscow on his way to France, Dong was given a cool welcome by the Soviets, who wished to show their discontent at Hanoi's warming relations with Western Europe and Washington, and at its quest for economic independence.[13] A NSC staffer reported his optimism:

> Vietnamese leaders appear to be scaling down their objectives vis-à-vis the United States. And in America the passions of war have cooled.... The uncertainties of future Sino-Soviet relations and the economic difficulties Hanoi faces give the Vietnamese practical incentives to explore an American "option" in their diplomacy.... Thus the stage has been set for realistic talks...[14]

The Department of State shared this optimism. Holbrooke noted that the Paris negotiations would "put the debris of the war behind us" and highlighted the "anniversaries and ironies" of such meetings. "It will be two years to the week that Saigon fell," he remarked, "and nine years to the month that ... Vance and I arrived in Paris [for the 1968 peace talks]. I was told then to get to know Phan Hien."[15] Holbrooke seemed to believe that a crucial breakthrough was about to take place. Vance publicly confirmed that the meetings would "explore the basis for ... normalization."[16] Washington signaled its goodwill on April 15, in allowing postcards, letters and small parcels to be mailed to Vietnam.[17]

Hanoi too welcomed the resumption of talks believing, again wrongly, that Washington was prepared to discuss aid. On April 19, Hanoi announced that the remains of a U.S. pilot downed in 1972 had been found and requested that Washington provide it with further information on more MIAs.[18] On April 27, a cable to Washington from the U.S. ambassador to Thailand quoted the Belgian ambassador to Hanoi as having said that the Vietnamese expected to obtain U.S. aid *after* normalization and "looked forward to the establishment of a small U.S. mission at the end of 1977."[19]

As Vietnam had understood the American reluctance to hear the issue of aid mentioned, Hanoi refrained from directly mentioning it explicitly; however, it remained an underlying theme in Vietnamese public declarations. Commenting on the upcoming talks, Pham Van Dong told French journalists that "if both sides are moved by good will in the present climate, considering the present context of the general situation and the respective situation of the United States and our country, I think it is possible to achieve results."[20] Upon his arrival, Phan Hien told French journalists that "the past and the future cannot be separated. That's why one must settle satisfactorily the problems left by the past. I come here with an attitude of good faith. For the time being, nothing can be said about the prospects of these negotiations." The United States, he concluded, should drop its "erroneous policy"[21]—a reference to aid in Vietnamese propaganda terminology. The day the talks opened, *Nhan Dan* and *Hanoi Radio* returned to linking normalization, the MIA issue and aid, claiming that resolving these three issues was the key to successful negotiations. Vietnam, they stressed, wanted "an overall, package deal solution."[22]

The Vietnamese, however, seemed prepared to adopt a harder stance than they had shown during the Woodcock mission. In an interview published in Japan, Central Committee member and *Nhan Dan* editor Hoang Tung commented that normalization "presumably will not become a reality within this year."[23] Such shifts in Vietnamese policy-making, although frequent in Hanoi's dialogue with Washington, betrayed a growing radical influence in the Politburo led by Le Duan and Le Duc Tho. The Vietnamese stance suggested that Hanoi had proven its goodwill to Woodcock by releasing remains of MIAs and adopting Washington's terminology—but not ideas—on aid, but would not be pushed into making unreciprocated concessions.

Other events touching upon Vietnamese relations within Indochina also affected the Vietnamese diplomatic mood. By 1977 Hanoi's concerns over its neighbors in Cambodia—rechristened "Democratic Kampuchea"—had come to the forefront of Vietnamese foreign policies.[24] Following the fall of Phnom Penh in April 1975, the new Cambodian dictator Pol Pot, and his authoritarian government "Angkar," had begun a vast campaign for economic reconstruction, a political mask for the perpetration of forced labor and ethnic cleansing, "with a hoe in one hand and a rifle in the other," according to the Khmer Rouge slogan.[25] This "auto-genocide" eventually led to the death of millions of Cambodians.[26]

Although Vietnamese-Cambodian border encroachments dated back to the seventeenth century, the ideological split between the two countries and a growing ethnic hatred, which had started with Pol Pot's discreet rapprochement with Peking in 1965, had laid the groundwork for the multiplication of skirmishes as soon as the war ended.[27] Immediately after the fall of Saigon, Cambodia had appealed to Vietnam to grant it the unilateral right to redefine borders as a compensation for territories lost to Vietnam over the course of history. Hanoi refused. Phnom Penh interpreted the Vietnamese refusal as growing ambition on Hanoi's part to take over all of Indochina, and eventually Southeast Asia, via the revival of Vietnam's alleged historical expansionist traditions. Unsurprisingly, former prime minister of Democratic Kampuchea, Khieu Samphan, dates the heightening of intense Cambodian paranoia towards Vietnam to December 1976, and to the VCP's declared intention, during the congress, to develop a "special relationship" with its Indochinese neighbors to guard it against Chinese threats.[28] As the dispute gathered momentum, border clashes multiplied and anti–Vietnamese purges were launched on Khmer territory from January 1977, as Cambodia began to promote its army and praise its strength.[29]

The first major Cambodian attack followed on April 30, forcing the evacuation of the border town Chau Doc. By choosing the second anniversary of the fall of Saigon for a large scale attack on Vietnam, Cambodia was openly claiming its independence from Hanoi and publicizing worldwide the hostility it harbored for its Vietnamese neighbors—an issue Hanoi had preferred to keep rather low-key since the fall of Saigon, considering the issue of border skirmishes an internal problem that might in the long-run attract international curiosity and create obstacles to the unification of Indochina.[30] The Cambodian invasion shocked Hanoi into realizing that Cambodian hostility was a greater problem than it had initially anticipated.

But the attack highlighted an even greater concern. While China had attempted to quiet the tumultuous Pol Pot since his coming to power, Hanoi's perception of Sino-Cambodian relations had come to see Peking as the supporter of Cambodian bullying and, by 1978, as its instigator.[31] Proposing a toast on the occasion of the second anniversary of the Khmer Rouge victory, two weeks before the Cambodian attack, Chinese foreign minister Huang Huain had declared "that in the future the Chinese and Cambodian peoples will unite still more closely, fight shoulder to shoulder, and advance together along the road of our common struggle." The statement did nothing to alleviate Vietnamese fears.[32] But China's interest in Cambodia reflected a wish to maintain a toehold in Indochina rather than an attempt to aggressively challenge Vietnam. Seeing that Vietnam, following the fall of Saigon, seemed ungrateful for Chinese support during the war and appeared to lean towards Moscow, Peking had turned instead to its other Indochinese allies in Cambodia, thus indirectly encouraging what it had attempted to prevent—a further Vietnamese tilt toward Moscow.

In early 1977 Vietnam had thus begun to upgrade its relations with Moscow, certainly more in an attempt to counter the danger of increasing Chinese influence in Indochina than to contain Pol Pot's military effervescence. While Hanoi had rejected Moscow's repeated invitations since 1975 to join COMECON, the Vietnamese requested membership, in mid–April, in the organization's International Bank for Economic Cooperation (IBEC) and in the International Investment Bank (IIB) also sponsored by Moscow. In the weeks that followed the Cambodian invasion, Hanoi also informed the Soviet Union that it had finally approved the Soviet demand to open a consulate in Hanoi. In mid–1977, Moscow's strategy of threatening to stop sending Soviet ships to Saigon if they were not provided the same consular facilities in Hanoi as the French, had proved successful. But Hanoi had responded less to Soviet threats than to the growing Vietnamese fear of a broader war with Cambodia. Therefore, Vietnam also hinted to Moscow that it would have to reevaluate its foreign policies and might accept the Soviet invitation to join COMECON.[33]

While Hanoi's fear of the Chinese grew, the Vietnamese did not entirely rule out the possibility of finding a discreet behind-the-scene solution to what it perceived as Chinese hostility. A month after opening the door to Moscow, Hanoi notified Peking that the Chinese too had been granted the authorization to open a consulate in the Vietnamese capital.[34]

Considering such shared misperceptions, the sudden shock and realization of the meaning of the April 30 Cambodian attack is understandable. The difficulties which Hanoi encountered with Cambodia, its apparent backing by Peking, and the need to counterbalance this hostility by granting greater weight to Hanoi's relations with Moscow, may have led the Vietnamese, and certainly Le Duc Tho, to consider other foreign policy issues as secondary matters, perhaps also including American-Vietnamese normalization.[35] Given the low-scale reception of Indochinese events in the Western press, one may suppose that the White House remained unaware of the major causes for Vietnamese diplomatic anxiety. Neither did the Vietnamese seem prepared to treat American domestic concerns on an equal footing. In fact, strikingly little appears in U.S. archives on the Vietnamese-Cambodian dispute before mid–1978, showing that the United States was only a little aware of inter–Indochinese states issues.

On May 3, Holbrooke reached the Vietnamese embassy in Paris for the first round of talks. "[I]n that first meeting," he recalled,

> we proposed ... that we proceed to normalization of relations, including the exchange of ambassadors. We said we were prepared to end our trade embargo contingent on the opening of an American Embassy and that we were prepared to agree to Vietnam's membership to the United Nations.[36]

Although this package did not include the aid issue the Vietnamese expected, it nevertheless signaled American willingness to engage in genuinely overt negotiations. Holbrooke's instructions were to hint to the Vietnamese "that they would never have a better chance to normalize with us, considering the current open attitude of the Administration toward them."[37]

As the talks opened, Holbrooke approached Hien and confidently proposed: "Mr. Minister, let's leave aside the issues that divide us. Let us go outside and jointly declare to the press that we have decided to normalize relations."[38] But to Holbrooke's surprise, Hien refused, insisting that such a move was impossible so long as the Americans had not first given a formal pledge towards the reconstruction of Vietnam as the Nixon letter and the peace agreement had stated. Unmistakably, Hanoi was clinging to Article 21, over whose "dead" body Washington had wished to step relatively discreetly. Holbrooke's offer to announce immediate normalization demonstrated that Carter considered the deal had been struck with Hanoi during the Woodcock mission, with only a few details to be arranged in Paris.

Holbrooke and the State Department had not expected the Vietnamese reply. They had misperceived the importance that Hanoi attached to aid—both as an economic and symbolic gesture. Their attempt to deprive the Vietnamese of their bargaining cards by reclassifying MIAs had remained fruitless.[39] Much as Hanoi was prepared to call aid "humanitarian" rather than "reparations," the renaming of MIAs as KIAs was little more than a matter of terminology to Hanoi.

Phan Hien brought up the issue of the secret Nixon letter, adding, as had been expressed to Woodcock, that whether Washington would provide direct economic aid or government-guaranteed credits was only "a question of form."[40] Similarly, "reparations" could be labeled "contributions" should it please Washington.[41] Holbrooke explained in 1979:

> The Vietnamese refused to accept our position and instead demanded that, linked to S.R.V. efforts to provide an accounting of our MIA's, the United States agree to provide direct economic assistance as part of any agreement to establish relations. This was their interpretation of the Paris accords. In addition the Vietnamese argued that the United States should unilaterally lift the trade embargo before relations were established.

Holbrooke, who had been instructed to seek mutual recognition without preconditions, impatiently dismissed the Vietnamese requests, explaining that neither Congress nor the administration would agree to such aid. Regarding the embargo, he highlighted that "the interests of all parties would be best served when commerce could be conducted in the context of normal diplomatic relations"—and rejected unconditionally lifting the embargo.[42] Robert Oakley, Holbrooke's deputy for Southeast Asia, further explained:

> Regarding the MIA issue, we stressed that we did not consider this as something to be bargained over, and that we would reject any Vietnamese attempt to link this question to aid or other possible aspects of the normalization process. We stressed that we believed the Vietnamese have a simple humanitarian obligation to resolve the MIA question.[43]

He again repeated that "the Paris accord was no longer valid in view of the massive North Vietnamese military attack on South Vietnam in 1975." This declaration went against Hanoi's belief during the Woodcock mission—that the Americans recognized that if the agreements were void, Washington renounced aid but also MIAs.[44]

Despite the irksome shift in Hanoi's position, Holbrooke asserted that, as a sign of goodwill, Washington would no longer oppose Vietnamese admission to the UN.[45] Again, his Vietnamese counterparts' response puzzled him. The Vietnamese delegates did not even thank him for this gesture. In fact, the Vietnamese had certainly grown impatient at the apparent reversal of the American position, and were demonstrating their displeasure. Furthermore, Hanoi probably considered this move part of Woodcock's misinterpreted pledges, a debt that Washington had denied for two years rather than a gift or a sign of diplomatic generosity. In return, however, Hien pledged to speed up and intensify efforts to account for MIAs, stressing that "this problem is being solved."[46]

While the negotiations were opening in Paris, Kissinger, during a speech at the U.S. Chamber of Commerce, reiterated his view that the U.S. had no commitment to supply reconstruction aid to Hanoi and that he would strongly object if such aid were the only aspect of the Paris Peace Accords to be fulfilled.[47] Two days later, on May 5, the State Department again confirmed that Washington did not plan on providing direct aid to Vietnam.[48] However, the administration hinted that it would develop and license the export of private humanitarian assistance which, since 1975, had totaled the equivalent of $6.6 million. This move would honor the U.S. pledge that it would allow indirect humanitarian aid.[49]

Meanwhile, Frank Sieverts and Vietnamese foreign ministry official for MIAs Vu Hoang held talks on MIAs. Although the Vietnamese did not provide Sieverts with any information on missing servicemen, they agreed to cooperate on several cases. Vu Hoang also agreed to the American suggestion that names of MIAs be kept secret until the remains had been positively identified, so as to spare the anguish of families, and accepted Sieverts' invitation to have Vietnamese representatives visit the Joint Casualty Resolution Center in Hawaii.[50] Talks were postponed for two weeks to allow Holbrooke's return to seek instructions in Washington on how to handle the Vietnamese position on aid.

"We think that there is some progress," reported U.S. spokesman Morton Smith, "but there is no schedule. I do not think that anyone can set forth a schedule at this time." Smith remained silent on the issue of aid and indicated that the administration was hoping for rapid diplomatic rapprochement.[51] In fact, Washington had decided to keep statements vague and refrain from outlining its negotiating position before Hanoi had had a chance to consider the U.S. proposals.[52] On the Vietnamese side, and although these negotiations had led to no major breakthrough, Phan Hien termed the talks "frank, friendly and very useful" and stressed that "both parties share the objective of early normalization."[53] However, he added that: "[t]he problem is complicated. It has human, political and psychological aspects."[54]

Among the psychological aspects to which Hien may have been referring was the impact of the MIA issue on American public opinion and especially on such lobby groups as the League of Families. In the absence of a satisfactory gesture from Vietnam on this issue, it would be difficult for Carter to justify diplomatic rapprochement with a former enemy. The issue of aid was certainly also at the forefront of Hien's thoughts. Congress and U.S. public opinion would object to the granting of direct aid that it would see as an acknowledgement of U.S. responsibility—or worse, an apology—for its involvement in Vietnam. Hanoi requested this economic aid as much out of financial considerations as out of a desire to trumpet its victory over American "imperialism."

Speaking to the American press on the aid issue, Phan Hien committed a diplomatic mistake that would soon play against Vietnam's interests, by, for the first time, disclosing Vietnam's continued insistence on aid, thus contradicting Carter's declarations after the Woodcock mission that Hanoi had dropped this issue. While Hien referred only to "contributions" rather than "reparations," signaling Hanoi's understanding of American reservations as to terminology, he nevertheless stuck to Vietnamese policy in announcing that "a dollar sent, regardless of how, is still a dollar."[55] Holbrooke knew that this sudden apparent reversal of the Vietnamese position would not fare well in the light of American public opinion.

While China refrained from referring to Hanoi's reassertion of the aid precondition for normalization, thus indicating that it encouraged Hanoi to reach a compromise with Washington and settle its disputes through normalization, Moscow highlighted Washington's need to fulfill its obligations to Vietnam. Although Hanoi favored Moscow's position, it recognized that the position demonstrated Soviet fear that American-Vietnamese normalization would diminish Hanoi's dependence on Soviet aid and therefore Soviet influence on Hanoi. Peking's promotion of American-Vietnamese rapprochement reflected China's wish to pull Hanoi away from Moscow.[56] The ASEAN countries, however, remained skeptical and presumably feared that American aid to Hanoi, whether through the implementation of the Paris Agreement or via a normal aid process following normalization, would strengthen Hanoi and encourage its aggressiveness.[57]

The Nixon Letter

Holbrooke's first meeting in Paris coincided with a debate on Capitol Hill over a $1.7-billion authorization bill for State Department foreign aid activities and contributions to international organizations. In this ill-timed context, news came of Hien's public acknowledgement that Hanoi still clung to the aid issue despite Carter's declarations as to the contrary.

In the House of Representatives meeting of May 4, Ohio Republican John Ashbrook angrily brandished a report of Holbrooke's talks and demanded a decision preventing the State Department from making any moves toward meeting the Vietnamese requirements.[58] After a debate of only ten minutes, the House voted to prohibit the granting of any aid to Vietnam. Ashbrook's amendment (HR 6689), banned even the negotiation of "reparation, aid or any other form of payment," clearly demonstrating to the executive branch that Congress did not want to see its authority overrun by unauthorized pledges in Paris.[59]

Ashbrook, who had run for president in 1972, until his poor campaigning results had led him to abandon the race in its early stages, was one of the most articulate anti-communists in Congress as well as a conservative—being both one of the founders of the American Conservative Union, and its chairman from 1966–1971. He would remain one of the leading, most vehement opposing figures to U.S. normalization with Vietnam in the postwar era.

Attempting to quiet Congress and save U.S. initiatives in Paris, Vance confirmed, during a press conference later that day, that Washington would continue to reject aid or "war reparations," and that normalization would remain impossible until Hanoi dropped such preconditions.[60] Montgomery, however, warned that the ban "could stop the negotiations that are going on at this time in Paris." "[If] that would stop the talks," replied Ashbrook, "it would be one-sided. It would be entirely on their part."[61]

That very day, Kissinger seized the opportunity to justify his previous stance and to reiterate that "[i]t would be absurd to claim that the Vietnamese have the right to economic aid after having brutally violated every provision of the 1973 peace agreement."[62] "Today," he added, "among the many claims on American resources, I would put those of Vietnam in alphabetical order."[63]

The Vietnamese soon committed a second mistake. On May 6, the foreign ministry released through *Nhan Dan*, along with a vehement article by "the commentator," believed to be a top party official, parts of the Nixon letter, Dong's reply to it, and a note, dated April 6, 1973, from Maurice Williams, chief U.S. delegate to the former U.S.-Vietnamese Joint Economic Commission.[64] The "commentator" claimed that the Carter administration's refusal to keep Nixon's promise "tramples upon the most elementary provision of international law." "If the present U.S. administration unilaterally denies any commitment made previously by the Nixon administration, what can guarantee that today's commitments will be valid tomorrow?"[65]

Hanoi certainly considered this partial release of the letter a final warning to the administration, hinting that if Washington did not agree to aid, the full text of the letter would be published, further rubbing salt on American wounds. But while a year earlier the American media, in the rush of the election campaign, had not noticed or reported the first publication in the Vietnamese press of excerpts of the Nixon letter, the publication of the full text of the letter in May 1977 would receive considerable attention and throw the U.S. into a fit of anger, which Hanoi had certainly not expected.

Moreover, this tactic betrayed Hanoi's profound misunderstanding of the new postwar political environment. While enjoying substantial international political leverage during the war and a geostrategic position between the three superpowers, playing one against the other to extract maximum advantages from all, the Vietnamese failed to understand that the end of the war had deprived them of these privileges and restored them to the flock of ordinary Third World states struggling to have their voices heard by western countries. Disregarding its precarious position, Hanoi failed to understand that arrogant Vietnamese rhetoric and threats were no longer appropriate in a dialogue with Washington.[66]

Of all U.S. institutions, the State Department was certainly the most disappointed by the Vietnamese stance. On May 9, Holbrooke, discussing the content of the Nixon letter, promised that no aid would be discussed with Vietnam without prior congressional approval and dismissed the letter as an "outmoded historical curiosity that keeps arising and complicating the discussion."[67]

But the release of excerpts of the letter also placed the administration in the uncomfortable situation of having to admit the existence of the document. When asked to produce the full text of the letter, Holbrooke denied its being in the State Department files, contrary to Kissinger's assertion of the opposite on March 10 in a letter to Lester L. Wolff, the new chairman of the House of Representative Subcommittee on Asian and Pacific Affairs.[68] Instead, Holbrooke suggested that it might be among the Nixon presidential papers.[69] The executive's decision to show the text of the letter to the Woodcock delegation, in the secrecy of the White House two months earlier, demonstrates that Holbrooke was keeping the truth from Congress in an effort to gain time.

Congress turned to Nixon. In late February, Wolff had requested the text of the letter from Nixon, Kissinger and former secretary of state Rogers. All had declined to provide it.[70] Wolff now shifted to harder lines, and, following Holbrooke's statement, threatened that Congress might subpoena Nixon should he fail to produce the letter. "If he [Nixon] can talk to a television guy," sneered Wolff referring to Nixon's series of televised interviews with David Frost during the month, "he can talk to Congress."[71]

On the same day, Wolff received a message from the former president, conveyed through his former military assistant Brent Scowcroft, in which Nixon informed Wolff that he would cooperate. Although Nixon did not provide Wolff with a copy of the secret letter to Hanoi, he acknowledged the existence of private correspondence with North Vietnam and declared that he would explain its "intent and purpose" in a private letter to Wolff.[72] This letter, written on May 14, would indeed reach Wolff a few days later.

The congressional ban and Holbrooke's statements on his return to Washington, designed to reassure congressional critics, angered Hanoi. The Vietnamese labeled the moves "premeditated expressions of U.S. policy towards Vietnam" reflecting Washington's "stubbornness and short-sightedness." The situation soured when, on May 11, *Nhan Dan* threatened that "there can be no normalisation of relations unless the U.S. meets its obligations and stops its hostility to Vietnam."[73] The same day a Vietnamese broadcast repeated this new position.

At the same time, in an attempt to induce one of America's most important lobby groups to pressure Washington for normalization, Hanoi informed American oil companies that if an agreement on normalization was reached, plans to develop Vietnam's offshore reserves would be approved within a week.[74]

But Congress clung to its position. On May 12, the House adopted another Ashbrook amendment forbidding the granting of economic aid to Vietnam or Cuba or the lifting of the trade embargo with either country.[75] Ashbrook contended that the U.S. "basic national purpose would be better served by not having aid in any form with Vietnam or Cuba."[76] In fact, two days earlier, Carter had approved a vote by the Senate Foreign Relations Committee allowing the sale of medical material and food to Cuba. This first breach in the seventeen-year trade embargo on Cuba had brought about some dissatisfaction amongst the most conservative members of Congress, triggering the fear that

Vietnam might also benefit from similar U.S. moves. Ashbrook and other strongly anticommunist members of Congress would, therefore, work towards countering all possibilities of aid or trade to both countries.

As legislation already prohibited funds to Vietnam these new amendments were mainly symbolic and signaled to the executive that Congress was now aware that aid was being discussed with Hanoi behind Congress' back. Reaffirming its authority, Congress nipped Carter's negotiating strategies in the bud depriving him of the possibility of granting humanitarian aid to Vietnam after normalization.[77]

Given these growing domestic tensions surrounding the issue of normalization, NSC top adviser on China and Indochina Michael Oksenberg suggested to Brzezinski that Carter's initial enthusiasm be tempered and that the president return to a more objective appreciation of the situation. "You might wish," he wrote, "to underscore to the President the desirability of toning down expectations" in his declarations on the Paris talks.[78] The remark suggested that the NSC believed that normalization had reached a stalemate and that the president should be advised to switch to unpublicized backchannel contacts, if not other matters. Such a stance had governed Washington's dealing with Cuba in 1977, leading to the signing of maritime agreements in April, and presented a lesser domestic risk than publicized talks.[79] Carter's rejection of the NSC's advice reflected his confidence that a breakthrough was still possible, and his sense that normalization represented an important healing symbol for his country.

However, Oksenberg's memorandum hinted at the beginning of an understanding between Brzezinski and Oksenberg that normalization with Vietnam might become counterproductive and that Carter should be persuaded to turn to other concerns.

A short note should be added about Michael Oksenberg, this intriguing character whose importance will grow in this narrative. Born in Belgium in 1938, Oksenberg had moved to the United States at the age of seven months. He became a member of the Trilateral Commission and interrupted his academic career to work on the Security Council. Perhaps due to their similar backgrounds, Oksenberg and Brzezinski's appraisal of global politics converged into a common hard-line anti–Sovietism. Over the following months, Brzezinski and Oksenberg, working in tandem, would counter what they saw as pro–Soviet initiatives—from SALT II to normalization with Vietnam—and strongly favor opening to China.

In his explanation letter to Wolff dated May 14, Nixon declared: "I want to be as helpful as I can in providing voluntarily my recollection of events surrounding the aid negotiation." His letter recalled the main lines of the 1973 negotiations and stressed that Washington had "no commitment of any kind" and that there was no "price" to pay for the release of information on MIAs. Nixon concluded:

> There is no commitment of any kind, moral or legal, to provide any aid whatever to the Hanoi Government. On the contrary, I can think of no action which would be less justified and more immoral than to provide any aid whatever to the Hanoi Government, in view of their flagrant violations of the peace accords.[80]

However, three days later, Hanoi's press agency repeated the content of the Nixon letter in a commentary in English.[81] On May 19, cornered between Vietnamese declarations and Wolff's insistence on obtaining the letter, the State Department released the text of the secret document. "Its author [Nixon] has indicated no objection to its release," declared the State Department. "In the light of all present circumstances, we have determined that the message is no longer deemed sensitive and it has been declassified."[82]

The release of the letter coincided with Nixon's third televised interview with David Frost on May 19 and was made even more theatrical by the televised "saga" of Nixon's responses on this issue. The interviews gave Nixon an opportunity to justify his actions during the Watergate scandal but also enabled him to respond to questions on the issue of the secret letter to North Vietnam as the details of this letter were progressively being discovered by the media through congressman Wolff. Nixon justified the existence of the letter by saying that he had been obliged to act forcefully against dissidents to extricate the country from Vietnam. He again repeated that he had warned Hanoi on February 12, 1973, that the granting of economic aid was contingent on Vietnam's strict implementation of the peace agreement and on congressional approval.[83]

In forcing the administration to declassify the document, Hanoi considered that it had gained the upper hand and would win congressional support. But if such a revelation may have shifted the support of public opinion and Congress towards Vietnam during the war, it had quite the opposite effect in the new political climate. With Congress no longer a liberal institution counterbalancing presidential conservatism, the end of the war had swayed the relationship between Congress and the administration into becoming just the opposite. Starting in the early 1970s Congress had begun to rebel against the executive, prohibiting certain military moves against Cambodia in 1970, then against all of Indochina in 1973, passing the War Powers Act and finally turning against the White House in the Watergate scandal. Despite being a democratic president in times of a Democratic congressional majority, Carter encountered difficulties in dealing with Capitol Hill, and Congress would not hesitate to have its opinion acknowledged by the administration, especially on the delicate issue of Vietnam. The Vietnamese leadership, immutable as it may have been, failed to understand the political changes in the United States and continued to address the Carter administration as it had with Nixon.

The Hanoi leadership, so remote from American political culture, could not understand that the head of state could have his hands tied by Congress, and perceived congressional bans as Carter's staging of an excuse to reject normalization and aid. The Vietnamese leadership remained blind to domestic changes on the U.S. political scene. It no longer enjoyed the sympathy of Congress and U.S. domestic opinion as it had during the war. This inability to dissociate the executive branch from the legislative would account for Hanoi's misperception that the most friendly ears lay not on Capitol Hill, nor in public opinion, but in the White House. In gambling on congressional and public support while it attacked the administration, Vietnam was undermining its own interests and feeding congressional hostility.[84] Again mutual misperceptions were at the root of the bogging down of bilateral initiatives.

On May 21, two days after the State Department's release of the text of the Nixon letter, the Vietnamese foreign ministry, in turn, officially released the full text of the letter, along with Pham Van Dong's answer to it, the note from Maurice Williams and excerpts of various joint communiqués.[85] The State Department remarked that Hanoi had omitted to publish the addenda to the letter in which Nixon stressed that aid would be subject to congressional approval. A *Nhan Dan* commentator article stressed that Washington could not use the "pretext" of an executive-legislative feud to escape its commitments.[86] On May 23, *Nhan Dan* recalled the "Ineluctable Obligation and Responsibility of the U.S. Government," while *Quan Doi Nhan Dan* declared the U.S. stance "obstinate ... [and] full of sophistry."[87] A series of low-level press commentaries on U.S. obligations flourished until the second round of bilateral talks in June.[88]

On May 26, intrigued by Vietnam's failure to include the addenda on the congressional role in the potential granting of aid, Wolff wrote to Nixon to request a private meeting.[89] Perhaps he feared that Nixon had linked the issue of aid to that of MIAs, which would have explained the continued Vietnamese insistence on linking the two issues.

Up to that date, the Vietnamese officials' constant references to Nixon's pledge on aid had been doubted and even dismissed as diplomatic nonsense by the Americans. Although *Nhan Dan* had published excerpts of this letter on April 16, 1976, which remained unnoticed by the American press, the full text had never been publicly released and the issue had up to then been confined to rather informal talks, referred to indirectly and kept away from the American public and Congress.[90] But, in a sudden reversal reminiscent of the Watergate era, the Vietnamese were now proudly brandishing the proof of their claim and throwing American public opinion off balance. Perhaps it was not a sense of having political secrets betrayed by the Vietnamese so much as the re-emerging foul scent of Watergate—and the feeling of wounded pride that the Vietnam debacle had been so cleverly orchestrated behind the nation's back—that threw the United States into such a fit of anger.

In view of the recent revelations, Wolff opened an investigation in which Kissinger and Rogers testified in open session.[91] On June 3, Nixon turned down Wolff's request for testimony on the grounds that the full text of the letter had been released and "all pertinent information [was] now available."[92] Wolff replied on June 7 that he was maintaining his request for a meeting, emphasizing that the letter was absent from State Department files and stressing his concern over Vietnamese declarations regarding the existence of further communications and working notes on the issue.[93] Nixon again refused to give formal testimony.[94]

Finally, in mid–June, Wolff received in his office four congressmen, including Congressman Gilman who had supported the National League of Families' dissatisfaction over the Woodcock report. The group telephoned Nixon for a private interview and, handing the telephone from one to the other, questioned him on the secret letter. Nixon stressed that Washington's commitment to provide aid had been annulled by Hanoi's incessant violations of the peace agreement, and stressed that the new administration should not yield to "blackmail for bodies."[95]

At the House of Representatives International Relations Subcommittee hearing, Kissinger reiterated Nixon's view that Vietnamese behavior since 1973 had relieved Washington of the letter's pledge, and stated that the claim by U.S. officials negotiating in Paris that they had been "surprised" by the revelation of the letter was "totally untrue." As for the $4.75 million mentioned in the letter, he explained, this had only constituted a "planning figure" on which negotiations were to begin.[96] Hanoi, he claimed, had "broken the [Paris Peace Agreement] and we owe them nothing."[97] "For them to try to hold us to an obligation when they have violated nearly every provision of the agreement," Kissinger added, "strikes me as an absurdity."[98]

However, the White House and congressional conservatives welcomed the release of the letter, hoping this would finally dismiss doubts that Vietnam still held any legitimate right to economic aid or to link the issue of aid to an accounting for MIAs. Relieved, Wolff declared that "[w]e never have believed that there was a link between reconstruction aid and the MIA issue."[99] As for aid, the Americans would by no means honor a secret promise made by a discredited president.

In Hanoi the release of the letter had not been intended as an impediment to negotiations, but rather as a catalyst to force Washington to concede to its obligations. Aid was considered a right, but also a prize which the victors of the war could take home in a final show of glory, and use to finance the reconstruction of their country. Reflecting on the issue in his memoirs, Kissinger questioned rhetorically how the North Vietnamese had transformed a "voluntary American offer" into a proclaimed right. Elaborating on this point, Kissinger underlined the frequent "mutual incomprehension"[100] which would often surface in negotiations between the two sides and would continue to hamper bilateral talks as the Vietnamese continued to insist on obtaining American reconstruction aid.

Although the Vietnamese indeed reshaped the U.S. offer into a "right" and conveniently removed the addendum making aid conditional on congressional approval, Kissinger's remark is at best cynical if one considers the history of the Nixon letter.

Background to the Nixon Letter

Given the political turmoil that the release of the letter created, one may wonder what Nixon had expected in drafting the secret letter to North Vietnam. Although many secondary sources have mentioned the existence of several secret letters from Nixon to South Vietnamese leader Nguyen Van Thieu, today, the Nixon letter to North Vietnam remains largely unknown to the public. In the case of the letters to South Vietnam, Nixon had pledged massive American military retaliation should Hanoi breach the cease-fire and continue its military activity in South Vietnam. "I can assure you that we will view any breach of faith on their part with the utmost gravity," wrote Nixon on October 16, 1972, and it would have "the most serious consequences."[101]

But the purpose of Nixon's pledges became clearer following his re-election. On November 14, 1972, only four days after his reelection to the White House, Nixon had again secretly written to Thieu:

> Far more important than what we say in the agreement on this issue is what we do in the event the enemy renews its aggression. You have my absolute assurance that if Hanoi fails to abide by the terms of the agreement, it is my intention to take swift and severe retaliatory action ... I repeat my personal assurances to you that the United States will react very strongly and rapidly to any violation of the agreement.[102]

Another letter, written on January 5, 1973, again promised a U.S. response in "full force."[103] In total, half a dozen letters were written to Thieu in 1972 and early 1973, aimed at assuring South Vietnam of continued American support and at bringing the reluctant South Vietnamese leader to the negotiating table for the signing of a peace agreement.

Unlike his secret pledges to South Vietnam, Nixon's letter to Pham Van Dong was written on February 1, following the signing of the Paris Peace Accords, and handed over to the Vietnamese during Kissinger's visit to Vietnam in February 1973. It could, therefore, not have been intended to bring North Vietnam to the negotiating table. Furthermore, the North Vietnamese had agreed to the signing of the Accords as early as October 1972, nearly four months before Nixon produced this last secret letter to Dong. Former CIA agent Frank Snepp argues that the North Vietnamese had agreed to the signing of the Accords but that Washington had delayed the signing to allow for Nixon's re-election and to persuade Thieu of the necessity of these Accords.[104] Recent studies indeed show that Saigon refused to sign the agreement in October, and that Washington postponed the signing judging that the timing was unfavorable for Saigon and U.S. domestic politics.[105] Kissinger also confirms that the U.S. bore responsibility for the delay to allow time to persuade Thieu to agree to the Accords so as not to create what Nixon termed a "shotgun marriage."[106] In addition, while Kissinger claims that delay was not intended to enhance Nixon's chances for re-election, it is undeniable that Nixon possessed a strong argument for re-election if the peace agreement were to be signed *after* rather than prior to the elections.

Irked by Washington's sudden refusal to proceed with the signing of the agreement, Hanoi began to introduce new requests for modification of the draft.[107] In Washington, North Vietnam took over the role of culprit in delaying the signing of the peace agreement. The Christmas bombings of December 1972 were therefore designed to impress Thieu with American military power and to prove to South Vietnam that Washington was indeed capable of "swift retaliatory action" against the Vietcong, as had been expressed in Nixon's letters to the South Vietnamese president. But the bombings would also show the American public that North Vietnam had been forced back into submission when, in fact, modern sources reveal it was South Vietnam that had initially delayed the signing of the peace document.[108]

However, Kissinger justified the utility of the Christmas bombing, claiming that "all significant concessions were made by Hanoi" from October "until the end of the negotiations."[109] In May 1973, Nixon explained to Congress:

> In mid–December ... we had little choice. Hanoi obviously was stalling for time, hoping that pressures would force us to make an unsatisfactory agreement. Our South Vietnamese friends, in turn, still had some strong reservations about the settlement. The more difficult Hanoi became, the more rigid Saigon grew. There was a danger that the settlement which was so close might be pulled apart by conflicting pressures. We decided to bring home to both Vietnamese parties that there was a price for continuing hostilities.[110]

The issue of the secret Nixon letter to North Vietnam is, however, more puzzling. What would be the use of pledging more than $4 billion in reconstruction aid to its enemy after the signing of the Paris Peace Agreement? If not a diplomatic carrot to bring the Vietnamese communists to the negotiating table, what purpose could this promise of aid have served?

Porter explains that the pledge for aid had initially been requested by Hanoi apparently to compensate for the damage caused by Nixon's Christmas bombing, and to complete Article 21 of the Paris Agreement which remained vague as to the details and organization of American postwar aid. But Nixon and Kissinger intended the letter to bear greater weight on their future dealings with Hanoi, despite Le Duc Tho's insistence that the letter should promise aid "without any political conditions."[111] Simply, the letter to Pham Van Dong would create an economic lever that would guarantee ongoing peace and North Vietnamese implementation of the accords, sealing two years of secret bilateral discussions with Hanoi with a formal pledge for aid.

Although Kissinger insisted that Washington had "taken the position that the problem of aid to North Vietnam would be discussed in the context of peace-time relations and not as the outcome of a negotiation to end the war," one may suppose that the secret letter represented a diplomatic reward for North Vietnam's signing of the peace document, which allowed official American military withdrawal.[112] In addition, threats of U.S. military retaliation would remind Hanoi of its pledges in the Agreement—until congressional prohibition of military attacks in Indochina deprived Nixon of this latter option. "Mr. Kissinger has two trump cards [in dealing with Hanoi]," wrote a senior French official commenting on the Paris meetings of 1973, "which, as always, are the carrot of economic aid and the stick of military reprisal."[113]

In fact, as South Vietnamese Senator Tran Van Lam disclosed in December 1973, a secret agreement had been reached between Washington and Hanoi in January 1973 according to which North Vietnamese troops were given fifteen days following the signing of the accord to pull out of Laos and Cambodia.[114] North Vietnam's withdrawal from Cambodia and Laos had already been provided for in Article 20 of the Paris Peace Accords but the linking of the aid issue to Vietnamese withdrawal demonstrated Washington's lack of belief in the relevance and reliability of the peace document.

Frank Snepp explains that Nixon's secret pledge for aid, which came only six days after the signing of the Accords, represented an economic lever to force the Vietcong out of the territory of their two Indochinese neighbors.[115] Kissinger had stressed that congressional approval for aid to communist Vietnam would certainly be dependent on a Vietnamese withdrawal from Cambodia. But the Vietnamese repeatedly refused to intervene in Phnom Penh claiming that they enjoyed no leverage on Cambodian leadership.[116]

Later, in 1974, Kissinger tried using the aid issue to halt the North Vietnamese military advance on South Vietnam.[117] "We were willing to extend aid because it had been promised by two administrations," Kissinger recalls in his memoirs, "and especially because we thought it useful as one of the inducements to encourage observance of the agreement."[118] But while the "two administrations" to which Kissinger refers include Nixon's, and Johnson's once failed attempt to tackle the issue in 1965, it seems that of Kissinger's two arguments the former was an excuse for the latter. Aid was tied to Vietnamese good behavior representing "an investment in peace" as Nixon had come to label it.[119]

But the letter was also engineered to bring about Hanoi's release of POWs and information on MIAs. In exchange for the letter in February 1973, Hanoi provided Kissinger with a list of ten civilian and military prisoners held in Laos—a disappointment to Washington, which had hoped for an accounting of a greater number of U.S. nationals.[120] Thus, as early as January 1973, Washington had already begun what would become an exchange of MIAs for dollars, setting the tone for a grim "blackmail for corpses" and Vietnam was engaged in a slow release of information on MIAs designed to extract maximum concessions from Washington.

By January 23, 1973, the main lines of the Nixon letter had been drafted but the aid figure still remained to be decided upon. Kissinger, who at first dismissed the issue as depending on congressional decision, finally yielded to Vietnamese pressure and agreed to a sum of $3.25 billion.[121] But the complex question of congressional approval remained.

Although the possibility of aid had been an issue since the 1960s, it only became official with the release of the text of the Paris Agreement on January 24, 1973.[122] President Johnson had been the first to mention the possibility of postwar U.S. aid to North Vietnam in April 1965 but Hanoi had made no reply. In 1969 Nixon took up the issue during a speech at the UN General Assembly but the Vietnamese again failed to respond.[123] Bilateral talks on the issue did not begin until 1971.[124]

Until 1973, the promise of aid had remained verbal, but on the day of the signing of the peace agreement, Le Duc Tho had insisted on receiving a formal pledge. After the issue had taken up three of the four hours of talks, Kissinger compromised by proposing that Washington initiate an exchange of secret notes, pledging aid in exchange for Hanoi's accounting of POWs in Laos. Kissinger further offered that the upcoming February talks in Hanoi be aimed at solving the details of the pledge.[125] The concept of linking aid to MIAs and POWs was therefore originally initiated by the American side, but rapidly picked up by the Vietnamese. Moreover, the episode shows that a major part of Nixon's secret diplomacy towards North Vietnam was in fact a Kissingerian product.

Nixon had rejected the term "reparations" in the peace agreement and opted instead for the more conciliatory phrase of "reconstruction aid" which would sound more palatable to Congress.[126] Kissinger explains that he "insisted that our offer was an application of traditional American principles; it was a voluntary act, not an 'obligation' to indemnify Hanoi. It may have been hairsplitting, but to us it involved a point of honor."[127] In writing the secret letter, the Vietnamese had insisted that the pledge of aid not be made conditional on congressional approval. Kissinger compromised that this mention would not be made in the main text of the letter but in a separate addendum stating that the pledge would "be implemented by each member in accordance with its own constitutional provisions."[128] As Kissinger recalls in his memoirs:

> Le Duc Tho, never lacking in chutzpah, presumed to instruct me in January [1973] as to what was appropriate to include in a communication from our President. He insisted that ... our obligation had to be unconditional. I pointed out that whatever the more convenient decision-making procedures of Hanoi, our legislative process [approval of Congress] was a fact of life. We "compromised" by stating the need for Congressional approval on a separate page, sent simultaneously and of equal weight. Le Duc Tho seemed to draw comfort from this.[129]

Neither the existence of the secret letter nor its pledge were suspected by Congress or the American public. "The commitment [to aid, in the peace agreement] was made only to discuss such a program with the North Vietnamese," Kissinger told the Senate on January 26, 1973, adding that aid was both a humanitarian act and a "concern for preserving the peace."[130] That same day, Kissinger assured the House that aid would "absorb the energies of the Vietnamese in the positive programs of reconstruction," insisting that "[s]uch a program would constitute in cost a small fraction of what would have been involved should the war continue."[131]

During his visit to Hanoi, from February 10 to 13, Kissinger handed Nixon's letter to Pham Van Dong. The issue of aid was not tackled until the last day of meetings and Kissinger again emphasized the need for congressional authorization. The Vietnamese communists, who had observed Washington's pouring of $200 billion into South Vietnam during the war, failed to understand how the American Congress could refuse Hanoi a modest $3.25 billion.[132] Rather, they believed that Congress was being used as an excuse to justify Nixon's delay in granting aid. Following the talks, a joint communiqué was issued on February 14 announcing the creation of a Joint Economic Commission to develop economic relations.[133] The communiqué stated that the two sides had "examined concrete steps which can be taken to normalize the relations between the two countries."[134]

As secret negotiations resumed in Paris in the spring of 1973, Washington began to link aid to the North Vietnamese presence in Laos and Cambodia, a linkage that Hanoi had refused to include in the peace agreement but which Washington now wished to counter using the economic bait of aid.[135]

The constant variations in U.S. conditions for the attribution of aid to Vietnam, linked to the release of prisoners, to an accounting for MIAs, to the maintaining of peace after the Paris Agreement and finally to the withdrawal of Vietnamese presence from its Indochinese neighbors, would supply Washington with a multitude of reasons to reject Hanoi's claims for aid after the fall of Saigon. In 1977, as the Nixon letter crisis was developing, Wolff recalled:

> Again, he [Kissinger] told the committee [on international relations during a private meeting in 1975] that the commitment of aid to North Vietnam had been conditioned on a cease-fire in Cambodia. This claim is flatly without basis because we failed to get an agreement with Hanoi that they would take responsibility for a cease-fire in Cambodia before the signing of the [Paris Peace] agreement.
> Now, this does certainly muddy the waters as to the background of where we stand with relationship to any request for assistance that is made by the North Vietnamese ... today.[136]

By March 27, 1973, an agreement had been reached on the mechanics of the attribution of aid.[137] Even then, Hanoi refused to withdraw from Laos and Cambodia. Nor did Washington cease its bombing of Vietnamese communist troops in Cambodia and, over a period of seven months, dropped a tonnage of bombs superior to that which the U.S. had inflicted on Japan during World War II.[138] Some critics underlined the violence of the conflict in naming it the "postwar war."[139]

By mid–April, Nixon had begun to be personally suspected in the Watergate scandal and the White House adopted a lower profile on Indochina.[140] On April 19, Washington suspended the talks in Paris.[141] On May 1, the Vietnamese delegation returned to Hanoi.[142]

Over the following months a series of fruitless meetings and a multiplication of promises did not alter Hanoi's determination for a communist victory. "Hit them hard on MIA accounting and on withdrawal from Cambodia as conditions for aid," Nixon instructed Kissinger on May 17.[143] But the Vietnamese were not to be manipulated nor would they renege their plans to take over the South.[144] Nor were they capable of imposing a Cambodian cease-fire.[145] During the House of Representatives International Relations Subcommittee hearing on July 19, 1977, Kissinger explained:

> The violations continued, however [despite U.S. efforts to find an aid program through the JEC], so by July of 1973 we had become convinced that they had no intention of adhering to

the agreement. We then dismantled the commission and at that point our aid commitment became moot.[146]

But contrary to Kissinger's claim in his 1977 testimony to the House of Representatives, the aid issue was not fully dismissed until December 1974, when Washington unilaterally renounced its pledge of aid to North Vietnam.[147] Hanoi, however, preserved Nixon's letter for future dealings with Washington while Kissinger, harassed by Congress in 1977 on the issue of the letter, repeatedly claimed that the commitment of aid had been conditioned on a cease-fire in Cambodia.[148] History and bad faith had turned his unofficial linkage into official policy.

In February 1973, while Kissinger was negotiating the withdrawal of Vietnamese troops from Laos and Cambodia and the terms for an economic agreement, Nixon was preparing public opinion and Congress in the event Hanoi should deserve the promised aid. Nixon refrained from mentioning aid in his fiscal 1974 budget, preferring to test the issue publicly first.[149] At the end of January, a Gallup poll indicated that public opinion opposed, by 51 to 40 percent, the granting of aid.[150] Granting reconstruction aid, Secretary of State Rogers dutifully reminded a journalist, would be "consistent with our traditional role to help after a war is ended."[151] Although the issue was discussed publicly, the exact amount of aid and the letter were kept secret. Congress would be asked to endorse the presidential proposal, unaware that it referred to an existing secret promise that Nixon had made without congressional support.

"I cannot give you that figure [on aid] now," explained Nixon at a press conference on January 31, "it is a matter that has to be negotiated and it must all be part of one pattern." He insisted, however, that "Congress has to support it."[152] The following day, in the privacy of the Oval Office, Nixon signed the letter promising $4.75 billion to Hanoi. That evening, Kissinger reiterated that "[a]ny projection we make would be fully discussed with the bipartisan leadership and fully discussed in public before it became our policy."[153] Press Secretary Ziegler pledged that no figure would be stated prior to congressional vote.[154] As for the drafting of the details of the aid accord—should it be reached with the Vietnamese—these seemed to imply that Nixon truly believed his plans workable. The money for North Vietnam, he stated, "will come out of the national security budget, which means the area of foreign assistance and defense—both."[155]

But the legislature seemed doubtful. During Rogers' testimony to a House Foreign Affairs Committee on February 8, several representatives questioned how Nixon could expect a vote on aid to Vietnam when domestic programs were being cut off.[156] A Congressional Research Service Report of February 22, 1973, stating that aid would indeed support peace in the region, also stressed that Hanoi did not deserve aid since, unlike Germany and Japan during World War II, it had not "surrendered unconditionally" and still denied its aggression on South Vietnam. Defeat by American forces seemed a precondition to aid and implied that, had Hanoi lost the war, Washington would have considered it natural to grant aid. Other reasons included inflation, the risk of slowing down U.S. "disengagement ... from Southeast Asia" and the unverified assurances from other countries that they would also participate in the aid program.[157]

On April 5, 1973, the Senate adopted an amendment introduced by Senator Robert C. Byrd (Democrat, West Virginia), forbidding any aid to Hanoi without prior congressional approval.[158] "I doubt the wisdom of embarking upon massive assistance to those countries [Indochina]," Byrd remarked, "at a time when they are in turmoil, and when the American taxpayer is so hard pressed to pay the bill for the obligations his government has already incurred."[159] "Our purpose," commented Senator Frank Church (Democrat, Idaho), "may well be ransom to give Hanoi a reason to keep the truce. Some may call it reparations and some may call it ransom, but neither fits my concept of peace with honor."[160] On May 3, Nixon pledged to "observe Constitutional requirements both in letter and spirit and consult closely with Congress at every step of the way."[161] As talks in Paris stalled, no official proposal was ever presented on Capitol Hill, nor figures submitted for congressional scrutiny.[162]

But the Nixon letter had led to the birth of a new kind of rhetoric and a linking of the aid issue to that of bilateral normalization. In February 1973, Kissinger stressed the purpose of his trip to Hanoi as "discussing the implementation of the agreement, [and] what forms normalization of relations might take"—hinting at a link between the two issues.[163] On January 14, 1974, Hanoi's foreign ministry issued a *White Book* on the United States which, for the first time, called for normalization, although it spelled out several preconditions. "The U.S.," it declared, "should totally end its military involvement and its interference in the internal affairs of South Vietnam, seriously fulfill its obligations regarding healing of the wounds of war in the DRV and strictly respect the fundamental national rights of the people of Laos and Cambodia."[164] While Kissinger linked aid to the Vietnamese withdrawal from Laos and Cambodia, Hanoi created its own linkage—attaching aid to normalization. Each had twisted the unofficial understanding into conflicting policies.

It is doubtful that Nixon had genuinely intended the strategy of the Paris Peace Accords to function in the long-run, and one is therefore led to wonder as to the true purpose of the peace agreement. As Khieu Samphan recalls in his memoirs:

> Although it may have brought some satisfaction to its signatories, from the moment of its signing, the limits of this agreement appeared to the eyes of most people acquainted with the question of Indochina.... To the Vietnamese communists, this agreement offered respite to prepare an assault against Saigon without having to face direct American military power. To the Americans, it allowed the withdrawal of the G.I.s, whilst also giving them the possibility of maintaining the South Vietnamese regime in the perspective of the "Nixon doctrine" and of the "vietnamization of the war."[165]

Simply, the president was attempting to gain time and the key to honorable peace.

Nixon had understood that congressional and public opposition to the war meant that victory could not be reached at the military level but that an honorable solution should be sought.[166] "I will not be the first President of the United States to lose a war" he had warned in 1969.[167] South Vietnam would eventually collapse but not during Nixon's time of office—a "decent interval," as initially thought out by Kissinger, should allow Nixon to be remembered as a master of foreign policy for bringing *peace* to a war-ravaged country.[168]

In May 1973, in a telegram to the French foreign ministry, the French embassy in Washington explained that "all in all, the Americans are only seeking to obtain from North Vietnam a paper for Congress and public opinion."[169] Nixon would be allowed to claim that he had achieved "peace with honor"—a phrase he repeated five times in announcing the signing of the Accords.[170]

By withdrawing its troops from Vietnam as agreed in an official peace treaty and waiting for Hanoi to breach the peace agreement, Washington was safely denying its responsibility for the upcoming events and making Hanoi the culprit. The signing of the Accords and the two-year "decent interval" between the withdrawal of American troops and the collapse of the Thieu regime placed Washington on the safe side of history. In 1976, Gareth Porter explained:

> Kissinger and Nixon refused to use their power to force a political change [in the South] because they found it more compatible with both domestic political needs and foreign policy objectives to lose militarily while playing the "good ally" than to actively seek a political solution to bring an end to the war.[171]

The pledge of aid in the secret letter would prolong this "decent interval." Nixon's claim, as reported by his biographer, Monica Crowley, that "[w]e won the war ... but then lost the peace" seems, at best, a hypocritical rewriting of history.[172]

However, one may also speculate that the swelling pressure, since July 1972, of the Watergate scandal, followed by that of the elections of November 1972 and of the congressional threat to cut off aid to South Vietnam in early January 1973 should a peace agreement not have been signed by then, may have contributed to the Americans' wish to accelerate peace negotiations.[173] In 1968, Nixon had claimed that a man incapable of ending the war in four years should not be elected president. The upcoming 1972 elections, arriving when no peace had been achieved in Indochina, had certainly placed him in an awkward position.[174] On October 26, a few days before the election of 1972, Kissinger had reassured Nixon's supporters that "peace is at hand," so that Nixon's past statements would not undermine his re-election.[175] A hasty American military withdrawal and a peace agreement, even if guaranteeing only a weak and temporary peace in Vietnam, might appear a political side step and save the president from the upcoming humiliating confrontation of Watergate in April 1973.

Although both North and South Vietnam eventually signed the peace agreement, it seemed rather unavoidable that the document would be as hollow as the pledges of its signatories. The agreement seemed barely a pretext for an American military withdrawal from Vietnam while neglecting to secure the needs of each Vietnamese state. While the United States had achieved an honorable peace and the Vietnamese communists had seen one of their military opponents withdraw, South Vietnam had gained the least from the accords which, of all absurdities, allowed North Vietnamese troops present in South Vietnamese territories to remain in the South.[176]

Only a few days before the signing of the agreement, Nixon had even sent Thieu a letter threatening that if Saigon refused to sign the Accords, Washington would proceed with the signing without the South Vietnamese.[177] Thieu yielded to American pressure. "I did not think that a Secretary of State like Mr. Kissinger," explained Thieu on resigning, "could not realize that it was an agreement leading the nation and country of Vietnam to its death. I believe he realized this."[178]

Kissinger's answer to Thieu came seven years later when, writing in his memoirs, he explained:

> I never believed that Hanoi would reconcile itself to the military balance as it emerged from the Paris Agreement without testing it at least once more ... we recognized that there might be gross breaches of the Agreement that could topple the military balance it ratified.[179]

"The record shows," writes Vietnam expert Larry Berman:

> that the United States *expected* that the signed treaty would be immediately violated and that this would trigger a brutal military response [by the U.S.]. Permanent war (air war, not ground operations) at acceptable costs was what Nixon and Kissinger anticipated from the so-called peace agreement.[180]

After fighting the French, the Japanese and the Americans for nearly forty years, one may doubt that the North Vietnamese would have kept to an incomplete peace treaty. It was merely allowing its enemies to leave.[181] Washington could not blind itself from such a fact.[182] And indeed, Washington's decision at the end of 1972 to send a massive shipment of weapons to South Vietnam and to train thousands of civilian military advisers indicated that the Nixon administration was well aware that peace in Indochina would only be temporary. In 2003, defending his Nobel Prize, Kissinger again rejected responsibility for the failure of the Peace Accords, complaining that the congressional bans of 1973 "and not the legal terms of the agreement, [had] ensured the collapse of Indochina." He further insisted that continued U.S. bombings of North Vietnamese troops infiltrating South Vietnam, once all U.S. grounds troops had been safely withdrawn, would have saved Saigon and its neighbor Indochinese capitals.[183] One may, however, question the American concept of "peace with honor," if "peace" were to include continued bombing.

Returning to the events of May 1977, until which date the text of the letter had been held secret, one may wonder about the circumstances that caused Hanoi to engage in what could be seen as a "sabotaging" of its own initiatives towards Washington in its apparently illogical and arrogant show of diplomatic force with the publication of the Nixon letter.

As has been shown, in Hanoi the release of the text of the letter was never intended as an obstacle to negotiations, but instead as a means of bringing Washington face-to-face with its obligations. Aid was considered as a right by Hanoi, promised by the American head of state. More importantly, this was a concession Hanoi could parade as a symbol of victory and—more concretely—use to accelerate economic reconstruction.

In his memoirs, Kissinger reports his irritation with the Vietnamese over their insistence that aid was a moral debt, and recalled Pham Van Dong's arrogance, in negotiating the aid issue during the peace talks of 1972–1973, when the North Vietnamese premier "almost made it seem that Hanoi was doing America a favor in accepting its money." In an act of bad faith, if one considers that for more than three years the Nixon administration had used the aid issue to extract greater concessions from the Vietnamese communists, Kissinger rhetorically asked:

> How we reached the point where a voluntary American offer became transmuted into a North Vietnamese "right" shows at least the degree to which the two societies were doomed to mutual incomprehension and at most the ability of the North Vietnamese to turn single-mindedness into an art form.[184]

His remark however, once drained of its sarcasm, calls to attention Hanoi's failure to understand the changes in American public opinion since the end of the war. In making Nixon's pledge public, Hanoi had sought to attract popular support for its cause, gambling that American public opinion, once aware of the deal struck between Nixon and Pham Van Dong, would immediately call on the government to fulfill its war-time promises. But Hanoi's mistake lay in its misperception of the popular and congressional moods in the United States which were no longer willing to lend a friendly ear to Vietnam's propaganda—even less so to consider another of Nixon's political blunders.

Still carried by the monolithic and immutable revolutionary ideologies that had motivated its people for more than fifty years, Hanoi had failed to comprehend that American antiwar sentiments could evaporate with the end of the war. Plus, added to the Vietnamese misconception that the antiwar movement had been pro–Vietnamese instead of simply against the war, Hanoi had created an ethnocentric understanding of world politics and, therefore, a state of political ignorance amongst Vietnamese leadership as to the new values now guiding its former enemy. Therefore, if the release of the Nixon letter during the war may have had the effect that Vietnam counted on, its release in 1977 created a reverse effect, shutting the door to American sympathy on Vietnam.

But this episode also sheds light on the inner mechanisms of the nebulous Vietnamese nucleus of the Hanoi leadership. As discussed earlier, factionalism within the VCP had developed since the Fourth Party Congress, leading to the growing influence of Le Duc Tho who, although in the background of the Vietnamese leadership, was certainly, according to his observers, the instigator of major foreign and domestic policies.[185] Certainly, it seems clear from Kissinger's memoirs that while the secret letter was addressed to Pham Van Dong, it was in fact Le Duc Tho and Kissinger who had planned its creation and orchestrated its writing.[186] Moreover, the letter was handed to Le Duc Tho rather than to the prime minister and one may suspect that it then remained in his possession.[187]

The release of the text of the letter may have originated with Le Duc Tho, a reportedly arrogant character who may have wanted to remind Hanoi's former enemy of Vietnamese superiority and punish Washington for not accepting Vietnamese terms for normalization.[188] Kissinger even hints in his memoirs that Le Duc Tho had insisted that the mention of a need for congressional approval be separated from the main text of the Nixon letter, stressing that this detail "would [later] enable Hanoi to publish the letter and to suppress the qualification ... earning itself for the gullible one more demonstration of [U.S.] duplicity."[189] Clearly the Nixon administration's sincerity not only regarding Hanoi but, perhaps more importantly, regarding its own people, is called into question.

The Paris Negotiations (June and December 1977)

The second round of the 1977 Paris talks were greatly affected by the theatrical release of the Nixon letter. Two weeks after the first talks, it was announced that the second round, initially planned for May 15, had been postponed to June 2. The American embassy of Paris was chosen to host these talks—an elegant move from Washington, as it would be the first time a Hanoi official had ever entered the embassy.[190] When Holbrooke addressed the Vietnamese, the entire context of the debate had changed. Hanoi was regarded with great suspicion following the release of the text of the secret

Nixon letter to Pham Van Dong. Shortly before leaving for Paris, Holbrooke had been given an FBI report stating that a spy, probably in the State Department, had been passing information to Hanoi. Holbrooke was uncertain of exactly how much the Vietnamese knew of his negotiating instructions.[191]

In addition, the Vietnamese had not grasped the nature of the scandal of the Nixon letter nor the extent to which its effect had reversed public and congressional opinion. Misunderstanding that the release of the letter had destroyed rather than upgraded the negotiating value of these documents, the Vietnamese now urged the granting of this promised economic crutch. Meanwhile, in Washington, congressional votes had renounced Nixon's pledge and dismissed the letter as yet another Nixonian political blunder. Neither side understood the other's position, and talks between Holbrooke and his Vietnamese counterpart stalled on the subject of aid.[192]

As for the meetings in May, Frank Sieverts held separate talks with Vu Hoang on MIAs. The Vietnamese had presented a list of twenty MIAs whose remains had been recovered and whose identities were being checked.[193] Two additional names of MIAs, including one civilian whose remains had previously been promised by Vietnam, were added to the list and the Vietnamese stated that the remains would be released in August.[194] Honoring the American request made in May, the Vietnamese refrained from publicly announcing the names of the servicemen until they had been fully identified. "[A]lthough much remains to be done," concluded Holbrooke, "I believe a start has finally been made in obtaining an accounting" and indeed the official press release stressed Washington's "appreciation for this positive action."[195]

Brzezinski also acknowledged the State Department's progress. But his preference for a more aggressive policy could already be observed. He reported to Carter:

> The release of information and remains suggests our strategy of decoupling the MIA and recognition issues is working. The Vietnamese perhaps are beginning to understand that withholding information yields no leverage. Deprived of incentive to hide information, they continue to release it. Now, in my opinion, we should continue to diffuse the MIA issue as an anti–Vietnam rallying point in the U.S.[196]

Brzezinski's recommended strategy to obtain greater concessions from Hanoi did not fit within the new president's initial aims of de-emphasizing the MIA issue. However, as Washington adopted this harder-line U.S. policy towards Hanoi the following year, reminiscent of Kissinger's own approach to the issue, and which was at the expense of the State Department's plans for American-Vietnamese normalization, one may speculate that the administration's slight cooling towards Vietnam, starting in June 1977, might have had as much to do with congressional pressures as with the growing influence of Brzezinski's skepticism about Carter. The cooling of U.S. relations with Hanoi also coincided with the completion of Presidential Review Memorandum 24 (PRM-24) in June 1977, a report recommending normalization with Vietnam's political adversary China—an issue which Brzezinski considered a priority.

Despite American self-congratulatory declarations that decoupling MIAs and normalization had led to fruitful results, Hanoi's declarations suggested that it still expected a link between the two issues. Hien had clearly hoped for a reciprocal move. While Holbrooke attempted to explain, once again, the complexities of the recent congressional vote opposing aid to Vietnam, Hien impatiently rejected Holbrooke's explanation, betraying Hanoi's lack of understanding of executive-legislative relations. "What would you do," he asked, "if I said the Vietnamese National Assembly had passed a law prohibiting searches for the MIAs?" The State Department, he concluded, "has not had the courage to tell the Congress or the public what they think about aid to Vietnam."[197] Instead, Hien requested a two-phase agreement—Washington would pledge aid at a later date and Hanoi would begin working on MIAs. Holbrooke insisted that such a promise was impossible but that Washington would consider the possibility of recommending Vietnam for aid programs in international institutions, only after normalization. Hien refused, requesting an American commitment prior to normalization.[198]

In fact, Hien's request was not unreasonable as it went along the lines of Carter's initial wish to normalize as a first step and to find a compromise on aid at a later stage. Hien would certainly have accepted an unofficial pledge of aid, as he would request from Holbrooke in December. But Carter's plans had been nipped by congressional bans on aid and Holbrooke could only offer aid through international institutions to counter the obstacle of Congress. A few days later, perhaps having heard of Holbrooke's offer, Congress would indeed attempt to ban U.S. aid in international institutions from reaching Vietnam.

After the meetings, a Vietnamese communiqué stressed that Hanoi had clearly expressed its views on the three issues of MIAs, aid and normalization, but that Washington "did not respond to this reasonable and logical attitude."[199] The Vietnamese press described the American position as "bargaining" for its dead and adopting an "arrogant" attitude.[200] Back in Washington, Holbrooke reported his disappointment to the House Committee on International Relations that "Vietnam has not accepted, thus far, our proposal for normalization of relations, on the ground that it fails to provide a commitment to provide U.S. reconstruction assistance, which they view as having been promised by past agreements." He continued:

> We have been at pains, in our talks in Paris, and in our public statements, to make clear our view that there is no such obligation, and that U.S. aid to Vietnam is prohibited by specific provisions of law enacted by the Congress. We continue to hope Vietnam will set aside its demand for such assistance and instead will join with us in looking toward a future in which such questions can be discussed and resolved under conditions of formal relations.[201]

The talks were postponed and due to resume "at a time and place" to be determined "later."[202]

As Vance politely summarized the situation: "The scars of war still exist on both sides. Both sides retain a residue of bitterness that must be overcome. But there is some progress."[203] However, listing Washington's recent efforts to reach diplomatic rapprochement with Hanoi, he publicly announced, in a declaration as much aimed at warning Hanoi as it was at reassuring Congress, that:

> These steps make clear that we seek to move forward in building a new relationship. Remembering the lessons of the past, neither side should be obsessed by them or draw the wrong conclusions. We cannot accept an interpretation of the past that imposes unfounded obligations on us.[204]

While the administration remained favorable toward normalization and still believed it possible, Congress seemed increasingly skeptical of the long-term advisability of this stance, and moved to make Holbrooke's offer of international aid impossible. The recent aggression in Vietnamese press statements confirmed congressional fears. In fact, congressional mood had changed considerably since the Woodcock mission and several figures of Congress voiced their open hostility toward American-Vietnamese rapprochement. In June, Assemblyman Dennis T. Gorski (Republican, New York), a former Vietnam War platoon leader, openly attacked the Vietnamese "use" of dead American servicemen to extricate reconstruction aid from Washington in a letter published [in] *The New York Times*.[205]

At the same time, the Senate reinforced its opposition to granting economic aid. On June 14, against the advice of the sponsoring committee, the Senate adopted a motion introduced by Senator Robert Dole (Republican, Kansas) requiring the government to oppose any aid to Vietnam by the World Bank or other international lending institutions such as the International Monetary Fund.[206] "I do not know of any taxpayer who wants to send money to Vietnam," explained the Senator.[207]

The amendment to foreign assistance bill HR 5262 provided that the appropriation for any international agency be reduced by the exact dollar amount of aid given to any of the three nations of Vietnam, Cambodia and Laos. As direct aid was already prohibited, Dole defended his new amendment by saying that it merely "closed the back door" on any possibility of delivering economic aid to Vietnam. He explained that "Vietnam is still such a controversial issue, from an emotional standpoint, with many constituents. My folks tell me they want no part of this so-called normalisation of relations with Vietnam."[208]

The next day, the Senate approved an amendment introduced by Senator John Glenn (Democrat, Ohio) to another foreign assistance bill HR 6714 barring all funds "for assistance to or reparations for" Vietnam, Cambodia and Laos, whether through international agencies or as bilateral assistance.[209] Impassively, Phan Hien reminded French journalists on June 21 that Hanoi remained "flexible" on the form of aid Washington should wish to provide, and that U.S. opposition to aid would only harm bilateral relations. Announcing Hanoi's willingness to resume talks, he stressed that the Vietnamese "want to know if it [Washington] really wants normal diplomatic relations with Vietnam."[210]

Phan Hien's statement points at the wavering Vietnamese position in dealing with Washington. While Hien declared himself "flexible" as to the form of aid Washington would supply, he had just refused an U.S. offer to provide aid through international institutions. It is doubtful that the Vietnamese vice-foreign minister had misunderstood Holbrooke's offer. It is more likely that Hanoi wanted a clear American commitment on aid as much out of financial need as out of a wish to trumpet Vietnam's success in forcing Washington to accept its responsibilities. Again this incident brings forth mutual misunderstandings and missed opportunities, while hinting at the first signs of growing radicalism and political aggressiveness in foreign policy within the Hanoi leadership—the consequences of which would affect Hanoi's foreign policies a few months later.

On June 22, the House of Representatives slashed almost $1 billion from the administration's fiscal 1978 Foreign Aid Bill (HR 7797). Through an amendment introduced by Florida Republican Representative Bill Young, it also forbade U.S. funds from being used "directly or indirectly" by international institutions to the profit of Vietnam or of six other countries.²¹¹ The same day, Wolff suggested the word "reparations" be added to the text of the already existing bills so as "to put to rest the question that was raised by the letter that President Nixon sent to the Vietnamese in 1973." Thus, in a 359–33 vote, the letter was formally renounced and the paying of reparations using any funds in the bill strictly forbidden.²¹² Congress approved the modified bills the next day despite Carter's personal appeal in a letter to the speaker.²¹³ Simultaneously, the House of Representatives opened a hearing on human rights in Vietnam, which Hanoi claimed was part of American "hostile arrogant acts to justify its erroneous policy."²¹⁴

On June 25, the White House described the congressional move to prevent international lending institutions from using U.S. contributions in Vietnam as "unworkable" and Press Secretary Jody Powell explained that limitations on direct or indirect aid to Vietnam might encourage other nations to impose their own vetoes and "politicize" lending institutions.²¹⁵ "If we adopt this amendment," warned David Obey (Democrat, Wisconsin), who led the opposition to the Young Amendment, "the international financial institutions apparently will not be able to accept our money. That will mean that the ability of those institutions to function will crumble."²¹⁶

Indeed in mid–July, World Bank President Robert McNamara declared that his institution "could not accept the [U.S.] funds, so conditioned."²¹⁷ Following McNamara's answer, Carter and the Senate opposed the House request for such restrictions and a House-Senate conference was called to resolve the issue.²¹⁸ In the final version of bill HR 5262, Congress called for U.S. representatives in international lending institutions to verify only that Vietnam, Laos and Cambodia were willing to provide a "more substantial accounting" of MIAs when their applications for loans were considered. During the conference, Carter was also requested to take all necessary measures to obtain a final accounting of POWs and MIAs of the Vietnam War.²¹⁹ Congress was reiterating its support for the families of MIAs.

After meeting congressional leaders on September 30, Carter sent an official letter to Representative Clarence Long (Democrat, Maryland), chairman of the House Foreign Operations Subcommittee, promising he would instruct U.S. representatives in international lending institutions "to oppose and vote against, through financial year 1978, any loans to the seven countries mentioned in the House amendments."²²⁰

In October, the House, by 229 votes to 195, rescinded its insistence that U.S. funds in international lending institutions not be used in loans to Vietnam or any of the six other countries recognized as those violating human rights.²²¹ Nevertheless, an amendment to the International Financial Institutions Authorization Bill for fiscal years 1978 to 1981, introduced by Senator Tom Harkin (Democrat, Iowa) passed, requiring the U.S. directors of some institutions, including the Inter-American Development Bank, to vote against aid to any government guilty of a "consistent pattern of gross violations of internationally recognized human rights ... unless such assistance will directly benefit the needy people in such country," including Vietnam. The same month, another amendment to the Foreign Assistance Appropriation Bill for fiscal year 1978, proposed by Representative Bill Young (Republican, Florida), was passed, forbidding any funds from going directly or indirectly to Vietnam, Cambodia, Laos or Uganda.²²²

On November 1, Carter signed the amended $6.2 billion Foreign Assistance Appropriation Bill.²²³ In practice, congressional barring of funds for Vietnam was impossible to achieve. But the message to the executive was clear: Congress strictly prohibited even discussing aid for Hanoi and renounced such a possibility even before the matter could emerge. The congressional move tied the executive's hands in denying both the use of direct economic aid to Vietnam and later that of indirect international aid, closing all doors on the possibility of an economic settlement.

Meanwhile, Hanoi was strengthening its position within Indochina, which proved a particularly successful strategy in Laos. Following the fall of Vientiane to the Pathet Lao in December 1975, Lao-Vietnamese relations had developed considerably. In February 1976, a Lao delegation to Hanoi announced that both countries would develop their economic ties and indeed several treaties on bilateral cooperation were signed, especially after the Vietnamese reunification.[224]

On July 17, 1977, Vietnam signed the Treaty of Friendship and Cooperation with Laos, which strengthened the suspicion and fear of the ASEAN countries that Hanoi sought "hegemonistic expansion" of its communist ideologies.[225] This treaty, signed in Laos by Lao People's Democratic Republic and Secretary-General of the Lao People's Revolutionary Party (LPRP) Kaysone Phomvihane during the visit of a Vietnamese delegation comprising Le Duan, Pham Van Dong, Vice-Premier Pham Hung and General Chu Huy Man, would regulate Lao-Vietnamese diplomatic exchanges over a period of twenty-five years.[226] The final joint declaration blamed the United States for "plotting to take advantage of the ASEAN [especially via Thailand and its military bases, they insisted] to oppose the trend toward genuine independence, peace and neutrality" in the region, signaling that Vientiane had drafted its policies towards Washington according to Hanoi's official position.[227] The joint communiqué, however, claimed each country's readiness "to establish and develop normal relations with the United States" should Washington "scrupulously carry out its pledge to contribute to healing the wounds of war and to postwar reconstruction in Vietnam and Laos."[228]

Viewed within the regional political context of the summer of 1977, this alliance clearly illustrated the growing uneasiness of Hanoi and Vientiane regarding the aggressive Pol Pot regime in Cambodia, and indirectly against the growing belief that China backed Phnom Penh's hostility towards Vietnam. The "special relationship," claimed the two signatory states, was designed to defeat those "who are trying to carry out many subtle and perfidious tricks and divisive schemes in order to weaken revolution in each country."[229] The treaty would aim "at reinforcing the defense capacity, preserving the independence and defending the people's peaceful labour against all schemes and acts of sabotage by imperialism and foreign reactionary forces." But the two signatory states refrained from uttering any direct attack on China, reserving all aggressive rhetoric for indirect allusions to Cambodia.

It is undeniable that the treaty had come as a direct response to the multiplication, in June 1975, of Chinese troops in northern Laos, and to increasing Chinese pressure on both Laos and Vietnam.[230] By the following September, the 24th Plenum of the Central Committee of the VCP had decided to "strengthen solidarity with Laos and Cambodia and realize lasting alliance and mutual assistance," of which the treaty with Laos was evidently the first step.[231] While the treaty sought to counter Chinese influence in Indochina, Peking and Moscow were referred to on an equal basis in the joint statement, which stressed that both countries would "do everything in their power to strengthen their militant solidarity and relations of cooperation with the USSR, China and other fraternal socialist countries."[232]

China was greatly displeased. The geographical realities of established borders already cut Peking from Phnom Penh, and the signing of the treaty and its inherent Vietnamese-Lao alliance would provide a new obstacle between China and its protégés.[233] In the light of this treaty and of the multiplication of Vietnam's border clashes with Cambodia, the Chinese journal for international propaganda *Peking Review* charged that Hanoi "dreams of becoming the overlord in Southeast Asia."[234]

China and Cambodia's description of the treaty as Vietnamese expansionism were not entirely irrelevant.[235] Along with this treaty, several military agreements provided a legal basis for the presence of more than 40,000 Vietnamese troops on Lao soil—unsurprisingly, mostly along the Lao-Cambodian border.[236] While Vietnam had initially tolerated the Cambodian determination to walk an independent line, Pol Pot's incessant provocations had exhausted Hanoi's patience. The Vietnamese no longer seemed willing to postpone the completion of the Indochinese "special relationship" and increasingly considered a military solution to its initially diplomatic goals, perhaps also wishing to limit Chinese influence on Cambodia.[237]

Following the end of the June talks with Holbrooke and the signing of the treaty with Laos, the Vietnamese launched several military assaults on the border front to intimidate their opponents.[238] The signing of the treaty had coincided with the adoption by the Vietnamese Party Committee for the Eastern Zone of a resolution recognizing that the border conflict "cannot be resolved," implying that another more permanent solution should be found.[239] A week later, Defense Minister General Vo Nguyen Giap called for combat readiness.[240] As Hanoi increasingly inclined towards a military solution, the need for international support increased.

Hanoi turned to the Soviet Union. In May and June 1977, Pham Van Dong flew to Moscow where he was later joined by Le Duc Tho. The Soviets immediately agreed to sign economic agreements and, in exchange, a Soviet military delegation was dispatched to Vietnam to visit several sites, including Cam Ranh Bay.[241] Far from being an ideological decision, Le Duc Tho maintained his wish to repulse Chinese influence from entering the region via Phnom Penh. Opening to Moscow was not a preferential course of action but a short-term solution to counter a growing Chinese threat; a resumption of the Vietnamese wartime strategy of counterbalancing influences to extract greater concessions from its allies.[242] Failed negotiations with the U.S. in spring and an apparent Sino-American rapprochement, represented by Vance's visit to China in August, encouraged the Vietnamese to look to Moscow. The first step toward attracting foreign support and alliances depended on obtaining prior international recognition, which Hanoi intended to find through Washington.

Despite congressional wrath during the June talks, Carter kept his promise not to oppose Vietnam's admission to the UN. More than a gesture of reconciliation, Carter's move signaled that the White House still hoped for rapprochement, despite recent setbacks, and would officially publicize American friendliness to Vietnam in the presence of the entire international community. On the domestic level, Carter's move also indirectly demonstrated his resistance to congressional hostility towards Vietnam and to the legislature's coalition against international aid to Hanoi. Certainly, the success of the signing of the Panama Canal treaties on September 7, three weeks before the Vietnamese admission, would soften the impact of this delicate issue on the American public and Congress.[243]

A friendly gesture would also ease the way for the Vietnamese release of information on MIAs. Speaking to the House Subcommittee on Asian and Pacific Affairs on July 27, Holbrooke confided:

> We do not know how much information [on MIAs] the Vietnamese have in total ... It is a reasonable assumption, and one that I make, that they have more information than they have given us. And although it is difficult for them to obtain still more information, they could obtain more. It is going to be a long process, and we are going to continue to press to get all the information.[244]

Considering Vietnam's application to the UN on July 19, Deputy U.S. Representative Donald McHenry declared that Washington was looking "forward to working with Vietnam, as with all other members of this body, to bring about a new era of peace, cooperation, and friendship, not only in our bilateral relations but in our work together in the United Nations." Thus, he declared, the "principle of universality of representation will be further advanced," ironically reversing the U.S. stance in 1975 that Vietnam's admission would mean only "selective universality" and went against UN principles.[245]

The next day, the Security Council voted to recommend Vietnam's application to the General Assembly.[246] Keeping to his usual declarations, Dinh Ba Thi, the Vietnamese observer, again seized the opportunity to emphasize that the U.S. should help in "healing the wounds of the war" further straining congressional patience.[247] Senator Dole stressed that the Security Council decision was an unfortunate step in Washington's premature normalization efforts.

Public opinion remained divided. By the end of July a poll indicated that 70 percent of Americans opposed direct economic aid to Vietnam, although a large proportion was not against providing food and medicine (66 percent) or industrial and agricultural equipment (49 percent) as a concomitant of normalization.[248]

Seeing the U.S. presidential winds blowing in a favorable direction, the Vietnamese made the friendly gesture of accepting, "in principle," Washington's invitation, initially issued by Woodcock and repeated during Holbrooke's first round of talks in May, to send Vietnamese experts to visit the Joint Casualty Resolution Center in Hawaii, where they would be introduced to modern methods in the identification of human remains.[249] A month later it was announced that an American delegation would travel to Vietnam to recover the twenty-two sets of remains promised during the June negotiations.[250] Hanoi was thanking Washington for yielding on the Vietnamese UN membership.

It had not escaped Vietnam's memory that Hanoi had been accused, during the previous UN General Assembly session, of inhumane behavior and lack of humanitarian concern, and the Vietnamese had cautiously prepared themselves for similar accusations during the 1977 session. In an official report, dated September 18, Vietnam announced that it had released more than 1,600 officials of the former Saigon regime in the course of the month, demonstrating its respect for human rights to the UN assembly.

A few days later, Vietnam was finally admitted as a full member of the UN.[251] A record 105 countries had co-sponsored Vietnam's application.[252] Its delegation, headed by Nguyen Duy Trinh, was greeted by thousands of people at the flag-raising ceremonies. Dinh Ba Thi attended a conference held by American humanitarian organizations which called for a U.S. contribution to the healing of Vietnamese war wounds.[253] A few dozen demonstrators, mostly Vietnamese refugees, protested outside.[254]

In his first speech at the General Assembly, Trinh placed Vietnam, with self-congratulatory zeal, at the forefront of all revolutionary forces, stating that:

> The victory of Viet Nam demonstrates this shining truth of our times: that a nation, however small, provided it is closely united and determined to fight accordingly to a correct line and provided that it enjoys the sympathy and the support of progressive mankind, is wholly capable of defeating all aggressors.[255]

While Hanoi rightly perceived its formal recognition by the international community as a major diplomatic success, rewarding Vietnamese perseverance, it also seemed to understand its recognition as a proof of American penitence, which Hanoi had earned the right to trumpet before its international audience. Had it not been for the "bloodiest neo-colonialist war" in history perpetrated by "imperialist aggressors," Trinh claimed, Vietnam would have been admitted to the UN as early as 1945.[256] "Our international community will never be deceived by those who loudly profess to be defenders of human rights but actually kindle wars of aggression and brutally trample underfoot the most sacred rights of nations and human beings."

However, Trinh reminded his audience that the Vietnamese government was nevertheless willing to normalize with Washington as a sign of Vietnamese goodwill, despite American policies and "imperialism."[257] Keeping within his new role as the "mentor" of the anti-colonial struggle, inherited by defeating the world's greatest military power, and appealing to the concept of self-determination, he claimed that American military bases were directed against the "valiant struggle" of the local population. Pointing his finger at the Pacific island of Guam, from which U.S. fighters planes had repeatedly launched bombing raids against North Vietnam during the war, he claimed that Hanoi supported

> unreservedly the struggle of peoples against imperialist military bases in other countries ... because those bases are not only designed for the subjugation of the colonial peoples in question but also constituted a threat to the peace and security of other peoples and countries.[258]

The General Assembly issued a resolution against the use of the Guam bases against the local population's right to self-determination and gave Vietnam a full sense of victory.

Despite the harshness of Vietnamese declarations, Vietnam rewarded American goodwill. In Hanoi, a convenient few days after Vietnam's admission to the UN, the twenty-two sets of MIA remains promised during the June negotiations were ceremonially handed over to Frank Sieverts on September 30, bringing to 61 the number of bodies released by Hanoi.[259] Sieverts handed back the remains of the misidentified Vietnamese soldier that had been given to Woodcock in April by mistake.[260] He also provided facts on a further 30 MIAs whose remains were to be sought.[261] The Vietnamese pointed out that time had come for normalization and the solving of "unresolved questions."[262]

III. Talks Turn Cold

U.S. ambassador to the UN Andrew Young had looked forward to improving relations between the southern, non-white regions of the world and the U.S. Shortly after his appointment he had announced that "[w]e look forward to working with Vietnam as with all other members of this body."[263] Upon Vietnamese admission to the UN, the American ambassador congratulated Trinh according to protocol, as he had received instructions to keep his contact with the Vietnamese, even during General Assembly meetings, to its strictest minimum. Young even had to refuse Trinh's invitation for a private and informal meeting.[264]

The Vietnamese admission, after two years of repeated U.S. vetoes, represented a delicate issue for the United States. Oksenberg had even suggested to Brzezinski that the U.S. discourage other nations supporting the Vietnamese admission to the UN from making too much of a show of this diplomatic victory. "This is a humiliating moment for us," he had privately written to the national security adviser; "no reason to add to the humiliation."[265]

Young therefore kept to formal comments on the Vietnamese admission. Vietnam's official entry into the UN, he declared, represented "a step in the struggle for peace, justice and prosperity which we now carry on together in the UN and in our own countries."[266] Washington, he added, would "look to the future."[267]

A few months later, on April 5, 1978, Representative Henry Gonzalez (Democrat, Texas), chairman of the House of Representatives Subcommittee on International Development, demanded an apology for what he had seen as too warm a welcome: "if I remember correctly Ambassador Young enthusiastically greeted the Vietnamese delegate and I think he either shook his hand or embraced him."[268] Again, the State Department had to intervene to counter the effects of the perceived breach of policy guidelines, and Holbrooke defended the ambassador saying that the Djibouti delegates, admitted simultaneously with Vietnam, had received the same greeting. Only a few days after the UN session, Carter included Dinh Ba Thi to his list of Asian diplomats for a luncheon organized by the White House.[269]

Vietnamese admission gave the opportunity to several nations, mainly Soviet-backed states, to express their view that Washington should contribute to the economic reconstruction of Vietnam.[270] Moscow reminded Washington of its duty to provide reconstruction aid following the American "war of aggression" in Vietnam, while China refrained from mentioning the issue and simply declared that Vietnam's admission represented the victory of justice.[271] Chinese restraint hinted at a cooling of relations between Hanoi and Peking that would turn icy over the following months.

In early October, forty-six states presented a resolution to the Economic Committee of the General Assembly requesting that Vietnam be added to the list of most seriously affected countries and that financial aid be provided to reconstruct its war-devastated economy. This proposal was submitted on the very day that Carter gave his written promise to Congress to instruct all U.S. representatives of international lending institutions to oppose aid to Vietnam. During the General Assembly debate, Young claimed he had not taken part in the Committee's decision due to this congressional barring of aid. The resolution was nevertheless adopted by the Committee without a vote and approved by the General Assembly on October 14.[272]

Events in Indochina barely allowed Hanoi time to savor its diplomatic victory in

New York. On September 24, only six days after Hanoi's admission, a second major Cambodian offensive marched into Vietnam along a 150-kilometer front. Three days later, while visiting Peking, Pol Pot shocked Hanoi by announcing, simultaneously, both the existence of the ruling Kampuchean Communist Party (KCP) and its seventeenth anniversary.[273] Whereas Hanoi had misperceived and downplayed Cambodian hostilities for a decade, hiding them from the international community, Pol Pot's speech revealed to the world its hostility towards Hanoi and its choice of Peking as a supporter, if not mentor. In response, chairman Hua Guofeng pledged that Peking would "always stand with Kampuchea" in its "just struggle" against imperialism (China's catchword for the United States) and hegemony (the Soviet Union).[274]

U.S. journalist and critic Elizabeth Becker argues that Pol Pot, under Chinese pressure, announced his belonging to the communist camp as a signal that his government had ceased to function as an obscure, undefined and disorganized guerrilla regime. China's open support for Cambodia, diplomatically and militarily, may have been made conditional on such a public disclosure of the true nature of the KCP. In an attempt to temper relations with both Cambodia and China, Hanoi sent a congratulatory message in honor of the anniversary of the KCP.[275] Doubt and anxiety were growing in Vietnam as the Sino-Cambodian axis formed, confronting the partly shaped Soviet-Vietnamese camp.

In September, the Cambodians mysteriously left their embassy in Moscow. Later, in October, the Cambodian embassy staff in Hanoi packed their bags and, escorted by Chinese delegates, boarded a Chinese commercial flight to Peking.[276] Although Hanoi had long observed Chinese support for Phnom Penh, the Vietnamese were now convinced that Peking was the instigator of Cambodian aggression.[277] Nor did Hanoi fail to see that, emboldened by Chinese support, the Cambodians were escalating attacks, which Hanoi's troops pushed back into Cambodian territory, occupying a few miles of Cambodian soil.[278]

Hanoi maintained low-scale unpublicized bombing of the border so as not to jeopardize talks with the Americans, simultaneously calling for a compromise with Phnom Penh. Le Duan reiterated that Vietnam did not wish to enter into large-scale battles with its communist neighbors and sought "to preserve and develop the special relationship between the [Vietnamese and Cambodian communist] parties and the people of Vietnam and Cambodia."[279] Meanwhile, Pol Pot took on his role of guest of honor for the Chinese National Day in Peking.[280] He reiterated his warning that Cambodia could turn to "a powerful friend" to protect its borders. The Chinese media, downplaying his vehemence, refrained from mentioning whether Pol Pot had met the Chinese defense minister.[281]

Hanoi turned to Peking to mediate with Cambodia as much to obtain a truce as to test Chinese reaction to the issue. By the end of October, Phan Hien had spent more than two weeks in Peking seeking a solution to the dispute but returned to Hanoi after most of the talks had been canceled.[282] During a Vietnamese visit to Peking in November, through which Hanoi hoped to find a solution to the conflict with Cambodia, China refused its assistance and demanded a withdrawal of Vietnamese troops from the eastern region of Cambodia before any negotiations might ensue.[283] The Chinese were showing their displeasure over the apparent warming of Hanoi's relations with Moscow and perhaps also with Vietnamese discussions on normalization with Washington.[284]

Le Duan responded to Chinese remarks on growing Soviet hegemony by provocatively calling on Peking "not to allow any exploiting class or reactionary force ... to cause new China to change color."[285] By the end of the visit, Le Duan was convinced that Khmer Rouge hostility was fueled by Peking.[286] When the Vietnamese delegation departed without holding the traditional reciprocal banquet for its hosts, it seemed that the Sino-Vietnamese diplomatic divorce had become official.

Hanoi finally went public on the issue, acknowledged the fighting and reported that 2,000 Vietnamese civilians had been killed or injured during Cambodian incursions.[287] Clearly Hanoi no longer believed that a diplomatic settlement was possible and was getting ready for severe retaliation by alerting international public opinion.[288] These clashes would set the scene for the Vietnamese invasion of Cambodia in 1978.

Meanwhile, the UN General Assembly session gave Holbrooke the opportunity to meet with Vietnamese officials and to discuss, once more, the issue of normalization. But Hanoi's difficulties with Cambodia and the growing fear of a Chinese threat had returned to the forefront of Vietnamese concerns. Phan Hien announced that the Vietnamese stance had not changed, and references to the Nixon promise failed to affect the American officials. Holbrooke again repeated that Washington had not altered its position.

During preliminary talks at the UN General Assembly on October 3, Nguyen Co Thach, a protégé of Le Duc Tho who was gradually replacing Hien and Trinh in negotiations with the West and genuinely favored normalization with Washington, suggested to Holbrooke that "about relations between our country and your country, before reaching diplomatic relations there might be a step of another kind."[289] He then suggested that both sides produce a program for normalization avoiding the political impediments imposed by each government. Holbrooke had seemed to favor the idea, considering it a positive gesture. The Vietnamese publicly commented at the end of the meetings that they would be expecting a breakthrough.[290]

Informal talks continued in November and the two officials chose to reconvene for a third round of Paris talks, from December 7 to 10. Washington requested that talks be held in Hanoi rather than Paris, but Vietnam objected, claiming that it preferred to wait until the issue of aid was settled before allowing any U.S. diplomatic presence in Hanoi.[291] Clearly the Vietnamese did not want to give in too quickly and waited for Washington to earn Hanoi's friendship. Thinking that normalization was in Washington's interest more than in its own, Hanoi continued to play Moscow and Washington against each other as it had during the war. But while Moscow seemed ready to continue wooing its long-term protégé with unquestioning economic aid, Hanoi misperceived its importance in the eyes of Washington in the postwar era, as it did in those of Peking.

In preparing for the December talks, Oksenberg, following the harder line of the NSC, attempted to persuade Holbrooke that another less conciliatory alternative be presented to Hanoi, encompassing the maintaining of the embargo and the opening of liaison offices rather than trade offices or embassies.[292] The recent congressional bans on Vietnam had made normalization more domestically risky than it had originally seemed, and the administration was now more cautious in its dealings with Hanoi. Carter did not want to risk a fight over Vietnam at a time when the Senate was debating the Panama Canal treaties and when he was attempting to obtain a breakthrough on SALT ratification, especially as Vietnam cared little to demonstrate its good faith through an act of cooperation. Vance was also instructed to keep a low profile on his visit to China in late August, and the trip was similarly downgraded for the same purpose of helping the Panama Canal treaties through the Senate.[293]

Hanoi too had adopted a stronger stance. In fact, heavy rain, floods, economic difficulties and corruption within the Vietnamese party in the South had brought about harsher living conditions. Industry was in a bad shape and the crop in the North had been destroyed by bitter cold, followed by a severe drought and, later, by heavy floods. Rice rations were reduced and the resulting food shortage weighed heavily on the population.[294] In Hanoi, economic difficulties had awakened an intense political debate between opposing factions through which a tougher political position was silently emerging. The problems Hanoi faced with Cambodia and China also stirred unease, accounting, as much as economic difficulties, for the increase in factional rivalries within the party.

Interestingly, the Vietnamese's rather cool attitude toward Holbrooke during the Paris talks in December may also have been partly due to Hanoi's suspicion of Sino-American backing of Cambodia's military incursions in Vietnam.[295] Perhaps Vance's trip to Peking in the summer was viewed as a confirmation of Sino-American collusion, betraying Hanoi's profound misreading of Sino-American relations. While these claims were proved wrong, they nevertheless hinted at the deep mistrust Hanoi felt for the United States and its profound uneasiness with the recent cooling of relations with its two neighbors.

Furthermore, the emergence of a Vietnamese spying affair in the U.S., and Washington's harsh reaction to the issue, may certainly have appeared to Vietnam as proof of American guilt. Vietnamese sources even insisted that Washington had used the issue to discredit Hanoi in the eyes of international organization at a time when Vietnam's problems with Cambodia were constantly escalating.[296]

Talks with Washington were postponed at Hanoi's request, probably to allow Vietnam time to decide on a course of action regarding Cambodia.[297] Meanwhile, Moscow, wooing Hanoi, reported on the opening of the third round of Paris talks by recalling Washington's "[s]abotaging the 1973 Paris agreement."[298]

The December talks proved hardly more fruitful than the earlier meetings. While Hien again requested a U.S. commitment on aid, Holbrooke repeated that such a pledge was impossible.[299] The State Department, he explained, favored the exchange of "interest sections" (a diplomatic office protecting the interests of a nation in a country with which the former has no formal relations, i.e., when no embassies have been exchanged) or "consulates" with the condition that the trade embargo would, according to Holbrooke's instructions, "remain intact as a bargaining chip in moving up to the embassy level later." The strategy was Oksenberg's, as the two men had prepared the December talks a few weeks earlier.

An interest section, argued Vance, would be less irksome to Congress than a consulate and would be a first step towards normalization. China, for instance, had agreed to the opening of a U.S. mission in Peking in 1973, which the United States was planning on expanding during the next fiscal year.[300] Likewise, in June, the Cubans had accepted the opening of interest sections and the State Department sought a similar breakthrough with Hanoi.[301] But the situation regarding Vietnam was complicated by the issues of MIAs and aid. While expecting a negative response from Hanoi, Vance noted that the U.S. proposal at least left "the door open to future discussion."[302] The Vietnamese rejected this proposition—as Washington expected—claiming that Hanoi "will never do what the Chinese did."[303]

This remark highlighted the gap between Washington and Hanoi's perceptions of each other. While Holbrooke's suggestion indicated that Washington had placed Vietnam and Cuba on the same level of Soviet client-states of moderate importance for U.S. geostrategic concerns, Hanoi compared itself to China and believed in its own inflated political importance in the eyes of Americans. Mutual misperceptions led to each country's distorted appraisal of both itself and the other.

During a break, Hien approached Holbrooke. Suddenly reversing the Vietnamese stance—now a recurrent strategy in Hanoi's dialogue with Washington—Hien offered to normalize, as a first step, and later let Washington independently declare that it would provide aid. To further prove the seriousness of his request, Hien produced a list of how Hanoi intended to spend U.S. aid. Clearly, Hien's orders had been to secure a pledge of aid, whether public or private, and Hien had prepared himself for both options. However, Holbrooke declined the proposal.[304]

But Hanoi was now too much in need of dollars to give up so rapidly, especially as prospects of a conflict with Cambodia might jeopardize Hanoi's future chances of aid. Hien insisted: "You just whisper in my ear the amount you'll offer and that is enough."[305] Ironically, the roles had been reversed and the once relatively malleable Americans who had offered normalization prior to any other commitments now had their hands tied by Congress and domestic pressures, while the Vietnamese, suddenly relaxing their demands, were now seeking normalization without any formal preconditions. While in May Holbrooke had offered to announce normalization and to solve all impending issues, including aid, at a later stage, he now rejected Hanoi's proposal for a similar timetable.

Holbrooke refused the offer and added that the trade embargo could not be lifted. Explaining that the American political arena had changed over the last two administrations and that Hanoi no longer benefited from the support of the anti-war element of U.S. public opinion, he also reminded Hien that Soviet-American normalization had taken seventeen years and that China remained unrecognized by Washington.[306] In Brzezinski's words, Carter had ordered that Washington should "leave the ball in Vietnam's court at the end of the meeting."[307] Holbrooke was warning Hien that Washington was in no hurry to normalize and that the next step should come from Hanoi.

Since the Vietnamese had previously declared that they would accept "humanitarian" aid, and Carter had succeeded in countering congressional opposition to prevent international institutions from lending aid to Vietnam, the administration could perhaps have found a loophole to enable humanitarian aid in the long-run. While American caution was legitimate considering congressional pressure, concerns for other foreign policy issues, and the dwindling trust in constant Vietnamese changes of policies, Holbrooke's sudden harsh stance might, in hindsight, appear a missed opportunity to bring a satisfactory conclusion to the issue within the year as Carter had intended. Washington now wanted Vietnam to drop the issue of aid altogether.[308]

In an attempt to prove Hanoi's goodwill, Hien repeated that a team of technicians would visit the Casualty Resolution Center in Hawaii, taking up the American invitation made nearly nine months earlier.[309] Hanoi also released three American yachtsmen and their boat, *The Brillig*, which had been captured 44 miles off the Vietnamese coast while sailing from Thailand to Borneo.[310] The three young Americans onboard had been charged with "violating Vietnamese territorial waters" and transporting marijuana.[311]

Holbrooke welcomed this gesture and, genuinely hoping that his tougher stance would bear fruit, seemed satisfied with the meetings. He described the talks as "useful, constructive and positive ... cordial and candid" and, noting that "progress" had been made, the two sides planned a new set of talks for February 1978.[312]

The Spying Affair

The February talks were never held. Events following the December 1977 talks halted negotiations and fed the growing American suspicion of Vietnam as bilateral relations stumbled over a strange affair.

The FBI report Holbrooke had been given in June, prior to the second round of Paris talks, and an investigation within the State Department, led to the arrest, on January 31, 1978, of two men—David Truong, the son of a South Vietnamese official in exile in the United States, and Ronald Humphrey, an evaluation officer in the U.S. Information Agency's Plans and Programs section—charged with communicating secret U.S. cables to Hanoi through the Vietnamese embassy in Paris in 1976 and 1977.[313] Allegedly, Humphrey had collaborated with the Vietnamese spy in order to obtain the release of his fiancée and her children from Vietnam.[314] But the news came as a shock to the American public. It was the first time an American had been charged with spying for Vietnam, as well as the first arrest in the United States, since the fall of Saigon, in connection with Vietnam.[315]

These stolen documents were of no great political value. Among the papers were a long report from the American consul-general in Hong Kong entitled "Vietnamese External Relations," focusing mainly on Chinese-Vietnamese relations, a report from the U.S. Ambassador to Bangkok on a coup attempt in Thailand, a cable from the American embassy in Laos on the arrival of Soviet advisers to Vientiane, and a report on the views of the Indian and Yugoslav diplomats posted in Hanoi.[316] One document, classified as "confidential" merely reported details of the Air France flights to Ho Chi Minh City over the period of a month.[317]

It was evident that Vietnam had required these documents in order to sound out the mood before the second round of Paris talks and to prepare its delegates more efficiently for the confrontation with Holbrooke. But, considering the content of such papers—unmistakably stolen by "amateur" spies—Hanoi could not have distilled much noteworthy information from their catch. Michael Tigar, David Truong and Ronald Humphrey's lawyer sarcastically pointed out during a meeting in New York on February 15 that: "This case does not involve what it must involve if the government is to succeed in an espionage case, and that is something called 'national defense.'"[318] "I've seen better leaks in *The New York Times* and *Aviation Week*," joked a senior Pentagon official.[319] Only one document entitled "U.S.-Vietnamese relations: Woodcock Commission" drafted by the American Embassy in Malaysia could have been of some interesting use to Hanoi, had Woodcock not already disclosed much of American reactions to the mission in personally sending his report to Hien upon his return to Washington.[320]

But American wrath had more to do with punishing the act of spying than redeeming the loss of national security documents. The two men were condemned to fifteen years' imprisonment.[321] The case would make an example, in which Vietnam had more to lose than it had gained, of capturing the official documents. "[T]he [Justice] Department wants blood on this one," confirmed an U.S. official.[322]

What could have remained a small-scale issue soon festered into an international scandal as Dinh Ba Thi's involvement in the affair came to light. Humphrey had been accused of passing information to Truong, who would then give it to the ambassador to communicate to Vietnam.[323] Michael Tigar, the men's lawyer, noted some discrepancies in the data used to prove Thi's involvement. In Vietnam, rumors circulated that the administration had looked for a "legal" way of expressing its hostility as it was too late to reverse the U.S. decision to allow Vietnam into the UN. The Vietnamese ambassador would be expelled, and although he would later be replaced, Washington had proven its point. For Hanoi, Thi's expulsion represented a diplomatic continuation of the Vietnam War.[324] The accusations against the ambassador are "fishy," commented the Soviet press, and charged that following its defeat in Vietnam, Washington had "set its mind on political revenge."[325]

However, it seemed doubtful that the administration, and especially the State Department, were truly at ease with this unfolding scandal, representing yet another obstacle to its normalization efforts. Vietnamese accusations that Washington had engineered it appeared even more dubious.

On February 1, attempting to solve the issue according to UN protocol, Washington requested a meeting with the Vietnamese Mission to the UN, which declined the offer. During further contacts with the Vietnamese embassy in Paris, the Americans emphasized that their insistence that Thi be expelled was only due to his involvement in the case and hoped that this would not affect bilateral relations.[326] On February 3, three days after the two men's arrest, Vance reluctantly expelled Thi from the U.S. on the grounds of his "abuse of the privileges of residence."[327]

That same day, Vietnam filed a complaint to the Committee on Relations with the Host Country rebuffing Washington's accusations and insisting that this would jeopardize normalization.[328] The affair, claimed *Nhan Dan*, was merely "A Vengeful U.S. Imperialist-Type Trick."[329] The Vietnamese foreign ministry condemned the charges against Thi as violations of the UN Charter, which jeopardized the entire organization. These accusations, stated Nguyen Duy Trinh, were a "sheer fabrication" creating "a dangerous precedent." This American move, he claimed, showed that Washington's calls for normalization had been "nothing but empty words."[330] Similar declarations on the Vietnamese stance were simultaneously issued in Moscow, hinting at a Soviet-Vietnamese rapprochement only a few days after the twenty-eighth anniversary of the Soviet-Vietnamese normalization.[331]

American intelligence reported that despite the Vietnamese press declarations that Washington should "cease such senseless fabrications if they really want to move toward normalizing relations," Hanoi's reactions were made "in a carefully measured fashion."[332] The accusations were no more vehement than the usual rhetoric of Cold War disputes over spying charges and suggested that Hanoi wished to reduce the impact of this affair on normalization prospects. The case embarrassed Hanoi as much as the State Department, and Vietnam toned down its accusations so as not to jeopardize the ongoing bilateral diplomatic dialogue, without appearing to lose face.

Thus, Hanoi's defense of Thi was symbolic. Denying his involvement, Thi refused to leave the U.S.[333] The ambassador personally requested Waldheim's intervention.[334] The matter was referred to the Committee on Relations with the Host Country, and no concrete evidence was produced in court linking Thi to the conspiracy. On February 5, he was recalled to Hanoi and replaced by former Vietnamese ambassador to Cuba Ha Van Lau.[335] The disgraced UN ambassador died in a car accident in Vietnam a few months later.[336] While it is still not clear where the ambassador stood in this affair, more important perhaps was its effect on bilateral relations.

Following Thi's expulsion, the State Department reiterated its hopes that the affair would not affect talks on normalization. But when Vietnam, through Deputy Foreign Minister Hoang Bich Son, once again addressed the UN at the Economic and Social Committee for Asia and the Pacific meeting in March, and renewed Hanoi's demand that Washington provide the promised postwar economic aid, Washington was no longer ready to lend a friendly ear to Hanoi's allegations.[337] Holbrooke stated that Washington remained "unequivocally ready" to normalize despite the recent affair, but not under Hanoi's conditions, and claimed that the negotiations had stalled over Hien's insistence that normalization be preceded by a U.S. commitment on aid.[338] Oksenberg felt that a "casualty of this [spy] affair ... is our effort to normalize with Vietnam ... I suspect that progress will be lost."[339]

Carter's wish to normalize with Hanoi during his first year in office had failed, and the short-term prospect of better relations had grown dim. Both Hanoi's insistence on obtaining aid and the spying scandal had eroded congressional support at a time when the president wished to spare congressional patience in order to push other policies, such as the Panama Canal treaties, through the Senate. While Congress had been the main initiator of contacts with Hanoi during the Ford years, Carter's failed overtures to Hanoi had triggered growing opposition in Congress. Carter had also failed to obtain a breakthrough with Cuba and, by fall 1977, Cuban involvement in the Horn of Africa had brought bilateral relations to a standstill. Vance's visit to China was also fruitless, as were his meetings on SALT in Moscow.[340] By early 1978, the administration reviewed its stance on these sensitive issues, understanding the need to encourage congressional patience until the ratification of the Panama Canal treaties. The Soviet-backed Cuban involvement in Africa may also have led Washington to reconsider its position towards Vietnam, where the pro–Soviet faction in the Politburo was gathering strength. The lack of bilateral contact in early 1978 suggested that Washington allowed the spying scandal to halt the bilateral dialogue, as perhaps it would not have done a few months earlier.

The scandal also coincided with the escalation of Vietnam's border conflict with Cambodia, which perhaps accounts for Holbrooke's remark that "[f]ollowing our request that Ambassador Thi leave the United States, there was considerable pause in communications from the Vietnamese."[341] Vietnam's restrained accusations against Washington suggest that the affair was not the main cause of the diplomatic silence of early 1978. The remark of an American observer that the case "just froze everything" is at best incomplete, as domestic issues were now at the top of each country's immediate agenda.[342]

IV

Cold War Clash

Brotherhood Turns Sour

On December 26, 1977, two weeks after the last Paris talks, Hanoi responded massively to border raids by pushing deeply into Cambodian territory and stopping only twenty-four miles from Phnom Penh. This counterattack was an impressive show of military power aimed at intimidating Cambodia.[1] However, the consequences were far from what Hanoi had predicted and did less to intimidate Pol Pot and Peking than to encourage Cambodian hostility. Its immediate effect was to brush away any of Peking's remaining doubts that Hanoi was pursuing regional hegemony on Moscow's behalf.[2]

But while Chinese perceptions of Vietnamese regional goals were relatively accurate, Peking's growing belief in direct Soviet responsibility seemed less convincing.[3] The resulting conflict, based as much on mutual misperceptions as self-fed fears, led Hanoi to opt for an alignment with Moscow in early 1978 to support its military aims regarding Cambodia, while at the same time renewing diplomatic initiatives with Washington. But by 1978, increasingly globalist views in Washington and similar opinions in Peking meant that international relations between these countries would be polarized along a Sino-Soviet axis, turning regional disputes into Cold War confrontation in late 1978.

Cambodian reaction to the invasion came swiftly. On December 31, 1977, while Nguyen Duy Trinh was beginning his tour around ASEAN countries to promote his country's friendliness, Cambodia broke off diplomatic ties with Vietnam, for its "large-scale unwarranted aggression [to] annex and swallow" its neighbors, and undermined Trinh's quest for international support. Phnom Penh had already cut off all contacts with Hanoi in August 1976 and the breaking off of formal diplomatic contact was more a symbolic gesture than an effective measure. At the same time, Cambodia launched a domestic propaganda campaign promoting ethnic hatred of the Vietnamese.[4]

The Cambodian decision to break ties was probably taken without Chinese consent to force Peking into taking sides, much to Peking's displeasure.[5] Even at the climax of the Sino-Soviet feud, the two communist giants had not broken off their diplomatic ties, and the Cambodian gesture made a striking break in the history of inter-communist relations. The Cambodian move illustrated the extreme tension between the two communist neighbors and justified the intense concern that Vietnam may have felt over the incident.[6]

While the Chinese leadership resented Vietnamese regional influence, convinced that Moscow stood behind Hanoi's hegemonic ambitions, China seemed unsure of the necessity to escalate into direct armed conflict. Peking thus immediately issued a press statement calling on both sides to hold talks and work towards a political compromise.[7] In order to show its non-involvement in Pol Pot's open attack on Hanoi, Chinese radio began to broadcast Hanoi's accusations that border skirmishes had originated on the Cambodian side. In addition, Peking also agreed to the signing of a trade agreement after only a remarkably short two weeks of negotiations in early January.[8] But the truce was temporary.

Hanoi, however, understood the Cambodian move as a Chinese initiative and noted that the breaking of ties had been announced in Peking during a speech by Pol Pot which journalists from the *Vietnam News Agency* were denied authorization to attend. Vietnam responded the same day that it agreed to talks "with the aim of resolving the border issues with all speed" but blamed Cambodia for initiating the border clashes.[9] As Southeast Asian expert Pao-Min Chang points out, Hanoi probably expected very little from such talks and thought that should Phnom Penh indeed concede to participating in them, Hanoi would seize the opportunity to exploit Sino-Cambodian antagonisms to pull Phnom Penh away from Chinese influence.[10] If Cambodia rejected such peace proposals, as it repeatedly did, Hanoi would have at least proven its goodwill to the international community.

On January 6, the Cambodian leadership again justified its hostility using the rhetoric of paranoia, claiming that "the border conflicts are but a pretext among many others for Vietnam to make aggression, to threaten, and to pressure Cambodia to join the 'Indochinese Federation'" pointing at the Lao-Vietnamese treaty to further explain its refusal to attend any talks with the Vietnamese if Hanoi persisted in its attempt to swallow Indochina.[11] Three months later, in an attempt to soothe Cambodian aggression and to reassure its ASEAN neighbors, Hanoi published a document entitled "The Truth About an 'Indochina Federation'" stating that the communist Vietnamese leadership had abandoned the concept in the mid–1950s and that it would not be taken up again.[12] Luu Van Loi, former assistant to the Vietnamese foreign minister, declared Cambodia's charges that Vietnam wished the establishment of an Indochina Federation "a great diplomatic scheme that went along with a genocidal plan envisaged inside Cambodia by the leaders of that country."[13] The Cambodian leadership, deeply imbedded in paranoia, convinced itself of the reality of its own fears.

Peking rapidly echoed Cambodian charges against Vietnam, understanding that Phnom Penh was an indispensable ally for Chinese ambitions in Indochina. Cambodia represented as much a geostrategic as a psychological token in Peking's duel with Moscow, a pro–Chinese sanctuary in China's geographical encirclement by pro–Soviet states.[14] Recalling his trip to China in 1973, Kissinger remarked that:

the Chinese leaders were beginning to understand that the domination of Indochina by Hanoi might be an ideological victory but a geopolitical defeat for China, as it would place at China's southern border a powerful state drawn to Moscow and with a record of historical enmity toward China.

Peking, he further explained, both wished and feared a "red" victory in Cambodia, preferring the emergence of a coalition government led by the Khmer Rouge but tempered by Prince Norodom Sihanouk, explaining their support for the prince during his exile in China and for his alliance with the Cambodian communists.[15]

In order to counter this possibility, Peking sided with Cambodia. But the prince's imprisonment by the Pol Pot regime shortly after the communist seizure of Phnom Penh led Peking to find a compromise with the Khmer Rouge. Only a month after the fall of Phnom Penh in April 1975, China had begun to seek the establishment of an alliance with the new Cambodian regime, receiving Pol Pot in a secret visit to Peking and offering him economic assistance, military and technical material, and training by Chinese officers.[16]

A few months later, Peking had suggested to Kissinger, during his visit to China in October 1975, that Washington seek diplomatic rapprochement with Cambodia with China's assistance.[17] Although Kissinger rebuffed the suggestion, he recognized China's eagerness to reinforce its power and Cambodia's influence in the region through the establishment of an unofficial Sino-Khmero-American axis, while sabotaging Hanoi's quest to establish diplomatic ties with the Americans. Cambodia, a country that Vietnam had perceived as a minor problem to be dealt with in the long run and probably without the use of military means, had, with the assistance of Peking, grown into an issue of deep concern to Hanoi.

By early 1978, China had fully emerged as a political supporter of Cambodia's claims and a harsh critic of Hanoi's policies.[18] As early as January 1978, the Vietnamese media began labeling the Peking leadership a bunch of "international reactionaries" who practiced socialism at home and "reactionary" policies abroad.[19] Not only would Cambodian attacks on Vietnam weaken and contain the Vietnamese but would also allow an indirect bullying of what the Chinese were now convinced represented a Soviet satellite. In the Vietnamese press Cambodia would be termed China's "second war front" on Vietnam while the Soviets nicknamed Cambodia China's "overseas province."[20] In the words of *Nhan Dan* editor Hoang Tung, Peking was attempting to "provoke a disease which is not fatal but [which would] keep us always sick."[21]

In response, Peking now highly publicized and denounced Vietnamese incursions into Khmer and Chinese territory and the Chinese media pointed an accusatory finger at Hanoi's violations of human rights and territorial integrity, not unintentionally playing on the favorite theme of the Carter administration. Questioning Thach about the reasons that were leading a weak country one-tenth of Vietnam's population to attack the Vietnamese, historian Wilfred Burchett, received the following answer:

> Why would Israel with a population of 3 million dare to invade Egypt with its population of 35 million? Because the Khmer Rouge are assured they have 800 million Chinese behind them, as Israel has the might of the United States to rely on.[22]

As the Vietnamese punitive strike against its Cambodian neighbors seemed unacceptable to the Chinese, starting in January 1978, Peking increased its shipments of arms to Cambodia, including long-range artillery and anti-tank equipment.[23] Simultaneously, Moscow began reporting the presence of Chinese military advisers in Cambodia and their participation in the shelling of Vietnamese border villages.[24] But Peking still sought to prevent military confrontation between its protégé and Vietnam, not so much out of a fear of further clashes between the two Indochinese rivals, as for increasing Soviet "meddling" into Indochinese and Asian affairs.[25]

A delegation, headed by Zhou Enlai's widow, Teng Ying-Chao, was rapidly dispatched to Phnom Penh to seek a solution to the issue.[26] But Mrs. Teng failed to persuade the Cambodian regime to sign a truce with Hanoi. However, she reiterated China's support for Cambodia and even affirmed that the "revolutionary friendship" that linked Peking and Phnom Penh meant that both sides would "always fight together, unite with each other and win victory together."[27] On her return to Peking she uttered China's first open accusation regarding Hanoi, declaring to visiting French premier Raymond Barre that Cambodia had fallen pray to "Vietnamese aggression."[28]

Concurrently, Peking multiplied its attacks on Moscow and blamed the Soviets for the military escalation in Indochina.[29] Hanoi responded to Chinese accusations with similar charges aimed at international propaganda. Thus, upon his return from Vietnam in 1979, a French official reported that Vietnamese officials were convinced that Peking had planned to take over Cambodia, possibly as a stepping-stone into Vietnam and Laos. According to this source Hanoi believed that Pol Pot had liquidated more than two million Cambodians in a "temporary depopulation" in the hope of repopulating the country with Chinese peasants and military.[30] While these accusations were largely based on fears and exaggerations regarding potential threats, they highlighted the growing tensions in the region and both countries' need to attract international sympathy and support.

On February 5, Vietnam offered a three-point peace treaty suggesting international supervision for a new demilitarized zone.[31] Deng replied that he wished the dispute could be resolved by "good negotiations" and asserted that China was not sitting in judgment over who was right or wrong.[32] In March, Phnom Penh accused Hanoi of once again uttering "sweet words" while its forces simultaneously continued to "commit barbarous aggression against Cambodia."[33] While declining Vietnam's peace offer, Phnom Penh declared it was ready to hold talks "at any time, at any level."[34] Another peace offer came from Hanoi in April and was equally rejected.[35]

On February 21, 1978, *Hanoi Radio* officially identified Peking as the source of Pol Pot's provisions of long-range heavy artillery.[36] Three weeks later a Chinese delegation was dispatched to Phnom Penh to reconstruct the railway line linking Kampong Som to the Cambodian capital—the main supply route for the delivery of Chinese aid.[37] Although the delegation reported that, once repaired, the line would transport only rice, the military attaché of the Chinese embassy in Phnom Penh greeted the Chinese delegates at the airport in person and the Chinese guests praised Pol Pot for "energetically defending Cambodia's independence, sovereignty and integrity."[38] At the same time, Peking supplied the Cambodians with a radar-based anti-aircraft defense system.[39]

Vietnam Changes Its Mind

By the early months of 1978, Hanoi realized that the mounting tension on its borders with China and Cambodia no longer enabled it to delay the normalization of relations with the West, and particularly Washington. Hanoi would have to take sides in the Sino-Soviet dispute and Peking's recent growing hostility left little option as to which camp to choose. Ironically, Peking's fear that Vietnam had already chosen to side with Moscow would turn Chinese fears into grim reality. "If the Chinese fear that Vietnam is a Soviet patsy," remarked a U.S. intelligence official, "their recent actions can only accelerate that trend."[40] China had acted as the catalyst for Soviet-Vietnamese rapprochement. While misunderstandings were repeatedly observed in American-Vietnamese relations since the fall of Saigon, it is interesting to notice how Sino-Vietnamese relations were also ruled by similar misperceptions that distorted each side's perception of the other. As hints of a Soviet-Vietnamese rapprochement multiplied in 1978, relations between Hanoi, Moscow, Peking and Washington would increasingly turn to Cold War diplomatic alliances and proxy confrontations.

In Vietnam, month after month of economic difficulties and the devastating loss of crops had resulted in the most severe food crisis in Vietnamese history, culminating in a shortage of 4.3 million tons of rice—a brutal defeat for the Five Year Economic Plan.[41] In Ho Chi Minh City, officials had declared that 83 percent of the winter rice crop was destroyed while the coming harvest would also be lost.[42] At Parkse, in the central Mekong, the river had reached its highest level in fifty-four years, and the UN Disaster Relief Organization estimated that four million people were affected by the flood that would not subside until mid–November.[43]

Ten divisions had been mobilized, to the border with Kampuchea, forcing the soldiers to stop their reconstruction work on various infrastructures in the country; and, while the refugee exodus had affected Hanoi's long-term credit rating in foreign capital and investment markets, it also had serious repercussions on the transport and engineering sectors.[44] Vietnam was also facing increasing hostility due to the refugee exodus. In addition, the failure of the socialist transformation in the South had brought the need for a reorganization of Vietnamese domestic policies to halt the pending social crisis.[45]

In early 1978, convinced of the heightening of Sino-Cambodian collusion, Hanoi opted for strengthening of its international ties to gain political support in the dispute. While overtures were later made to the ASEAN countries and Washington, Hanoi's immediate attention turned towards the Soviet bloc. Ironically, Chinese fears of Hanoi's tilt towards Moscow were accelerating Vietnam's opening to the Soviet Union in 1978. After refusing to side openly with Moscow for more than a decade, Hanoi had given up hope of improving relations with China and, reversing its strategy, sent COMECON a formal letter requesting permanent admission to the organization.[46]

A Department of State report stated that "a decision [to invade Cambodia] was probably made sometime early in 1978."[47] In fact, the decision to support an insurgency organization had first arisen just following Cambodia's decision to cut off ties with Hanoi, during a secret meeting of the Central Committee in late January and early February. Le Duc Tho, who headed the debate, had introduced the concept.[48] The Soviets suggested toppling Pol Pot with a quick and forceful intervention, much as they had in Czechoslovakia in 1968, but Hanoi opted for the use of a clandestine army patched together from groups of defectors, Cambodian refugees in Vietnam and Khmer Krom—or ethnic Cambodians living in Vietnam.[49] Following the Politburo decision, Le Duan and Le Duc Tho met with Cambodian refugees and former cadres in exile in Saigon to brief them on the new Vietnamese policy and to launch a vast recruitment campaign. Tho took personal charge of their training.[50]

Hanoi had already begun to initiate contacts with Cambodian rebels as early as November 1977 and hopes had centered around So Phim, a former member of the Indochinese Communist Party, now head of the Eastern region, and who enjoyed the post of vice-chairman of the Cambodian State Presidium. Disillusioned with Pol Pot's policies So Phim had lent a friendly ear to Vietnamese callings for a general uprising. However, he had been under close scrutiny by Kampuchean authorities since 1976 and, in hindsight, seemed a precarious basis for Vietnamese plans.[51] Understanding that a permanent solution needed to be found for its problems with Cambodia, Hanoi simultaneously opted for the recruitment of Cambodian refugees in the southern provinces to create a guerrilla force on its territory.[52]

In finally withdrawing from Cambodia in early January 1978 after the Christmas offensive, Vietnamese forces escorted hundreds of Cambodian refugees into Vietnamese territory, recruiting a number of them to fill the ranks of its budding guerrilla army. From January to April, Cambodian-Vietnamese border areas witnessed the erection of several training camps as Vietnamese broadcasts encouraged more Khmer Rouge refugees to defect and join the insurgents. In parallel, starting in April, Vietnamese broadcasts encouraged more Khmer Rouge to defect and join the insurgent army.[53] Phnom Penh's accusations that Vietnam was trying to set up a parallel Cambodian communist party in an attempt to overthrow Pol Pot's regime with "a handful of Khmer traitors and hooligans" were therefore correct.[54] "[E]nemies of all stripes," announced *Radio Phnom Penh*, "still nurture designs to topple our Cambodian revolution ... and to make Cambodia their new colony."[55]

But Vietnam also needed to obtain further international backing and understood that the Soviet world offered potential allies. On the sixtieth anniversary of the Soviet army in February, commander of the Cambodian-Vietnamese border military region, General Tran Van Tra had traveled to Moscow, presumably to discuss impending military issues regarding Cambodia.[56] By April, COMECON had appointed a study group whose goal was to reflect upon the possible coordination of economic programs to Vietnam.[57] While Brezhnev and his defense minister Ustinov visited the Asian extremity of Soviet territory and witnessed joint Soviet forces perform a mock battle along the Sino-Soviet border, Le Duan was reviewing Vietnamese forces along Vietnam's border with Cambodia.[58] Hints as to the building of a Soviet-Vietnamese alliance against Cambodia and China multiplied and, if confirmed by Hanoi's formal admission to COMECON, would ensure Hanoi of greater protection against its two agitated neighbors and allow a more permanent and military "solution" to the issue.

In Hanoi, the hard-line majority of the Vietnamese Politburo led by Le Duc Tho and Le Duan was gathering strength and increasingly urged military intervention in Cambodia as well as a pro–Soviet tilt to obtain foreign support for their plans against Cambodia.[59] During the early days of August *Nhan Dan* was flooded with a deluge of articles reporting the ideological and political debates in motion since the beginning of the year, which had resulted in the purge of the moderate minority led by Truong Chinh, and to a shift toward the more orthodox Soviet line, replacing the moderates' Marxist-Leninist-Maoist ideology.[60] Considering Le Duan and Le Duc Tho's personalities and ideologies, one may argue that their "pro–Soviet" stands had more to do with their wish to obtain foreign support for their nationalist ambitions than with a genuine belief in Soviet socialist superiority. Owing partly to Confucian tradition—helped by Moscow's patience and generosity in providing aid to serve its own interests in enhancing Soviet influence in Asia—the Vietnamese favored an opening to the "bigger" of its two communist "brothers," much like Le Duan and Le Duc Tho expected to force Laos and Cambodia to turn unquestioningly to their "bigger" Vietnamese "brothers."[61]

In Prime Minister Khieu Samphan's words, which illustrate the Cambodian fear of Vietnam in the aftermath of the Vietnam war:

> The Vietnamese considered themselves the legitimate leaders of the communist movements in the three countries of Indochina [and] considered that the communist khmers leaders had been encouraged by the Chinese to violate "proletarian internationalism" and thus to create havoc in Indochina by refusing the leading role of the Vietnamese communist party.[62]

But the Vietnamese Politburo would not simply open to the Soviet Union. It also labeled China its new enemy. During the February 5 Central Committee secret meeting, which had made a decision to create a popular uprising in Cambodia, the VCP, lead by Le Duan, adopted a resolution that crucially affected Vietnamese policies over the next fifteen years. According to Vietnamese VCP defector Hoang Van Hoan the resolution:

> stated that China was the immediate deadly enemy of the Vietnamese people; that it was imperative to overthrow the reactionary pro–Mao leadership clique in Beijing; that it was essential to help the progressive forces in China come to power; that it was necessary to criticize Mao Zedong Thought in every field of endeavour; and that it was necessary to persuade all countries in Southeast Asia to oppose China.[63]

The same resolution also provided for the purging of the ethnic Chinese, or Hoas, in Vietnam, beginning with Cholon. This move would give the last blow to the Hoa oligarchy, which blocked the socialist transformation in the South, where the annual inflation rate had reached nearly 80 percent and only 30 percent of trade was conducted by State agencies.[64] Beyond presenting an economic obstacle to South Vietnamese welfare, Hoas, who had refused assimilation into the Vietnamese population and were still profoundly attached to their motherland, were seen as a security risk now that China and Vietnam were official enemies.

The Hoa Crisis

By the end of the war, the Hoa population, or ethnic Chinese, in Vietnam numbered 1.2 million, 85 percent of which resided in the South, especially in Cholon near Saigon.[65] As Sino-Vietnamese relations worsened, Hanoi's concern with the Hoas increased. The Vietnamese were increasingly convinced that the Chinese community presented a potential security risk in the event of a serious conflict with Peking. Furthermore, many Hoas were known to have family in Taiwan—an ally of the United States—and Hanoi reportedly feared a renewal of American influence via the ethnic Chinese community.[66]

Hanoi's dealings with the Hoas was a mixture of fear, xenophobia and disdain for diverging ideologies. In utter disregard for the VCP's concern about revolutionary ideals, Hoas had taken up trading and, by 1961, controlled 80 percent of the total retail trade and 75 percent of all South Vietnamese commercial activities, which represented a serious obstacle to Hanoi's postwar wish for socialist construction.[67] This prosperous population, enjoying no common ideological link with Hanoi, had thus turned Cholon into "an unreformed capitalist heart beating within the socialist body of Vietnam," as the *Far Eastern Economic Review*, a Western-oriented weekly based in Hong Kong, had expressed.[68] In fact, the Hoas, still officially registered as Chinese rather than Vietnamese citizens despite the passing of several generations, enjoyed many privileges and lacked the incentive to be recognized as Vietnamese. For instance, Hoas were allowed to vote in Vietnamese elections but were not subject to military draft, a valuable prerogative during the war that had certainly further embittered the nationalist Vietnamese.

On the morning of September 11, 1975, a fourteen-point declaration signed by Prime Minister Huynh Tan Phat was published in the Saigon news media announcing a series of measures aimed at boosting the Vietnamese industry and economy, and at putting down "compradore capitalists who have monopolized and illegally hoarded goods and disrupted markets." As a result, armed forces raided the homes of the Hoas in Cholon, marking the beginning of their ethnic persecution.[69]

In January 1976, Hanoi requested all Hoas in the South to register their citizenship, but to its great surprise most declared themselves "Chinese."[70] In fact, in 1955, the Central Committees of both the Chinese and Vietnamese Communist parties had agreed that Hoas would be encouraged to adopt Vietnamese nationality after "sustained and patient persuasion and ideological education" and nearly all Hoas would have had to accept Vietnamese nationality.[71] But the 1976 census had demonstrated the persistence of the Hoas' irritating nationalist pride and that the community's loyalty remained not in Hanoi but in Peking. Hanoi became increasingly distressed by the existence of this inner society on the Vietnamese homeland.

In February, the Hoas were again requested to register their nationality, but only as it had already been declared following the 1955 campaign.[72] Those who still persisted in declaring themselves Chinese would undergo severe repression.

In the summer of 1976, Hanoi further tightened its grasp on the Hoas by issuing a decree declaring that all businesses that had made more than 10 percent profit since the fall of Saigon would be subject to a tax rate of 80 percent.[73] By September 1976, all the Chinese newspapers and Chinese schools in South Vietnam had been shut down.[74] In December 1976, while redefining the new "Socialist Man" and reorienting political and ideological trends of Vietnamese policies towards more pro–Soviet lines, the Fourth National Congress was deciding to neutralize the potential danger of Hoas.

In 1977, Vietnamese authorities in the North urged the Hoas living near the Sino-Vietnamese border to adopt Vietnamese citizenship, but many refused and crossed the border into China.[75] Vietnamese repression increased in proportion to its distrust of China and with increasing evidence of Chinese backings of Khmer Rouge attacks against Vietnam. However, Peking expressed little concern over the plight of their overseas citizens.

But by early 1978 Peking renewed its interest in overseas Chinese, realizing that their skills, energy and wealth would be a serious boost to the "four modernizations" program. On January 4, the Pekinese press hailed the overseas Chinese as an integral "part" of China "with their destiny closely linked with that of the motherland." The statement convinced Hanoi that the Hoas were manipulated by Peking and consequently represented a true threat to national security given the recent cooling of relations with China. Thus, Hanoi turned down three requests to allow a Chinese official to visit the Chinese community in Cholon fearing a conspiracy between Peking and its overseas citizens.[76] In early March 1978, a demonstration led by Hoas holding portraits of Mao persuaded Hanoi that the ethnic Chinese should be neutralized on a more permanent basis.[77]

On March 24, 1978, the Vietnamese police conducted a two-day raid against Cholon. Thousands of Hoas were turned out of their houses and saw their belongings confiscated by the police and army, while simultaneously the radio announced the abolition of "bourgeois trade" in the South.[78] Hoas were instructed to move to NEZs, to find some "productive" occupations, or to return to China.[79] The raid was followed by an announcement by the *Vietnam News Agency* that Hanoi would rid the country of the few remaining capitalists, and quoted a statement by the Saigon People's Council forbidding private enterprise, speculation, black-marketing and the hoarding of goods.[80] Hanoi stressed that the operation had not been directed at the Chinese community but against "bourgeois traders ... regardless of nationality or religion."[81] Yet the repression had been mainly aimed at intimidating Hoas. Although the Vietnamese fear of the Hoas was not economic but political, economic considerations became a pretext for ethnic persecution. Overall, the raid on Cholon marked the end of more than 30,000 Hoa businesses.

In Peking's eyes, the Vietnamese persecution of Hoas had come at the behest of Moscow, as had Hanoi's expansionist ambitions in Indochina. Hanoi saw China as the main instigator behind Cambodian provocations and the Chinese populations as a national security threat. Moscow had also picked up on Vietnam's view of Hoas as a potential threat to peace in Vietnam, and began referring to the Hoas as China's "fifth column."[82] The similar terminologies and aligned accusations revealed the recent rapprochement between Vietnam and the Soviet Union. But although Hanoi had previously refrained from openly endorsing Soviet views, the Vietnamese were beginning to publicize their alignment with Moscow. Thus, Hanoi reciprocated Moscow's gesture of support regarding the Hoa issue by stressing Vietnamese support for Soviet ambitions in Africa and developed its criticism of Chinese policies along preferred Soviet lines.[83]

In Peking, the concern for Hoas became more a political than humanitarian issue, and a means of raising international support for China's anti–Vietnamese policies. On May 1, 1978, the newly established Overseas Chinese Affairs Office warned that Peking was "concerned" about the sudden flight of "large numbers" of Hoas from Vietnam, but refrained from uttering any accusations as to the causes of the exodus.[84]

On May 3, reinforcing its previous move against Chinese trade in Cholon, the VCP introduced a new national currency, aimed not only at replacing the separate monetary denominations of the North and South that had survived the reunification with one unique national currency, but also at wiping out the last savings of the Hoas.[85] Later, the Vietnamese authorities would announce the prohibition of "all illegal activities" of open-air markets in Saigon.[86] By mid–May, as the panic among the Hoas gathered momentum, Xuan Thuy, secretary of the Vietnamese Communist Party invited the overseas

Chinese in Vietnam to seek exit visas. Hundreds of them besieged the Chinese embassy in Hanoi.[87]

Peking issued its strongest attack yet, accusing Hanoi of "ostracizing, persecuting and expelling" Hoas from Vietnam.[88] On May 12, China announced the cancellation of twenty of its aid projects to Vietnam and called back 800 of its personnel. This move, explained Peking, would "divert funds and materials to making arrangements for the life and productive work of the returned Chinese."[89] Vietnamese sources reported that China had called back its key miners and technicians to slow down the construction of vital links and infrastructures and indirectly sabotage the Vietnamese economy.[90]

As Sino-Vietnamese relations deteriorated, and border skirmishes with China increased along with Cambodian-Vietnamese border disputes, Hanoi began military construction work along its border with China, helped by Soviet advisers disguised as geological surveyors.[91] Concurrently, Hanoi placed its forces on nationwide alert and began recruiting one division of self-defense militia for each of its 500 districts.

Beyond its purely humanitarian dimension, the Hoa issue proved a timely pretext for Peking to come out openly against Vietnam, punishing Hanoi for its preference for Soviet friendship. China therefore began using the Hoa issue as a tool to direct international criticisms at Hanoi. In addition, Peking certainly hoped that the Hoa crisis would divert Hanoi's attention from its alleged expansionist ambitions in the region and relieve Cambodia of Vietnamese military pressure along the border. Placing Vietnam in the international spotlight would undermine Vietnamese capacity to respond too aggressively to Cambodian provocations. In addition, the voicing of Chinese open support for such an embarrassing ally as Pol Pot hardly seemed advisable in the light of international indignation over the mass murders and human rights violations perpetrated by the Khmer Rouge. And the persecution of the Hoas provided Peking with an official and legitimate excuse to publicize its irritation with Hanoi. In his memoirs, Khieu Samphan recalls that:

> In particular, after the death of Mao Tsé Toung in September 1976, Chinese attitude towards the C.P.K. seemed no longer beaconed by ideological considerations, but rather followed a strict realpolitik that found the radicalism of the latter [the Cambodian leadership] rather embarrassing and disadvantageous for it on the international level.[92]

Behind the scene, however, Chinese support for Phnom Penh was unwavering. In early May, and for the first time since 1975, long-range artillery and armored vehicles began to appear along the Cambodian-Vietnamese border—evidence of Chinese generosity towards Phnom Penh.[93] Encouraged by the new Chinese position, the Cambodian foreign ministry sent a note to Hanoi in which it declared that only if Hanoi accepted Phnom Penh's position on the border issue, abandoned its designs to create an Indochina federation and agreed to halt all hostilities for a period of seven months, would the Cambodians be ready to negotiate. Hanoi rejected the proposal.[94]

The Cambodian accusation that Vietnam was attempting to create an Indochina federation testified to the intense paranoia of the Cambodian leadership. In fact, the end of the Vietnam War had revived fears among Hanoi's neighbors that North Vietnam might seek regional and ideological expansion.[95] Once North and South Vietnam had been reunified, ran the rumors, Vietnam would exercise "hegemony" on its Indochinese neighbors before extending its political influence onto Thailand, the Philippines, Indonesia, Singapore and the region.[96]

During the French colonial rule in Indochina, Vietnam had played the role of the older brother, the head of the Indochinese trio that exercised regional influence and centralized sociopolitical life of the colony, reorganized into a federation of states. The contemporary concept of a renewed Indochina federation, therefore, appeared to be a hybrid born from Asian and American appraisals of international politics—a mixture of the former French colonial regrouping of the Indochinese territories, the Southeast Asian countries' fear of communist expansionism, Sino-Soviet rivalry for influence in the region, and the American belief in the domino theory.

While Cambodia was the first to accuse Vietnam of attempting to set up an Indochinese federation as early as 1975, Peking adopted similar terminology in 1978, accusing Vietnam of seeking regional hegemony for the sake of Soviet expansionism in the world.[97] Vietnam's alleged clandestine military support to communist guerrillas in its neighbor countries reinforced the rumors of Hanoi's quest for regional domination.[98]

The United States too seemed ready to believe in Vietnamese regionalist ambitions, as Kissinger hinted in his memoirs. "Lacking the humanity of their Laotian neighbors and the grace of their Cambodian neighbors," he recalls, the Vietnamese "strove for dominance by being not attractive but single-minded."[99] Kissinger's cold feelings for the Vietnamese communists would remain unchanged throughout his tenure as secretary of state.

True Vietnamese ambitions remain impossible to determine given the absence of Vietnamese archival material. However, several testimonies, not only from dissidents of the Vietnamese regime but also from close observers, reveal that the creation of an Indochina federation may indeed have been envisaged in the aftermath of the Second Indochina War and especially following the Fourth Party Congress of December 1976. A Vietnamese diplomat, interviewed in early 2002 but who prefers to remain unnamed, confirmed this piece of information regarding Hanoi's wish to create an Indochinese federation in the aftermath of the Vietnam war.[100] In the words of Hoang Van Hoan, a former member of the Vietnamese leadership who defected to China in 1979, "instead of showing concern for the welfare of the people, [Le Duan] made use of people's force to turn Viet Nam into a power dominating part of the world."[101]

The Fourth Party Congress had indeed witnessed the reemergence of the concept of a "special relationship" between the three Indochinese states, and which Phnom Penh rapidly began criticizing as a dissimulated Vietnamese quest for regional expansion. The term, however, explained Phan Hien a few years later, referred to these countries' "long history under the same colonialism," to their past sharing of common enemies, and to the fact that Indochinese states "must be close to each other, although each country is independent."[102] But while Hanoi claimed that such a principle did not go against each country's right for self-determination, it would simultaneously refuse to abide by Cambodia's refusal to join such an organization. While the Congress adopted a resolution for a tougher response to its growing border dispute with Cambodia, which had started immediately after the victory of the communist regimes in both countries in 1975, it also clearly resolved, as Le Duan expressed during the Congress, to have "the three countries stand shoulder to shoulder for ever."[103]

The concept, however, was not new, and dated back at least to the existence of the Indochinese Communist Party before it was dissolved in 1951. Tho himself had been at the head of a Politburo committee focusing on Cambodia as early as 1966 and by the second half of 1970s was clearly the originator of Vietnamese policies toward Cambodia.[104] Reportedly, from 1970 to 1972, in the early days of Vietnamese-Cambodian animosity, Hanoi had even seriously considered taking over the country but had renounced, perhaps in order not to jeopardize the ongoing peace talks in Paris.[105]

Writing on the Paris Peace Accords negotiations in 1972 and 1973, Kissinger had referred to Tho as "clearly the Politburo's expert on the other countries of Indochina" and was intrigued by Tho's insistence that Hanoi be given "the entire package [of economic aid] that [the U.S.] had earmarked for *all* of Indochina."[106] While Kissinger dismissed this insistence as Vietnamese greed and self-attribution of all U.S. aid, it seems upon closer look to point to Tho's wish to enhance Hanoi's control over its Indochinese neighbors by centralizing their policies in Hanoi. Le Duc Tho had even remarked to Kissinger, when he was the chief VCP negotiator at the Paris Peace Accords from 1968 to 1973, that it was "Vietnam's destiny to dominate not only Indochina but all of Southeast Asia" and Pham Van Dong had obediently echoed Tho's line of thought in claiming that the Vietnamese were "the Prussians of Southeast Asia."[107] Kissinger also noted that Le Duc Tho's role seemed to prevail over Dong's. While discussing the negotiations Kissinger remarked that Dong often "deferred" to Tho before responding to questions from the U.S. side and that, at one point: "amazingly, [Dong] was disavowed by Le Duc Tho, who sought a private meeting with me to suggest that henceforth Cambodia and Laos be discussed by him and me alone since his Prime Minister was not familiar with all the nuances."[108] Tho's power within the Politburo, although in the shade of other political figures, was nevertheless increasing, as was his growing interest in reuniting Indochina.[109]

Therefore, although no undeniable proof exists to corroborate the Cambodian accusations of Vietnamese regionalist ambitions, there are enough signs in the aftermath of the Vietnam War, and particularly by 1978, to support the possibility of Vietnamese quest for expansionism. One may remember that following the end of the war, Hanoi seemed reluctant to withdraw its forces from Lao and Cambodian territory, and only yielded after Chinese diplomatic intervention. Nor had Hanoi withdrawn its troops from Laos following the signing of the 1954 Geneva agreement.[110] Considering the continued presence of Vietnamese troops in Laos, Hanoi's intentions concerning the creation of an Indochina federation may understandably have fed the fears of a Cambodian leadership already destabilized by the intense political paranoia common to totalitarian dictatorial states.

Largely unaware of—or unconcerned by—the geopolitical forces at play behind the regional bickerings, American reactions were limited to press articles, despite Chinese efforts to stir U.S. attention. On May 17, in view of Brzezinski's upcoming visit to China, the Chinese foreign ministry had handed a protest note to Hanoi's ambassador to Peking, Nguyen Trong Vinh, calling on Vietnam to stop its persecution of Hoas. The Vietnamese foreign ministry responded on May 18 that Hoas had always enjoyed the same treatment as the Vietnamese and hinted that Peking should instead show its concern for Hoas who "have been subjected to blatant repression, mass evictions and massacres" in Cambodia. While denouncing Chinese accusations as "sheer fabrications," Hanoi called for the holding of talks "in a spirit of friendship."[111]

During Brzezinski's visit to Peking in May, a deluge of accusations against Hanoi flooded the Chinese media. In the same issue as the one retracing Brzezinski's visit, *Peking Review* published a lengthy article by Lien Kuan entitled "History of Overseas Chinese and Their Glorious Traditions."[112] The most flagrant attack, on May 24, condemned Hanoi for "unwarrantedly ostracizing and persecuting Chinese residents in Vietnam and expelling many of them back to China." The accusation officially brought the conflict to international light.[113]

Following Brzezinski's return to Washington, and seeing, through him, that Washington favored the Chinese position, Peking encouraged American concern for the humanitarian problem of the Hoa exodus, hoping to increase its influence on Washington. Hanoi and Peking, once claiming that their people were "as close as lips and teeth," were now openly waging diplomatic war.[114] Hoas seemed more of a diplomatic tool to justify Chinese hostility and arouse worldwide indignation than a true humanitarian concern to China, which, after all, had ignored the persecution of more than half a million Hoas in Cambodia.[115]

Sino-Vietnamese mutual accusations increased following Brzezinski's visit to Peking as each country put on a show of self-victimization and claimed its innocence. On May 27, Vietnam issued an oblique accusation, later confirmed by Moscow, that Peking had sent agents to Vietnam who "threatened and coerced Hoa people to leave Vietnam."[116] A Chinese source retorted that the same day Vietnamese troops had opened fire on Hoas crossing the border.[117]

Vietnam replied that Peking had spread rumors of an upcoming Khmero-Vietnamese military confrontation and urged the return to the homeland of all Hoas in Vietnam.[118] If they didn't return, ran the rumors, they would be seen as having chosen the Vietnamese side over the Sino-Cambodian camp in the confrontation.[119] Hanoi further stressed that Peking encouraged the exodus and that Chinese border guards guided the fleeing Hoas towards the frontier with loudspeakers.[120] The Vietnamese press, however, insisted that Hanoi wished to preserve its friendship with Peking despite the fact that China was deliberately distorting the dispute for nationalistic purposes.[121] A Hoa personally reported that propaganda tracts were being spread in the North so as to encourage mass Hoa emigration into China and to induce Southern Hoa populations to follow.[122]

But Peking rebuked these accusations and claimed that these rumors had originated in Moscow as a joint Soviet-Vietnamese effort to humiliate China.[123] The Chinese communist newspaper *Wen Wei Pao* swiftly added that Vietnam was persecuting Hoas at Soviet instigation, as part of the Soviet policy of encirclement, which the Vietnamese almost immediately denied.[124]

On May 30, China canceled fifty-one aid projects due to Hanoi's maltreatment of Hoas, which brought the total of withdrawn projects to seventy-two, valued at about $1 billion. Only eight were still officially in operation although most, like the Thang Long bridge over the Red River, were paralyzed by lack of material.[125]

In a show of force, and mostly to play out on the international scene how the massive exodus revolted China, Peking followed its accusations by sending humanitarian ships to "bring the victimized Chinese emigrants home."[126] Vietnam retorted that talks should be held prior to any evacuation. Concurrently, China submitted a proposal calling on Hanoi to recognize its description of Hoas as "Chinese residents who are victims of ostracism, persecution and expulsion" while Vietnam had labeled them "Vietnamese of Chinese descent [who] wish to leave Vietnam for China."[127] However, the talks stalled on this terminological issue and the ships were not granted permission to enter Vietnamese waters, much to the advantage of Peking, which held onto the proof that its attempt to negotiate had been refused by Hanoi. The ships were finally allowed to enter Vietnamese waters on June 5.[128] A series of Sino-Vietnamese meetings were held until the end of the year without any satisfactory resolution to the Hoa issue.[129]

In June, the conflicts with China and the Khmer Rouge were growing in intensity, further urging Hanoi to seek international support. By mid-June 1978, 133,000 Hoas had fled Vietnam at a rate of 4,000 per day.[130] Chen Chih-fang, Peking's ambassador to Vietnam, returned to China allegedly "because of illness," and two days later a Vietnamese radio broadcast announced that Peking had ordered Hanoi to close its consulates in three Chinese cities.[131] Vietnam charged that the closing of the Vietnamese consulates, while intelligence reports in Hong Kong announced the presence of a substantial Chinese fleet in the Tonkin Gulf, was part of Chinese policy regarding its border disputes and was visible proof of Peking's support for Pol Pot.[132] Hanoi mirrored the Chinese move by informing Peking that Vietnam had returned to its decision of November 1977 to allow the opening of Chinese consulates in Saigon and Haiphong, which had postponed the opening of the consulates to October. In response, China recalled its consulate staff who had been waiting in Hanoi for the opening of Chinese consulates since April. However, it also signaled Peking's displeasure with Hanoi's rapprochement with the Soviet Union.[133]

Chinese claims were soon echoed by other countries, mainly ASEAN states, which saw their beaches invaded by Vietnamese boat people, and turned to Washington for support, hoping American diplomatic aid would mop up the outflow of Vietnamese refugees spilling into Southeast Asian countries. The moralistic Carter, who greatly emphasized respect for human rights and peace, was the perfect interlocutor for Peking. Refugees carried with them the stories of Hanoi's "human trafficking scheme" through which refugees bought, at a very high cost, their way to freedom, which discredited Vietnam.[134] As Vietnam and China engaged in a competition of international propaganda to obtain maximum leverage on Washington, the refugee exodus would eventually turn into a fatal obstacle in Vietnamese dealings with Washington.

Vietnam's Dual Opening to Moscow and Washington

In Hanoi, Nguyen Co Thach had been appointed, since the last round of Paris talks, to replace Nguyen Duy Trinh in negotiations with Washington. While he was considered one of Tho's protégés, Thach was an educated man who grasped the importance of giving entrée to the West, particularly to Washington. During the war, as Bui Tin recalls, Thach had been one of the engineers of the manipulation of U.S. public opinion and understood American moods better than any other member of the Politburo.[135] While he was personally not in favor of the invasion of Cambodia, Thach also understood that diplomatic rapprochement had to be reached prior to the Vietnamese military intervention.[136] Vietnam began to play on both stages, wooing both Moscow and Washington, prodding the Soviets into making greater concessions by waving the American card, and concealing its regional and international ambitions from Washington to attract American concessions.

During a congressional visit to Japan in March 1978, the Japanese, increasingly worried over the mounting tensions between Vietnam and China, had urged Washington to normalize with Vietnam. A congressman had replied in referring to the constant Vietnamese request for aid that "[t]here can be absolutely no restoration of ties if it means admitting, even in the slightest way, that America was wrong."[137] "We are not discussing giving economic assistance to the Vietnamese, nor do we believe that we have an obligation based upon the past to do so." Holbrooke echoed this reply during a congressional hearing in March, stating that "we are not discussing giving economic assistance to the Vietnamese, nor do we believe that we have an obligation based upon the past to do so." The hard-line Vietnamese stance during the Paris talks and the spying affair had cooled bilateral relations. "It is my judgment," explained Holbrooke in a cooler and more detached tone than usual,

> that these negotiations [in Paris] have improved the relationship between the former bitter adversaries and that 1977 was a year when haltingly, step by step, slowly, there was slight but significant improvement in relations.... So while our progress has been limited, it exists. We will continue to be ready to talk to the Vietnamese about issues of mutual concern in Paris or elsewhere as appropriate at any time. At this time ... we do not have any meeting currently scheduled, but we are not averse to a meeting later in the year, perhaps later in the spring, if the other side wishes one. We may end up requesting one ourselves, if we see some value in it.
> In short ... we are prepared to move forward with the Vietnamese on the basis that I have outlined.[138]

Holbrooke's intended spring meeting did not occur for several reasons, including Hanoi's growing friendship with Moscow, but perhaps most importantly, due to the administration's growing interest in normalizing with China, following Soviet involvement in the Horn of Africa, and the establishment of Marxist regimes in Afghanistan and Yemen which had forced Carter to reevaluate his perception of the "Soviet threat."[139] When asked when normalization with Hanoi would occur, Holbrooke enigmatically replied: "I try not to use the word normalization with regard to Vietnam because it is a word associated with China and the issues are so different. What we are talking about is the step-by-step process of putting behind us a difficult and tortured past.... *However it will take time.*"[140]

A short note should also be made on the ambivalent personality of Richard Holbrooke, the main actor in post–1975 American-Vietnamese contacts. Although Holbrooke had genuinely wished to act as the initiator of a U.S. rapprochement with Hanoi in 1977, his insistence on American-Vietnamese normalization had relapsed by 1978. While disillusion over the failed efforts of 1977 and the spying affair at the UN may account for much of Holbrooke's change of emphasis, the young diplomat's concern for his own career may also have played an important part in his change of position.

By early 1978, NSC-favored positions, such as normalization with China, had begun to gain precedence in the White House over State Department initiatives, including any regarding Vietnam. Despite his earlier initiatives for normalization with Vietnam, Holbrooke's statements starting in late 1977 indicated an increasing distancing from the issue and a growing interest in normalization with China. By switching to supporting political themes upheld by the NSC, Holbrooke perhaps hoped to hint to the NSC that it had found an ally within the State Department, winning Brzezinski's confidence and eventually advancing his own career.

While Holbrooke would continue to work towards normalization with Vietnam for the State Department, his attention would increasingly turn towards the NSC during 1978.[141] Although Holbrooke's self-motivated strategy eventually failed to impress the NSC, which turned a deaf ear to Holbrooke's wooing, it may account for much of the State Department's hovering and indecision over Vietnamese overtures during the summer of 1978 to the benefit of the China issue.

Consequently, while Holbrooke, in late 1977, had mentioned holding a meeting with Vietnam, the significant event in the spring was instead Brzezinski's trip to China, in which the young diplomat would also take part.

Such an American response came as no surprise to Thach. While he believed that normalization was in Vietnam's interest, he also understood that the only way to obtain it was to lift the aid precondition that had so angered Congress and the American public. Other economic benefits would be reaped from normalization through what Carter had termed a "normal aid process."[142] Normal diplomatic relations would remove the trade embargo and allow the development of foreign businesses, both American and Western European, which had shown great interest in Vietnamese trade possibilities. Hanoi would also have access to the $75 million of the former Thieu regime, blocked in the United States until normalization, and which would enable Vietnam to pay back part of its debts. The amount would quadruple Vietnam's reserves in foreign currencies at a time when foreign businesses were unable to set up in Vietnam.[143] Moreover, such aid would compensate for the loss of Chinese aid projects. In addition, Hanoi understood that a dual opening to both Washington and Moscow would counterbalance and neutralize each country's influence on Vietnam, much as Chinese and Soviet pressures had neutralized each other during the war.

"Our position," recalled Thach the following fall, was "that the normalization of relations ... is in the interests of both countries and in the interests of peace and stability [in] Southeast Asia."[144] Thach therefore waived the last obstacle to normalization. The aid issue was about to be dropped.

During a speech in Honolulu on May 10, Vice-President Mondale commented on the five months of silence that had elapsed since the December 1977 talks and the halting of negotiations due to the spying affair. "[W]e have made a fair offer," he explained, "that we are ready to establish diplomatic relations without preconditions. But Hanoi is still demanding a prior commitment of ... aid, something which the American people cannot accept."[145] A few days later, as the Hoa crisis was raging and China announced the cutting of its aid projects, Hanoi sent a discreet message to Washington through the U.S. embassies in Japan and India. Vietnam wished to normalize as soon as possible, and was ready to drop its request for aid.[146]

This offer surprised Washington. The State Department publicly denied having received any message. Hanoi, not wishing to add any pressure on the Americans, did not contradict this claim.[147] While the executive considered the sudden change in Hanoi's stance with great caution, it was perhaps as much intrigued by its purpose as uncertain of the potentially negative effect it could shed on growing Sino-American relations. Meanwhile, Hanoi encouraged independent U.S. initiatives to prove its friendliness to Washington. In spring, Vietnam welcomed a visit by the Church World Service and, on May 25, responded positively to a request by Montgomery to visit Vietnam.[148]

Unaware of the true Vietnamese position, such humanitarian organizations and lobby groups were ready to take Hanoi's friendship for granted. "Vietnam's biggest problems are political rather than economic," reported a member of the Church World Service, returning from Vietnam in May.[149] Hanoi, added delegation member Cora Weiss, "is not looking for enemies, whether they are Cambodian or Chinese." She stressed that no evidence exists of Vietnamese mistreatment of Hoas.[150] The delegation's report to Carter repeated Hanoi's wish to resume discussions and its decision to drop the aid precondition.[151]

In early June, Senator Kennedy urged the administration to normalize and provide reconstruction aid.[152] On June 21, never slow in manipulating the strings of American public opinion, Hanoi informed Kennedy, as former chairman of the Senate Subcommittee on Refugees, that it would allow a small group of ten Vietnamese wives and nineteen children of American citizens to join their relatives in the United States.[153]

However, Washington, and especially the State Department, misunderstood the sudden Vietnamese change in attitude. Hanoi's policy shift was neither an attempt to seek protection from Cambodian attacks through international diplomatic means, nor to shield Hanoi from the danger of Soviet influence, which Vietnam had already deliberately sought.[154] Rather, it aimed at reaping the benefits of American friendship before it would be made impossible by the upcoming move on Cambodia.[155] Perhaps Hanoi also hoped that it would nip in the bud China's growing links with Washington, confining Peking to diplomatic solitude to the benefit of the pro–Soviet block, and deterring any risk of Chinese response to Vietnam's action against Cambodia. While confiding its ambitions to Moscow, Hanoi was concealing its true motives from Washington, encouraging U.S. belief in the Vietnamese need for American protection and support, by publicizing Cambodian attacks and Chinese hostility to visiting U.S. delegations, echoed in the Soviet press for greater emphasis.

As Chinese accusations multiplied, the dispute headed the front page of most American newspapers. Until 1978, there had been little public awareness in the U.S. of the growing Sino-Vietnamese hostility, and the sudden refugee exodus had greatly affected public opinion. Since 1975, Hanoi had sought to keep clashes with Cambodia away from the eyes of international public opinion and had constantly downplayed border confrontations, promoting the image of friendly neighbors. By 1978 such a policy had proved counterproductive. After failing to attract Cambodian friendship, the Vietnamese switched to a sudden denunciation of Cambodian aggressions, revealing to the world Khmer atrocities. Not only did this reversal undermine the credibility of Vietnamese declarations but it confirmed Peking and Cambodia's ever-increasing warnings regarding Hanoi at a time when the Vietnamese were more than ever in need of international support.[156]

In May further doubts arose as to Vietnamese intentions when Washington received a warning from its embassy in Bangkok that Vietnam was preparing to invade Cambodia.[157] During the summer of 1978, the State Department never seemed to grasp the full meaning of all the forces at play behind the unfolding Indochinese conflict.

While some conservative Americans saw this new Indochinese conflict as justifying past U.S. military intervention and as the consequence of an all too early American military withdrawal from Indochina, Washington refused any involvement in Indochinese affairs.[158] In a lumping together of Vietnam, Cambodia and all Indochinese conflicts, Nixon later claimed that "[f]ewer people were killed during the anti–Communist war than during the Communist peace," and, in the words of his biographer Monica Crowley, Nixon "felt that a conclusive moral judgement could be rendered" from such facts.[159]

On the contrary, liberal American sources and postwar doves accused Washington of having cleared the way for the coming to power of the barbaric Khmer Rouge, claiming that the U.S. "can only wring its hands—not wash them of its share of responsibility—over the new horrors of Indochina."[160] All in all, the U.S. domestic debate over the situation in Cambodia remained largely self-centered as hawks and doves found new arguments to justify their past positions during the Vietnam War.

Such comments illustrated the American lack of understanding of the real historical, ethnic and nationalist issues in Indochina. Instead, the conflict was transformed to fit domestic needs for self-justification or blame, for defending one's past positions on the Vietnam War that had tainted so many reputations and careers over the last fifteen years.[161] The realities of history, past and present, seemed a side issue. Ironically, the Sino-Vietnamese and Cambodian-Vietnamese conflicts were proving the domino theory wrong, at least in Southeast Asia, since the communist countries, fuelling their own internal dissensions, were now turning against each other rather than uniting to impose Marxism onto neighboring countries.[162]

One may regret that the continuation of past debates on the justifications of the Vietnam War among American intellectuals and thinkers, and the weighing of each other's responsibility in the issue, blinded the United States from assessing the true nature of events in Indochina. The constant rehashing of past positions over the causes and history of the Vietnam War, on which many careers had been built, resulted in the sidestepping of realities in the post–Vietnam war era and the U.S. failure to propose concrete actions for intervention in the unfolding conflict.

During congressional testimony in July 1977, Holbrooke reported that Cambodian purges may have claimed more than a million victims, but dismissed the possibility of diplomatic intervention, claiming that neither "the United States, the United Nations, nor any Western European nation has the leverage to affect the human rights situation in Cambodia." Instead, he promised that Washington would continue to assist Indochinese refugees through UN programs.[163] The following April, Carter labeled the Pol Pot regime "the world's worst violators of human rights" during a conference on Cambodia in Oslo, which would lead to an investigation by the UN High Commission on Refugees on human rights violations in Cambodia, as requested by Britain.[164] Despite Carter's pledges to promote human rights, the administration did not wish to jeopardize its relations with China, or risk another conflict in Indochina, and refrained from taking action.

Brzezinski's Growing Influence and His Visit to China

Meanwhile, Washington and Peking were developing bilateral contacts—a budding friendship would have an undeniable impact on American responses to Vietnam's overtures in late 1978 and contribute to the shift from U.S. regionalist to globalist perceptions of foreign policy.

Nixon had reinitiated bilateral relations with China in 1971 with the Shanghai Communiqué.[165] He had claimed his one-week visit to China to be "the week that changed the world," leading to the signing of the Shanghai Communiqué. The document, pledging a concordance of views over international order, had set the tone for future negotiations on the normalization of Sino-American relations.[166] The Vietnamese, viewing the American move on China with a suspicious eye, had seen Nixon's visit as a sabotage of their liberation struggle, and had feared that in return for Washington's acquiescence to Chinese policy over Taiwan, China would reduce its commitments to Vietnam and let the Americans have their war in Indochina.[167] "If out of the narrow interests of one's nation," *Nhan Dan* had charged in August 1972, "one tries to help the most reactionary forces, avert the dangerous blows just like throwing a life-belt to a drowning pirate, that is a cruel reconciliation beneficial to the enemy."[168] Although the president had claimed that his visit was "not directed against any other nation," it seemed that the USSR had much to lose in this new relationship.[169]

After Nixon had placed the first cornerstone in the building of diplomatic relations with China, Ford and Kissinger furthered the initial contact by visiting Peking in 1975.[170] Ford, however, realized that his trip, if exclusively limited to a visit to Peking, would flatter China as bearing too great emphasis in U.S. foreign policy. The trip was thus rearranged to include a few stops in Southeast Asian countries, which the Chinese perceived as a "downgrading" of Nixon's previous 1971 move to open to China.[171]

In fact, neither party was greatly impressed by the other and Ford's trip to Peking, after Nixon, was sarcastically compared by the Asian press to a second man's visit to the moon.[172] Ford also knew that, after the humiliating collapse of the American-backed Saigon regime, American public opinion was not ready to see Washington drop its allies in Taiwan, which China incessantly insisted should be a precondition to normalization. An American official, pointing at the fall of Saigon, sarcastically explained: "We have used up our ration for betrayals this year."[173] The Chinese rapidly concluded that the United States "had not made up its mind."[174]

Relations stalled in 1976, with the death of Premier Zhou Enlai on January 8, and of Chairman Mao Zedong on September 9. Political and economic dilemmas, linked to the arrest of the Gang of Four and to the new modernization plans, which were to make China a modern economy by the year 2000, further postponed American efforts to pursue normalization. However, the Chinese still manifested their interest in the matter by symbolically inviting Nixon to Peking in February 1976.[175] Kissinger rapidly understood that, between Washington and the "cold, pragmatic bastards" in Peking, no breakthrough would occur under Ford.[176]

As his rival Kissinger—in historian James Mann's words, the "godfather" of American secret policies toward China—had failed to oversee normalization, Chinese affairs seemed all the more appealing to Brzezinski.[177] After describing Kissinger as "an acrobat when what we need is an architect," and accusing him of "creating uneasiness and overselling détente" with Moscow, Brzezinski seemed ready to challenge and surpass Kissinger's accomplishments.[178] Rather than playing one communist power against the other according to Kissinger's strategy, Brzezinski's version of confrontationalism would opt for an alliance with the lesser of the two, leaving the second in forced isolation.[179]

Furthermore, Brzezinski, an advocate of "Cold War orthodoxy," attributed the post–Vietnam War decline in U.S. credibility and prestige to détente.[180] In an interview in mid–1976, he explained that Nixon's 1971 rapprochement "has been somewhat impaired by the Chinese belief that the United States' weakness constitutes appeasement of the Soviet Union designed to deflect Soviet hostility from the West on to China."[181] Brzezinski's role would be to reaffirm American interest in Sino-American friendship in the midst of SALT negotiations with Moscow, which China both distrusted and violently criticized.

Brzezinski understood that China was the perfect card to play against the Soviets to challenge "their very existence."[182] He shared the Chinese view that détente represented a diplomatic hoax with which Moscow was manipulating Washington. He viewed SALT II with growing skepticism as tension with Moscow increased in early 1978 over the Soviet- and Cuban-backed conflicts in Africa, despite Vance's claims that negotiations should continue and that losing SALT would be "the worst thing that could happen."[183] As an American official put it: "Zbig likes to poke the [Soviet] bear through the bars of his cage."[184] Some international observers would even charge that the national security adviser hoped that Chinese nuclear warheads would turn to the other side, towards the USSR.[185]

Although Brzezinski stresses that the phrase "China card" originated in the Soviet press, Moscow claimed that it opposed both the phrase and the concept.[186] Neither Brzezinski nor Moscow wished to have the NSC advisor's name associated with it. In a rather cool response to the article "Playing the China Card" published in *Time* in November 1978, the NSC press secretary strongly denied that Brzezinski had ever used this phrase.[187]

In fact, the concept had first been uttered at the beginning of the 1970s in the early phase of the Sino-American rapprochement and was merely being taken up by the U.S. press as bilateral relations gathered momentum under Carter.[188] But while the expression itself may not have originated with Brzezinski, the concept was strongly reminiscent of the views of the national security adviser. In his memoirs, Brzezinski explains:

> The Soviet dimension [of opening to China] was one of those considerations of which it is sometimes said, "Think of it at all times but speak of it never." I, for one, thought of it a great deal, even though I knew that publicly one had to make pious noises to the effect that U.S.-Chinese normalization had nothing to do with U.S.-Soviet rivalry.[189]

As Garthoff says, the "card intended initially by Carter to retaliate for Soviet and Cuban actions in Africa was converted by Brzezinski into a long-term strategic relationship binding the United States and China more closely."[190]

In early 1977 Carter requested the drafting of Policy Review Memorandum PRM-24 to study possible Sino-American normalization. The study, completed in June 1977, sided with State Department views that Washington should continue to engage in a policy of even-handedness between Moscow and Peking, refraining from favoring either so as not to jeopardize Washington's relations with Moscow over the SALT treaty or exacerbate Sino-Soviet animosity. The report advised against gestures of U.S. friendliness towards Peking that could appear as provocative to Moscow, such as the endorsement of Chinese anti–Soviet criticisms or the sale of military equipment to Peking.[191]

Regarding bilateral relations, it recommended that Tokyo's dealings with Peking become a model for Sino-American normalization. The "Japan formula" encompassed the breaking of ties with Taiwan and the formal ending the Mutual Defense treaty paired with the withdrawal of U.S. troops from Taiwan.[192]

In August 1977, while Holbrooke and Phan Hien were preparing for a third round of Paris talks, Vance was dispatched to Peking to test the Chinese on normalization. But Carter wished to maintain a low profile during the Senate debate over the Panama Canal treaties, and instructed Vance to remain restrained.[193] The Chinese were evidently disappointed and called for a more aggressive anti–Soviet view as Vance disclosed Washington's negotiation strategy, based along the lines of PRM-24.[194] During the visit, Hua Guofeng quoted Lenin as having said that it is necessary "to take advantage of every, even the smallest, opportunity of gaining a mass ally, even though this ally could be temporary, vacillating, unstable, unreliable and conditional"—a strong and direct criticism of Washington's weakness in refusing to oppose Moscow openly.[195] Peking was signaling, in unflattering metaphors, that it envisaged friendship with the United States as a necessity rather than as a genuine appreciation of U.S. policies. The criticism was designed to punish Washington for its wavering signals to Peking over the last few years.

Nor did Peking welcome Washington's "interventionist" strategy in its domestic affairs, as the Chinese leadership described the Taiwan issue. The *People's Daily* commented that to "liberate Taiwan is the internal affair of China and no one has the right to intervene."[196] Deng told a Japanese delegation that bilateral negotiations had suffered a "major setback" during Vance's visit.[197] Also, Washington had not renounced its conditions for normalization or endorsed Chinese hostility towards Moscow. Deng later qualified the American position as "playing with two cards."[198]

Vance rejected the aggressiveness behind the concept of "playing the China card" against Moscow, and considered Peking more a political and economic power that could no longer be neglected, than a geopolitical stage on which to nag Moscow.[199] While Carter later dubbed Vance's trip a "disappointing failure," the visit confirmed that an ideological and bureaucratic competition had begun between Vance and Brzezinski.[200] Carter attempted to redeem Vance's "failure" and to regain Peking's attention with a series of friendly gestures, including sending his own son, Chip, as part of a congressional delegation to China and making several statements about his wish to share the details of the SALT talks with Peking.[201]

An unfortunate leak to the U.S. press that China had been malleable during the talks triggered an outburst of rage in Peking, and Vance suspected that this rumor had been designed by the NSC as a deliberate sabotage of his trip.[202] He had already repeatedly noticed that some reports and summaries of NSC meetings, which Brzezinski presented to the president, contained "discrepancies, occasionally serious ones."[203]

According to an American source, Brzezinski indeed spent more time alone with Carter than his secretaries of state and defense put together.[204] Every morning Brzezinski met Carter in the Oval Office and briefed him on intelligence reports.[205] Peter Bourne describes the weathering of Carter's initial appraisals of foreign policies under Brzezinski's influence as "Chinese water torture." Since both men were early risers, Brzezinski took advantage of his one-to-one morning meetings with Carter to impress on the president his own anti–Soviet views, relying on the dropping of subtle hints on a daily basis rather than in occasional all-out attacks that would have aroused the President's suspicion. Little by little, Brzezinski's anti–Soviet thinking colored Carter's judgment and accounted for much of his growing harshness in dealing with matters concerning Moscow.[206]

The national security adviser's influence on Carter had grown—much to the State Department's discontent—and Brzezinski became more of an engineer of foreign policies than an adviser, bypassing the State Department and encouraging bilateral secrecy with the president.[207] As all information relating to advice on policy-making was filtered through the national security adviser, Vance complained that Brzezinski "had the power to interpret the thrust of discussion" and forward it to Carter.[208] "The United States has ... two secretaries of State competing with one another," commented Chairman of the Senate Foreign Relations Committee Senator Frank Church (Democrat, Idaho) a few months later.[209] However, Brzezinski rejected the rumors of his competition with Vance as a myth and explained in an interview with *Newsweek* in May 1977:

> I consider it an aberration that so many people seem to think that doing somebody in, intriguing against colleagues, has to be the routine and that the ability to cooperate decently is either only something very transitional or ... a sham.[210]

By early 1978, the initial enthusiasm of public opinion for the president had vanished and Carter told his top staff that it was time for him to adopt a "stronger" image. At the same time, since the development of the Soviet and Cuban involvement in the wars raging between Ethiopia and Somalia, then in Angola and Zaire, the NSC versus State Department competition had reached a breaking point as Brzezinski urged a strong stance against Moscow, against the advice of the State Department.[211] As Carter's perception of the "global community" was altered into a more globalist appraisal of foreign policy, in which Moscow was perceived as a threat, he opted for Brzezinski's "hard-nosed" approach to foreign policy contrasting with the State Department's diplomatic "pussyfooting."[212]

Meanwhile, the Chinese Fifth National Congress had adopted a new constitution in March depicting Moscow in increasingly harsher terms and denouncing the "subversion and aggression by social-imperialism, imperialism and their lackeys."[213] This concomitant similarity of views set the tone for Brzezinski's favoring rapid rapprochement with Peking.

Brzezinski's turn to woo Peking came soon. At a reception in November 1977, a Chinese official had asked him if he intended to visit China. Brzezinski, who longed to copy Kissinger in negotiating with Peking, pulled out his diary and requested the Chinese official to "name the date."[214] By mid–November, Brzezinski had written to chief of the Chinese liaison office in Washington, Huang Chen, reiterating his acceptance of the invitation to visit China, and requesting the setting of "mutually satisfactory arrangements" for the trip. The national security adviser stressed that normalization was "a historical necessity."[215]

Reportedly, Brzezinski also requested Oksenberg's help in initiating an invitation from the Chinese.[216] The recent ratification of the Panama Canal treaties, shelved for several months so as not to jeopardize the administration's efforts to push these treaties through the Senate, had opened the way for the resumption of negotiations with Peking.[217] Oksenberg recalls:

One day after the Administration won the vote on the first [Panama Canal] treaty, the Chinese were informed of Brzezinski's desire to accept the invitation they had extended in the winter, and the precise date for his visit was set on the day following the vote on the second treaty.[218]

Oksenberg represented Brzezinski's best ally in the administration and strongly favored normalization with China. In 1976, he had presented a report to the House declaring that "time had come to establish full diplomatic relations with ... China." The report's conclusions presented the same anti–Soviet lines as commonly found in Brzezinski's discourse:

> [A]s to the fear of Soviet reactions to the development of sounder Chinese-American ties, so be it. I do not believe our China policy should be dictated by Moscow. By proclaiming a policy of maintaining an equal distance from China and the USSR we in effect enable the Soviets to determine, to an extent, our relations with the PRC. By keeping us at arm's length and by indicating displeasure if we undertake certain activities with the Chinese, in effect the Soviets inhibit closer United States-Chinese ties. But we have important long-term interests in reducing Chinese and American isolation from each other, and if the people in the Kremlin do not understand the long-run danger of an isolated, economically poor China, that is their deficiency, not ours.

In his report, Oksenberg had listed five American actions designed "to enhance our attractiveness to the Chinese." These included:

> Maintenance of a firm, credible military posture in the Western Pacific and into the Indian Ocean as a counterweight to the Soviet thrust...
> Determination more generally to prevent Soviet domination of key strategic points around the world and to resist Soviet attempts to establish a new empire.
> Expediting the flow of technology to China, including computer and petroleum technology, to hasten China's economic development.
> Extending most favored nation status to the PRC.
> Responding positively but selectively to Chinese requests to purchase military equipment which would enhance their defensive capabilities vis-à-vis the USSR.[219]

From mid–1978, U.S. policies towards China would keep remarkably close to Oksenberg's five suggestions, indicating that his and Brzezinski's views were largely concordant. However, less concessions would be requested of China than Oksenberg had originally planned, as NSC views considerably hardened against Moscow and found a similarity of opinions in Peking. The association of these two masterminds would lead to the growing influence of the national security adviser on White House foreign policy-making.

Upon hearing of Brzezinski's visit, Vance opposed the trip that he saw as an NSC attempt to further compete with the State Department.[220] "Though ... Brzezinski [was] very eager to go to Peking," recalls Carter in his memoirs:

> Secretary Vance was insisting that any negotiations be carried out through him. I presumed that the State Department professionals were still smarting over Secretary William Rogers' having been bypassed when Henry Kissinger, as Nixon's National Security Adviser, played such a major role in preparing for the President's visit to China and in negotiating the Shanghai communiqué.[221]

Brzezinski outmaneuvered his rival by organizing his trip while Vance was visiting Moscow, and Vance could do nothing to prevent it.[222] Noting Kissinger and Brzezinski's similar taste for secrecy, Hamilton Jordan sneered that this was "foreign policy déjà vu."[223]

The trip would demonstrate Brzezinski's supremacy over Vance. Brzezinski's visit to China and Vance's visit to Moscow can be seen as a competition over who would return with the greater gains. Brzezinski even managed to exclude Holbrooke from his discussion team with Chinese leaders to include solely NSC staff members in the meetings. Holbrooke appealed to Woodcock, requesting his help to force Brzezinski into accepting his presence for the negotiations with the Chinese. But his efforts were in vain.[224] Following the meetings, the NSC team trumpeted the fact that they had obtained more time with the Chinese than the Vance delegation the previous year.[225]

"The President ... is determined to join you in overcoming the remaining obstacles in the way of full normalization," Brzezinski told his hosts during his toast on May 22. "The U.S. has made up its mind on this issue."[226] The national security adviser had been charged with giving Peking a piece of moon rock as well as a Chinese flag that had been to the moon, as a symbolic pledge for future technological cooperation—perhaps also to remind the Chinese that the Americans had won the race to the moon against the Soviets.[227] A note from Carter stressed that the present was "symbolic of our quest for a better future."[228]

But Brzezinski had brought other presents and, much as Kissinger had given Peking U.S. reconnaissance satellite pictures of Soviet military material and troop deployments along the Sino-Soviet border during his secret visit of July 1971, Brzezinski had similar tokens with which to gain Chinese friendship and prove mutual anti–Soviet ideologies.[229] NSC official Samuel Huntington discussed the top secret "Presidential Review Memorandum 10" with the Chinese, an assessment of where Washington stood in the world balance of power in relation to the Soviets, which Huntington had drafted for the president in mid–1977. The report predicted that Moscow would encounter long-term domestic difficulties eventually leading to its weakening both economically and militarily, and that Washington would emerge as the stronger power.

Vance had probably also briefed the Chinese on the conclusions of PRM-10 during his trip but his reading of the report diverged from Brzezinski's. While the State Department stressed that the report allowed Washington to seek rapprochement with Moscow and a new SALT treaty, the NSC considered that Washington should take advantage of Moscow's weakening to extract greater concessions from the Soviets.[230] While Vance's position on PRM-10 may have irritated Peking, Brzezinski's interpretation of the report seemed more to Chinese taste.[231]

Huntington also informed the Chinese officials that Washington would no longer oppose the sale of "dual-use" technology or arms from its allies.[232] As proof of Washington's goodwill, Deputy Assistant Secretary of Defense for International Security Morton Abramowitz provided recent intelligence on Soviet military deployments along the Sino-Soviet border.[233] Concurrently, Benjamin Huberman, Carter's assistant science and technology adviser, briefed the Chinese on global security.[234] Brzezinski intentionally leaked details of these talks to the press, further adding to Soviet uneasiness.[235]

Brzezinski was clearly delighted at finding and sharing such similar views with Vice-Chairman Deng Xiaoping.[236] He, whom Kissinger had once named "a nasty little man," had found a true diplomatic partner in the national security adviser.[237] Deng was "a living example of the survival of the fittest," as had declared Thai politician Kukrit Pramoj, recalling Deng's survival of the recent political reshuffling of the Chinese leadership.[238] Brzezinski, who often charged that Vance tended to "shy away from the unavoidable ingredient of force," admired his host and hoped that some of Deng's "cold and even ruthless appreciation of the uses of power" would rub off on the State Department. According to Carter, Brzezinski had been "seduced" by his Chinese hosts.[239]

Likewise, Deng seemed to enjoy Brzezinski's company much more than he had ever liked "The Doctor"—Henry Kissinger.[240] At the Great Wall, Brzezinski challenged his hosts to a race: "whoever [reaches] the top second would be sent off to Ethiopia to confront the Cubans."[241] In asking a group of sailors to join him for a picture in front of the Great Wall, Brzezinski even chanced the joke that they were standing next to an "imperialist." But the sailors joked back that they were being photographed with a "polar bear tamer," which became Brzezinski's Chinese nickname.[242] Russian sources bitterly noted Brzezinski's "dubious joke" of pretending he had seen a "polar bear" outside the Great Wall.[243] Brzezinski's show seemed staged to oppose Moscow.

American public opinion did not fully welcome Brzezinski's endorsing of Peking's global view nor his openly anti–Soviet attitude, and Carter had to call him back to order after Moscow protested that the "visit signified a sharp zig-zag in the policy of the Carter [A]dministration from a relatively considered and even-handed 'triangular diplomacy' to a single-minded pro–Peking and anti–Soviet orientation."[244]

Peking was delighted to have found an ally at so opportune a moment, when what the Vietnamese termed "Peking's neurotic obsession with Moscow" was at its height, with mounting Chinese alarm over continued Soviet successes in Africa, the escalation of the clashes with Vietnam and territorial disputes with Japan.[245] Only eleven days before Brzezinski's visit, the Soviets had made a border incursion into China, which Moscow had intended as a warning against Sino-American collusion.[246] Peking widely publicized Moscow's "grave, calculated step," during Brzezinski's visit.[247] "We absolutely must be prepared to wage war," declared Hua Guofeng. "There is no time to be wasted."[248]

On his way back Brzezinski took the initiative to stop in Tokyo, without having secured prior presidential authorization.[249] The aim of his short visit was to urge the Japanese, upon Chinese request, to sign a treaty with Peking. Tokyo yielded to Brzezinski's pressure and the two countries would eventually sign this treaty on August 12. But more importantly, the incident demonstrated Brzezinski's readiness to act as a mediator and supporter of Chinese views both domestically and abroad.

In his final toast in Peking, Brzezinski pledged that he would work towards "friendship and normalization," which he depicted as "vital."[250] Woodcock, now head of the Chinese liaison office in Peking, commented that Brzezinski's visit had represented a "substantial push" towards normalization. By August, Holbrooke reported that Washington was "convinced that normalization is an essential objective for our new Asian policy."[251] Talks began in June in Peking, and while Woodcock had at first rejoiced in opening a dialogue between Washington and Hanoi, he was now working towards opening the door to Peking—and thus indirectly closing it on Hanoi.[252]

Brzezinski's successful visit to Peking created permanent changes within the U.S. administration, marking the ascendancy of his influence on Carter, eventually leading to Vance's resignation several months later. The visit undermined Vance's efforts in Moscow already bogged down by the slowness of the SALT negotiations, and in the U.S. press the Moscow trip remained in the shadow of the colorful photographs of Brzezinski at the Great Wall. Brzezinski's victory over State Department policies eventually spilled over into Carter's own appraisal of foreign policy, encouraging him to adopt a stronger stance with Moscow.

During a speech on June 7, only a few days after Brzezinski's return to Washington, Carter remarked that détente had experienced recent setbacks and warned that Moscow "can choose either confrontation or cooperation.... The United States is prepared to meet either choice."[253] Carter had not intended his declaration to appear as a direct provocation to Moscow but simply to urge the Soviets to cooperate. However, his speech represented a clumsy cut-and-paste of two drafts, composed by Vance and Brzezinski respectively, representing their diverging ideas. The final draft revealed Carter's attempt to walk the middle-line between both views in the ongoing competition between State Department and NSC, although the influence of Brzezinski's hardline approach had already gained precedence over State Department views.[254] But in Moscow, Carter's speech was understood as a half-veiled diplomatic threat.

Consequences of the Brzezinski Trip to China on the NSC Perception of the Sino-Cambodian-Vietnamese Conflicts

Carter had also requested Brzezinski to raise the issue of Cambodian human right violations with his Chinese hosts, which provided Deng with an opportunity to lecture his guests on the dangers of Vietnamese hegemony and reinforced Brzezinski's belief in the "proxy" nature of the conflict.[255] Deng warned that the Hanoi "hooligans," "puppet aggressor"[256]—or, privately, "dogs"—would soon give in to total Soviet authority.[257] China began referring with faithful regularity to Vietnam as an "Asian Cuba," first in newspapers in Hong Kong and later in Peking during Brzezinski's visit. The recent war in the Horn of Africa provided a precedent to convince Washington of Soviet expansionist ambitions, and the Chinese media warned that "tomorrow wars such as those in Angola and the Horn of Africa will occur in other areas of the world," encouraging Washington to engage in the Chinese struggle against the spreading of Soviet influence.[258] Deng stressed that he perceived Vietnam's influence in Southeast Asia as copying the disruptive role of the Cubans in Africa.

Peking's occasional nicknaming of the U.S. as a "paper tiger" for not challenging the Soviets pricked Brzezinski's pride. In a banquet speech during his visit to Peking, Brzezinski stated that the U.S. would "recognize—and share—China's resolve to resist the efforts of any nation which seeks to establish global [Soviet] regional [Vietnamese] hegemony."[259] "Only those aspiring to dominate others have any reason to fear the further development of American-Chinese relations," he added.[260] This speech, drafted by Oksenberg, who had once named Vietnam "a cesspool of civilization," reflected that the two men shared an anti–Soviet, and consequently anti–Vietnamese, worldview.[261]

Again, Peking's views coincided with those of Brzezinski, who, as early as January 1978, had already begun to see the Vietnamese-Cambodian conflict within the framework of Soviet expansionism.[262] When questioned during an interview in January 1978 on recent clashes between Vietnamese and Cambodian forces, Brzezinski answered: "I find it very interesting, primarily because it is the first case of a proxy war between China and the Soviet Union."[263] Moscow responded that Brzezinski wished to "see that Soviet-Chinese relations remain spoiled ... [and] to poison the international atmosphere."[264] But Brzezinski's appraisal of the situation had more to do with his own animosity towards Soviet goals and his ambition of normalizing with China, making rapprochement with Hanoi counterproductive in attaining his set goals. In early February, the Soviet press concluded that the "Vietnamese-Cambodian conflict suits the interests of the U.S. policy."[265] At the UN, Ha Van Lau charged that Brzezinski's statement showed that armed conflicts suited some U.S. circles more than peace.[266]

In fact, the NSC cared little about true Vietnamese regional aims and sought to take advantage of the situation. While disagreeing with Brzezinski's appraisal of the causes behind the Khmero-Vietnamese conflict, Oksenberg warned Brzezinski to be more discreet on the issue:

> [W]e gain little either in Peking or Moscow by characterizing it as a "proxy war." Our description marginally affects events. We want this conflict to fester. We create subtle pressures upon participants to settle if we prematurely reveal that we consider the developments as favorable to us.[267]

What mattered to the NSC was the fact that the conflict fit within the larger issue of opposing Moscow. Historians Lawrence Caldwell and Alexander Dallin's claim that Brzezinski's labeling of the Cambodian-Vietnamese conflict as a "proxy war" was one example of his "engrained reluctance ... to acknowledge diversity among communists and their clients" thereby urging him to "opt for a view that posits excessive neatness in hierarchical dependence" while failing to perceive the finer tones of motivations and ideologies behind the apparent spectrum, seems incomplete.[268]

The State Department's appraisal of the situation was far different from Brzezinski's, and based on a more regionalist approach than his and Oksenberg's globalist reading of local conflicts. In his testimony to Congress two months later, Holbrooke urged the rapid establishment of U.S.-Vietnamese relations, stressing that seeing the Vietnamese-Cambodian border war as a proxy war represented a "serious misinterpretation."[269] For Vance and Holbrooke, these border wars were to be perceived through the prism of individual power-craving states and diverging nationalist ideologies rather than through the all-too-schematic East-West conflict.

Neither NSC nor State Department appraisals were totally accurate, or entirely dismissible. While the State Department was correct in its understanding of the forces behind the Sino-Cambodian-Vietnamese dispute, it had been too much involved in short-term discourses on normalization with Hanoi and on human rights violations in Cambodia to perceive the more global dimensions of the conflict. Starting as a bilateral dispute between Vietnam and Cambodia, initiated by the Cambodians, China's fear that the dispute might be turning into a "proxy war" transformed the border conflict into a war of influence between Moscow and Peking. China stepped up its support for Cambodia against what it perceived as a Soviet ally. Hanoi, cornered between Phnom Penh and Peking, and encouraged by its own ambitions, turned towards Moscow for support, which happily accepted its role as a mentor. While both the NSC and the State Department based their policies on incomplete perspectives of the conflicts, Brzezinski's views would soon dominate the White House.

Focusing on the geopolitical aspects of the issue, Brzezinski saw the conflict as a confirmation of his anti–Soviet views and of the need to adopt a hard-line approach toward Moscow.[270] Siding with Peking seemed an accessible solution to countering Soviet influence, either directly or by opposing Vietnam, and recent American history in Vietnam had endowed the Americans with an uncommon predisposition to the latter. When Murray Hiebert, of the Indochina Project in Washington, suggested to Oksenberg that Washington could quiet the geopolitical conflict in Indochina by reducing the economic pressures that had propelled so many people into such a massive exodus, Oksenberg coldly replied: "The Vietnamese are stewing in their own juice and I can't think of a more deserving people."[271]

Following Brzezinski's return from Peking, the NSC and the State Department formulated two different foreign policy programs on normalization with Vietnam and China. Peking had warned against American plans to recognize Vietnam, as Oksenberg recalled:

> We knew that the Chinese had obviously soured on the Vietnamese but it was much worse than we had thought. Earlier we had told them that we were thinking of normalizing relations with Vietnam and they had said, essentially, it was our business. This time they were vehement against the Vietnamese and normalization.[272]

Brzezinski would therefore advocate normalization with China only, rejecting Hanoi as an irritant for Peking that would uselessly jeopardize Sino-American talks: "I ... repeatedly mentioned to the president that such an action would be interpreted by the Chinese as a 'pro–Soviet, anti–China move.'"[273]

Meanwhile, Vance and Holbrooke, fearing the national security adviser's growing anti–Soviet line would affect Soviet-American relations and indeed push Vietnam toward Moscow, urged normalization with both Vietnam and China, which they also considered an "essential objective" to U.S. foreign policy albeit for different ideological and geopolitical reasons.[274] Brzezinski recalled:

> For reasons which I could never quite understand from a policy standpoint, but which perhaps may be better explained by the psychologically searing impact of the Vietnamese war tragedy, both Vance and, even more, Holbrooke seemed determined at this time to initiate a diplomatic relationship with Vietnam. They did not propose a formal interagency Policy Review Memorandum, but simply preferred to keep the initiative in the State Department, with Vance communicating with the President on this subject primarily through evening notes.[275]

Such a strategy would later allow Brzezinski to dismiss normalization with Hanoi as a State Department rather than presidential objective, which consequently need not be pushed into policy.[276] Concurrently, starting in mid–1978, the China issue became an NSC issue, closely followed by Carter, and with his secret understanding that negotiating instructions sent to Woodcock in Peking be issued without State Department screening.[277] This strategy of secrecy, reminiscent of Kissinger-Nixon tactics, suggested that Carter increasingly sided with Brzezinski.[278] The two institutions spent the summer and fall competing for presidential approval for their opposing views.[279]

V

REVERSAL IN U.S. FOREIGN POLICY

Vietnam's American Card

As Vietnam's conflict with its neighbors heightened, Hanoi hastened its openings to both Moscow and Washington.

So Phim, one of the main actors of the Vietnamese planned coup against Pol Pot, had been executed by the Khmer Rouge during spring 1978, which forced Hanoi to reevaluate its plans during the Fifth Plenum of the VCP in mid-June. Now that the death of So Phim had considerably jeopardized the chances of a popular uprising from within Cambodia, Hanoi would have to rely on its own means and opted for direct military attack against Cambodia.[1] The remaining rebels in Cambodia would provide the Vietnamese with a semblance of legitimacy with which to establish a new Cambodian leadership, but the fighting would be performed mainly by Vietnamese troops.[2] The Plenum, having now formally decided to overthrow Pol Pot, ordered the beginning of a military build-up. By late June, Hanoi had intensified its military incursions into Cambodia, including several air raids over Cambodian territory. By July, all attempts to negotiate with Cambodia had been abandoned.[3]

This decision to opt for direct military intervention, taken by the Politburo and ratified by the National Assembly, pointed at the prevailing influence of Le Duc Tho.[4] Sources suggest that the decision had given rise to much controversy within the Vietnamese leadership, with a clashing of factions and ideologies. Shortly after the Plenum, *Nhan Dan* launched harsh criticism of certain members of the party, claiming that the party should "leave behind and discard weak elements incapable of enduring trials or bent on giving up or betraying the cause."[5]

Other issues could also account for growing Vietnamese uneasiness. During the Fifth Plenum, the Politburo, which, in January baptized Peking its "Number 3 enemy" behind the U.S. and Cambodia, decided to "clearly identify China as the main enemy of Vietnam."[6] Contrary to what Douglas Pike asserted in 1987, it seems today highly improbable that "the deterioration [in Sino-Vietnamese relations] could have been reversed" during the summer of 1978.[7] Rather, if a breaking point was never completely reached nor diplomatic relations broken, as had occurred between Cambodia and Vietnam in December 1977, it seemed more out of a concern for saving face in the eyes of international public opinion, and avoiding an act potentially proving one's guilt, than of lack of animosity.

The Plenum also provided for the increase of efforts to strengthen and make official Vietnamese economic and military ties with Moscow, including entering COMECON. It was also decided that Hanoi would multiply its efforts to reach normalization with Washington, a rapprochement that would become impossible once the invasion of Cambodia had started. Beyond the economic advantages—even without the granting of direct U.S. aid—siding with Washington would counterbalance Soviet influence on Hanoi, while allowing the manipulation of Sino-American antagonisms to extract maximum concessions from both sides. Rapprochement with the ASEAN countries would also be sought.[8]

On June 15, in a secret message to the Kremlin, Hanoi requested that a meeting be arranged urgently between Le Duan and Brezhnev over the following week.[9] No records exist of this meeting, but in the light of future events one may speculate that the two sides agreed on Vietnam's admission to COMECON. Hanoi also briefed Moscow on its decision to overthrow Pol Pot with its own military forces and seek Soviet support for its plans. Although Moscow criticized Chinese policies towards Vietnam, the Soviets were secretly pleased with Hanoi's conflicts with Cambodia and China, which drew the Vietnamese away from Peking and closer into the Soviet orbit—Vietnam's admission into COMECON being the first in a series of official diplomatic steps paving the path towards Moscow.[10]

It is possible that the idea of signing a treaty providing for mutual defense may have originated in Hanoi, but Moscow, considering the risks of war with China which Hanoi's military coup in Cambodia might involve, preferred a treaty of friendship and cooperation, minimizing the level of Soviet support in the Vietnamese offensive.[11] Or, it may have been Moscow that insisted on signing a treaty, which it had attempted to push on Vietnam for several years, as the price for support of Hanoi's military plans.[12] In any event, the treaty would be signed in November, after Hanoi's last attempts to obtain a rapprochement with Washington had failed. Hanoi had perhaps also requested military aid from Moscow which might explain the presence of Deputy Military Chief of Staff Van Tien Dung's presence during the meeting and later General Vo Nguyen Giap's secret flight to Moscow with a shopping list of weapons, and the delivery of large shipments of Soviet weapons in August.[13]

Meanwhile, Hanoi continued its two-sided diplomacy. On June 20, Vietnam announced that a group of twenty-five Vietnamese women and children holding American passports would soon be allowed to join their families in the United States. Hanoi had previously objected to this move, claiming that such contacts could only take place after normalization. But as difficulties grew in Hanoi's relationship with its neighbors, the Vietnamese understood the need to tone down their attitude toward Washington.[14]

A few days later, on June 27, Hanoi finally took up the American invitation, issued the previous summer but postponed due to the spying affair, to send a Vietnamese delegation of experts to visit Hawaii in July. The invitation had been extended so that Vietnamese officials could observe procedures for identifying human remains, which the Americans hoped would speed up the accounting of MIAs.[15]

At the same time, Hanoi engaged in a show of humanitarian concern designed to prove its guiltless intentions to Washington in the light of constant Chinese accusations as to Vietnamese persecutions of Hoas and human rights violations. In mid–June, despite the reclassification of China as its immediate enemy, Hanoi announced that it was launching an "orderly departure program" for Hoas wishing to return to their homeland, and highly publicized the event for broader international attention. But the operation was soon canceled as 30,000 Hoas flooded the Chinese embassy in Saigon for exit visas while others arrived in uncontrollable numbers.[16]

On June 29, Vietnam became the first country in Southeast Asia, and the second Asian country after Mongolia, to join COMECON.[17] Hanoi certainly intended this move to show that the Chinese role in aiding Vietnam, left vacant by Peking's withdrawal of most of its aid projects from Vietnam in May, had been replaced for the better by the Soviet group. Indirectly, it signaled to Washington that American indecisiveness might trigger Vietnam's more permanent tilting into friendship with Moscow. Making the message clearer to Washington, Thach claimed that "without the cutting off of [Chinese] aid, this would not have been necessary" and added that Vietnam's aim had solely been "to find assistance"—playing on the belief that U.S. "assistance" may still save Hanoi from an overwhelming Soviet embrace.[18] Despite the delight of Soviet delegates, most of the European members had not hoped for Vietnam's entry and feared that Vietnam, like Cuba or Mongolia, would absorb a large portion of Soviet funds.[19] By August, the group had agreed to help in ten of the eighty projects that China had abandoned.

On July 3, Peking announced the formal end of its last eight economic projects in Vietnam that ended Chinese aid to Vietnam after two decades and $10 to $18 billion in assistance.[20] Although, in 1973, Zhou Enlai had pledged to provide Hanoi with economic and military aid at the 1973 level for another five years, in 1975 China stopped offering non-refundable aid. Peking's last move, in July 1978, now canceled all its last projects in Vietnam.[21]

Vietnam was charged with having "created a foul atmosphere of vilifying and inciting antagonism against China," and the last Chinese technicians were called home. Vietnamese students were also expelled from Chinese universities.[22] Although this move was presented as a Chinese response to Hanoi's persecution of Hoas, its timing indicates that it responded instead to Vietnam's entry into COMECON. Vietnam was clearly aware of this fact.[23] "The only thing wrong," Deng Xiaoping explained to a group of visiting Thai journalists inquiring about the cooling of Chinese relations with Vietnam, "is that we have given Viet Nam too much," in a direct reference to apparent Vietnamese ungratefulness over Chinese support during the war.[24]

A Soviet commentator condemned Peking's move of July 3 as "downright blackmail."[25] *Nhan Dan* added that it had come as a direct consequence of Hanoi's refusal to curb its policies and ideologies to fit the Chinese model.[26] Starting in July 1978, Hanoi's media began an all-out attack against Peking, which would not cease until the late

1980s.[27] Both Hanoi and Peking would feed American beliefs with mutual accusations and toy with the Carter administration's deep feelings for human rights in adopting a rhetoric designed more to fit U.S. concerns than to reflect Hanoi and Peking's own humanitarian inclinations. While Hanoi pointed at Khmer Rouge genocides, Peking accused Vietnam of xenophobic violence.

On July 11, after seeing its economy in Yunnan Province deeply strained by the flows of refugees, Peking ordered the closing of its land border with Vietnam, alleging that Hanoi was sending spies and "other bad elements" to Chinese southern provinces.[28] Permission to enter Chinese territory would be granted only to refugees holding Chinese embassy certificates as well as exit visas issued by Hanoi. This move demonstrated Peking's lack of true concern for the well being of Hoas, and countered Hanoi's accusations that Peking was encouraging the exodus. Armed border incidents multiplied as illegal Hoas attempted to cross into China, often forced by Vietnamese troops made restless from the clogging of the region by Hoas trapped on their side of the border. Such clashes fed Peking's charges that Vietnam was violating its land borders.[29]

In September, a congressional report concluded that the issue of Hoas was no more than a "sideshow." "China is using the issue of the Chinese exodus from Vietnam, whatever its origins, as a means of discrediting Vietnam internationally and as a pretext for making clear moves in the direction of an open break."[30] Six months later the conclusions of the report eventually proved correct.

On July 5, after an independent American delegation had visited Vietnam and reported Vietnam's wish to normalize with Washington, Phan Hien traveled to Tokyo and repeated that Vietnam would not consider aid as a precondition to normalization.[31] "If the U.S. and Vietnam reach agreement as to the understanding that normalization will help secure peace and stability in Southeast Asia," he declared, "we will be able to settle the matter without attaching any pre-conditions."[32] Five days later he added that "a new, forward-looking attitude is being shown by the Vietnamese side."[33]

Rather than submitting a direct request for the resumption of bilateral meetings, Hanoi wished to verify that Washington, after Brzezinski's declarations in Peking, still favored normalization. Hien called on Washington to suggest when and where meetings could be held.[34] "[I]f [the Americans] come with something in their hands," Hien declared, "they will be more welcomed than if they come with empty hands ... Even if the U.S. Congress rejects the reconstruction aid we look forward to establishing full diplomatic relations."[35] Hien also expressed hopes that new developments come out of the MIA talks in Honolulu. He seemed eager to normalize and alluded to a "new phase" in Hanoi's political situation with its neighbors.[36] Hien had "meant what he said," reported the Soviet political counselor in Tokyo to U.S. embassy officers, which the East German ambassador to Japan later confirmed.[37] Although Japanese officials reported Hien's proposition to normalize without precondition, the U.S. press noted that the subject was not raised during Hien's final news conference. A State Department spokesman gave the obscure reply that Washington had not yet received official notification of Hanoi's change in stance, but claimed that the State Department remained willing to normalize without precondition at any time.[38]

Hien continued his tour of the Pacific. In Canberra, he twice called for the resumption of talks "at any time and in any place," in a direct reply to the State Department's previous announcement.[39] He again repeated the new Vietnamese position.[40] The Australian foreign affairs minister Andrew Peacock, in an interview with Nayan Chanda, recalled: "Before Hien arrived, I already had two, if not three, telephone conversations with Dick [Holbrooke] about Vietnam's new position. I called him again after our meeting. He was quite optimistic because they dropped the precondition."[41] Hien reiterated his offer four days later in New Zealand, stressing that if "no one raises preconditions and the two sides have good will, the problem can be solved."[42]

In mid–July, Frank Sieverts welcomed the Vietnamese delegation in Honolulu and the Vietnamese were brought to the U.S. Army's Central Identification Laboratory (CILHI).[43] Hanoi had planned the meeting to be more than technical, and the relative secrecy of the visit provided both sides with the opportune atmosphere in which concessions could be made. After visiting the laboratory, the group was brought to visit the Marine zoo.

Vu Hoang, the senior foreign ministry official heading the delegation took State Department official Frederick Brown aside and repeated that Hanoi had dropped its aid precondition and was eager to normalize with Washington "by Labor Day or at the latest Thanksgiving," even suggesting that the giant C-5A aircraft be used to transport what Washington would need to open an embassy in Hanoi "with a big commercial section. U.S. Navy Seabees would be welcome to oversee the construction."[44] This, undoubtedly, was a reference to Holbrooke's proposition, during the Paris talks in May 1977, that Washington was ready to exchange embassies with Hanoi.[45]

Vu Hoang proposed a scenario for the establishment of relations. Normalization would be announced and a date set for the exchange of embassies. Several trade agreements and scientific and technical exchange programs would be signed simultaneously and take effect after the opening of the embassies. As for economic aid, the issue would be shelved, at least for the present. A U.S. information memorandum reported that, in "tones that hinted of quiet desperation," Vu Hoang urged the Americans to accept this proposal, insisting that Hanoi had shown its flexibility and seriousness and that the commercial and technical agreements would allow it to save face despite its many concessions to Washington.

The U.S. side suggested that meetings be held during the UN session in September, to which the Vietnamese agreed, adding their wish for rapid progress.[46] Brown went over to a pay phone and immediately conveyed Vu Hoang's informal message to Holbrooke, who seemed very pleased.[47] The State Department, although cautious and aware that diplomatic winds turned rapidly in Vietnam, as it had experienced the previous year, was pleased with Hanoi's yielding to the U.S. position on aid.

Hanoi's choice to inform Washington of its shift in policy through informal communication channels had not obliged the Americans to give an official response, and as Washington refused immediate talks, Hanoi did not get a chance to put the proposition formally to the Americans. As a State Department spokesman pointed out during Hien's visit to Tokyo, Washington had not yet been officially informed that Hanoi was ready to normalize without aid and hinted that Washington would respond favorably to such a move.[48] "Vietnamese statements in this regard were somewhat ambiguous," explained Holbrooke almost a year later. "There were no official communications on the subject."[49]

However, the Vietnamese note, sent indirectly to Washington through the U.S. embassies in Japan and India in May, and requesting normalization without precondition, contradicts this claim. In fact, Holbrooke's statement supports the view of some U.S. observers that, in the summer of 1978, his attention had turned to attempting to woo the higher spheres of Washington, and particularly the NSC, which enjoyed greater leverage on the White House than the State Department. Following his personal ambitions, Holbrooke's statements show that he had increasingly begun to adopt positions that suited Brzezinski and Oksenberg, such as his position on China, and to demonstrate less interest for issues unilaterally supported by the State Department—mainly normalization with Vietnam.

In addition, although no documents are yet available to support this point, one may speculate that the State Department did not want to face another humiliation as had occurred the previous year, when, understanding through Woodcock that Vietnam had dropped the aid precondition, the White House had enthusiastically announced the opening of talks. The memory of the bogging down of the talks and of the ensuing severe congressional backlash against Vietnam and Carter's initiatives regarding this country were not going to be forgotten by the administration. The upcoming congressional elections increased the administration's need for caution in tackling this sensitive issue. As Stephen Barber, the American foreign policy specialist for the *Far Eastern Economic Review*, commented in fall 1978: "The reasons for dawdling over mending relations despite the Vietnamese overtures now appear to have more to do with priorities than concrete objections at this stage."[50]

But the Vietnamese also remembered the humiliation of the Paris talks when the aid that they believed had been promised by Woodcock was eventually denied to them. While they were now taking the first step to restore a dialogue with Washington, and waited for an American response so as not to undergo further humiliation, the State Department, for similar reasons, awaited a formal Vietnamese declaration.[51] In the words of a U.S. official, Washington appeared to be "hard of hearing."[52]

The State Department was losing precious time in its competition with Brzezinski. His influence on Carter was growing, and he now warned the President that "moving ahead on relations with Vietnam would only be an irritant to expanding our understanding with China."[53] In the State Department, Vance and Holbrooke favored parallel recognition of Peking and Hanoi to reduce Soviet influence in Vietnam and diminish the risk of military clashes in the region.[54] American-Vietnamese talks, recalled State Department official Frederick Brown, "became enmeshed in the bureaucratic infighting with the National Security Council staff."[55]

In Peking, Woodcock, who had once supported normalizing with Vietnam, followed Brzezinski's encouragement to woo the Chinese into rapid normalization. Now head of the new American liaison office in Peking, Woodcock held talks with the Chinese from July to December 1978, and proved a skilful diplomat. U.S. science adviser Frank Press's visit in July, followed by Energy Secretary James Schlesinger and Agriculture Secretary Bob Bergland, had reminded Washington of the important capacity for trade offered in China, and Peking was now discussing the purchase of a $30 million communications satellite system, supposedly aimed at developing Chinese domestic telephone and television services, and presumably, although it was denied, for defense command purposes. These U.S. gestures, opposing the recommendations of both PRM-24 and the State Department that Washington refrain from selling dual-use technology to China so as not to exacerbate Sino-Soviet tensions, suggested the growing influence of Brzezinski's views on Carter, at the expense of the State Department.[56]

Understanding the long-term implications of these visits, and especially Schlesinger's trip, Moscow warned:

> By kneeling before the neutron bomb idol put up by the Pentagon and by trying to set the Western apostles of the neutron bomb against the Soviet Union, the Maoists are once again exposing themselves as the enemies of peace and security of the people.[57]

James Schlesinger's visit to China coincided on July 15 with the sharpest attack against the Chinese yet published in *Nhan Dan*. Hanoi's Fifth Plenum decision to identify Peking as its utmost enemy was being put into practice, warning Washington and the international community against Peking. The article stated that although Pol Pot was the head of the "large-scale, systematic, ferocious, and barbaric genocide" in Cambodia, "the bigger criminals, the main culprits are the Chinese rulers who are running headlong down the road of expansionism, and are full of hegemonistic ambitions."[58]

The Chinese *People's Daily* replied, as an indirect warning to Washington against the dangers of normalizing with Hanoi, that Vietnam's victory against the U.S. and its capture of large amounts of U.S. weapons had "made the Vietnamese authorities' heads swell and their hands itch to get more." The article further warned that Hanoi sought to "subdue and gobble up Kampuchea by force" in its "dream of rigging up an Indochina Federation." Accusations against Vietnamese ambitions to create an "Indochina Federation" had become a recurrent theme in the chorus of Chinese newspapers and Cambodian speeches.[59]

Hanoi requested another Paris meeting in August but Washington rejected the proposal.[60] Holbrooke later explained that Washington could not have accepted Hanoi's offer of a publicized meeting in the light of the growing conflict between China and Vietnam, which would have put the administration in an ambiguous position. Instead, Holbrooke reiterated the offer to hold quieter talks when Vietnamese officials visited New York in September for the UN General Assembly.[61] The State Department certainly preferred the safety of unpublicized meetings and understood that it should not repeat the mistake made during the 1977 Paris talks. Vance and Holbrooke knew that the repetition of a similar mistake would irritate Congress and provide Brzezinski with the leverage he sought to shut down talks and shelve normalization. Hanoi should first be tested privately and an understanding secured secretly before Washington could risk going public.[62] State Department hesitations and the postponing of direct contact would, however, benefit Brzezinski's own initiatives in China, at the expense of Vietnam.

One may notice the striking parallel between this episode and the failed "Pennsylvania" peace initiatives in 1967 as recounted by McNamara. While both parties had been willing to negotiate, the peace initiatives had collapsed over mutual misreading of bilateral signs. Washington, recalls McNamara, "was sloppy and disorganized, but Hanoi was defensive and rigid"—characteristics which still applied more than a decade later. The missed opportunity of 1967 was due to a "lack of secret, high-level channel of communication ... with sustained face-to-face discussions." He recalled:

[W]hat was really lacking was the kind of nuanced understanding of the adversary that can occur only through repeated, direct contacts.... We didn't talk to each other directly; we were misinformed in basic ways about each other; we relied much too heavily on intermediaries and hit-or-miss contacts between lower-level officials to represent each leadership.[63]

The "mistakes" of war also applied to peace. By relying only on informal communications, third party contacts and discussions with lower-rank officials, Hanoi was giving Washington a chance to gain time before answering the Vietnamese overtures, allowing Brzezinski to develop his own efforts vis-à-vis China.[64]

In the light of Peking's incessant accusations, Washington investigated Chinese claims that Cam Ranh Bay had been handed to the Soviets. In July, Holbrooke requested a CIA report on Soviet military activities in Vietnam. When he received the conclusion that no Soviet presence had been detected in Vietnam, the Department of State notified Hanoi, through the Australian government, that Washington accepted its statement that no military bases had been leased to Moscow. Gareth Porter reported that this greatly pleased Hanoi, which saw this acknowledgement as a positive step toward normalization, and as a victory over Chinese hostility and competition to woo Washington.[65]

While armed clashes and mutual accusations multiplied in the Indochinese region, Washington was still struggling to define the position it should adopt regarding the unfolding conflict and its stance toward Hanoi. In late July, Senator Kennedy announced that a five-member American delegation, sponsored by the Red Cross and the UN, would be dispatched the following month to arrange for the reunion of families with the persons Hanoi had agreed to release in June.[66] In setting the tone for the encounter with this delegation, VCP secretary Xuan Thuy announced, on July 30, that Hanoi would welcome normalization despite the fact that Washington had not yet agreed to provide aid.[67] Although he referred to American responsibility to provide aid, he neither quoted Article 21 nor linked the issue to normalization. The secretary referred to the Vietnamese visit to Honolulu as proof of Hanoi's seriousness and hinted that Washington should reciprocate.[68]

When the delegation met with Pham Van Dong in Hanoi on July 31, he confirmed that Vietnam wanted "not only a reconciliation" with Washington but normalization and "indeed friendship."[69] "We received the clear impression," remarked a delegation member, "that there has been a substantial change of policy in Hanoi on the subject of relations with Washington."[70] Hanoi reiterated its new position, suggesting that Washington's lifting of the trade embargo would be enough of an indication of U.S. willingness to normalize. This suggestion of "reciprocity" indicated that Hanoi wished to soften its stance without altogether appearing to sell off its own interests. It was well aware that the embargo presented less emotional impetus than aid and could more easily be managed through Congress.[71] The Vietnamese repeated this new stance several times over the delegation's stay.

Hanoi also expressed readiness to speed up the reunion of American-Vietnamese families, promised its "full cooperation" in attempting to solve other humanitarian issues inherited from the war, and reiterated its pledge that no conditions would be imposed.[72] Foreign ministry official in charge of MIAs Vu Hoang hinted that similar moves could be repeated in the future, nevertheless stressing that difficulties might arise in attempting to unite some families, as relatives could not always be located.[73] By mid–August some twenty-nine people had joined their families in the U.S., including the last known American citizens left behind in April 1975, and pictures of these emotional reunions flooded the U.S. press.[74]

Impressed by Hanoi's efforts, Kennedy reported that not only had Vietnam released "the original list of persons we had requested, but also additional family members"—a move which "clearly demonstrates that the government of Vietnam is anxious to work for a reconciliation between our two nations."[75] This move, commented Kennedy, had been "an extraordinary act of human rights" and there "is every indication that they will continue this process."[76] What Kennedy termed humanitarianism appeared, in hindsight, more Hanoi's attempt to shift U.S. opinion toward favoring normalization.

To temper Kennedy's argument and undermine his enthusiasm, Sieverts emphasized that, despite the success of the Kennedy mission, there were still about 300 relatives of U.S. citizens held in Vietnam, and that a further 5,000 relatives of Vietnamese refugees also wished to join their families in the U.S.[77] Again, it seemed that the State Department remained hesitant and evaded having to reply to Hanoi while simultaneously assuring U.S. public opinion that Washington remained firm in dealing with Vietnam—an important message only three months before congressional elections.[78] Instead, the State Department chose to test the new Vietnamese stance through informal channels, keeping to the unofficial level which Hanoi used to communicate its new position to Washington, and cooperating with Democratic congressmen as it would with Montgomery a few weeks later.

Kennedy's emphasis on Hanoi's concern for human rights appeared as a direct response to a report entitled "Repression in Vietnam," issued a few days earlier by the American Conservative Union's Education and Research Institute, which had criticized Hanoi's disregard for human rights.[79] Rumors had developed in the U.S., accusing Hanoi of detaining POWs. On August 9, in a letter to Sieverts, Vu Hoang refuted these accusations and repeated that all POWs had been released.[80]

Kennedy brought home Hanoi's message.[81] His report to the Senate Judiciary Committee, two weeks later, called for normalization, the granting of aid according to "the humanitarian traditions of our country" and the lifting of the embargo. Moreover, it clearly stated that the Vietnamese had "now given every indication that they are prepared to immediately establish diplomatic relations ... and to resolve all outstanding issues between our two countries through that diplomatic process—with no preconditions mentioned."[82] His report stressed that:

> Indeed, we have arrived to a historic decision point in our foreign policy ... where we now have an opportunity to do through peaceful means what we sought to do so long through war: to protect U.S. national interests in Southeast Asia by assuring Vietnam's independence from the domination of an outside power [the Soviet Union].[83]

Archbishop Philip Hannan added that Vietnam would accept assistance in food and medicine from official or private sources, to quench its growing thirst for foreign support against expanding economic, social and political difficulties.[84] The ball now lay in the administration's court.

Meanwhile the NSC and the State Department continued to draft their policy programs. On August 2, interviewed by a journalist, Oksenberg "sought to guide him away" from the issue of Vietnam, declaring that although Washington was aware of recent Vietnamese statements, he "did not foresee any immediate developments."[85] The NSC had its attention on other concerns.

On August 4, Vance provided a more positive appraisal of the situation and again repeated Washington's position that it had not yet received any formal communication from Hanoi—a statement intended as a request for Hanoi to make the first official move. But Vietnam considered that it had done enough to woo Washington and would not condescend to repeating its offer in a more articulate form. The next day, questioned on Vance's declaration, Ngo Dien refrained from condemning American political deafness and called on Washington to show goodwill.[86]

On August 10, following Kennedy's return to Washington, Holbrooke again commented that the State Department had not been "officially informed" of Hanoi's shift in attitude. "We are attentively following the situation," he explained. "We hope to resume talks with Hanoi by the end of this year although no date and time have been set."[87] Facing Congress, however, Holbrooke remained quiet on the issue, using the excuse that "time [would] not permit" him to discuss the subject of Vietnam, safely refraining from taking chances with congressional sensitivity. He added that "we have made a reasonable offer [in 1977] to establish diplomatic relations and to lift the trade embargo."[88] His discretion suggested that the administration certainly wished to remain cautious on the issue so as not to stir opposition shortly before congressional elections, but also hinted that his attention had steered away from Vietnam.

Meanwhile, although it officially denied contact with Hanoi to avoid awakening Republican opposition in Congress and perhaps also the sabotaging of its initiatives by the pro–China members of the NSC, the State Department was secretly working toward the resumption of bilateral talks. A few days before the departure of the Kennedy delegation in early August, during a meeting between congressional leaders and a delegation of foreign ministers from the ASEAN countries, the administration expressed its interest in "informal" talks with Hanoi.[89] The *Far Eastern Economic Review*, impressed by Hanoi's efforts regarding MIAs, confirmed that Washington had agreed to the resumption of talks in Paris in September, but had insisted that no ambassadors would be exchanged before spring 1979. However, the administration was considering the lifting of the embargo.[90]

Intriguingly, no other source corroborates this point. The September talks in Paris would never be held but would instead be replaced by secret talks in New York during the next UN General Assembly session that provided a more discreet medium than highly publicized negotiations in France. While no primary sources shed light on this point, one may suggest that plans to resume talks with the Vietnamese encountered opposition within the administration—either from Brzezinski, who later prided himself in having shut down the September talks with Hanoi, or from the executive's fear that the public re-emergence of normalization would jeopardize Democratic chances in the congressional elections. In addition, the State Department certainly doubted Vietnamese sincerity in the light of the rumors of an upcoming Vietnamese attack on Cambodia, and the ongoing plight of refugees, and delayed talks accordingly. The State Department, therefore, chose to continue discreet contacts through several Democratic congressmen, as it had through Kennedy.

A fortnight later, a congressional delegation, largely staffed by Democrats and headed by Montgomery, visited Vietnam to further the investigation on MIAs that the Montgomery Committee had begun under Ford. But this eight-member delegation was also to start informal discussions with Hanoi.[91] The presence of seven Democrats and only one Republican, representative Henson W. Moore (Republican, Louisiana), suggested that the delegation may also have been intended to demonstrate the Democratic party's continued concern for MIAs, to mobilize public and electoral support. Simultaneously, on August 18, Carter signed a resolution designating July 18, 1979, as National POW-MIA Day, signaling to Hanoi but more importantly to U.S. public opinion that accounting for MIAs remained a priority.[92]

Montgomery had been planning this visit for nearly five months with the help of the State Department. He had first expressed his interest in visiting Vietnam on April 28, in a personal correspondence with Phan Hien.[93] This initiative fitted nicely within the Vietnamese decision to improve relations with Washington in its new quest for international support. Unsurprisingly, Hien accepted the initiative on May 25, immediately after So Phim's death and at a time when the VCP was beginning to consider a Vietnamese invasion of Cambodia. He informed Montgomery that Hanoi welcomed such contacts that would "contribute to our mutual understanding" and "be beneficial to the process of normalization."[94]

Montgomery had requested that State Department and White House officials join the delegation and make his trip an "historic" visit, as he had personally assured Hien.[95] The State Department agreed to send two escort officers to accompany the congressional delegation.[96] Vance himself participated in the organization of the trip, certainly hoping that such congressional visits would place Congress in a more favorable mood for the resumption of ties than it had been the previous year.[97] Kennedy's earlier experience had stirred congressional interest in State Department initiatives that opened up new possibilities for bilateral contacts. Cooperation with Congress would also prove to Capitol Hill that the administration was not acting behind congressional backs, while congressional support would mean that the State Department had won one lap in the race against the NSC.

Montgomery also telephoned the NSC to request the appointment of an officer to join the delegation, but the agency was unenthusiastic.[98] When asked to accompany the delegation, Assistant to the President Hamilton Jordan, who shared much of Brzezinski's thoughts, declined the invitation.[99] The NSC did not share the congressman's concern for Vietnam: "No need to encourage him [Montgomery], I should think," Oksenberg wrote to Brzezinski in June, at a time when NSC attention had begun to focus almost entirely on Peking.[100] In fact, it appeared that it was Brzezinski who had urged Jordan to reject the offer, explaining that he thought "this is the right level of representation. Anything higher or White House representation would convey the wrong signals"—to Hanoi and to U.S. opinion.[101] Neither the White House nor the NSC would be represented, hinting at the growing influence of the NSC on the executive branch and the isolation of the State Department.

The delegation arrived in Ho Chi Minh City to a warm welcome. The Vietnamese acceptance to welcome Americans to South Vietnam for the first time since April 1975 was a highly symbolic move and a testimony to Vietnamese willingness to set aside times of hostility to the benefit of peace-time diplomacy.[102] Tran Quang Co, the Vietnamese head of North American affairs of Hanoi's foreign ministry warmly greeted his guests and expressed his "hope that we can move to a new stage in relations."[103] Similarly, Pham Van Dong's pledge for "friendship" was reflected by his choice that one of the three members of the Vietnamese delegation should be National Assembly member Madame Ngo Ba Thanh, who had spent a year in prison under the former American-backed Saigon regime. Thus, her presence symbolized that Hanoi was willing to forget the past dispute between the two countries while at the same time provocatively highlighting the past sufferings of Vietnam during the American war.

Washington had insisted on "informal" meetings to test Hanoi on normalization, much as it had in early 1977 through the Woodcock mission. "We cannot make policy or negotiate" on normalization, Montgomery told Hien, "we will take back what we learn to the President and the Congress."[104] The Vietnamese repeated that Hanoi had shelved the aid precondition and urged normalization—preferably before the rice harvest in November, added Phan Hien.[105] As the Vietnamese invasion of Cambodia was planned to start following the rice harvest, Hien's insistence for normalization prior to the harvest suggests that Vietnam was well aware that Washington would no longer agree to normalize following Hanoi's move on Cambodia.

During the first meeting, Dong and Hien pledged that Vietnam would return eleven sets of remains, only eight of which had been identified, bringing to 38 the number of MIAs delivered to Washington since the end of the war.[106] Vu Hoang received from the U.S. delegation 20 files on 37 more MIA cases and promised Hanoi's help.[107] "I am confident," Dong told his guests, "that, provided we have good will, everything will be fine between us." The eleven sets of remains were handed over to the Americans the following weekend, along with an additional four sets provided by Vientiane—interestingly the first four MIAs which Laos had ever accounted for. The fifteen sets of remains were sent to Hawaii for further identification.[108]

Dong asserted to Representative Henson Moore (Republican, Louisiana) that a full-time committee had been appointed to search for MIA remains.[109] Hien also agreed to study Montgomery's request that MIA families be allowed to visit Hanoi and speak with MIA officials.[110] The release of a number of remains more generous than usual Vietnamese "signs of goodwill," Hanoi's efforts to obtain information on MIAs in Laos, and the contrast with its coldness in the 1977 Paris talks, indicated the extent of Hanoi's concern that normalization be concluded rapidly, and before Vietnam's attack on Cambodia. When Montgomery suggested that Hien visit Washington for talks, he accepted with great pleasure.[111]

When Montgomery returned to Washington his admiration for the Vietnamese was clear. He termed them a proud and independent nation and concluded that "[w]e have to look ahead. We can't look behind."[112] The congressman rejected the rumors that Hanoi was considering allowing the Soviets to establish military bases on its territory. Although the delegation was refused access to Cam Ranh Bay, he reported that reliable sources had informed them that the Soviets had never used the base. Montgomery also reiterated his certainty, first voiced in 1976, that no MIAs remained alive.[113] Representative George Danielson (Democrat, California) confirmed that the congressional group would recommend that all servicemen listed as MIAs be reclassified as killed, confirming the findings of both the Committee on Missing Persons in Southeast Asia and of the Woodcock mission.[114]

The delegation reported "dramatic and fundamental change" in Hanoi's attitude, informing the administration that Vietnam had shelved the aid promised by Nixon and was ready to normalize without precondition.[115] "[The Vietnamese] are anxious to resume negotiations," remarked Representative John P. Murtha (Democrat, Pennsylvania), because "they are afraid of the Chinese."[116] "They want to normalize relations so badly, they can taste it," he commented, pointing at Hanoi's growing feud with China and Cambodia.[117] He even enthusiastically commented that the report was the "piece of paper" that was required for Washington to acknowledge Hanoi's new position.[118] The report indeed urged normalization and the simultaneous lifting of the embargo.[119] Clearly, Hanoi also considered the Montgomery visit a success and brought several visiting U.S. humanitarian delegations to visit the building in Hanoi where the United States would open its embassy after normalization.[120]

Representative Moore—the only Republican of the delegation—filed a "minority report" which greeted Hanoi's new position, albeit with less enthusiasm than the Democrats. Given the recent evidence of clashes on the Cambodian-Vietnamese border, he explained during a hearing in September, Washington should make sure "that we are not giving legitimacy to a carefully clocked plan of theirs to extend their influence ... I am not so terribly sure at this point we ought to run and embrace whatever that [Vietnamese plan] might be." Relations, he continued, should start "at a low level," perhaps by the lifting of the trade embargo, "and eventually work up to full relations." On aid, he explained that the Vietnamese "are looking for trade, they are looking for aid, but they are smart enough not to say that." Trade and humanitarian aid, they knew, would come as a logical step following normalization.[121] Moore's appraisal, both on Vietnamese ambitions and regarding the aid issue, was by far the most accurate.

In explaining the delay in Washington's response to Vietnam during a hearing with the House Subcommittee on Asian and Pacific Affairs on June 13, 1979, Holbrooke stated that Montgomery's delegation was the first that "was able to elicit a direct statement that the Vietnamese were no longer demanding an advance commitment on aid."[122] While there seem to have been no direct and official contacts from Hanoi to Washington, Vietnam had repeatedly announced its new position to foreign diplomats and visiting U.S. delegations.

Holbrooke's assertions seem highly dubious as the record shows that responsibility for the slowing of the negotiation process lay mainly with Washington. The administration, still weighing the State Department's program against Brzezinski's seems to have favored caution during the congressional elections. The bureaucratic slowness of the State Department, growing competition between State and NSC recommendations, and uncertainties over the often-fluctuating Vietnamese positions and short-term ambitions in Indochina, may also have contributed to U.S. hesitations. Ironically, Washington had been last to recognize Hanoi's policy shift, behind France and China, both of which already openly reported on the new Vietnamese stance. Even Cambodia, understanding the underlying reasons behind Vietnam's efforts, reported Hanoi's "abject" "kowtowing" and "mendicancy" in "selling out the national honor ... to kneel down and lick the feet of U.S. imperialism."[123]

In August, Peking attempted to counter growing Soviet pressure in Asia through a Sino-Japanese treaty, whose signing had been encouraged by Brzezinski during his improvised visit to Tokyo on his return from Peking in May.[124] In the words of the Soviet international propaganda journal *New Times*, the United States had served as a "catalyst" in the establishment of the new Sino-Japanese relationship, which indeed it had.[125]

The treaty included an anti-hegemony clause—the Chinese catchword for Moscow—directed against the Soviets and to which the Japanese, up to then, had objected. But following Brzezinski's improvised visit to Japan, Peking had dropped its insistence that a treaty with Japan condemn "hegemony" on a general basis and had yielded to Tokyo's request that the treaty not be directed at "any third nation"—an important concession for Peking, which signaled its growing distress and urgency.[126] The agreement would create a Sino-Japanese-American resistance front against Soviet influence, and prove to be a first sign of U.S. alignment on Chinese anti–Soviet policies. The *People's Daily* in China proclaimed that the treaty was "a thorn in the flesh for the Soviet Union ... [which] flies into rage at the very word 'anti-hegemonism,' fully revealing its rage at the very word 'anti-hegemonism,' fully revealing its sordid features."[127]

In a cycle of mutual paranoia, the signing of the Sino-Japanese treaty in turn reinforced Vietnamese fears of China. Shortly after its signing, an unusually high-level team of Vietnamese officials, headed by Le Duan and Pham Van Dong, departed for Moscow to assess the impact of this new alliance on the geopolitical situation in Asia.[128]

At the same time, Cambodian-Vietnamese border clashes escalated during Cambodian deputy prime minister for national defense Son Sen's visit to Peking.[129] Understanding that being officially associated with such an embarrassing ally would be counterproductive in wooing Washington or ASEAN, Peking had refrained from openly voicing any commitment to Cambodia, and stressed to Pol Pot that although China would privately continue to support the KCP and increase military aid, it would not defend Cambodia militarily in the event of a Vietnamese attack.[130] Cambodia was repeatedly advised to opt for a guerrilla war, which Peking saw as a way of securing its position.[131] Peking-based observers repeatedly stressed that China would not prevent the fall of Phnom Penh.[132]

The Chinese leadership had ruled out a direct siding with the Pol Pot regime. Instead, however, Peking had come to consider the possibility, as early as July 1978, of teaching a "lesson" to Vietnam in the event it should attack Cambodia—a concept initially suggested by Deng and later agreed upon by the CCP.[133] By then, Hanoi was still five months away from its military coup in Cambodia and the plan for a Chinese military gesture could be seen more as a punishment for Hanoi's blatant disregard for Chinese warnings than as a true concern for Cambodian welfare. More importantly, it would show Moscow that Asia was not a Soviet playground.

But the Sino-Vietnamese conflict cannot be explained only as a bilateral dispute between Hanoi and Peking and a Chinese fear of the Soviet proxy of Vietnam. In fact, the record shows that Peking never separated the issue of a possible Chinese attack against Vietnam from its prospects of normalizing with Washington. A careful study of the sequence of dates for all important Chinese decisions on its invasion of Vietnam in 1979 reveals that Chinese plans were made on a step-by-step basis each time progress was recorded on Sino-American normalization. Rapprochement with Washington would secure the Chinese position in the international arena and ensure reliable diplomatic backing for the Chinese move. Therefore, Peking certainly viewed Sino-American normalization not as Washington's "China Card" on the Soviet Union along Brzezinski's formula, but as China's "American Card" on the USSR and insurance for war against Vietnam.

While a Vietnamese attack on Cambodia was scarcely a respectable reason for a Chinese intervention in Vietnam, Peking opted for a more distinguished excuse to justify an attack. R.S. Ross argues that Peking, playing on Cambodian accusations of Vietnamese border violations, initiated border clashes along the Sino-Vietnamese frontier, first to divert Vietnamese attention from Cambodia and later to justify the need to "punish" Vietnam for violating Chinese territorial integrity.[134] In fact, Chinese troops had been held in combat readiness along the Sino-Vietnamese border since May 1978.[135] While Cambodia used its own border dispute with Hanoi to justify military incursions on Vietnamese territory, Peking exacerbated its border dispute with Hanoi in 1978, increasing the pressure as the Cambodian-Vietnamese conflict escalated. Cambodia, the initiator of the third Indochina conflict, had become a pretext for the eruption of a broader war of interests.[136]

On August 25, as the Montgomery delegation was returning to Washington, serious border clashes were reported at "Friendship Gate," along the Sino-Vietnamese border.[137] On August 31, Hanoi's foreign ministry accused Peking of preparing an attack against Vietnam.[138] Already in February, following two Sino-Vietnamese border clashes, Vietnamese troops had been instructed to prepare for a possible Chinese attack.[139] While the issue had remained silent since 1974, the Chinese press began reporting that 2,000 incidents had taken place along its border with Vietnam since 1975.[140]

As discussed earlier, China had demonstrated its uneasiness with the emergence of a stronger Vietnam, at the war's end, by re-emphasizing the historical border disputes which had existed since antiquity, when China—after dominating Vietnam for nearly a thousand years, since the tenth century—had annexed large bands of Vietnamese land and Vietnam's South China Sea islands.[141] At first, the Sino-Vietnamese dispute, which would eventually be fuelled by both sides, seemed little more than an attempt by Peking to intimidate Vietnam and remind Hanoi, like an unruly child whose growing strength gave cause for concern, that Chinese authority prevailed in the region.

But as China's fear of Vietnam grew and the Cambodian-Vietnamese bickering had grown to the level of border war, the Chinese leadership saw in its own border dispute with Vietnam the means of more aggressive designs. While the Khmer Rouge used their own border dispute with Hanoi to justify military incursions into Vietnamese territory until Vietnam's violent backlash in late 1978 provided a permanent solution to the issue, Peking would exacerbate its own border dispute with Hanoi in 1978, increasing the pressure as the Cambodian-Vietnamese conflict gained momentum. This strategy would later allow Peking to justify its "punishment" of Hanoi, not as a response to Vietnam's invasion of Cambodia, which would have repelled Chinese chances of obtaining international support, but as a "punishment" for Vietnamese violations of Chinese territorial integrity. At the end of August, Moscow began to equip Vietnamese bases along the Sino-Vietnamese border with offensive missiles pointed towards China while simultaneously launching a hasty and massive airlift of military materials.[142]

Washington remained divided and confused in its appraisal of the Indochina situation. While the NSC ignored Hanoi and raced towards a breakthrough with Peking, the State Department worked towards normalization with Hanoi. The congressional position regarding Vietnam had also changed. Having furiously tied the administration's hands in 1977, Congress seemed more favorable to normalization, especially now that Hanoi had dropped the original reason for congressional fury—Nixon's promise of aid.

At the end of August, a bipartisan group of congressmen named the members of Congress for Peace through Law and numbering 175 Senate and House members, issued a report calling on Washington to improve relations with Vietnam and warning against a too hasty rapprochement with Peking. The report stressed that:

> The unfortunate irony may be that the very Soviet influence which the "China Card" global strategy is designed to ward off will be increased in Southeast Asia by a short-sighted play of the card, vis-à-vis our relations with Vietnam.... Vietnam is almost certain to appeal to the Soviet Union for greater support in order to neutralize the increased Chinese pressure.

Failure to halt this evolution would create a new and dangerous Cold War in Asia.[143] Some representatives believed that mounting economic and political tensions meant that Vietnam was increasingly in need of normalizing with Washington, and cleansing its image in the eyes of its neighbors.[144]

This report, advising against Brzezinski's "China Card" program to the benefit of the State Department's softer policies, illustrates the extent to which Congress and the State Department misunderstood the forces at play in Southeast Asia. It suggests that Congress wrongly believed in Vietnam's passive bowing to Soviet authority, whereas the record shows that Hanoi had deliberately chosen to side with Moscow not only to resist Chinese hostility but mainly to fulfill its political ambitions in the region.

Furthermore, the authors of the report believed that improving bilateral relations would draw Hanoi away from the Soviets and alleviate tensions between Vietnam, Cambodia, China and, indirectly, the ASEAN countries. Hanoi, however, did not wish to be "rescued" from the Soviet embrace but hoped to secure normalization with Washington for its own domestic agenda, before the invasion of Cambodia made this move impossible.

While the report stressed that Washington could be the active force in defusing hostility in Southeast Asia, it seemed that both China and Vietnam considered Washington a passive element in the dispute and wished to play the "American Card" against each other. The report's conclusion that the American playing of the "China Card" would entail a Cold War confrontation in the region, eventually proved correct as the outbreak of the Third Indochina War in late 1978 would show.

Washington, unsure of the situation in Indochina and haunted by its past experience in the region, refrained from taking any concrete steps toward solving the problem of human rights violations in Cambodia over the summer. However, it would support efforts by the UNHCR to investigate Cambodian human right violations in 1979, although the UN agency too seemed hesitant and postponed action, granting Cambodia the benefit of the doubt and a delay to explain the situation.[145]

In Washington, the issue was taken up only through individual efforts, mainly by Representative Stephen Solarz (Democrat, New York) and Senator George McGovern

(Democrat, South Dakota). McGovern, who had run against Nixon in 1972 as an antiwar Democratic presidential candidate, pronounced Cambodian massacres "a clear case of genocide" and felt that Hanoi, which held a "popularly supported regime," would be within its rights to intervene. McGovern even hinted at the potential need for armed intervention in Cambodia similar to that in the Middle East.[146] Pointing out that "the Nazis look very tame in comparison" he asked whether Washington should "sit on the sidelines and watch a population slaughtered or ... marshal military force and put an end to it?"[147] On August 26, he received an angry letter from Phnom Penh criticizing his "campaign of calumnies and disparagements."[148]

The executive branch's silence was due to its fear that accusations against Cambodia would jeopardize its relations with China. In July, Carter received a letter from seventeen congressmen requesting him to take action in promoting the respect for human rights in Cambodia, primarily by demanding significant Chinese diplomatic intervention in Phnom Penh as a precondition to Sino-American normalization.[149] After pondering the situation for more than a month, Carter answered that such a precondition would be a "mistake." However, he pledged continued U.S. condemnation of human rights violations in Cambodia.[150] Unfortunately, no Cambodian lobby group existed in the United States at that time that could have pressed the White House for direct action in Indochina. Not only had lobbies disappeared following the withdrawal of U.S. forces from Indochina in 1973, but the United States, whether through public opinion, Congress or the executive, was little inclined to turn its attention once again to the area. Only in mid–1979 would the issue be adopted by a Jewish lobby, drawing an awkward parallel between the Jewish plight in the 1940s and that of the Cambodians in the late 1970s.[151]

A foreign service report in late August concluded that Vietnam indeed sought to create an "Indochina Federation" although it was in no hurry to launch such a campaign just yet.[152] Other warnings emanating from Southeast Asia, such as Filipino foreign minister Carlos Romulo's claim that "the precise relationship between the two conflicts [Vietnamese-Cambodian and Sino-Vietnamese] remains to be defined, but there is reason to believe that they are not necessarily separate," confirmed the executive's doubts.[153] By mid-summer, the most common reason Hoa refugees gave for their mass exodus was their fear of a possible Sino-Vietnamese warfare in which they would undoubtedly be caught.[154] "We need to know clearly and precisely just what the Vietnamese really want," concluded a State Department official following Montgomery's return to Washington, "and then take a long look at the situation."[155]

The Thach Delegation to New York

According to UNHCR figures, the number of refugees leaving Vietnam for other parts of Southeast and East Asia since January, around 75 percent of whom were Hoas, reached a total of nearly 40,000 by September. The State Department was increasingly concerned over reports claiming that as many as half of them died at sea.[156] The United States had accepted 172,000 Vietnamese refugees after the war and looked upon the exodus with growing impatience.[157] A report from the United Nations High Commissioner for Refugees, issued in early June, stated that more than a million people had fled the

Cambodian-Vietnamese border due to the escalation of military attacks.[158] Although the fleeing of Hoas was certainly the most publicized refugee movement of its time in Southeast Asia, other ethnic groups, such as Chinese residents in Cambodia, were also cause for concern but failed to benefit from as much attention from the West. While China publicized its indignation over the Hoa issue, it carefully suppressed all remarks about victims of the Khmer Rouge rule.

While endorsing the Chinese claim that Hanoi was urging Hoas to depart, the ASEAN countries had also begun blaming the United States for indirectly encouraging the refugees to leave Vietnam by painting an enticing image of what could be found in the capitalist world rather than in the poverty of South Vietnamese dilapidated cities. As a Muslim country, Malaysia had first agreed to abide by its religious tenets in accepting the early flow of refugees but, by the autumn of 1978, had found itself caught among religious principles, social difficulties and political realities that did not permit it to take in a greater number of refugees. After receiving 20,000 refugees, the greatest number in the ASEAN group, Malaysia had begun referring to them as "illegal immigrants" to justify its recent policy of turning ships of refugees away from its coast.[159]

Likewise, Singapore, where 75 percent of its population were of Chinese extraction, refused all refugees, claiming that its territory was too small to absorb such numbers of people. Hong Kong, which happened to be on one of the direct maritime routes of the refugees, was also crawling with Vietnamese refugees and had to refuse the landing of some ships. Meanwhile, China was sending its chief negotiator Chung Hsi-tung to and fro between Peking and Hanoi to discuss the Hoa issue.[160]

In an attempt to soothe the ASEAN countries' growing discontent at the sight of so many refugees disembarking on their beaches, and to repeat Hanoi's pledge of non-aggression, Hanoi had decided to adopt a friendly policy toward its ASEAN neighbors, probably to undermine rumors of Vietnamese expansionist ambitions. At a dinner he hosted in New York in spring during the UN Conference for Disarmament and Peace, Vietnamese foreign deputy Vo Dong Giang had proposed to the ASEAN diplomats the turning of Southeast Asia into a region of "peace, independence and neutrality."[161] Vo Dong Giang was re-invoking, with a slight twist in terminology, the seven-year-old ASEAN proposal that the area become a region of "peace, freedom and neutrality," which up to then had been criticized by the Vietnamese as an indirect maneuver from ASEAN to place Southeast Asia under camouflaged American control. Although the proposal was again repeated at the ASEAN annual meeting in Pattaya, the ASEAN countries found the Vietnamese term "independence" suspicious and perhaps rather offensive to the Chinese.[162] When at the end of July, Phan Hien visited Malaysia, where the initial concept of a region of "peace, freedom and neutrality" had originated, the ASEAN group was still reluctant to accept the proposition.[163]

As it faced the escalation of clashes on its borders, Hanoi was determined to find allies in the region, especially those who could induce Washington to engage in friendlier policies. During the summer, Vietnamese embassy officials were insistent that their Premier tour ASEAN countries in September. Dong's tour of the region would not only reinforce Hanoi's diplomatic push toward Washington with a simultaneous wooing of the ASEAN nations, many of which were U.S. allies, but also secure ASEAN's siding with Hanoi, or their neutrality, over the Sino-Vietnamese feud. Dong's visit would demonstrate Vietnamese goodwill to Washington prior to the resumption of negotiations, and to the ASEAN countries before Deng Xiaoping had had a chance to convince them to side with China during his own tour of the region in November. After shunning ASEAN and criticizing Chinese influence in these countries, Hanoi had understood that its interests lay in opening to these nations and now privately sought membership to the organization, hoping diplomatically to isolate Peking.[164] Hanoi had planned to complete the visit before the opening of the United Nations General Assembly when secret talks were to be held with the Americans in New York, perhaps to address the Americans with a complete assessment of the situation and of the Vietnamese position in Southeast Asia.[165]

On September 8, while Dong was wooing the ASEAN nations, Vietnamese forces delivered a massive retaliatory attack against the Khmer Rouge. These air strikes dealt a serious blow to Dong's credibility in promoting Hanoi's peace-loving policies. Although a joint communiqué was issued at the end of Dong's visit to Thailand, the other ASEAN countries received him with great cynicism and more out of diplomatic politeness than out of a genuine desire to host the Vietnamese.[166]

While Washington had first refused to respond to Vietnamese overtures, dismissing them as "unofficial," Washington now agreed to informal and unpublicized talks with the Vietnamese. The administration had insisted that talks should take place preferably before November 7, the polling day in the mid-term congressional elections, and had suggested the use of the UN building as a venue to disguise bilateral negotiations. In addition to the administration's fear that publicized meetings might undermine Democratic chances in the congressional elections, at the international level, this wish to avoid publicity reflected Washington's belief that American-Vietnamese normalization would irk Peking and jeopardize Sino-American normalization, as Brzezinski and Oksenberg repeatedly warned.[167] If indeed the NSC appraisal proved correct, the State Department did not want to give Brzezinski the upper hand by needlessly irritating Peking, which he might use to justify the shelving of American-Vietnamese normalization.

Peking, however, had never imposed this precondition in negotiating with Washington.[168] Although Deng had voiced his surprise, following the Paris talks, over the American effort to normalize with a nation that had defeated the United States in war, Carter recalls that: "[d]uring the early part of 1978, the Chinese sent word to me that they would welcome our moving toward Vietnam in order to moderate that country's policies and keep it out of the Soviet camp."[169] In fact, while the Chinese had encouraged American-Vietnamese normalization in 1977 thinking it would draw Hanoi away from Moscow, they had become more prudent and suspicious by the fall of 1978.[170] In Peking's view, American-Vietnamese normalization would ease Vietnamese economic pressure on Moscow and relieve the Soviets of a heavy weight.

Following a meeting between Vance and Japanese foreign minister Sunao Sonoda in September 1978, the Chinese inquired of the Japanese whether Washington would grant reconstruction aid to Vietnam. Although the minister had privately encouraged Vance to opt for rapprochement with Hanoi, he answered that his primary concern was to avoid Sino-Soviet war in that region.[171] By the end of September, Washington had concluded that Peking considered American-Vietnamese normalization—in Oksenberg's words—a "U.S. decision," although they warned that it would mainly benefit the Soviets.[172]

In Hanoi, the Vietnamese understood that Sino-American rapprochement would signal growing Chinese influence in Southeast Asia.[173] Clearly China and Vietnam both hoped that normalizing with Washington would help contain the threat posed by the other. While Peking hoped for normalization to contain the Soviet threat (and that of Vietnam in Indochina), Vietnam sought normalization to counter Sino-Cambodian pressure. As for the ASEAN countries, they feared both Vietnam and China's expansionist policies and seemed to judge normalization and U.S. aid to Vietnam as "necessary for the sake of peace," a sentiment similarly expressed by the foreign minister of Indonesia.[174]

In the United States, opinions were less clear-cut. On September 14, the members of Congress for Peace through Law again spoke out and read a report on U.S. policies towards Vietnam and China authored by representatives Jonathan Bingham, Paul McCloskey and Anthony Beilenson, three of the most productive speakers on Vietnam in the House of Representatives. The report spoke against the concept of playing the China Card and encouraged U.S. rapprochement with Hanoi to ensure the stability of the region. It stressed:

> The danger is that the United States will drift into a *de facto* alignment with China against Vietnam which would, in turn, force Vietnam into an exclusive alliance with the Soviet Union.... American-Vietnamese diplomatic relations and a Vietnam equidistant from the superpowers could be the keystone for a more peaceful and stable political order in a Southeast Asia where both Soviet and Chinese influence would be lessened and where the development of each nation could be determined by internal policies rather than external pressures. American influence in the region would increase.[175]

On the same day, probably fearing that the above report would encourage the executive branch to opt for normalization with Hanoi, several senators wrote to the president arguing that normalization would not halt Hanoi's claim to U.S. aid, agreeing with China that "[a]ssistance from the United States can only ease the burden now borne by the Soviets" which "does not appear to be in our national interest." The letter further stressed that the senators would oppose all aid to Vietnam "whether or not it is identified as 'war reparations.'" As for Hanoi's efforts on MIAs, "they reflect what ought to be the appropriate and routine response of civilized nations everywhere in dealing with humanitarian problems" and therefore need not be rewarded by economic aid.[176] Given the lack of uniformity of views around him, Carter simply ordered Brzezinski, in early September, to work towards a "simultaneous recognition" of both Peking and Hanoi.[177]

The administration had, however, slightly softened its position. The International Monetary Fund, funded 20 percent by the United States, had granted a $28 million loan to Hanoi in June, and in August Vietnam had received another $60 million from the World Bank for irrigation work, despite some grumbling in Congress.[178] By mid–1978 Vietnam now benefited from five loans from the World Bank, touching on industrial and energy projects, mining and railways worth a total of $160 million.[179] In early September, a trade council including private companies was set up between Washington and Hanoi to study possible trade cooperation.[180] But Carter remained prudent. "We're still moving ahead on Vietnam," explained a senior American official, "We're just not leaping forward.... [The Vietnamese] want us to jump into their arms, but we don't think that's justified.... We don't want to give the Chinese a veto, but we do want to go very carefully."[181]

Despite some overtures and easing of economic pressures, Carter refrained from giving up his bargaining cards. Consequently, on September 9, the president sent a memorandum to Vance and the secretary of commerce informing them that the embargo on Vietnam would be extended for a year, unless specific political changes occurred. Similarly, Vietnamese bank deposits in the U.S. would remain frozen.[182] Carter seemed no longer to be prepared to make unilateral concessions to Hanoi as he had in 1977 in allowing Vietnamese admission to the UN in the hope of a reciprocal friendly gesture from Vietnam.

That day, during his visit to Thailand, Dong formally invited the U.S. ambassador to Bangkok to a dinner and informed him that although Vietnam no longer insisted on aid as a precondition, it had not renounced the issue altogether but would solve the problem following normalization.[183] In an interview on September 10, when asked if Hanoi had indeed dropped its request for aid, Dong ignored the question and responded that "actions spoke louder than words."[184] The ambiguous Vietnamese declarations demonstrate Vietnam's difficulty in keeping to one position, perhaps due to the presence of competing factions within the VCP leadership, and may in part explain American hesitation over Hanoi's call for normalization.

However, Carter's attention soon shifted to Peking. A week before the September meetings were to be held, Egyptian president Anwar Sadat and Israeli premier Menachem Begin proposed to celebrate the triumph of the Camp David summit with a ceremony on Mount Sinai, where Moses had received the tablets of the Ten Commandments. Enthusiastic and God-loving Carter had replied that this would make wonderful Christmas television in the United States.[185] Carter started looking more actively into normalizing with China, which would make a perfect second Christmas gift to the American public.[186] A Harris poll had in fact indicated that 66 percent of Americans favored Sino-American normalization while only 25 percent opposed it.[187] The president intended SALT II, which Carter also hoped to complete before Christmas, to counterbalance the gesture toward China.[188]

In the meantime, Hanoi was continuing its double-play. In early September, before the opening of the New York talks, Le Duan confided to the Soviet ambassador in Hanoi that the VCP had decided to "solve fully" its problems with Cambodia by early 1979.[189] According to a Yugoslav diplomat, Hanoi had similarly informed the Yugoslavian government that Pol Pot's regime would need to be overthrown.[190] On September 21 and 22, while the Vietnamese delegation was preparing to meet Holbrooke, Tho met secretly with Cambodian insurgents in Vietnam and decided to launch the invasion in December.[191]

While Washington was delaying its response to the Vietnamese, the influence of the radicalist faction, led by Le Duan and Le Duc Tho, had grown in Hanoi. Washington now faced a harder line from Hanoi, which it perhaps might have avoided had it accepted Hanoi's offer of talks in Paris in early August. By the time Holbrooke and Nguyen Co Thach met at the UN American mission on September 22, after secret arrangements had been made to prevent the media from suspecting that talks were being resumed, Vietnam's position had changed. Thach reiterated Hanoi's previous insistence that aid, MIAs and normalization were interrelated. Irritated, Holbrooke produced a file containing a list of Hanoi's official and unofficial statements uttered since July 1978, that Hanoi sought unconditional normalization, but Thach would not drop the aid precondition. Holbrooke impatiently replied that since Hanoi's position on aid had not changed since 1977 there was little else to talk about. The Vietnamese requested a tea break.[192]

But when negotiations resumed, the Vietnamese had softened their stance. Thach understood that Hanoi was playing its last chance for normalization and possibly took it upon himself to deviate from his negotiating instructions and propose a compromise.[193] The Vietnamese acknowledged the U.S. position that linking MIAs, aid and normalization would not be accepted and inquired more broadly about U.S. aid, loan and credit policies. They also questioned Holbrooke about how rapidly normalization could be established and when the trade embargo could be lifted. Holbrooke refrained from providing direct answers to these questions, claiming that Washington would have to reflect on these issues. At the end of the meeting the Vietnamese acknowledged that the ball was now in their court.[194]

Thach proposed to arrange for a second session of talks at the Vietnamese mission to the United Nations and Holbrooke, certain that this meant Thach would officially drop the aid precondition during the next meeting, accepted with renewed hope. Thach may have suggested reconvening talks through this new meeting to gain time to request new instructions and convince Hanoi to accept a compromise on normalization. His inquiries on aid betrayed his understanding that, contrary to the opinion of the Vietnamese leadership, Hanoi needed normalization more than Washington, and that even if Vietnam dropped the aid precondition it would benefit from economic aid through the normal aid process.[195]

Holbrooke telephoned Oksenberg to report on his meeting with Thach, and invited the China expert to attend the upcoming talks. Holbrooke's "adrenalin was obviously flowing," noted Oksenberg. For Oksenberg's first meeting with a Vietnamese, Holbrooke offered his bureaucratic rival the chance to hear, in person, Hanoi's formal renunciation of aid and to witness the success of Holbrooke's efforts for rapprochement with Vietnam. Oksenberg reported to Brzezinski:

> I believe the Vietnamese are going to drop their demand for aid and we are going to be in the unpleasant position of having little bargaining room left. We may find ourselves, by pushing these negotiations forward, normalizing relations with Vietnam before we do so with China and complicating our normalization process with China immeasurably.

"[T]ake part," replied Brzezinski, "and monitor."[196] According to Oksenberg, Brzezinski had requested him to "keep an eye on Holbrooke."[197]

Talks resumed on September 27. But Thach had returned to his former cooler stance and the Vietnamese clung to the aid issue as they had during the first meeting. Holbrooke, disappointed and vexed that his plans had failed, especially in Oksenberg's presence, rose from his chair and announced that talks had "reached the end of the road."[198]

Whether Hanoi had intended to test the Americans in returning to a harder stance and retracting if Washington did not give in, or whether Thach unilaterally offered a compromise thinking that aid would follow normalization through normal processes, is not known.[199] But seeing that his counterpart was about to leave the negotiation table, Thach, suddenly shifting to a softer-line policy, proposed immediate normalization.[200]

Other issues, he claimed, could be solved "step by step."[201] "I'll tell you what you want to hear," Thach said. "We will defer other problems until later. Let's normalize our relations without preconditions" and, pointing to a typewriter, suggested that a memorandum be signed immediately.[202]

Thach's offer was a direct reference to Holbrooke's proposition during the Paris talks in 1977 that they should immediately and publicly announce normalization while the exact terms would be settled later, which was sure to please Holbrooke.[203] However, the assistant secretary of state declined the offer, probably preferring that such a step be made after the congressional elections, or once a move had been made on China. He warmly expressed his satisfaction over Thach's return to a more reasonable position and promised that he would urge Carter to formalize the understanding.[204] The two sides agreed to the appointment of a working group to draft a joint communiqué and to arrange for the visit of a Vietnamese delegation for the final signing of an agreement. Thach even proposed that the text of a joint communiqué he had written before the meeting be used—betraying that his initial return to imposing the aid precondition had merely been aimed at testing Washington.[205]

Thach announced to his U.S. counterparts that the former American consulate in Hanoi had been covered with a fresh coat of paint and was now ready to be returned to the Americans. Holbrooke replied that the former embassy of the Republic of South Vietnam in Washington was also ready for a new Vietnamese ambassador. As the conversation reached the point where the two sides were discussing members of the new ambassadorial staffs, the Americans were even offered a "Jerusalem formula" in which the United States would be granted permission to reopen their former embassy in Ho Chi Minh City instead of their former consulate in Hanoi that had not been touched since the days of French colonial rule.[206] Holbrooke instructed a working group to find the plans of the former consulate and a Vietnamese-speaking officer was scheduled to visit Hanoi in December. Oksenberg "was astonished to see the voluminous materials they had prepared dealing with practical aspects of normalization—the frozen assets question, the question of embassy location, communications—the whole works."[207] Even the National League of Families accepted the grounds for normalization and joined the effort, insisting that the new embassy, once open, should prioritize the search for MIAs.[208]

Holbrooke and Oakley stressed their "belief that the Vietnamese could and should be doing more to resolve the MIA question."[209] Thach obediently promised greater efforts on the issue.[210] The Vietnamese expressed their hope that the signing would be completed the first week of October, while Nguyen Duy Trinh was in New York—Thach himself would stay until October 20. However, Holbrooke declined to set a date and indicated that another meeting might be possible after the congressional elections of November 7. Finally, Holbrooke warned Thach that Vietnam's developing of relations with Moscow and its problems with Cambodia might "complicate the normalization process," and talks were adjourned.[211]

The Vietnamese diplomat seemed pleased with the outcome of the meeting. Reportedly, Thach had been "favorably impressed" with Holbrooke and normalization seemed close at hand.[212]

But the talks had shown that the American position on Vietnam had hardened since the initial 1977 talks. Congressional wrath over the release of the secret Nixon letter and congressional prohibition of both humanitarian and direct aid to Vietnam meant that normalization represented a far more complex and controversial task than Carter had originally expected when coming into office in 1977. Holbrooke explained:

> We have worked very hard to remove hostility without doing something that Congress would destroy us for—providing direct American aid. Vietnam has all the problems, and it is being driven toward Moscow. We've done everything we can to show that we are not hostile.[213]

Beyond purely seeking normalization with Washington, Hanoi may also have been using the talks with Washington to extract greater concessions from Moscow in view of the upcoming invasion of Cambodia. The following day, fearing that Vietnam might stray from Soviet influence, Moscow announced that it had reestablished a committee on aid to Vietnam, and issued a violent statement on Chinese diplomatic and military provocations against its Vietnamese protégé.[214]

Thach, visibly pleased with the negotiations, announced that the talks had been "very useful" and eagerly shared his enthusiasm with the U.S. media:

> We think that the first issue, which is normalization of relations, can be settled first. As for the second problem, we have willingness to help the M.I.A. families get information. We have been doing this but it is not a very easy job. After all, your country still has M.I.A. problems from the Second World War. We think that the aid problem can be settled in the long run, too. Even now we are benefiting from the good will of the American people for humanitarian purposes, and the United States government is willing to facilitate that relief.[215]

The Vietnamese "are panting to lock up the deal," Oksenberg reported to Brzezinski following the second meeting with Thach. "One could sense Vietnam's weakness during the discussions. Their economic difficulties, their conflict with Cambodia and their tensions with China place them in a very disadvantageous position."[216] "Hanoi's urge to normalize with the U.S.," confirmed an NSC report a few days later, "is only marginally based on a desire to gain advantage vis-à-vis Peking."[217] "But we should not be lulled into thinking that the Vietnamese harbor anything but hostile feelings toward us," continued Oksenberg a week later, sharing his antipathy toward the Vietnamese with Brzezinski. "Until yesterday's meeting, I never thought I would meet any people who would surpass the Chinese in the art of false flattery, but the Vietnamese make the Chinese look like pikers."

Remarking that Washington's Vietnam policy remained unofficial and had "been set through the Secretary's Evening Items and the President's marginalia," Oksenberg further recommended that Brzezinski "obtain from State an options paper on Vietnam policy which has been coordinated with DOD, CIA, and where pertinent, Treasury and Commerce."[218] Oksenberg was suggesting that the NSC contain State Department initiatives and control the issue by requesting a formal report on State Department intentions, recommendations and proposed timing for their normalization program. "The ball is now in our court to decide the pace of forward movement," he concluded.[219]

That evening, in a report to Carter on Holbrooke's talks with the Vietnamese, Vance recommended that, following congressional elections, Washington proceed towards normalization along the lines agreed with Thach. Reviewing Vance's report before its submission to Carter—as was customary on all reports reaching the president—Brzezinski added his own recommendation that no move be made before securing a deal with Peking.[220] The next day Brzezinski noted in his diary:

> I pointed out to the President that his comments on the evening notes from Cy [Vance] last night might imply that he is now giving the green light to the rapid establishment of diplomatic relations with Vietnam. This in my judgement could prejudice our efforts with the Chinese. The President, though somewhat reluctantly, wrote in the margins of the evening notes an additional sentence: "Please first give me the reactions of the Chinese," I hope this will slow things down somewhat.[221]

The negotiations on Vietnam had run against Brzezinski's China plans.[222] "I think Holbrooke went there [to the meetings with Thach] to suggest that they do that in order to facilitate normalization," he later confided to Chanda, proudly adding, "and I shot it down."[223] It appears, from sources within the White House, that Brzezinski indeed intervened to stall normalization, fearing it might upset Peking, and lobbied Carter into ordering the State Department to delay normalization, at least as long as was required to test Peking on the subject.[224]

A few days after the second meeting between Thach and Holbrooke, Vance received an angry warning from Chinese foreign minister Huang Hua underlining Peking's unhappiness at possible American-Vietnamese rapprochement.[225] The State Department was less inclined to yield to Chinese whims than the NSC and wished to counter the obstacle by normalizing first with Peking and then with Hanoi. Thus, Peking could not use the issue to delay its own rapprochement with Washington, and the State Department believed that once Sino-American normalization had taken place the Chinese would tolerate American-Vietnamese normalization.[226]

Meanwhile, Carter's attention was turning to Peking. On September 19, Carter met with Chinese delegates to discuss normalization and achieved a breakthrough on Taiwan.[227] By early October, as many as twenty different Chinese delegations were visiting the United States.[228] At a dinner on October 3, the Chinese, who had up to then repeatedly accused the American delegates of stubbornness for refusing to give up their relations with Taiwan—the only obstacle to normalization—finally accepted a new round of talks with Woodcock in Peking, and Brzezinski knew that an agreement would soon be reached.[229] The talks with the Chinese had been so strenuous that Oksenberg, Vance and Holbrooke had never tested Peking on the issue of simultaneous normalization with Vietnam. After the difficulties of reaching an agreement with the Chinese, the administration simply did not wish to raise the issue of Chinese consent or opposition to U.S.-Vietnamese normalization, which Washington feared Peking might turn into a precondition for Sino-American normalization.[230]

On October 11, seeing that talks with China were reaching a stalemate, Carter asked Woodcock and Brzezinski for a private meeting on China in the Oval Office. At Brzezinski's request Vance was not invited to join the discussions.[231] In his own account of this meeting, Brzezinski recalls that he had instructed Woodcock to bring up the issue of normalization with Hanoi during the meeting with the president. Therefore, when Carter asked his aides' view regarding normalization with Hanoi, both dismissed the issue as a question that would uselessly jeopardize negotiations with the Chinese. Consequently, Carter had replied that the U.S. "would not move on Vietnam."[232]

Woodcock, who had initially allowed the opening to Vietnam and favored American-

Vietnamese normalization, had now utterly reversed his position, preferring rapprochement with Peking and confining Vietnam to diplomatic isolation. At the time of his dealing with Vietnam in early 1977, Hanoi's tilt towards Moscow had been less flagrant and American interests in opening to Peking had not yet been enhanced by Brzezinski's visit to China. Recent months had brought about changes in the international diplomatic context that had reversed his appraisal of the utility of a rapprochement with Vietnam. Constant Chinese warnings that Vietnamese expansionism was carrying Soviet "hegemony" to Southeast Asia, combined with Brzezinski's anti–Soviet stand and ideological infatuation with Peking may have been sufficient to convince Woodcock of the diplomatic strategic superiority of opening solely to China. By fall 1978, Woodcock had already repeatedly and personally voiced his position to Carter.[233]

Consequently, during this meeting of October 11, Carter decided to concentrate his efforts on Peking. According to Oksenberg and Carter's accounts, the president shelved the issue of normalization with Hanoi until after an agreement had been secured with the Chinese.[234] "The China move was of paramount importance," Carter explains in his memoirs, "so after a few weeks of assessment, I decided to postpone the Vietnam effort until we had concluded an agreement with Beijing."[235]

Neither Peking nor Hanoi was informed of this decision.[236]

Fearing opposition from Vance and Holbrooke, Brzezinski convinced Carter that the decision should be kept secret from the State Department, which still hoped for the mutual recognition of both countries and which was already far too absorbed in planning the opening of an embassy in Vietnam.[237] Two decades later, Carter explained:

> I did not feel that I had full support there [in the State Department] and it was and is an enormous bureaucracy that is unable and sometimes unwilling to keep a secret. It seemed obvious to me that premature public disclosure of our intensifying diplomatic effort could arouse a firestorm of opposition from those who thought that Taiwan should always be the "one China." I decided that no negotiating instructions to Ambassador Leonard Woodcock would ever be channeled through the State Department; they would be sent directly from the White House.[238]

By October this mutual distrust had tilted the presidential scales in favor of the NSC staff. The State Department would remain largely unaware of the details of Sino–American talks and that normalization with Vietnam had been permanently shelved — as opposed to Carter's stated intent of opting for a temporary postponement, until Washington had pushed through on normalization with China. In fact, it appears that Vance and Holbrooke were not informed of the presidential decision before mid–November, being led to think that, according to Vance's recommendations to Carter, Washington was gaining time and would act only once the November elections were over.[239] The decision was also kept from both Peking and Hanoi, possibly to counter any leaks that might appear through Chinese boastings of diplomatic success or Vietnamese protests against U.S. policies.[240] When the Vietnamese requested a date for further bilateral discussions, Holbrooke responded that his timetable did not allow any immediate meetings.[241]

Two weeks after the secret presidential decision of October 11, the U.S. press was still announcing that negotiations with Hanoi had reached a point "where the principal subjects being discussed are a timetable and ways and means of aiming toward a normal relationship."²⁴² However, the same article noted that while the Indochinese refugee exodus was fuelling talks at the UN, the White House had not yet made any decision concerning the exchange of ambassadors with Hanoi, and that Peking's reaction to this issue was unknown.

During his trip to Malaysia, one of the last stops on his ASEAN tour, Dong attempted to leverage ASEAN sympathy and to partly lift the humanitarian weight of the refugee issue off Thach's negotiation efforts in New York, by vowing that he felt "very wicked" about the burden that the refugee exodus was imposing on ASEAN.²⁴³ That day, Robert Oakley met Thach to discuss the setting up of embassies and observed that the Vietnamese diplomat was increasingly impatient, insisting that an agreement should be concluded "right away."²⁴⁴ Oakley resisted Vietnamese pressure, stressing that some details still remained to be negotiated.

The following month Cambodian foreign minister Ieng Sary toured ASEAN countries, competing with Dong for regional support for the Cambodian dispute with Vietnam. In Thailand, Ieng Sary announced that Cambodia would cease its support of communist insurgent groups within the ASEAN nations and pledged no more Cambodian incursions in Thai territory.²⁴⁵

Stopping in New York for the UN meetings, the Cambodian minister continued his international propaganda campaign, distributing copies of the Cambodian "Black Paper" on Vietnam, listing Hanoi's violations of human rights and disregard for Cambodian independence and sovereignty.²⁴⁶ He formally invited UN Secretary General Kurt Waldheim to visit Cambodia and to personally investigate alleged human rights violations. The secretary general agreed, on the condition that Hanoi accept a similar visit in Vietnam so as not to favor one country over the other.²⁴⁷ Hanoi, too busy preparing its attack on Cambodia which would have been difficult to conceal from its UN visitors, refused, declining its last chance to secure international backing. The Vietnamese seemed confident that despite present complaints, international public opinion would support its overthrow of the Pol Pot regime, and understood that a too early UN involvement would be an impediment to its plans.

Hanoi perhaps also took normalization with Washington for granted, which would account for Hanoi's refraining from seeking UN support. Again, as it had during the war, Vietnam was gambling on the support of U.S. and international public opinion, pushing its luck beyond the realities of its position in the new world order.

While waiting in New York, Thach had also attempted to defend his country's position on the border conflicts with its neighbors in an interview in *The New York Times*, by charging that Hanoi's relations with Peking were based solely on how useful Vietnam was to Chinese strategic interests. Thach declared that the present conflict, which he claimed had been initiated by the Chinese, dated far back in history and was totally independent of Soviet-Vietnamese relations.²⁴⁸ Thach also seized his chance to warn the United States that Vietnam's border conflict with China would probably soon escalate.

> We hope, of course, for peace. But if we were to assume an ostrich posture, we would certainly end up with a war on our back. We have to prepare for the worst.... There was a joke in the Western press during the war that the Chinese would fight to the last Vietnamese. American journalists could have no idea how true that joke was.²⁴⁹

Although Vietnam had pushed back more powerful adversaries over the last seven centuries, this was a clear hint that an American move toward Hanoi would be more than welcome at this point. A few days later, Deng retorted that Hanoi had increased Vietnamese troop strength on the border and that the Soviets had been granted access to Cam Ranh Bay from which they would infiltrate Southeast Asia as they had the "Asian Cuba."[250]

In the meantime, Nguyen Duy Trinh had come and left again, and Thach had been patiently waiting to receive the final U.S. decision. But after spending four weeks in New York, Thach left the U.S. on October 20 without having been informed of the American decision.

A week later, on October 27, Le Duan and Pham Van Dong announced their intention to visit Moscow "in the near future." While the visit to Moscow would seek Soviet support, the early announcement and the fear it would trigger of closer Soviet-Vietnamese relations was certainly intended as a diplomatic carrot to speed up the Americans' decision. But if Hanoi intended this strategy to function, the outcome was far from a success.

Le Duan and Dong left Hanoi on October 29.[251] The next day, Robert Oakley informed Tran Quang Co, a Vietnamese foreign ministry representative in charge of Vietnamese relations with North America, that Washington had postponed its decision to normalize with Hanoi in the light of the problems of refugees, the developing of Soviet-Vietnamese relations and of Vietnam's hostility to Cambodia.[252]

The Drawing of Lines

While the Vietnamese and the Soviets were meeting in Moscow, Vietnamese military forces drove back two Chinese attacks. Hanoi's border negotiations with China were suspended, the frontiers closed, and the *Voice of Vietnam* pronounced the situation "critical."[253] On November 1, while the occasional clashes with China were turning into intense fighting, Le Duan stood up in the Kremlin and charged "the reactionary clique in the Peking ruling circles" of attempting to "form a new alliance with imperialism and its fascist henchmen."[254]

Meanwhile, tensions were also growing between Moscow and Peking. "[W]ar with the Soviet Union is inevitable," had declared the Chinese defense minister in May, and the issue had since become a main theme of Chinese anti–Soviet propaganda.[255] On November 1, Yeh Chien-ying repeated this assertion during a conference on Chinese airforce defense, which both Deng and Hua Guofeng were attending.[256] By then, Moscow had spread over a quarter of its army and one-fifth of its air force over Mongolia and along its border with China.[257]

On November 3, while Peking and Hanoi were exchanging accusations following a border incident, Pham Van Dong and Le Duan, knowing that the time had come for Hanoi to further seek support and protection by its allies, signed a treaty of friendship and cooperation with the USSR.[258] The treaty, linking the two countries for a period of twenty-five years, was signed along with six economic agreements.[259] "The Soviet Union has long been trying to draw Vietnam into its orbit," commented a diplomat in

Asia. "This treaty dots the i's and crosses the t's."[260] The U.S. conservative *National Review* agreed with this view and termed the treaty a "bear hug."[261] The *Far Eastern Economic Review*, observing Asian politics from Hong Kong, claimed that the treaty had driven "the Soviet hook further into Vietnam," which thus became the second Soviet foothold in the region after India.[262]

Considering that the Vietnamese had signaled their intention to enter COMECON prior to initiating overtures to the United States and had joined the organization before resuming negotiations with Washington, such criticisms blaming Washington for the Soviet-Vietnamese rapprochement attributed disproportionate responsibility to the U.S. side. Hanoi had already made its decision to side with Moscow before potential normalization with Washington had been given a clear chance, and the treaty merely confirmed this tilt. Nevertheless, it is possible that Moscow had insisted on signing a treaty as the price for Soviet support in the Vietnamese move on Cambodia, which may explain why its signing took place in November rather than June.[263] Postponement may also have been requested by Hanoi so as not to jeopardize its chances for a last-minute normalization with Washington. Doubts will remain until the opening of new sources.

The Soviet-Vietnamese treaty had also originated from Moscow's wish to restore a balance of power in Southeast Asia following the warming of Sino-American relations and the signing of Peking's treaty with Tokyo in August. The strategic triangle linking China, Tokyo and the United States, added to Chinese and Cambodian provocations against Moscow's protégé, had greatly disturbed Moscow and the Soviets would not give up their foothold in Southeast Asia.[264] Vietnamese newspapers had abandoned their claims to ideological neutrality to the benefit of pro–Soviet slogans. "Union with the USSR," now claimed *Việtnam*, "has always been a fundamental policy, and a question of principle, for the Party of the Vietnamese state.... Vietnamese-Soviet solidarity has become a beautiful tradition."[265]

But when facing a Western audience the Vietnamese seemed less enthusiastic and again played on the heartstrings of their interlocutors. Much as Thach had attributed the Vietnamese entry into COMECON to American unwillingness to normalize, the signing of the treaty was portrayed along similar lines, and Hanoi stressed that it would now be forced to make a series of concessions to its larger comrade—stirring the international fear that Cam Ranh Bay be handed over to the Soviets. Answering questions on the implications of the recent treaty, a senior Vietnamese diplomat encouraged the American guilt-trip in responding: "We survived French conquest. We survived American hostility. We can survive Russian friendship."[266] By the eighties, however, Hanoi would realize the full implications of its past decisions, and come to call the Soviets "Americans without dollars."[267]

Despite Hanoi and Moscow's declarations that the treaty was "not intended to oppose any third country" (Article 7), Article 6 stated that "the two parties ... shall actively oppose all schemes and maneuvers of imperialism and reactionary forces"[268]— Hanoi's catchword for Peking. During the banquet celebrating the signing of the treaty, Soviet leader Leonid Brezhnev thus stressed:

> At this complicated moment when the policy of the Chinese leadership has created new and considerable difficulties for socialist construction on Vietnamese soil, the strength of our friendship holds special significance.[269]

But the treaty did not make Soviet intervention automatic in the case of an attack on Vietnam, unlike, for instance, the agreement that linked East Germany to the Soviet Union. It only planned, in Article 6, that the two parties consult each other in the event of an attack, and Hanoi and Moscow would "immediately begin mutual consultations for the purpose of removing that threat and taking appropriate effective measures to ensure the peace and security of their countries."[270]

The Soviet press failed to mention whether Vietnamese Army chief-of-staff general Van Tien Dung, who replaced Vo Nguyen Giap in the Politburo in 1980, and Soviet defense minister Dmitry Ustinov had met or decided upon measures.[271] But the mere presence of the Vietnamese general indicated that Hanoi intended to discuss military issues, and while Giap had resented a military intervention in Cambodia, Dung sided with Le Duc Tho in favor of it.[272] Reportedly, vivid negotiations between Dung and his Soviet counterparts, presumably on the upcoming attack, had postponed the signing of the treaty for a few days.[273] Given such facts, Stephen Morris' claim that, as for the Tet Offensive of 1968, Moscow had not been forewarned of the upcoming attack, seems highly questionable.[274]

The Chinese reported to American visitors that Peking had been distraught by the signing of the Soviet-Vietnamese treaty.[275] The Chinese immediately disclosed that senior Vietnamese officials had claimed Pol Pot's days were "numbered" and "would be toppled before the end of the year."[276] The following month, the Vietnamese radio would indeed publicly utter and repeat such threats.[277]

Peking responded to the treaty with great scorn and bitterness, portraying it as a threat to peace in Asia. Although *Pravda* termed Peking's reaction "absolute nonsense," it is undeniable that the treaty, through which Hanoi was tying itself to the Soviet Union, clearly went against Pham Van Dong's recent proposition to the ASEAN countries to create a zone of "peace, freedom and neutrality."[278] Despite the fact that the treaty scrupulously avoided terms such as "neutrality" and "non-alignment," it was evident that Hanoi now stood fully by Moscow's side, allowing Deng Xiaoping to score a few extra points against Vietnam as he toured the ASEAN countries in November and pledged that he would "not copy Pham Van Dong in lying," adding that "sincerity is the prerequisite for good relations among states."[279] *Nhan Dan* retorted that Deng was merely giving out "'beginners' lessons in politics" and that the ASEAN countries "had enough intelligence and wisdom to perceive the danger awaiting them."[280]

It came as little surprise that, on the day following the signing of the treaty, the highest-ranking Chinese delegation yet dispatched to Cambodia arrived in Phnom Penh, headed by CCP Politburo member Wang Dongxing. No longer a veiled support to the Khmer Rouge regime, the visit was officially publicized as a direct response to the Soviet-Vietnamese treaty. Peking was now certain of Vietnam's intentions regarding Cambodia.

However, Peking still rejected Pol Pot's request that Chinese troops be stationed in Cambodia, for fear that open Chinese backing of such an embarrassing ally might both damage Peking's international image and place China in a difficult position vis-à-vis the Soviet-Vietnamese front.[281] China also made it clear that it would not intervene militarily to rescue the Cambodian regime. Peking also seemed convinced that Cambodia would be defeated should Vietnam attack. The delegation therefore again recommended that, in the event of a war with Vietnam, the Cambodian leadership be prepared to leave the capital, and wage a "protracted guerrilla war" in the countryside.[282] Publicly, therefore, the Chinese simply repeated their "unconditional support" for Cambodia's "just struggle" and returned to Peking.[283]

As evidence of an upcoming Vietnamese move on Cambodia gathered, Peking understood the need to secure international support, mainly in Washington, and manifested its haste to achieve Sino-American normalization. On the day following the signing of the treaty, China allowed a breakthrough on its negotiations with Washington in accepting Woodcock's draft for normalization and January 1 as the date for its official announcement.[284]

While refusing to intervene militarily, China was considering other means of retaliation, and prepared an independent response to the Vietnamese attack. After Peking had given new impetus to negotiations with Washington, its leadership began a series of meetings on Cambodia. While it confirmed that Peking would not intervene militarily to defend Cambodia, it agreed to support the Cambodian regime on the diplomatic level. Furthermore, according to Vietnamese official Luu Van Loi, Peking began to reflect on the possibility of an independent military action against Vietnam.[285] From then on, Peking would never separate the issue of a possible Chinese attack against Vietnam from its prospects of normalization with Washington.

The Chinese continued publicizing their diplomatic support for Phnom Penh and accused Hanoi of moving its troops southward in preparation for an attack on Cambodia.[286] "History has proved," warned the CCP Central Committee delegation visiting Cambodia, "and will continue to prove that those who commit expansion and aggression against other countries may run wild for a while, but they can never escape from the fate of final defeat."[287] However, China persisted in its refusal to pledge a military intervention to defend Cambodia in the event of a Vietnamese attack.

On November 24, Cambodian prime minister Khieu Samphan wrote to chairman of the Standing Committee of the Chinese National People's Congress Yeh Chien-ying to inquire about China's reaction should Vietnam launch a military attack against Cambodia. Again, China refused to grant official military support to Phnom Penh.

On December 5, after the Vietnamese formal announcement of the existence of a Cambodian insurgent army in Vietnamese territory, Yeh Chien-ying once again asserted that Peking would "fully support" Phnom Penh but refrained from making any other commitments.[288]

Ironically, the signing of Le Duan and Pham Van Dong's treaty with Moscow coincided with the State Department's first public acknowledgement that Hanoi had officially dropped its aid precondition to normalization with the United States.[289] In Tokyo, which had lately become an important center of informal communication between the Americans and the Vietnamese, after Vance had asked Sonoda in September to help prevent Vietnam from falling to Moscow, Hanoi's ambassador to Japan Nguyen Giap immediately assured Japanese deputy vice-minister Masuo Takashima that despite the signing of the treaty, Hanoi still clung to its policy of independence and still sought normalization with Washington.[290] Hanoi, reported an official Vietnamese source, expected normalization to occur in 1979. While refraining from presenting the aid issue as a precondition, however, the official stated that Washington "must provide something as a symbolic gesture" to represent its responsibility for the war damages in Vietnam, but added that Washington could choose the nature and the amount of aid.[291]

Concurrently, Hanoi attempted to reassure its ASEAN neighbors by providing the Thai Ambassador to Hanoi with a copy of the treaty, hoping that this would prevent Deng, who had just arrived in Thailand, from spreading rumors of a Soviet-Vietnamese military pact against ASEAN.[292] However, the prospect of an unofficial Soviet-Vietnamese rapprochement raised fears amongst Vietnam's neighbors that the Soviets would be granted access to Cam Ranh Bay and Da Nang, from which they would be able to overfly the Philippines and the U.S. fleet in both the Gulf of Thailand and the Pacific.[293]

Vance knew that the treaty represented a major blow to normalization prospects and would deepen congressional hostility already greatly influenced by growing conservatism.[294] The NSC sided with the CIA's view that this treaty might represent "a prelude to an attack on Cambodia" and added that it "should have some impact on our thinking about normalization."[295] "That treaty," confirmed a State Department official, "gave Brzezinski and Oksenberg all the ammunition they needed."[296] While the decision to shelve normalization with Hanoi had been made three weeks earlier, the NSC would use the treaty as a pretext for justifying the hardening of the administration's policies towards Vietnam.

The situation further festered when Peking notified Energy Secretary James Schlesinger, then on a visit to China, that it formally stood against American-Vietnamese normalization, stressing that Washington would be providing "Vietnam [with] economic assistance beyond what it is getting from the Russians."[297] Again, Brzezinski's and China's plans took precedence over the State Department's as the Chinese declaration confirmed the NSC's belief that Peking opposed U.S.-Vietnamese normalization. The White House officially announced that it was lifting the ban on military equipment sales to Peking as Brzezinski had promised Peking in May.[298] "[I s]pent the morning with journalists," Oksenberg reported to Brzezinski. "They all sniffed a China story."[299]

With Peking willing to proceed toward normalization, Washington now had to dispose of the issue of normalizing with Vietnam. The congressional elections were over and Hanoi was expecting an answer. Carter informed Vance that, in the light of recent events and of the administration's decision to open to China, normalization with Vietnam had been permanently shelved, and instructed the secretary to formally condemn the Vietnamese on the refugee exodus as a reason to renounce normalization. Brzezinski, knowing that Holbrooke would give a speech on U.S. Asian policy on November 16, immediately set out to inform the State Department of Carter's decision.[300] In so doing, the NSC adviser—while refraining from too early an announcement of the Sino-American rapprochement—had undercut Holbrooke and signaled to the State Department that it should temper its declarations on relations with Vietnam.

Meanwhile, the Cambodian-Vietnamese border was noticeably quiet and Vietnamese forces refrained from trespassing too far onto Cambodian territory in pushing back Khmer Rouge attacks. Hanoi probably intended its military restraint to be read in Washington as a sign of peacefulness and goodwill.[301] But when negotiations resumed after the congressional elections, Vance instructed Oakley to inform Hanoi that Washington was stopping bilateral talks in view of the number of intelligence reports that had reached Washington on the persecution of Hoas in Vietnam. In a last attempt to salvage the situation, Oakley advised against Hanoi's continuing hostilities with Cambodia and China, and recommended that Hanoi agree to a UN solution on these issues. Irked by weeks of waiting for a positive U.S. response to Vietnamese overtures, Hanoi rejected Oakley's advice.[302]

Holbrooke's ensuing dialogue with the Vietnamese was no more than justification of Washington's withdrawal from the negotiating table. The State Department now insisted on Vietnamese military restraint in Cambodia as a pretext for postponing normalization.[303] Holbrooke explained this reversal as a direct reaction to the daily TV news reports showing hundreds of Indochinese refugees, which greatly upset viewers, and pulled out an intelligence report on Vietnamese military preparations for an attack on Cambodia.[304] Holbrooke explained a few months later:

> We requested that the Vietnamese inform us of their intentions toward Kampuchea, given the massive buildup then underway along their border with that country. We also asked for clarification of the implications of the November S.R.V.-Soviet Treaty of Peace, Friendship and Cooperation in light of previous Vietnamese assurances that they would follow an independent foreign policy and never allow any foreign bases on their territory ... [and] we expressed deep concern over the growing refugee exodus from Vietnam.[305]

The Vietnamese insistence that Hanoi had no intention of invading Cambodia and would provide all details on human rights and re-education camps, failed to bring Washington back to the negotiating table.[306] Washington had decided to shelve normalization, and the Vietnamese answers to Holbrooke's face-saving humanitarian pretexts for delaying rapprochement could not alter Carter's decisions.

More importantly perhaps, it signaled that Brzezinski's policies had outweighed the State Department's in the Oval Office. Rather than naming the State-NSC competing programs as one of the explanations for the shelving of normalization, Holbrooke later justified American refusal to normalize by pointing to Vietnamese failure to provide satisfactory resolution to the issues of Vietnamese refugees and Hanoi's rapprochement with Moscow. "In the light of these responses," he explained, "movement toward normalization came to a halt, as we awaited further developments."[307] One can only speculate on whether this statement was made out of genuine conviction, as Elizabeth Becker suggests, or in a self-serving desire to hide the internal clashes, which appears the most plausible explanation in the light of recently released archival sources. Hurst's explanation that "the two key factions within the administration concurred in the decision to shelve normalisation, albeit for different sets of reasons" appears a serious misinterpretation.[308]

Washington had carefully weighed the phrasing of its new stance on the events in Southeast Asia. Whereas Brzezinski had urged the immediate announcement that the Soviet-Vietnamese treaty had come as an unquestionable and permanent obstacle to normalization plans with Hanoi, the State Department argued that Washington could not interfere in Hanoi's bilateral affairs with another country and requested that Vietnam be asked for "clarification" of the treaty.[309] On November 20, listing obstacles to normalization, Oksenberg remarked to Brzezinski that "the Vietnamese matter is now under control."[310]

In an interview with Seymour Hersh, in August 1979, Nguyen Co Thach explained that the agreement reached with Holbrooke on September 27, 1978, had been broken by Washington, which had instead announced normalization with China, and later blamed the failure of bilateral talks on Hanoi's behavior vis-à-vis the refugee exodus, possible Vietnamese military involvement in Cambodia and the signing of the Soviet-Vietnamese treaty.[311] In Hanoi's eyes, human rights had become a pretext to justify the diplomatic freeze.[312] The State Department even charged Hanoi with forcing refugees to give away their gold and buy their way out of Vietnam.[313] Following the closure of the November meetings, the Vietnamese representatives to the UN were notified that normalization had become impossible.[314] By the end of the month the State Department declared that the embargo could only be lifted after normalization and that no aid would be provided to Hanoi.[315]

Hanoi was also correct in viewing the shelving of normalization within the context of Sino-American rapprochement. In his book, published in 2002, Luu Van Loi stated that "the Carter Administration shifted to establishing strategic relations with China to cope with the Soviet Union"—a view which analysts seem to favor, and with which this book sides.[316] However, while Sino-American rapprochement and intra-administration feuds account for much of the failure of the negotiations, one may suppose that the issue of Hoa and Vietnamese designs on Cambodia had triggered genuine concern within the State Department, preventing it from pushing more vigorously for simultaneous recognition of Peking and Hanoi as it had originally planned.

Overall, the refugee crisis had greatly affected American public opinion. By January 1978 a Louis Harris poll indicated that 57 percent of Americans opposed the entry of more Indochinese refugees into the United States, and in early March the Carter administration, finding itself unable to agree on an overall comprehensive policy on this issue, was forced to cancel a press conference for the third time in three weeks.[317] Finally, by the end of March, Carter agreed to accept Vietnamese boat-people who had been refused asylum elsewhere as well as refugees in camps who had relatives in the United States.[318] As the number of refugees fleeing Vietnam reached more than 5,000 a week in November, Washington grew increasingly displeased with Hanoi.[319]

During the International Conference on Refugees organized by the UN High Commission for Refugees in Geneva, Australian minister of immigration Michael Mackellar, backed by Malaysia and Thailand, accused Vietnam of closing its eyes on and even fostering the illegal exodus of refugees in fishing boats in return for payments in gold and foreign currencies.[320] Ironically such practices, already in existence in 1978, multiplied in 1979, following the conference and the U.S. refusal to normalize with Vietnam. According to Southeast Asian expert Pao-Min Chang, during the month of April 1979 alone an estimated $242 million sent by overseas Chinese to finance their relatives' departure from Vietnam, traveled through Hong Kong's banks on the way to Saigon, representing the equivalent of 50 percent of the total value of Vietnamese exports for 1978.[321]

The American delegation at the conference highly publicized its indignation and joined the chorus of nations condemning Vietnam's shameful treatment of refugees, pledging to modify present legislation in order to absorb a greater number of refugees in the coming months.[322] A few days following the end of the conference, Trinh charged that Washington was using the refugee issue as a means of delaying the establishment of normal diplomatic relations with Hanoi.[323] In early December, State Department official John Cannon explained that although Washington was still interested in normalization, several factors had slowed down the negotiations.[324] The pretext had become the official face-saving policy line.

Meanwhile, tensions toward Vietnam by its neighbors were growing daily. On November 30, Hanoi issued a letter to UN Secretary General Waldheim accusing Peking of using "the Cambodian ruling clique to cause the border war against Vietnam," depicting this as a first step towards broader Chinese expansionism in Southeast Asia. Both Cambodia and China had separately replied on December 11 and suggested that these accusations be turned on Hanoi.[325]

Hanoi made a last attempt to woo Washington. A Vietnamese diplomat disclosed in 2002 that during a meeting with Holbrooke in Hawaii in early December—only two weeks before Vietnam's offensive on Cambodia—the Vietnamese representatives had played their last card in wooing Washington by signing a document declaring that Hanoi officially renounced its claim to the reconstruction aid promised by Nixon.[326] This striking gesture represented a total reversal of Hanoi's bold and unwavering stance during the first Paris talks of 1977. It was renouncing aid—the main issue that had governed its policies toward Washington since 1975. Hanoi's readiness to make this important concession reveals Vietnam's understanding that normalization would become impossible after its invasion of Cambodia and suggests that Hanoi may have sought normalization with Washington to protect it against Chinese retaliation—which Hanoi probably expected.

This point sheds light on the Sino-Vietnamese competition to secure U.S. protection before pushing their respective plans into policy. While Vietnam intended to use the "American Card" against the Chinese to "contain" the risk of Chinese military retaliation, Peking intended to use the "American Card" against Vietnam to counter the Vietnamese and Soviet expansionist threat in the region. Eventually Peking, supported by Brzezinski, won the upper hand. But this also reveals Washington's passivity and misperception of the issues at stake in the Sino-Vietnamese conflict, again leading observers to speculate that Washington's "China Card" against the USSR was in fact China's "American Card" against the Soviet Union, in which Washington represented little more than a geostrategic "joker" in a Cold War "card game."

Despite Vietnamese efforts no agreement on normalization was achieved. A week later, Washington officially announced that it would normalize with China.

Normalization with Peking

Meanwhile, Washington was cozying up to Peking and arranging the final details of normalization. After American euphoria following the Camp David summit in September had quieted down, and Middle East peace talks seemed to have stalled, it appeared that Carter was looking forward to rapid normalization with China in an effort to bolster his popularity rating.[327] After spending nearly three decades repelling Chinese influence from Indochina, Washington was now eager to normalize with China, and sided with Peking against the Vietnamese and the Soviets.[328]

Peking too was looking forward to normalization. Washington understood this eagerness within the context of the domestic opposition Deng Xiaoping faced from his rival Hua Guofeng, a more moderate political figure who favored a partial withdrawal of Chinese troops from the Sino-Soviet border to encourage the recent signs of a thaw between Peking and Moscow.[329] In August, following his meeting with CIA analysts, Oksenberg reported that "[s]hould [Deng's] policies fail to pay off, a number of people are poised to attack him, probably including Hua Guofeng. The consensus among analysts is that Deng needs some quick and relatively uncontroversial victories."[330] In December, a cable from the U.S. consulate in Hong Kong again warned that Deng's problems within the Chinese leadership had grown.[331] Therefore, the administration understood Deng's urge for normalization as a way of securing his position at home through diplomatic "victories" when Peking was in fact considering a military "victory" against Vietnam after securing normalization with Washington.[332] While mutual misperceptions and misunderstandings plagued Washington's negotiations with Hanoi, it seemed that American relations with China were based on similar misjudgments.

On December 13, Woodcock met Deng and completed the last details of normalization. Deng had finally agreed to proceed with the announcement of the upcoming normalization of relations and Woodcock reported his amazement at sudden Chinese impatience to proceed with the signing of the document.[333] Woodcock also conveyed Carter's invitation to Deng to visit the United States, which Deng gladly accepted. "My God, they've accepted," Woodcock cabled Carter on his return from a meeting with Deng, "I think we've got something."[334]

Deng had long hoped for a summit in Washington. During Brzezinski's visit to China in the spring, Deng had informed his guest of his wish to visit the United States within three years—possibly hinting that his position in Chinese domestic politics, then in jeopardy, may be secured by such a diplomatic move.[335] The Chinese vice-premier's wish was a surprising break from China's earlier refusal to send Peking's premiers to visit the United States as long as Washington maintained ties with Taiwan. Brzezinski had therefore enthusiastically pronounced himself in favor of such a visit, adding that he would invite the Chinese leader to his home for dinner.[336] In preparing his visit Deng would later admit: "I have been wishing for this trip for at least several years" and the Chinese vice-premier indeed seemed to appreciate his American tour.[337]

While Woodcock attributed Chinese sudden haste to normalize to Deng's longing for an invitation—which was however certainly partly true—and Brzezinski pointed at growing Sino-Soviet hostility, the White House seemed unaware of the Chinese wish to secure political backing for Peking's possible attack on Vietnam. Chinese impatience to seal a formal alliance with Washington through normalization had certainly more to do with Peking's short-term ambitions than with Deng's personal inclination for tourism.

Thus, the same day, Peking issued its first direct warning to Hanoi that Vietnam "must be responsible for the consequences" of its acts.[338] As Sanjay Lodha remarks, Washington's reaching of an agreement with the Chinese coincided with the massive build-up of Vietnamese forces along the border with Cambodia as all three countries were becoming increasingly restless.[339] Only the United States seemed, as yet, largely unsuspecting of the motivations of their Chinese counterparts.

In fact, the Oval Office was preoccupied with other issues. During a visit to Tokyo,

Deng had already let his Japanese hosts know that secret negotiations with Washington were under way, expecting such a revelation to arouse domestic support for his initiatives in China.[340] But Carter feared that leaks might awaken congressional attention and jeopardize the initiative. In fact, Congress was in the midst of its winter recess, which meant that the theatricality and surprise of such a disclosure would not be bogged down by lengthy congressional debates.[341] "If we wait until January 1," the President told his aides, "it will leak," and he cabled Deng to bring forward the date of the announcement, to which the Chinese agreed.[342]

Carter's doubts had probably arisen from Deng's rejection of the White House's request that China refrain from publicizing the upcoming normalization, and the Chinese leader had declared that "it is easier to keep a secret in China than in the United States," adding to Woodcock that "if this great problem is solved during your excellency's tenure, I believe that our two peoples will be grateful to you."[343]

But while most press reports later stated that forwarding the announcement would prevent possible opposition to normalization from pro–Taiwanese factions in the United States, journalist Patrick Tyler suggests that Brzezinski and Carter "would use the China announcement just as Kissinger had in 1971: to build a fire under Brezhnev" just before the upcoming SALT talks, and had rejected Vance's argument that normalization with China should come only after a SALT agreement had been reached. As had become routine within the administration, Brzezinski's anti–Soviet views were dominating U.S. foreign policy-making, leading the White House to reverse its initial priorities to the benefit of globalist concerns.[344]

To prevent any leaks to the press before the announcement that could alert Taiwan supporters in the United States and jeopardize Sino-American normalization, only four members of the White House staff—Brzezinski, Vance, Woodcock, and Hamilton Jordan—at that time, were aware that secret negotiations were under way with the Chinese.[345] But Vance was the last to be warned that an agreement had been reached. The president ordered his secretary to cut short his negotiations with Egyptian president Anwar Sadat and Israeli premier Menachem Begin, and to return urgently to Washington.[346] "The matter that the five of us have been working on is coming to a rapid conclusion," Carter enigmatically told him over the telephone. "I need you back here."[347] All U.S. officials involved in the issue were ordered to maintain secrecy and Vance simply told his aides that the president was awaiting his return for foreign policy matters.[348]

The day before the announcement of its official rapprochement with Washington, and perhaps more importantly, the day following the exchange in Hanoi of the instruments of ratification of the Soviet-Vietnamese treaty, China proceeded, along its northwestern border with the Soviet Union, to its second atmospheric nuclear test in the year and its fifth in twenty-six months—certainly intended to intimidate Moscow.[349]

On the morning of December 15, Carter telephoned former president Ford to inform him of the upcoming announcement.[350] He also dispatched Oksenberg to brief Nixon on the issue and received the former president's congratulations for his "tough" dealings with the Chinese.[351] A few hours later, speaking from the Oval Office, Carter announced that normalization with China would take effect as of January 1, 1979, while a simultaneous announcement was made in Peking.[352] Carter was delighted. Following his declaration and unaware that a microphone was still on, he exclaimed: "Massive applause throughout the nation."[353]

But the success was largely Brzezinski's. Later that day, the national security adviser proudly claimed that "[w]hat we are doing in our relations with China should have been done anyway, whether our relations with the Soviet Union were much better or much worse"—with an obvious criticism of Kissinger's preference for détente over rapprochement with Peking.[354] After seven years, and three administrations, the United States and China had achieved normalization.

As historian John Dumbrell stresses, Sino-American normalization signaled the victory of Brzezinski's anti–Soviet views over the State Department's softer policies and confirmed his influence on the White House.[355]

Brzezinski chose to trumpet his success over the Soviets in warning Moscow himself of the impending normalization shortly before the joint communiqué was released. In the afternoon of December 15, shortly before the official announcement, Soviet Ambassador Anatoly Dobrynin called at the national security adviser's office. In his memoirs, Brzezinski recalls the episode with obvious delight:

> Dobrynin arrived full of cheer at 3 p.m. I tipped Jody [Powell] off and he in turn tipped some newsmen off, so they were all outside photographing him. Our hope was to divert newspapermen into thinking that maybe something involving American-Soviet relations would be announced in the evening by the President. By the time Dobrynin arrived, it was known that we had requested television time for 9 p.m. At first I chatted pleasantly ... and then out of the blue I informed him that we were announcing tonight initiation of diplomatic, full-scale relations with the Republic of China. He looked absolutely stunned. His face turned kind of grey and his jaw dropped. He didn't say anything but then he recouped and thanked me for the information. I added that it wasn't directed against anyone and that American relations with China would then have as normal a character as Soviet relations with China. Formally, a correct observation; but substantively, a touch of irony.[356]

On his leaving Brzezinski's office, the journalists asked Dobrynin the subject of his interview with the national security adviser. The Soviet ambassador replied that the meeting had involved the discussion of "chess."[357] Brzezinski had just laid down its China Card. A few hours after the official announcement, Moscow calmly replied that Brezhnev hoped Washington would not give up its interest in SALT II.[358]

The press communiqué issued in both countries to announce Sino-American normalization was strangely worded. Unlike Carter's clumsy and double-edged speech of June 7, 1978, calling on the Soviet Union to choose between confrontation or cooperation, which had been drafted with a hodgepodge of State Department and NSC views, the press communiqué confirmed the dominance of NSC ideology over State Department positions. The terminology of the resulting document demonstrated great Chinese-inspired anti–Soviet influence, especially in its reference to "regional hegemony"—the Peking leadership's catchword to describe Vietnamese foreign policy ambitions.[359] The president and his national security adviser had brushed aside Vance's objection to the use of this tendentious phrase, and Brzezinski had succeeded in excluding the State Department from the writing of the communiqué, much as Kissinger, in 1972, had kept the secretary of state from participating in the drafting of the Shanghai Communiqué.[360] On December 13, Woodcock had initially proposed that no such phrases be used in joint declarations but rather in separate Chinese statements so as not to fully endorse Peking's provocations against the USSR.³⁶¹ But Brzezinski had played on Vance's absence from Washington during the last days of Sino-American negotiations, to convince Carter to include "anti-hegemony phraseology" in the joint communiqué. Upon his return to Washington, the secretary of state could no longer prevent the anti–Soviet phrases. Again the phrasing of Brzezinski's anti–Soviet ideology in U.S. foreign policy formulation underlined NSC domination of Washington's policy-making, signaling to Moscow that Washington had chosen to prioritize its relations with the Chinese and to endorse Peking's position over Moscow.³⁶²

Overall, the diplomatic victory of Sino-American normalization was Chinese more than American. At a press conference in Peking, Hua Guofeng announced that the move would "contribute to the anti-hegemony struggle" and that China "would continue to struggle against both big and small hegemonists, both global and regional hegemony."³⁶³ Dobrynin immediately asked to see Vance, expressing his concern over the communiqué and requesting clarification of its meaning.³⁶⁴ His move confirmed that Moscow saw Sino-American normalization as an anti–Soviet gesture and proof of how predominance of Brzezinski's views in the White House jeopardized Soviet-American bilateral relations, as his earlier conversation with the national security adviser had already made clear.

Brzezinski's globalist appraisal of foreign policy had eroded Carter's interest in regionalist policies such as normalization with Third World powers, including Vietnam, leading to the prioritization of the East-West conflict over regional affairs. Sino-American normalization was viewed within the framework of the containment of the Soviet threat and the prioritizing of military security over diplomacy. In historian James Mann's words, Washington viewed China "not so much [as] a country as a military strategy" which it "linked intrinsically to America's immediate needs in the Cold War."³⁶⁵ Vietnam seemed no longer a regionalist issue to be dealt with independently. Rather, as the administration had shifted to a bipolar worldview, the NSC lumped Vietnam together with the Soviet bloc, and the possibility of American-Vietnamese normalization was sacrificed on the altar of Cold War rivalries.³⁶⁶

Far from being a purely diplomatic move, Sino-American normalization had sealed the Carter-Brzezinski complicity. In sending his New Year greetings to Brzezinski, Carter congratulated the adviser for his "high standard of ethics" and added, in a handwritten remark at the bottom of the page: "It's good to have you as my partner—J."³⁶⁷ Congratulating the national security adviser following the announcement of Sino-American normalization, Carter identified his adviser as "the driving force behind the whole effort" and thanked him for his support. "Whenever I wavered," said the president congratulating Brzezinski following the announcement of Sino-American normalization, "you pushed me and pressed me to go through with this."³⁶⁸ More than Carter, it was Brzezinski's realist policies that had won China and defeated Vietnam.

The USSR refrained from criticizing Sino-American normalization so as not to jeopardize their own relations with Washington. Normalization, as Brzezinski had expected, had struck Moscow as a blow. In an interview on December 19, Carter explained that Brehzhnev had expressed "his understanding that our commitment is to peace in the entire world ... [and acknowledged] the fact that the proper relationship between major sovereign nations is to have full diplomatic relations." Carter termed Brezhnev's message "very positive in tone," and, in a misperception of Soviet irritation, sought to persuade his audience as well as himself that the Soviet congratulations were genuine.[369]

Publicly, Brzezinski denied the anti–Soviet dimension of normalization with China. "We see no fundamental incompatibility between a better relationship with China and a better relationship with the Soviet Union," explained Brzezinski in an interview with *Time* in late December.[370] But in the privacy of the White House, Brzezinski appeared more vehement, pushing his authority more than his position allowed.

During a SALT II meeting in Geneva a week later, Gromyko showed his displeasure over the recent Sino-American rapprochement by rejecting Vance's proposals regarding the treaty. When the secretary of state telephoned Washington from the meeting room on an open and audible line to request new instructions, Brzezinski bluntly told him to maintain a hard line with Moscow, which did nothing to diminish Soviet irritation. The talks stalled and the Carter-Brezhnev meeting was put off.[371] Brezhnev's visit to the United States to discuss the SALT II agreement, planned for January 15, was later canceled.[372] Much like Ford had been nicknamed the "second man on the moon" during his visit to China in 1975, Brezhnev refrained from endorsing the rather humiliating role of being the "second" man to travel to the United States, after Deng's announced visit in January 1979.[373]

The Japanese press reported that Phan Hien, General Vo Nguyen Giap and Nguyen Duy Trinh, then on a visit to Tokyo, had been "surprised" by the Sino-American normalization that announced the destruction of their last prospects for normalization with Washington.[374] Trinh "hardened his face and refused to comment" and Giap "waved his hands as if to ask that no more questions be asked." Later that day, recovering from the shock of the announcement, Hien declared that he welcomed Sino-American normalization if it were truly aimed at promoting peace, but declined to comment on how this would affect Asian politics.[375] However, he recalled that American-Vietnamese talks had stalled due to U.S. insistence on new preconditions after Hanoi had dropped its own, illustrating Washington's use of pretexts to justify shelving normalization.[376] He added that Vietnam was still ready to normalize with Washington without preconditions and that "pending bilateral problems" could be discussed after normalization was established. "[I]t is up to them to decide," he explained.[377] Privately, however, Hien declared, "We know enough about the Chinese and the Americans"—bitterly expressing Hanoi's growing fears of the pact.

Publicly, Trinh also politely termed the event a "logical step."[378] The Vietnamese minister repeated Hien's call for normalization, stressing that Hanoi had dropped the aid issue, and bitterly pointed at the recent U.S. introduction of new preconditions into its negotiations with Vietnam.[379] Simultaneously, vice-consul of the SRV embassy in France, Le Tho, declared that Hanoi did not consider Sino-American normalization an obstacle to American-Vietnamese normalization.[380]

A month later, a triumphant Brzezinski was briefing American businessmen on trade opportunities in China, in what seemed to be more of a lecture on geopolitical strategy than on international trade:

> Normalisation ... is an act rooted in historical optimism and political realism.... For a generation, we said "no" to the reality of East Asia. We refused to recognize reality, we sought to isolate China, and we lived by myths—with two wars and with incalculable cost to the region and to us.
>
> Now, we say "yes" to reality.[381]

Ironically, Brzezinski seemed to imply that the Vietnam War—and the Korean War—had been fought at a time when the United States was disconnected from reality and that the success of normalization with China had erased past political mistakes and military defeats. In Peking, *People's Daily* issued a series of seven articles depicting U.S. consumer society, no longer portrayed as decadent capitalism, and demonstrating a significant change in China's attitude toward a social system it had so highly claimed to disdain. "We should learn the good points of advanced capitalist countries," explained an article, "and at the same time screen out all the corruption.... Since we have the superior social system, we should be able to avoid the evils of capitalism."[382]

A few days before Woodcock's December 13 meeting with Deng during which both sides had agreed to January 1 as the date of effective normalization, the Fourth Plenum of the Chinese Central Committee had gathered for a special meeting to discuss future Sino-American relations and the details of a possible attack against Vietnam.[383] While Chinese leadership was aware that the Pol Pot regime would be unable to stand up militarily to invading forces, it understood the need for such Vietnamese actions to not remain unpunished. The announcement of Sino-American normalization opened the way for a military option and Peking approved the decision for a military attack after Vietnam had moved against Cambodia.

It was decided that, to counter negative international reactions, the Chinese attack would not be linked to Hanoi's move against Cambodia but rather would be portrayed as a self-defensive move. The constant border skirmishes that had multiplied over the summer would provide a legitimate excuse for Chinese anger. This strategy would also diminish the risk of Soviet retaliation. The Chinese leadership, however, agreed that the attack should be limited in space and time so as not to delay China's "four modernizations" plans. As the Plenum agreed to these points, China mobilized its troops in its five border regions with Vietnam.[384]

VI

WINNING THE THIRD VIETNAM WAR

Vietnam Invades Cambodia

On December 3, 1978 *Hanoi Radio* announced the creation of the Kampuchean National United Front for National Salvation (KNUFNS), headed by Heng Samrin.[1] In its first declaration the Front made an eleven-point proposal to the Cambodian people and expressed its wish to create a "region of peace, independence, freedom, neutrality, stability and prosperity," a phrase strongly reminiscent of Vietnam's proposal to the ASEAN countries in October to create a region of "peace, independence and neutrality."[2] Those thoughts, goals and terminologies undoubtedly suggested that Hanoi had given birth to a new Vietcong-style organization, although its labeling as "Kampuchean" provided it with a cloak of legitimacy, allowing the organization to appear to be a self-led Cambodian force attempting a coup on its own government.[3] The liberation army had officially come into being.

In an indirect warning to China, the Front's first declaration stressed that "no international force, however perfidious it may be, can exterminate the heroic Kampuchean people," demonstrating Vietnamese anxiety over Chinese reactions.[4] Hanoi publicized its support for the new Cambodian insurgents by highlighting the atrocities committed by the Khmer Rouge. The Vietnamese media clamored that since 1977 Cambodian damage to Vietnam had destroyed 121 towns and villages, and needed to be stopped. Vietnamese charges were not unfounded as contemporary estimates show that more than 257,000 people had lost their homes and that several hundreds had been killed by Khmer Rouge incursions on Vietnamese territory.[5] Concurrently, *Hanoi Radio* reported that more than two million Cambodians had been executed by Khmer Rouge forces—a figure that the West denounced as vastly exaggerated but which recent sources quote as minimal.[6] Hanoi had already begun to justify the upcoming invasion and to prepare the overthrow of the Pol Pot regime.

The opportunity soon arose. The multiplication of border clashes with Cambodia, leading to the forced evacuation of several villages and NEZs, urged Vietnam to respond urgently to the escalation of the situation. On December 22, nineteen Cambodian divisions launched a large-scale attack against Vietnam.[7] This provided Hanoi with a pretext to launch its invasion, allowing the claim that the KNUFNS was, in the words of Luu Van Loi, merely "using the right of legitimate self-defense."[8] On December 25, 100,000 Vietnamese troops and 20,000 Khmer insurgents began what Hanoi termed an "historic mission" of stopping "the aggressive war of the reactionary clique in Phnom Penh."[9]

While the attack was coordinated by Hanoi, the Vietnamese stressed that they were merely supporting "Cambodian people and the revolutionary forces under the leadership of" the KNUFNS.[10] This was hardly needed as rumors of an upcoming invasion had been circulating for several months. Phnom Penh emphasized the link between the invasion and the signing of the Soviet-Vietnamese treaty in charging that as many as 8,000 Soviet and Cuban military advisers helped coordinate the Vietnamese effort.[11] U.S. intelligence services confirmed the presence of 12,000 Soviet advisers but reported that these were not directly involved in military operations.[12] The Vietnamese bitterly denied these reports, requesting that their critics "recall that the Vietnamese did not accept military advisers from foreign countries during the Vietnam war against the Americans."[13]

In fact, the Soviets lent several ships and AN-22 transport planes to carry Vietnamese troops and ammunition from Haiphong to Saigon and also provided Vietnam with spare parts.[14] The amount of Soviet aid to Vietnam, reported an analyst, had reached its maximum since the end of the war.[15] The political report of the Vietnam's Fifth Party Congress would later praise Hanoi's relationship with Moscow as "the keystone of the foreign policy" and added that this relation "joined in an important manner to the independence of the three Indochinese countries and to the peace and stability in the area."[16] Similarly, Hanoi reported that more than 10,000 Chinese advisers in civilian clothing were conducting the Khmer Rouge defense.[17]

Following the orders of General Van Tien Dung, said to be Hanoi's most skilled military tactician, the Vietnamese forces crossed the border into Cambodia, finding very little resistance from the weakening Khmer Rouge and causing the desertion of nearly 80 percent of Pol Pot's troops. On January 4, the Vietnamese had reached Hanoi's initial objective of securing a large area east of the Mekong which now stood as a buffer zone protecting Vietnam, but seeing the crumbling of Khmer forces, the Vietnamese decided to push further into Cambodia. After two weeks of fighting, the Vietnamese captured Phnom Penh on January 7. Heng Samrin was named head of the new government, and proclaimed the land the People's Republic of Cambodia.[18] Cambodia, announced the Vietnamese media, had been taken back from "the ogres with a human face" and had returned to being "the property of its people."[19]

Following the capture of the city, recalled Bui Tin, Le Duc Tho headed for the former royal palace and sat on the throne, fully savoring the Vietnamese victory.[20] He was later appointed by the Politburo to oversee the building of a new Cambodian party and government and moved into a large villa behind the palace from which he orchestrated Cambodian political life.[21] If Tho had wished for the creation of a Vietnamese-led Cambodian regime and the taking over of Phnom Penh, his ambition was now satisfied.

Despite Chinese warnings, the Cambodian regime had not anticipated that Phnom Penh would fall so rapidly to the lightning attack of the Vietnamese. Surprised by the rapidity of the Vietnamese troops, the Chinese Ambassador was forced to reach the frontier by car. Meanwhile 25,000 fleeing Khmer Rouge were hurrying toward the Thai frontier, along with 625 Chinese and 49 North Korean diplomats.[22] By the time the Vietnamese entered the capital, Pol Pot had already fled to the countryside.

Foreseeing the collapse of their Cambodian allies, the Chinese had requested Thai assistance to arrange for the repatriation of Chinese personnel from Cambodia.[23] Peking had encouraged Pol Pot to prepare a refuge in the jungle near the Thai border and, once the Vietnamese invasion had begun, requested Bangkok authorization to host the Pol Pot government's exile on Thai territory in exchange for a Chinese pledge that it would temper the Thai Communist Party since it threatened the Thai leadership.[24] Abandoning Phnom Penh, as soon as the Vietnamese stepped into the area, was part of Peking's wish to better highlight Hanoi's "aggressive designs."[25]

Soon after the Vietnamese takeover, the Chinese *People's Daily* warned that Pol Pot's government "is still around and exercising all functions as the sole legal representative of the Kampuchean people."[26] In early January, a new radio program named *Voice of Democratic Kampuchea* began broadcasting anti–Vietnamese propaganda from China; and a few days later, Peking announced the creation of the Democratic Patriotic Front for National Salvation.[27] At the same time, Peking took care to warn its neighbors of Hanoi's "expansionist ambitions," commenting, in the *People's Daily* that "like a gambler maddened by one loss after another, the Vietnamese authorities have decided to throw in all their stakes and overrun Kampuchea so as to lay the cornerstone for their future 'great empire.'"[28] Criticizing Hanoi's "Nazi-like" behavior, China called on the United States and the western world to reject Vietnamese requests for recognition and aid.[29]

Peking's international propaganda campaign proved successful. Giving in to pressure from Washington, the World Bank also suspended all assistance to Vietnam and canceled its aid for 1980.[30] The EEC Council of Ministers also suspended its aid programs to Vietnam, on the grounds that the presence of Vietnamese troops in Cambodia represented a violation of Cambodia's right to internal sovereignty and a military affront to its independence, and all shipments of food, medicine and commodities were halted until 1984 for fear they should fall into Vietnamese hands and not profit the needy.[31]

On February 19, Heng Samrin and Pham Van Dong signed a twenty-five-year Treaty of Peace, Amity and Cooperation legalizing the presence of 180,000 Vietnamese troops in Cambodia. Much like Hanoi's treaties with Vientiane and Moscow, the Vietnamese-Cambodian treaty provided for mutual support in the event of an attack, but also reiterated each nation's wish for peace and friendship with their ASEAN neighbors.[32] However, Article 2 of the treaty, stating that the two countries agreed "to lend mutual support and aid in every field and in all necessary forms to strengthen their defense capacities" hinted at a broader military agreement.[33] Similarly, the presence of the south–Lao military commander at the signing of a five-year Lao-Cambodian pact in March, pledging economic, cultural and technical cooperation between the two governments, aroused even greater suspicions as to the possibility of an informal military understanding between the three Indochinese countries.[34]

The invasion had a major impact on Hanoi's relations with Washington that would indirectly reinforce Sino-American relations. The State Department condemned the invasion, called for the withdrawal of Vietnamese troops and expressed its concerns over the "danger of a wider conflict."[35] Washington, expressed a State Department spokesman, "takes great exception to [Pol Pot's] human rights record ... [and] as a matter of principle does not feel that a unilateral intervention against that regime by a third power is justified."[36]

Asked whether this would affect American-Vietnamese talks, Assistant Secretary of State for Public Affairs Hodding Carter declared it "clearly does not help at all."[37] On January 9, the State Department declared the official halt of bilateral talks and Hanoi was informed that normalization had been postponed "indefinitely."[38] "Under the [present] circumstances," declared Oakley during a Senate hearing, "there is no question of any movement toward normalization of relations with Vietnam at this time."[39] A congressional visit to Vietnam, which Wolff had planned for January, was called off for fear it would be seen as an approval of the Vietnamese attack.[40]

On January 27, Hanoi's ambassador to Thailand paid an official visit to the U.S. embassy in Bangkok. The Vietnamese ambassador heard Washington's position on the invasion, and although the content of the meeting was not disclosed, the U.S. press speculated that the ambassadors had mentioned Washington's fear that the conflict might spill over into Thailand—possibly also discussing U.S. refusal to normalize.[41] On February 6, Carter declared that Washington remained "intensely interested and deeply committed" to the inviolability of Thai borders.[42] Washington had accepted the Chinese belief that Hanoi may not restrict itself to expansionism within Indochina and seek regional influence beyond Cambodia into Thai territory. In the space of 22 months Washington's position toward Vietnam had reverted from open offers of reconciliation to the distrustful opposition that had characterized the Ford years.

By early 1979, Washington had reversed its former position of rejecting all preconditions for normalization to demanding the total withdrawal of Vietnamese troops from Cambodia as a precondition to the resumption of talks.[43] Holbrooke explained:

> In so doing we made clear that we were not taking sides in Vietnam's dispute with Kampuchea, that we ourselves had long been at the forefront of those nations denouncing the Pol Pot government for its terrible human rights abuses, and that we were not supporting that regime. We stressed, however, that even that regime's unparalleled crimes would not justify a Vietnamese military violation of Kampuchean sovereignty and replacement of the government by force. We urged that the dispute be settled peacefully.[44]

This position represented an attempt to save face regarding relations with Vietnam and justifying past U.S. inaction over the Cambodian genocide. This statement was a serious blow to any further chances of normalizing with Hanoi. It also appeared as an awkward first opening of American support for Pol Pot.[45] Although, during the negotiations the previous fall, Washington had repeatedly asked the Vietnamese not to intervene in Cambodia despite Cambodian human rights violations, the administration had crossed the line into echoing China's accusations on Hanoi and, later, would support Pol Pot keeping his seat at the United Nations. As an observer commented in 1979, "Since the Khmer Rouge were pushed out of Phnom Penh ... they have found themselves thrust into the same political bed as the Western imperialists which, as a government, they had so violently condemned."[46] The roles seemed now reversed, with the U.S. diplomatically backing insurgents against a foreign-backed regime.

Deng's Visit to the United States

The Vietnamese offensive hastened Chinese preparations for war. Within a week, Hanoi reported the presence of Chinese warships in Vietnamese waters and the multiplication of clashes along its northern border with China.[47] In the midst of these preparations, Deng's visit to Washington and the postponing of direct Chinese reaction to the Vietnamese invasion of Cambodia had more to do with the seeking of strategic alliances and the preparation of the Vietnamese "punishment" than with public politeness. Signs of an upcoming Chinese retaliation increased, as well as justifications for China's publicizing of military clashes along the Sino-Vietnamese border initiated by Peking.

On January 5, speaking to twenty-seven American journalists visiting Peking for the press coverage of Sino-American normalization, Deng explained the situation in Vietnam with the following words:

> The flagrant large-scale aggression against Kampuchea by the Vietnamese is not an isolated event, but part of the global strategy of great-power hegemonism [in Moscow]. Its impact is definitely not limited to Vietnam and Kampuchea, nor even to the Asian and Pacific region. It has an impact on the world situation as a whole ... it has been our consistent stand to support Kampuchea against Vietnamese aggression. While attacking Kampuchea, the Vietnamese constantly commit provocations against China, in an attempt to realize the strategic designs of great-power hegemonism.[48]

Peking's charges were certainly directed more toward Moscow than the Vietnamese. In response, the Soviets had already begun increasing concentration of troops along the Sino-Soviet border, reaching one million men in combat readiness. But in the light of Hanoi's recent economic and political weakening, Washington seemed to fear the spilling over of the Khmero-Vietnamese conflict into a war between China and the Soviet Union.[49]

On January 6, American intelligence sources began reporting the increase of Chinese troops along its border with Vietnam.[50] On January 18, the Chinese foreign ministry complained to the Vietnamese embassy that, in the first three weeks of 1979, Vietnamese troops had violated the border thirteen times, killing four Chinese border guards and wounding four others.[51] The next day U.S. intelligence sources released a second "alert memorandum" regarding the Chinese build-up along China's frontier with Vietnam.[52] Shortly after, the *New China News Agency* prophesized: "Having overrun Phnom Penh, they [the Vietnamese] regard it as a landmark of victory, but actually it is a landmark of doom."[53] At the end of January, an analyst predicted that the "Chinese may be polite enough to wait until [D]eng returns from the U.S., but they are not going to hold off for very much longer."[54]

On the eve of the Chinese leader's visit to Washington, Vance said that Moscow should not be alarmed by Deng's visit as Washington's policy toward these two countries "will be balanced and there will be no tilts one way or the other," but Brzezinski had decided otherwise.⁵⁵ Contradicting Vance's declarations, Deng announced that his visit would "lead to an alliance between the United States and China and other countries against the Soviet Union."⁵⁶ The Premier's visit rapidly turned into what the U.S. press dubbed "bearbaiting."⁵⁷

If Sino-American normalization confirmed the predominance of Brzezinski's globalist and anti–Soviet views, and highlighted the extent to which the national security adviser's influence had grown in the White House, Deng Xiaoping's visit illustrated this shift.⁵⁸ More than Carter, it was Brzezinski who staged and managed the Chinese leader's visit to the United States and publicized it to prick Soviet pride.⁵⁹ Carter even allowed Brzezinski to bypass official protocol and play the host, on January 28, the first night of Deng's stay, by inviting the Chinese vice-chairman to a dinner at his own home in McLean, Virginia, as the national security adviser had promised Deng during his visit to Peking in May.⁶⁰

Brzezinski was delighted by Carter's one-night abdication from his presidential privilege, and seized the opportunity to place himself on the same diplomatic level as Deng.⁶¹ Boasting in front of Vance, Woodcock, Oksenberg and Holbrooke, of his success in bringing about Sino-American normalization, Brzezinski pulled out a bottle of vodka offered by Brezhnev, and greatly amused his Chinese guest by toasting Sino-American friendship with the Soviet gift.⁶² Photographs of the dinner were later sent to Vance as nagging souvenirs.⁶³ Amidst all the merry toasts celebrating normalization, Deng took Brzezinski aside and asked him to arrange a private meeting between him and Carter. Brzezinski happily obliged.⁶⁴

On the evening of January 30, Carter received Deng at the White House for the private meeting that the Chinese Vice-Premier had requested. Earlier that day, Deng had reminded his hosts of the recent escalation of problems in Southeast Asia, which he attributed to Hanoi's misbehavior, and declared that "both the United States and China had long and unpleasant contacts with the Vietnamese."⁶⁵ This brief introduction was only a hint of what Deng would privately reveal.

During the private meeting, in the presence of Brzezinski, Mondale, Vance and Secretary of Defense Harold Brown, Deng explained that "[Peking] consider[s] it necessary to put a restraint on the wild ambitions of the Vietnamese and to give them an appropriate limited lesson." Knowing that Washington had chosen to maintain its distance from the Cambodian-Vietnamese conflict and, under Brzezinski's ideological lead, had turned its attention to more globalist concerns, Deng added that, beyond the regional aspect of such a move, the lesson would "disrupt Soviet strategic calculations." The vice-premier was asking for "moral support." In order to reassure Carter, he added that the lesson would be limited in time and scope and was not aimed at promoting direct Sino-Soviet confrontation.⁶⁶ China was seeking Carter's unofficial support to punish Hanoi and, indirectly, Moscow, to minimize the risk of Soviet military reprisals but also to guarantee that this move would not jeopardize China's seat at the United Nations.⁶⁷

Carter only weakly attempted to dissuade his guest of his plans, and enquired whether it would not be preferable to push Moscow and Hanoi into geopolitical isolation rather than to take up military action. The Chinese attack might "arouse sympathy for [the Vietnamese] and cause some nations to brand China as a culprit."⁶⁸ Deng disagreed, arguing that Soviet threat could be extracted from Vietnam only by forcing

Hanoi and Moscow closer together, which would enhance their ideological and political incompatibilities and break up their alliance. However, as years of Soviet domination of Eastern Europe had shown, it seemed highly improbable that the Vietnamese would, once under total dependence, have the slightest chance of causing "friction" with Moscow without being crushed in return. Carter refrained from giving a direct answer and informed his guest that he would first have to privately consult his aides to weigh the situation.[69]

During the reception given in his honor at the Kennedy Center on January 29, Deng prepared U.S. public opinion for the upcoming Chinese move on Vietnam. He reminded the press that the two nations were "duty bound" to help both peace and stability in the world, adding that he and the Carter administration had entirely agreed as to where the dangers to peace might lie. The statement threw the secretary of state, who up to then had always made a point of maintaining an equilibrium between Washington's dealings with Peking and with Moscow, into considerable embarrassment.[70]

In an interview with Hedley Donovan in the *Washington Star* Deng had pronounced the Soviet Union a "hotbed of war" and assured the reporter that the United States was in "strategic retreat."[71] "If we really want to be able to place curbs on the polar bear," he continued, "the only thing is for us to unite."[72] Keeping within the same rhetoric, Deng explained to a group of journalists, on January 31, that the United States, China, Japan, Western Europe and Third World countries should unite against the Soviet threat.[73] "The threat to international peace, security and stability," Deng explained, "comes from the Soviet Union so the thing that we can all do is that we should try to hamper whatever they do, undermine whatever they do and frustrate what they try to do in any part of the world."[74] In Southeast Asia for instance, Deng explained, Peking supported Cambodia's efforts to defeat the Vietnamese—and, through it—Soviet aggression. Deng even publicly admitted that Peking was supplying Pol Pot's forces with both weapons and ammunition to continue their resistance to Hanoi's expansionism.[75]

Brzezinski was more than ever infatuated with Deng's "single most impressive demonstration of raw power politics," and did not wish his guest to think the U.S. weak and shy when facing exterior provocations.[76] Despite his yielding to Brzezinski's influence, Carter did not wish to use Sino-American normalization as an irritant to Moscow and reportedly hesitated to back Peking's plans.[77] "I was worried," Brzezinski recalls in his memoirs, "that the President might be persuaded by Vance to put maximum pressure on the Chinese not to use force, since this would simply convince the Chinese that the United States was a 'paper tiger.'"[78] Brzezinski did his best to convince Carter to support the Chinese move.

In their next meeting on the morning of January 31, Carter supplied Deng with a handwritten letter presenting a synopsis of the reasons why the administration opposed the Chinese invasion of Vietnam. After listing nine reasons for Chinese restraint, mainly the risk of an escalation of the conflict on a regional scale, Carter concluded that the Chinese plans would represent a "serious mistake," but his objections were expressed in a remarkably weak tone:

> Because of these reasons the United States could not support such action, and I strongly urge you not to approve it. In my opinion, Vice Premier Deng, a concerted effort through the United Nations or other international force could prove to be much more damaging to Viet Nam and her allies.[79]

This mildly worded letter amounted to a U.S. discharge of responsibility in an affair that it did not condemn. Rather than rejecting the concept of a lesson on Vietnam, Washington agreed to it in principle, but expressed restraint as to the means by which it should be carried out. "I felt that this was the right approach," noted Brzezinski, "for we could not collude formally with the Chinese in sponsoring what was tantamount to overt military aggression."[80] Carter was giving a green light to Peking while denying Washington's complicity.

In an attempt to distance himself from responsibility, Carter records in his memoirs that Deng "claimed to be still considering the issue, but my impression was that the decision had already been made. Vietnam would be punished."[81] However, the record shows that each Chinese step in preparing for the invasion always followed a push-through in Sino-American relations. Therefore the accuracy of Carter's claim remains doubtful as Chinese caution seems to indicate that the invasion may not have occurred had Washington refrained from offering its support.

Whereas the president's memoirs point to the probability that Peking would have acted without Washington's support, Brzezinski claims that it seemed doubtful that Peking would have engaged in a military strike against Vietnam had Washington refused its support.[82] While one cannot confirm what Peking's decision would have been, it seems nevertheless clear that the decision to back China originated with Brzezinski.

In Hanoi's opinion, Brzezinski's involvement in the Chinese plans went even farther, as Luu Van Loi explained:

> Carter said that war might exert a negative influence on the U.S. and the world public opinion, China should review its plans. But Carter's close entourage, on the contrary, encouraged China to give Vietnam a "lesson." Security Adviser Brézinski said China should deal a strong blow that would not last long.[83]

While in the United States, Deng also engaged in a loud propaganda campaign against Moscow and Hanoi, stressing the need to counter Soviet influence either politically or through other means. Speaking to eighty-five leading members of Congress on January 30, the vice-premier found that most were ready to side with China against Vietnam. Deng charged the Soviet Union of backing Vietnam's attack on Cambodia in order to fulfill their expansionist ambitions in Southeast Asia and warned that the "zealous pushing of a global strategy for world domination by the hegemonists cannot but increase the danger of a new world-war."[84] However, the "Chinese people suffered amply from the miseries of war," he explained, "We do not wish to fight a war unless it is forced upon us. We are firmly against a new world war"—implying that Peking was acting as a responsible, peace-loving country and that provocations originated in Moscow.[85] Deng later added that he could not dismiss the possibility of using military force to help secure Chinese borders against Vietnam using Vietnam's invasion of Cambodia to justify Chinese fears.[86] He explained that China needed to act "appropriately" in response to Vietnam's move on Cambodia:

> We call the Vietnamese the Cubans of the Orient. If you don't teach them some necessary lessons ... their provocations will increase.... Naturally we are also concerned about the security of our borders. There have been necessary troop movements and you are aware of this. But as to what actions to take, we will have to wait and see. I can say two things: one, we Chinese mean what we say; and two, we do not act rashly.[87]

Peking Review reported this statement in rather different words, adding, at the end of Deng's speech, his remark that "as to what measures we will adopt ... a question like that is not something to be decided by us alone."[88] The nuance in these two versions of Deng's remarks hinted that China had expected Washington's support for the invasion and—as Brzezinski had claimed—might not have attempted the military move had Washington categorically refused to back Peking. Overall, Congress seemed impressed by his zeal and Senator Kennedy reported that Deng had made "a hell of an impression."[89]

In the meantime, Vietnamese forces gathered on the border in an effort to protect their country against air-strikes, while, on the other side of the frontier, some 100,000 Chinese troops were starting to assemble. The Vietnamese foreign ministry sent a protest note to the Chinese embassy charging that Chinese troops were provoking clashes by barging into Lai Chau province. The next day Hanoi further accused Peking of sending troops to attack a Vietnamese sugar mill, destroying several houses and wounding Vietnamese workers.[90]

Reports on Vietnamese protests to Chinese accusations failed to attract the attention of the U.S. press, which focused on Deng's visit. For nearly a week Deng was on all the television shows, newspapers and magazines and even featured in *Time* magazine as "Man of the Year."[91] As one observer noted, Deng "turned out to be a master of U.S.-style political campaigning."[92] "It's a good thing you're not an American," Mondale jokingly told Deng, "because you could be elected to any office you sought."[93] Carter, seduced by the Chinese vice-premier, would call Deng's visit "one of the delightful experiences of [his] Presidency."[94]

Deng's success lay in portraying Washington as siding with Peking against Moscow. Vance, who feared that Deng's visit, and especially any mention of Soviet "hegemonism," would provoke Soviet wrath, attempted to convince Carter to not issue a joint communiqué, but Carter impatiently rejected Vance's proposal after ironically asking the secretary whether "that [was] another apology" to the Soviets.[95] This point, emphasized by Gaddis Smith, suggests that not only was policy-making set upon the lines of Brzezinski's anti–Soviet ideologies, but that Vance's role had declined from once being advisory to the executive branch to becoming the spokesman of apologies to the Soviet Union.

Vance could no longer compete with Brzezinski's influence. His ideas were no longer heard, and his duty—largely self-imposed—was now to buffer the effects of the new U.S. policy lines on Soviet ears. Carter and Deng issued a joint communiqué, bearing a familiar Chinese flavor, stating that the two countries "are opposed to efforts by any country or group of countries to establish hegemony or domination over others." This threw Vance into even greater embarrassment when Dobrynin requested to meet him to seek yet another explanation of U.S. intentions.[96] Brzezinski even succeeded in convincing Carter to withdraw the disclaimer of the two previous Sino-American statements, carefully stating that relations between the two countries were "not directed at other states."[97]

On February 1, Soviet news agency *Tass* commented:

> All this calls for clarification. For in statements by the American side it was said that the talks with Deng revealed the existence of "many common perspectives," that the two sides could facilitate the attainment of "analogous aims" and even that the sides had agreed to

"conduct regular consultations on questions of common interest." The Chinese understanding of perspectives, aims and strategic interest is known....[98]

On February 8, supporting Moscow, *Nhan Dan* simultaneously warned that the Sino-American collusion was doomed to failure.[99] Science Adviser Frank Press, then on a visit to Moscow, heard Prime Minister Kosygin's views that Carter should have objected to Deng's anti–Soviet declarations when in the United States, which had constituted a "declaration of war."[100]

Asked whether he endorsed Deng's anti–Soviet statements, Carter informed journalists, during a press conference on February 12, that he had "never tried to exercise censorship on a head of state" visiting the U.S. and therefore could not prevent Deng from presenting his views. However, he added that there were "some areas where we disagree with the assessment of the Soviet Union as expressed by Mr. Deng.... I don't have any inclination," he added, "to condemn the Soviets as a people or even as a government."[101] Hanoi would later interpret Washington's failure to oppose Deng's claims of an impending "lesson" on Vietnam as an authorization of the attack.[102]

Brzezinski supervised Deng's departure and again performed presidential duties. He noted that "as a particular gesture of friendship, I went out to the helipad near the Washington Monument to bid goodbye to Deng personally. I wanted to underline presidential support and Deng gave me the impression of being quite pleased."[103]

While stopping in Tokyo on his way back from the United States, Deng again repeated his threat regarding Vietnam in an increasingly confident tone, insisting that it would not be a rash action.[104] The Chinese move would simply be "punitive."[105] Carter's restraint on the issue had reassured Peking of U.S. backing. Later, he privately confided to the Japanese prime minister Takeo Fakuda that "[i]t is wise for China to force the Vietnamese to stay in Kampuchea, because that way they will suffer more."[106] Cambodian sovereignty seemed not a justification but a tool.

The Chinese lesson also aimed to teach Washington to adopt a stronger stance in future exchanges with Moscow, as Brzezinski also wished, bringing the U.S. from the level of "paper tiger" to that of a superpower ready to stand up to Moscow. "The measures the United States has taken in Iran and in dealing with Cuba are not good," Deng explained during a stop in Japan. "The Soviet Union will never be impressed by halfway positions."[107] The "lesson" would teach Moscow that Peking did not fear the Soviet giant, and lecture Washington on how Peking felt that foreign policy and international conflicts should be handled.[108]

Following his return to Peking, Deng chaired a CCP Military Commission that decided to launch the attack.[109] The conference, from February 9 to 12, led to the appointment of a general military command, including Deng and three other important figures for the southern front against Vietnam, and provided for the creation of a northern front in the event of Soviet retaliation against China.[110] One may further speculate that the Commission also decided that the attack should be launched soon after Deng's return from the United States, in the hope that the tight timing of events would induce uncertainty over a potential Sino-American collusion and prevent the Soviets from launching a counter-offensive. Peking seemed to care little that the short delay would undermine U.S. claims that Washington had played no part in the Chinese decision.[111]

China's Lesson on Vietnam

On February 16, Deng held a last explanatory meeting in Peking, aimed at instructing high-ranking cadres of the necessity of the war, insisting that it represent a gesture of self-defense over Vietnamese incursions beyond the Sino-Vietnamese border.[112] That day, Washington received a message from Peking, informing the White House that China was in the course of preparing necessary "self-defense" measures. Washington then drafted a message to be delivered to Moscow revealing when the armed conflict might start, requesting that no military measures be taken in response to the Chinese move.[113] Counting on the American discreet message to Moscow, Deng predicted that the Soviet response would be limited to small-scale skirmishes along the Sino-Soviet border.[114] The vice-premier dispatched his close aide Commander Xu Shiyou to head the operations.[115]

China called its troops to full alert in Sinkiang province, its border region with the Soviet Union, and evacuated local civilians.[116] Seventy to eighty Chinese divisions were already facing Soviet troops on the border.[117] Intelligence sources revealed that two weeks before the invasion of Vietnam the Soviet Union discreetly had delivered two Petya II class frigates to Vietnam.[118] Six days after the start of the attack, Moscow had begun the airlift of military supplies to Vietnam and dispatched a naval task force towards Vietnamese waters. By February 27, Moscow had scattered seven intelligence-gathering ships and a cruiser in the Southeast Asian seas, and guided-missile cruiser *Admiral Senyavin* was making her way to East Asian waters.[119] A few days later, several Soviet vessels had docked for the first time in a Vietnamese port in Danang then in Haiphong to deliver logistic supplies and missiles.[120]

In Washington, Brzezinski closely followed the Chinese move. During the morning staff meeting, Brzezinski commented that the Cambodian-Vietnamese conflict had, in the words of Oksenberg, "been essentially beneficial to [U.S.] interests, for it has exacerbated Sino-Soviet tensions." Although Oksenberg had usually agreed with the national security adviser's views, the Chinese expert appeared skeptical.[121]

Despite U.S. claims of neutrality on the Sino-Vietnamese war, the United States dispatched several U.S. military ships in the West Pacific in a half-veiled show of force to discreetly remind Moscow of the U.S. wish for non interference in the Chinese offensive against Vietnam. The U.S. aircraft-carrier *Constellation*, with its long-range patrol aircraft equipped with radars, as well as the *Midway*, were sailing north to engage in a "military exercise" off the coast of South Korea. Concurrently, the Seventh Fleet had taken to following a Soviet squadron of eleven ships in the South China Sea while the destroyer *Richard S. Edwards* followed a Soviet missile cruiser.[122] Washington intended their presence to discourage Soviet military maneuvers against China.[123]

While the Chinese attack was intended to punish Vietnam for invading Cambodia and drawing closer to Moscow, Peking publicly endorsed the safer stand, decided during the CCP Committee meeting of December, of portraying the attack as a response to Vietnamese violations of Chinese territory. Officially, China was not getting involved in the war between Vietnam and Cambodia, which would have made the Chinese position difficult to justify, and legitimized its right to attack Vietnam by claiming instead that it was merely protecting its own territory and sovereignty. Peking seemed little troubled by the conflict between its border claims and Deng's repeated warnings that Hanoi deserved to be punished for its move against Cambodia—a point Washington would fail to notice once the war began, clumsily adopting Deng's position while in the U.S. that Peking was responding to the attack on Cambodia. Although the mention of an upcoming lesson on Vietnam only became part of Chinese rhetoric following the overthrow of Pol Pot, Peking understood that support for a barbaric regime would be both embarrassing and diplomatically unproductive.[124]

Thus, starting in mid–1978, the Chinese press began to publicize China's indignation over the multiplication of Sino-Vietnamese border skirmishes, which were possibly exacerbated by Peking to justify its new stance. The strategy later allowed Peking to present the attack on Vietnam as a self-defense measure. In early February, the Chinese foreign ministry issued a protest note to the Vietnamese embassy stating that, from mid–January to February 7, seventy Chinese military and civilians had been killed along the Sino-Vietnamese border. The following day Vice-Premier Li Hsien-nien warned Hanoi to halt its provocations.[125]

Four days later, on February 11, Nguyen Duy Trinh sought United Nations support and reported to Waldheim and Security Council President Abdulla Bishara that sixty Chinese incursions on Vietnamese territory had occurred in the first week of February and informed the UN that Peking was "feverishly preparing for war."[126] On February 16, one day before the Chinese attack, in preparing justifications for self-defense, the Chinese foreign ministry again formally protested to the Vietnamese embassy that Hanoi was sending "large numbers of armed personnel to encroach upon Chinese territory."[127] The Vietnamese press mirrored Chinese accusations in issuing a series of warnings that the "Chinese expansionists were preparing a dangerous trap for humanity, like the [N]azis during the Second World War."[128]

The invasion started at dawn on February 17 coinciding with the Vietnamese signing of the Treaty of Friendship with the new Cambodian regime. One hundred thousand Chinese troops poured out of Yunnan and Kwangsi into Vietnam's six northern provinces. Another 150,000 troops and 800 aircraft remained behind the border, some of which had been demobilized from their previous position, facing Taiwan, to reinforce Chinese forces pressing against the Vietnamese border.[129]

In Phnom Penh, during the preparatory meeting about the Cambodian-Vietnamese friendship treaty with the new Cambodian authorities, a Vietnamese official came to whisper the news of the Chinese attack in Pham Van Dong's ear. But Dong barely raised an eyebrow and proceeded to the signing of the document, commenting that Vietnam's plans would not be interrupted.[130] Nor were Vietnamese troops mobilized to counter the offensive.[131] Vietnam understood that, to save face, Peking could not remain silent on the Vietnamese move in Cambodia. Consequently, the attack was symbolic and its scope would remain limited. In fact, Hanoi called for mobilization only on the day Peking announced its withdrawal. In Le Duan's own words, Hanoi was showing that it was not "scared" of China.[132] The war was mainly one of face.[133] Thus, on February 27, addressing American newsmen in Peking, Deng confided that China had had "no other aims than to explode the myth that is Vietnam's claim to be the third strongest military power in the world."[134]

After capturing four of the six capitals of the border provinces, the Chinese troops headed toward the town of Lang Son.¹³⁵ But the Chinese invasion had become more costly than Peking had expected and the Chinese rapidly found themselves outweighed by the well-trained Vietnamese resistance troops. Although a diplomatic victory, the Chinese attack represented a military flop. In fact, the Vietnamese regional militia troops had contained Peking's forces with only half their number of men.¹³⁶ The Chinese operation, explained a diplomat in Peking, had been consistent with Deng's personality: "hastily conceived, ill tempered and poorly thought out."¹³⁷

By February 20, three to six Chinese main force divisions had come to reinforce the positions of the fifteen or seventeen already in Vietnam, followed two days later by another three, amounting to a total of 320,000 men.¹³⁸ Vietnamese ambassador to the UN Ha Van Lau remarked that the concentration of Chinese troops on Vietnamese territory was now superior to that of U.S. troops at the highest point of the American war in Indochina.¹³⁹ Such analogies with the American experience in Indochina confirmed that Hanoi was aware of Washington's backing of the Chinese attack and called for U.S. restraint.

As the Chinese were fighting their way into entering Lang Son and encountering increasing Vietnamese resistance, Peking judged that it had proven its point and announced on March 5 that it had "attained the goals set for them" and was withdrawing its forces from Vietnam.¹⁴⁰ It is estimated that from the Vietnamese invasion of Cambodia in 1978 to the final withdrawal of its troops in 1989, Hanoi had suffered 60,000 casualties.¹⁴¹ This "war of face" had produced as many Chinese and Vietnamese casualties as the Vietnam war had American victims.¹⁴²

The Vietnamese press proudly announced that the Chinese lesson on Vietnam had turned into a Vietnamese lesson on Peking—a theme that the Western press promptly adopted.¹⁴³ American sources drew an obvious parallel to Washington's history in Vietnam. Pointing at Deng's recent difficulties within the Chinese leadership, *Saturday Review* inscribed Peking's military misfortune to "statesmen who feel they can best justify their station not by acknowledging their errors but by asserting their power at bombast."¹⁴⁴

As the invasion began, the State Department called a meeting in which the U.S. official stance was decided.¹⁴⁵ Carter adopted a two-fold policy, condemning both Vietnam's invasion of Cambodia and China's invasion of Vietnam. On February 20, only three days after the start of the Chinese offensive, Carter stressed that Washington was "deeply concerned" by the events in Southeast Asia. "[I]n the last few weeks," he declared, "we have seen the Vietnamese invasion of Cambodia and, *as a result*, a Chinese border penetration into Vietnam.... We have opposed both military actions."¹⁴⁶ Carter's declaration set Washington's official position: the Chinese attack was a response to the Vietnamese offensive against Cambodia. The strategy placed the U.S. in safe neutrality, publicly condemning both actions while discreetly supporting the Chinese move.

As had become common in the administration, this policy had been engineered by Brzezinski. But, more importantly, it demonstrated that the national security adviser was now remarkably close to occupying the role of policy-maker in the White House:

> I wanted to avoid a situation in which we would be pressured, both by world opinion and by the State Department, to condemn the Chinese as aggressors. Accordingly, I developed a proposal that the United States should criticize the Chinese for their military action but

should couple that criticism with a parallel condemnation of the Vietnamese for their occupation of Cambodia, and demand that both China and Vietnam pull out their forces. I knew that such a proposal would be totally unacceptable to the Vietnamese and to the Soviets, and hence would provide a partial diplomatic umbrella for the Chinese action without associating the United States with it, thereby permitting the United States to adopt publicly a somewhat critical position.[147]

In so doing he contradicted China's claim that its invasion of Vietnam was the result of Vietnamese provocations along the Sino-Vietnamese border.[148] While Peking stressed the regional details of the conflict and the border clashes to legitimize its attack, Washington's position failed to mention this point. This omission suggests that the only element now of importance to Washington was the geopolitical anti–Soviet dimension of the conflict. Seen through globalist eyes, regional concerns hardly mattered.

It was also decided, during the staff meeting that, officially, Washington would deny having been informed of the attack during Deng's visit.[149] As American "interests are not threatened" publicly explained an official, Washington would remain politically aloof.[150] Carter further stressed that Washington "will not get involved in conflict between Asian Communist nations."[151] During a press conference, State Department spokesman Hodding Carter repeated that Washington was "committed to the territorial integrity of all nations."[152] "It's not our war," repeatedly echoed U.S. officials.[153]

A second staff meeting, held on the day of the invasion, was to study possible Soviet reaction—the issue that lay at the heart of Sino-American concerns.[154]

Congressional opinion seemed split over the issue and while some members of Congress called for a hard position on Vietnam, others had understood that too early a withdrawal of the Vietnamese military would destabilize the region. In a letter to the president, Representative Solarz, one of the main Jewish-American voices to speak out in favor of Vietnam, argued that Washington should not pressure Hanoi to withdraw from Cambodia as this would undoubtedly secure Pol Pot's return to power.[155]

The two-week delay between Deng's return to Peking and the Chinese military offensive meant that the Carter administration would have a difficult time justifying the timing of these events, and that Moscow and Hanoi could undoubtedly deduce that a Sino-American collusion existed behind the Chinese move on Vietnam. On the very day of the Chinese invasion, Carter telephoned Brezhnev and called for Soviet restraint.[156] An official message from the White House repeated this appeal in "the spirit of dedication to preserving peace, as exemplified in our mutual effort to limit strategic arms"—an indirect threat that a Soviet move would jeopardize the establishment of a new SALT treaty.[157] In his reply to Carter, Brezhnev pointed out that only two weeks had elapsed since Deng's return from the United States before the Chinese attack on Vietnam, and rhetorically asked: "And is this a simple coincidence? We and others must, of course, draw from this the appropriate conclusions."[158]

The Soviet press pointed to Brzezinski as the main initiator of the recent events. "[I]t was no accident," claimed a Soviet radio broadcasting in Mandarin to Peking's attention, "that Deng Xiaoping lunched with Brzezinski immediately upon his arrival in the United States." The radio further accused Peking and Washington of having planned the attack as early as May, during Brzezinski's visit to Peking.[159] "[N]o propaganda twists and turns," claimed *Pravda*, "will help cover up the responsibility of those circles in the U.S.A. that facilitated, directly or indirectly, Peking's actions."[160] Vietnam agreed with the Soviet analysis. Hanoi charged that Deng had "won the approval and support of the United States in Japan" and that both governments "knew in advance about the entire plan of this attack"—a statement State Department observers labeled "the strongest political swipe ... to date."[161]

On February 17, a State Department spokesman answered these accusations, declaring that while Deng had indeed mentioned that "unspecified types of action" would be directed against Vietnam, Carter had strictly stated that he objected to further military confrontations in the area.[162] The next day, Washington cabled Tokyo and several European leaders, assuring them that the U.S. bore no responsibility in the conflict and repeating Peking's pledge that the invasion would be limited in both time and scope.[163] On February 23, Holbrooke again repeated that Carter had made clear to Deng that Washington "would not support such an action" and accused Moscow of spreading rumors for its own propaganda needs.[164]

On February 22, in order to prove non-involvement in the conflict, the United States requested an urgent meeting of the United Nations Security Council to study the events in Southeast Asia—calling for the simultaneous withdrawal of Chinese forces from Vietnam, and Vietnamese forces from Cambodia.[165] Vance rejected the idea that an immediate American draft resolution on the Sino-Vietnamese conflict be presented to the UN, and suggested that a third country be contacted and requested to introduce a resolution on which the United States would follow up.[166] When the issue was brought up during Security Council meetings, Andrew Young repeated the State Department position, rejecting rumors of Sino-American collusion, and "urged restraint on all parties." Behind the solely humanitarian aspect of such a decision, Young explained that it was "important for us [the United States] to push a resolution to demonstrate to the world that we are not in complicity with this invasion."[167]

The Vietnamese press remarked that Washington was repeating Peking's "propaganda lines" and "deliberately belittling the seriousness and minimizing the great danger of this aggression" to "confuse public opinion."[168] "The reaction of the U.S. Administration," further asserted *Pravda*, "appears, if not as approval, then at least most definitely as indirect encouragement." No resolution would, however, be adopted due to China's warnings that it would veto any resolution that condemned its move on Vietnam, and Moscow's declaration that it would veto any resolution that failed to condemn China.[169]

In the meantime, however, Sino-American links were developing, fueling additional rumors fed to the Soviet and Vietnamese press. On February 20, Carter had declared that the Chinese military move would not jeopardize Sino-American normalization, which was now "an accomplished fact and could not be altered."[170] Moscow renewed its accusations, pointing at Washington's dubious inconsistency in condemning the Chinese invasion while refusing to postpone Treasury Secretary Michael Blumenthal's visit to China only a few days after Peking's military move on Vietnam.[171] The Vietnamese press portrayed the visit as blinding proof of Sino-American "collusion" and a political "duet" aimed at weakening Hanoi.[172]

In fact, Vance had firmly objected to the visit, claiming that it would be seen as an approval of the Chinese move on Vietnam. Congressman Wolff's congressional trip to

Hanoi had been canceled the previous month to boycott the Vietnamese invasion of Cambodia. But Brzezinski had countered the obstacle, stating that postponing the trip would disappoint the Peking leadership and confirm China's remark that the United States was a "paper tiger," in view of American softness towards Moscow. "If Blumenthal can visit Moscow while the Soviets ... back a Vietnamese invasion of Cambodia," had argued Oksenberg to NSC Military Adviser General William Odom, "he ought to be able to visit Peking. A final argument is that to pull Blumenthal back would expose the President's China policy as vacillating and inconsistent and having suffered a setback."[173]

Carter sided with the NSC, and chose to proceed with Blumenthal's visit. But upon arriving in Peking, the secretary warned the Chinese that "even limited invasions risk wider wars and turn public opinion against the transgressor."[174] Brzezinski immediately cabled him to cease such declarations and to focus on the promotion of Sino-American trade.[175] However, the United States was also keen on making a public show of Washington's disapproval of the Chinese offensive, a face-saving position to wave at international opinion. On February 27, Blumenthal handed Deng a letter from Carter calling for an immediate cease-fire. The invasion of Vietnam, the Treasury Secretary later explained, presented "risks that are unwarranted."[176]

Hanoi noted that despite Carter's letter to Deng, Washington had concluded several trade agreements that represented a "spiritual and material encouragement to the Chinese authorities' adventures against neighboring countries." The ceremony for the opening of the U.S. embassy and the hoisting of the American flag while China was at war, commented the Vietnamese press, stood as further proof of Sino-American collusion.[177] Carter's announcement, on the same day, that he hoped to obtain congressional approval to extend most-favored-nation trade status, to both Peking and Moscow, certainly came as an added source of bitterness to the Vietnamese.[178]

As Peking had predicted, the Soviet response to Peking's provocations was limited. Moscow uttered a series of harsh articles promising Soviet support, which it would eventually never provide, and warnings that Peking was attempting to "plunge the world into a war," playing on the American fear of nuclear confrontation between the two communist giants.[179] In fact, Moscow understood that Peking's action was more of a show of diplomatic arrogance than a real threat to Soviet allies or expansionist ambitions in Asia. Moreover, the Soviet-Vietnamese treaty merely provided that mutual consultation be held in case of an attack and did not include the need for automatic Soviet military intervention. Nor did the Soviet Union wish to risk nuclear war with China or to jeopardize its negotiations on SALT with Washington. And, indeed, Moscow openly signaled its intentions to Peking. While the Soviet press warned Peking to "stop before it is too late," Moscow dismissed any intention that it wished to engage in direct confrontation with China and expressed its confidence that the "heroic Vietnamese people ... [are] capable of standing up for [themselves]" without Soviet interference.[180] The Soviet response had been carefully crafted so as to openly support Vietnam without risking direct confrontation with China. Rather than warning China not to go any further, Moscow simply called on China to "stop before it is too late" without stressing where exactly the limit to Soviet tolerance stood.[181]

The Kremlin briefed foreign diplomats in Moscow on the Soviet choice for restraint should China also keep its pledge of limited intervention, knowing that this message would be passed on to Peking.[182] Other declarations would merely be directed at intimidating Peking and saving face in front of Hanoi. Speaking on Soviet television Brezhnev denounced the Chinese "brazen, bandit attack on a small neighboring country" and demanded Chinese withdrawal "to the last soldier" without, however, stating what consequences Chinese disobedience would entail.[183]

Hanoi and Moscow were not far from the truth in emphasizing Washington's involvement in the Chinese attack. Not only had Washington been informed of the Chinese plan to attack Vietnam, but it had also supported it. During the offensive, Brzezinski met every evening with Chinese ambassador Chai Zemin to inform him of Soviet military deployments along the Sino-Soviet border, and produced satellite intelligence material otherwise unavailable to Peking.[184] As much as the invasion was labeled "Deng's war" in China, it could have been labeled "Brzezinski's war" in Washington, both in indirectly confronting Moscow and gaining supremacy over Vance. Brzezinski proudly declared that "the new American-Chinese relationship had weathered its baptism of fire."[185]

Although Brezhnev boasted, on March 5, during the Chinese withdrawal from Vietnam that the Chinese move had failed to affect Soviet-American relations and expressed his hope that a summit would soon be held between Carter and himself, Peking had reasons for rejoicing.[186] While protesting angrily against the Chinese attack, Moscow had not engaged in a military response. While newspapers mentioned the political existence of a China Card, the world was witnessing Peking's American Card on the Soviets.[187] More than Washington, it was Peking that extracted immediate gains from Sino-American collusion. The Chinese victory in Vietnam, despite military difficulties, was diplomatic. Peking had humiliated Moscow in the eyes of the world, downgrading the political and military value of the Soviet-Vietnamese treaty, consolidating Deng's position in the government, and bringing out anti–Soviet sentiments in its new American allies. Peking had shown Moscow and the ASEAN countries that, in Asia, China remained the greater power, guarding its smaller Asian brothers from invading Soviet influence. Failure to draw Hanoi away from the Soviet orbit or to free Cambodia—the stated goals of the Chinese "lesson"—were hardly an issue.

After witnessing Hanoi's plunge into the Soviet orbit, Washington had allowed Peking to inflict on Hanoi and Phnom Penh what some historians labeled "Vietnam's Vietnam" and what the *Congressional Quarterly* termed a "New Vietnam War."[188] The analogy was correct only in its globalist dimension, to the extent this new war once again aimed at containing a big communist power's influence upon a smaller country. The roles, however, had been reversed.

As James Mann explained, "U.S. support for China's invasion was also a remarkable demonstration of just how much America's role in Asia had changed" since the early 1960s. While Washington had justified its fifteen-year involvement in Vietnam with the need to counter the prospects of Chinese expansionism into Indochina through its friendly Vietnamese communist neighbors, the U.S. now realized that Peking and Hanoi were neither friends nor allies. The "crowning irony," explained Mann, was that Washington was now siding with its former adversary by helping the Chinese, through unofficial channels, to attack a country Washington had sought to protect from Chinese grasp during four administrations.[189]

Given the Carter administration's shift from regionalist to globalist concerns in 1978, Vietnam was no longer viewed as an independent nation-state but as a "proxy" of the Soviet camp in a world defined by superpower rivalry. Vietnam's regionalist ambitions of creating an "Indochina Federation" were inflated into a globalist perception of Soviet hegemonistic designs aimed at provocatively confronting both Washington and Peking. For the second time in two decades—albeit for different reasons—Vietnam had become the arena of Cold War confrontation, and American-Vietnamese normalization turned into a diplomatic casualty of the superpower struggle.

Conclusion

Reflecting upon postwar American-Vietnamese relations, a Vietnamese official concluded: "There have been many missed opportunities for a political rapprochement during those years [1975–1979]. On both sides," he added pensively.[1] John McAuliff agreed. "The first mistake was Vietnamese," he explained, "the second was American."[2]

Following the fall of Saigon, the U.S. and Vietnam continued hostilities on a diplomatic front, each failing to understand or consider the other's position. Hanoi noisily trumpeted and requested reparations as much as a token of American acceptance of Vietnamese superiority as an economic necessity. Washington rejected all claims of postwar American responsibilities and defensively counterattacked Hanoi with the MIA issue.

Ford's use of MIAs for political ends was not new. It had begun as early as 1969 with Nixon's "go public" campaign, initiated to portray the Vietcong as "inhumane" in their refusal to account for MIAs, and to pull U.S. public opinion towards supporting the war.[3] Nixon had justified the continued U.S. military presence in South Vietnam by arguing that Americans could not leave as long as POWs remained in North Vietnam. He had also introduced the issue of POWs and MIAs into the Paris Peace talks only five days after his 1968 election.[4] By the end of the 1960s, MIAs had become a national priority and while the executive branch had used POWs as an excuse for continued U.S. involvement in Vietnam, MIAs became the reason justifying continued American hostility in the postwar era.

Ford followed on his predecessor's approach, refusing to consider Hanoi's call for aid while at the same time requesting Hanoi's collaboration on the "humanitarian" issue of MIAs after Washington had accused Hanoi of an inhumane attitude for nearly six years. Hanoi opposed Ford's labeling the Peace Accords "void" whenever Vietnam tackled the issue of aid provided in Article 21, while calling on Hanoi to implement Article 8b on MIAs. While Ford argued that Washington simply wished to recover missing men and not promote animosity towards Vietnam, his vetoes on Vietnamese admission to the UN in 1975 and 1976, and his use of MIAs to promote his presidential campaign, point in the opposite direction. The unrealistic demand for a complete resolution of the MIA issue as a precondition to any negotiations on normalization with Hanoi was an excuse to postpone normalization in addition to being a lever for domestic electoral support. Furthermore, Hanoi's insistence that aid be provided prior to normalization led to a diplomatic dead-end. While no secondary writings focus on the Ford years, and most studies keep to the geostrategic squabble of the Carter years, the study of the Carter administration's dealings with Vietnam cannot be fully understood if one fails to contrast it with Ford's policies.

The complexity of bilateral relations grew further as the Fourth Party Congress in December 1976, following Vietnamese reunification, confirmed the increasing authority of a radical faction within the Politburo, led by Le Duc Tho and Le Duan, and the reorganization of Vietnamese priorities. The myth of an "Indochina Federation" in turn promoted Cambodian and Chinese fear of Soviet-backed Vietnamese "hegemonism." The importance of Le Duc Tho and Le Duan has been disregarded in modern analyses. As much as one cannot separate U.S. policies from the geopolitical context and domestic pressures, the story of American-Vietnamese relations is distorted if not viewed within the context of Vietnamese Politburo rivalries and the clash of ideologies.

Carter, intent on pushing towards the end of the Cold War, aimed at normalizing with all nations with which Washington did not enjoy diplomatic relations, and tackled the most controversial issue first—Vietnam—in order that, should this fail, time would allow dust to settle on this issue before his next presidential campaign. This study confirms that Carter dropped the American precondition for normalization from a "total" to a more subjective "satisfactory" accounting, and initiated an opening to Vietnam through the Woodcock mission aimed at promoting dialogue and at de-emphasizing MIAs at the domestic level by suggesting their reclassification into KIAs. The controversy surrounding this visit and the ensuing reclassification of MIAs have seldom been examined. Their importance lies in the fact that this issue remained a delicate topic to be handled with care if Washington did not wish it to backfire on Carter's initiatives towards Vietnam. The impact of MIAs on the U.S. domestic arena explains the importance of this episode on subsequent U.S. perceptions of Vietnam. In Hanoi, Woodcock's exchange of views with the Vietnamese was sufficiently vague to allow each side to interpret the meaning of the other in ways that best suited each country's expectations; and while Washington believed that Hanoi had dropped the aid precondition, the Vietnamese understood that Washington was prepared to pledge aid renaming it "humanitarian" rather than the more aggressive Vietnamese catchwords of "reconstruction," "reparations" or "obligations." Although misperceptions were shared, Vietnam may have been aware of the American mistake and may have sought to further mislead Washington to extract a pledge of aid.

The new Vietnamese leadership had appeared sufficiently friendly during the Woodcock mission to allow the organization of talks in Paris in May, June and December 1977. In May, however, the two sides understood that neither had modified its initial position, despite the seemingly positive dialogue during the Woodcock mission. The Vietnamese had returned to their earlier hard-line stance and the publication of the text of Nixon's secret letter triggered considerable wrath on Capitol Hill, as

Congress formally renounced Nixon's pledge, prohibited the granting of reconstruction aid, and barred the use of U.S. funds for Vietnam, imposing a legislative straightjacket on future initiatives, whether diplomatic or humanitarian, bilateral or international. Interpretations vary on the motivations behind the release of the letter and some authors fail to analyze the underlying reasons for the Vietnamese publication of this document. Chanda and Becker, two of the most distinguished Indochina observers, mention the event but fail to expand on Vietnamese aims in releasing this document.[5] In the light of recently declassified materials and interviews with political actors, this book shows how Vietnamese intentions in releasing the letter lay both in deliberately nagging Washington and in seeking to promote rapprochement in a clumsy fashion by appealing to American opinion, which no longer stood at Hanoi's side. By mid–1977, Hanoi did not truly seem to wish for normalization and believed that Washington, more than Hanoi, longed for diplomatic rapprochement. This letter negatively affected the signing of the Paris Accords and left a long-term impact on bilateral relations.

Further talks in Paris in June and December 1977 did not convince the Vietnamese to change their negotiating tactics; they did not renounce their claim for the implementation of the provisions of the Nixon letter and failed to offer a satisfactory accounting of MIAs. Consequently, the talks did not succeed in calming congressional anger. Carter misunderstood the Vietnamese mood and kept to his friendly approach of seeking mutual concessions and, in September 1977, refrained from vetoing the admission of Vietnam to the UN—further breaking with Ford's policy of opposing Vietnamese membership at all cost.

By the end of 1977 the administration's enthusiasm dwindled as months went by without favorable Vietnamese responses. The White House began to question the necessity of risking further confrontation with Congress over Vietnam when Hanoi was giving only a little slack to ease negotiations. Other concerns had also arisen, such as the ratification of the Panama Canal treaties, SALT, and the completion of PRM-24, giving birth to renewed American interest in normalizing with Peking. Talks stalled as the Vietnamese ambassador to the UN was expelled following his alleged involvement in a spying affair on the U.S. government in early 1978. The U.S. shift away from Vietnam was gradual, starting in late 1977, contrary to Hurst's claim that it occurred in 1978, mainly due to a reorientation of U.S. priorities. Hurst's claim is true, although incomplete. This book shows how Carter's initial wish to normalize became cornered between Vietnamese diplomatic rigidity, congressional bans and the mutually embarrassing scandal of the spying affair, halting all immediate chances of progress in late 1977. In light of the Vietnamese hard-line, Carter turned to securing congressional support for other foreign policy matters, and temporarily shelved normalization with the uncooperative Vietnamese so as not to needlessly irritate Congress. Hurst's appraisal of the late 1977 period, lacking the domestic context and focusing solely on bilateral relations, offers a distorted perspective of the political forces at play, and neglects bilateral tensions in offering an interpretation rooted in Carter's turn from regional to global priorities. This book shows that postwar relations cannot be summarized into such a simplistic pattern.

By 1978, the growth of global conflicts and superpower rivalry dominated the international stage, promoting the expansion of superpower-backed regional conflicts in Indochina and bypassing the now secondary issue of American-Vietnamese relations.

The "proxy war" on the Cambodian-Vietnamese border, opposing Soviet-backed Vietnam to Chinese-backed Cambodia, could be described as a degenerating of the Vietnamese urge for a "special relationship" with Cambodia which, encouraged by Chinese beliefs, Cambodian paranoia and mutual provocation, would lead to the Vietnamese toppling of the Cambodian regime. From then on, regional and bilateral interactions were absorbed into the globalist quagmire of superpower rivalry.

This book confirms suggestions by Funnell, Heder, Elliott, Porter, Becker, Duiker and others, that by early 1978 Vietnam had secretly come to the conclusion that Pol Pot would need to be overthrown.[6] But among these sources only Morris provides a full account of Vietnamese overtures to Moscow to seek international backing for its new goals in Cambodia and developed its links with the Soviet block, culminating in the signing of the Treaty of Friendship and Cooperation on November 3. This book supports Morris' suggestions by showing how Hanoi simultaneously opened to Washington starting in January 1978, proposing normalization without preconditions in a striking shift from its previous stance. Vietnam, knowing that Washington would refuse normalization after the invasion of Cambodia, intended to push towards normalization prior to the invasion, without letting Washington know of Vietnamese intentions towards Cambodia. This accounted for Hanoi's sudden impatience for rapprochement with Washington, which it considered largely an independent issue. Given this new insight, this book rejects claims by Smith and Evans and Rowley, who attribute the failure of normalization mainly to American diplomatic clumsiness while downplaying Vietnamese responsibility. Nor would normalization have altered Vietnamese plans regarding Cambodia. In fact, Hanoi knowingly sided with Moscow for political and military support, while playing on the American belief that it was being drawn towards Moscow due to Washington's failure to normalize, and harping on the U.S. liberal sense of guilt to attract American sympathy and protection against China. Thus, this analysis confirms Funnell's claim of a Soviet-Vietnamese marriage of convenience, allowing the former to contain China and the latter to contain Cambodia.[7]

While Rosati and Dumbrell date Carter's shift from a regionalist to a globalist appraisal of foreign policy in 1979, this work confirms Westad's and Jackson's opinion that the shift began in early 1978 following the Soviet-backed conflict in the Horn of Africa.[8] Given these new concerns, Washington no longer viewed Hanoi as an independent regional power but as an element of Soviet expansionism in which American-Vietnamese normalization had become irrelevant. Garthoff's parallel between the shelving of normalization with Vietnam and the simultaneous bogging down of American relations with Cuba after the Cuban involvement in Africa is particularly accurate and draws to attention the striking similarities in U.S. policies on these two countries.[9]

In May 1978, Brzezinski found a similarity of views on foreign policy in the Chinese leadership regarding Moscow and its "Asian Cuba" of Vietnam. In so doing, he also endorsed Peking's view that Hanoi stood as a proxy Soviet-backed power in Southeast Asia, and of the potential threat that this represented to Chinese interests and security. This visit confirmed his wish to work towards the establishment of diplomatic relations with Peking while resisting the State Department's plans to seek simultaneous normalization with both Hanoi and Peking.

Brzezinski prevailed over Vance and Holbrooke, as his influence on Carter steadily increased. From then on, Washington's relations with Hanoi shifted from a regionalist focus to a globalist framework. American-Vietnamese talks in New York in September 1978 only confirmed the impossibility of normalization following the reorganization of each country's priorities. The description of inter-administrative feuds and opposed ambitions points to the improbability of Hurst's view that the NSC and the State Department "concurred" in shelving normalization. It stresses instead the clash of opposing diplomatic programs between the two institutions and suggests that the preponderance of Brzezinski's views in the White House led to the shelving of normalization, and that the State Department justified the new policy by stressing the face-saving pretext of humanitarian issues in Indochina.[10] Whether Vance and Holbrooke convinced themselves of the validity of this reason or used it to hide the decline of presidential trust in State Department programs can only be speculated upon until the opening of archives.

The failure of American-Vietnamese normalization, the establishing of Sino-American relations and the "moral" backing of the Chinese invasion of Vietnam had more to do with global and geopolitical considerations than with regional or bilateral concerns or with the need to punish Vietnam for its attack on a rather barbaric and embarrassing neighbor. This study supports the claim that, in the international arena, the Chinese attack confirmed the anti–Soviet dimension of the Sino-American alliance, much as, on the U.S. domestic stage, it confirmed the predominance of Brzezinski's influence in the White House, as Dumbrell suggested.[11]

Washington misunderstood Vietnamese aims and Hanoi's only partial interest in improving bilateral relations. The lack of high-level visits, due to the constant pressure which Congress and public opinion imposed on the executive branch, did little to improve Carter's grasp of Vietnamese moods. McNamara notes misperceptions and the failure to open a comprehensive dialogue in his study of the failed peace initiatives during the war, and this book argues that his conclusions can be equally applied to the postwar era.[12] While normalization may have been possible in 1976, prior to the reorganization of the VCP during the Fourth Party Congress, Hanoi had come to the conclusion in 1977 that it had other priorities and returned to favoring normalization only when its regional priorities required American support. After opening the dialogue with Washington, Hanoi accepted and rejected American gestures as suited Vietnamese foreign policies. Meanwhile, at the height of its conflict with Vietnam, China, helped by Brzezinski, pressed Washington for Sino-American normalization.

While Morris' claim that Vietnam invaded Cambodia without informing Moscow of the details of the attack seems unrealistic, as shown in this study, his portrayal of mutual misunderstanding and self-fuelled paranoia among the four communist countries is confirmed.[13] While Vietnam defended its territory from Cambodian attacks and initially preferred to achieve a "special relationship" with Cambodia through diplomatic rather than military means, China believed in Soviet instigation of Vietnamese counterattacks to gain political influence in the region. In turn, Chinese animosity led to Vietnamese hostility towards the ethnic Chinese and to a further siding with Moscow, which in turn strengthened the Chinese belief in Soviet-Vietnamese collusion. Through this cause-and-effect circular policy, the Cambodian-Vietnamese conflict presented the full color of a "proxy war" by mid–1978, despite the American State Department's allegations. The Chinese "lesson" was as much aimed at Moscow as it was at Hanoi, punishing Soviet "hegemonistic" ambitions via an attack on Vietnam. Ironically, it seemed that none of the actors truly understood the aims and motivations of the others.

A new understanding of the U.S. role in the Cold War may emerge from this study. In the last chapter, this work investigated whether Washington's China card against Moscow was not in fact Peking's American card against Moscow, after Hanoi had failed to play the American card against China in obtaining American-Vietnamese normalization. Washington was not the conductor of policies but the diplomatic tool that both Hanoi and Peking had first snubbed and later raced to obtain to use against each other, but on which Peking finally won the upper hand. This new perspective places Washington no longer as an active protagonist of Cold War confrontation as it was in Europe, but as a relatively passive card with which Moscow and Peking sought to outweigh each other in Southeast Asia. Further studies are needed to determine whether this could be said of other areas and Third World countries.

Yet, the findings of this work encourage a different approach to existing Cold War literature. David Reynolds, and Melvyn Leffler and David Painter, mention the need for modern scholars to concentrate on peripheral issues to the Cold War—which they reject as being a bilateral, bipolar one—and call for the study of other "sides" of the Cold War, including their focus on the "European-American connexion." The exploration of American-Vietnamese relations demonstrates their impact on bipolar Cold War contacts, and *vice versa*, and confirms these authors' view that regional conflicts shaped triangular relationships between Washington, Moscow and China, halting or encouraging progress on these countries' relations with regional powers in the constant need to adapt their policies to each other's stances, and to assume a bold posture. In turn, such policies shaped the two powers' response to regional countries depending on Washington and Moscow's own requirements in their bipolar confrontation.[14] Indeed, the U.S. strategy of containing Moscow in the Far East, at least during the Carter years, crystallized into a strategic alliance with China and an American endorsement of Chinese foreign policy views.

One should note that this study is by no means exhaustive and several points are still left unclarified for want of archival material. Vietnamese archives, once opened, will shed light on Hanoi's perceptions of bilateral relations that have only been briefly sketched in this book. For instance, the access to Vietnamese papers will allow broader analysis of the birth of the Nixon letter and Kissinger-Nixon initial intentions regarding this document, and of the precise motives behind Hanoi's decision to release its text in May 1977. This would also allow further insights on the state of Hanoi's domestic policies, enabling scholars to inspect the details of factionalist conflicts in Hanoi and judge their impact on Vietnamese foreign policies, not only towards Washington but also towards Phnom Penh, China and the Soviet Union—issues on which historians have had to rely solely on second-hand sources, mainly memoirs and oral histories, that are as distorted—although differently—as the empty rhetoric of official Vietnamese propaganda.

The opening of French archives may perhaps offer a third-party approach to bilateral relations, as Paris has enjoyed an observer-status of Vietnamese affairs since 1954 and was used as a venue for American-Vietnamese talks since the 1960s. Such an approach may shed light not only on the 1977 talks, but also on bilateral relations during the Ford years. This source could, for example, add to the knowledge of the reasons surrounding the American vetoes in the UN, which had led France to request postponement of the consideration of the Vietnamese application in 1976, or to a fuller understanding of the exchange of notes between Washington and Hanoi via Paris in 1976—and to Montgomery's first postwar direct contact with Vietnamese officials in Paris.

Most importantly, the opening of the Ford and Carter Presidential Libraries collections yet unavailable, and of the State Department archives, would allow a better understanding of the Vance-Brzezinski feud that plagued bilateral relations by 1978. A careful study of this phenomenon, and its comparison to the American cooling of relations with Hanoi, might allow a more precise dating of the bogging down of bilateral relations and explain American reluctance to enter into a dialogue with the Vietnamese in summer 1978. Such sources would also enable scholars to analyze the striking shift in Carter's new reprioritizing of foreign policies in fall 1978, leading to the October 11 decision to shelve normalization with Hanoi. The details of how this decision was broken to the State Department and how, in turn, the State Department justified this shift to Hanoi and brought Hanoi to sign a formal document in December 1978, stating that Vietnam renounced its claim for aid, would also be of importance for a better understanding of the failure of normalization. It would also be of value to investigate whether the drafting of PRM-24 in June 1977 affected the administration's agenda and pushed normalization with Hanoi down on the list of U.S. priorities while increasing the advisability of Sino-American normalization—thus leading to a closer study of how the prospects of Sino-American normalization affected American and Chinese policies towards Vietnam. Many further points could be listed but will remain unanswered until the opening of such archives.

* * *

In the late 1970s and early 1980s the U.S. refused to recognize the new Vietnamese-backed Cambodian regime, preferring to support the Khmer Rouge at the UN rather than allow its being passed on to the new Cambodian authorities.[15] The withdrawal of Vietnamese troops from Cambodia and the Paris Accords on Cambodia in 1989 handed the issue over to UN supervision.

Therefore, American-Vietnamese normalization, made conditional on a Vietnamese withdrawal from Cambodia, had to wait until the mid–1990s, following the collapse of the Soviet Union. In 1983, Vietnam veteran Jan Scruggs saw his initiative of building a commemorative monument completed as the Great Wall of the Vietnam Veterans Memorial was inaugurated in Washington. Meanwhile, following the openly hostile policies of Ronald Reagan, who pledged to start "World War III" in Vietnam if proof was given that U.S. servicemen remained alive in Indochina, the myth that POWs were still held captive in Vietnam developed in the late 1980s.[16] By 1991, 69 percent of Americans still believed that U.S. servicemen were being held captive in Vietnam.[17]

In 1992, Washington lifted the embargo on telecommunications on Vietnam followed two years later by the lifting of the trade embargo. In July 1995, Washington and Hanoi normalized relations.

"We can now move on to common ground," declared Clinton during his visit in 2000. "Whatever divided us before, let us consign to the past."[18] Twenty-five years had elapsed since the fall of Saigon. The fruitless toil of a generation of diplomats, the repetitive shelving of dusty files recounting the forgotten history of aborted negotiations, and the war wounds' endless pinpricking of each country's pride had finally ceased and brought the two former enemies onto the more fertile soil of reconciliation.

Appendix 1

Message from the President of the United States to the Prime Minister of the Democratic Republic of Vietnam,[1] February 1, 1973

The President wishes to inform the Democratic Republic of Vietnam of the principles which will govern United States participation in the postwar reconstruction of North Vietnam. As indicated in Article 21 of The Agreement on Ending the War and Restoring Peace in Vietnam signed in Paris on January 27, 1973, the United States undertakes this participation in accordance with its traditional policies. These principles are as follows:

1) The Government of the United States of America will contribute to postwar reconstruction in North Vietnam without any political conditions.

2) Preliminary United States studies indicate that the appropriate programs for the United States contribution to postwar reconstruction will fall in the range of $3.25 billion of grant aid over five years. Other forms of aid will be agreed upon between the two parties. This estimate is subject to revision and to detailed discussion between the Government of the United States and the Government of the Democratic Republic of Vietnam.

3) The United States will propose to the Democratic Republic of Vietnam the establishment of a United States-North Vietnamese Joint Economic Commission within 30 days from the date of this message.

4) The function of this Commission will be to develop programs for the United

States contribution to reconstruction of North Vietnam. This United States contribution will be based upon such factors as:

(a) The needs of North Vietnam arising from the dislocation of war;
(b) The requirements for postwar reconstruction in the agricultural and industrial sectors of North Vietnam's economy.

5) The Joint Economic Commission will have an equal number of representatives from each side. It will agree upon a mechanism to administer the program which will constitute the United States contribution to the reconstruction of North Vietnam. The Commission will attempt to complete this agreement within 60 days after its establishment.

6) The two members of the Commission will function on the principle of respect for each other's sovereignty, non-interference in each other's internal affairs, equality and mutual benefit. The offices of the Commission will be located at a place to be agreed upon by the United States and the Democratic Republic of Vietnam.

7) The United States considers that the implementation of the foregoing principles will promote economic, trade and other relations between the United States of America and the Democratic Republic of Vietnam and will contribute to insuring a stable and lasting peace in Indochina. These principles accord with the spirit of Chapter VIII of The Agreement on Ending the War and Restoring Peace in Vietnam which was signed in Paris on January 27, 1973.

Addenda

Understanding Regarding Economic Reconstruction Program:

It is understood that the recommendations of the Joint Economic Commission mentioned in the President's note to the Prime Minister will be implemented by each member in accordance with its own constitutional provisions.

Note Regarding Other Forms of Aid:

In regard to other forms of aid, United States studies indicate that the appropriate programs could fall in the range of 1 to 1.5 billion dollars depending on food and other commodity needs of the Democratic Republic of Vietnam.

APPENDIX 2

MESSAGE OF THE PRIME MINISTER OF THE DEMOCRATIC REPUBLIC OF VIET NAM TO THE PRESIDENT OF THE UNITED STATES OF AMERICA (FEBRUARY 23, 1973)[1]

The Prime Minister of the Democratic Republic of Viet Nam has received the February 1st, 1973 message of the President of the United States of America on the principles governing U.S. participation in post-war reconstruction in North Viet Nam. During the stay in Ha Noi of Dr. Henry A. Kissinger, Assistant to the President of the United States from February 10 to 13, 1973, the Democratic Republic of Viet Nam side and the United States side have exchanged views on the manner in which the United States will contribute to healing the wounds of war and post war reconstruction in North Viet Nam.

The Government of the Democratic Republic of Viet Nam takes note of the following:

1) As indicated in Article 21 of the Agreement on Ending the War and Restoring Peace in Viet Nam, the United States of America will contribute to post-war reconstruction in Viet Nam. This contribution is without any political conditions.

2) The grant aid by the United states over five years amounts to $3.25 billion, on the basis of the value of the dollar on February 1st, 1973, the date of the message of the President of the United States to the Prime Minster of the Democratic Republic of Viet

Nam. The above-mentioned sum will be distributed according to the needs of the Democratic Republic of Viet Nam to various branches of the economy, such as communication and transportation, industry, agriculture, construction of civilian installations and residential areas etc. The Democratic Republic of Viet Nam will use the greater part of this money to buy goods from the United States and a part for purchases from other countries.

3) A Democratic Republic of Viet Nam—United States Joint Economic Commission will be established by the two sides on March 1st, 1973.

4) The function of this Commission will be to develop programs for the United States contribution on the basis of such factors as:

   a) The needs of North Viet Nam arising from the dislocation of war.
   b) The requirements for post-war reconstruction in different sectors of North Viet Nam's economy.

The programs which will be developed will be directed and administered by the Democratic Republic of Viet Nam.

5) The delegation of each side to the Joint Economic Commission will comprise three delegates.

The two sides will agree upon a work schedule and set targets for the Commission to endeavor to achieve in a determined period.

6) The two members of the Commission will function on the principle of respect for each other's sovereignty, non-interference in each other's internal affairs, equality and mutual benefit.

The offices of the Commission will be located in Paris.

7) The Democratic Republic of Viet Nam considers that the contribution of the United States to healing the wounds of war and post-war reconstruction in Viet Nam will promote economic, trade and other relations between the Democratic Republic of Viet Nam and the United States, and contribute to ensuring a stable and lasting peace in Viet Nam and Indochina, in accordance with the spirit of Chapter VIII of the Agreement on Ending the War and Restoring Peace in Viet Nam which was signed in Paris on January 23, 1973.

Appendix 3

U.S.-Vietnamese Exchanges of Six Diplomatic Notes, 1976

Note from U.S. Secretary of State Henry Kissinger to DRV Minister for Foreign Affairs Nguyen Duy Trinh (March 26, 1976)[1]

Dear Mr. Minister,

Congressman G.V. Montgomery, chairman and other members of the Select Committee on Missing Persons in Southeast Asia of the United States House of Representatives have informed me about their recent visit to your country and have asked me to express their appreciation for the hospitality shown the committee by your government. Representative Montgomery has also told me of expressions by members of your government of interest in discussion looking toward eventual normalization of relations between Vietnam and the United States. The United States expressed its willingness to look to the future in its relationships with Vietnam.

I believe that the interests of peace and security will benefit from placing the past behind us and developing the basis for a new relationship between our two countries. We are prepared to open discussion with your government in pursuit of this objective. I would appreciate receiving your views on such discussion and on what you believe might be the procedures and issues involved.

Best regards,
Henry A. Kissinger

Note of DRV Minister for Foreign Affairs Nguyen Duy Trinh to U.S. Secretary of State Henry Kissinger (April 10, 1976)

Mr. Secretary,

I acknowledge receipt of your message dated March 26, 1976. The Government of the Democratic Republic of Vietnam has on many occasions stated that it was prepared to discuss with the Government of the United States an early settlement of the outstanding questions concerning Vietnam and the United States in the postwar period as provided for in the Paris agreement on Vietnam, such as the U.S. contribution to healing the wounds of war and to postwar reconstruction in the two zones of Vietnam, the seeking of the Americans missing in action, the exhumation and repatriation of the remains of the dead Americans... On this basis, the Democratic Republic of Vietnam would normalize relations with the United States in the spirit of Article 22 of the Paris agreement on Vietnam.

Through practical deeds, the Government of the Democratic Republic of Vietnam has constantly shown its good will and serious intent in implementing this very reasonable and sensible policy. It is much to be regretted that the U.S. side has so far refused to fulfill its obligation to contribute to healing the wounds of war and to postwar reconstruction in Vietnam. It has gone so far as taking hostile actions against the Vietnamese people and using discourteous and slanderous terms towards the Government of the Democratic Republic of Vietnam. Should your government really desire to hold talks to normalize relations with the Democratic Republic of Vietnam, the United States would have to show the same good will and serious intent as the Democratic Republic of Vietnam.

The Government of the Democratic Republic of Vietnam is prepared to consider any concrete proposal of your government.

Sincerely yours,
Nguyen Duy Trinh

Note of the U.S. State Department to the DRV Ministry of Foreign Affairs (May 8, 1976)

The Department of State presents its compliments to the Ministry of Foreign Affairs of the Democratic Republic of Vietnam and has the honor to confirm receipt of the letter of April 10 from Minister of Foreign Affairs Nguyen Duy Trinh to Secretary of State Henry A. Kissinger. The department reaffirms the willingness of the United States Government to enter into discussions with the Government of the Democratic Republic of Vietnam at an early date. In doing so, it wishes to point out that talks on the basis of the selective application of past agreements, which appears to be the objective of the Democratic Republic of Vietnam, would not be fruitful and would only lead to sterile debate rather than constructive discussion.

The United States believes that it would be more useful for representatives of the two governments to discuss issues affecting future relations between our two countries. The humanitarian concern of a full accounting for our missing men will be one of the primary issues of the United States in such discussions. Until this issue is substantially resolved, there can be no real progress towards normalization of relations between our two countries.

At the same time the Democratic Republic of Vietnam will be free to raise any issue of concern to it. The United States invites the Government of the Democratic Republic of Vietnam to indicate whether it considers a meeting to discuss outstanding issues useful.

The Department of State takes this opportunity to renew to the Ministry of Foreign Affairs of the Democratic Republic of Vietnam the assurances of its highest consideration.

Department of State

Note of the DRV Foreign Ministry to the U.S. State Department (June 19, 1976)

The Foreign Ministry of the DRV has received the U.S. State Department's note dated May 8, 1976.

Since the complete liberation of South Vietnam, the Foreign Ministry of the DRV has on repeated occasions made clear its views on the Paris agreement on Vietnam. The unilateral U.S. denunciation of the agreement is aimed at evading the pledges it has solemnly undertaken in signing the agreement, especially under Article 21 thereof which provides for a U.S. obligation to contribute to healing the wounds of war and to postwar reconstruction in Vietnam and Indochina without setting any political conditions.

On the other hand, the United States demands that the Democratic Republic of Vietnam implement Article 8 (B) of the agreement as a condition for a normalization of relations between the two countries. Obviously, it wants to renege on its obligation under the Paris agreement on Vietnam while demanding that the other side implement another article of the same [agreement]. This completely runs counter to international law and practices.

For its part, the Democratic Republic of Vietnam has expressed its willingness to discuss with the United States a settlement of the postwar issues that concern Vietnam and the United States such as the U.S. contribution to healing the wounds of war and to postwar reconstruction in the two zones of Vietnam, the search for information about Americans missing in the war, the exhumation and repatriation of the remains of the dead Americans. The Government of the Democratic Republic of Vietnam has made and will continue to make efforts to relieve the anxiety of those American families whose relatives have died or are still considered missing in Vietnam.

Once again the Government of the Democratic Republic of Vietnam affirms its attitude of seriousness and good will. It holds that the two sides should resolve the issues of interest of each of them, thus creating favorable conditions for a normalization of relations between the two countries. As an initial step, the Democratic Republic of Vietnam representative is prepared to meet with the U.S. representative in Paris for an exchange of views. If it really wants early discussions with the DRV Government with a view to normalization of relations between the two countries, the U.S. Government itself should adopt an attitude of seriousness and good will.

The Foreign Ministry of the Democratic Republic of Vietnam takes this opportunity to renew to the U.S. State Department the assurances of its high consideration.

Note of the U.S. State Department to the DRV Foreign Ministry (July 19, 1976)

The Department of State has received the note dated June 19 of the Ministry of Foreign Affairs of the Democratic Republic of Vietnam. The United States agrees that discussions between representatives of our two governments in Paris would be appropriate and useful. The United States would expect to be represented at any such meeting by the deputy chief of mission of its Embassy in Paris, and suggests that it be held in the American Embassy or at another mutually agreed upon site.

The United States welcomes the assurances of the Vietnamese Government that it will undertake efforts to relieve the anxiety of those American families whose relatives have died, or are still considered missing in Vietnam.

A full accounting for those Americans missing-in-action and the return of the remains of those killed is a matter of primary concern to the United States. Resolution of this basic humanitarian issue will be a fundamental consideration of the United States in any discussions.

The United States does not consider that it has an obligation to provide reconstruction assistance to Vietnam, as the Ministry of Foreign Affairs alleges in its note. As the United States has made clear many times, it intends to look to the future rather than the past as far as its relations with Vietnam are concerned. The relations should develop on the basis of reciprocal interests.

If the above suggestions for a meeting are satisfactory, the United States would be prepared to discuss and work out a mutually convenient date for our representatives to meet, as well as procedures for such a meeting.

Department of State

Note of the SRV Foreign Ministry to the U.S. State Department (August 27, 1976)

The Ministry of Foreign Affairs of the Socialist Republic of Vietnam acknowledges receipt of the July 19, 1976, note of the State Department of the United States of America. The Government of the Socialist Republic of Vietnam has on many occasions made clear its viewpoint on the Paris agreement and on the normalization of relations between Vietnam and the United States. This view has also been affirmed clearly in its June 19, 1976 note sent to the United States.

Concerning the meeting of representatives of the two sides in Paris, the Socialist Republic of Vietnam suggests as follows:

The representative of the Socialist Republic of Vietnam will be the counsellor of the Vietnamese Embassy in Paris. The meeting site will be outside the embassy of either side; the two sides will arrange for it in rotation. If the U.S. side agrees to the above-mentioned suggestions, liaison officials of both sides will meet to exchange views on the date and site for the first meeting.

Appendix 4

Letter from President Jimmy Carter to Chinese Vice Premier Deng Xiaoping (January 30, 1979)[1]

To Vice Premier Deng Xiaoping:

You asked my opinion about a possible punitive strike against the Viet Namese. I think it would be a serious mistake for the following reasons:

a) Success would be unlikely if one of the objectives is to interrupt the action of the Viet Nam invading forces now in Kampuchea. A token action would not be considered a significant "punishment."

b) The peaceful image of the PRC and the aggressive invader image of Viet Nam would both be changed. Now—for the first time—Viet Nam stands condemned by most of the nations of the world. The Soviet Union and Cuba are seen as co-conspirators.

c) The long range result of this U.N. and worldwide condemnation will have some significant adverse effect on Viet Nam provided a concerted effort is made among industrialized nations to curtail economic aid and among the "non-aligned" nations to take U.N. action and to invoke sanctions.

d) A serious incident may escalate into regional conflict.

e) Plans for a brief and limited action may have to be abandoned if China is given an ultimatum to withdraw. This would make it very difficult to withdraw.

f) Armed conflict initiated by China would cause serious concern in the United States concerning the general character of China and the future peaceful settlement of the Taiwan issue. Our claim of peace and stability resulting from normalization would be refuted to some extent.

g) The Kampucheans seem to be doing better than expected as guerilla fighters.

h) Your border threats can create problems for Viet Nam even without intrusion into Viet Nam.

i) Such action may create an additional excuse for greater Soviet pressure in Viet Nam.

Because of these reasons the United States could not support such action, and I strongly urge you not to approve it.

In my opinion, Vice Premier Deng, a concerted effort through the United Nations or other international force could prove to be much more damaging to Viet Nam and her allies.

Respectfully,
Jimmy Carter

CHAPTER NOTES

Abbreviations: **CPL** Carter Presidential Library (Atlanta, Georgia). **FMoFA** French Ministry of Foreign Affairs. **FPL** Ford Presidential Library (Ann Arbor, Michigan). **Lib. of Cong.** Library of Congress (Washington, DC). **N.A. II** National Archives II (College Park, Maryland). **UBIA** University of Berkeley Indochina Archives (Berkeley, California).

Introduction

1. *Libération*, November 17, 2000, p. 2; *The International Herald Tribune*, November 17, 2000, p. 5; *Time*, November 27, 2000, p. 30. All references to *Time* refer to the European edition unless otherwise noted.
2. Le Kha Phieu, head of the VCP, published some remarks on the war clearly identifying the United States as "imperialists [having] invaded to get colonies" (*The International Herald Tribune*, November 20, 2000, p. 7).
3. The identity of this official was not revealed (*Ibid.*).
4. However, the Vietnamese would continue to use Saigon as its official name (CIA report on "Trends in Communist Propaganda," April 30, 1975, Computerized CIA Collection: Record Group 263, N.A. II). Also: *Keesing's Contemporary Archives*, 1975, p. 27203.
5. A.J. Dommen, 2001, pp. 112, 127–9.
6. *Department of State Bulletin*, February 12, 1973, p. 158.
7. USIS Report on U.S. post-war economic aid to the DRV, February 1974, File: 833. Ceasefire (incl. January 1973), SRV-U.S. Foreign Relations, Douglas Pike Collection, UBIA.
8. Committee on Veterans' Affairs, "Americans Missing in Southeast Asia," U.S. House of Representatives, 100th Congress (Washington D.C.: U.S. Government Printing Office, 1988), p. 228.
9. J. Portes, 1993, p. 254.
10. Author's correspondence with Pr. Larry Berman, February 1, 2003.
11. H. Kissinger, 2003, p. 493.
12. *Far Eastern Economic Review*, May 23, 1975, p. 12.
13. *Asia Yearbook*, 1976, p. 312.
14. See: M. Brown and J.J. Zasloff, "Laos in 1975: People's Democratic Revolution—Lao Style," *Asian Survey*, February 1976, pp. 193–9.
15. Most Vietnamese and occasionally Western authors, such as Bui Tin, Hoang Van Hoan, Larry Berman, Nayan Chanda, Elizabeth Becker and many others, could rightly argue that no peace ever came to Vietnam, for reasons which will later be explained. Therefore the concept of "peace," as used in this work, refers only to the ending of the American involvement in Indochina and the collapse of U.S.-backed regimes in Saigon, Phnom Penh and Vientiane.
16. USIS Report on U.S. post-war economic aid to the DRV, February 1974, File: 833. Ceasefire (incl. January 1973), SRV-U.S. Foreign Relations, Douglas Pike Collection, UBIA.
17. Senator G. McGovern, "Vietnam: 1976: A Report by Senator George McGovern to the Committee on Foreign Relations, United States Senate," March 1976 (Washington D.C.: U.S. Government Printing Office, 1976), p. 3.
18. Author's interview with former BBC journalist and Indochina specialist Judith Stowe, October 26, 2002. Also: W. Burchett, 1981, p. 165; M. Bradley and R.K. Brigham, "Vietnamese Archives and Scholarship on the Cold War Period: Two Reports," Cold War International History Project, Working Paper no. 7, September 1993, pp. 6 and 9.
19. Correspondence from David Aaron to the author, August 23, 2001.
20. Author's telephone interview with General William Odom, June 10, 2002.
21. R. Garthoff, 1994, pp. 636–40.
22. O.A. Westad, 1997, pp. 9–10; J. Ehrman, 1995, p. 98.
23. See: J. Dumbrell, 1995, p. 198; J. Rosati, 1987, pp. 59–63 and 75; S. Hurst, 1996, p. 89; O.A. Westad, 1997, p. 21; D.R. Jackson, 2002, pp. 152–8.
24. See: N. Chanda, 1988, pp. 273–82; E. Becker, 1998, p. 388–90.
25. S. Hurst, 1996, p. 3.
26. Ben Kiernan similarly noted Morris' dubious stand on the Cambodian-Vietnamese conflict and the ensuing occupation of Cambodia by Vietnamese forces. He adds that Morris stood against the Vietnamese presence in Cambodia and supported the return of the Khmer Rouge, even protesting in the 1990s against the plans to bring former Khmer Rouge leader Khieu Samphan to justice

under charges of genocide. See: B. Kiernan, "Bringing the Khmer Rouge to Justice," *Human Rights Review*, April-June 2000, pp. 92–108.
27. S.J. Morris, 1999, p. 6.

I. Ford and Vietnam's Peace

1. *Far Eastern Economic Review*, January 17, 1975, p. 11.
2. *Far Eastern Economic Review*, July 14, 1978, p. 16.
3. Estimates for the years 1961 to 1975 (*Vietnam Info*, May 22, 1975, p. 17 and *Asia Yearbook*, 1976, p. 311). See also: J. Lacouture and S. Lacouture, 1976, p. 54 ; E. Becker, 1998, p. 1.
4. *Far Eastern Economic Review*, June 27, 1975, p. 13.
5. CIA report on "Trends in Communist Propaganda," May 7, 1975, Computerized CIA Collection: Record Group 263, N.A. II.
6. *The New York Times*, May 1, 1976, p. 19; *Far Eastern Economic Review*, June 27, 1975, p. 13. See also: *Keesing's Contemporary Archives*, 1975, p. 27494 ; *Keesing's Contemporary Archives*, 1976, p. 27896.
7. Letter from Congress to the president, September 14, 1978, File: DRV—Foreign Relations U.S. 1950/1973, Douglas Pike Collection, UBIA.
8. *Far Eastern Economic Review*, September 12, 1975, p. 39.
9. Amnesty International, "Viet Nam: renovation (Doi Moi), the law and human rights in the 80's," 1990, p. 33.
10. *Asia Yearbook*, 1976, p. 311. Also: W.M. Bagby, 1999, p. 292. See also: *Vietnam International*, January-February-March 1976, p. 7.
11. Nguyen Van Canh and E. Cooper, 1983, p. 135. Also: *Vietnam Southeast Asia International*, October-November-December 1978, p. 5.
12. *Vietnam Southeast Asia International*, January 1977, pp. 2–3 and *Vietnam Southeast Asia International*, October-November-December 1978, p. 12.
13. M. Beresford, 1988, pp. 146–7; *Vietnam Broadsheet*, Autumn 1983, p. 4.
14. *Vietnam Broadsheet*, Autumn 1983, p. 4.
15. *Vietnam Southeast Asia International*, July-August-September 1977, p. 2.
16. *Far Eastern Economic Review*, August 1, 1975, p. 19.
17. *The New York Times*, May 3, 1975, p. 12.
18. *Vietnam Info*, May 1976, p. 15.
19. *Keesing's Contemporary Archives*, 1976, pp. 27647–8.
20. S. Lodha, 1997, p. 249; R.S. Ross, 1988, p. 121.
21. Figures from: D. Pike, 1987, p. 127.
22. *The New York Times*, April 10, 1975, p. 50.
23. *The New York Times*, April 24, 1975, p. 19.
24. *Chicago Tribune*, May 6, 1975, p. 13.
25. *Far Eastern Economic Review*, December 26, 1975, p. 22.
26. N. Chanda, 1988, p. 143.
27. Report from the *Hanoi Liberation Radio*, May 25, 1975, File: 1975/2, SRV-U.S. Foreign Relations, Douglas Pike Collection, UBIA. Also: *Department of State Bulletin*, June 9, 1975, p. 760; *Asia Yearbook*, 1976, p. 312.
28. Author's correspondence with Judith Stowe, March 15, 2003.
29. *Department of State Bulletin*, May 19, 1975, p. 629. See also: *The New York Times*, April 30, 1975, p. 16.
30. *Keesing's Contemporary Archives*, 1975, p. 27496; *The New York Times*, May 1, 1975, p. 14; *Far Eastern Economic Review*, December 26, 1975, p. 22.
31. *Far Eastern Economic Review*, July 4, 1975, p. 13.
32. Report entitled "DRV line follows moderate line on U.S. policies, U.S.-DRV Relations," unattributed, June 13, 1975, File: 1975/2, SRV-U.S. Foreign Relations, Douglas Pike Collection, UBIA. Also: CIA report on "Trends in Communist Propaganda," June 4, 1975, Computerized CIA Collection: Record Group 263, N.A. II.
33. Report from *Hanoi International Service*, May 22, 1975, File: 1975/2, SRV-U.S. Foreign Relations, Douglas Pike Collection, UBIA.
34. *Keesing's Contemporary Archives*, 1975, p. 27496.
35. Committee on International Relations, "United States Embargo of Trade with South Vietnam and Cambodia," Hearing before the Subcommittee on International Trade and Commerce, House of Representatives, 94th Congress, 1st session, June 4, 1975 (Washington D.C.: U.S. Government Printing Office, 1975), p. 1.
36. *The New York Times*, May 8, 1975, p. 14.
37. *Far Eastern Economic Review*, July 4, 1975, p. 13.
38. *Vietnam Southeast Asia International*, October-November 1975, p. 15. See also: Committee on International Relations, "United States Embargo of Trade with South Vietnam and Cambodia," Hearing before the Subcommittee on International Trade and Commerce, House of Representatives, 94th Congress, 1st session, June 4, 1975 (Washington D.C.: U.S. Government Printing Office, 1975).
39. *Far Eastern Economic Review*, July 4, 1975, p. 13.
40. D.H. Allin, 1995, p. 52.
41. Memorandum for G.S. Springsteen from Staff Secretary Jeanne W. Davis, July 9, 1975, File: Vietnam (27), National Security Adviser: Presidential Country Files for East Asia and the Pacific, Box 20, FPL.
42. Committee on International Relations, "Export Licensing of Private Humanitarian Assistance to Vietnam," hearing before the Subcommittee on International Trade and Commerce, House of Representatives, 94th Congress, 1st session, September 9, 1975 (Washington D.C.: U.S. Government Printing Office, 1975), p. 36.
43. *The New York Times*, July 29, 1975, p. 32.
44. Committee on International Relations, "Export Licensing of Private Humanitarian Assistance to Vietnam," hearing before the Subcommittee on International Trade and Commerce, House of Representatives, 94th Congress, 1st session, September 9, 1975 (Washington D.C.: U.S. Government Printing Office, 1975), pp. 1 and 45.
45. *The New York Times*, September 27, 1975, p. 16.
46. Committee on International Relations, "Export Licensing of Private Humanitarian Assistance to Vietnam," hearing before the Subcommittee on International Trade and Commerce, House of Representatives, 94th Congress, 1st session, September 9, 1975 (Washington D.C.: U.S. Government Printing Office, 1975), p. 33.
47. *Congressional Record*, Senate, September 14, 1978, p. 29453.
48. See: E. Becker, 1998, pp. 373–5.
49. Cable from the U.S. Embassy in Stockholm to Kissinger, May 7, 1975, File: Vietnamese War–"Camp David" File—(2), 3/24/75–12/11/75, National Security Adviser : Kissinger-Scowcroft West Wing Office Files: 1969–1977, Box 34, FPL.
50. Foreign Minister Nguyen Duy Trinh's speech at the National Assembly, May 1975, File: 1975/2, SRV-U.S. Foreign Relations, Douglas Pike Collection, UBIA.
51. Report from *Agence France Presse*, May 22, 1975, File: 1975/2, SRV-U.S. Foreign Relations, Douglas Pike Collection, UBIA.
52. *The Washington Star*, May 14, 1975, p. 13.
53. Memorandum from Brzezinski to the President, July 20, 1977, NSA Brzezinski Files, Box 85, CPL.
54. *Keesing's Contemporary Archives*, 1975, p. 27395. Also: P. Langlet and Quach Thanh Tâm, 2001, p. 43.
55. Memorandum from Brzezinski to the President, July 20, 1977, NSA Brzezinski Files, Box 85, CPL.
56. *The New York Times*, July 8, 1975, p. 4.
57. Report from the *Vietnam News Agency*, June 3, 1975, File: 1975/2, SRV-U.S. Foreign Relations, Douglas Pike Collection, UBIA.
58. *The New York Times*, June 12, 1975, p. 4.
59. On World War II and the Korean War see: G.R.

Hess, 1990, p. 160; H.B. Franklin, 1992, p. 11. On French MIAs: J.S. Olson and R. Roberts, 1991, p. 279. On Vietnamese MIAs see: *Libération*, November 20, 2000, p. 10.
60. E. Becker, 1998, p. 462.
61. For an analysis of Nixon's use of the "go public" campaign on MIAs, see: H.B. Franklin, 1992, p. 49.
62. Report entitled "DRV line follows moderate line on U.S. policies, U.S.-DRV Relations," unattributed, June 13, 1975, File: 1975/2, SRV-U.S. Foreign Relations, Douglas Pike Collection, UBIA.
63. CIA report on "Trends in Communist Propaganda," June 4, 1975, Computerized CIA Collection: Record Group 263, N.A. II.
64. *Keesing's Contemporary Archives*, 1975, p. 27276.
65. CIA report on "Trends in Communist Propaganda," June 11, 1975, Computerized CIA Collection: Record Group 263, N.A. II. Also: Document entitled "Vietnamese statements on settling problems with the United States," November 25, 1975, File: 1975/4, SRV-U.S. Foreign Relations, Douglas Pike Collection, UBIA.
66. *Baltimore Sun*, June 12, 1975, p. 4.
67. S. Hurst, 1996, p. 19.
68. *The New York Times*, June 5, 1975, p. 8. Also : *Far Eastern Economic Review*, July 4, 1975, p. 13.
69. Memorandum from W.R. Smyser to Kissinger, June 9, 1975, File: Vietnamese War–'Camp David File'–(2), 3/24/75–12/11/75, National Security Adviser : Kissinger-Scowcroft West Wing Office Files: 1969–1977, Box 34, FPL.
70. Memorandum from General Scowcroft to Colonel Oveson, June 11, 1975, File: Vietnamese War–'Camp David File'–(2), 3/24/75–12/11/75, National Security Adviser: Kissinger-Scowcroft West Wing Office Files: 1969–1977, Box 34, FPL.
71. *Hanoi Radio* commentary, June 41, 1975, File: 1975/2, SRV-U.S. Foreign Relations, Douglas Pike Collection, UBIA.
72. Report from the Hanoi International Service, June 13, 1975, File: 1975/2, SRV-U.S. Foreign Relations, Douglas Pike Collection, UBIA. See also: *The New York Times*, June 15, 1975, p. 5.
73. Document entitled "Vietnamese statements on settling problems with the United States," November 25, 1975, File: 1975/4, SRV-U.S. Foreign Relations, Douglas Pike Collection, UBIA.
74. *The New York Times*, June 12, 1975, p. 4.
75. *The New York Times*, June 12, 1975, p. 4.
76. *The New York Times*, June 15, 1975, p. 5.
77. Number of dead or wounded: Ford, 1979, pp. 278 and 284.
78. Report from the Hanoi Diplomatic Information Service on a June 21 article in *Nhan Dan*, June 21, 1975, File: 1975/4, SRV-U.S. Foreign Relations, Douglas Pike Collection, UBIA. Also: *Far Eastern Economic Review*, July 4, 1975, p. 13.
79. *The New York Times*, June 19, 1975, p. 1.
80. *Far Eastern Economic Review*, July 4, 1975, p. 13.
81. CIA report on "Trends in Communist Media," June 25, 1975, Computerized CIA Collection : Record Group 263, N.A. II.
82. *Vietnam News Agency*, July 7, 1975, File: 1975/3, SRV-U.S. Foreign Relations, Douglas Pike Collection, UBIA.
83. *The New York Times*, July 8, 1975, p. 4.
84. *Keesing's Contemporary Archives*, 1975, p. 27276.
85. S. Hurst, 1996, p. 20.
86. *The New York Times*, May 9, 1975, p. 11.
87. *The New York Times*, June 21, 1975, p. 2.
88. CIA report on "Trends in Communist Propaganda," July 23, 1975, Computerized CIA Collection: Record Group 263, N.A. II. Also: *Keesing's Contemporary Archives*, 1975, p. 27345.
89. News briefing, May 5, 1975, "Vietnam—Secret Understandings," Counsel to the president Philip Buchen Files 1974–1977, Box 64, FPL.
90. *The New York Times*, July 20, 1975, p. 7.
91. *The New York Times*, July 31, 1975, p. 4.
92. *Asia Yearbook*, 1976, p. 39.
93. *The New York Times*, July 30, 1975, p. 6; *Far Eastern Economic Review*, December 12, 1975, p. 34.
94. *Keesing's Contemporary Archives*, 1976, pp. 27977–9.
95. Telegram from Daniel Moynihan to Kissinger, July 1975, "Admission of Vietnam to the United Nations," NSC Institutional Files: Selected Documents (1973) 1974–1977, Boxes 24 and 57, FPL.
96. H. Kissinger, 1999, p. 106; J. Ehrman, 1995, pp. 86–90.
97. D.P. Moynihan, 1978, p. 146.
98. Douglas Pike's personal notes on U.S. policy and Indochina, File: 1975/3, SRV-U.S. Foreign Relations, Douglas Pike Collection, UBIA.
99. For an excellent appreciation of Moynihan's views see: J. Ehrman, 1995, p. 64.
100. Moynihan's emphasis (D.P. Moynihan, 1978, pp. 142–3).
101. D.P. Moynihan, 1978, p. 145.
102. *Keesing's Contemporary Archives*, 1975, p. 27345.
103. *The New York Times*, August 7, 1975, p. 1 and August 10, 1975, p. 4.
104. *Keesing's Contemporary Archives*, 1975, p. 27345.
105. *The Nation*, October 4, 1975, p. 292.
106. *U.N. Chronicle*, November 1975, p. 13.
107. Telegram from Daniel Moynihan to Kissinger, July 1975, "Admission of Vietnam to the United Nations," NSC Institutional Files: Selected Documents (1973) 1974–1977, Boxes 24 and 57, FPL.
108. Dinh Ba Thi and Nguyen Van Luu's statement of August 6 1975, undated, File: 1975/3, SRV-U.S. Foreign Relations, Douglas Pike Collection, UBIA.
109. *Keesing's Contemporary Archives*, 1975, p. 27496; *The New York Times*, August 6, 1975, p. 30.
110. Report from the Saigon *Liberation Press Agency*, August 7, 1975, File: 1975/3, SRV-U.S. Foreign Relations, Douglas Pike Collection, UBIA.
111. Moynihan's statement to the Security Council on August 6 1975, undated, File: 1975/3, SRV-U.S. Foreign Relations, Douglas Pike Collection, UBIA. Also: *Department of State Bulletin*, September 15, 1975, p. 421.
112. *Far Eastern Economic Review*, August 22, 1975, p. 20.
113. *The New York Times*, August 7, 1975, p. 1 and August 8, 1975, p. 29.
114. *The Nation*, October 4, 1975, p. 292.
115. Report from the Hanoi *Vietnam News Agency*, August 8, 1975, File: 1975/3, SRV-U.S. Foreign Relations, Douglas Pike Collection, UBIA.
116. Memorandum from W.L. Stearman to Kissinger entitled "Approach to DRV on MIAs," File: MIA/Amnesty/National League of Families (2), June 27, 1975, National Security Adviser: Presidential Subject Files 1974–1977, Box 10, FPL. Also: *Department of State Bulletin*, August 16, 1976, p. 250.
117. *The New York Times*, August 11, 1975, p. 7.
118. *Agence France Press* report on an article in *Giai Phong*, August 9, 1975, File: 1975/3, SRV-U.S. Foreign Relations, Douglas Pike Collection, UBIA.
119. Department of State Telegram from Moynihan to the State Department on his August 11 statement, undated, File: 1975/3, SRV-U.S. Foreign Relations, Douglas Pike Collection, UBIA. Also: *U.N. Chronicle*, December 1976, p. 16; *Far Eastern Economic Review*, September 10, 1976, p. 11. Costa Rica is the only country that voted against the admission of the Vietnamese states. For this vote, as for all until the admission to the UN in 1977 of unified Vietnam, the Vietnamese would benefit from a large support from Third World countries, the Soviet

Union, China and communist countries. Also: *Vietnam International*, July-August 1976, p. 13.
120. See Moynihan's speech during the Security Council meeting of August 11 in: *Department of State Bulletin*, September 15, 1975, pp. 421–2. See also: *Keesing's Contemporary Archives*, 1975, p. 27345.
121. *The New York Times*, August 12, 1975, p. 1. See also the editorial of: *The New York Times*, August 13, 1975, p. 32.
122. *Hanoi Liberation Radio* (PRG) in South Vietnam, August 16, 1975, File: 1975/3, SRV-U.S. Foreign Relations, Douglas Pike Collection, UBIA.
123. *Department of State Bulletin*, August 16, 1976, p. 250. The remains were eventually returned to American authorities the following December.
124. D.P. Moynihan, 1978, pp. 145–6 and 148.
125. *Peking Review*, August 29, 1975, p. 15. *Peking Review* is a Chinese international propaganda journal, written in English for a larger audience.
126. Statement of the Foreign Ministry of South Vietnam as reported by *Hanoi Liberation Radio* on August 12, 1975, File: 1975/3, SRV-U.S. Foreign Relations, Douglas Pike Collection, UBIA. Also: CIA report on "Trends in Communist Media," August 13, 1975, Computerized CIA Collection : Record Group 263, N.A. II.
127. *The New York Times*, August 13, 1975, p. 9; *The Nation*, October 4, 1975, p. 292.
128. *The Nation*, October 4, 1975, p. 292.
129. Report from the Hanoi *Vietnam News Agency*, September 15, 1975, File: 1975/3, SRV-U.S. Foreign Relations, Douglas Pike Collection, UBIA.
130. Statement by the Foreign Ministry, September 14, 1975, File: 1975/2, SRV-U.S. Foreign Relations, Douglas Pike Collection, UBIA.
131. Document entitled "Vietnamese statements on settling problems with the United States," November 25, 1975, File: 1975/4, SRV-U.S. Foreign Relations, Douglas Pike Collection, UBIA.
132. CIA report on "Trends in Communist Media," August 20, 1975, Computerized CIA Collection: Record Group 263, N.A. II.
133. *The New York Times*, August 15, 1975, p. 3.
134. *Peking Review*, June 16, 1978, pp. 13–7. Also: S.J. Hood, 1992, p. 34 and Qiang Zhai, 2000, p. 213.
135. CIA report on "Trends in Communist Media," August 20, 1975, Computerized CIA Collection: Record Group 263, N.A. II; *The New York Times*, August 17, 1975, p. 9. Also: O.A. Westad, Chen Jian, S. Tonneson and al., "77 Conversations Between Chinese and Foreign Leaders on the Wars in Indochina, 1964–1977," Cold War International History Project, Working Paper no. 22, May 1998, pp. 192–3.
136. CIA report on "Trends in Communist Media," September 4, 1975, Computerized CIA Collection: Record Group 263, N.A. II.
137. Nayan Chanda in: A. R. Isaacs, 1997, p. 177. Qiang Zhai offers the same remark: Q. Zhai, 2000, p. 220.
138. Ton That Thien, 1989, p. 111.
139. *The New York Times*, 4 July 1978, 4. Also: M. Beresford, 1988, p. 144; Q. Zhai, 2000, p. 136; I.V. Gaiduk, 1996, pp. 64–67.
140. See: D. Pike, 1987, p. 53.
141. Ton That Thien, 1989, p. 130.
142. *Congressional Record*, Senate, September 14, 1978, 29451.
143. I.V. Gaiduk, 1996, p. 217.
144. D. Pike, 1987, p. 2.
145. I.V. Gaiduk, 1996, pp. 96–7.
146. D. Pike, 1987, p. 180.
147. Eugene K. Lawson, 1984, pp. 309–11.
148. *Vietnam Southeast Asia International*, October-November-December 1977, p. 13.
149. *Far Eastern Economic Review*, June 20, 1975, p. 17.
150. *Far Eastern Economic Review*, August 8, 1975, p. 21.
151. Newspaper cutting of an article by Tin Sang among Douglas Pike's personal notes, September 5, 1975, File: 1975/3, SRV-U.S. Foreign Relations, Douglas Pike Collection, UBIA. Also: *Far Eastern Economic Review*, November 7, 1975, p. 14.
152. *Keesing's Contemporary Archives*, 1976, p. 27908.
153. *The New York Times*, September 3, 1975, p. 3.
154. *Far Eastern Economic Review*, September 26, 1975, p. 10.
155. *U.N. Chronicle*, December 1976, p. 16; *Far Eastern Economic Review*, September 10, 1976, p. 11. See also: *Keesing's Contemporary Archives*, 1975, p. 27428.
156. S. Hurst, 1996, p. 20.
157. See Moynihan's speech to the General Assembly on September 19: *Department of State Bulletin*, October 20, 1975, pp. 604–5.
158. *The New York Times*, September 20, 1975, p. 9.
159. *The New York Times*, October 3, 1975, p. 4.
160. *The New York Times*, July 29, 1975, p. 32.
161. Committee on International Relations, "U.S. Trade Embargo of Vietnam: Church Views, Hearing Before the Subcommittee on International Trade and Commerce," House of Representatives on HR 9503 amending the Trading with the Enemy Act to repeal the embargo on U.S. trade with North and South Vietnam, 94th Congress, 1st session, November 17, 1975 (Washington D.C.: U.S. Government Printing Office, 1976), p. 12.
162. *Peking Review*, September 26, 1975, pp. 5–7.
163. *The New York Times*, November 9, 1975, p. 23.
164. *The New York Times*, August 18, 1975, p. 24.
165. O.A. Westad, Chen Jian, S. Tonneson et al., "77 Conversations Between Chinese and Foreign Leaders on the Wars in Indochina, 1964–1977," Cold War International History Project, Working Paper no. 22, May 1998, pp. 192–3.
166. S. Lodha, 1997, p. 270.
167. *Peking Review*, September 26, 1975, pp. 5–7; *The New York Times*, September 23, 1975, p. 9. Also: S. J. Morris, 1999, p. 173; R.S. Ross, 1988, pp. 64–5.
168. *The Nation*, September 9, 1978, p. 210; *The New York Times*, September 30, 1975, p. 11; *Far Eastern Economic Review*, July 14, 1978, p. 8. See also: *Keesing's Contemporary Archives*, 1976, p. 27909.
169. D. Pike, 1987, pp. 201–2.
170. O.A. Westad, Chen Jian, S. Tonneson, et al., "77 Conversations Between Chinese and Foreign Leaders on the Wars in Indochina, 1964–1977," Cold War International History Project, Working Paper no. 22, May 1998, p. 192.
171. A. Gilks, 1992, p. 151–2.
172. *Ibid.*, p. 143; *Peking Review*, August 22, 1975, pp. 3–4.
173. *The Nation*, June 9, 1979, p. 700.
174. See: S.W. Simon, "Peking and Indochina: The Perplexity of Victory," *Asian Survey*, May 1976, pp. 401–410.
175. *The New York Times*, September 24, 1975, p. 1.
176. See Moynihan's speech to the Security Council on September 26: *Department of State Bulletin*, October 20, 1975, pp. 605–6. Also: *The New York Times*, September 27, 1975, p. 13.
177. *The New York Times*, September 30, 1975, p. 11.
178. See Moynihan's statement to the Security Council on September 30 in: *Department of State Bulletin*, October 20, 1975, p. 606. See also: *U.N. Chronicle*, December 1976, p. 16; *Keesing's Contemporary Archives*, 1975, p. 27428; *The New York Times*, October 1, 1975, p. 5; *Far Eastern Economic Review*, September 10, 1976, p. 11.
179. *Peking Review*, October 10, 1975, pp. 28–29.
180. Joint Letter of the PRG and DRV Permanent Observers circulated as a UN General Assembly Document,

September 30, File: 1975/2, SRV-U.S. Foreign Relations, Douglas Pike Collection, UBIA.
181. CIA report on "Trends in Communist Media," October 1, 1975, Computerized CIA Collection: Record Group 263, N.A. II.
182. Remarks by Peter Florin and Tiamiou Adjibade, U.N. Ambassadors of the German Democratic Republic and Dahomey respectively (*U.N. Chronicle*, November 1975, p. 14).
183. *Far Eastern Economic Review*, November 7, 1975, p. 18.
184. CIA report on "Trends in Communist Media," November 5, 1975, Computerized CIA Collection: Record Group 263, N.A. II.
185. Joint declaration signed by Brezhnev and Le Duan on October 30, 1975, File: 1975/2, SRV-U.S. Foreign Relations, Douglas Pike Collection, UBIA.
186. *The New York Times*, November 9, 1975, p. 23.
187. *Far Eastern Economic Review*, November 21, 1975, p. 22. *Peking Review*, September 12, 1975.
188. *Keesing's Contemporary Archives*, 1976, p. 27909; *The New York Times*, October 31, 1975, p. 6. Also: D. Pike, 1987, p. 128. Also: *Far Eastern Economic Review*, November 28, 1975, p. 30–31.
189. CIA report on "Trends in Communist Media," November 5, 1975, Computerized CIA Collection: Record Group 263, N.A. II.
190. *The New York Times*, November 9, 1975, p. 23.
191. N. Chanda, 1988, p. 181; A. Gilks, 1992, p. 153. V. Funnell quotes a $3.2 billion contribution from Moscow (V. Funnell in: M. Light, 1993, p. 88). See also: *The New York Times*, December 23, 1975, p. 39.
192. *Far Eastern Economic Review*, November 28, 1975, p. 30–31. Also: *The New York Times*, November 8, 1975, p. 3.
193. *The New York Times*, November 9, 1975, p. 23. See also: S.J. Morris, "The Soviet-Chinese-Vietnamese Triangle in the 1970's: The View From Moscow," Cold War International History Project Working Paper no. 25, April 1999, pp. 28–32.
194. *Far Eastern Economic Review*, November 14, 1975, p. 15. Schlesinger was reportedly dismissed probably due to his feud with Kissinger. Colby had begun cooperating with Senator Frank Church's committee on CIA assassination plots which was certainly a nagging reminder of Ford's predecessor's involvement with the CIA. De-emphasizing Kissinger's power probably responded to popular pressure for his dismissal following the fall of Saigon although Ford insisted that Kissinger remain Secretary of State if he should win the upcoming elections. On this issue see: A.H. Cahn, 1998, p. 123.
195. G. Ford, 1979, pp. 355–356.
196. *Far Eastern Economic Review*, March 19, 1976, p. 36.
197. M.A. Niehaus, "U.S. Policy toward the Socialist Republic of Vietnam," The Library of Congress Congressional Research Service, July 18, 1977, File: 7–9/1977, SRV-U.S. Foreign Relations, Douglas Pike Collection, UBIA. Also: *Department of State Bulletin*, June 30, 1975, p. 919.
198. Summary entitled: "DRV releases bodies; Pham Van Dong sees Congressmen," undated, File: 1975/4, SRV-U.S. Foreign Relations, Douglas Pike Collection, UBIA. Also: *Far Eastern Economic Review*, December 26, 1975, p. 22.
199. Memorandum of Conversation between Kissinger and Members of the House Select Committee on Missing Persons in Southeast Asia, November 14, 1975, File: POW-MIA (2), National Security Adviser: NSC East Asian and Pacific Affairs Staff Files, (1969) 1973–1976, Box 16, FPL.
200. Committee on International Relations, "U.S. Trade Embargo of Vietnam: Church Views," Hearing before the Subcommittee on International Trade and Commerce on HR 9503 amending the Trading with the Enemy Act to repeal the embargo on U.S. trade with North and South Vietnam, House of Representatives, 94th Congress, 1st session, November 17, 1975 (Washington D.C.: U.S. Government Printing Office, 1976), pp. 1 and 12. *Far Eastern Economic Review*, January 9, 1976, p. 20; *The New York Times*, November 15, 1975, p. 9.
201. *Far Eastern Economic Review*, July 2, 1976, p. 54.
202. *The New York Times*, November 19, 1975, p. 42.
203. *The New York Times*, November 15, 1975, p. 9.
204. Briefing for Kissinger's meeting with members of the House Select Committee on MIA's, undated, File: MIA/Amnesty/National League of Families (3), National Security Adviser: Presidential Subject Files 1974–1977, Box 10, FPL.
205. *Congressional Quarterly Weekly Report*, September 20, 1975, p. 2019. The appointment of this committee was first proposed in resolution H. Res.380 on April 8, 1975 by Montgomery in a letter to Dr. Tedd Marrs from Congressman Montgomery, April 15, 1975, File: POW-MIA (1), National Security Adviser: NSC East Asian and Pacific Affairs Staff Files, (1969) 1973–1976, Box 16, FPL.
206. Author's emphasis. Committee on Veterans' Affairs, "Americans Missing in Southeast Asia," U.S. House of Representatives, 100th Congress (Washington D.C.: U.S. Government Printing Office, 1988), p. 1.
207. *Ibid.*, p. 9.
208. Memorandum of Conversation between Kissinger and Members of the House Select Committee on Missing Persons in Southeast Asia, November 14, 1975, File: POW-MIA (2), National Security Adviser: NSC East Asian and Pacific Affairs Staff Files, (1969) 1973–1976, Box 16, FPL.
209. Author's telephone interview with John McAuliff, March 15, 2002 (Former member of the American Friends Service Committee and current Executive Director of the Fund for National Reconciliation and Development).
210. Committee on Veterans' Affairs, "Americans Missing in Southeast Asia," U.S. House of Representatives, 100th Congress (Washington D.C.: U.S. Government Printing Office, 1988), p. 9.
211. Memorandum of Conversation between Kissinger and Members of the House Select Committee on Missing Persons in Southeast Asia, November 14, 1975, File: POW-MIA (2), National Security Adviser: NSC East Asian and Pacific Affairs Staff Files, (1969) 1973–1976, Box 16, FPL.
212. *The Nation*, July 3, 1976, p. 22.
213. Committee on Veterans' Affairs, "Americans Missing in Southeast Asia," Hearings before the House Select Committee on Missing Persons in Southeast Asia, 94th Congress, 2nd session, Part 5, June 17, 25, July 21 and September 21, 1976 (Washington D.C.: U.S. Government Printing Office, 1976), p. 56.
214. Memorandum of Conversation between Kissinger and Members of the House Select Committee on Missing Persons in Southeast Asia, November 14, 1975, File: POW-MIA (2), National Security Adviser: NSC East Asian and Pacific Affairs Staff Files, (1969) 1973–1976, Box 16, FPL.
215. *The New York Times*, November 15, 1975, p. 9.
216. Committee on Veterans' Affairs, "Americans Missing in Southeast Asia," U.S. House of Representatives, 100th Congress (Washington D.C.: U.S. Government Printing Office, 1988), pp. 9–10.
217. Document entitled "DRV-U.S. Relations: Vietnamese Refugee Issue May–December 1975," undated, File: 1975/3, SRV-U.S. Foreign Relations, Douglas Pike Collection, UBIA. They eventually returned to Vietnam in November.
218. *The New York Times*, October 12, 1975, p. 7.

219. CIA report on "Trends in Communist Media," December 10, 1975, Computerized CIA Collection: Record Group 263, N.A. II.
220. *Keesing's Contemporary Archives*, 1975, p. 27496. See also: *The New York Times*, November 23, 1975, p. 7.
221. Transcript of Kissinger's address before the Economic Club of Michigan, November 24, File: 1975/4, SRV-U.S. Foreign Relations, Douglas Pike Collection, UBIA. Also: *Far Eastern Economic Review*, December 26, 1975, p. 22; *Far Eastern Economic Review*, July 2, 1976, p. 54; *The Nation*, July 3, 1976, p. 22; *The New York Times*, November 25, 1975, p. 5.
222. Document entitled: "DRV, PRG Media ignore Kissinger remarks on improved relations," December 3, 1975, File: 1975/4, SRV-U.S. Foreign Relations, Douglas Pike Collection, UBIA. This silence was also reported by the CIA: CIA report on "Trends in Communist Media," December 3, 1975, Computerized CIA Collection: Record Group 263, N.A. II.
223. Letter from Senator E. Kennedy to Nguyen Duy Trinh, November 17, 1975, File: 1-2/1976, SRV-U.S. Foreign Relations, Douglas Pike Collection, UBIA.
224. Report from Hanoi *Vietnam News Agency*, January 2, 1976, File: 1-2/1976, SRV-U.S. Foreign Relations, Douglas Pike Collection, UBIA.
225. Analysis of recent *Nhan Dan* articles on the aid issue written by D. Pike, January 28, 1976, File: 1-2/1976, SRV-U.S. Foreign Relations, Douglas Pike Collection, UBIA.
226. Letter from Nguyen Duy Trinh responding to letters from Montgomery of December 26, 1975 and January 17, 1976, February 25, 1976, File: 1-2/1976, SRV-U.S. Foreign Relations, Douglas Pike Collection, UBIA.
227. *Far Eastern Economic Review*, December 19, 1975, p. 17.
228. Committee on Veterans' Affairs, "Americans Missing in Southeast Asia," U.S. House of Representatives, 100th Congress (Washington D.C.: U.S. Government Printing Office, 1988), p. 10.
229. *Ibid.*, p. 10.
230. *Keesing's Contemporary Archives*, 1976, p. 27908.
231. Cable from the U.S. Embassy in Bangkok to Kissinger on Montgomery's press conference of December 23 in Bangkok, File: 1975/4, SRV-U.S. Foreign Relations, Douglas Pike Collection, UBIA.
232. Telegram from the U.S. Embassy in Paris to Kissinger, December 1976, File: Vietnamese War—'Camp David File'—(3), 12/12/75-12/15/76, National Security Adviser: Kissinger-Scowcroft West Wing Office Files: 1969-1977, Box 34, FPL.
233. Committee on Veterans' Affairs, "Americans Missing in Southeast Asia," U.S. House of Representatives, 100th Congress (Washington D.C.: U.S. Government Printing Office, 1988), p. 10; *The New York Times*, December 7, 1975, p. 22. The pilots were Navy Commander Jesse Taylor, Jr. (declared missing in 1965), Air Force Lieutenant Crosley James Fitton (declared missing in 1968) and Air Force Captain Ronald Dwight Perry (declared missing in 1972). (See: *The New York Times*, December 22, 1975, p. 3).
234. Report from the Hanoi *Vietnam News Agency*, December 9, 1975, File: 1975/2, SRV-U.S. Foreign Relations, Douglas Pike Collection, UBIA.
235. *The Nation*, October 9, 1976, p. 334.
236. *Far Eastern Economic Review*, December 19, 1975, p. 17. Also: Montgomery's press release of December 8, 1975, File: 1975/2, SRV-U.S. Foreign Relations, Douglas Pike Collection, UBIA.
237. News release by the State Department on Ford's "Pacific Doctrine" statement in Hawaii, December 7, 1975, File: 1975/4, SRV-U.S. Foreign Relations, Douglas Pike Collection, UBIA.
238. *Keesing's Contemporary Archives*, 1976, p. 27557.

239. *Sudestasie information*, *Viet-Nam Info*, May-June 1978, p. 5. On Thai-American negotiations on military bases see: *Keesing's Contemporary Archives*, 1976, pp. 27843-4 and p. 28101.
240. Title of an article in *Quan Doi Nhan Dan*, December 10, 1975, File: 1975/4, SRV-U.S. Foreign Relations, Douglas Pike Collection, UBIA.
241. *Vietnam International*, January-February-March 1976, pp. 16-17.
242. CIA report on "Trends in Communist Media," December 10, 1975, Computerized CIA Collection: Record Group 263, N.A. II.
243. *Far Eastern Economic Review*, December 19, 1975, p. 24; *Keesing's Contemporary Archives*, 1976, p. 27557.
244. Notes on presidential statements, undated, File: 6-8/1976, SRV-U.S. Foreign Relations, Douglas Pike Collection, UBIA.
245. *Far Eastern Economic Review*, December 26, 1975, p. 21.
246. J. Mann, 1999, pp. 68-71.
247. *Far Eastern Economic Review*, January 9, 1976, p. 20.
248. M.A. Niehaus, "U.S. Policy toward the Socialist Republic of Vietnam," The Library of Congress Congressional Research Service, July 18, 1977, File: 7-9/1977, SRV-U.S. Foreign Relations, Douglas Pike Collection, UBIA. Also: *The New York Times*, December 21, 1975, p. 7.
249. The remains were flown to the United States on February 22, 1976 (*Keesing's Contemporary Archives*, 1976, p. 27908). See also: *The New York Times*, December 22, 1975, p. 3.
250. Committee on Veterans' Affairs, "Americans Missing in Southeast Asia," U.S. House of Representatives, 100th Congress (Washington D.C.: U.S. Government Printing Office, 1988), pp. 11-12.
251. Memorandum of Conversation between Ford and the Montgomery Committee, December 17, 1975, File: December 17, 1975—Ford, Scowcroft, Representatives Montgomery, Gilman and McCloskey, National Security Adviser: Memoranda of Conversations, 1973-1977, Box 17, FPL.
252. Committee on Veterans' Affairs, "Americans Missing in Southeast Asia," U.S. House of Representatives, 100th Congress (Washington D.C.: U.S. Government Printing Office, 1988), pp. 11-12.
253. Report to the President of the United States by the Montgomery Committee, undated, File: MIA/Amnesty/National League of Families (3), National Security Adviser: Presidential Subject Files 1974-1977, Box 10, FPL.
254. Briefing for Kissinger's meeting with Members of the House Select Committee on MIA's, undated, File: MIA/Amnesty/National League of Families (3), National Security Adviser: Presidential Subject Files 1974-1977, Box 10, FPL.
255. Memorandum of Conversation between the President and the Montgomery Committee, January 26, 1976, File: January 26 1976—Ford, House Select Committee on MIAs, National Security Adviser: Memoranda of Conversations, 1973-1977, Box 17, FPL.
256. Memorandum of Conversation between Kissinger and the Montgomery Committee, March 12, 1976, File: Vietnam-Nixon-Pham Van Dong Exchange on Reconstruction (1), National Security Adviser: Presidential Country Files for East Asia and the Pacific, Box 20, FPL.
257. Report to the President of the United States by the Montgomery Committee, undated, File: MIA/Amnesty/National League of Families (3), National Security Adviser: Presidential Subject Files 1974-1977, Box 10, FPL.
258. *Far Eastern Economic Review*, January 9, 1976, p. 20.
259. *The New York Times*, December 24, 1975, p. 5.
260. Report to the President of the United States by the

Montgomery Committee, undated, File: MIA/Amnesty/National League of Families (3), National Security Adviser: Presidential Subject Files 1974–1977, Box 10, FPL.
261. Transcript of the meeting between Phan Hien and the American Friends Service, January 1977, File: 3–4/1977, SRV-U.S. Foreign Relations, Douglas Pike Collection, UBIA.
262. Report to the President of the United States by the Montgomery Committee, undated, File: MIA/Amnesty/National League of Families (3), National Security Adviser: Presidential Subject Files 1974–1977, Box 10, FPL.
263. Memorandum of conversation between the President and the Montgomery Committee, January 26, 1976, File: January 26 1976 — Ford, House Select Committee on MIAs, National Security Adviser: Memoranda of Conversations, 1973–1977, Box 17, FPL. List provided by Hanoi to Montgomery in December 1975, File: 1976, SRV-U.S. Foreign Relations, Douglas Pike Collection, UBIA.
264. *Far Eastern Economic Review*, January 9, 1976, p. 20.
265. Message from the President of the United States to the Prime Minister of the Democratic Republic of Vietnam, February 1, 1973, File: Vietnam (1), National Security Adviser: Presidential Country Files for East Asian and the Pacific, Box 18, FPL. See also: *The New York Times*, May 20, 1977, p. 17; *Vietnam Southeast Asia International*, May-June 1977, p. 8. Also: B.H. Franklin, 1992, p. 125.
266. Committee on Veterans' Affairs, "Americans Missing in Southeast Asia," U.S. House of Representatives, 100th Congress (Washington D.C.: U.S. Government Printing Office, 1988), p. 11. Also: Memorandum of Conversation between Kissinger and the Montgomery Committee, March 12, 1976, File: Vietnam-Nixon-Pham Van Dong Exchange on Reconstruction (1), National Security Adviser: Presidential Country Files for East Asia and the Pacific, Box 20, FPL.
267. Committee on Veterans' Affairs, "Americans Missing in Southeast Asia," Hearings before the House Select Committee on Missing Persons in Southeast Asia, 94th Congress, 2nd session, Part 5, June 17 and 25, July 21 and September 21, 1976 (Washington D.C.: U.S. Government Printing Office, 1976), p. 56.
268. Committee on Veterans' Affairs, "Americans Missing in Southeast Asia," U.S. House of Representatives, 100th Congress (Washington D.C.: U.S. Government Printing Office, 1988), p. 11.
269. *Ibid.*, p. 115.
270. Letter from Scowcroft to Montgomery, November 29, 1976, File: Vietnam-Nixon-Pham Van Dong Exchange on Reconstruction (2), National Security Adviser: Presidential Country Files for East Asia and the Pacific, Box 20, FPL.
271. *The New York Times*, December 24, 1975, p. 5.
272. R.S. McNamara, J.G. Blight and R.K. Brigham, 1999, p. 392.
273. Document from the State Department Bureau of Public Affairs entitled: "United States relations with Viet-Nam," December 31, 1975, File: 1975/4, SRV-U.S. Foreign Relations, Douglas Pike Collection, UBIA.
274. Memorandum from R. Holbrooke to C. Vance, April 25, 1977, NSA Brzezinski Files, Box 85, CPL.
275. F. Joyaux, 1988, p. 361.
276. *Keesing's Contemporary Archives*, 1975, p. 27496.
277. CIA report on "Trends in Communist media," November 19, 1975, Computerized CIA Collection: Record Group 263, N.A. II.
278. *The New York Times*, June 8, 1975, p. 6. Amongst the members of the new Cabinet were General Vo Nguyen Giap (Defense Minister), Nguyen Duy Trinh (Foreign Minister), Le Tanh Nghi (State Planning), and Ton Duc Thang (President).

279. *Newsweek*, November 24, 1975, p. 35. All references to *Newsweek* refer to the European edition unless otherwise noted.
280. *The New York Times*, June 9, 1975, p. 1.
281. *The New York Times*, July 16, 1975, p. 3.
282. A. Gilks, 1992, p. 149. See also: C.A. Thayer, "North Vietnam in 1975: National Liberation, Reunification and Socialist Construction," *Asian Survey*, January 1976, pp. 14–23; W.J. Duiker, "Ideology and Nation-Building in the Democratic Republic of Vietnam," *Asian Survey*, May 1977, pp. 413–431.
283. Luu Van Loi, 2002, p. 9.
284. *The New York Times*, October 6, 1975, p. 32.
285. *Far Eastern Economic Review*, September 12, 1975, p. 12.
286. CIA reports on "Trends in Communist Media," November 19, 1975, and December 3, 1975, Computerized CIA Collection: Record Group 263, N.A. II. Also: *The New York Times*, November 10, 1975, p. 9 and November 16, 1975, p. 16.
287. See: *Keesing's Contemporary Archives*, 1975, pp. 27496-7.
288. *The New York Times*, November 22, 1975, p. 1. See also: *Far Eastern Economic Review*, January 23, 1976, p. 21.
289. *The New York Times*, November 9, 1975, p. 22.
290. *The New York Times*, December 29, 1975, pp. 1 and 5.
291. S. Lodha, 1997, p. 239; R.S. Ross, 1988, p. 69.
292. M.A. Niehaus, "U.S. Policy toward the Socialist Republic of Vietnam," The Library of Congress Congressional Research Service, July 18, 1977, File: 7–9/1977, SRV-U.S. Foreign Relations, Douglas Pike Collection, UBIA.
293. See: *Keesing's Contemporary Archives*, 1976, p. 27917-9. Also: *Far Eastern Economic Review*, May 7, 1976, pp. 6–7.
294. *The New York Times*, July 4, 1976, p. 10.
295. *Asia Yearbook*, 1977, p. 37. The official acknowledgement of the VCP's position as the leading political organ would however only occur in 1980 with the writing of the new constitution. Vague allusions to its leading role existed in the constitution of 1959 but had not been openly stated in order to maximize popular support for the Party (W. Duiker, 1989, p. 82).
296. *The New York Times*, July 4, 1976, p. 10.
297. S.J. Morris, "The Soviet-Chinese-Vietnamese Triangle in the 1970's: The View From Moscow," Cold War International History Project, Working Paper no. 25, April 1999, pp. 22 and 26–8.
298. Author's interview with Judith Stowe, October 26, 2002. Bui Tin explains that although Le Duan was born in a town North of Hue he was considered a southerner for having lived in the South almost all his life (Bui Tin, 1999, pp. 32–3).
299. *Far Eastern Economic Review*, May 21, 1976, p. 30.
300. *The Nation*, September 9, 1978, p. 211. Also: S. Lodha, 1997, pp. 232–3.
301. E. Palmujoki, 1997, p. 65; R.S. Ross, 1988, p. 26.
302. W.J. Duiker, 1986, pp. 60–1.
303. E.K. Lawson, 1984, p. 281.
304. *Vietnam Southeast Asia International*, July-August-September 1978, p. 4. See also: Quang Loi, Le Minh Nghia and Vu Phi Hoang, *Les Archipels Hoàng Sa et Truòng Sa (Paracels et Spratly)*, Dossier II, (Hanoi: Le Courrier du Vietnam, 1984).
305. See: G. Evans and K. Rowley, 1990, pp. 46–8.
306. W.J. Duiker, 1986, pp. 60–1.
307. *Newsweek*, August 2, 1976, p. 5.
308. *Newsweek*, June 20, 1977, p. 21.
309. *Far Eastern Economic Review*, May 5, 1978, p. 11. *Peking Review*, December 12, 1975, pp. 10–15.
310. Accusation in *Nhan Dan* against the Chinese, *in*:

Notes—Chapter I

Far Eastern Economic Review, July 7, 1978, p. 8. For a summary of the Sino-Vietnamese dispute over these islands see: *Keesing's Contemporary Archives*, 1976, p. 27872; *Keesing's Contemporary Archives*, 1978, p. 28913; *Keesing's Contemporary Archives*, 1979, pp. 29869–70.

311. Luu Van Loi, 2002, p. 29.
312. *The New York Times*, July 13, 1976, p. 1 and July 14, 1976, p. 6.
313. *Newsweek*, July 26, 1976, p. 35.
314. *Keesing's Contemporary Archives*, 1978, pp. 28862–3; *The New York Times*, July 13, 1976, p. 1; July 14, 1976, p. 6; August 7, 1976, p. 1; August 25, 1976, p. 3. Hanoi had already enjoyed diplomatic relations with Indonesia since 1964, and with Malaysia and Singapore since the signing of the Paris Peace Agreement in 1973.
315. *The New York Times*, August 25, 1976, p. 3.
316. *Far Eastern Economic Review*, July 2, 1976, p. 54.
317. Report from the Saigon *Liberation Press Agency*, January 16, 1976, File: 1–2/1976, SRV-U.S. Foreign Relations, Douglas Pike Collection, UBIA. Also: *The New York Times*, December 25, 1975, p. 31.
318. Senator McGovern's remarks in: *The Nation*, July 3, 1976, p. 21.
319. Report from the Hanoi *Vietnam News Agency*, January 19, 1976, File: 1–2/1976, SRV-U.S. Foreign Relations, Douglas Pike Collection, UBIA.
320. See: Senator McGovern's remarks in: *The Nation*, July 3, 1976, pp. 21–2.
321. Analysis of recent *Nhan Dan* articles on the aid issue written by D. Pike, January 28, 1976, File: 1–2/1976, SRV-U.S. Foreign Relations, Douglas Pike Collection, UBIA.
322. Report from the Hanoi *Vietnam News Agency*, January 19, 1976, File: 1–2/1976, SRV-U.S. Foreign Relations, Douglas Pike Collection, UBIA; *Vietnam Info*, June-July 1976, p. 24.
323. Analysis of recent *Nhan Dan* articles on the aid issue written by D. Pike, January 28, 1976, File: 1–2/1976, SRV-U.S. Foreign Relations, Douglas Pike Collection, UBIA.
324. Report from the *Saigon Domestic Service*, February 4, 1976, File: 1–2/1976, SRV-U.S. Foreign Relations, Douglas Pike Collection, UBIA.
325. Report from *Agence France Presse*, February 12, 1976, File: 1–2/1976, SRV-U.S. Foreign Relations, Douglas Pike Collection, UBIA.
326. Senator G. McGovern, "Vietnam: 1976: A Report by Senator George McGovern to the Committee on Foreign Relations United States Senate," March 1976 (Washington D.C.: U.S. Government Printing Office, 1976). Also quoted in: *The Christian Century*, April 7, 1976, p. 323; *Vietnam Info*, May 1976, p. 19 and June/July 1976, p. 24. See also McGovern's interesting remarks on Vietnam's request for admission to the United Nations in: *U.S. News & World Report*, October 25, 1976, pp. 49–50.
327. Statements on the MIA issue in D. Pike's notes, January 1976, File: 1–2/1976, SRV-U.S. Foreign Relations, Douglas Pike Collection, UBIA.
328. *The Nation*, July 3, 1976, p. 22.
329. Status Memo on Vietnamese-U.S. Negotiations by Douglas Pike, February 26, 1976, File: 1976, SRV-U.S. Foreign Relations, Douglas Pike Collection, UBIA.
330. Memorandum of Conversation between Kissinger and the Montgomery Committee, March 12, 1976, File: Vietnam-Nixon-Pham Van Dong Exchange on Reconstruction (1), National Security Adviser: Presidential Country Files for East Asia and the Pacific, Box 20, FPL. See also: *Keesing's Contemporary Archives*, 1976, p. 27908.
331. Committee on Veterans' Affairs, "Americans Missing in Southeast Asia," U.S. House of Representatives, 100th Congress (Washington D.C.: U.S. Government Printing Office, 1988), p. 11. The Memorandum of the ensuing conversations may be found in the following: File: January 26 1976—Ford, House Select Committee on MIAs, National Security Adviser: Memoranda of Conversations, 1973–1977, Box 17, FPL.
332. NSC Memorandum for Scowcroft from T.J. Barnes on "Possible Approaches to Vietnam," February 11, 1976, File: Vietnam (28), National Security Adviser: Presidential Country Files for East Asia and the Pacific, Box 20, FPL.
333. Memorandum of Conversation between Kissinger and the Montgomery Committee, March 12, 1976, File: Vietnam-Nixon-Pham Van Dong Exchange on Reconstruction (1), National Security Adviser: Presidential Country Files for East Asia and the Pacific, Box 20, FPL.
334. Memorandum of Conversation between Ford and the Montgomery Committee, January 26, 1976, File: January 26 1976—Ford, House Select Committee on MIAs, National Security Adviser: Memoranda of Conversations, 1973–1977, Box 17, FPL.
335. Letter from Scowcroft to Senator Sparkman, March 25, 1976 on the Nixon letter to North Vietnam, File: Vietnam-Nixon-Pham Van Dong Exchange on Reconstruction (1), National Security Adviser: Presidential Country Files for East Asia and the Pacific, Box 20, FPL.
336. Committee on Veterans' Affairs, "Americans Missing in Southeast Asia," U.S. House of Representatives, 100th Congress (Washington D.C.: U.S. Government Printing Office, 1988), pp. 11–12.
337. Committee on Veterans' Affairs, "Americans Missing in Southeast Asia," Hearings before the House Select Committee on Missing Persons in Southeast Asia, 94th Congress, 2nd session, Part 5, June 17 and 25, July 21 and September 21, 1976 (Washington D.C.: U.S. Government Printing Office, 1976), pp. 47–8 and 52.
338. Kissinger's meeting with members of the House of Representatives, January 26, 1973, File: January 1973, SRV-U.S. Foreign Relations, Douglas Pike Collection, UBIA.
339. Unattributed, "Summary of Statutes and Regulations Affecting or Restricting Trade, Travel and Other Dealings with North Vietnam Given to DRV Representative at Paris Economic Talks, August 1973"; Unattributed, "U.S. Background Paper on U.S. Foreign Aid Handed [to] DRV Representatives in Paris, August, 1973"; "Congressional Statements on U.S. Economic Aid (Handed [to] DRV Representative in Paris, August, 1973"; File: May-June 1973, SRV-U.S. Foreign Relations, Douglas Pike Collection, UBIA.
340. See Appendix 3 for the full text of the six letters.
341. Cable from Kissinger to the American Embassy in Paris, March 26, 1976, File: 1976, SRV-U.S. Foreign Relations, Douglas Pike Collection, UBIA. Also: *Department of State Bulletin*, August 16, 1976, p. 250; *Vietnam Info*, April 1976, p. 4; *Keesing's Contemporary Archives*, 1977, p. 28280.
342. Author's emphasis. *The New York Times*, March 27, 1976, p. 5.
343. *Far Eastern Economic Review*, November 26, 1976, p. 14.
344. *Keesing's Contemporary Archives*, 1976, p. 27909.
345. *Asia Yearbook*, 1977, p. 33.
346. *Keesing's Contemporary Archives*, 1976, p. 27909.
347. Telegram from the U.S. Embassy in Paris to Kissinger, April 1976, File: Vietnamese War—'Camp David File'—(3), 12/12/75–12/15/76, National Security Adviser: Kissinger-Scowcroft West Wing Office Files: 1969–1977, Box 34, FPL. Also: *Keesing's Contemporary Archives*, 1977, p. 28280.
348. Document dated 14 September 1976, "Foreign Ministry Spokesman reveals U.S.-SRV Notes," File: 4/1975, SRV-U.S. Foreign Relations, Douglas Pike Collection, UBIA. See Appendix 3 for the full text of the diplomatic note.
349. Report on a *Nhan Dan* article of April 12, 1976,

File: 1976, SRV-U.S. Foreign Relations, Douglas Pike Collection, UBIA.
350. *Keesing's Contemporary Archives*, 1976, p. 27909.
351. *Asia Yearbook*, 1977, p. 33.
352. Memorandum from D. Pike, unreferenced, undated, File: 1976, SRV-U.S. Foreign Relations, Douglas Pike Collection, UBIA.
353. News dispatch from the *Reuters* agency, April 27, 1976, File: 3-5/1976, SRV-U.S. Foreign Relations, Douglas Pike Collection, UBIA.
354. Report from *Quan Doi Nhan Dan*, April 16, 1976, File: 3-5/1976, SRV-U.S. Foreign Relations, Douglas Pike Collection, UBIA.
355. Report on the Hanoi media's publicizing of the exchange of notes, April 21, 1976, File: 3-5/1976, SRV-U.S. Foreign Relations, Douglas Pike Collection, UBIA.
356. Comments and news report from D. Pike to Kissinger on a *Hanoi Radio* broadcast, April 16, 1976, File: 1976, SRV-US Foreign Relations, Douglas Pike Collection, UBIA.
357. Intelligence report dated April 16, 1979, File: 4/1975, SRV-U.S. Foreign Relations, Douglas Pike Collection, UBIA.
358. *Keesing's Contemporary Archives*, 1976, p. 27909. Also: *Vietnam Info*, November 1977, p. 25 and *Vietnam Info*, May 1976, pp. 18-19. The text of this letter would again be published several times in the following years.
359. Committee on Veterans' Affairs, "Americans Missing in Southeast Asia," U.S. House of Representatives, 100th Congress (Washington D.C.: U.S. Government Printing Office, 1988), p. 12.
360. A.H. Cahn, 1998, p. 46.
361. *Vietnam International*, July-August 1976, p. 13. Ford's strengthening of his policies also applied to other foreign policy issues.
362. Ford's interview at Lenoir Rhyne College, North Carolina, March 20, 1976, File: MIA/Amnesty/National League of Families (3), National Security Adviser: Presidential Subject Files 1974-1977, Box 10, FPL. See also: *Far Eastern Economic Review*, July 2, 1976, p. 54; *Le Monde*, March 30, 1976, p. 1.
363. Press report on Vietnamese reactions to Ford's campaign statements in North Carolina, March 31, 1976, File: 3-5/1976, SRV-U.S. Foreign Relations, Douglas Pike Collection, UBIA.
364. Report on Do Thanh's phone call to the U.S. Embassy in Paris, March 30, 1976, File: 3-5/1976, SRV-U.S. Foreign Relations, Douglas Pike Collection, UBIA.
365. *Department of State Bulletin*, April 12, 1976, p. 465.
366. See: D. Caldwell in: O.A. Westad, 1997, p. 98; A.H. Cahn, 1998, p. 47.
367. Ford quoted in: Committee on Veterans' Affairs, "Americans Missing in Southeast Asia," Hearings before the House Select Committee on Missing Persons in Southeast Asia, 94th Congress, 2nd session, Part 5, June 17 and 25, July 21 and September 21, 1976 (Washington D.C.: U.S. Government Printing Office, 1976), p. 51.
368. P. Udell's interview with Ford in Indianapolis, April 22, 1976, File: Foreign Relations (6), President Ford Committee Records, 1975-76, Box H37, FPL.
369. Ford's interview at the Indiana Broadcasters Association Statewide Convention, Indianapolis, April 23, 1976, File: MIA/Amnesty/National League of Families (3), National Security Adviser: Presidential Subject Files 1974-1977, Box 10, FPL. Also: *Keesing's Contemporary Archives*, 1976, p. 27909; *The New York Times*, April 24, 1976, p. 10.
370. Carter's words as recorded in the *Washington Post*, April 25, 1976, File: Vietnam, President Ford Committee Records 1975-1976, Box H34, FPL.
371. Carter's words as recorded in *Newsweek*, May 10, 1976, File: Vietnam, President Ford Committee Records 1975-1976, Box H34, FPL.
372. See: D. Caldwell in: O.A. Westad, 1997, p. 98.
373. Memorandum from D. Pike to W. Lord, April 13, 1976, File: 1976, SRV-U.S. Foreign Relations, Douglas Pike Collection, UBIA.
374. Memorandum from D. Pike to Kissinger, April 22, 1976, File: 1976, SRV-U.S. Foreign Relations, Douglas Pike Collection, UBIA.
375. Telegram from Kissinger to the U.S. Embassy in Paris, May 1976, File: Vietnamese War—'Camp David File'—(3), 12/12/75-12/15/76, National Security Adviser: Kissinger-Scowcroft West Wing Office Files: 1969-1977, Box 34, FPL. Also: *Keesing's Contemporary Archives*, 1977, p. 28280. See the full text of the diplomatic note in Appendix III.
376. *Vietnam Info*, June-July 1976, p. 4.
377. Kissinger's interview with Barbara Walters on the "Today" show, May 17, 1976, File: MIA/Amnesty/National League of Families (3), National Security Adviser: Presidential Subject Files 1974-1977, Box 10, FPL. Also: *Far Eastern Economic Review*, May 28, 1976, p. 13 and July 2, 1976, p. 54.
378. Committee on Foreign Relations, "Hearing before the Committee on Foreign Relations on Accounting for U.S. Prisoners of War and Missing in Action in Southeast Asia," U.S. Senate, 93rd Congress, 2nd session, January 28, 1974 (Washington D.C.: U.S. Government Printing Office, 1974), p. 55. Also: *The Nation*, October 9, 1976, pp. 331-2. Roger Shields was also the chief Pentagon official for MIA affairs.
379. *Department of State Bulletin*, August 16, 1976, p. 252. Also in: *Far Eastern Economic Review*, September 24, 1976, p. 20.
380. H. Kissinger, 1982, pp. 372-3.
381. Original emphasis (*The Nation*, October 9, 1976, p. 332).
382. See: M. Hiebert, "Playing Politics with the MIAs: Both sides have used the MIA issue as a negotiating tool," *Southeast Asia Chronicle*, August 1982, pp. 14-18.
383. Commentary from D. Pike to Kissinger (?), October 1976, File: 1976, SRV-U.S. Foreign Relations, Douglas Pike Collection, UBIA.
384. W.I. Cohen, 1993, p. 198.
385. Cable from the U.S. Embassy in Paris to Kissinger, June 21, 1976, File: 1976, SRV-U.S. Foreign Relations, Douglas Pike Collection, UBIA. Also: *Keesing's Contemporary Archives*, 1977, p. 28280.
386. Report from the Hanoi *Vietnam News Agency*, September 13, 1976, File: 1976, SRV-U.S. Foreign Relations, Douglas Pike Collection, UBIA.
387. Cable from the U.S. Embassy in Paris to Kissinger, June 21, 1976, File: 1976, SRV-U.S. Foreign Relations, Douglas Pike Collection, UBIA.
388. M.A. Niehaus, "U.S. Policy toward the Socialist Republic of Vietnam," The Library of Congress Congressional Research Service, July 18, 1977, File: 7-9/1977, SRV-U.S. Foreign Relations, Douglas Pike Collection, UBIA.
389. Report from the Hanoi *Vietnam News Agency*, September 13, 1976, File: 1976, SRV-U.S. Foreign Relations, Douglas Pike Collection, UBIA. Also: *Keesing's Contemporary Archives*, 1977, p. 28280. See the full text of this diplomatic note in Appendix III.
390. Committee on Veterans' Affairs, "Americans Missing in Southeast Asia," Hearings before the House Select Committee on Missing Persons in Southeast Asia, 94th Congress, 2nd session, Part 5, June 17 and 25, July 21 and September 21, 1976 (Washington D.C.: U.S. Government Printing Office, 1976), p. 47.
391. *Keesing's Contemporary Archives*, 1976, p. 27919.
392. Committee on Veterans' Affairs, "Americans Missing in Southeast Asia," Hearings before the House Select Committee on Missing Persons in Southeast Asia, 94th Congress, 2nd session, Part 5, June 17 and 25, July 21 and

Notes—Chapter I

September 21, 1976 (Washington D.C.: U.S. Government Printing Office, 1976), p. 94.

393. *Congressional Quarterly Weekly Report*, July 31, 1976, p. 2035. For a short summary of the creation of this League refer to: *The Nation*, October 9, 1976, p. 332.

394. *Department of State Bulletin*, August 16, 1976, p. 248; *Congressional Quarterly Weekly Report*, July 31, 1976, p. 2035.

395. *The Nation*, October 9, 1976, p. 332.

396. *The New York Times*, July 26, 1976, p. 6. Although he had lost the primaries, Reagan also sent a telegram to the convention.

397. *Far Eastern Economic Review*, May 28, 1976, p. 13.

398. *Far Eastern Economic Review*, July 30, 1976, pp. 11–12.

399. *Far Eastern Economic Review*, August 6, 1976, p. 5.

400. Report from the Hanoi *Vietnam News Agency*, July 31, 1976, and State Department dossier entitled "Vietnamese release 50 American civilians: 8/76," File: 6–8/1976, SRV-U.S. Foreign Relations, Douglas Pike Collection, UBIA. Also: *Asia Yearbook*, 1977, p. 37; *The New York Times*, August 2, 1975, p. 1 and August 8, 1976, p. 3.

401. *The New York Times*, August 8, 1976, p. 3 and August 12, 1976, p. 5.

402. Memorandum from D. Pike to Kissinger, August 13, 1976, April 22, 1976, File: 1976, SRV-U.S. Foreign Relations, Douglas Pike Collection, UBIA. Also: *The New York Times*, August 9, 1976, p. 26.

403. *Asia Yearbook*, 1977, p. 38.

404. M.A. Niehaus, "U.S. Policy toward the Socialist Republic of Vietnam," The Library of Congress Congressional Research Service, July 18, 1977, File: 7–9/1977, SRV-U.S. Foreign Relations, Douglas Pike Collection, UBIA. Also: *The New York Times*, August 18, 1976, p. 7.

405. Statements by the Vietnamese Premier, August 1976, File: 6–8/1976, SRV-U.S. Foreign Relations, Douglas Pike Collection, UBIA.

406. *The New York Times*, August 20, 1976, p. 3.

407. *U.N. Chronicle*, October 1976, p. 12; *The New York Times*, August 21, 1976, p. 11.

408. Congressional statements, August 26, 1976, File: 6–8/1976, SRV-U.S. Foreign Relations, Douglas Pike Collection, UBIA.

409. *The New York Times*, August 22, 1976, p. 3.

410. Newspaper cutting of an article by Tin Sang among Douglas Pike's personal notes, September 5, 1975, File: 1975/3, SRV-U.S. Foreign Relations, Douglas Pike Collection, UBIA. Also: *Far Eastern Economic Review*, November 7, 1975, p. 14.

411. Report from the Hanoi *Vietnam News Agency*, September 13, 1976, File: 1976, SRV-U.S. Foreign Relations, Douglas Pike Collection, UBIA. See the full text of this diplomatic note in Appendix 3.

412. Cable from the U.S. Embassy in Paris to Kissinger, August 28, 1976, File: 1976, SRV-U.S. Foreign Relations, Douglas Pike Collection, UBIA.

413. *Keesing's Contemporary Archives*, 1977, p. 28280.

414. Memorandum of Conversation between Ford, Kissinger and Scowcroft, August 30, 1976, File: August 30, 1976—Ford, Kissinger, National Security Adviser: Memoranda of Conversations, 1973–1977, Box 20, FPL.

415. The violence of these demonstrations increased until the Thai coup of October 6, 1976.

416. *The New York Times*, September 2, 1976, p. 6.

417. Kissinger and Secretary Waldheim's remarks to the press following their meeting at the U.N., September 2, 1976, File: 9–11/1976, SRV-U.S. Foreign Relations, Douglas Pike Collection, UBIA. Also: *Department of State Bulletin*, September 27, 1976, p. 400.

418. *The New York Times*, September 3, 1976, pp. 2 and 4.

419. Memorandum from D. Pike to Kissinger, July 26, 1976, File: 6–8/1976, SRV-U.S. Foreign Relations, Douglas Pike Collection, UBIA. Other options included: "Abstain and thereby permit Vietnamese entry" and letting Hanoi know through backchannels that the U.S. vote would depend on their efforts on producing an accounting but "leaving our position ambiguous" until the final vote.

420. Telegram from the U.S. Embassy of Paris to the State Department, September 6, 1976, File: Vietnamese War—'Camp David File'—(3), 12/12/75–12/15/76, National Security Adviser: Kissinger-Scowcroft West Wing Office Files: 1969–1977, Box 34, FPL.

421. *Asia Yearbook*, 1977, p. 38; *The New York Times*, September 7, 1976, p. 2. These servicemen were: Elwyn Rex Capling, William M. Roark, James H. Metz, Thomas C. Kolstad, William Blue Klenert, Stephen W. Diamond, Curtis Abbot Eaton, Samuel Edwin Jr. Waters, Roy Howard Bowling, Bruce Chalmers A. Ducat, Lawrence H. Goldberg, Guy David Johnson.

422. *Keesing's Contemporary Archives*, 1977, p. 28280.

423. Cable from Kissinger to the U.S. Embassy in Paris, September 6 (?), 1976, File: Vietnamese War—'Camp David File'—(3), 12/12/75–12/15/76, National Security Adviser: Kissinger-Scowcroft West Wing Office Files: 1969–1977, Box 34, FPL.

424. Cable from Kissinger to the USUN, September 11, 1976, File: 6–8/1976, SRV-U.S. Foreign Relations, Douglas Pike Collection, UBIA.

425. Cable from Kissinger to the U.S. Embassy in Paris, September 6 (?), 1976, File: Vietnamese War—'Camp David File'—(3), 12/12/75–12/15/76, National Security Adviser: Kissinger-Scowcroft West Wing Office Files: 1969–1977, Box 34, FPL. Also: *Keesing's Contemporary Archives*, 1977, p. 28280.

426. *Department of State Bulletin*, October 4, 1976, p. 418; *Far Eastern Economic Review*, September 24, 1976, p. 5 ; *The New York Times*, September 8, 1976, p. 20.

427. *Keesing's Contemporary Archives*, 1977, p. 28280.

428. *The Nation*, October 9, 1976, p. 333.

429. Cable from the USUN to Kissinger (?), September 7, 1976, File: 9–11/1976, SRV-U.S. Foreign Relations, Douglas Pike Collection, UBIA.

430. Telegram from the U.S. Embassy in Bangkok to the State Department on a radio broadcast from Hanoi, September 13, 1976, File: Vietnamese War—'Camp David File'—(3), 12/12/75–12/15/76, National Security Adviser: Kissinger-Scowcroft West Wing Office Files: 1969–1977, Box 34, FPL.

431. Commentary from D. Pike to Kissinger (?), October 1976, File: 1976, SRV-U.S. Foreign Relations, Douglas Pike Collection, UBIA.

432. Reports by the Hanoi International Service, September 11, 1976, and by the Hanoi *Vietnam News Agency*, September 11, 1976, File: 12/1976, SRV-U.S. Foreign Relations, Douglas Pike Collection, UBIA.

433. *U.N. Chronicle*, October 1976, p. 12; *The New York Times*, September 11, 1976, p. 22.

434. *U.N. Chronicle*, December 1976, p. 16; *The New York Times*, September 14, 1976, p. 1 and 16.

435. *The New York Times*, September 14, 1976, p. 16.

436. *Keesing's Contemporary Archives*, 1977, p. 28280; *The Nation*, October 9, 1976, p. 333.

437. Interview with Scranton on the North Lawn, September 13, 1976, File: Material not released to the Press—Remarks of Administration Officials, Ronald H. Nessen Press Secretary to the President Files: 1974–1977, Nessen Subject Files 1974–77, Box 40, FPL.

438. Scranton recalling Kissinger's words at the conference (*Department of State Bulletin*, December 20, 1976, p. 741).

439. *U.N. Chronicle*, December 1976, p. 18.

440. *U.S. News & World Report*, October 25, 1976, pp. 49–50.

441. Criticisms were uttered by various countries of

different political and ideological background, including Sri Lanka speaking for the Non-Aligned Movement, Singapore (usually one of the most vehement ASEAN states on Indochinese affairs), Western states such as France, and a wide number of other countries (including a majority of communist powers) including: the USSR and China, Czechoslovakia, German Democratic Republic, Mongolia, Bulgaria, Lao People's Democratic Republic, Romania, Ukrainian SSR, Byelorussian SSR, Cuba, Syrian Arab Republic, Somalia, Mauritius, the Lybian Arab Republic, Yugoslavia (and Cyprus and Malta speaking through Yugoslavia). The United Kingdom sided with Washington (*U.N. Chronicle*, December 1976, pp. 16–7; *Far Eastern Economic Review*, September 24, 1976, p. 20).

442. *The New York Times*, September 14, 1976, p. 1.

443. Telegram from the U.S. Embassy of Paris to the State Department, October 1, 1976, File: Vietnamese War–'Camp David File'–(3), 12/12/75–12/15/76, National Security Adviser: Kissinger-Scowcroft West Wing Office Files: 1969–1977, Box 34, FPL.

444. *Vietnam International*, July-August 1976, p. 13; *Vietnam International*, December 1976, p. 1.

445. *Keesing's Contemporary Archives*, 1977, p. 28280; *U.N. Chronicle*, October 1976, p. 12; *Newsweek*, September 27, 1976, p. 22; *The Nation*, October 9, 1976, p. 333.

446. *The New York Times*, September 15, 1976, pp. 1 and 44.

447. Telegram from the U.S. Embassy of Paris to the State Department, October 1, 1976, File: Vietnamese War–'Camp David File'–(3), 12/12/75–12/15/76, National Security Adviser: Kissinger-Scowcroft West Wing Office Files: 1969–1977, Box 34, FPL.

448. See also: *The New York Times*, September 24, 1976, p. 24.

449. *Far Eastern Economic Review*, September 24, 1976, p. 20. Also quoted in: *Newsweek*, September 27, 1976, p. 22.

450. *The New York Times*, October 8, 1976, p. 19.

451. Statement by the Foreign Ministry of Vietnam as reported by the *Hanoi Domestic Service* and *Hanoi Vietnam News Agency*, September 13, 1976, File: 1976, SRV-U.S. Foreign Relations, Douglas Pike Collection, UBIA. Also: *The New York Times*, September 14, 1976, p. 16.

452. Telegram from the U.S. Embassy in Paris to Kissinger, April 1976, File: Vietnamese War–'Camp David File'–(3), 12/12/75–12/15/76, National Security Adviser: Kissinger-Scowcroft West Wing Office Files: 1969–1977, Box 34, FPL.

453. Telegram from the U.S. Embassy of Paris to the State Department, September 13, 1976, File: Vietnamese War–'Camp David File'–(3), 12/12/75–12/15/76, National Security Adviser: Kissinger-Scowcroft West Wing Office Files: 1969–1977, Box 34, FPL.

454. *The New York Times*, September 14, 1976, p. 16.

455. Telegram from the U.S. Embassy in Bangkok to the State Department on a radio broadcast from Hanoi, September 13, 1976, File: Vietnamese War–'Camp David File'–(3), 12/12/75–12/15/76, National Security Adviser: Kissinger-Scowcroft West Wing Office Files: 1969–1977, Box 34, FPL.

456. *Far Eastern Economic Review*, November 12, 1976, p. 13. See also: *The Nation*, September 25, 1976, pp. 260–1.

457. *The Nation*, October 9, 1976, p. 333.

458. M.A. Niehaus, "U.S. Policy toward the Socialist Republic of Vietnam," The Library of Congress Congressional Research Service, July 18, 1977, File: 7–9/1977, SRV-U.S. Foreign Relations, Douglas Pike Collection, UBIA. Also: *Keesing's Contemporary Archives*, 1976, p. 28004; *Far Eastern Economic Review*, October 1, 1976, p. 5; *Vietnam International*, April-May-June 1976, pp. 29–30.

459. *Far Eastern Economic Review*, February 25, 1977, p. 18.

460. *The New York Times*, September 21, 1976, p. 26.

461. *The New York Times*, September 25, 1976, p. 9 and G. Ford, 1979, p. 417.

462. *The Christian Century*, May 26, 1976, p. 507.

463. Carter's speech in Buffalo, New York, October 1, 1976, File: January 1977, President Ford Committee Records 1975–76, Box H28, FPL. Also: Committee on International Relations, "Americans Missing in Action in Southeast Asia," Hearings before the House Subcommittee on Asian and Pacific Affairs, 95th Congress, March 31, July 27, October 5, 27, 1977, and February 2, 1978 (Washington D.C.: U.S. Government Printing Office, 1976), p. 22.

464. *The New York Times*, October 7, 1976, p. 38. Also: L. Bitzer and T. Rueter, 1980, p. 320.

465. Analysis written by Pike for Kissinger, October 22, 1976, File: 1976, SRV-U.S. Foreign Relations, Douglas Pike Collection, UBIA.

466. Hanoi *Diplomatic Information Service* report on an article in *Nhan Dan*, October 29, 1976, File: 9–11/1976, SRV-U.S. Foreign Relations, Douglas Pike Collection, UBIA.

467. *Hanoi International Service* report, October 27, 1976, File: 12/1976, SRV-U.S. Foreign Relations, Douglas Pike Collection, UBIA.

468. *Time*, October 18, 1976, p. 22.

469. G. Ford, 1979, p. 429. On the pardon see: *The New York Times*, August 7, 1975, p. 31.

470. Carter's words as recorded by the *Chicago Tribune* of March 16, 1976, File: Kissinger, Henry, President Ford Committee Records 1975–76, Box H28, FPL.

471. *Time*, November 8, 1976, pp. 23–24.

472. *Newsweek*, October 18, 1976, p. 30.

473. Analysis written by D. Pike for Kissinger (?), October 22, 1976, File: 1976, SRV-U.S. Foreign Relations, Douglas Pike Collection, UBIA.

474. Report entitled "1976: U.S. relations," undated, File: 1976, SRV-U.S. Foreign Relations, Douglas Pike Collection, UBIA.

475. State Department note to Henry Kissinger, October 22, 1976, File: 4/1975, SRV-U.S. Foreign Relations, Douglas Pike Collection, UBIA.

476. *Department of State Bulletin*, November 15, 1976, pp. 606–611. Also: *The New York Times*, October 25, 1976, p. 5 and October 26, 1976, p. 12.

477. Report entitled "1976: U.S. relations," undated, File: 1976, SRV-U.S. Foreign Relations, Douglas Pike Collection, UBIA.

478. Telegram from the U.S. Embassy in Paris to the State Department, November 2 (?), 1976, File: Vietnamese War–'Camp David File'–(3), 12/12/75–12/15/76, National Security Adviser: Kissinger-Scowcroft West Wing Office Files: 1969–1977, Box 34, FPL.

479. Telegram from the U.S. Embassy in Paris to Kissinger, November 3, 1976, File: 1976, SRV-U.S. Foreign Relations, Douglas Pike Collection, UBIA.

480. Author's emphasis (Telegram from the U.S. Embassy in Paris to Kissinger on a "flash summary of the November 12 meetings," November (12?) 1976, File: Vietnamese War–'Camp David File'–(3), 12/12/75–12/15/76, National Security Adviser: Kissinger-Scowcroft West Wing Office Files: 1969–1977, Box 34, FPL).

481. Telegram from the U.S. Embassy in Paris to Kissinger, April 1976, File: Vietnamese War–'Camp David File'–(3), 12/12/75–12/15/76, National Security Adviser: Kissinger-Scowcroft West Wing Office Files: 1969–1977, Box 34, FPL.

482. Telegram from U.S. Embassy in Paris to Kissinger on the declaration of the Vietnamese representatives during the Paris talks, November 12(?) 1976, File: Vietnamese War–'Camp David File'–(3), 12/12/75–12/15/76, National Security Adviser: Kissinger-Scowcroft West Wing Office Files: 1969–1977, Box 34, FPL.

483. *Vietnam Info*, November 1977, p. 24.
484. Telegram from the U.S. Embassy in Paris to Kissinger on a "flash summary of the November 12 meeting," November (12?) 1976, File: Vietnamese War—'Camp David File'—(3), 12/12/75–12/15/76, National Security Adviser: Kissinger-Scowcroft West Wing Office Files: 1969–1977, Box 34, FPL.
485. *Keesing's Contemporary Archives*, 1977, p. 28280.
486. *The New York Times*, November 13, 1976, pp. 1 and 6.
487. *Newsweek*, September 27, 1976, p. 22.
488. *The New York Times*, November 13, 1976, pp. 1 and 6.
489. *The New York Times*, November 14, 1976, p. 1.
490. See Scranton's November 15 speech at the U.N. Security Council in: *Department of State Bulletin*, December 20, 1976, pp. 740–1. Also: *Keesing's Contemporary Archives*, 1977, p. 28280; *The New York Times*, November 16, 1976, p. 1. The vote was 14–1.
491. *U.N. Chronicle*, December 1976, p. 19.
492. *The Christian Century*, December 1, 1976, p. 1067; *U.N. Chronicle*, December 1976, pp. 16 and 22.
493. *Department of State Bulletin*, August 16, 1976, pp. 249–253.
494. *Far Eastern Economic Review*, September 24, 1976, p. 20.
495. *U.N. Chronicle*, December 1976, p. 3 and 17. The Swedish Ambassador to the U.N. had openly argued in favor of Vietnam's admission in order to obtain the release of information on MIAs (*Far Eastern Economic Review*, November 26, 1976, pp. 14–17). See the other countries' reactions in: *U.N. Chronicle*, December 1976, pp. 16 and 18–23.
496. *U.N. Chronicle*, December 1976, p. 17.
497. *Keesing's Contemporary Archives*, 1977, p. 28280. The United States' political allies preferred to avoid the issue and West Germany, Israel and the United Kingdom abstained.
498. *Department of State Bulletin*, December 20, 1976, pp. 741–2.
499. *U.N. Chronicle*, December 1976, pp. 3 and 17; *The New York Times*, November 27, 1976, p. 5.
500. *U.N. Chronicle*, December 1976, p. 17.
501. *Far Eastern Economic Review*, November 26, 1976, p. 14; *The New York Times*, November 17, 1976, p. 9.
502. Author's translation. In French: "abus de pouvoir" (*Vietnam Info*, November 1977, p. 24).
503. *Far Eastern Economic Review*, November 26, 1976, p. 14.
504. *The New York Times*, November 21, 1976, p. 9.
505. *Far Eastern Economic Review*, November 26, 1976, pp. 14–17.
506. *Vietnam Info*, December 1976/January 1977, p. 26; *The New York Times*, November 30, 1976, p. 27.
507. *Far Eastern Economic Review*, September 24, 1976, p. 5.
508. *The New York Times*, November 30, 1976, p. 27.
509. Report entitled "1976: U.S. relations," undated, File: 1976, SRV-U.S. Foreign Relations, Douglas Pike Collection, UBIA.
510. Telegram from the U.S. Embassy in Paris to Kissinger, November 1976, File: Vietnamese War—'Camp David File'—(3), 12/12/75–12/15/76, National Security Adviser: Kissinger-Scowcroft West Wing Office Files: 1969–1977, Box 34, FPL.
511. Telegram from the U.S. Embassy in Paris to Kissinger, December 1976, File: Vietnamese War—'Camp David File'—(3), 12/12/75–12/15/76, National Security Adviser: Kissinger-Scowcroft West Wing Office Files: 1969–1977, Box 34, FPL.
512. Report entitled "1976: U.S. relations," undated, File: 1976, SRV-U.S. Foreign Relations, Douglas Pike Collection, UBIA.

II. The Advent of the Carter Years

1. *Asia Yearbook*, 1977, p. 38.
2. M.A. Niehaus, "U.S. Policy toward the Socialist Republic of Vietnam," The Library of Congress Congressional Research Service, July 18, 1977, File: 7–9/1977, SRV-U.S. Foreign Relations, Douglas Pike Collection, UBIA.
3. Remarks by Bui Tin (Bui Tin, 1999, pp. 65–7, 98 and 122). Bui Tin, formerly a colonel in the North Vietnamese army, a member of the VCP and assistant editor of the Communist Party daily *Nhan Dan*, was expelled from the VCP in March 1991 for criticizing the Party and revealing details on inner-party rivalries. His memoirs, first published in Vietnamese in the United States in 1991, were censored in Vietnam where they continue to circulate clandestinely. Bui Tin has been living in France since 1990.
4. W.J. Duiker, 1989, pp. 36–7.
5. M.A. Niehaus, "U.S. Policy toward the Socialist Republic of Vietnam," The Library of Congress Congressional Research Service, July 18, 1977, File: 7–9/1977, SRV-U.S. Foreign Relations, Douglas Pike Collection, UBIA. Also: *Asia Yearbook*, 1978, p. 336.
6. *The New York Times*, December 21, 1976, p. 3.
7. P.J. Honey, 1966, pp. 32–5; Bui Tin, 1999, pp. 29–33. Also: Author's correspondence with Judith Stowe, November 13, 2002.
8. Bui Tin, 1999, p. 32.
9. See: Hoang Van Hoan, "Distortion of Facts About Militant Friendship between Viet Nam and China is Impermissible," *Peking Review*, December 7, 1979, p. 11. Hoang Van Hoan, clearly a pro–Chinese member of the Party. He was dismissed from the Politburo during the Fourth Party Congress for "age reasons" and defected to China in 1979 where he published several articles attacking Le Duan and Vietnamese policies, then wrote his memoirs in 1988. See also: Hoang Van Hoan, *A Drop in the Ocean: Hoang Van Hoan's Revolutionary Reminiscences* (Beijing: Foreign Languages Press, 1988). Also: W.J. Duiker, 1983, p. 93.
10. Bui Tin, 1999, p. xiii.
11. Hoang Van Hoan, 1988, p. 312 and Preface.
12. Remark by Bui Tin (Bui Tin, 1999, p. 72).
13. Stein Tonneson in the introduction to: C. Goscha, "Le Duan and the Break with China," Cold War International History Project, Dossier 3. See also: W.J. Duiker, 1996, p. 305.
14. Author's correspondence with Judith Stowe, November 13, 2002.
15. Author's interview with Judith Stowe, October 26, 2002.
16. P.J. Honey, 1966, p. 27.
17. Bui Tin, 1999, p. 78.
18. A. Gilks, 1992, p. 164.
19. *Vietnam International*, August-September 1975, p. 6.
20. Nguyen Van Canh and E. Cooper, 1983, p. 145.
21. *Vietnam International*, December 1976, p. 3.
22. *The Nation*, June 9, 1979, p. 700.
23. *Time*, January 3, 1977, p. 55.
24. *The New York Times*, December 13, 1976, p. 6; *Peking Review*, December 17, 1976, p. 8.
25. Gareth Porter commenting in: *The Nation*, June 9, 1979, p. 700.
26. *Asia Yearbook*, 1978, p. 329.
27. *Far Eastern Economic Review*, November 12, 1976, p. 13.
28. *Far Eastern Economic Review*, December 3, 1976, pp. 15–16.
29. *Far Eastern Economic Review*, December 31, 1976, pp. 11–12. See also: *Keesing's Contemporary Archives*, 1977, pp. 28277–9.
30. *Far Eastern Economic Review*, February 2, 1979, p. 17.

31. J. Guiloineau, 1980, pp. 29–30.
32. *Pravda* quoted in: T. Hopf, 1997, p. 52.
33. S. Lodha, 1988, p. 249.
34. G. Evans and K. Rowley, 1990, p. 46.
35. *The New York Times*, December 3, 1976, p. 8. However, the Soviets would be denied access to the bay until spring 1979, after the failure of normalization talks with Washington and the signing of the Soviet-Vietnamese treaty (J.W. Garver in: J.C. Hsiung, 1983, p. 92; V. Funnell in: M. Light, 1993, p. 96).
36. S.J. Morris, 1999, pp. 180–1.
37. This term was originally used in French: "nordmalisation du Sud." Author's interview with Judith Stowe, October 26, 2002.
38. *Far Eastern Economic Review*, December 24, 1976, pp. 23–4.
39. See also: E. Palmujoki, 1997, p. 79.
40. *The New York Times*, February 12, 1977, p. 1.
41. *Vietnam Southeast Asia International*, October-November-December 1978, p. 2.
42. *The New York Times*, December 17, 1976, p. 14; January 16, 1977, p. 9. Also: G. Evans and K. Rowley, 1990, p. 38.
43. A.J. Dommen, 2001, p. 961.
44. W. Duiker, 1989, pp. 64 and 87.
45. P. Langlet and Quach Thanh Tâm, 2001, p. 40.
46. W. Duiker, 1989, p. 201.
47. S. Hurst, 1996, pp. 37–9; Nguyen Van Canh and E. Cooper, 1983, p. 233.
48. G. Smith, 1986, p. 242.
49. *Indian Express* quoted in: *Time*, November 22, 1976, p. 14.
50. The Carter Museum, Carter Presidential Center, Atlanta.
51. *Newsweek*, November 15, 1976, pp. 7–10.
52. *Keesing's Contemporary Archives*, 1976, p. 27974–5.
53. The Carter Museum, Carter Presidential Center, Atlanta.
54. *Newsweek*, March 14, 1977, pp. 30–32 and March 28, 1977, pp. 32–34. Also: R.A. Melanson, 1996, pp. 91–92.
55. G. Ford, 1979, p. 378. See also: R.E. Osgood, "Vietnam: Implications and Impact" in: P. Braestrup, 1984, pp. 135–144.
56. *Keesing's Contemporary Archives*, 1977, p. 28245; *Newsweek*, January 31, 1977, pp. 8–13.
57. Original emphasis. Jimmy Carter campaign poster. (The Carter Museum, Carter Presidential Center, Atlanta).
58. See: J.S. Olson and R. Roberts, 1991, p. 276. The pardon did not apply to deserters (J. Dumbrell, 1997, p. 11).
59. *Keesing's Contemporary Archives*, 1977, p. 28270.
60. *Time*, May 31, 1976, p. 25. See also: L. Bitzer and T. Rueter, 1980, p. 134.
61. *Time*, January 17, 1977, pp. 24–25.
62. Report from *Nhan Dan*, January 22, 1977, File: 3-4/1977, SRV-U.S. Foreign Relations, Douglas Pike Collection, UBIA. Also in: *Far Eastern Economic Review*, February 11, 1977, p. 31.
63. *The New York Times*, November 4, 1976, p. 26.
64. Report on Vietnamese perceptions of the U.S., undated, unattributed, File: 1976, SRV-U.S. Foreign Relations, Douglas Pike Collection, UBIA.
65. Report from *Quan Doi Nhan Dan*, January 26, 1977, File: 3-4/1977, SRV-U.S. Foreign Relations, Douglas Pike Collection, UBIA.
66. *Asia Yearbook*, 1977, p. 329.
67. W.I. Cohen, 1993, p. 207; T. Smith, 1994, pp. 6–7.
68. O.A. Westad, 1997, p. 23.
69. D.H. Allin, 1995, p. 68; J. Dumbrell, 1995, p. 2; R.D. Schulzinger, 1998, p. 317.
70. Carter's speech at the 31st Annual Meeting of the Southern Legislative Conference in Charleston, South Carolina, July 21, 1977, Public Papers of the Presidents of the United States: Jimmy Carter 1977, Vol. II (Washington D.C., United States Government Printing Office, 1977), p. 1310.
71. *Time*, February 7, 1977, p. 22.
72. On this issue see Steven Hurst's excellent drawing of definitions and his discussion of the regionalist versus globalist approach to foreign policy in the Carter era, including Carter's own shift in early 1978 (S. Hurst, 1996, pp. 10–2).
73. Handwritten memorandum from Jimmy Carter to C. Vance, January 28, 1977, Name File—C. Vance, CPL.
74. J. Carter, 1982, p. 195. See also: J.A. Rosati, 1987, pp. 52–7, 59–60.
75. *Department of State Bulletin*, June 13, 1977, p. 625. On the concept of "global community" see Carter's speech at the U.N. General Assembly: *Department of State Bulletin*, October 24, 1977, pp. 547–552.
76. Memorandum from Brzezinski to Carter, January 12, 1978, File: Weekly Reports, 42–52 (1/78–3/78), Z. Brzezinski Donated Historical Material, Box 41, CPL.
77. S. Hurst, 1996, p. 28.
78. *Congressional Quarterly Weekly Report*, April 2, 1977, p. 613; *Far Eastern Economic Review*, March 18, 1977, p. 28. See also: J. Carter, 1982, p. 195.
79. Japanese press report from Hanoi quoting Vietnamese Committee for Cultural Relations official Vu H Quooc Juy, March 5, 1977, File: 3-4/1977, SRV-U.S. Foreign Relations, Douglas Pike Collection, UBIA.
80. *Keesing's Contemporary Archives*, 1977, pp. 28246–7. On the appointment of the administration members see: J. Carter, 1982, pp. 41–55.
81. W.M. Bagby, 1999, p. 298.
82. *U.S. News & World Report*, January 3, 1977, p. 29.
83. *Far Eastern Economic Review*, July 2, 1976, p. 39. A. Yoder, 1986, p. 160.
84. J. Dumbrell, 1997, p. 15.
85. *U.S. News & World Report*, May 22, 1978, p. 42.
86. *Far Eastern Economic Review*, May 19, 1978, p. 23.
87. *Foreign Affairs*, September-October 1999, p. 94. Also: J. Carter, 1982, p. 52.
88. S. Hurst, 1996, p. 15; J.T. Patterson, 1996, pp. 744–6. Ford's description of Kissinger: G. Ford, 1979, p. 129.
89. J. Carter, 1982, pp. 51–3.
90. H. Jordan, 1982, p. 46. In fact, while Brzezinski is thanked in the first line of the acknowledgements of Carter's memoirs, Vance's name does not even appear on the page (J. Carter, 1982, p. 597).
91. C. Vance, 1983, p. 35.
92. *Newsweek*, June 12, 1978, p. 12. On this issue: M Berger, "Vance and Brzezinski: Peaceful coexistence or guerrilla war?" *The New York Times Magazine*, February 13, 1977, pp. 19–25. On the Kissinger-Rogers feud see Cahn's descriptions of their "petty bureaucratic games" in: A.H. Cahn, 1998, pp. 21–2.
93. H. Kissinger, 1979, p. 265. Kissinger congratulated Carter for appointing so "exceptionally well-qualified" a man to replace him in the State Department (*Newsweek*, December 13, 1976, p. 38).
94. J. Dumbrell, 1997, p. 15.
95. *Newsweek*, December 13, 1976, p. 38. On average, however, the American press described him as rather dull (*U.S. News & World Report*, December 13, 1976, p. 15). See a short biography of Vance in: *Keesing's Contemporary Archives*, 1977, pp. 28245–6.
96. J. Carter, 1982, p. 50. See also: J. Fromm, "What Vance Appointment Means for Foreign Policy," *U.S. News & World Report*, December 13, 1976, p. 27.
97. See: J. Fromm, "What Vance Appointment Means for Foreign Policy," *U.S. News & World Report*, December 13, 1976, p. 27.
98. *U.S. News & World Report*, January 3, 1977, p. 29.

Peter Bourne, one of Carter's biographers and intimate friends, adds that this counterbalancing effect had not been intentional (author's interview with Peter Bourne, February 18, 2003).
99. J. Dumbrell, 1995, pp. 110–1.
100. Memorandum from Brzezinski to Vance, August 16, 1977, Country Files, Box CO-17, CPL.
101. C. Vance, 1983, p. 122.
102. R.D. Schulzinger, 1998, p. 316.
103. Document entitled "Hanoi Notes Vance Role at Paris Talks," December 6, 1976, File: 12/1976, SRV-U.S. Foreign Relations, Douglas Pike Collection, UBIA.
104. Committee on Foreign Relations, "Vance Nomination," Hearing before the Committee on Foreign Relations on Nomination of Hon. Cyrus R. Vance to be Secretary of State, U.S. Senate, 95th Congress, 1st session, January 11, 1977 (Washington D.C.: U.S. Government Printing Office, 1977), p. 15.
105. L. Césari, 1995, p. 254.
106. *The New York Times Magazine*, February 13, 1977, p. 25.
107. C. Vance, 1983, p. 450.
108. Committee on Veterans' Affairs, "Americans Missing in Southeast Asia," U.S. House of Representatives, 100th Congress (Washington D.C.: U.S. Government Printing Office, 1988), pvii. Also in: *Far Eastern Economic Review*, March 11, 1977, p. 11; *The New York Times*, December 16, 1976, p. 1. Also: Nguyen Van Canh and E. Cooper, 1983, p. 232.
109. *The New York Times*, December 17, 1976, p. 4.
110. *The New York Times*, December 18, 1976, p. 2.
111. Author's telephone interview with John McAuliff, March 15, 2002.
112. *Far Eastern Economic Review*, July 21, 1978, p. 19 and February 11, 1977, p. 31; *The New York Times*, December 28, 1976, p. 5.
113. Committee on Foreign Relations, "Nomination of Hon. Andrew Young as U.S. Representative to the U.N.," Hearing before the Committee on Foreign Relations, U.S. Senate, 95th Congress, 1st session, January 25, 1977 (Washington D.C.: U.S. Government Printing Office, 1977), p. 25.
114. Author's correspondence with Z. Brzezinski, February 5, 2002.
115. See: Z. Brzezinski, 1983, p. 439; J. Carter, 1982, p. 491. For an analysis of Young's revisionist views, see: J. Erhman, 1995, pp. 103–4, 110–1 and 125–6.
116. *The New York Times*, January 27, 1977, p. 10.
117. *The New York Times*, January 28, 1977, p. 3.
118. *The New York Times*, January 7, 1977, p. 1.
119. *The New York Times*, January 12, 1977, p. 1.
120. *Far Eastern Economic Review*, February 18, 1977, p. 13.
121. *Far Eastern Economic Review*, November 12, 1976, p. 11.
122. *Time*, October 18, 1976, p. 10.
123. Z. Brzezinski, 1983, p. 200. Also: J. Mann, 1999, pp. 78–9.
124. Author's telephone interview with John McAuliff, March 15, 2002.
125. *Far Eastern Economic Review*, December 17, 1976, p. 5.
126. *Newsweek*, April 25, 1977, p. 23. One should note the gap between Carter's initial stated goal and the actual outcome. While he intended to normalize with Hanoi in 1977 and with China in 1980 or later, American-Vietnamese normalization efforts failed in 1977, Sino-American normalization occurred two years ahead of the initial schedule and contributed to the bogging down of subsequent bilateral talks with Hanoi. The following chapters will shed light on the domestic, bilateral and geopolitical reasons for these events.
127. D. Caldwell in: O.A. Westad, 1997, p. 105.
128. O.A. Westad, 1997, pp. 9–10.
129. E. Becker, 1998, p. 382; S. Hurst, 1996, p. 31.
130. R.L. Garthoff, 1994, p. 637.
131. *The New York Times*, January 30, 1977, p. 5. See also: *Vietnam Southeast Asia International*, February-March-April 1977, p. 1.
132. *Congressional Quarterly Weekly Report*, April 2, 1977, p. 614.
133. Transcript of Phan Hien's meeting with the American Friends Service Committee, January 1977, File: 3–4/1977, SRV-U.S. Foreign Relations, Douglas Pike Collection, UBIA.
134. Letter from W.T. Collett to the President with the Committee's report, March 9, 1977, WHCF, Box ND-14, CPL.
135. *Time*, February 28, 1977, p. 20.
136. *The New York Times*, February 26, 1977, p. 4; Committee on Veterans' Affairs, "Americans Missing in Southeast Asia," U.S. House of Representatives, 100th Congress (Washington D.C.: U.S. Government Printing Office, 1988), p. 235.
137. Report from Hanoi *Vietnam News Agency*, February 4, 1977, File: 1–2/1977, SRV-US Foreign Relations, Douglas Pike Collection, UBIA. Also: Nguyen Van Canh and E. Cooper, 1983, p. 231.
138. Analysis of Vo Van Sung's statements, by D. Pike (?), February 9, 1977, File: 1–2/1977, SRV-US Foreign Relations, Douglas Pike Collection, UBIA.
139. R.S. Ross, 1988, pp. 127–8.
140. Report from the Hanoi *Vietnam News Agency*, February 3, 1977, File: 1–2/1977, SRV-US Foreign Relations, Douglas Pike Collection, UBIA.
141. Report from the Hanoi *Vietnam News Agency*, February 9, 1977, File: 1–2/1977, SRV-US Foreign Relations, Douglas Pike Collection, UBIA.
142. Report from *Agence France Press* in Hong-Kong, February 7, 1977, File: 1–2/1977, SRV-US Foreign Relations, Douglas Pike Collection, UBIA.
143. Letter from the National League of Families to the President, January 31, 1977, WHCF, Box ND-14, CPL. Also: Newspaper cutting of the *Congressional Record* of January 26, 1977, WHCF, Box ND-14, CPL. See also: *Keesing's Contemporary Archives*, 1977, p. 28280.
144. Moscow *TASS* report, February 19, 1977, File: 1–2/1977, SRV-US Foreign Relations, Douglas Pike Collection, UBIA.
145. *The New York Times*, February 22, 1977, p. 15.
146. *Time*, February 28, 1977, p. 20.
147. *The New York Times*, February 13, 1977, p. 2.
148. *Time*, February 28, 1977, p. 20; *The New York Times*, February 18, 1977, p. 4.
149. *Department of State Bulletin*, March 21, 1977, p. 258.
150. *Time*, February 28, 1977, p. 20; *The New York Times*, February 26, 1977, p. 1.
151. E. Becker, 1998, 378. Carter had initially offered Woodcock the post of Secretary of Health, Education and Welfare which Woodcock had turned down. Woodcock's appointment as head of Carter's first mission to Vietnam would therefore come as a reward, later completed by his appointment as head of the American mission in Peking (author's interview with Peter Bourne, February 18, 2003).
152. Memorandum for the record of the meeting between the President and the National League of Families, February 11, 1977, WHCF, Box ND-14, CPL.
153. *Department of State Bulletin*, March 21, 1977, p. 258.
154. Committee on Veterans' Affairs, "Americans Missing in Southeast Asia," U.S. House of Representatives, 100th Congress (Washington D.C.: U.S. Government Printing Office, 1988), pvii.
155. Committee on International Relations, "Americans Missing in Action in Southeast Asia," Hearings before the Subcommittee on Asian and Pacific Affairs, House of Representatives, 95th Congress, 1st session, July

27, 1977 (Washington D.C.: U.S. Government Printing Office, 1978), p. 48.
156. Committee on Veterans' Affairs, "Americans Missing in Southeast Asia," U.S. House of Representatives, 100th Congress (Washington D.C.: U.S. Government Printing Office, 1988), pvii. The report was dated December 13, 1976 and made public three days later on December 16.
157. Letter from the White House to C. Bates, March 16, 1977, Country Files, Box CO-66, CPL.
158. N. Chanda, 1988, p. 140–1.
159. C. Vance, 1983, p. 450.
160. *Department of State Bulletin*, March 21, 1977, p. 258.
161. *Department of State Bulletin*, April 18, 1977, p. 365.
162. *Time*, March 28, 1977, pp. 35–6.
163. Letter from C. Bates to Brzezinski, February 18, 1977, WHCF, Box ND-14, CPL.
164. *Far Eastern Economic Review*, July 30, 1976, p. 5; *Far Eastern Economic Review*, December 31, 1976, p. 5; Committee on Veterans' Affairs, "Americans Missing in Southeast Asia," U.S. House of Representatives, 100th Congress (Washington D.C.: U.S. Government Printing Office, 1988), pvii.
165. *The New York Times*, November 14, 1976, p. 1.
166. Memorandum from H. Brown to the President, May 26, 1977, WHCF, Box ND-14, CPL.
167. H.B. Franklin, 1992, pp. 13–4.
168. Author's telephone interview with John McAuliff, March 15, 2002.
169. Committee on Foreign Relations, "Vance Nomination," Hearing before the Committee on Foreign Relations on Nomination of Hon. Cyrus R. Vance to be Secretary of State, U.S. Senate, 95th Congress, 1st session, January 11, 1977 (Washington D.C.: U.S. Government Printing Office, 1977), pp. 16–7.
170. Committee on Foreign Relations, "Nomination of Hon. Andrew Young as U.S. Representative to the U.N.," Hearing before the Committee on Foreign Relations, U.S. Senate, 95th Congress, 1st session, January 25, 1977, (Washington D.C.: U.S. Government Printing Office, 1977), p. 25.
171. Letter from C. Bates (head of the League of Families) to Brzezinski, February 18, 1977, WHCF, Box ND-14, CPL. Also: *Time*, February 28, 1977, p. 20.
172. Letter from Montgomery to the President, February 2, 1977, WHCF, Box ND-14, CPL.
173. Letter from Frank Moore to Senator Roth, March 28, 1977, WHCF, Box ND-14, CPL.
174. Author's emphasis (*Department of State Bulletin*, March 21, 1977, p. 258).
175. S. Hurst, 1996, pp. 40–1.
176. Analysis of the Hanoi announcement of March 3, 1977, by D. Pike (?), undated, File: Woodcock trip: 3/1977, SRV-U.S. Foreign Relations, Douglas Pike Collection, UBIA.
177. Hanoi *Vietnam News Agency*, March 3, 1977, File: 3–4/1977, SRV-U.S. Foreign Relations, Douglas Pike Collection, UBIA. Also: *Far Eastern Economic Review*, April 1, 1977, p. 22.
178. M.A. Niehaus, "U.S. Policy toward the Socialist Republic of Vietnam," The Library of Congress Congressional Research Service, July 18, 1977, File: 7–9/1977, SRV-U.S. Foreign Relations, Douglas Pike Collection, UBIA. *Keesing's Contemporary Archives*, 1977, pp. 28280 and 28356.
179. The Woodcock Commission Report.
180. *Time*, May 9, 1977, pp. 22–3.
181. *The New York Times*, March 6, 1977, p. 1.
182. Committee on International Relations, "Americans Missing in Action in Southeast Asia," Hearings before the House Subcommittee on Asian and Pacific Affairs, 95th Congress, 1st session, March 31, 1977 (Washington D.C.: U.S. Government Printing Office, 1976), p. 12.

183. These senior and highly respected figures of the U.S. media were: John Hart from NBC, Willis Brown from CBS, Strobe Talbott from *Time Magazine*, Peter Arnett from AP and Richard Growald from UPI. The Vietnamese objected to receiving more than five journalists (The Woodcock Commission Report).
184. *The New York Times*, March 13, 1977, p. 8.
185. Coverage of the Woodcock mission by journalist P. Arnett, March 15, 1977, File: Woodcock trip: 3/1977, SRV-U.S. Foreign Relations, Douglas Pike Collection, UBIA. Also: *Time*, March 28, 1977, p. 35.
186. Coverage of the Woodcock mission by journalist P. Arnett, March 16, 1977, File: Woodcock trip: 3/1977, SRV-U.S. Foreign Relations, Douglas Pike Collection, UBIA.
187. Unreferenced press report on the Woodcock Mission, March 16, 1977, Country Files, Box CO-66, CPL.
188. E. Becker, 1998, p. 379.
189. M.W. Bell's interview with Leonard Woodcock, August 21, 1994 in: M.W. Bell, 1995, pp. 9–10.
190. Coverage of the Woodcock mission by journalist P. Arnett, undated, File: Woodcock trip: 3/1977, SRV-U.S. Foreign Relations, Douglas Pike Collection, UBIA.
191. *The New York Times*, March 18, 1977, p. 4.
192. Coverage of the Woodcock mission by journalist P. Arnett, March 17, 1977, File: Woodcock trip: 3/1977, SRV-U.S. Foreign Relations, Douglas Pike Collection, UBIA. Also: *Time*, March 28, 1977, p. 35.
193. *Newsweek*, March 28, 1977, p. 29.
194. The Woodcock Commission Report. Also: Draft letter from Carter to Pham Van Dong acknowledging the receipt of the Vietnamese letter of March 12, 1977, undated, WHCF, Box ND-14, CPL.
195. Coverage of the Woodcock mission by journalist P. Arnett, March 17, 1977, File: Woodcock trip: 3/1977, SRV-U.S. Foreign Relations, Douglas Pike Collection, UBIA.
196. Report from *Agence France Presse* in Hong-Kong, March 17, 1977, File: Woodcock trip: 3/1977, SRV-U.S. Foreign Relations, Douglas Pike Collection, UBIA.
197. *Department of State Bulletin*, September 12, 1977, p. 359.
198. The Woodcock Commission Report.
199. *Time*, March 28, 1977, p. 36.
200. Coverage of the Woodcock mission by journalist P. Arnett, March 17, 1977, File: Woodcock trip: 3/1977, SRV-U.S. Foreign Relations, Douglas Pike Collection, UBIA.
201. M.B. Young, 1991, p. 303.
202. M.W. Bell's interview with Leonard Woodcock, August 21, 1994 in: M.W. Bell, 1995, p. 10.
203. Coverage of the Woodcock mission by journalist P. Arnett, undated, File: Woodcock trip: 3/1977, SRV-U.S. Foreign Relations, Douglas Pike Collection, UBIA. Also: N. Chanda, 1988, p. 140.
204. Author's emphasis (E. Becker, 1998, p. 380).
205. Coverage of the Woodcock mission by journalist P. Arnett, undated, File: Woodcock trip: 3/1977, SRV-U.S. Foreign Relations, Douglas Pike Collection, UBIA.
206. Phan Hien interviewed in *Vietnam Info*. Author's translation from French: "les trois questions abordées ont entre elles une corrélation" (*Vietnam Info*, May 1977, p. 33).
207. The Woodcock Commission Report.
208. Phan Hien interviewed in *Vietnam Info*. Author's translation from French: "En ce qui concerne la question de normalisation des relations entre le Vietnam et les Etats-Unis, nous avons dit clairement à la partie américaine que nous sommes prêts à regarder vers l'avenir mais que nous ne saurions trancher totalement l'avenir du passé: car celui-ci a laissé un certain nombre de problèmes qui, sans une solution satisfaisante, créeront des obstacles sur la voie de normalisation des relations entre les deux pays" (*Vietnam Info*, May 1977, p. 32).

209. *Far Eastern Economic Review*, May 6, 1977, p. 19.
210. S. Hurst, 1996, pp. 33–4.
211. R.S. McNamara, J.G. Blight and R.K. Brigham, 1999, pp. 376–7.
212. Committee on International Relations, "Americans Missing in Action in Southeast Asia," Hearings before the House Subcommittee on Asian and Pacific Affairs, 95th Congress, 1st session, March 31, 1977 (Washington D.C.: U.S. Government Printing Office, 1976), p. 3. Also: *Department of State Bulletin*, April 18, 1977, pp. 366–374. Also: *Far Eastern Economic Review*, June 3, 1977, p. 13.
213. Author's emphasis (See: Luu Van Loi, 2002, p. 30).
214. Letter from Oksenberg to Republican Representative H.W. Moore, April 18, 1977, WHCF, Box ND-14, CPL.
215. Phan Hien interviewed in *Vietnam Info*. Author's translation from French: "Au cours des entretiens, la délégation américaine a dû reconnaître que, si l'Accord de Paris sur le Vietnam n'est plus valable, les Articles 8B et 21 ne le sont pas non plus, cela est incontestable" (*Vietnam Info*, May 1977, p. 33).
216. *Department of State Bulletin*, April 18, 1977, p. 366.
217. Hien's interview with the Hanoi *Vietnam News Agency*, March 26, 1977, File: Woodcock trip: 3/1977, SRV-U.S. Foreign Relations, Douglas Pike Collection, UBIA.
218. Committee on International Relations, "Americans Missing in Action in Southeast Asia," Hearings before the House Subcommittee on Asian and Pacific Affairs, 95th Congress, 1st session, March 31, 1977 (Washington D.C.: U.S. Government Printing Office, 1976), p. 17. Also: *Vietnam Info*, May 1977, p. 33.
219. *Far Eastern Economic Review*, April 1, 1977, p. 22.
220. Coverage of the Woodcock mission by journalist P. Arnett, undated, File: Woodcock trip: 3/1977, SRV-U.S. Foreign Relations, Douglas Pike Collection, UBIA.
221. *Time*, March 28, 1977, p. 35; *The New York Times*, March 19, 1977, p. 1 and March 23, 1977, p. 18.
222. E. Becker, 1998, p. 381.
223. Committee on International Relations, "Americans Missing in Action in Southeast Asia," Hearings before the House Subcommittee on Asian and Pacific Affairs, 95th Congress, March 31, 1977 (Washington D.C.: U.S. Government Printing Office, 1976), p. 9.
224. M.W. Bell, 1995, p. 11.
225. N. Chanda, 1988, p. 141.
226. Peking *New China News Agency*, March 19, 1977, File: Woodcock trip: 3/1977, SRV-U.S. Foreign Relations, Douglas Pike Collection, UBIA. Also: *Far Eastern Economic Review*, April 1, 1977, p. 22.
227. *Time*, March 28, 1977, p. 35.
228. *The New York Times*, March 23, 1977, p. 18.
229. Department of State telegram to the U.S. Embassy in Paris, undated, File: Woodcock trip: 3/1977, SRV-U.S. Foreign Relations, Douglas Pike Collection, UBIA.
230. *Department of State Bulletin*, September 12, 1977, p. 359.
231. *Department of State Bulletin*, April 18, 1977, pp. 363–4.
232. *Congressional Quarterly Weekly Report*, April 2, 1977, p. 613. See also: *Department of State Bulletin*, October 1979, p. 39.
233. *Department of State Bulletin*, April 18, 1977, p. 363; *The New York Times*, March 24, 1977, p. 1.
234. *Congressional Quarterly Weekly Report*, April 2, 1977, p. 613; *The New York Times*, March 24, 1977, pp. 1 and 12.
235. *Department of State Bulletin*, April 18, 1977, p. 374.
236. Outgoing Department of State telegram from the President to U.S. Embassy in Paris, March 23, 1977, File: Woodcock trip: 3/1977, SRV-U.S. Foreign Relations, Douglas Pike Collection, UBIA. Comment repeated during a press conference, see: *Department of State Bulletin*, April 18, 1977, pp. 363–4.
237. Memorandum from M. Hornblow to M. Armacost, April 11, 1977, NSA Staff Material Far East, Box 2, CPL.
238. E. Becker, 1998, p. 383.
239. *Department of State Bulletin*, April 18, 1977, p. 369. Also: M.W. Bell, 1995, p. 10.
240. Intelligence report, unattributed, undated, File: 3–4/1977, SRV-U.S. Foreign Relations, Douglas Pike Collection, UBIA.
241. E. Becker, 1998, p. 383; S. Hurst, 1996, p. 35.
242. *Congressional Quarterly Weekly Report*, April 2, 1977, p. 614. Also: *Keesing's Contemporary Archives*, 1978, p. 28912.
243. *The New York Times*, May 4, 1977, p. 13.
244. N. Cawthorne, 1991, pp. 124–6. On the militancy of the National League of Families, see: B.H. Franklin, 1992, p. 131.
245. Woodcock's joint press conference with President Carter (*Department of State Bulletin*, April 18, 1977, p. 364–5).
246. The Woodcock Commission Report. Also: Committee on Veterans' Affairs, "Americans Missing in Southeast Asia," U.S. House of Representatives, 100th Congress (Washington D.C.: U.S. Government Printing Office, 1988), p. 238.
247. Committee on International Relations, "Americans Missing in Action in Southeast Asia," Hearings before the House Subcommittee on Asian and Pacific Affairs, 95th Congress, 1st session, March 31, 1977 (Washington D.C.: U.S. Government Printing Office, 1976), p. 25–9.
248. J. Le Boutillier, 1989, p. 52. Representative John Le Boutillier's book, published in 1989, is dedicated "[t]o the hundreds of American Prisoners of War, still held against their will, who will be freed only when there is a new relationship between Washington and Hanoi." In this book, prefaced by Nixon, he therefore calls for rapid normalization as a means of obtaining information from the Vietnamese on the fate of potential American POWs still held in Indochina.
249. *Congressional Quarterly Weekly Report*, April 2, 1977, p. 613.
250. News release, August 16 1977, WHCF, Box ND-14, CPL. Also: *The New York Times*, August 17, 1977, p. 11.
251. *Far Eastern Economic Review*, March 18, 1977, p. 28.
252. Committee on Veterans' Affairs, "Americans Missing in Southeast Asia," U.S. House of Representatives, 100th Congress (Washington D.C.: U.S. Government Printing Office, 1988), p. 165.
253. Memorandum from Oksenberg to Brzezinski, March 16, 1977, Country Files Box CO-66, CPL.
254. *The New York Times*, September 3, 1977, p. 2.
255. *The New York Times*, September 9, 1977, p. 15.
256. *The New York Times*, Septemlber 24, 1977, p. 8.
257. The Woodcock Commission Report.
258. Committee on Veterans' Affairs, "Americans Missing in Southeast Asia," U.S. House of Representatives, 100th Congress (Washington D.C.: U.S. Government Printing Office, 1988), p. 238.
259. Committee on International Relations, "Americans Missing in Action in Southeast Asia," Hearings before the House Subcommittee on Asian and Pacific Affairs, 95th Congress, 1st session, July 27, 1977 (Washington D.C.: U.S. Government Printing Office, 1976), pp. 38–9.
260. *Time*, March 28, 1977, p. 36.
261. Committee on International Relations, "Americans Missing in Action in Southeast Asia," Hearings before the House Subcommittee on Asian and Pacific Affairs, 95th Congress, 1st session, July 27, 1977 (Washington D.C.: U.S. Government Printing Office, 1976), p. 49.

262. J. Mann, 1999, p. 78.
263. Letter from Jimmy Carter to Montgomery, March 25, 1977, Name File—Montgomery, CPL.
264. Letter from Carter to Woodcock, March 25, 1977, Country Files, Box CO-66, CPL.
265. Mike Mansfield, also a member of the Woodcock delegation, would be named Ambassador to Japan (*Far Eastern Economic Review*, May 6, 1977, p. 5).

III. Talks Turn Cold

1. *The New York Times*, April 15, 1977, p. 3.
2. E. Becker, 1998, p. 382.
3. *Far Eastern Economic Review*, January 6, 1978, p. 16.
4. *Time*, May 9, 1977, p. 22.
5. *Congressional Quarterly Weekly Report*, April 2, 1977, p. 613.
6. Phan Hien's interview in French in *Vietnam Info*. Author's translation from French: "Les perspectives des prochaines négociations dépendent de ce que les Etats-Unis renoncent ou non à leur ancienne politique érronée vis-à-vis du peuple vietnamien ... Si les Etats-Unis continuent d'empêcher l'entrée du Vietnam à l'O.N.U. ou tentent d'associer ce fait avec d'autres problèmes pour marchander, ils commettront une grosse erreur et cela ne leur sera que préjudiciable" (*Vietnam Info*, May 1977, p. 33). See also: N. Chanda, 1988, p. 141.
7. *Department of State Bulletin*, September 12, 1977, p. 359.
8. F. Snepp, 1978, p. 324.
9. M.W. Bell, 1995, p. 7.
10. H. Kissinger, 1999, p. 532.
11. Report from the *Paris Domestic Service*, April 29, 1977, File: 3-4/1977, SRV-U.S. Foreign Relations, Douglas Pike Collection, UBIA.
12. M.A. Niehaus, "U.S. Policy toward the Socialist Republic of Vietnam," The Library of Congress Congressional Research Service, July 18, 1977, File: 7-9/1977, SRV-U.S. Foreign Relations, Douglas Pike Collection, UBIA. Also: *Keesing's Contemporary Archives*, p. 28912; *The New York Times*, May 1, 1977, p. 21.
13. A. Gilks, 1992, p. 165.
14. Report entitled: "EAST ASIA: Where Do We Stand? Where Are We Going?" in a memorandum from M. Armacost to Brzezinski, April 7, 1977, NSA Staff Material Far East, Box 2, CPL.
15. *Time*, May 9, 1977, p. 23.
16. Letter from Oksenberg to T.E. Kaiser, June 8, 1977, WHCF, Box ND-14, CPL.
17. M.A. Niehaus, "U.S. Policy toward the Socialist Republic of Vietnam," The Library of Congress Congressional Research Service, July 18, 1977, File: 7-9/1977, SRV-U.S. Foreign Relations, Douglas Pike Collection, UBIA.
18. Report from Hanoi *Vietnam News Agency*, April 22, 1977, File: 3-4/1977, SRV-U.S. Foreign Relations, Douglas Pike Collection, UBIA.
19. N. Chanda, 1988, p. 151.
20. Transcript of Dong's comments, *Paris Domestic Service*, April 29, 1977, File: 3-4/1977, SRV-U.S. Foreign Relations, Douglas Pike Collection, UBIA.
21. Report from the Hanoi *Vietnam News Agency*, April 30, 1977, File: 3-4/1977, SRV-U.S. Foreign Relations, Douglas Pike Collection, UBIA.
22. *The New York Times*, May 4, 1977, p. 1; *Far Eastern Economic Review*, June 3, 1977, p. 13.
23. Report from Tokyo *Asahi Shimbun*, April 15, 1977, File: 3-4/1977, SRV-U.S. Foreign Relations, Douglas Pike Collection, UBIA.
24. *Department of State Bulletin*, September 5, 1977, pp. 323-4.
25. *Time*, April 16, 1976, p. 17. Also quoted by French journalist Jacques Decornoy in: *Le Monde*, July 18, 1975. On Democratic Kampuchea, see also: K.M. Quinn, "Cambodia 1976: Internal Consolidation and External Expansion," *Asian Survey*, January 1977, pp. 43-54. For 1977 see: K.D. Jackson, "Cambodia in 1977: Gone to Pot," *Asian Survey*, January 1978, pp. 76-90; *Keesing's Contemporary Archives*, 1978, pp. 29269-76. For 1978, see: K.D. Jackson, "Cambodia 1978: War, Pillage, and Purge in Democratic Kampuchea," *Asian Survey*, January 1979, pp. 72-84; S.W. Simon, "Barbarism in a Small State Under Siege," *Current History*, December 1978, pp. 197-201, 227.
26. Jean Lacouture quoted in: *The Nation*, April 2, 1977, p. 388. Also in: D.P. Chandler, 1999, p. vii.
27. T. Engelbert and C.E. Goscha, 1995, pp. v-viii.
28. Khieu Samphan, 2004, pp. 91-94.
29. For a complete history of Vietnamese-Cambodian relations with regard to the dispute over border lines, see: G. Evans and K. Rowley, 1990, pp. 81-107. Also: *Asia Yearbook*, 1978, p. 155. For a view of the Cambodian position on the border dispute see: Khieu Samphan, 2004, pp. 84-91.
30. Author's interview with Judith Stowe: October 26, 2002.
31. S.J. Morris, 1999, pp. 98 and 112.
32. N. Chanda, 1988, p. 91.
33. R.S. Ross, 1988, p. 122.
34. *Asia Yearbook*, 1980, p. 340; *Far Eastern Economic Review*, May 13, 1977, p. 5.
35. Author's interview with Judith Stowe, October 26, 2002.
36. *Department of State Bulletin*, September 12, 1977, p. 359. This corresponds with Holbrooke's negotiating instructions in: Memorandum from C. Vance to the President on the attitude the U.S. should adopt during the Paris meetings, April 27, 1977, NSA Brzezinski Files, Box 85, CPL. Also: Memorandum from R. Holbrooke to Vance, April 25, 1977, NSA Brzezinski Files, Box 85, CPL.
37. Memorandum from M. Armacost to Brzezinski on the attitude the U.S. should adopt during the Paris meetings, April 12, 1977, NSA Staff Material Far East, Box 2, CPL.
38. M. B. Young, 1991, p. 303.
39. S. Hurst's interview with Holbrooke in: S. Hurst, 1996, pp. 35 and 44.
40. *Far Eastern Economic Review*, May 13, 1977, pp. 12-3. Also: *Congressional Quarterly Weekly Report*, May 7, 1977, p. 884.
41. *Newsweek*, May 16, 1977, p. 29.
42. *Department of State Bulletin*, October 1979, p. 34; *Keesing's Contemporary Archives*, 1978, p. 28912.
43. R. Oakley's statement of February 15, 1979, File: 1-3/1978, SRV-U.S. Foreign Relations, Douglas Pike Collection, UBIA.
44. *Department of State Bulletin*, October 1979, p. 39.
45. Joint Communiqué of May 4, 1977 in *Far Eastern Economic Review*, May 13, 1977, p. 5. Also: *Newsweek*, May 23, 1977, pp. 24-25.
46. *Vietnam Info*, November 1977, pp. 24-5. Also: Joint Communiqué of May 4, 1977 in *Far Eastern Economic Review*, May 13, 1977, p. 5.
47. *The New York Times*, May 4, 1977, p. 13.
48. Letter from Oksenberg to T.E. Kaiser, June 8, 1977, WHCF, Box ND-14, CPL.
49. Draft letter from the NSC to J.A. Peacock, undated, WHCF, Box FO-32, CPL.
50. *Department of State Bulletin*, September 12, 1977, p. 360.
51. Report from the Hanoi *Vietnam News Agency*, May 6, 1977, File: 5-6/1977, SRV-U.S. Foreign Relations, Douglas Pike Collection, UBIA.
52. Memorandum from R. Holbrooke to Vance, April 25, 1977, NSA Brzezinski Files, Box 85, CPL.

53. Reports from Hanoi *Vietnam News Agency*, May 4, 1977 and May 5, 1977, File: 5-6/1977, SRV-U.S. Foreign Relations, Douglas Pike Collection, UBIA. Also: *Vietnam Info*, November 1977, p. 24. Also: *Newsweek*, May 16, 1977, p. 29.
54. *Far Eastern Economic Review*, June 24, 1977, p. 32.
55. *The New York Times*, May 5, 1977, p. 1.
56. R.S. Ross, 1988, p. 128.
57. S. Lodha, 1997, p. 251.
58. *Congressional Quarterly Weekly Report*, May 7, 1977, p 884. Also: N. Chanda, 1988, p. 153.
59. Ashbrook Amendment to the Foreign Relations Authorization Bill (HR 6689) adopted by 266–131 (Document of the "Coalition for a New Foreign and Military Policy," undated (1977), File: 1-2/1977, SRV-US Foreign Relations, Douglas Pike Collection, UBIA). Also: *Far Eastern Economic Review*, June 3, 1977, p. 12.
60. M.A. Niehaus, "U.S. Policy toward the Socialist Republic of Vietnam," The Library of Congress Congressional Research Service, July 18, 1977, File: 7-9/1977, SRV-U.S. Foreign Relations, Douglas Pike Collection, UBIA. Also: *The New York Times*, May 6, 1977, p. 1.
61. *Congressional Quarterly Weekly Report*, May 7, 1977, p. 884.
62. *Ibid.*, p. 884; *Keesing's Contemporary Archives*, 1978, p. 28912.
63. Transcript of Kissinger's press conference, PR202/13, May 4, 1977, File: 5-6/1977, SRV-U.S. Foreign relations, Douglas Pike Collection, UBIA.
64. The text of the secret Nixon letter to North Vietnam is reproduced in Appendix 1.
65. *Far Eastern Economic Review*, June 3, 1977, p. 12.
66. E. Becker, 1998, p. 384.
67. *Keesing's Contemporary Archives*, 1978, p. 28912.
68. Report entitled "Chronology of U.S. Aid to Vietnam: 1965–1977," File: 7-9/1977, SRV-U.S. Foreign Relations, Douglas Pike Collection, UBIA.
69. SEPTEL report of Holbrooke's testimony of March 10, 1977, File: Woodcock trip: 3/1977, SRV-U.S. Foreign Relations, Douglas Pike Collection, UBIA. Also: *The New York Times*, May 10, 1977, p. 19.
70. Request from Representative Wolff to Former President Nixon Concerning the February 1, 1973 Letter, February 22, 1977, File: 1-2/1977, SRV-US Foreign Relations, Douglas Pike Collection, UBIA. Also: Report entitled "Chronology of U.S. Aid to Vietnam: 1965–1977," File: 7-9/1977, SRV-U.S. Foreign Relations, Douglas Pike Collection, UBIA.
71. *The New York Times*, May 10, 1977, p. 19.
72. *The New York Times*, May 11, 1977, p. 16.
73. *Far Eastern Economic Review*, June 3, 1977, p. 12; May 20, 1977, p. 5.
74. M.A. Niehaus, "U.S. Policy toward the Socialist Republic of Vietnam," The Library of Congress Congressional Research Service, July 18, 1977, File: 7-9/1977, SRV-U.S. Foreign Relations, Douglas Pike Collection, UBIA.
75. Ashbrook Amendment to the International Development and Food Assistance Authorization (HR556) adopted by 288–119 (Document of the "Coalition for a New Foreign and Military Policy"), undated (1977), File: 1-2/1977, SRV-US Foreign Relations, Douglas Pike Collection, UBIA). Also: *Keesing's Contemporary Archives*, 1978, p. 28912; *The New York Times*, May 13, 1977, p. 5.
76. *Congressional Quarterly Weekly Report*, May 21, 1977, p. 1001.
77. S. Hurst, 1996, p. 42.
78. Memorandum from Oksenberg to Brzezinski, May 25, 1977, Country Files, Box CO-66, CPL.
79. R.L. Garthoff, 1994, p. 637.
80. Douglas Pike's personal notes on Nixon's statements on aid, undated, File: February 1973, SRV-U.S. Foreign Relations, Douglas Pike Collection, UBIA. The full text of this letter appears in: Committee on International Relations, "Hearing before the Subcommittee on Asian and Pacific Affairs," House of Representatives, 95th Congress, 1st session, July 19, 1977 (Washington D.C.: U.S. Government Printing Office, 1979), Appendix 4, pp. 27–28. Also: *The New York Times*, May 20, 1977, p. 17.
81. Report from the *Hanoi International Service*, May 17, 1977, File: 5-6/1977, SRV-U.S. Foreign Relations, Douglas Pike Collection, UBIA.
82. Cable from the U.S. Embassy in Paris to the White House, May 19, 1977, NSA Brzezinski Files, Box 85, CPL.
83. Committee on International Relations, "Hearing before the Subcommittee on Asian and Pacific Affairs," House of Representatives, 95th Congress, 1st session, July 19, 1977 (Washington D.C.: U.S. Government Printing Office, 1979), Appendix 4, pp. 27–8. Also: *The New York Times*, May 20, 1977, pp. 1 and 17; *Keesing's Contemporary Archives*, 1978, p. 28912.
84. E. Becker, 1998, p. 384; S.E. Ambrose and D.G. Brinkley, 1997, p. 244. See also: T.E. Yarbrough, "Carter and the Congress" in: M.G. Abernathy, D.M. Hill and P. Williams, 1984, pp. 165–191.
85. Report from the *Hanoi Domestic Service*, May 21, 1977, File: 5-6/1977, SRV-U.S. Foreign Relations, Douglas Pike Collection, UBIA. Also: Report from Hanoi *Vietnam News Agency*, May 21/22, 1977 in: Committee on International Relations, "Hearing before the Subcommittee on Asian and Pacific Affairs," House of Representatives, 95th Congress, 1st session, July 19, 1977 (Washington D.C.: U.S. Government Printing Office, 1979), Appendix 8, p. 33. Also: *The New York Times*, May 22, 1977, p. 11; *Vietnam Info*, November 1977, p. 25.
86. Analyses of the Vietnamese release of the Nixon letter, May 22, 1977 and May 25, 1977, File: 5-6/1977, SRV-U.S. Foreign Relations, Douglas Pike Collection, UBIA.
87. Reports from the *Hanoi Domestic Service*, May 23, 1977 and from the *Hanoi International Service*, May 24, 1977, File: 5-6/1977, SRV-U.S. Foreign Relations, Douglas Pike Collection, UBIA.
88. Analysis of Vietnamese articles on the Nixon letter, May 25, 1977, File: 5-6/1977, SRV-U.S. Foreign Relations, Douglas Pike Collection, UBIA.
89. Letter from Wolff to Nixon, May 26, 1977 in: Committee on International Relations, "Hearings before the Subcommittee on Asian and Pacific Affairs," House of Representatives, 95th Congress, 1st session, July 19, 1977 (Washington D.C.: U.S. Government Printing Office, 1979), Appendix 6, p. 31.
90. *Vietnam Info*, November 1977, p. 25.
91. Kissinger's testimony in: Committee on International Relations, "Hearings before the Subcommittee on Asian and Pacific Affairs," House of Representatives, 95th Congress, 1st session, July 19, 1977 (Washington D.C.: U.S. Government Printing Office, 1979), Appendix 6, pp. 3–22.
92. Letter from Nixon's secretary J.V. Brennan to L.L. Wolff, June 3, 1977, File: 5-6/1977, SRV-U.S. Foreign Relations, Douglas Pike Collection, UBIA.
93. Letter from Wolff to Nixon, June 7, 1977, Committee on International Relations, "Hearings before the Subcommittee on Asian and Pacific Affairs," House of Representatives, 95th Congress, 1st session, July 19, 1977 (Washington D.C.: U.S. Government Printing Office, 1979), Appendix 9, p. 40.
94. Selected U.S. press articles in: Committee on International Relations, "Hearings before the Subcommittee on Asian and Pacific Affairs," House of Representatives, 95th Congress, 1st session, July 19, 1977 (Washington D.C.: U.S. Government Printing Office, 1979), Appendix 10, p. 41.
95. Transcript of an unidentified article, June 17, 1977,

File: 5–6/1977, SRV-U.S. Foreign Relations, Douglas Pike Collection, UBIA.
96. *Keesing's Contemporary Archives*, p. 28912; *The New York Times*, July 20, 1977, p. 5. For the full report see: Committee on International Relations, "Hearing before the Subcommittee on Asian and Pacific Affairs," House of Representatives, 95th Congress, 1st session, July 19, 1977 (Washington D.C.: U.S. Government Printing Office, 1979), pp. 3–22.
97. *Asia Yearbook*, 1978, p. 346; *Far Eastern Economic Review*, July 29, 1977, p. 5.
98. *The New York Times*, July 20, 1977, p. 5.
99. *Far Eastern Economic Review*, June 10, 1977, p. 20.
100. H. Kissinger, 1982, p. 37; H. Kissinger, 2003, p. 446.
101. Letter from Nixon to Thieu, October 16, 1972, NSA Brzezinski Files, Box 85, CPL.
102. Letter from Nixon to Thieu, November 14, 1972, NSA Brzezinski Files, Box 85, CPL.
103. *Keesing's Contemporary Archives*, 1975, p. 27201.
104. F. Snepp, 1978, pp. 18–30.
105. P. Asselin, 2002, pxiii; A.J. Dommen, 2001, pp. 815–6.
106. H. Kissinger, 1979, p. 1377; H. Kissinger, 2003, pp. 356 and 425.
107. H. Kissinger, 1979, pp. 1395–1446; H. Kissinger, 2003, pp. 372–408.
108. F. Snepp, 1978, pp. 18–30. See the works of Larry Berman, Arthur Dommen, Frank Snepp, Pierre Asselin, and Gareth Porter.
109. H. Kissinger, 2003, p. 455: This statement does not appear in Kissinger's previous memoirs.
110. Richard Nixon, "United States Foreign Policy for the 1970's: Shaping a Durable Peace, A Report to Congress," *Department of State Bulletin*, June 4, 1973, p. 744.
111. G. Porter in: *The Nation*, April 30, 1977, p. 519.
112. Kissinger's interview with CBS News, February 1, 1973, File: February 1973, SRV-U.S. Foreign Relations, Douglas Pike Collection, UBIA.
113. Author's translation from French: "M. Kissinger a deux atouts qui sont, comme toujours, la carotte de l'aide économique et le bâton de la riposte militaire." Report on the Kissinger-Le Duc Tho Paris meetings by Henri Froment-Meurice, December 18, 1973, Dossier: Vietnam-Conflit, 1960–1975, Collection Asie-Océanie, Box 279, FMoFA.
114. *The Times* (London), December 21, 1973, p. 6c.
115. F. Snepp, 1978, pp. 63–4; G. Porter, 1975, p. 237; A.J. Dommen, 2001, p. 839.
116. H. Kissinger, 1982, p. 36; H. Kissinger, 1979, p. 1383; H. Kissinger, 2003, p. 363. See also: G. Porter, "Kissinger's Double-Cross for 'Peace': The Broken Promise to Hanoi," *The Nation*, April 30, 1977, pp. 519–21.
117. *The Sunday Times*, March 10, 1974, p. 9; *Asian Survey*, January 1975, p. 63.
118. H. Kissinger, 1982, p. 39; H. Kissinger, 2003, p. 447.
119. Nixon's Press Conference no. 29, January 31, 1973, File: January 1973, SRV-U.S. Foreign Relations, Douglas Pike Collection, UBIA. Also: *Department of State Bulletin*, February 19, 1973, p. 194.
120. H. Kissinger, 1982, p. 39; H. Kissinger, 2003, p. 448; P. Asselin, 2002, p. 181.
121. H. Kissinger, 1982, pp. 38–9; H. Kissinger, 2003, p. 447–8; G., Porter in: *The Nation*, April 30, 1977, p. 519.
122. *Congressional Digest*, June-July 1973, p. 163.
123. H. Kissinger, 1982, p. 38; H. Kissinger, 2003, p. 447.
124. M. Niehaus, "A Chronology of Selected Statements by Administration Officials on the Subject of Postwar Reconstruction Aid to Indochina: April 7, 1965–April 4, 1973," April 4, 1973, File: March 1973, SRV-U.S. Foreign Relations, Douglas Pike Collection, UBIA). Also: P. Asselin, 2002, p. 28.
125. While, in his memoirs, Kissinger mentions Tho's sudden insistence on aid, he refrains from stating that any secret pledge was given (H. Kissinger, 1979, p. 1472; H. Kissinger, 2003, pp. 429–30). P. Asselin, 2002, pp. 162–3, 174–5.
126. Press report from Japanese journalist S. Usami, February 15, 1973, File: February 1973, SRV-U.S. Foreign Relations, Douglas Pike Collection, UBIA.
127. H. Kissinger, 1982, p. 39; H. Kissinger, 2003, p. 447.
128. A.R. Isaacs, 1983, p. 133. See Appendix 1.
129. H. Kissinger, 1982, p. 40. This statement was deleted from Kissinger's new book *Ending the Vietnam War* (2003).
130. Kissinger's meeting with members of the Senate, January 26, 1973, File: January 1973, SRV-U.S. Foreign Relations, Douglas Pike Collection, UBIA.
131. Kissinger's meeting with the House of Representatives, January 26, 1973, File: January 1973, SRV-U.S. Foreign Relations, Douglas Pike Collection, UBIA.
132. A.J. Dommen, 2001, p. 839.
133. *Congressional Digest*, June-July 1973, p. 168.
134. Text of the Joint Communiqué between Hanoi and Washington as reported by the USIS Taipei News Backgrounder, File: February 1973, SRV-U.S. Foreign Relations, Douglas Pike Collection, UBIA.
135. F. Snepp, 1977, pp. 63–4.
136. Committee on International Relations, "Americans Missing in Action in Southeast Asia," Hearings before the House Subcommittee on Asian and Pacific Affairs, 95th Congress, March 31, 1977 (Washington D.C.: U.S. Government Printing Office, 1976).
137. G. Porter, 1975, p. 237.
138. J.T. Patterson, 1996, p. 766.
139. G.C. Herring, 1986, p. 257.
140. H. Kissinger, 1982, p. 324; H. Kissinger, 2003, pp. 463–469.
141. M. Niehaus, "A Chronology of Selected Statements by Administration Officials on the Subject of Postwar Reconstruction Aid to Indochina: April 7, 1965–April 4, 1973," April 4, 1973, p. 2, File: March 1973, SRV-U.S. Foreign Relations, Douglas Pike Collection, UBIA.
142. Immediate press release from the *Vietnam News Agency*, May 1, 1973, File: May-June 1973, SRV-U.S. Foreign Relations, Douglas Pike Collection, UBIA.
143. Letter from Nixon to Wolff, May 14, 1977, Committee on International Relations, "Hearing before the Subcommittee on Asian and Pacific Affairs," House of Representatives, 95th Congress, 1st session, July 19, 1977 (Washington D.C.: U.S. Government Printing Office, 1979), Appendix 4, pp. 27–8. Also: *The New York Times*, May 20, 1977, p. 17
144. S.E. Ambrose and D.G. Brinkley, 1997, p. 246.
145. G. Porter in: *The Nation*, April 30, 1977, p. 521.
146. *The New York Times*, July 20, 1977, p. 5.
147. Press report from Washington, December 4, 1974, unattributed, File: 833.Ceasefire (incl. January 1973), SRV-U.S. Foreign Relations, Douglas Pike Collection, UBIA. See also: *Keesing's Contemporary Archives*, 1975, p. 27276; *Asia Yearbook*, 1975, p. 242.
148. Committee on International Relations, "Americans Missing in Action in Southeast Asia," Hearings before the House Select Committee on Missing Persons in Southeast Asia, 94th Congress, 2nd session, Part 5, June 17, 25; July 21 and September 21, 1976 (Washington D.C.: U.S. Government Printing Office, 1976), p. 12.
149. *Congressional Quarterly Weekly Report*, February 24, 1973, p. 405.
150. Library of Congress Congressional Research Service Report on "U.S. Reconstruction aid to North Viet Nam: A Brief Listing of Major Pro-Con Arguments," by M. Niehaus, February 22, 1973, File: February 1973, SRV-U.S. Foreign Relations, Douglas Pike Collection, UBIA.

151. *Department of State Bulletin*, April 2, 1973, p. 377.
152. Nixon's Press Conference no. 29, January 31, 1973, File: January 1973, SRV-U.S. Foreign Relations, Douglas Pike Collection, UBIA. Also: *Department of State Bulletin*, February 19, 1973, p. 194.
153. Committee on Veterans' Affairs, "Americans Missing in Southeast Asia," U.S. House of Representatives, 100th Congress (Washington D.C.: U.S. Government Printing Office, 1988), p. 114.
154. USIA Press Report, February 1, 1973, File: February 1973, SRV-U.S. Foreign Relations, Douglas Pike Collection, UBIA.
155. *Department of State Bulletin*, March 26, 1973, p. 349.
156. *Congressional Quarterly Weekly Report*, February 24, 1973, p. 404.
157. Library of Congress Congressional Research Service Report on "U.S. Reconstruction aid to North Viet Nam: A Brief Listing of Major Pro-Con Arguments" by M. Niehaus, February 22, 1973, File: February 1973, SRV-U.S. Foreign Relations, Douglas Pike Collection, UBIA.
158. This was passed by an 88–3 vote. (M. Niehaus, "A Chronology of Selected Statements by Administration Officials on the Subject of Postwar Reconstruction Aid to Indochina: April 7, 1965–April 4, 1973," April 4, 1973, File: March 1973, SRV-U.S. Foreign Relations, Douglas Pike Collection, UBIA). See also: *Congressional Digest*, June-July 1973, p. 169; *The Times*, April 6, 1973, p. 9.
159. Douglas Pike's personal notes on congressional reactions to aid, File: March 1973, SRV-U.S. Foreign Relations, Douglas Pike Collection, UBIA.
160. M. Niehaus, "A Chronology of Selected Statements by Administration Officials on the Subject of Postwar Reconstruction Aid to Indochina: April 7, 1965–April 4, 1973," April 4, 1973, p. 2, File: March 1973, SRV-U.S. Foreign Relations, Douglas Pike Collection, UBIA.
161. Nixon's report to Congress on May 3, 1973: Richard Nixon, "United States Foreign Policy for the 1970's: Shaping a Durable Peace, A Report to Congress," *Department of State Bulletin*, June 4, 1973, pp. 747–8.
162. *Congressional Digest*, June-July 1973, p. 163.
163. *Department of State Bulletin*, March 19, 1973, p. 318.
164. Report on the Vietnamese *White Book* from *Agence France Press*, Paris, January 16, 1974, File: 833. Ceasefire (incl. January 1973), SRV-U.S. Foreign Relations, Douglas Pike Collection, UBIA. Also: *White Book*, File: Vietnam-Conflit, 1960–1975, Collection Asie-Océanie, Box 280, FMoFA. See also: *Asian Survey*, January 1975, p. 63.
165. Author's translation from French: "[B]ien qu'il ait pu procurer certaines satisfactions à ses signataires, le caractère limité de cet accord est apparu dès le moment de sa signature à la plupart des yeux avertis de la question de l'Indochine ... Aux communistes vietnamiens, cet accord offrait un répit pour se préparer à un assaut contre Saigon sans avoir à faire face directement à la puissance militaire américaine. Aux Américains, il a permis le retrait des GIs, tout en leur donnant la possibilité de maintenir le régime du Sud-Vietnam dans la perspective de la "doctrine Nixon" et de la "vietnamisation de la guerre." (Khieu Samphan, 2004, p. 125).
166. S.E. Ambrose and D.G. Brinkley, 1997, p. 236.
167. J.T. Patterson, 1996, p. 750.
168. Arthur Dommen adds that the theory, first set to last eight then two years, initiated by Kissinger (A.J. Dommen, 2001, p. 754). On the theory of "decent interval," see also: A.R. Isaacs, 1983, p. 333.
169. Author's translation from French: "Les Américains ne cherchent, dans le fond, qu'à obtenir des Nord-Vietnamiens un papier pour le congrès et l'opinion publique." Telegram from the French embassy in Washington to the French Ministry of Foreign Affairs, Mai 25, 1973, File: Vietnam-Conflit, 1960–1975, Collection Asie-Océanie, Box 135, FMoFA.
170. J.T. Patterson, 1996, p. 766.
171. *The Christian Century*, April 7, 1976, p. 323.
172. M. Crowley, 1998, p. 256.
173. P. Asselin, 2002, pp. 155–6; A.J. Dommen, 2001, p. 821. Kissinger confirms that the congressional threat to stop aid was indeed a concern to the Nixon administration (H. Kissinger, 1979, p. 1386 and 1461; H. Kissinger, 2003, pp. 366 and 419).
174. W.I. Cohen, 1993, p. 191.
175. Speech by Kissinger, October 27, 1972, File: Vietnam-Conflit, 1960–1975, Collection Asie-Océanie, Box 233, FMoFA.
176. See: N. Chomsky, "Endgame: The Tactics of Peace in Vietnam," *Ramparts*, no. 11, April 1973. Also: G. Kolko, "Nixon's Vietnam Strategy," *Commonwealth*, March 23, 1973.
177. H. Kissinger, 1979, pp. 1382 and 1469; H. Kissinger, 2003, p. 361 and 427. Also: G. Porter, 1975, p. 180; P. Asselin, 2002, p. 167.
178. *Keesing's Contemporary Archives*, 1975, pp. 27200–1; *U.S. News and World Report*, May 5, 1975, p. 20.
179. H. Kissinger, 1982, p. 303.
180. Original emphasis (L. Berman, 2001, p. 9).
181. W.J. Duiker, 1996, p. 325.
182. A.R. Isaacs, 1983, pp. 68–9; G. Porter, 1975, p. 278. Gareth Porter captured the profound distrust between all four signatory parties in describing how, after having proofread the American's transcript of the text of the agreement before its signing, the Vietnamese had noticed that the separate page due to hold the signatures had not been numbered and suspected the Americans of having planned this trick in order to later deny the validity of the document (G. Porter, 1975, pp. 172–3). Kissinger further adds that the South Vietnamese PRG and the DRV signed together on one page while the Saigon regime and the U.S. signed on another. "In a final paranoiac gesture," Kissinger adds, "the North Vietnamese insisted that, on completion, each text be bound by string and the string sealed—to prevent the American delegation from deviously slipping in new pages overnight" (H. Kissinger, 1979, p. 1465 and 1472; H. Kissinger, 2003, pp. 423 and 429).
183. H. Kissinger, 2003, p. 455.
184. H. Kissinger, 1982, p. 37; H. Kissinger, 2003, p. 446.
185. Author's interview with Judith Stowe, October 26, 2002.
186. H. Kissinger, 1982, p. 39; H. Kissinger, 2003, p. 448.
187. Author's interview with Bui Tin, October 30, 2002.
188. Author's interview with Judith Stowe, October 26, 2002, and author's interview with Bui Tin, October 30, 2002.
189. H. Kissinger, 1982, p. 40. This paragraph was deleted from Kissinger's latest revised version of his dealings with Hanoi in his last memoirs: *Ending the Vietnam War* (2003).
190. *The New York Times*, May 24, 1977, p. 5.
191. *Vietnam Info*, April 1978, p. 23; N. Chanda, 1988, p. 154.
192. *The New York Times*, June 4, 1977, p. 1.
193. Report from the Hanoi *Vietnam News Agency*, June 4, 1977, File: 5–6/1977, SRV-U.S. Foreign Relations, Douglas Pike Collection, UBIA.
194. *The New York Times*, June 7, 1977, p. 9. The remains were eventually returned in October.
195. *Department of State Bulletin*, September 12, 1977, pp. 360–1; Unattributed cable on the U.S. press release following the second round of talks, June 3 (?), 1977, File:

10–12/1977, SRV-U.S. Foreign Relations, Douglas Pike Collection, UBIA.
196. Memorandum from Brzezinski to the President on the release of MIA names in June 1977, undated, WHCF, Box ND-14, CPL.
197. N. Chanda, 1988, p. 154.
198. S. Hurst, 1996, p. 42.
199. *Keesing's Contemporary Archives*, 1978, p. 28912.
200. *Vietnam Info*, November 1977, p. 25.
201. *Department of State Bulletin*, September 12, 1977, p. 360.
202. Cable from the U.S. Embassy in Paris to the Department of State on the press conference held by Phan Hien and Holbrooke on June 3, 1977, File: 10–12/1977, SRV-U.S. Foreign Relations, Douglas Pike Collection, UBIA. Also: *Keesing's Contemporary Archives*, 1978, p. 28912.
203. Vance's address before the Asia Society on June 29, 1977. Compiled by E.P. Adam, 1979 (a), p. 396.
204. *The New York Times*, June 30, 1977, p. 9. Also: E.P. Adam, 1979 (a), p. 396.
205. *The New York Times*, June 21, 1977, p. 32.
206. *Congressional Quarterly Weekly Report*, June 18, 1977, p. 1205; *Far Eastern Economic Review*, June 17, 1977, pp. 106–111; Dole Amendment to the International Financial Institutions Authorization Bill (HR 5262) adopted by 58–32 (Document of the "Coalition for a New Foreign and Military Policy," undated (1977), File: 1–2/1977, SRV-US Foreign Relations, Douglas Pike Collection, UBIA). Also: *Congressional Quarterly Weekly Report*, June 11, 1977, p. 1175.
207. *Congressional Quarterly Weekly Report*, August 13, 1977, p. 1740.
208. *Far Eastern Economic Review*, June 17, 1977, p. 111.
209. Glenn Amendment to International Development Assistance Authorization Bill (HR 6714) (Document of the "Coalition for a New Foreign and Military Policy," undated (1977), File: 1–2/1977, SRV-US Foreign Relations, Douglas Pike Collection, UBIA). Also: *The New York Times*, June 16, 1977, p. 14.
210. Report from Paris *Agence France Presse*, June 21, 1977, File: 5–6/1977, SRV-U.S. Foreign Relations, Douglas Pike Collection, UBIA.
211. Young Amendment to the Foreign Assistance Appropriations Bill (HR 7797) adopted by 295–115 (Document of the "Coalition for a New Foreign and Military Policy," undated (1977), File: 1–2/1977, SRV-US Foreign Relations, Douglas Pike Collection, UBIA). The six other countries were Uganda, Cambodia, Laos, Cuba, Angola and Mozambique. The African countries and Cuba were later added to the list of the three Southeast Asian nations. In a tightening of its policies, the House also refused to cut military aid to South Korea and voted to keep a close eye on Indonesia, Thailand and the Philippines for future sanctions. The amendment was approved by a 295–115 vote (*Far Eastern Economic Review*, July 15, 1977, p. 23). The *Congressional Weekly* reports that: "liberals went along because of human rights violations by these countries. Conservative support was assured because all but one of the governments was Marxist and because of general displeasure with foreign aid" (*Congressional Quarterly Weekly Report*, June 17, 1978, p. 1533).
212. Wolff Amendment to the Foreign Assistance Appropriations Bill (HR 7797) adopted by 359–33 (Document of the "Coalition for a New Foreign and Military Policy," undated (1977), File: 1–2/1977, SRV-US Foreign Relations, Douglas Pike Collection, UBIA). Also: *Congressional Quarterly Weekly Report*, June 25, 1977, p. 1282.
213. *Keesing's Contemporary Archives*, 1978, p. 28912.
214. Report from the *Hanoi International Service*, June 24, 1977, File: 5–6/1977, SRV-U.S. Foreign relations, Douglas Pike Collection, UBIA.
215. *Asia Yearbook*, 1978, p. 345; *Far Eastern Economic Review*, July 8, 1977, p. 5; *The New York Times*, June 26, 1977, p. 1.
216. *Congressional Quarterly Weekly Report*, June 25, 1977, p. 1281.
217. *Far Eastern Economic Review*, October 28, 1977, p. 44.
218. The Senate voted 47–52 to delete the House proposal (*Congressional Quarterly Weekly Report*, August 13, 1977, pp. 1731 and 1738; *Congressional Quarterly Weekly Report*, October 22, 1977, p. 2255).
219. *Congressional Quarterly Weekly Report*, August 6, 1977, pp. 1662–3.
220. *Far Eastern Economic Review*, October 28, 1977, p. 44; *Congressional Quarterly Weekly Report*, October 22, 1977, p. 2255.
221. *The New York Times*, October 19, 1977, p. 10.
222. *Far Eastern Economic Review*, November 4, 1977, pp. 45–6. Later, two other representatives added Mozambique, Angola and Cuba to the existing list of countries. See also: *The New York Times*, October 20, 1977, p. 5.
223. *Keesing's Contemporary Archives*, 1978, p. 28912.
224. *Keesing's Contemporary Archives*, 1978, p. 28769.
225. *Far Eastern Economic Review*, July 29, 1977, p. 14. Also: *The New York Times*, July 20, 1977, p. 5.
226. *The New York Times*, July 20, 1977, p. 5. For a summary of the evolution of Lao-Vietnamese relations and of Lao policies see: M. Brown and J.J. Zasloff, "Dependency in Laos," *Current History*, December 1978, pp. 202–207. See also: *Keesing's Contemporary Archives*, 1978, pp. 28765–70.
227. *Far Eastern Economic Review*, July 29, 1977, p. 14.
228. *Keesing's Contemporary Archives*, 1978, p. 28769; *The New York Times*, July 20, 1977, p. 5.
229. *Far Eastern Economic Review*, July 29, 1977, p. 14.
230. E.K. Lawson, 1984, p. 281.
231. Luu Van Loi, 2002, p. 24.
232. *Keesing's Contemporary Archives*, 1978, p. 28769.
233. N. Regaud, 1992, p. 17.
234. *The Nation*, September 9, 1978, p. 209.
235. On China's endorsement of Cambodian accusations against Vietnam, see: A. Gilks, 1992, p. 164.
236. *The New York Times*, July 20, 1977, p. 5. Also: F. Joyaux, 1988, p. 370; S. Lodha, 1997, p. 232.
237. W.J. Duiker, 1989, pp. 200–1.
238. A. Gilks, 1992, p. 179.
239. *The Nation*, June 9, 1979, p. 700.
240. *Asia Yearbook*, 1978, p. 347.
241. N. Chanda, 1988, pp. 188–9; G. Evans and K. Rowley, 1990, p. 55.
242. Author's interview with Judith Stowe, October 26, 2002. The same pattern of a dual opening to Moscow and Washington was repeated in 1978, when it was clear that Hanoi had decided to tilt openly towards Moscow.
243. J.A. Rosati, 1987, p. 118.
244. Committee on International Relations, "Americans Missing in Action in Southeast Asia," Hearings before the House Subcommittee on Asian and Pacific Affairs, 95th Congress, July 27, 1977 (Washington D.C.: U.S. Government Printing Office, 1976), p. 38.
245. *Department of State Bulletin*, August 29, 1977, p. 283.
246. *U.N. Chronicle*, October 1977, p. 6.
247. *The New York Times*, July 21, 1977, p. 3.
248. *The New York Times*, July 29, 1977, p. 22.
249. *The New York Times*, July 28, 1977, p. 9.
250. *Vietnam Info*, November 1977, p. 24; *The New York Times*, September 3, 1977, p. 2.
251. *Far Eastern Economic Review*, September 30, 1977, p. 5; *Vietnam Info*, November 1977, p. 24.
252. *Newsweek*, October 3, 1977, p. 14.
253. Reports from Hanoi *Vietnam News Agency*, September 26 and 27, 1977, File: 7–9/1977, SRV-U.S. Foreign Relations, Douglas Pike Collection, UBIA.

254. *The New York Times*, September 26, 1977, p. 2.
255. E. Palmujoki, 1997, p. 121.
256. *Keesing's Contemporary Archives*, 1977, p. 28638.
257. *The New York Times*, September 22, 1977, p. 3.
258. See the summary of Trinh's speech in: *U.N. Chronicle*, October 1977, p. 7. Also: E. Palmujoki, 1997, p. 122.
259. *Keesing's Contemporary Archives*, 1978, p. 28912.
260. Report from *Agence France Presse* in Hong-Kong, September 30, 1977, File: 7–9/1977, SRV-U.S. Foreign Relations, Douglas Pike Collection, UBIA.
261. *The New York Times*, October 1, 1977, p. 3.
262. Report from *Agence France Presse* in Hong-Kong, September 30, 1977, File: 7–9/1977, SRV-U.S. Foreign Relations, Douglas Pike Collection, UBIA.
263. *Department of State Bulletin*, August 29, 1977, p. 283. Also: R.D. Schulzinger, 1998, p. 316.
264. M.W. Bell, 1995, pp. 13–4.
265. Handwritten memorandum from Oksenberg to Brzezinski, undated, NSA Brzezinski Files, Box 85, CPL.
266. *Newsweek*, October 3, 1977, p. 14.
267. *U.N. Chronicle*, October 1977, p. 8.
268. M.W. Bell, 1995, p. 14.
269. *The New York Times*, October 7, 1977, p. 9.
270. *Newsweek*, October 3, 1977, p. 14.
271. *U.N. Chronicle*, October 1977, pp. 8–9; *New Times*, July 1977, no. 31, p. 16. *New Times* is a Soviet international propaganda journal, written in English for a larger audience.
272. *U.N. Chronicle*, December 1977, p. 57; *Keesing's Contemporary Archives*, 1978, pp. 28912 and 28843; *The New York Times*, October 7, 1977, p. 9. On the implementation of this resolution see: *U.N. Chronicle*, April 1978, p. 61.
273. D.P. Chandler in: D.P. Chandler and B. Kiernan, 1983, p. 37.
274. *Peking Review*, October 7, 1977, pp. 9–13 and 46.
275. S.J. Morris, 1999, p. 99.
276. *Far Eastern Economic Review*, January 13, 1978, pp. 10 and 13.
277. S.J. Morris, 1999, p. 112; Khieu Samphan, 2004, p. 96.
278. W.J. Duiker, 1986, p. 69.
279. E. Palmujoki, 1997, pp. 93–94.
280. *Far Eastern Economic Review*, October 7, 1977, p. 5; *Keesing's Contemporary Archives*, 1978, pp. 28807–8.
281. *Far Eastern Economic Review*, October 14, 1977, pp. 30–32. See also: *Peking Review*, October 7, 1977, pp. 9–13 and 22–30.
282. *Far Eastern Economic Review*, January 13, 1978, p. 12.
283. *Peking Review*, November 25, 1977, p. 3 and 8. Also: W.J. Duiker, 1986, p. 69.
284. Author's interview with Peter Bourne, February 18, 2003.
285. R.S. Ross, 1988, p. 149.
286. N. Chanda, 1988, p. 215.
287. *Newsweek*, January 16, 1978, p. 22.
288. S.J. Morris, 1999, p. 102.
289. Memorandum from Brzezinski to the President, undated, NSA Brzezinski Files, Box 85, CPL.
290. Report from Hanoi *Vietnam News Agency*, November 25, 1977, File: 10–12/1977, SRV-U.S. Foreign Relations, Douglas Pike Collection, UBIA. Also: *The New York Times*, November 25, 1977, p. 17.
291. Report from Hanoi *Vietnam News Agency*, November 24, 1977, File: 10–12/1977, SRV-U.S. Foreign Relations, Douglas Pike Collection, UBIA.
292. Memorandum from Oksenberg to Brzezinski, November 29, 1977, NSA Brzezinski Files, Box 85, CPL.
293. M. Oksenberg in: *Foreign Affairs*, Fall 1982, pp. 182–3. Also: J. Carter, 1982, pp. 191–3; J. Mann, 1999, pp. 82–3; R.L. Garthoff, 1994, pp. 638 and 664–5.
294. *Newsweek*, August 1, 1977, p. 18.
295. *The Nation*, October 20, 1979, p. 366.
296. *Vietnam Info*, April 1978, p. 23.
297. Report from the Hanoi *Vietnam News Agency*, December 6, 1977, File: 10–12/1977, SRV-U.S. Foreign Relations, Douglas Pike Collection, UBIA.
298. Soviet broadcast in Vietnamese to Vietnam, December 19, 1977, File: 10–12/1977, SRV-U.S. Foreign Relations, Douglas Pike Collection, UBIA.
299. N. Chanda, 1988, p. 156.
300. *Far Eastern Economic Review*, May 27, 1977, p. 5.
301. R.L. Garthoff, 1994, p. 637; C. Vance, 1983, pp. 131–2; J.A. Rosati, 1987, p. 119.
302. Memorandum from Vance to the President, November 29, 1977, NSA Brzezinski Files, Box 85, CPL.
303. N. Chanda, 1988, pp. 156–7.
304. *Ibid.*, p. 157.
305. M.B. Young, 1991, p. 304.
306. E. Becker, 1998, pp. 384–5.
307. Memorandum from Brzezinski to Vance, December 1, 1977, NSA Brzezinski Files, Box 85, CPL.
308. While no documents corroborate this view, one may speculate that Washington, understanding that normalization with Vietnam represented a more complicated task than Carter had initially expected, may already have turned its attention to China after the completion of PRM-24 in June 1977. This could account for the increasingly hardening U.S. stance on Vietnam in the second half of 1977.
309. Report from Hanoi *Vietnam News Agency*, December 21, 1977, File: 10–12/1977, SRV-U.S. Foreign Relations, Douglas Pike Collection, UBIA.
310. Letter from V. Wirt to the President, November 2, 1978, WHCF, Box FO-32, CPL.
311. Report from *Agence France Presse* in Hong-Kong, October 17, 1977, and: Report from *Hanoi International Service*, December 24, 1977, File: 10–12/1977, SRV-U.S. Foreign Relations, Douglas Pike Collection, UBIA. Also: *Keesing's Contemporary Archives*, 1978, pp. 28912–3; *The New York Times*, December 20, 1977, p. 8.
312. *Far Eastern Economic Review*, January 6, 1978, p. 16 and February 17, 1978, p. 12.
313. Report from Hanoi *Vietnam News Agency*, February 2, 1978, File: 1–3/1978, SRV-U.S. Foreign Relations, Douglas Pike Collection, UBIA. Also: *Newsweek*, February 13, 1978, p. 21–2.
314. *Newsweek*, February 13, 1978, p. 21. She and her children indeed obtained exit visas in July 1977.
315. *The New York Times*, February 1, 1978, p. 1.
316. *Far Eastern Economic Review*, February 17, 1978, p. 12.
317. N. Chanda, 1988, p. 268.
318. *Vietnam Southeast Asia International*, April-May-June 1978, p. 4.
319. *Newsweek*, February 13, 1978, p. 21.
320. N. Chanda, 1988, p. 268. Also: E. Becker, 1998, pp. 390–1.
321. *Keesing's Contemporary Archives*, 1978, p. 29311.
322. *The Nation*, February 25, 1978, p. 195.
323. *Far Eastern Economic Review*, February 17, 1978, p. 12.
324. *Vietnam Info*, April 1978, p. 23.
325. Soviet broadcast in English to North America, February 8, 1978, File: 1–3/1978, SRV-U.S. Foreign Relations, Douglas Pike Collection, UBIA.
326. *U.N. Chronicle*, April 1978, p. 92.
327. *New Times*, February 1978, no. 7, p. 9; *The New York Times*, February 4, 1978, p. 1.
328. *U.N. Chronicle*, April 1978, p. 71.
329. Report from *Hanoi Domestic Service*, February 20, 1978, File: 1–3/1977, SRV-U.S. Foreign Relations, Douglas Pike Collection, UBIA.
330. Report from *Hanoi Domestic Service*, February 4, 1978, File: 1–3/1978, SRV-U.S. Foreign Relations, Douglas Pike Collection, UBIA.

331. Moscow *TASS* report dated February 4, 1978, and Soviet broadcast in Vietnamese to Vietnam dated January 30, 1978, File: 1-3/1978, SRV-U.S. Foreign Relations, Douglas Pike Collection, UBIA.
332. Analysis of Vietnamese press reports on the spy affair, February 8, 1978, File: 1-3/1978, SRV-U.S. Foreign Relations, Douglas Pike Collection, UBIA.
333. *Ibid.* Also: *Vietnam Southeast Asia International*, April-May-June 1978, pp. 1–9.
334. Report from *Hanoi Domestic Service*, February 4, 1978, File: 1-3/1978, SRV-U.S. Foreign Relations, Douglas Pike Collection, UBIA. Also: *Keesing's Contemporary Archives*, 1978, p. 28913.
335. Soviet broadcast in Vietnamese to Vietnam, February 6, 1978, File: 1-3/1978, SRV-U.S. Foreign Relations, Douglas Pike Collection, UBIA.
336. *Vietnam Info*, December 1978, p. 6.
337. *The New York Times*, February 6, 1978, p. 4 and *The New York Times*, March 9, 1978, p. 10.
338. M.A. Niehaus, "Vietnam: problems of normalizing U.S.-Vietnamese relations," The Library of Congress Congressional Research Service, reworked copy of March 8, 1977, File: 4-6/1978, SRV-U.S. Foreign Relations, Douglas Pike Collection, UBIA. Also: *The New York Times*, March 15, 1978, p. 7.
339. Memorandum from Oksenberg to Brzezinski, January 30, 1978, NSA Brzezinski Files, Box 85, CPL.
340. R.L. Garthoff, 1994, pp. 636–40. On Vance's trip to China see: *Department of State Bulletin*, September 19, 1977, pp. 365–74; *Keesing's Contemporary Archives*, 1979, p. 29533.
341. See Holbrooke's testimony before the Subcommittee on Asian and Pacific Affairs of the House Committee on Foreign Affairs on June 13, 1979 in: *Department of State Bulletin*, October 1979, p. 34.
342. Author's telephone interview with John McAuliff, March 15, 2002. Also: N. Chanda, 1988, pp. 268–9; M.B. Young, 1991, p. 304.

IV. Cold War Clash

1. S.J. Morris, 1999, p. 102.
2. Pao-Min Chang, 1987, p. 55.
3. S.J. Morris, 1999, p. 17.
4. *Far Eastern Economic Review*, January 13, 1978, p. 10. Also: Luu Van Loi, 2002, p. 63; B. Kiernan, 1996, p. 386.
5. N. Regaud, 1992, p. 20.
6. H. Kamm, 1998, p. 148.
7. *Peking Review*, January 6, 1978, pp. 25–27.
8. *Newsweek*, January 23, 1978, pp. 17–8.
9. *New Times*, January 1978, no. 2, p. 9.
10. Pao-Min Chang, 1987, p. 58.
11. Luu Van Loi, 2002, p. 64. Also: *Peking Review*, January 13, 1978, pp. 23–24; *New Times*, February 1978, no. 7, p. 12.
12. *New Times*, April 1978, no. 16, p. 11.
13. Luu Van Loi, 2002, p. 52.
14. S.J. Morris, 1999, p. 85.
15. H. Kissinger, 2003, pp. 474–5.
16. W.J. Duiker, 1986, p. 67.
17. G. Porter in: D.W.P. Elliott, 1982, p. 78.
18. See: *Keesing's Contemporary Archives*, 1978, p. 29275. Also: W. Burchett, 1981, p. 149.
19. *Far Eastern Economic Review*, June 9, 1978, p. 14.
20. *The Nation*, June 9, 1979, p. 701; *New Times*, December 1978, no. 52, p. 14.
21. *The Nation*, September 9, 1978, p. 212.
22. W. Burchett, 1981, p. 149.
23. *The Nation*, September 9, 1978, p. 211. Also: S. Lodha, 1997, pp. 302–3, 308. S.P. Heder in: D.W.P. Elliott, 1982, p. 49.
24. *Peking Review*, January 27, 1978, pp. 24–5; *New Times*, July 1978, no. 27, p. 11.
25. R.S. Ross, 1988, p. 165.
26. See: *Peking Review*, January 27, 1978, p. 4.
27. *Newsweek*, January 30, 1978, p. 18.
28. *Time*, February 6, 1978, p. 19.
29. *Newsweek*, January 30, 1978, p. 18.
30. In French: "dépopulation momentanée" (Sudestasie information supplement, *Vietnam Info*, May-June 1979, p. 5).
31. *Vi*ệ*tnam*, March 1978, p. 1.
32. *Far Eastern Economic Review*, November 11, 1977, p. 32.
33. *Far Eastern Economic Review*, April 14, 1978, p. 40.
34. *Newsweek*, February 6, 1978, p. 26.
35. *Vietnam Southeast Asia International*, April-May 1979, p. 9.
36. *Far Eastern Economic Review*, March 17, 1978, p. 10.
37. *Far Eastern Economic Review*, July 14, 1978, p. 7; R.S. Ross, 1988, p. 156.
38. See also the Vietnamese bombing of this line during the invasion: *Far Eastern Economic Review*, January 12, 1979, p. 14.
39. S. Heder in: D.W.P. Elliott, 1982, p. 51. Also: Pao-Min Chang, 1987, p. 59.
40. *Newsweek*, July 3, 1978, p. 16.
41. *Asia Yearbook*, 1979, p. 321.
42. *Far Eastern Economic Review*, November 17, 1978, p. 9.
43. Report from U.N.D.R.O, October 5, 1978, WHCF, Box FO-32, CPL. Also: *Far Eastern Economic Review*, October 20, 1978, p 13.
44. *Far Eastern Economic Review*, October 20, 1978, p. 14.
45. M. Niehaus, "Vietnam 1978: The Elusive Peace," *Asian Survey*, January 1979, pp. 85–94.
46. S.J. Morris, 1999, p. 209–10.
47. Department of State Briefing Memorandum for the Secretary, January 8, 1979, NSA Brzezinski Files, Box 86, CPL.
48. N. Chanda, 1988, p. 215.
49. *Far Eastern Economic Review*, January 26, 1979, pp. 11–13. Also: V. Funnell in: M. Light, 1993, p. 89.
50. N. Chanda, 1988, pp. 217 and 340.
51. S.P. Heder in: D.W.P. Elliott, 1982, p. 56; G. Porter in: *Ibid.*, pp. 97–8. Also: W.J. Duiker, 1986, pp. 69 and 73–4.
52. E. Becker, 1998, p. 309. Also: S.J. Morris, 1999, pp. 100–1.
53. S.P. Heder in: D.W.P. Elliott, 1982, pp. 51–2. Also: S.J. Morris, 1999, pp. 102–105; W.J. Duiker, 1989, pp. 161–2.
54. *Far Eastern Economic Review*, April 21, 1978, p. 17; *Newsweek*, January 16, 1978, p. 23. See also: *Keesing's Contemporary Archives*, p. 28805; pp. 29270–1 and p. 29274.
55. *Newsweek*, January 9, 1978, p. 23.
56. *Far Eastern Economic Review*, March 3, 1978, p. 13.
57. S.J. Morris, 1999, p. 209–10; R.S. Ross, 1988, pp. 175 and 190.
58. R.S. Ross, 1988, pp. 175 and 190.
59. Author's interview with Bui Tin, October 30, 2002.
60. *Far Eastern Economic Review*, October 6, 1978, p. 32–34.
61. Author's interview with Bui Tin, October 30, 2002. This theme of brotherhood has been largely depicted by Nayan Chanda in *Brother Enemy* (1986) and G. Evans and K. Rowley in *Red Brotherhood at War* (1990) (see bibliography). Also: Bui Tin, 1999, p. 127.
62. Author's translation from French: "Les Vietnamiens se considéraient comme les leaders légitimes des mouvements communistes dans les trois pays d'Indochine ... Les dirigeants vietnamiens considéraient que les dirigeants communistes khmers avaient été encouragés par les Chi-

nois à violer l'"internationalisme prolétarien" et ainsi troubler l'ordre en Indochine en refusant le rôle dirigeant du parti communiste vietnamien" (Khieu Samphan, 2004, p. 96).
63. Hoang Van Hoan, 1988, p. 356.
64. *Far Eastern Economic Review*, February 23, 1979, p. 33; *Far Eastern Economic Review*, April 14, 1978, p. 12. Also: G. Evans and K. Rowley, 1990, pp. 51–2.
65. *Far Eastern Economic Review*, April 14, 1978, p. 12.
66. *Far Eastern Economic Review*, October 10, 1975, pp. 28–29.
67. E. Palmujoki, 1997, p. 74. A Vietnamese source reported that 90 percent of the 20 million overseas Chinese lived in Southeast Asia, representing 75 percent of Singapore's population, 43 percent of Malaysia's, 11.3 percent of Thailand's, 5.5 percent of Kampuchea's, 3 percent of Vietnam's, 2.7 percent of Indonesia's, and 0.6 percent of Laos.' These populations, living in very introverted communities, hold the larger part of each country's economy and trade. As these communities keep in close contact with their relatives in their homeland, to which they send much of their earnings, much to the discontent of the governments of their host countries (Sudestasie Information supplement, *Vietnam Info*, May–June 1979, p. 11).
68. *Far Eastern Economic Review*, April 14, 1978, p. 12.
69. *Far Eastern Economic Review*, October 17, 1975, pp. 31-2.
70. *Peking Review*, July 7, 1978, p. 29.
71. *Việtnam*, June 1978, p. 1; G. Evans and K. Rowley, 1990, pp. 49–50.
72. *Peking Review*, July 7, 1978, p. 29. See also: Pao-Min Chang, 1982, p. 17.
73. *The New York Times*, August 26, 1976, p. 13.
74. E. Palmujoki, 1997, p. 75.
75. G. Evans and K. Rowley, 1990, p. 50.
76. *Far Eastern Economic Review*, May 5, 1978, p. 10.
77. Pao-Min Chang, 1982, pp. 25–7.
78. *Far Eastern Economic Review*, April 14, 1978, p. 12. Also: N. Chanda, 1988, p. 232.
79. *The New York Times*, May 3, 1978, p. 6; *Vietnam Southeast Asia International*, Appendix to Vol. XIV, January-February-March 1980, p. 2.
80. *The New York Times*, March 26, 1978, p. 8.
81. *Far Eastern Economic Review*, April 14, 1978, p. 12.
82. *Peking Review*, June 23, 1978, p. 25; *Newsweek*, June 12, 1978, p. 23. Also: S.J. Morris, 1999, p. 175.
83. *Asia Yearbook*, 1979, p. 320.
84. *Newsweek*, June 5, 1978, p. 25.
85. G. Evans and K. Rowley, 1990, p. 52.
86. *The New York Times*, April 18, 1978, p. 29.
87. *The New York Times*, May 10, 1978, p. 8.
88. *Vietnam*, June 1978, p. 1.
89. Min Chen, 1992, p. 141. Also: S. Lodha, 1997, p. 264.
90. *Việtnam Southeast Asia International*, April–May 1979, p. 9.
91. *Far Eastern Economic Review*, June 16, 1978, p. 11.
92. Author's translation from French: "En particulier après la mort de Mao Tsé Toung en septembre 1976, l'attitude chinoise envers le P.C.K. ne semblais plus guidée par des considérations idéologiques, mais relevait plutôt d'une stricte realpolitik qui trouvait le radicalisme de ces derniers plutôt embarrassant et désavantageux sur le plan international" (Khieu Samphan, 2004, p. 89).
93. Pao-Min Chang, 1987, p. 59; S. Lodha, 1997, p. 308.
94. *Peking Review*, June 30, 1978, p. 28. Also: Luu Van Loi, 2002, p. 66; G. Porter, in: D.W.P. Elliott, 1982, p. 104.
95. *The New York Times*, 22 June 1975, p. 15.
96. *The New York Times*, 11 May 1975, p. 11.
97. See: J. Glaubitz, "Anti-Hegemony Formulas in Chinese Foreign Policy," *Asian Survey*, March 1976, pp. 205–215.
98. *Keesing's Contemporary Archives*, 1976, p. 27844; *Keesing's Contemporary Archives*, 1977, p. 28511.
99. H. Kissinger, 1982, 12; H. Kissinger, 2003, p. 434.
100. Bui Tin also mentions the Vietnamese leadership's "determination to create a federation" (Bui Tin, 1999, p. 127). Former BBC journalist Judith Stowe also shares this view (author's interview with Judith Stowe, October 26, 2002).
101. Hoang Van Hoan, 1988, Preface.
102. *The Nation*, June 9, 1979, p. 699.
103. W.J. Duiker, 1989, p. 129; Pao-Min Chang, 1982, p. 21.
104. N. Chanda, 1988, pp. 224 and 340.
105. Pao-Min Chang, 1987, pp. 33–4.
106. Original emphasis. H. Kissinger, 1982, pp. 38–9. Also: H. Kissinger, 2003, pp. 445 and 447.
107. Ton That Thieu, 1989, p. 156.
108. H. Kissinger, 1982, pp. 33, 36–37. Also: H. Kissinger, 2003, p. 446.
109. Author's interview with Judith Stowe, October 26, 2002.
110. S.J. Morris, 1999, p. 93; H. Kissinger, 2003, p. 455.
111. *Time* (U.S. edition), June 12, 1978, p. 45; *Việtnam*, June 1978, pp. 2–3.
112. *Peking Review*, May 26, 1978, pp. 12–7.
113. *Far Eastern Economic Review*, June 9, 1978, p. 10–14; *Việtnam*, August 1978, p. 3; *The Nation*, September 9, 1978, p. 211. See also: Pao-Min Chang, 1987, p. 30.
114. *Time* (U.S. edition), June 12, 1978, p. 44. This term was first used during the American escalation of the war in Vietnam (R.S. Ross, 1988, p. 25).
115. *New Times*, September 1978, no. 36, p. 20; *Time* (U.S. edition), June 12, 1978, p. 45.
116. *Far Eastern Economic Review*, June 9, 1978, p. 12.
117. *Peking Review*, June 9, 1978, p. 17.
118. Shih-Fu Lo, 1980, p. 9.
119. *Việtnam*, June 1978, p. 1; *New Times*, June 1978, no. 23, p. 9; *Peking Review*, June 16, 1978, pp. 17–21.
120. Shih-Fu Lo, 1980, p. 7.
121. Report from *Hanoi Domestic Service*, August 4, 1978, File: 7–8/1978, SRV-U.S. Foreign Relations, Douglas Pike Collection, UBIA.
122. *New Times*, July 1978, no. 28, p. 14.
123. *Peking Review*, June 23, 1978, p. 24.
124. *The New York Times*, June 1, 1978, p. 14; *The New York Times*, June 6, 1978, p. 4.
125. Min Chen, 1992, p. 142. Also: *Việtnam*, August 1978, p. 3; *Far Eastern Economic Review*, July 7, 1978, p. 8.
126. *New Times*, July 1978, no. 28, p. 15; *The New York Times*, May 28, 1978, p. 1.
127. *The New York Times*, June 23, 1978, p. 3.
128. *Việtnam*, August 1978, p. 3.
129. *Peking Review*, 1978, October 6, 1978, p. 33; *Keesing's Contemporary Archives*, 1979, p. 29468. See also: J.K. Kallgren, "China 1978: The New Long March," *Asian Survey*, January 1979, pp. 1–19.
130. *Time* (U.S. edition), June 12, 1978, p. 44; M.B. Young, 1991, p. 306. Also: *Peking Review*, June 2, 1978, p. 15; *Peking Review*, June 9, 1978, p. 16.
131. *The New York Times*, June 18, 1978, p. 8; *Việtnam*, August 1978, p. 3; *Asia Yearbook*, 1979, p. 340; *The New York Times*, June 20, 1978, p. 8.
132. *The New York Times*, June 21, 1978, p. 1.
133. In November 1977, the Vietnamese had initially approved the Chinese plans of late 1976 to open consulates in Saigon and Haiphong—but not in Danang as the Chinese had also requested (Pao-Min Chang, 1987, pp. 23 and 41). Also: *Far Eastern Economic Review*, June 30, 1978, p. 8. See also: R.S. Ross, 1988, p. 185.
134. On this point see: Nguyen Van Canh and E. Cooper, 1983, p. 128–134. Nguyen Van Canh is himself a South Vietnamese refugee.

135. Bui Tin, 1999, p. 160. Trinh would officially be ruled out of the Politburo during the Fifth Party Congress in 1982.
136. Author's interview with Judith Stowe, October 26, 2002.
137. *Vietnam Southeast Asia International*, April-May-June 1978, p. 6. This source does not identify this congressman.
138. Committee on International Relations, "Foreign Assistance Legislation for Fiscal Year 1979 (Part 6): Economic and Security Assistance in Asia and the Pacific," Hearings before the Subcommittee on Asian and Pacific Affairs, House of Representatives, 95th Congress, 2nd session, March 7, 9, 14, 16, 21 and 22, 1978 (Washington D.C.: U.S. Government Printing Office, 1978), p. 108.
139. O.A. Westad, 1997, p. 20.
140. Committee on International Relations, "Foreign Assistance Legislation for Fiscal Year 1979 (Part 6): Economic and Security Assistance in Asia and the Pacific," Hearings before the Subcommittee on Asian and Pacific Affairs, House of Representatives, 95th Congress, 2nd session, March 7, 9, 14, 16, 21 and 22, 1978 (Washington D.C.: U.S. Government Printing Office, 1978), p. 112.
141. Author's interview with Professor Ngo Vinh Long (University of Maine), May 2003.
142. *Far Eastern Economic Review*, July 21, 1978, p. 19.
143. *Far Eastern Economic Review*, May 20, 1977, p. 17.
144. *The New Yorker*, October 23, 1978, p. 30.
145. E.P. Adam, 1979 (b), p. 408.
146. *Far Eastern Economic Review*, May 19, 1978, p. 5.
147. *Far Eastern Economic Review*, July 21, 1978, p. 19.
148. Letter from Phan Hien to Montgomery, May 25, 1978, Name File—Montgomery, CPL.
149. *U.S. News & World Report*, July 10, 1978, p. 30.
150. Report from Hanoi *Vietnam News Agency*, May 30, 1978, File: 4-6/1978, SRV-U.S. Foreign Relations, Douglas Pike Collection, UBIA.
151. Report from the World Church Service to the President, June 8, 1978, Country Files, Box CO-66, CPL.
152. Report from *Hanoi Domestic Service*, June 4, 1978, File: 4-6/1978, SRV-U.S. Foreign Relations, Douglas Pike Collection, UBIA.
153. Press release from the Office of Senator Kennedy, August 10, 1978, File: 7-8/1978, SRV-U.S. Foreign Relations, Douglas Pike Collection, UBIA. Also: *The New York Times*, June 21, 1978, p. 2.
154. V. Funnell in: M. Light, 1993, p. 89.
155. S. Hurst, 1996, p. 69.
156. W. Burchett, 1981, p. 153.
157. E. Becker, 1998, p. 389.
158. *The Nation*, April 2, 1977, p. 388.
159. M. Crowley, 1998, p. 256.
160. *The Nation*, January 20, 1979, p. 35.
161. E. Becker, 1998, p. 375.
162. S.E. Ambrose and D.G. Brinkley, 1997, p. 250.
163. *Department of State Bulletin*, September 5, 1977, pp. 323-4.
164. W. Shawcross in: D.P. Chandler and B. Kiernan, 1983, pp. 243-4.
165. H. Kissinger, 1979, p. 1053-1087.
166. *Far Eastern Economic Review*, March 18, 1977, p. 30.
167. *Vietnam Southeast Asia International*, July-August-September 1978, p. 3.
168. *Far Eastern Economic Review*, June 9, 1978, p. 12-13.
169. P.Y.C. Chang in: J.C. Hsiung and W. Chai, 1981, p. 111.
170. H. Kissinger, 1999, pp. 874-886 and 886-894.
171. *Far Eastern Economic Review*, November 21, 1975, p. 28-30.
172. *Far Eastern Economic Review*, December 12, 1975, p. 17.
173. *Far Eastern Economic Review*, December 5, 1975, p. 24.
174. Z. Brzezinski, 1983, p. 197.
175. M. Schaller, 1990, p. 197-202. Also: *Far Eastern Economic Review*, February 27, 1976, p. 34.
176. W. Burr, 1998, p. 406. On the Kissingerian legacy on the China issue see: J.C. Hsiung, "U.S. Relations with China in the Post-Kissingerian Era: A Sensible Policy for the 1980s," *Asian Survey*, August 1977, pp. 691-710. See also: J. Mann, 1999, pp. 75-77.
177. J. Mann, 1999, p. 79.
178. *The New York Times Magazine*, February 13, 1977, p. 21; *Time*, December 27, 1976, p. 24. On this issue see: M. Berger, "Vance and Brzezinski: Peaceful coexistence or guerrilla war?" *The New York Times Magazine*, February 13, 1977, pp. 19-25. See also: J. Mann, 1999, p. 85. Also: P. Tyler in: *Foreign Affairs*, September-October 1999, p. 107.
179. E. Becker, 1998, p. 388. See also: J. Mann, 1999, p. 85-6.
180. The phrase first appeared in: J. Dumbrell, 1995, p. 198.
181. *Far Eastern Economic Review*, July 2, 1976, p. 39.
182. W.M. Bagby, 1999, p. 300.
183. Minutes of the SCC meeting, March 2, 1978, File: Meetings: SCC 61 (3/2/1978), Z. Brzezinski Donated Historical Material, Box 28, CPL.
184. *Far Eastern Economic Review*, May 19, 1978, p. 23.
185. *Vietnam Southeast Asia International*, June-July 1979, p. 5.
186. Author's correspondence with Z. Brzezinski, February 5, 2002; *Time* (U.S. edition), November 6, 1978, p. 48. A selection of articles on the rhetoric of the "China Card" might include: Unattributed, "China Card," *National Review*, January 5, 1978, p. 13; Unattributed, "The China Card," *New Republic*, January 6, 1979, pp. 5-6; Unattributed, "Peeking at the Chinese Card," *Time*, May 22, 1978, pp. 18-9; Unattributed, "Limits to Brzezinski's China Card," *Business Week*, August 14, 1978, p. 43; B. Levin, S. Liu and A.M. Field, "The Peking Card," *Newsweek*, August 21, 1978, p. 14; H.J. Morgenthau, "Gambling on China: Should we play the Chinese Card?" *Current*, September 1978, pp. 53-4; E.N. Luttwak, "Against the China Card," *Commentary*, October 1978, pp. 37-43; S. Talbott, "Playing the China Card," *Time*, November 6, 1978, p. 45; Unattributed, "That China Card," *America*, November 18, 1978, p. 346; Unattributed, "Carter Stuns the World: Thwarted in the Middle East, he suddenly plays the China Card," *Time* (U.S. edition), December 25, 1978, pp. 16-20; Unattributed, "Exposing the China Card," *National Review*, February 2, 1979, pp. 135-6.
187. Letter from J.L. Schecter to the Editors of *Time Magazine*, November 1, 1978, Country Files, Box CO-17, CPL.
188. Author's interview with Peter Bourne, March 21, 2002.
189. Z. Brzezinski, 1983, p. 196.
190. R.L. Garthoff, 1994, p. 662.
191. B. Garrett in: K.A. Oye, D. Rothchild, R.J. Lieber, 1979, pp. 238-9.
192. P. Tyler in: *Foreign Affairs*, September-October 1999, p. 99.
193. R.L. Garthoff, 1994, p. 763.
194. B. Garrett in: K.A. Oye, D. Rothchild, R.J. Lieber, 1979, p. 239.
195. *Far Eastern Economic Review*, September 2, 1977, p. 8.
196. *Newsweek*, July 11, 1977, p. 17.
197. *Newsweek*, September 26, 1977, p. 25.
198. *Asia Yearbook*, 1978, p. 349. See also: J. Mann, 1999, p. 83-4.
199. M.B. Young, 1991, p. 308.

200. Letter from Jimmy Carter to the editors in: *Foreign Affairs*, November-December 1999, p. 164.
201. B. Garrett in: K.A. Oye, D. Rothchild and R.J. Lieber, 1979, p. 236.
202. N. Chanda, 1988, p. 275.
203. C. Vance, 1983, p. 37; J. Dumbrell, 1997, p. 51.
204. *U.S. News & World Report*, May 22, 1978, p. 42.
205. J. Carter, 1982, p. 51.
206. Author's interview with Peter Bourne, February 18, 2003.
207. See: M. Berger, "Vance and Brzezinski: Peaceful Coexistence or Guerrilla War?" *The New York Times Magazine*, February 13, 1977, pp. 19–25. Also: G. Smith, 1986, p. 88.
208. C. Vance, 1983, p. 37.
209. *U.S. News & World Report*, March 19, 1979, pp. 25–7.
210. See Brzezinski's interview in: *Newsweek*, May 9, 1977, p. 35.
211. *Newsweek*, June 12, 1978, pp. 12–3. Also: S. Hurst, 1996, p. 79; J. Mann, 1999, p. 85.
212. Z. Brzezinski, 1983, p. 204. The second quote is Stephen Barber's phrase in: *Far Eastern Economic Review*, May 19, 1978, p. 24. See also: M.B. Young, 1991, pp. 308–9.
213. *Asia Yearbook*, 1979, p. 168–70; *Peking Review*, March 17, 1978, pp. 5–14.
214. *Far Eastern Economic Review*, May 19, 1978, p. 24.
215. Letter from Brzezinski to Huang Chen, November 14, 1977, Country Files, Box CO-17, CPL.
216. P. Tyler in: *Foreign Affairs*, September-October 1999, p. 104.
217. R.L. Garthoff, 1994, p. 772. Also: M. Oksenberg in: *Foreign Affairs*, Fall 1982, pp. 182–4. See also: P. Tyler in: *Foreign Affairs*, September-October 1999, p. 105.
218. M. Oksenberg in: *Foreign Affairs*, Fall 1982, p. 184.
219. Committee on International Relations, "United States-Soviet Union-China: The Great Power Triangle," Hearings before the Subcommittee on Future Foreign Policy Research and Development, House of Representatives, 94th Congress, Part I, March 10, 1976 (Washington D.C.: U.S. Government Printing Office, 1976), pp. 120 and 124.
220. M.B. Young, 1991, pp. 308–9; G. Smith, 1986, p. 88; J. Mann, 1999, p. 87–8.
221. J. Carter, 1982, p. 193.
222. *Time*, May 22, 1978, p. 19. See also: Z. Brzezinski, 1983, pp. 202–9.
223. H. Jordan, 1982, p. 49.
224. P. Tyler in: *Foreign Affairs*, September-October 1999, p. 106. In a letter to the editors of *Foreign Affairs*, Brzezinski indirectly confirms this information: Brzezinski's letter to the editors, *Foreign Affairs*, November-December 1999, p. 166.
225. J. Mann, 1999, pp. 87–8.
226. *National Review*, June 23, 1978, p. 768. Also: Z. Brzezinski, 1983, p. 217.
227. *Far Eastern Economic Review*, June 2, 1978, p. 22.
228. Z. Brzezinski, 1983, p. 208.
229. B. Garrett in: K.A. Oye, D. Rothchild, R.J. Lieber, 1979, p. 231.
230. J. Dumbrell, 1995, p. 125; S. Hurst, 1996, pp. 82–3.
231. B. Garrett in: K.A. Oye, D. Rothchild and R.J. Lieber, 1979, pp. 239–40, 244. Also: L.T. Caldwell and A. Dallin in: K.A. Oye, D. Rothchild and R.J. Lieber, 1979, pp. 217–8. See also: J. Mann, 1999, p. 87.
232. N. Chanda, 1988, p. 279. Also: P. Tyler in: *Foreign Affairs*, September-October 1999, p. 99.
233. J. Mann, 1999, pp. 86–87.
234. Memorandum of conversation between Huberman, Gleysteen and Chinese officials, May 21, 1978, Microfiche collection of recently declassified material, Fiche 29, declassified in 2000, Library of Congress.
235. B. Garrett in: K.A. Oye, D. Rothchild and R.J. Lieber, 1979, p. 244.
236. G. Smith, 1986, p. 88.
237. *Time*, December 15, 1975, p. 19 and January 19, 1976, p. 17. Also: J. Mann, 1999, p. 70.
238. *Far Eastern Economic Review*, November 24, 1978, p. 32. On the Gang of Four see: J. Domes, "China in 1976: Tremors of Transition," *Asian Survey*, January 1977, pp. 1–17; P.R. Moody, "The Fall of the Gang of Four: Background Notes on the Chinese Counterrevolution," *Asian Survey*, August 1977, pp. 711–723; J. Domes, "China in 1977: Reversal of Verdict," *Asian Survey*, January 1978, pp. 1–16; *Keesing's Contemporary Archives*, 1977, p. 28717.
239. J. Carter, 1982, p. 196; Z. Brzezinski, 1983, p. 25.
240. H. Kissinger, 1999, p. 871.
241. Z. Brzezinski, 1983, p. 210. See also: R.L. Garthoff, 1994, p. 770–775.
242. *Time*, June 5, 1978, p. 29; *Newsweek*, June 5, 1978, p. 26. See also: *Far Eastern Economic Review*, June 2, 1978, p. 22.
243. *New Times*, June 1978, no. 23, p. 10. See also the report on Brzezinski's visit to China in: *Peking Review*, May 26, 1978, pp. 4–6.
244. R.L Garthoff, 1994, p. 780.
245. *Far Eastern Economic Review*, March 3, 1978, p. 12.
246. *Far Eastern Economic Review*, May 26, 1978, p. 15; *Peking Review*, May 26, 1978, pp. 20–21.
247. *Time*, May 22, 1978, p. 18. Also: R.S. Ross, 1988, p. 181.
248. *New Times*, June 1978, no. 23, p. 15.
249. See also: B. Levin, B. Came and S. Liu, "The Peking Card," *Newsweek*, August 21, 1978, p. 14.
250. *Time*, June 5, 1978, p. 29.
251. *Keesing's Contemporary Archives*, 1979, p. 29533; *Department of State Bulletin*, August 1978, p. 4.
252. M. Oksenberg in: *Foreign Affairs*, Fall 1982, p. 184.
253. *Department of State Bulletin*, July 1978, pp. 14–6. Also: E.P. Adams, 1979 (b), pp. 25–6 and 204–210.
254. R.L. Garthoff, 1994, pp. 665–7.
255. S.M. Neuringer, 1993, p. 30; E. Becker, 1998, p. 389.
256. *Vietnam Southeast Asia International*, August-September-October 1979, p. 23.
257. M.B. Young, 1991, p. 308. Keeping to this animal imagery, the Chinese later termed Hanoi's final Soviet tilt: "the Russian bear has had a cub" (*Far Eastern Economic Review*, June 9, 1978, p. 11). Also: A.R. Isaacs, 1997, p. 171.
258. R.S. Ross, 1988, p. 175.
259. *Far Eastern Economic Review*, July 7, 1978, p. 9.
260. *Time*, June 5, 1978, p. 29. For a compendium of Brzezinski's anti-Soviet remarks during his visit to China refer to: *Keesing's Contemporary Archives*, 1979, p. 29533.
261. *Vietnam Southeast Asia International*, April-May-June 1980, p. 1; *The Nation*, October 20, 1979, p. 366 ; M.B. Young, 1991, p. 309.
262. See: B. Gwertzman "Indochina Conflict Seen as 'Proxy War'" (Author's emphasis) in: *The New York Times*, January 9, 1978, p. 3.
263. G. Smith, 1986, p. 97. Also: *Newsweek*, January 23, 1978, p. 15; *Time*, January 23, 1978, p. 14. In his memoirs Carter uses a similar expression, calling Vietnam a "puppet" and "surrogate" of the Soviet Union (J. Carter 1982, pp. 195 and 235).
264. Commentary from *TASS* in: *Washington Star*, January 9, 1978, p. 4.
265. Soviet broadcast in Vietnamese to Vietnam, February 8, 1978, File: 1-3/1978, SRV-U.S. Foreign Relations, Douglas Pike Collection, UBIA.
266. Report from *TASS*, Moscow, January 17, 1978, File: 1-3/1978, SRV-U.S. Foreign Relations, Douglas Pike Collection, UBIA.
267. Memorandum from Oksenberg to Brzezinski, January 9, 1978, NSA Brzezinski Files, Box 85, CPL.

268. L.T. Caldwell and A. Dallin in: K.A. Oye, D. Rothchild and R.J. Lieber, 1979, p. 220.
269. *The Nation*, October 20, 1979, p. 367.
270. S. Hurst, 1996, pp. 79–90.
271. *Vietnam Southeast Asia International*, April-May-June 1980, p. 2.
272. E. Becker, 1998, p. 389.
273. Z. Brzezinski, 1983, p. 228. Also: S. Hurst, 1996, p. 93.
274. Holbrooke speaking to Congress about "Changing perspectives of U.S. Policy in East Asia," *Department of State Bulletin*, August 1978, p. 4. See also: J. Mann, 1999, p. 90.
275. Z. Brzezinski, 1983, p. 228. See also: J. Carter, 1982, p. 194.
276. Oksenberg quoted in: E. Becker, 1998, p. 391.
277. Letter from Jimmy Carter to the editors: *Foreign Affairs*, November-December 1999, pp. 164–5.
278. On this issue see: J. Dumbrell, 1995, p. 198.
279. S. Hurst, 1996, p. 91.

V. Reversal in U.S. Foreign Policy

1. W.J. Duiker, 1989, p. 162; R.S. Ross, 1988, p. 189.
2. W.J. Duiker, 1986, p. 78.
3. Pao-Min Chang, 1987, p. 67.
4. Author's interview with Judith Stowe, October 26, 2002.
5. *Far Eastern Economic Review*, September 1, 1978, p. 9. Also: W.J. Duiker, 1986, p. 78.
6. *Far Eastern Economic Review*, June 16, 1978, p. 10; *Newsweek*, June 12, 1978, p. 22; G. Evans and K. Rowley, 1990, p. 53.
7. D. Pike, 1987, p. 184.
8. G. Porter in: D.W.P. Elliott, 1982, p. 105. Also: S. Hurst, 1996, p. 69. See also Hoang Van Hoan's statement in: *Peking Review*, September 7, 1979, p. 25.
9. S.J. Morris, 1999, p. 108.
10. Min Chen, 1992, p. 138. Also: G. Porter in: *The Nation*, June 9, 1979, p. 701. Also: G. Férier, 1993, p. 145.
11. S.J. Morris, 1999, p. 108.
12. W.J. Duiker, 1986, p. 79.
13. G. Evans and K. Rowley, 1990, p. 56; S.J. Morris, 1999, p. 212.
14. *The New York Times*, June 21, 1978, p. 2.
15. *Department of State Bulletin*, October 1979, p. 34; *The New York Times*, June 28, 1978, p. 3.
16. Pao-Min Chang, 1987, pp. 40 and 47.
17. *Far Eastern Economic Review*, July 14, 1978, p. 9.
18. W.J. Duiker, 1989, p. 183.
19. *Far Eastern Economic Review*, August 18, 1978, p. 9–11.
20. *Việtnam*, August 1978, p. 3; *The New York Times*, July 4, 1978, p. 1.
21. *Far Eastern Economic Review*, June 9, 1978, p. 13.
22. *Far Eastern Economic Review*, July 14, 1978, p. 9; *The New York Times*, July 4, 1978, p. 1; *Time*, July 31, 1978, p. 16.
23. *Vietnam Info*, December 1978, p. 9.
24. *Time* (U.S. edition), July 3, 1978, p. 30.
25. *New Times*, June 1978, no. 25, p. 16.
26. *New Times*, July 1978, no. 29, p. 17.
27. E. Palmujoki, 1997, p. 78.
28. *Việtnam*, August 1978, p. 3; *Asia Yearbook*, 1979, p. 340; *The New York Times*, July 15, 1978, p. 3. See also: W. Burchett, 1981, pp. 189–90.
29. Pao-Min Chang, 1987, p. 46 and 50.
30. Report entitled "Vietnam and China: An American Diplomatic Opportunity," by Representatives Jonathan Bingham (Democrat, New York), Paul McCloskey (Republican, California) and Anthony Beilenson (Democrat, California), members of Congress for Peace through Law (*Congressional Record*, Senate, September 14, 1978, p. 29452).
31. *The New York Times*, July 2, 1978, p. 8 and July 11, 1978, p. 6.
32. Committee on International Relations, Hearing before the Subcommittee on Asian and Pacific Affairs, House of Representatives, 95th Congress, 1st session, July 19, 1977 (Washington D.C.: U.S. Government Printing Office, 1979), Appendix 13, p. 56.
33. Report from Tokyo *Kyodo*, July 10, 1978, File: 7–8/1978, SRV-U.S. Foreign Relations, Douglas Pike Collection, UBIA. Reprinted in: Committee on International Relations, Hearing before the Subcommittee on Asian and Pacific Affairs, House of Representatives, 95th Congress, 1st session, July 19, 1977 (Washington D.C.: U.S. Government Printing Office, 1979), Appendix 13, p. 56. Also: N. Chanda, 1988, p. 270.
34. *The Nation*, October 20, 1979, p. 367.
35. Report from Tokyo *Kyodo*, July 10, 1978, File: 7–8/1978, SRV-U.S. Foreign Relations, Douglas Pike Collection, UBIA. Reprinted in: Committee on International Relations, Hearing before the Subcommittee on Asian and Pacific Affairs, House of Representatives, 95th Congress, 1st session, July 19, 1977 (Washington D.C.: U.S. Government Printing Office, 1979), Appendix 13, p. 56. Also: N. Chanda, 1988, p. 270.
36. *The Japan Times*, July 11, 1978, p. 1.
37. Memorandum from Platt to Aaron, evening report, July 24, 1978, NSA Staff Material Far East, Box 1, CPL.
38. *The New York Times*, July 11, 1978, p. 6.
39. Report from *Agence France Presse* in Hong-Kong, July 14, 1978, File: 7–8/1978, SRV-U.S. Foreign Relations, Douglas Pike Collection, UBIA; Memorandum from Oksenberg to Brzezinski, evening report, July 17, 1978, NSA Staff Material Far East, Box 1, CPL. Also: Committee on International Relations, Hearing before the Subcommittee on Asian and Pacific Affairs, House of Representatives, 95th Congress, 1st session, July 19, 1977 (Washington D.C.: U.S. Government Printing Office, 1979), Appendix 13, p. 56.
40. Memorandum from Oksenberg to Brzezinski, evening report, July 17, 1978, NSA Far East Box 1, CPL.
41. N. Chanda's interview with Andrew Peacock in: N. Chanda, 1988, p. 270.
42. Committee on International Relations, Hearing before the Subcommittee on Asian and Pacific Affairs, House of Representatives, 95th Congress, 1st session, July 19, 1977 (Washington D.C.: U.S. Government Printing Office, 1979), Appendix 13, p. 56.
43. Report from Hanoi *Vietnam News Agency*, July 11, 1978, File: 4–6/1978, SRV-U.S. Foreign Relations, Douglas Pike Collection, UBIA. Also: *The New York Times*, July 12, 1978, p. 3.
44. F. Brown, 1989, p. 29; L.M. Stern, 1995, p. 25; N. Chanda, 1988, p. 270.
45. *The New York Times*, May 6, 1977, p. 1.
46. Unidentified information memorandum on Vietnamese views in Honolulu, December 1978, File: 9–12/1978, SRV-U.S. Foreign Relations, Douglas Pike Collection, UBIA.
47. L.M. Stern, 1995, p. 25; N. Chanda, 1988, p. 270. A reference to this conversation appears in: Memorandum from Oksenberg to Brzezinski, evening report, July 18, 1978, NSA Staff Material Far East, Box 1, CPL.
48. *The New York Times*, July 11, 1978, p. 6.
49. *Department of State Bulletin*, October 1979, p. 34.
50. *Far Eastern Economic Review*, October 13, 1978, p. 13.
51. S. Hurst, 1996, pp. 71–2.
52. *The Nation*, October 20, 1979, p. 367.
53. Z. Brzezinski, 1983, Annex II, p. 562. See also: M.B. Young, 1991, p. 309.

54. *Business Week*, August 14, 1978, p. 43.
55. F. Brown, 1989, p. 29; L.M. Stern, 1995, p. 25.
56. B. Garrett in: K.A. Oye, D. Rothchild, R.J. Lieber, 1979, pp. 238–9. Also: P. Tyler in: *Foreign Affairs*, September-October 1999, p. 99.
57. Unidentified Russian radio quoted in: *Far Eastern Economic Review*, November 10, 1978, p. 14.
58. Pao-Min Chang, 1987, p. 63.
59. *Peking Review*, July 21, 1978, p. 8; *Far Eastern Economic Review*, July 28, 1978, p. 26.
60. L.M. Stern, 1995, p. 25.
61. N. Chanda, 1988, p. 271. See also the statement made by Robert B. Oakley to the Subcommittee on Asian and Pacific Affairs of the House Committee on Foreign Affairs in May 1979 in: *Department of State Bulletin*, October 1979, p. 39.
62. S. Hurst, 1996, p. 95.
63. R.S. McNamara, J.G. Blight and R.K. Brigham, 1999, pp. 302 and 310–1.
64. For a discussion on the lack of communications and exchanges in the post-war era see: M.W. Bell, "'Healing the Wounds': US-Vietnamese Diplomacy after the Fall of Saigon" (Leicester: University of Leicester Press, 1995).
65. G. Porter in: *The Nation*, October 20, 1979, p. 367.
66. Press release from the Office of Senator Kennedy, August 10, 1978, File: 7–8/1978, SRV-U.S. Foreign Relations, Douglas Pike Collection, UBIA. The five members of the delegation were: Dr. Jean Mayer of Tufts University (Massachusetts), Archbishop Philip M. Hannan (New Orleans), Dr. LaSalle Leffall of the American Cancer Society of Howard University Hospital (Washington), Ms. Mildred Kaufman of the American Public Health Association (University of North Carolina), and Mr. Jerry Tinker from the Senate Committee on the Judiciary.
67. *Asia Yearbook*, 1979, p. 340.
68. Report from Hanoi *Vietnam News Agency*, July 30, 1978, File: 7–8/1978, SRV-U.S. Foreign Relations, Douglas Pike Collection, UBIA.
69. *Far Eastern Economic Review*, August 18, 1978, p. 11.
70. *Newsweek*, August 21, 1978, p. 15.
71. *Congressional Record*, Senate, August 24, 1978, ppS14348.
72. Press release from the Office of Senator Kennedy, August 10, 1978, File: 7–8/1978, SRV-U.S. Foreign Relations, Douglas Pike Collection, UBIA. The press release does not specify what these other "humanitarian issues" although they seem to refer to MIAs.
73. *The New York Times*, August 8, 1978, p. 93.
74. *Asia Yearbook*, 1979, p. 340. See the illustration in: *The New York Times*, August 8, p. 1, of an American citizen embracing his wife and son after a three-year separation.
75. Press release from the Office of Senator Kennedy, August 10, 1978, File: 7–8/1978, SRV-U.S. Foreign Relations, Douglas Pike Collection, UBIA.
76. *Newsweek*, August 21, 1978, p. 15.
77. *The New York Times*, August 10, 1978, pp. 25–6.
78. S. Hurst, 1996, p. 95.
79. *National Review*, August 18, 1978, p. 1006.
80. Report from Hanoi *Vietnam News Agency*, August 11, 1978, File: 7–8/1978, SRV-U.S. Foreign Relations, Douglas Pike Collection, UBIA.
81. *Far Eastern Economic Review*, August 18, 1978, p. 11.
82. *Congressional Record*, Senate, August 22, 1978, ppS14007-9.
83. N. Chanda, 1988, p. 272.
84. *The New York Times*, August 8, 1978, p. 3.
85. Memorandum from Oksenberg to Brzezinski, evening report, August 2, 1978, NSA Staff Material Far East, Box 1, CPL.
86. Report from Hanoi *Vietnam News Agency*, August 5, 1978, File: 7–8/1978, SRV-U.S. Foreign Relations, Douglas Pike Collection, UBIA.
87. Report from Hanoi *Vietnam News Agency*, August 10, 1978, File: 7–8/1978, SRV-U.S. Foreign Relations, Douglas Pike Collection, UBIA.
88. *Department of State Bulletin*, August 1978, p. 5.
89. *Far Eastern Economic Review*, August 18, 1978, p. 11.
90. Report from *Agence France Presse* in Hong-Kong quoting the *Far Eastern Economic Review*, July 27, 1978, File: 7–8/1978, SRV-U.S. Foreign Relations, Douglas Pike Collection, UBIA. Also: *Far Eastern Economic Review*, August 4, 1978, p. 5. As this was reported in the intelligence section of the *Review* it may have originated from an U.S. leak. The *Far Eastern Economic Review* intelligence reports are usually reliable.
91. The members of this delegation included: Congressman Montgomery (Democrat, Mississippi), and Representatives James T. Broyhill (Democrat, North Carolina), George Danielson (Democrat, California), John P. Murtha (Democrat, Pennsylvania), Sam Hall (Democrat, Texas), Ike Skelton (Democrat, Missouri), W. Henson Moore (Republican, Louisiana), and Antonia Borja Won Pat (Democrat, Guam). (Press release from the Committee on International Relations, Subcommittee on Asian and Pacific Affairs, September 11, 1978, File: 9–12/1978, SRV-U.S. Foreign Relations, Douglas Pike Collection, UBIA). Although he was the only Republican member of the delegation, Moore was certainly concerned about the MIA issue, as several letters from him suggest (UBIA).
92. Draft letter to R.E. Bauman, undated, WHCF, Box ND-14, CPL.
93. Letter from Montgomery to Phan Hien, April 28, 1978, WHCF, Box ND-14, CPL.
94. Letter from Phan Hien to Montgomery, May 25, 1978, Name File—Montgomery, CPL.
95. Letter from Montgomery to H. Jordan dated July 13, 1978, and letter from Montgomery to Phan Hien dated July 13, 1978, WHCF, Box FO-48, CPL.
96. These officers were Warren Magruder, Press Assistant in the East Asia Bureau's Public Affairs Section and Michael Eiland, interpreter in the Regional Affairs Section of EA (Letter from Hamilton Jordan to Montgomery, August 3, 1978, WHCF, Box FO-48, CPL).
97. Letter from the Speaker of the House of Representatives to Vance, June 29, 1978, WHCF, Box FO-48, CPL.
98. Hand-written note on a memorandum from Oksenberg to Brzezinski, August 1, 1978, WHCF, Box FO-48, CPL.
99. Letter from H. Jordan to Montgomery, June 29, 1978, WHCF, Box FO-48, CPL (Also in: Name File—Montgomery, CPL).
100. Memorandum from Oksenberg to Brzezinski, June 12, 1978, WHCF, Box FO-48, CPL.
101. Memorandum from Brzezinski to H. Jordan, August 3, 1978, WHCF, Box FO-48, CPL.
102. Report from Hanoi *Vietnam News Agency*, August 23, 1978, File: 7–8/1978, SRV-U.S. Foreign Relations, Douglas Pike Collection, UBIA.
103. *Time*, September 4, 1978, p. 18.
104. Report from *New China News Agency*, August 27, 1978, File: 7–8/1978, SRV-U.S. Foreign Relations, Douglas Pike Collection, UBIA.
105. Report of the Special Committee on Southeast Asia, House of Representatives, 95th Congress, 2nd session, September 7, 1978 (Washington D.C.: U.S. Government Printing Office, 1978), p. 6. Also: *The New York Times*, August 25, 1978, p. 61.
106. Report from *New China News Agency*, August 27, 1978, File: 7–8/1978, SRV-U.S. Foreign Relations, Douglas Pike Collection, UBIA.
107. Report of the Special Committee on Southeast

Asia, House of Representatives, 95th Congress, 2nd session, September 7, 1978 (Washington D.C.: U.S. Government Printing Office, 1978), p. 2.
108. *The New York Times*, August 29, 1978, p. 15.
109. *Time*, September 4, 1978, p. 18; *The New York Times*, August 29, 1978, p. 43.
110. Report of the Special Committee on Southeast Asia, House of Representatives, 95th Congress, 2nd session, September 7, 1978 (Washington D.C.: U.S. Government Printing Office, 1978), p. 3.
111. *The New York Times*, August 25, 1978, p. 61.
112. *Time*, September 4, 1978, p. 23.
113. Report of the Special Committee on Southeast Asia, House of Representatives, 95th Congress, 2nd session, September 7, 1978 (Washington D.C.: U.S. Government Printing Office, 1978), pp. 3 and 5. Also: *Far Eastern Economic Review*, October 13, 1978, p. 13.
114. *The New York Times*, September 1, 1978, p. 59.
115. Report of the Special Committee on Southeast Asia, House of Representatives, 95th Congress, 2nd session, September 7, 1978 (Washington D.C.: U.S. Government Printing Office, 1978), p. 6. Also: *The New York Times*, August 29, 1978, p. 43.
116. N. Chanda, 1988, p. 271.
117. *Philadelphia Inquirer*, August 28, 1978, p. 1.
118. *The New York Times*, August 29, 1978, p. 43.
119. Report of the Special Committee on Southeast Asia, House of Representatives, 95th Congress, 2nd session, September 7, 1978 (Washington D.C.: U.S. Government Printing Office, 1978), p. 7.
120. Unreferenced report from the Singapore press, September 1978, File: 9-12/1978, SRV-U.S. Foreign Relations, Douglas Pike Collection, UBIA.
121. Committee on International Relations, "Americans Missing in Action in Southeast Asia," Hearings before the Subcommittee on Asian and Pacific Affairs, 95th Congress, 2nd session, Part 2, August 9 and September 13, 1978 (Washington D.C.: U.S. Government Printing Office, 1978), p. 52.
122. Holbrooke's statements to the House Subcommittee on Asian and Pacific Affairs, June 13, 1979 (*Department of State Bulletin*, October 1979, p. 34).
123. Report from *Phnom Penh Domestic Service*, August 25, 1978, File: 7-8/1978, SRV-U.S. Foreign Relations, Douglas Pike Collection, UBIA.
124. See: *Keesing's Contemporary Archives*, 1978, p. 29378; *Far Eastern Economic Review*, March 10, 1978, p. 25 and August 25, 1978, p. 11.
125. *Peking Review*, September 8, 1978, pp. 3-4; *New Times*, August 1978, no. 34, pp. 8-9.
126. R.S. Ross, 1988, p. 193.
127. *Far Eastern Economic Review*, September 22, 1978, p. 20.
128. *Far Eastern Economic Review*, November 10, 1978, p. 13.
129. *New Times*, August 1978, no. 32, p. 7.
130. *Far Eastern Economic Review*, January 19, 1979, p. 12. Also: W.J. Duiker, 1986, p. 78.
131. *Far Eastern Economic Review*, December 22, 1978, p. 17.
132. *Far Eastern Economic Review*, January 12, 1979, p. 14.
133. L. Césari, 1995, p. 260.
134. R.S. Ross, 1988, pp. 216-7.
135. See: *Far Eastern Economic Review*, May 26, 1978, pp. 9-10.
136. The Pol Pot regime published a *Black Book* on Vietnam in 1978, listing, with an utmost xenophobia, all conflicts which had opposed the two countries. Vietnam responded with the publication in October 1979 of a *White Paper*—on China—presenting Peking as one of the main players in the Vietnamese-Cambodian struggle. The *Black Book* was first given to *Washington Post* reporter Elizabeth Becker a few days after the fall of Phnom Penh (See: *The New York Times*, January 11, 1979, p. 21). On the *White Paper* see: Ton That Thien, 1989, pp. 123-4. Also an excellent analysis in: G. Evans and K. Rowley, 1990, pp. 134-137.
137. *The New York Times*, August 27, 1978, p. 17.
138. *New Times*, September 1978, no. 37, p. 2.
139. *Far Eastern Economic Review*, June 16, 1978, p. 11.
140. China claimed that about 400 of such incidents had taken place in 1975, with roughly 700 and 900 more in the years 1976 and 1977 respectively (*Peking Review*, March 30, 1979, p. 19). Vietnamese figures were largely the same (*Vietnam Courier*, March 1979, p. 8). Also: R.S. Ross, 1988, p. 243.
141. Nguyen Van Canh and E. Cooper, 1983, p. 240.
142. Pao-Min Chang, 1987, pp. 68-9.
143. Report drafted by "Members of Congress for Peace Through Law": *Congressional Record*, Senate, August 24, 1978, pp. S14345-8.
144. Committee on International Relations, "Hearings before the Subcommittee on Asian and Pacific Affairs," House of Representatives, 95th Congress, 1st session, July 19, 1977 (Washington D.C.: U.S. Government Printing Office, 1979), p.v.
145. S.M. Neuringer, 1993, p. 35.
146. Transcript of McGovern's speech to the Senate, undated, File: 7-8/1978, SRV-U.S. Foreign Relations, Douglas Pike Collection, UBIA. Also: *Far Eastern Economic Review*, October 13, 1978, p. 13; *Time*, September 4, 1978, pp. 18-23.
147. G.R. Hess, 1990, pp. 153-4.
148. *Congressional Record*, Senate, September 21, 1978, p. S15680.
149. Letter from James Hanley and 16 other members of Congress to Carter, July 6, 1978, WHCF, Box CO-40, CPL.
150. Letter from Douglas J. Bennett to James Hanley, August 17, 1978, WHCF, Box CO-40, CPL.
151. See: W. Shawcross, "Cambodia: Some Perceptions of a Disaster," in: D.P. Chandler and B. Kiernan, 1983, pp. 230-258.
152. Draft statement by D. Pike on the Indochina situation, August 21, 1978, File: 4-6/1978, SRV-U.S. Foreign Relations, Douglas Pike Collection, UBIA.
153. *Far Eastern Economic Review*, June 30, 1978, p. 20.
154. *The New York Times*, August 15, 1978, p. 17.
155. *Time*, September 4, 1978, p. 18.
156. *Far Eastern Economic Review*, November 10, 1978, p. 27. Also: R. Oakley's statement to the House on August 15, 1978, File: 7-8/1978, SRV-U.S. Foreign Relations, Douglas Pike Collection, UBIA.
157. *The New York Times*, July 6, 1978, p. 7.
158. *Asia Yearbook*, 1979, p. 340.
159. *Far Eastern Economic Review*, October 27, 1978, pp. 9-13 and *Far Eastern Economic Review*, December 15, 1978, p. 15.
160. *The New York Times*, September 5, 1978, p. 67.
161. *Far Eastern Economic Review*, June 30, 1978, p. 19.
162. Memorandum from Oksenberg to Brzezinski, evening report, July 18, 1978, NSA Far East Box 1, CPL.
163. *Far Eastern Economic Review*, August 4, 1978, p. 8.
164. *Asia Yearbook*, 1979, p. 321.
165. *Far Eastern Economic Review*, September 15, 1978, p. 21.
166. *Far Eastern Economic Review*, September 22, 1978, pp. 10 and 28-30; *Time*, January 23, 1978, pp. 13-4. See the account of Dong's trip in: *Vietnam*, November 1978, pp. 1-3.
167. Memorandum from Brzezinski to the President, October 21, 1978, Country Files, Box CO-17, CPL. Also: *Business Week*, August 14, 1978, p. 43; *Far Eastern Economic Review*, October 13, 1978, p. 13. See also: S. Hurst, 1996, p. 95.

168. L. Césari, 1995, p. 262.
169. *The Nation*, October 20, 1979, p. 367. Also: J. Carter, 1982, p. 194.
170. Author's interview with Judith Stowe, October 26, 2002.
171. NSC memorandum from N. Platt to Brzezinski, September 26, 1978, Microfiche collection of recently declassified material, Fiche 31, declassified in 2000, Library of Congress.
172. Memorandum from Oksenberg to Brzezinski, evening report, September 26, 1978, NSA Staff Material Far East, Box 1, CPL.
173. S.J. Hood, 1992, p. 49.
174. See the interview of Adam Malik, Foreign Minister of Indonesia in: *Newsweek*, June 20, 1977, pp. 19–20.
175. Report entitled "Vietnam and China: An American Diplomatic Opportunity," by Representatives Jonathan Bingham (Democrat, New York), Paul McCloskey (Republican, California) and Anthony Beilenson (Democrat, California), (*Congressional Record*, Senate, September 14, 1978, pp. 29450–1).
176. Letter from several senators to the President, September 14, 1978, File: 1950/1973, DRV—U.S. Foreign Relations, Douglas Pike Collection, UBIA. (Also in: WHCF, Box FO-32, CPL). These senators, senior representatives of both parties, were Robert C. Byrd (Democrat, West Virginia), Barry Goldwater (Republican, Arizona), Lloyd Bentsen (Democrat, Texas), John Tower (Republican, Texas), Edward Zorinsky (Democrat, Nebraska), Robert Morgan (Democrat, North Carolina), Birch Bayh (Democrat, Indiana), Thomas McIntyre (Democrat, New Hampshire), Jennings Randolph (Democrat, West Virginia), William Proxmire (Democrat, Wisconsin), Milton R. Young (Republican, North Dakota) and Pete V. Domenici (Republican, New Mexico). See also: *The New Yorker*, October 23, 1978, pp. 31–2.
177. Z. Brzezinski, 1983, p. 228. See also: M.B. Young, 1991, p. 309.
178. *Far Eastern Economic Review*, October 13, 1978, p. 13. Also: Letter from Congressman C.W.B. Young, June 14, 1978, WHCF, Box IT-3, CPL.
179. *Congressional Quarterly Weekly Report*, June 17, 1978, p. 1533.
180. Report from Hanoi *Vietnam News Agency*, September 6, 1978, File: 9–12/1978, SRV-U.S. Foreign Relations, Douglas Pike Collection, UBIA.
181. *Newsweek*, September 18, 1978, p. 27.
182. The extension of the U.S. embargo also affected other countries including Cuba and North Korea. Report from Moscow *TASS*, September 9, 1978, File: 9–12/1978, SRV-U.S. Foreign Relations, Douglas Pike Collection, UBIA. The full document was printed as: "Determination under the Trading with the Enemy Act: Communication from the President of the United States," 95th Congress, 2nd Session, September 11, 1978 (Washington: Government Printing Office, 1978).
183. Intelligence report, September 1978, File: 9–12/1978, SRV-U.S. Foreign Relations, Douglas Pike Collection, UBIA.
184. Report from *Agence France Presse* in Hong-Kong, September 10, 1978, File: 9–12/1978, SRV-U.S. Foreign Relations, Douglas Pike Collection, UBIA.
185. *Far Eastern Economic Review*, October 6, 1978, p. 16.
186. For a brief synopsis on the development of Sino-American trade from the signing of the Shanghai Communiqué to 1980, see: K. Holly Maze Carter, 1989, p. 114–117.
187. *Time* (U.S. edition), December 25, 1978, p. 17.
188. M. Oksenberg in: *Foreign Affairs*, Fall 1982, p. 187.
189. S.J. Morris, 1999, pp. 108–9.
190. *Keesing's Contemporary Archives*, 1979, p. 29616. Also: Young Jin Choi, 1987, p. 287.
191. N. Chanda, 1988, p. 255; L. Césari, 1995, p. 260.
192. Memorandum from Oksenberg to Brzezinski, September 22, 1978, NSA Brzezinski Files, Box 85, CPL. Also: N. Chanda, 1988, p. 264.
193. Judith Stowe's speculations based on having observed this episode from Thailand while working for the BBC (Author's interview with Judith Stowe, October 26, 2002).
194. Memorandum from Oksenberg to Brzezinski, September 22, 1978, NSA Brzezinski Files, Box 85, CPL.
195. Author's interview with Judith Stowe, October 26, 2002. This is based on her observations as a journalist for the BBC.
196. Memorandum from Oksenberg to Brzezinski, September 22, 1978, NSA Brzezinski Files, Box 85, CPL.
197. Memorandum from Oksenberg to Brzezinski, September 28, 1978, NSA Brzezinski Files, Box 85, CPL.
198. *The Nation*, October 20, 1979, p. 367.
199. Judith Stowe supposes that the sudden change in the Vietnamese position was certainly Thach's personal initiative (Author's interview with Judith Stowe, October 26, 2002).
200. E. Becker, 1998, p. 393.
201. *The New Yorker*, October 23, 1978, p. 30.
202. N. Chanda, 1988, p. 266.
203. See Holbrooke's statement to the Subcommittee on Asian and Pacific Affairs of the House Committee on Foreign Affairs in June 1979, in: *Department of State Bulletin*, October 1979, pp. 34–5.
204. M.B. Young, 1991, p. 309–10.
205. Author's interview with Judith Stowe, October 26, 2002. Also: *The Nation*, October 20, 1979, p. 367.
206. M. William Bell, 1995, p. 15–16.
207. N. Chanda, 1988, p. 284; M.B. Young, 1991, p. 310.
208. S. Hurst, 1996, p. 108.
209. *Department of State Bulletin*, October 1979, p. 39.
210. *The New Yorker*, October 23, 1978, p. 31.
211. *The Nation*, October 20, 1979, p. 367.
212. Report on a meeting in Paris between the Vietnamese Embassy and the Association of Vietnamese in France on October 30, 1978, File: 9–12/1978, SRV-U.S. Foreign Relations, Douglas Pike Collection, UBIA.
213. *The New Yorker*, October 23, 1978, p. 31.
214. *New Times*, October 1978, no. 41, p. 7.
215. *The New Yorker*, October 23, 1978, p. 30.
216. Memorandum from Oksenberg to Brzezinski, September 28, 1978, NSA Brzezinski Files, Box 85, CPL.
217. Memorandum from East Asia to Brzezinski, evening report, October 2, 1978, NSA Staff Material Far East, Box 1, CPL.
218. Memorandum from Oksenberg to Brzezinski, September 28, 1978, NSA Brzezinski Files, Box 85, CPL.
219. Memorandum from Oksenberg to Brzezinski, evening report, September 28, 1978, NSA Staff Material Far East, Box 1, CPL.
220. E. Becker, 1998, p. 393.
221. Z. Brzezinski, 1983, p. 228.
222. S. Hurst, 1996, pp. 97–8.
223. N. Chanda, 1988, p. 287.
224. *Vietnam Southeast Asia International*, April-May-June 1980, p. 3.
225. J. Mann, 1999, p. 90.
226. S. Hurst, 1996, p. 93.
227. *Time* (U.S. edition), December 25, 1978, p. 17; *Keesing's Contemporary Archives*, 1979, p. 29534.
228. *U.S. News & World Report*, December 11, 1978, p. 36.
229. *Keesing's Contemporary Archives*, 1979, p. 29534.
230. N. Chanda, 1988, pp. 288–9.
231. Patrick Tyler in: *Foreign Affairs*, September-October 1999, p. 112.
232. Z. Brzezinski, 1983, p. 229.
233. *Ibid*.

234. M. Oksenberg in: *Foreign Affairs*, Fall 1982, p. 186. Several secondary sources corroborate this point: N. Chanda, 1988, pp. 288–90; L. Césari, 1995, p. 263; J. Mann, 1999, p. 90. Gareth Porter, in an article in October 1979, claims that this meeting took place on October 1, 1978 (*The Nation*, October 20, 1979, p. 368). However, all other sources and the relevant memoirs date this meeting to October 11.
235. J. Carter, 1982, pp. 194–5.
236. M. Oksenberg in: *Foreign Affairs*, Fall 1982, p. 186; L. Césari, 1995, p. 263.
237. N. Chanda, 1988, p. 289.
238. Letter from Jimmy Carter to the editors in: *Foreign Affairs*, November-December 1999, p. 165. Brzezinski confirms this point in his memoirs but states that briefings reaching Woodcock were sent jointly by Vance and himself (Z. Brzezinski, 1983, p. 225–6).
239. Z. Brzezinski, 1983, pp. 228–9; N. Chanda, 1988, p. 290.
240. M. Oksenberg in: *Foreign Affairs*, Fall 1982, p. 186.
241. E. Becker, 1998, p. 393.
242. *The New York Times*, October 26, 1978, p. 80.
243. *The New York Times*, October 17, 1978, p. 63.
244. N. Chanda, 1988, p. 290.
245. E. Becker, 1998, p. 397.
246. See: *Livre Noir: Faits et preuves des actes d'agression et d'annexion du Vietnam contre le Kampuchéa* (Phnom Penh: Ministère des Affaires Étrangères du Kampuchéa Démocratique, September 1978).
247. E. Becker, 1998, pp. 322–3. Also: McGovern on "Meet The Press," October 15, 1978, File: 9–12/1978, SRV-U.S. Foreign Relations, Douglas Pike Collection, UBIA.
248. *The New York Times*, October 8, 1978, pp. 28–31.
249. *The New York Times*, February 20, 1979, p. 6; *New Times*, November 1978, no. 46, p. 5; *Vietnam Info*, December 1978, p. 10.
250. *The New York Times*, October 22, 1978, p. 13. Deng's accusations were wrong as the Soviets would only be granted access to Vietnamese military bases in 1979.
251. Washington time or the morning of October 30 in Vietnam. Also: N. Chanda, 1988, p. 291.
252. N. Chanda, 1988, p. 290. Chanda's sources on this point are his own interviews with senior Vietnamese officials.
253. *The New York Times*, November 3, 1978, p. 19.
254. *Far Eastern Economic Review*, November 17, 1978, pp. 8–9.
255. *National Review*, June 23, 1978, p. 768.
256. *Vietnam Info*, December 1978, p. 22.
257. *Commentary*, October 1978, p. 37.
258. *America*, November 18, 1978, p. 346. See: V. Funnell in: M. Light, 1993, p. 82–109.
259. *Keesing's Contemporary Archives*, 1979, p. 29473. See also: D. Pike, 1987, p. 130.
260. *Newsweek*, November 13, 1978, p. 36.
261. *National Review*, July 21, 1978, p. 882.
262. Commentary in: *Far Eastern Economic Review*, February 2, 1979, p. 20.
263. W.J. Duiker, 1989, p. 163.
264. A. Haselkorn, "Impact of the Sino-Japanese Treaty on the Soviet Security Strategy," *Asian Survey*, June 1979, pp. 558–573; V. Funnell in: M. Light, 1993, p. 89.
265. Author's translation from French: "[L]'union avec l'URSS est depuis toujours une politique fondamentale, ayant un caractère de principe, du Parti et de l'État vietnamiens ... la solidarité vietnamo-soviétique est devenue une belle tradition" (*Việtnam*, December 1978, p. 1).
266. *Asian Survey*, December 1979, p. 1159. Also quoted in: D. Pike, 1987, pxvi.
267. J.S. Olson and R. Roberts, 1991, p. 277.
268. Appendix A to a Defense Intelligence note no. 478, November 1978, File: 9–12/1978, SRV-U.S. Foreign Relations, Douglas Pike Collection, UBIA. Also: *Far Eastern Economic Review*, November 17, 1978, p. 8.
269. *Newsweek*, November 13, 1978, p. 36; *Far Eastern Economic Review*, November 17, 1978, p. 13; *The New York Times*, November 4, 1978, p. 16.
270. *Keesing's Contemporary Archives*, 1979, p. 29473. Also: W.T. Tow, 1991, p. 185. Douglas Pike, however, states that he "was told by a former SRV official who had defected that a secret protocol to the treaty was signed in Moscow in November 1978 under which the USSR is automatically authorized to intervene militarily in Vietnam in the event the current government is replaced by non-Communists or is toppled in a coup d'état by a pro-Chinese faction. The existence of such a protocol is highly questionable." (D. Pike, 1987, p. 186). No evidence has been found of such a protocol, but this may explain Moscow's restraint and warnings to Peking.
271. *Far Eastern Economic Review*, November 17, 1978, p. 8.
272. Author's interview with Judith Stowe, October 26, 2002. This is based on Judith Stowe's observations at the time.
273. D. Pike, 1987, p. 184.
274. S.J. Morris, 1999, pp. 215–6.
275. Memorandum from Oksenberg (East Asia) to Brzezinski, evening report, November 9, 1978, NSA Far East Box 1, CPL.
276. *Peking Review*, November 10, 1978, pp. 22–23.
277. N. Sihanouk, 1980, p. 98.
278. *Far Eastern Economic Review*, November 24, 1978, p. 11.
279. *Far Eastern Economic Review*, November 17, 1978, pp. 10–12; *Newsweek*, November 20, 1978, p. 47.
280. Author's translation from French: "les leçons de politiques pour débutants dispensés par Mr. [D]eng: on se croirait transporté des siècles en arrière, à l'époque des royaumes combattants de la Chine antique ... [A]ujourd'hui, à l'époque de l'éveil des peuples, ceux-ci ont assez d'intelligence et de sagesse pour savoir discerner le danger qui les menace" (*Vietnam Info*, December 1978, p. 8).
281. Luu Van Loi, 2002, pp. 67 and 73.
282. *Far Eastern Economic Review*, November 24, 1978, p. 11; December 15, 1978, p. 34; January 12, 1979, p. 14.
283. *Peking Review*, November 10, 1978, p. 4; *Keesing's Contemporary Archives*, 1979, p. 29583. Also: R.S. Ross, 1988, p. 214.
284. *Keesing's Contemporary Archives*, 1979, p. 29534. Also: R.L. Garthoff, 1994, p. 776.
285. Luu Van Loi, 2002, p. 75.
286. *The New York Times*, November 6, 1978, p. 31.
287. *Peking Review*, November 10, 1978, p. 4.
288. *Peking Review*, December 15, 1978, p. 3.
289. *Vietnam Southeast Asia International*, June-July 1979, p. 4. Also: *Asia Yearbook*, 1979, p. 20; *The New York Times*, November 4, 1978, p. 16.
290. *Far Eastern Economic Review*, November 17, 1978, p. 11.
291. Unattributed piece of intelligence, November 1978, File: 9–12/1978, SRV-U.S. Foreign Relations, Douglas Pike Collection, UBIA.
292. *The New York Times*, November 6, 1978, p. 1.
293. K.J. Conboy, 1987, p. 4.
294. *Far Eastern Economic Review*, November 17, 1978, p. 11, p. 13.
295. Memorandum from Oksenberg (East Asia) to Brzezinski, evening report, November 3, 1978, NSA Staff Material Far East, Box 1, CPL.
296. *The Nation*, October 20, 1979, p. 368.
297. *Newsweek*, November 13, 1978, p. 36.
298. G. Evans and K. Rowley, 1990, p. 141.
299. Memorandum from Oksenberg to Brzezinski, evening report, November 1, 1978, NSA Staff Material Far East, Box 1, CPL.

300. Z. Brzezinski, 1983, p. 228–9.
301. Pao-Min Chang, 1987, p. 76.
302. E. Becker, 1998, p. 394.
303. M.B. Young, 1991, p. 310.
304. N. Chanda, 1988, p. 292.
305. *Department of State Bulletin*, October 1979, p. 35.
306. Report on a meeting in Paris between the Vietnamese Embassy and the Association of Vietnamese in France on October 30, 1978, File: 9–12/1978, SRV-U.S. Foreign Relations, Douglas Pike Collection, UBIA.
307. *Department of State Bulletin*, October 1979, p. 35. See also Robert B. Oakley's statement (*Department of State Bulletin*, October 1979, pp. 39–40).
308. S. Hurst, 1996, p. 3.
309. *The Nation*, October 20, 1979, p. 368.
310. Memorandum from Oksenberg to Brzezinski, evening report, November 20, 1978, NSA Staff Material Far East, Box 1, CPL.
311. *The New York Times*, August 7, 1979, p. 1. These were indeed the three reasons raised by Holbrooke during his congressional hearing of June 13, 1979 (*Department of State Bulletin*, October 1979, p. 35).
312. Report by *Hanoi International Service* in Thai entitled "Why Have They Brought Up The Human Rights Issue Against the SRV?" File: 9–12/1978, SRV-U.S. Foreign Relations, Douglas Pike Collection, UBIA.
313. *Asia Yearbook*, 1979, p. 340.
314. *The Nation*, October 20, 1979, p. 368.
315. *Vietnam Info*, December 1978, p. 6.
316. Luu Van Loi, 2002, p. 30; E. Becker, 1998, pp. 394; N. Chanda, 1988, pp. 273–93.
317. *The New York Times*, January 2, 1978, p. 10 and *The New York Times*, March 2, 1978, p. 2.
318. *The New York Times*, March 31, p. 1.
319. *The Nation*, October 20, 1979, p. 368.
320. *The New York Times*, December 12, 1978, p. 4.
321. Pao-Min Chang, 1982, pp. 56–7. The refugee exodus would continue until the mid-1990s. An estimated 859,251 boat people survived, with thousands perishing at sea (A.J. Dommen, 2001, p. 961).
322. *The New York Times*, December 16, 1978, p. 22.
323. *The New York Times*, December 20, 1978, p. 15.
324. Report from *Peking Domestic Service*, December 8, 1978, File: 9–12/1978, SRV-U.S. Foreign Relations, Douglas Pike Collection, UBIA. This source does not specify whom Cannon was addressing.
325. *Keesing's Contemporary Archives*, 1979, p. 29613.
326. Author's interview with a Vietnamese diplomat who prefers to remain unnamed. Vance briefly mentions that the Vietnamese "approached us again in December" but does not expand on the issue (C. Vance, 1983, pp. 122–3).
327. *Far Eastern Economic Review*, December 29, 1978, p. 12.
328. *Vietnam Southeast Asia International*, April-May-June 1980, p. 3.
329. M. Oksenberg in: *Foreign Affairs*, Fall 1982, p. 185; G. Evans and K. Rowley, 1990, p. 142; W.I. Cohen, 2000, pp. 201–2.
330. Memorandum from Oksenberg to Brzezinski, evening report, August 7, 1978, NSA Far East Box 1, CPL.
331. Cable from the U.S. Consulate in Hong Kong to the Secretary of State, December 1978, NSA Far East Box 1, CPL.
332. J. Mann, 1999, p. 91.
333. Cable from Woodcock to Vance and Brzezinski with a transcript of his exchange with Deng, December 13, 1978, Microfiche collection of recently declassified material, Fiche 11, declassified in 2000, Library of Congress. See also: J. Mann, 1999, pp. 90–1.
334. Cable from Woodcock to Vance and Brzezinski, December 13, 1978, Microfiche collection of recently declassified material, Fiche 11, Library of Congress. Also: *Newsweek*, January 1, 1979, p. 8.
335. *Time* (U.S. edition), December 25, 1978, p. 17.
336. P. Tyler in: *Foreign Affairs*, September-October 1999, p. 109.
337. *Newsweek*, January 15, 1979, p. 19. Also: J. Carter, 1982, p. 198.
338. W.J. Duiker, 1986, p. 83.
339. S. Lodha, 1997, pp. 322–3.
340. *Far Eastern Economic Review*, December 29, 1978, p. 12.
341. *National Review*, January 5, 1979, p. 13.
342. *Time* (U.S. edition), December 25, 1978, p. 20.
343. Cable from Woodcock to Vance and Brzezinski, December 13, 1978, Microfiche collection of recently declassified material, Fiche 11, Library of Congress.
344. P. Tyler in: *Foreign Affairs*, September-October 1999, pp. 116–7.
345. G. Evans and K. Rowley, 1990, p. 142; J. Mann, 1999, p. 91; J. Carter, 1982, p. 199.
346. *Far Eastern Economic Review*, December 29, 1978, p. 12.
347. *Newsweek*, January 1, 1979, pp. 4 and 8.
348. *Time* (U.S. edition), December 25, 1978, p. 18.
349. *Việtnam*, February 1979, p. 27; *Keesing's Contemporary Archives*, 1979, p. 29473; *New Times*, December 1978, no. 52, p. 11.
350. *New Republic*, January 6, 1979, p. 9.
351. R. Madsen, 1995, p. 124.
352. Report from *Hanoi International Service*, December 16, 1978, File: 9–12/1978, SRV-U.S. Foreign Relations, Douglas Pike Collection, UBIA. The full texts of the joint communiqué of the United States and the People's Republic of China, as well as the President's address and remarks are reprinted in: *Department of State Bulletin*, January 1979, pp. 25–6. See Carter's message to Deng and Deng's message to Carter on January 1, 1979, in: *Department of State Bulletin*, February 1979, pp. 6–23. See also: K. Holly Maze Carter, 1989, Appendix pp. 202–203.
353. *Time* (U.S. edition), December 25, 1978, p. 20; *Newsweek*, January 1, 1979, p. 8. See also: *Department of State Bulletin*, January 1979, p. 26.
354. *Time* (U.S. edition), December 25, 1978, p. 19.
355. J. Dumbrell, 1995, p. 196.
356. Z. Brzezinski, 1983, p. 232.
357. *Time* (U.S. edition), December 25, 1978, p. 18.
358. *Far Eastern Economic Review*, December 29, 1978, p. 13.
359. K. Holly Maze Carter, 1989, Appendix p. 203.
360. P. Tyler in: *Foreign Affairs*, September-October 1999, pp. 117–20.
361. Cable from Woodcock to Vance and Brzezinski, December 13, 1978, Microfiche collection of recently declassified material, Fiche 11, Library of Congress.
362. J. Mann, 1999, p. 91.
363. Report by *Hanoi International Service*, December 17, 1978, File: 9–12/1978, SRV-U.S. Foreign Relations, Douglas Pike Collection, UBIA. Also: *Far Eastern Economic Review*, December 29, 1978, p. 14.
364. *Newsweek*, February 12, 1979, p. 22. See also Vance's interview on "Meet the Press" on December 17, 1978, in: *Department of State Bulletin*, February 1979, pp. 14–7.
365. J. Mann, 1999, pp. 96–7.
366. See Steven Hurst's excellent appraisal of globalist and regionalist ideologies as applied in Vietnam: S. Hurst, 1996, pp. 11–7. Also: J. Mann, 1999, pp. 90–2; J. Dumbrell, 1995, p. 196–8.
367. Letter from Jimmy Carter to Brzezinski, December 22, 1978, Name File—Brzezinski, CPL.
368. Z. Brzezinski, 1983, p. 233.
369. *Department of State Bulletin*, February 1979, p. 6; *New Republic*, January 6, 1979, p. 10. Also: R. Garthoff, 1994, p. 684.

370. *Time* (U.S. edition), December 25, 1978, p. 19.
371. C. Vance, 1983, pp. 110-19.
372. *New Republic*, January 6, 1979, p. 10.
373. *Newsweek*, February 19, 1979, p. 40.
374. Author's interview with Judith Stowe, October 26, 2002.
375. Report from Tokyo *Kyodo*, December 16, 1978, File: 9-12/1978, SRV-U.S. Foreign Relations, Douglas Pike Collection, UBIA.
376. Memorandum from the East Asia Office to Brzezinski, evening report, December 18, 1978, NSA Staff Material Far East, Box 1, CPL.
377. Report from Tokyo *Kyodo*, December 18, 1978, File: 9-12/1978, SRV-U.S. Foreign Relations, Douglas Pike Collection, UBIA.
378. *Far Eastern Economic Review*, December 29, 1978, p. 14-15.
379. Trinh's conference in Tokyo reported by *Agence France Press* in Hong-Kong, December 19, 1978, File: 9-12/1978, SRV-U.S. Foreign Relations, Douglas Pike Collection, UBIA.
380. Report of Le Tho's conference with the Association of Vietnamese in France, December 1978, File: 9-12/1978, SRV-U.S. Foreign Relations, Douglas Pike Collection, UBIA. While the news of Sino-American normalization certainly greatly surprised Hanoi, Bruce D. Porter's claims, in his early study of this issue, that it had contributed to Hanoi's decision to attack Cambodia, is certainly untrue since the Vietnamese invasion of Cambodia was decided at least six months prior to Sino-American normalization (B.D. Porter, 1985, p. 33).
381. *Far Eastern Economic Review*, March 16, 1979, p. 83.
382. *U.S. News & World Report*, December 11, 1978, pp. 39-40.
383. J. Carter, 1982, pp. 197-8; W.J. Duiker, 1989, p. 185.
384. Luu Van Loi, 2002, p. 75. Also: *Current History*, December 1979, p. 197. Wilfred Burchett reports: "In early 1979 the Laotian government discovered that a road which the Chinese had contracted to build as an 'aid project' for Laos had changed its course. Instead of heading almost due south from the Chinese border ... it was swinging east towards the Vietnamese frontier at a point near the highly strategic Dien Bien Phu valley ... The Laotian government ordered the suspension of the road-building work and asked that all Chinese personnel be withdrawn." China had been preparing its attack on Vietnam (W. Burchett, 1981, p. 224-5).

VI. Winning the Third Vietnam War

1. *New Times*, December 1978, no. 52, pp. 15 and 30-2.
2. *Far Eastern Economic Review*, December 15, 1978, p. 35; *Far Eastern Economic Review*, June 30, 1978, p. 18.
3. *Keesing's Contemporary Archives*, 1979, pp. 29582-3.
4. *Far Eastern Economic Review*, December 15, 1978, p. 35.
5. *Vietnam Broadsheet*, Summer 1985, p. 6.
6. *Keesing's Contemporary Archives*, 1979, p. 29582. In a report to the Senate, Senator George McGovern estimated the number of Cambodian victims to be around two million (transcript of McGovern's report to the Senate, undated, File: 7-8/1978, SRV-U.S. Foreign Policy, Douglas Pike Collection, UBIA.) The total number of people killed in such purges is not well known. Heng Samrin, who became president after the fall of Pol Pot in 1979, estimated the number of victims to be around three million, out of a total population of seven million (*Far Eastern Economic Review*, March 2, 1979, p. 22), while a report from Amnesty International estimated that between one and two million people had perished of malnutrition and disease with a further 300,000 victims of Khmer Rouge mass executions (Amnesty International, 1987, p. 16). More recent sources seem to confirm the figure of three million dead (S.M. Neuringer, 1993, p. 6; R.D. Schulzinger, 1998, p. 311). See also: B. Kiernan, *The Pol Pot Regime: Race, Power, and Genocide in Cambodia under the Khmer Rouge: 1975-1979*, (New Haven: Yale University Press, 1996); V. Kaonn, *Cambodge 1975-1995: la nuit sera longue*, (Paris: Association d'Aides au Cambodge, 1996).
7. *Vietnam Broadsheet*, Summer 1985, p. 6.
8. Luu Van Loi, 2002, pp. 68, 77 and 92.
9. *Far Eastern Economic Review*, January 19, 1979, p. 10; *Asia Yearbook*, 1980, p. 46. Kiernan's numbers are higher, with 150,000 troops and 30,000 Khmer insurgents (B. Kiernan, 1996, p. 450).
10. Luu Van Loi, 2002, p. 68.
11. *Newsweek*, December 18, 1978, p. 23 and *Newsweek*, January 22, 1979, p. 23.
12. Department of State Briefing Memorandum to the Secretary, April 25, 1979, NSA Box 86, CPL.
13. Comment by Trinh in a report by Tokyo *Kyodo*, December 19, 1978, File: 9-12/1978, SRV-U.S. Foreign Relations, Douglas Pike Collection, UBIA.
14. Nguyen Van Canh and E. Cooper, 1983, p. 229.
15. *Newsweek*, January 22, 1979, p. 23.
16. Nguyen Van Canh and E. Cooper, 1983, p. 139.
17. *The Nation*, September 9, 1978, p. 211.
18. See: J.M. Van der Kroef, "Cambodia: From 'Democratic Kampuchea' to 'People's Republic,'" *Asian Survey*, August 1979, pp. 731-50. N. Chanda, 1988, pp. 344-346; G. Evans and K. Rowley, 1990, pp. 109-110; *Asia Yearbook*, 1980, p. 47; *Vietnam Broadsheet*, Summer 1985, pp. 6-7.
19. Author's translation from French: "la propriété du peuple" and "des ogres à face humaine" (*Viêtnam*, January 1979, pp. 7-9).
20. Author's interview with Bui Tin, October 30, 2002.
21. Bui Tin, 1999, p. 122.
22. *Far Eastern Economic Review*, January 19, 1979, p. 11; *Keesing's Contemporary Archives*, 1979, p. 29614. Also: Yun Shui, "An Account of Chinese Diplomats Accompanying the Government of Democratic Kampuchea's Move to the Cardamon Mountains," *Critical Asian Studies*, December 2002, pp. 497-501; N. Chanda, "China and Cambodia: In the Mirror of History," *Asia-Pacific Review*, November 2002, p. 1.
23. N. Sihanouk, 1980, p. 90.
24. W.J. Duiker, 1986, p. 99.
25. *Far Eastern Economic Review*, December 15, 1978, p. 34.
26. *Far Eastern Economic Review*, January 26, 1979, p. 10.
27. *Asian Survey*, August 1979, pp. 731-50; *Asia Yearbook*, 1980, p. 47.
28. *Far Eastern Economic Review*, January 19, 1979, p. 13.
29. *Asia Yearbook*, 1980, p. 301.
30. *The New York Times*, July 1, 1979, p. 8.16
31. *Vietnam Broadsheet*, Summer 1985, p. 7.
32. *Asia Yearbook*, 1980, p. 312.
33. Ton That Thien, 1989, pp. 154-5.
34. G. Evans and K. Rowley, 1990, p. 168.
35. Report from Peking *Xinhua*, January 8, 1979, File: 1-3/1979, SRV-U.S. Foreign Relations, Douglas Pike Collection, UBIA.
36. *Newsweek*, January 15, 1979, pp. 16-7.
37. Report from Peking *Xinhua*, January 9, 1979, File: 1-3/1979, SRV-U.S. Foreign Relations, Douglas Pike Collection, UBIA.
38. Report from Peking *Xinhua*, January 10, 1979, File: 1-3/1979, SRV-U.S. Foreign Relations, Douglas Pike

Notes—Chapter VI

Collection, UBIA. Also: *Vietnam Southeast Asia International*, April-May-June 1980, p. 3.
39. R. Oakley's statement of February 15, 1979, File: 1–3/1978, SRV-U.S. Foreign Relations, Douglas Pike Collection, UBIA.
40. Unreferenced newspaper cutting, January 11, 1979, File: 1–3/1979, SRV-U.S. Foreign Relations, Douglas Pike Collection, UBIA. Due to the Vietnamese occupation of Cambodia, the visit was eventually postponed for eighteen months.
41. Report from *Agence France Presse*, January 27, 1979, File: 1–3/1979, SRV-U.S. Foreign Relations, Douglas Pike Collection, UBIA.
42. *The New York Times*, February 7, 1979, p. 1. Also: R.G. Sutter in: D.W.P. Elliott, 1982, p. 187–8.
43. *Vietnam Southeast Asia International*, April-May-June 1980, p. 3; *The Nation*, October 20, 1979, p. 368.
44. *Department of State Bulletin*, October 1979, p. 35.
45. *Far Eastern Economic Review*, January 12, 1979, p. 15.
46. Robert Whymant, *The Guardian*, November 24, 1979, p. 19.
47. *The New York Times*, January 15, 1979, p. 6.
48. *U.S. News & World Report*, January 22, 1979, p. 37.
49. *Ibid.*, p. 45.
50. *Asia Yearbook*, 1980, p. 44.
51. *Far Eastern Economic Review*, February 2, 1979, p. 5.
52. N. Chanda, 1988, p. 350.
53. *Far Eastern Economic Review*, January 19, 1979, p. 17.
54. *Newsweek*, February 12, 1979, p. 22.
55. N. Chanda, 1988, p. 351.
56. Report from *Hanoi Domestic Service*, January 31, 1979, File: 1–3/1979, SRV-U.S. Foreign Relations, Douglas Pike Collection, UBIA.
57. *Newsweek*, February 12, 1979, p. 22.
58. J. Dumbrell, 1995, p. 196.
59. O.A. Westad in: O.A. Westad, 1997, p. 22.
60. *U.S. News & World Report*, February 12, 1979, p. 26; *Newsweek*, February 12, 1979, p. 24.
61. Carter only refers to this dinner at the end of his subchapter on Deng's visit and does not mention that the dinner was held on Deng's first day in the United States (J. Carter, 1982, p. 210).
62. Z. Brzezinski, 1983, p. 405. See the picture of the toast in Brzezinski's memoirs opposite page 398.
63. Letter from Vance to Brzezinski, March 6, 1979, Name File—C. Vance, CPL.
64. Z. Brzezinski, 1983, p. 406. See also: J. Mann, 1999, pp. 98–9.
65. N. Chanda, 1988, p. 351.
66. Z. Brzezinski, 1983, pp. 409–10.
67. J. Mann, 1999, pp. 98–100; Luu Van Loi, 2002, p. 74; J. Dumbrell, 1997, p. 46; G. Smith, 1986, p. 98; M.B. Young, 1991, pp. 310–1.
68. Z. Brzezinski, 1983, p. 410; J. Carter, 1982, p. 206.
69. M.B. Young, 1991, p. 309; Min Chen, 1992, pp. 143–4.
70. *Far Eastern Economic Review*, February 9, 1979, p. 11. See also Deng's remark at the Kennedy Center in: *Department of State Bulletin*, March 1979, p. 4.
71. *Far Eastern Economic Review*, February 9, 1979, p. 11.
72. *Keesing's Contemporary Archives*, 1979, p. 29537.
73. *U.S. News & World Report*, February 12, 1979, p. 24; *Keesing's Contemporary Archives*, 1979, p. 29537.
74. *Peking Review*, February 9, 1979, p. 13.
75. *Far Eastern Economic Review*, February 16, 1979, p. 29.
76. Z. Brzezinski, 1983, p. 25. See also: *The New York Times*, February 4, 1979, p. 19.
77. For Carter's position on the implications of Sino-American normalization see: R.L. Garthoff, 1994, p. 684.
78. Z. Brzezinski, 1983, p. 409.
79. Letter from Carter to Deng Xiaoping, January 30, 1979, Brzezinski Collection Geographic Files, Box 9, File: China-President's Meeting with Deng Xiaoping, CPL. See Appendix 4 for the full text of this letter.
80. Z. Brzezinski, 1983, p. 410.
81. J. Carter, 1982, pp. 208–9.
82. Author's correspondence with Z. Brzezinski, February 5, 2002.
83. Luu Van Loi also blamed Congress for supporting the Chinese in their decision to invade Vietnam—a doubtful point which may be justified by Deng's declarations to Congress (Luu Van Loi, 2002, p. 74).
84. *Far Eastern Economic Review*, February 9, 1979, p. 11.
85. *Peking Review*, February 9, 1979, p. 10.
86. *The New York Times*, January 31, 1979, p. 1 and *The New York Times*, February 1, 1979, p. 16.
87. *Peking Review*, February 9, 1979, p. 13; *U.S. News & World Report*, February 12, 1979, p. 24. Also: N. Chanda, 1988, p. 354.
88. *Peking Review*, February 16, 1979, p. 17.
89. *The New York Times*, February 1, 1979, p. 17.
90. *The New York Times*, February 3, 1979, p. 3; *The New York Times*, February 4, 1979, p. 5.
91. M. Schaller, 1990, p. 208.
92. *Far Eastern Economic Review*, February 16, 1979, p. 19 and 24.
93. *U.S. News & World Report*, February 12, 1979, p. 26.
94. J. Carter, 1982, p. 202.
95. See: G. Smith, 1986, p. 93.
96. *Department of State Bulletin*, March 1979, p. 11. Also: R.L. Garthoff, 1994, p. 789. See also: Z. Brzezinski, 1983, p. 408.
97. N. Chanda, 1988, p. 351.
98. *Keesing's Contemporary Archives*, 1979, p. 29537.
99. Report from Hanoi *Vietnam News Agency*, February 8, 1979, File: 1–3/1979, SRV-U.S. Foreign Relations, Douglas Pike Collection, UBIA.
100. *Newsweek*, February 19, 1979, p. 40.
101. *Department of State Bulletin*, March 1979, p. 33; *Keesing's Contemporary Archives*, 1979, p. 29537.
102. Luu Van Loi, 2002, p. 74.
103. Z. Brzezinski, 1983, pp. 410–1.
104. *Far Eastern Economic Review*, February 16, 1979, p. 10.
105. *Time*, March 5, 1979, p. 6.
106. *Vietnam Southeast Asia International*, January-February-March 1980, p. 8.
107. *Newsweek*, February 19, 1979, p. 40. See also: Nguyen Manh Hung, "The Sino-Vietnamese Conflict: Power Play Among Communist Neighbors," *Asian Survey*, November 1979, pp. 1037–1052.
108. J. Guillermaz, "La politique américaine de Pékin," *Politique Internationale*, no. 16, summer 1982, pp. 191–206.
109. Report from *Hanoi Domestic Service*, March 1, 1979, File: 1–3/1979, SRV-U.S. Foreign Relations, Douglas Pike Collection, UBIA.
110. Luu Van Loi, 2002, p. 78.
111. S. Lodha, 1997, p. 327.
112. Luu Van Loi, 2002, p. 78.
113. Schedule of February 15–18, 1979, Brzezinski Collection Geographic File, Box 10, CPL. Also: Z. Brzezinski, 1983, p. 412.
114. R.S. Ross, 1988, p. 230.
115. *Asia Yearbook*, 1980, p. 44; Luu Van Loi, 2002, p. 78.
116. Report of the Special Coordination Meeting, February 18, 1979, Brzezinski Collection Geographic Files, Box 10, CPL. Also: Report of the National Security Council Meeting, February 16, 1979, Z. Brzezinski Donated Historical Material, Box 10, CPL. See also: *Time*, February 26, 1979, p. 21.
117. *U.S. News & World Report*, February 5, 1979, p. 27.
118. *Far Eastern Economic Review*, December 22, 1978, p. 18.

Notes—Chapter VI

119. *Newsweek*, March 5, 1979, p. 8; *Asia Yearbook*, 1980, pp. 45.
120. *Keesing's Contemporary Archives*, 1979, p. 29872; *Asia Yearbook*, 1980, p. 319; *Newsweek*, March 19, 1979, p. 33; *Time*, March 5, 1979, p. 6.
121. Memorandum from Oksenberg to Brzezinski, January 16, 1979, NSA Box 86, CPL.
122. Report from *Hanoi International Service*, March 2, 1979, File: 1–3/1979, SRV-U.S. Foreign Relations, Douglas Pike Collection, UBIA. Also: *The New York Times*, February 28, 1979, p. 1; *Time*, February 26, 1979, p. 21; *Newsweek*, March 12, 1979, p. 24.
123. Report of the National Security Council Meeting, February 16, 1979, Z. Brzezinski Donated Historical Material, Box 10, CPL.
124. R.S. Ross, 1988, pp. 215–7.
125. *Peking Review*, February 16, 1979, p. 17.
126. *Asia Yearbook*, 1980, p. 319; *New Times*, March 1979, no. 10, p. 7.
127. Report from Beijing *Xinhua* in English, February 16, 1979, Z. Brzezinski Donated Historical Material, Box 10, CPL.
128. Author's translation from French: "les hégémonistes chinois ... préparent pour l'humanité un piège dangereux comme les nazis dans la deuxième guerre mondiale" (*Việtnam*, June 1979, p. 27).
129. *U.S. News & World Report*, March 12, 1979, p. 28; *Time*, February 26, 1979, p. 21; *Time*, March 5, 1979, p. 6.
130. Author's interview with Bui Tin, October 30, 2002.
131. *Asia Yearbook*, 1980, p. 319.
132. See: Goscha, C., "Le Duan and the Break with China," *Cold War International History Project Bulletin*, no. 12/13, fall/winter 2001, p. 275.
133. Author's interview with Bui Tin, October 30, 2002.
134. *U.S. News & World Report*, March 12, 1979, p. 30.
135. *Asia Yearbook* 1980, p. 45.
136. *Việtnam*, April 1979, p. 1; *Time*, March 12, 1979, p. 14.
137. *Newsweek*, March 12, 1979, p. 27.
138. *Asia Yearbook*, 1980, p. 44.
139. *New Times*, March 1979, no. 10, p. 7.
140. *Newsweek*, March 19, 1979, p. 32; *The Nation*, March 24, 1979, p. 296; *Keesing's Contemporary Archives*, 1979, pp. 29873–4; *Asia Yearbook*, 1980, p. 319.
141. A.J. Dommen, 2001, p. 977.
142. Considering these countries' capacity to sacrifice such large numbers of lives on the altar of national pride one may understand, in hindsight, the Vietnamese failure to appreciate Washington's concern for an amazingly small number of missing servicemen—not to mention that 3 million Vietnamese had either died or been wounded during the American involvement in Vietnam as compared with the 57,000 American death casualties.
143. See: Unattributed, "La leçon vietnamienne," *Việtnam*, May 1979, pp. 2–3; J.N. Wallace, "Now China Learns a Lesson in Vietnam," *U.S. News & World Report*, March 12, 1979, pp. 27–30.
144. See: N. Cousins, "China, Vietnam and the U.S.," *Saturday Review*, April 28, 1979, p. 8.
145. Memorandum from Oksenberg to Brzezinski on Vance's briefing memorandum on U.S. attitude in the light of the Sino-Vietnamese conflict, February 17, 1979, Brzezinski Collection Geographic File, Box 10, CPL.
146. Author's emphasis (*Department of State Bulletin*, March 1979, p. 22).
147. Z. Brzezinski, 1983, p. 411.
148. *Far Eastern Economic Review*, March 2, 1979, pp. 12–3.
149. Report from the Special Coordinating Meeting, February 17, 1979, Brzezinski Collection Geographic File, Box 10, CPL.
150. *Newsweek*, February 26, 1979, p. 29.
151. *Department of State Bulletin*, March 1979, p. 22; *Far Eastern Economic Review*, March 2, 1979, p. 12.
152. *Time*, February 26, 1979, p. 21.
153. *Newsweek*, March 5, 1979, p. 13.
154. Memorandum from Brzezinski to the President, February 17, 1979, Brzezinski Collection Geographic File, Box 10, CPL.
155. Letter from Representative Solarz to Carter, February 22, 1979, WHCF, Box CO-66, CPL.
156. *Newsweek*, March 5, 1979, p. 8.
157. Letter from Carter to Brezhnev, February 17, 1979, Z. Brzezinski Donated Historical Material, Box 10, CPL.
158. Letter from Brezhnev to Carter translated by Brzezinski, February 18, 1979, Z. Brzezinski Donated Historical Material, Box 10, CPL.
159. Report from Moscow *Radio Peace and Progress* in Mandarin to China, February 19, 1979, Brzezinski Collection Geographical File, Box 10, CPL.
160. *Time*, March 5, 1979, p. 12.
161. Report from *Hanoi Domestic Service* dated March 1, 1979 and an analysis of Hanoi's press statements dated March 1979, File: 1–3/1979, SRV-U.S. Foreign Relations, Douglas Pike Collection, UBIA.
162. *Keesing's Contemporary Archives*, 1979, p. 29872.
163. Cable from the White House to London, Paris and Berlin, February 18, 1979, Brzezinski Collection Geographic File, Box 10, CPL and Wire from the White House to Prime Minister Ohira, February 18, 1979, Z. Brzezinski Donated Historical Material, Box 10, CPL.
164. *The New York Times*, February 23, 1979, p. 3.
165. State Department statement, February 22, 1979, File: 1–3/1979, SRV-U.S. Foreign Relations, Douglas Pike Collection, UBIA and Unreferenced cable on the approved text for the American statement at the U.N., February 20, 1979, File: 1–3/1978, SRV-U.S. Foreign Relations, Douglas Pike Collection, UBIA. Also: *Department of State Bulletin*, June 1979, p. 63.
166. Report of the Special Coordination Committee Meeting, February 17, 1979, Brzezinski Collection Geographic File, Box 10, CPL.
167. Cable from the U.S.U.N. to U.S. embassies abroad, February 27 (?), 1979, File: 1–3/1979, SRV-U.S. Foreign Relations, Douglas Pike Collection, UBIA.
168. Report from *Hanoi Domestic Service*, March 1, 1979, File: 1–3/1979, SRV-U.S. Foreign Relations, Douglas Pike Collection, UBIA.
169. *Keesing's Contemporary Archives*, 1979, pp. 29872–3.
170. *Ibid.*, p. 29872.
171. *U.S. News & World Report*, March 12, 1979, p. 27.
172. Report from *Hanoi Domestic Service*, March 1, 1979, File: 1–3/1979, SRV-U.S. Foreign Relations, Douglas Pike Collection, UBIA.
173. Memorandum from Oksenberg and Odom to Brzezinski, February 19, 1979, Z. Brzezinski Donated Historical Material, Box 10, CPL.
174. *Keesing's Contemporary Archives*, 1979, p. 29872.
175. Z. Brzezinski, 1986, p. 414.
176. *Newsweek*, March 12, 1979, p. 23.
177. Report from *Hanoi International Service*, March 2, 1979, File: 1–3/1979, SRV-U.S. Foreign Relations, Douglas Pike Collection, UBIA.
178. *The New York Times*, February 28, 1979, p. 4.
179. *Time*, March 5, 1979, p. 6.
180. *The Nation*, March 24, 1979, pp. 295–6; *Newsweek*, February 26, 1979, p. 28.
181. N. Regaud, 1992, p. 51.
182. W.J. Duiker, 1989, p. 189.
183. *Newsweek*, March 12, 1979, p. 22; *Keesing's Contemporary Archives*, 1979, p. 29872; *Asia Yearbook*, 1980, p. 319.
184. J. Mann, 1999, p. 100; N. Regaud, 1992, p. 51.
185. Z. Brzezinski, 1983, p. 414.
186. Min Chen, 1992, p. 154.

187. *The Nation*, February 17, 1979, p. 163; *Asian Survey*, August 1979, p. 804. Also: Min Chen, 1992, p. 151.
188. S.W. Simon, "Kampuchea: Vietnam's Vietnam," *Current History*, December 1979, pp. 197–8 and 221–3. Also: Ton That Thien, 1989, p. 155; *Congressional Quarterly Weekly Report*, March 3, 1979, p. 352.
189. J. Mann, 1999, p. 100.

Conclusion

1. This piece of information was reported by a Vietnamese diplomat interviewed for the writing of this thesis but who prefers to remain unnamed.
2. Author's telephone interview with John McAuliff, March 15, 2002.
3. H.B. Franklin, 1992, p. 49.
4. K.A. Hass, 1998, p. 113.
5. N. Chanda, 1988, pp. 152–3; E. Becker, 1998, pp. 383–4.
6. V. Funnell in: M. Light, 1993, p. 89; S.P. Heder in: D.W.P. Elliott, 1982, pp 51–6; G. Porter in: D.W.P. Elliott, 1982, pp. 97–8; W.J. Duiker, 1986, pp. 69, 73–4; E. Becker, 1998, p. 309; S.J. Morris, 1999, pp. 100–9; W.J. Duiker, 1989, pp. 160–3.
7. V. Funnell in: M. Light, 1993, p. 90.
8. J. Dumbrell, 1995, p. 198; J. Rosati, 1987, pp. 59–63 and 75; O.A. Westad, 1997, p. 21; D.R. Jackson, 2002, pp. 152–8.
9. R.L. Garthoff, 1994, pp. 636–40.
10. S. Hurst, 1996, p. 3.
11. J. Dumbrell, 1995, p. 196.
12. R.S. McNamara, J.G. Blight, R.K. Brigham, 1999, pp. 302, 310–1, 376–7 and 392.
13. S.J. Morris, 1999, pp. 215–6.
14. See: D. Reynolds, "The Origins of the Cold War: The European Dimensions, 1944–1951," *Historical Review*, vol. 28, no. 2, June 1985, pp. 497–515. Also: M.P. Leffler and D.S. Painter, 1994, pp. 125–198.
15. P. Langlet and Quach Thanh Tâm, 2001, p. 48.
16. H.B. Franklin's analysis of this phenomenon, in which he labels MIA "Mythmaking In America," is an excellent study explaining the political benefits of maintaining such a myth (H.B. Franklin, 1992, p. 138).
17. K.A. Hass, 1998, p. 105.
18. A.R. Isaacs, 1997, p. 174.

Appendix 1

1. Message from the President of the United States to the Prime Minister of the Democratic Republic of Vietnam 1 February 1973, File: Vietnam (1), National Security Adviser: Presidential Country Files for East Asian and the Pacific, Box 18, FPL.

Appendix 2

1. Message from the President of the United States to the Prime Minister of the Democratic Republic of Vietnam 1 February 1973, File: Vietnam (1), National Security Adviser: Presidential Country Files for East Asian and the Pacific, Box 18, FPL.

Appendix 3

1. The texts of these notes were found in: Document dated 14 September 1976, "Foreign Ministry Spokesman reveals U.S.-SRV Notes," File: 4/1975, SRV-U.S. Foreign Relations, Douglas Pike Collection, UBIA.

Appendix 4

1. Letter from Jimmy Carter to Deng Xiaoping, 30 January 1979, File: China-President's Meeting with Deng Xiaoping, Brzezinski Donated Material, Geographical File, Box 9, CPL.

BIBLIOGRAPHY

Primary Sources

Archival Material

—UNITED STATES OF AMERICA:

Carter Presidential Library (Atlanta, Georgia):
- Brzezinski Collection Geographic Files
- Country Files (Vietnam: CO-17 and CO-66)
- Name File—C. Vance
- Name File—Montgomery
- NSA Brzezinski Files
- NSA Staff Material Far East
- White House Central Files
- Z. Brzezinski Donated Historical Material

Ford Presidential Library (Ann Arbor, Michigan):
- Congressional Relations Office Loen and Leppert Files
- Counsel to the President Philip Buchen Files: 1974–1977
- National Security Adviser: Kissinger-Scowcroft West Wing Office Files: 1969–1977
- National Security Adviser: Memoranda of Conversations; 1973–1977
- National Security Adviser: Presidential Country Files for East Asia and the Pacific
- National Security Adviser: Presidential Subject Files: 1974–1977
- National Security Adviser: NSC East Asian and Pacific Affairs Staff Files: (1969)1973–1976
- National Security Adviser Staff Assistant John K. Metheny Files: 1969–1976
- Nessen Subject Files: 1974–1977
- NSC Information Liaison with Commissions and Committees Files: 1975–1976
- NSC Institutional Files: Selected Documents (1973)1974–1977
- President Ford Committee Records: 1975–1976

United States of America Library of Congress (Washington D.C.):
- Microfiche collection of recently declassified material

United States of America National Archives I and II (Washington D.C.):
- Computerized CIA Collection: Record Group 263
- Department of State Collection: Record Group 273

University of California, Berkeley, Indochina Archives (Berkeley, California):
- Douglas Pike Collection: 1975–1979

—FRANCE:

Ministère des Affaires Etrangères (Paris):
- Asie-Océanie: Vietnam Conflit 1960–1975

Archives d'Histoire Contemporaine, Centre d'histoire de l'Europe du vingtième siècle (Paris):
- Fonds Jean Sainteny (Vietnam 1961–1973)

U.S. Congressional Reports and Hearings

Committee on Foreign Relations. "Hearing before the Committee on Foreign Relations on Accounting for U.S. Prisoners of War and Missing in Action in Southeast Asia." U.S. Senate, 93rd Congress, 2nd session, January 28, 1974. Washington D.C.: U.S. Government Printing Office, 1974.

Committee on Foreign Relations. "Nomination of Hon. Andrew Young as U.S. Representative to the U.N.," Hearing before the Committee on Foreign Relations, U.S. Senate, 95th Congress, 1st session, January 25, 1977. Washington D.C.: U.S. Government Printing Office, 1977.

Committee on Foreign Relations. "Vance Nomination." Hearing before the Committee on Foreign Relations on Nomination of Hon. Cyrus R. Vance to be Secretary of State, U.S. Senate, 95th Congress, 1st session, January 11, 1977. Washington D.C.: U.S. Government Printing Office, 1977.

Committee on International Relations. "Export Licensing of Private Humanitarian Assistance to Vietnam." Hearing before the Subcommittee on International Trade and Commerce, House of Representatives, 94th Congress, 1st session, September 9, 1975. Washington D.C.: U.S. Government Printing Office, 1975.

Committee on International Relations. "Foreign Assistance Legislation for Fiscal Year 1979 (Part 6): Economic and Security Assistance in Asia and the Pacific." Hearings before the Subcommittee on Asian and Pacific Affairs, House of Representatives, 95th Congress, 2nd session, March 7, 9, 14, 16, 21 and 22, 1978. Washington D.C.: U.S. Government Printing Office, 1978.

Committee on International Relations. Hearings before the Subcommittee on Asian and Pacific Affairs. House of Representatives, 95th Congress, 1st session, July 19, 1977. Washington D.C.: U.S. Government Printing Office, 1979.

Committee on International Relations. "United States Embargo of Trade with South Vietnam and Cambodia. Hearing before the Subcommittee on International Trade and Commerce. House of Representatives, 94th Congress, 1st session, June 4, 1975. Washington D.C.: U.S. Government Printing Office, 1975.

Committee on International Relations. "United States-Soviet Union-China: the Great Power Triangle." Hearings before the Subcommittee on Future Foreign Policy Research and Development, House of Representatives, 94th Congress, Part I, March 10, 1976. Washington D.C.: U.S. Government Printing Office, 1976.

Committee on International Relations. "U.S. Trade Embargo of Vietnam: Church Views." Hearing before the Subcommittee on International Trade and Commerce on HR 9503 amending the Trading with the Enemy Act to Repeal the Embargo on U.S. Trade with North and South Vietnam, House of Representatives, 94th Congress, 1st session, November 17, 1975. Washington D.C.: U.S. Government Printing Office, 1976.

Committee on Veterans' Affairs. "Americans Missing in Southeast Asia." Hearings before the House Select Committee on Missing Persons in Southeast Asia, 94th Congress, 2nd session, Part 5, June 17, 25; July 21 and September 21, 1976. Washington D.C.: U.S. Government Printing Office, 1976.

Committee on Veterans' Affairs. "Americans Missing in Southeast Asia." U.S. House of Representatives, 100th Congress. Washington D.C.: U.S. Government Printing Office, 1988.

Report of the Special Committee on Southeast Asia, House of Representatives, 95th Congress, 2nd session, September 7, 1978. Washington D.C.: U.S. Government Printing Office, 1978.

Senator G. McGovern. "Vietnam: 1976: A report by Senator George McGovern to the Committee on Foreign Relations United States Senate." March 1976. Washington D.C.: U.S. Government Printing Office, 1976.

Official Publications

Congressional Digest
Congressional Quarterly Weekly Report
Congressional Record
Department of State Bulletin
Public Papers of the Presidents of the United States: Gerald Ford. Washington, D.C., United States Government Printing Office, 1975–1976.
Public Papers of the Presidents of the United States: Jimmy Carter. Washington, D.C., United States Government Printing Office, 1977–1979.
UN Chronicle
U.S. Congress Committee Reports

Periodicals (extensive or sporadic use)*

Asia Yearbook (Hong-Kong)
Beijing Review (China)
Current (U.S.A.)
Current History (U.S.A.)
Far Eastern Economic Review (Hong-Kong)
Keesing's Contemporary Archives (U.S.A.)
The Nation (U.S.A.)
National Review (U.S.A.)
New Times (Russia)
The New York Times (U.S.A.)
The New Yorker (U.S.A.)
Newsweek (U.S.A.)†
Peking Review (China)
Saturday Review (U.S.A.)
Time (U.S.A.)‡
U.S. News and World Report (U.S.A.)
Việtnam (Hanoi)
Vietnam Broadsheet (U.K.)
Vietnam Courier (Hanoi)
Vietnam Info (France)
Vietnam International (U.K.)
Vietnam South-East Asia International (U.K.)

Interviews and Correspondence

David Aaron: Deputy Assistant to National Security Affairs to President Carter. Correspondence dated August 23, 2001.

Elizabeth Becker: New York Times journalist and author of When the War Was Over: Cambodia and the Khmer Rouge Revolution (New York: Public Affairs, 1986). Telephone interview on February 8, 2002.

Larry Berman: Professor of American Politics and International Relations at the University of California. Conference in Paris on March 27, 2002, and ongoing correspondence and meetings.

Peter Bourne: Special Assistant to President Carter and liaison officer between the White House and the United Nations. Telephone interview on March 21,

---

*Not all articles used for this book can be listed here. For practical reasons, only the most important ones have been quoted in the bibliography.
†European edition (occasional issues of the American edition have been used, as stipulated in the footnotes).
‡European edition (occasional issues of the American edition have been used, as stipulated in the footnotes).

2002; interviewed in Oxford on February 18, 2003; and ongoing correspondence.

Robert Brigham: Professor of History at Vassar College (New York), currently working on the writing of a book on the Carter Administration and Vietnam. Ongoing correspondence.

Zbigniew Brzezinski: NSC Adviser to President Carter. Correspondence dated February 5, 2002.

Bui Tin: Former North Vietnamese colonel and VCP member who participated in the battle of Dien Bien Phu, the taking of Saigon in 1975 and the invasion of Cambodia in 1979. As a journalist and assistant editor of *Nhan Dan* he witnessed the signing of the Paris Peace Accords and was the only journalist reporting from Phnom Penh in 1979. Interviewed in Paris on October 30, 2002.

Steven R. Ekovich: American Vietnam veteran and former professor at "Ecole Polytechnique" (Paris). He is now a professor in the Department of Politics and International Affairs of The American University of Paris. Interviewed in Paris on April 10, 2001.

Michel Fournié: Son of a French prisoner in Dien Bien Phu, and Director of the Department of Vietnamese Studies at the "Institut National de Langues et Civilisations Orientales de Paris." Interviewed in Cambridge on March 9, 2001.

William Gleysteen: Senior China expert of the State Department in the Carter Administration. Correspondence dated April 22, 2002.

Jean Lacouture: French journalist during the Vietnam War and author of several books on Chinese and Southeast Asian politics. Telephone interview on December 23, 2000.

John McAuliff: Former member of the American Friends Service Committee and current executive director of the Fund for National Reconciliation and Development. Telephone interview on March 15, 2002.

Gillespie "Sonny" Montgomery: U.S. Congressman from 1967–1997 and head of the House Select Committee on Missing Persons in Southeast Asia. Telephone interview on February 8, 2002, and ongoing correspondence.

General William Odom: Military advisor to the NSC during the Carter Administration. Telephone interview on June 10, 2002.

Mrs. Pham Thi Thieu Tu: Member of the French association "Franternité Europe-Asie" and, formerly, of "SudestAsie" a publishing company for the French Vietnamese community. Interviewed in Paris on November 22, 2001.

Ken Quinn: Special Assistant to the Secretary for Southeast Asian and Pacific Affairs Richard Holbrooke from January 1977 to August-September 1978. Telephone interview on April 1, 2002.

Alain Ruscio: French historian who specializes in Vietnam, and who lived in Hanoi from 1978 to 1980 and met Nguyen Co Thach on several occasions. Interviewed in Paris on February 14, 2002.

Judith Stowe: Former British Foreign Office staff member and BBC correspondent for Southeast Asia and Vietnam from 1972 to 1994. Interviewed in London on October 26, 2002, January 11, 2003, and ongoing correspondence and meetings.

A Senior Vietnamese diplomat interviewed for the writing of original thesis but who prefers to remain unnamed. Interviewed in January 2002.

Memoirs and Autobiographies

Brown, Frederick Z. *Second Chance: The United States and Indochina in the 1990's*. New York: Council on Foreign Relations Press, 1989.

Brzezinski, Zbigniew. *Power and Principle: Memoirs of the National Security Advisor 1977–1981*. London: Weidenfeld and Nicolson, 1983.

Bui Tin. *Following Ho Chi Minh: Memoirs of a North Vietnamese Colonel*. Honolulu: University of Hawaii Press, 1999.

Carter, Jimmy E. *Keeping Faith: Memoirs of a President*. London: Collins, 1982.

Crowley, Monica. *Nixon in Winter: His Final Revelations About Diplomacy, Watergate, and Life out of the Arena*. New York: Random House, 1998.

Ford, Gerald R. *A Time To Heal: The Autobiography of Gerald R. Ford*. New York: Harper & Row Publishers, 1979.

Hoang Van Hoan. *A Drop in the Ocean: Hoang Van Hoan's Revolutionary Reminiscences*. Beijing: Foreign Languages Press, 1988.

Jordan, Hamilton. *Crisis: The Last Year of the Carter Presidency*. New York: Putnam's, 1982.

Khieu Samphan. *L'Histoire récente du Cambodge et mes prises de position*. Paris: L'Harmattan, 2004.

Kissinger, Henry. *Ending the Vietnam War: A History of America's Involvement in and Extrication from the Vietnam War*. New York: Simon & Schuster, 2003.

Kissinger, Henry. *The White House Years*. London: Weidenfeld and Nicolson, 1979.

Kissinger, Henry. *Years of Renewal*. London: Weidenfeld and Nicolson, 1999.

Kissinger, Henry. *Years of Upheaval*. London, Weidenfeld and Nicolson, 1982.

Lacouture, Jean and Lacouture, Simone. *Vietnam: Voyage à travers une victoire*. Paris: Seuil, 1976.

Moynihan, Daniel P. and Weaver, Suzanne. *A Dangerous Place*. Boston: The Atlantic Monthly Press, 1978.

Sihanouk, Norodom. *War and Hope: The Case for Cambodia*. New York: Pantheon Books, 1980.

Snepp, Frank W. *Decent Interval: An Insider's Account of Saigon's Indecent End Told by the CIA's Chief Strategy Analyst in Vietnam*. New York: Random House, 1978.

Sokha, Boun. *Cambodge: La Massue de l'Angkar*. Collection: Les Droits de l'Homme. Paris: Atelier Marcel Jullian, 1979.

Vance, Cyrus. *Hard Choices—Critical Years in American Foreign Policy*. New York: Simon and Schuster, 1983.

Secondary Sources

Articles and Unpublished Sources*

Amnesty International. "Kampuchea: Political Imprisonment and Torture." London: Amnesty International Publications, 1987.

Amnesty International. "Political Imprisonment in the People's Republic of China: An Amnesty International Report." London: Amnesty International Publications, 1978.

Volume numbers are quoted in arabic numerals or roman, as they originally appeared in the publications.

Amnesty International. "Viet Nam: 'Renovation' (Doi Moi), the Law and Human Rights in the 1980s." London: Amnesty International Publications, 1990.

"Asian Equations." *America*, March 17, 1979.

Bell, Martin W. "'Healing the Wounds': U.S.-Vietnamese Diplomacy After the Fall of Saigon." Discussion paper no. 3. Leicester: Center for the Study of Diplomacy, Diplomatic Studies Programme, University of Leicester Press, 1995.

Berger, Marilyn. "Vance and Brzezinski: Peaceful Coexistence or Guerrilla War?" *The New York Times Magazine*, February 13, 1977.

Bradley, Mark, and Robert K. Brigham. "Vietnamese Archives and Scholarship on the Cold War Period: Two Reports." Cold War International History Project, Working Paper no. 7, September 1993.

Brown, MacAlister, and Joseph J. Zasloff. "Dependency in Laos." *Current History*, December 1978, vol. 75, no. 442.

Brown, MacAlister, and Joseph J. Zasloff. "Laos in 1975: People's Democratic Republic Revolution—Lao Style." *Asian Survey*, vol. XVI, no. 2, February 1976.

Buchan, Alistair. "The Indochina War and World Politics." *Foreign Affairs*, vol. 53, no. 4, July 1975.

Burnham, James. "Breaching the Great Wall: The Protracted Conflict." *National Review*, June 23, 1978.

Carter, Jimmy E., and Zbigniew Brzezinski. "Letters to the Editor: Jimmy Carter and Zbigniew Brzezinski correct history ..." *Foreign Affairs*, vol. 78, no. 6, November/December 1999.

"Carter's Big Spy Case." *The Nation*, February 25, 1978.

"Carter's Plan to Pressure Russia." *Business Week*, June 12, 1978.

Chanda, Nayan. "China and Cambodia: In the Mirror of History." *Asia-Pacific Review*, November 2002.

Chang, Parris H. "The Passing of the Maoist Era." *Asian Survey*, vol. XVI, no. 11, November 1976.

"The China Card." *National Review*, January 5, 1979.

Chomsky, Noam. "Endgame: The Tactics of Peace in Vietnam." *Ramparts*, April 1973.

Clubb, Edmund. "China Drops a Stone on Its Own Foot." *The Nation*, March 24, 1979.

Conboy, Kenneth J. "The U.S. and Vietnam: Twelve Years After the War." Washington D.C.: Heritage Foundation, 1987.

Cousins, Norman. "China, Vietnam and the U.S." *Saturday Review*, April 28, 1979.

Darling, Frank C. "Political Functions of the United States Embassy in Thailand." *Asian Survey*, vol. XVIII, no. 1, November 1978.

Domes, Jürgen. "China in 1976: Tremors of Transition." *Asian Survey*, vol. XVII, no. 1, January 1977.

Domes, Jürgen. "China in 1977: Reversal of Verdict." *Asian Survey*, vol. XVIII, no. 1, January 1978.

Donnell, John C. "South Vietnam in 1975: The Year of Communist Victory." *Asian Survey*, vol. XVI, no. 1, January 1976.

Duiker, William J. "Ideology and Nation-Building in the Democratic Republic of Vietnam." *Asian Survey*, vol. XVII, no. 5, May 1977.

Fairbank, John K. "The Consequences of Cultural Ignorance." *Current*, no. 174, July-August 1975.

"Fallen Domino." *The Nation*, January 20, 1979.

Féray, Pierre-Richard. "Nouvelles problématiques d'une histoire devenue 'sans modèle.'" Paris: *Vietnam Contemporain*, 1975.

Fifield, Russell H. "The Third Years War in Indochina: A Conceptual Framework." *Asian Survey*, vol. XVII, no. 9, September 1977.

"For Deng—Coke and Hegemony." *The Nation*, February 17, 1979.

Ghebhart, Alexander O. "Soviet and U.S. Interests in the Indian Ocean." *Asian Survey*, vol. XV, no. 8, August 1975.

Glaubitz, Joachim. "Anti-Hegemony Formulas in Chinese Foreign Policy." *Asian Survey*, vol. XVI, no. 2, February 1976.

Goscha, Christopher. "Le Duan and the Break with China." *Cold War International History Project Bulletin*, nos. 12/13, fall/winter 2001.

Grinter, Laurence E. "How They Lost: Doctrines, Strategies and Outcomes of the Vietnam War." *Asian Survey*, vol. XV, no. 12, December 1975.

Guillermaz, Jacques. "La Politique américaine de Pékin." *Politique Internationale*, no. 16, summer 1982.

Haselkorn, Avigdor. "Impact of the Sino-Japanese Treaty on the Soviet Security Strategy." *Asian Survey*, vol. XIX, no. 6, June 1979.

Hiebert, Murray. "Playing Politics with the MIAs: Both sides have used the MIA issue as a negotiating tool." *Southeast Asia Chronicle*, August 1982.

Hoang Van Hoan. "Distortion of Facts About Militant Friendship Between Viet Nam and China Is Impermissible." *Beijing Review*, December 7, 1979.

Horelick, Arnold L. "Soviet Policy Dilemmas in Asia." *Asian Survey*, vol. XVII, no. 6, June 1977.

Horn, Robert C. "China and Russia in 1977: Maoism Without Mao." *Asian Survey*, vol. XVII, no. 10, October 1977.

Horn, Robert C. "Soviet Influence in Southeast Asia: Opportunities and Obstacles." *Asian Survey*, vol. XV, no. 8, August 1975.

"How Hanoi's Cadaver Diplomacy Shames the U.S." *Business Week*, August 27, 1978.

"How the Hanoi-Peking Face-Off Endangers the U.S." *Business Week*, June 19, 1978.

Jackson, Donna R. "The Carter Administration and the Horn of Africa." (unpublished PhD. thesis, University of Cambridge, 2002).

Jackson, Karl D. "Cambodia in 1977: Gone to Pot." *Asian Survey*, vol. XVIII, no. 1, January 1978.

Jackson, Karl D. "Cambodia 1978: War, Pillage, and Purge in Democratic Kampuchea." *Asian Survey*, vol. XIX, no. 1, January 1979.

Jacobsen, Carl G. "Sino-Soviet Crisis in Perspective." *Current History*, vol. 77, no. 450, October 1979.

Jarvis, Helen. "Trials and Tribulations: The Latest Twists in the Long Quest for Justice for the Cambodian Genocide." *Critical Asian Studies*, December 2002.

Jencks, Harlan W. "China's 'Punitive' War on Vietnam: A Military Assessment." *Asian Survey*, vol. XIX, no. 8, August 1979.

Jespersen, Christopher. "The Bitter End and the Lost Chance in Vietnam: Congress, the Ford Administration, and the Battle Over Vietnam, 1975–76." *Diplomatic History*, vol. 24, no. 2, spring 2000.

Kallgren, Joyce K. "China 1979: The New Long March." *Asian Survey*, vol. XIX, no. 1, January 1979.

Kiernan, Ben. "Bringing the Khmer Rouge to Justice." *Human Rights Review*, April-June 2000.

Kirsch Leighton, Marian. "Perspectives on the Vietnam-Cambodian Border Conflict." *Asian Survey*, vol. XVIII, no. 5, May 1978.

Kolko, Gabriel. "Nixon's Vietnam Strategy." *Commonwealth*, March 23, 1973.

"The Korean Connection." *The Nation*, October 4, 1975.

Le Hoang Trong. "Survival and Self-Reliance: A Vietnamese Viewpoint." *Asian Survey*, vol. XV, no. 4, April 1975.

Levine, Steven I. "China Policy During Carter's Year One." *Asian Survey*, vol. XVIII, no. 5, May 1978.

"The Limits to Brzezinski's 'China Card.'" *Business Week*, August 14, 1978.

Lo, Shih-Fu. "L'éxode des réfugiés du Vietnam: ses causes et ses effets." Chapitre Chine et la Ligue Anticommuniste des Peuples d'Asie (Republique of China: *La Ligue Anticommuniste Mondiale*, December 1980).

Luttwak, Edward N. "Against the China Card." *Commentary*, vol. 66, no. 4, October 1978.

McGovern, George. "A Friendly Visit: Peacetime in Vietnam." *The Nation*, July 3, 1976.

Ménétrey-Monchau, Cécile. "The *Mayaguez* Incident as an Epilogue to the Vietnam War and its Reflection of the Post-Vietnam Political Equilibrium in Southeast Asia." *Cold War History*, vol. 5, no. 3, August 2005.

"MIA: The Heartless Ploy." *The Nation*, September 25, 1976.

"Monsters in our Footsteps." *The Nation*, April 2, 1977.

Moody, Peter R., Jr. "The Fall of the Gang of Four: Background Notes on the Chinese Counterrevolution." *Asian Survey*, vol. XVII, no. 8, August 1977.

Morgenthau, Hans J. "Gambling on China: Should We Play the Chinese Card?" *Current History*, no. 205, September 1978.

"The Morning After the China Thaw." *Business Week*, February 12, 1979.

Morris, Stephen J. "The Soviet-Chinese-Vietnamese Triangle in the 1970's: The View from Moscow." Woodrow Wilson Center, Cold War International History Project, Working Paper no. 25, April 1999. Available online at http://wwics.si.edu/topics/pubs/ACFB2E.pdf.

Musil, Robert K. "The Politics of Cynicism: Manipulating the MIAs." *The Nation*, October 9, 1976.

Nash, Jesse W. "Vietnamese values: Confucian, Catholic, American." PhD dissertation (Anthropology), UMI Dissertation Information Service (Ann Arbor), 1992.

Niehaus, Marjorie. "Vietnam 1978: The Elusive Peace." *Asian Survey*, vol. XIX, no. 1, January 1979.

Nguyen Manh Hung. "The Sino-Vietnamese Conflict: Power Play Among Communist Neighbors." *Asian Survey*, vol. XIX, no. 11, November 1979.

"Observer from Vietnam: Nguyen Co Thach." *New Yorker*, October 23, 1978.

Oksenberg, Michael. "A Decade of Sino-American Relations." *Foreign Affairs*, fall 1982, vol. 61, no. 1.

Osborne, John. "White House Watch: Carter and China." *New Republic*, January 6, 1979.

Pike, Douglas. "The USSR and Vietnam: Into the Swamp." *Asian Survey*, vol. XIX, no. 12, December 1979.

Pike, Douglas. "Vietnam in 1977: More of the Same." *Asian Survey*, vol. XVIII, no. 1, January 1978.

Porter, Gareth. "Asia's New Cold War." *The Nation*, September 9, 1978.

Porter, Gareth. "Kissinger's Double-Cross for 'Peace': The Broken Promise to Hanoi." *The Nation*, April 30, 1977.

Porter, Gareth. "The Sino-Vietnamese Conflict in Southeast Asia." *Current History*, vol. 75, no. 442, (December 1978).

Porter, Gareth. "U.S. and Vietnam—The Missed Chance." *The Nation*, October 20, 1979.

Porter, Gareth. "Why Vietnam Invaded Cambodia." *The Nation*, June 9, 1979.

Quang Loi, Le Minh Nghia, and Vu Phi Hoang. "Les Archipels Hoàng Sa et Trùong Sa (Paracels et Spratly), Dossier II." Hanoi: *Le Courrier du Vietnam*, 1984.

Quinn, Kenneth M. "Cambodia 1976: Internal Consolidation and External Expansion." *Asian Survey*, vol. XVII, no. 1, January 1977.

Ravenal, Earl C. "Consequences of the End Game in Vietnam." *Foreign Affairs*, vol. 53, no. 4, July 1975.

"Rencontre avec Philippe Devillers de retour du Vietnam et du Cambodge." *Sudestasie Information/* Supplement to *Viet-nam Info* no. 18, June 1979.

Reynolds, David. "The Origins of the Cold War: The European Dimensions, 1944–1951." *Historical Review*, vol. 28, no. 2, June 1985.

Shaplen, Robert. "Southeast Asia—Before and After." *Foreign Affairs*, vol. 53, no. 3, April 1975.

Silverman, Jerry M. "The Domino Theory: Alternatives to a Self-Fulfilling Prophecy." *Asian Survey*, vol. XV, no. 11, November 1975.

Simon, Sheldon W. "Cambodia: Barbarism in a Small State Under Siege." *Current History*, vol. 75, no. 442, December 1978.

Simon, Sheldon W. "China, Vietnam and ASEAN: The Politics of Polarization." *Asian Survey*, vol. XIX, no. 12, December 1979.

Simon, Sheldon W. "Kampuchea: Vietnam's Vietnam." *Current History*, vol. 77, no. 452, December 1979.

Simon, Sheldon W. "Peking and Indochina: The Perplexity of Victory." *Asian Survey*, vol. XVI, no. 5, May 1976.

"That China Card." *America*, November 18, 1978.

Thayer, Carlyle A. "North Vietnam in 1975: National Liberation, Reunification and Socialist Construction." *Asian Survey*, vol. XVI, no. 1, January 1976.

"The Truth About Vietnam-China Relations Over the Last Thirty Years." Vol. 15, nos. 11/79. Hanoi: *Vietnam Courrier*, November 1979.

Tyler, Patrick. "The (Ab)normalization of U.S.-Chinese Relations." *Foreign Affairs*, September/ October 1999, vol. 78, no. 5.

Van der Kroef, Justus M. "Cambodia: From 'Democratic Kampuchea' to 'People's Republic.'" *Asian Survey*, vol. XIX, no. 8, August 1979.

"Vietnam Round-Up." *National Review*, August 18, 1978.

Wall, James M. "Moving Toward U.S.-Vietnam Dialogue." *The Christian Century*, April 7, 1976.

Wall, James M. "Playing Games at the U.N." *The Christian Century*, December 1, 1976.

Wall, James M. "Shaping Public Perceptions." *The Christian Century*, May 26, 1976.

Westad, Odd A., Jian Chen, Stein Tonneson, Nguyen Vu Tungand and James G. Hershberg. "77 Conversations Between Chinese and Foreign Leaders on the Wars in Indochina, 1964–1977." Cold War International History Project, Working Paper no. 22, May 1998.

"What Right to Judge?" *The Nation*, February 12, 1977.

Yun Shui. "An Account of Chinese Diplomats Accompanying the Government of Democratic Kampuchea's Move to the Cardamom Mountains." *Critical Asian Studies,* December 2002.

Zagoria, Donald S. "The Soviet Quandary in Asia." *Foreign Affairs,* vol. 56, no. 2, January 1978.

Books

Abernathy, Glenn M., Dilys M. Hill, and Phil Williams. *The Carter Years: The President and Policy Making.* London: Frances Pinter, 1984.

Adam, Elaine P., ed. *American Foreign Relations: 1976: A Documentary Record.* A Council on Foreign Relations Book. New York: New York University Press, 1978.

Adam, Elaine P., ed. *American Foreign Relations: 1977: A Documentary Record.* A Council on Foreign Relations Book. New York: New York University Press, 1979. (a)

Adam, Elaine P., ed. *American Foreign Relations: 1978: A Documentary Record.* A Council on Foreign Relations Book. New York: New York University Press, 1979. (b)

Adam, Elaine P., and Richard P. Stebbins, eds. *American Foreign Relations: 1975: A Documentary Record.* A Council on Foreign Relations Book. New York: New York University Press, 1977.

Allin, Dana H. *Cold War Illusions: America, Europe and Soviet Power, 1969–1989.* Basingstoke: Macmillan, 1995.

Ambrose, Stephen E., and Douglas G. Brinkley. *Rise to Globalism: American Foreign Policy Since 1938.* 8th ed. New York: Penguin Books, 1997.

Amter, Joseph A. *Vietnam Verdict: A Citizen's History.* New York: Continuum, 1984.

Asselin, Pierre. *A Bitter Peace: Washington, Hanoi and the Making of the Paris Agreement.* Chapel Hill: University of North Carolina Press, 2002.

Bagby, Wesley M. *America's International Relations Since World War I.* Oxford: Oxford University Press, 1999.

Becker, Elizabeth. *When the War Was Over: Cambodia and the Khmer Rouge Revolution.* 2nd ed. New York: Public Affairs, 1998.

Beresford, Melanie. *Vietnam: Politics, Economics and Society.* London: Pinter, 1988.

Berman, Larry. *No Peace, No Honor: Nixon, Kissinger, and Betrayal in Vietnam.* New York: The Free Press, 2001.

Bernkopf Tucker, Nancy. *Taiwan, Hong Kong, and the United States, 1945–1992: Uncertain Friendships.* New York: Twayne Publishers, 1994.

Bill, James A. *George Ball: Behind the Scenes in U.S. Foreign Policy.* London: Yale University Press, 1997.

Bitzer, Lloyd, and Theodore Rueter. *Carter vs. Ford: The Counterfeit Debates of 1976.* Madison: The University of Wisconsin Press, 1980.

Bizot, François. *Le Portail.* Paris: La Table Ronde, 2000.

Blanchard, Michel. *Vietnam-Cambodge: Une frontière contestée.* Points sur l'Asie. Paris: L'Harmattan, 1999.

Blanchard, William H. *Neocolonialism American Style: 1960–2000.* London: Greenwood Press, 1996.

Bourne, Peter G. *Jimmy Carter: A Comprehensive Biography from Plains to Postpresidency.* New York: Scribner, 1997.

Braestrup, Peter. *Vietnam as History: Ten Years After the Paris Peace Accords.* A Wilson Center Conference Report. Washington D.C.: University Press of America, 1984.

Brinkley, Douglas G. *The Unfinished Presidency: Jimmy Carter's Journey Beyond the White House.* New York: Viking, 1998.

Brown, Michael E., Owen R. Cote, Sean M. Lynn-Jones, and Steven E. Miller. *America's Strategic Choices.* London: The MIT Press, 1997.

Bundy, William. *A Tangled Web: The Making of Foreign Policy in the Nixon Presidency.* London: I.B. Tauris, 1998.

Burchett, Wilfred. *The China-Cambodia-Vietnam Triangle.* Chicago: Vanguard Books, 1981.

Burr, William, ed. *The Kissinger Transcripts.* New York: The New York Press, 1999.

Butler, David. *The Fall of Saigon: Scenes From the Sudden End of a Long War.* New York: Simon and Schuster, 1985.

Cahn, Ann H. *Killing Détente: The Right Attacks the CIA.* University Park: Pennsylvania University Press, 1998.

Cawthorne, Nigel. *The Bamboo Cage: The Full Story of the American Servicemen Still Held Hostage in South-East Asia.* London: Leo Cooper Publishers, 1991.

Cecil, Paul F. *Herbicidal Warfare: The Ranch Hand Project in Vietnam.* New York: Praeger, 1986.

Césari, Laurent. *L'Indochine en guerres, 1945–1993.* Paris: Belin, 1995.

Chanda, Nayan. *Brother Enemy: The War After the War.* London: Harcourt Brace Janovich, 1988.

Chandler, David P. *Voices from S-21: Terror and History in Pol Pot's Secret Prison.* Berkeley: University of California Press, 1999.

Chandler, David P., and Ben Kiernan. *Revolution and its Aftermath in Kampuchea: Eight Essays.* Yale University Southeast Asia Studies, Monograph Series No. 25. New Haven: Yale University Press, 1983.

Chang, Pao-Min. *Beijing, Hanoi and the Overseas Chinese.* China Research Monograph no. 24. Berkeley: Center for Chinese Studies, Institute of East Asian Studies, University of California, 1982.

Chang, Pao-Min. *Kampuchea Between China and Vietnam.* 2nd ed. Kent Ridge: Singapore University Press, 1987.

Chang, Tsan-Kuo. *The Press and China Policy: The Illusion of Sino-American Relations: 1950–1984.* The Communication and Information Science Series. Norwood: Ablex Publishing Corporation, 1993.

Chen, Jie. *Ideology in U.S. Foreign Policy: Case Studies in U.S.-China Policy.* London: Praeger, 1992.

Clarke, Duncan L., Daniel B. O'Connor, and Jason D. Ellis. *Send Guns and Money: Security Assistance and U.S. Foreign Policy.* London: Praeger, 1997.

Cobb Jr., William W. *The American Foundation Myth in Vietnam: Reigning Paradigms and Raining Bombs.* Lanham: University Press of America, 1998.

Cohen, Warren I. *America's Response to China: A History of Sino-American Relations.* 4th ed. New York: Columbia University Press, 2000.

Cohen, Warren I. *The Cambridge History of American Foreign Relations: America in the Age of Soviet Power, 1945–1991.* vol. IV, Cambridge: Cambridge University Press, 1993.

Colby, William. *Lost Victory: A Firsthand Account of America's Sixteen-Year Involvement in Vietnam.* Chicago: Contemporary Books, 1989.

Dittmar, Linda, and Gene Michaud. *From Hanoi to Hollywood: The Vietnam War in American Film.* 2nd ed. New Brunswick: Rutgers University Press, 1997.

Dobbs, Charles M. *The United States and East Asia since 1945*. Lampeter: The Edwin Mellen Press, 1990.

Dommen, Arthur J. *The Indochinese Experience of the French and the Americans: Nationalism and Communism in Cambodia, Laos, and Vietnam*. Indianapolis: Indiana University Press, 2001.

Duiker, William J. *China and Vietnam: The Roots of Conflict*. Indochina Research Monographs no. 1. Berkeley: Institute of East Asian Studies, 1986.

Duiker, William J. *The Communist Road to Power in Vietnam*. 2nd ed. Boulder: Westview Press, 1996.

Duiker, William J. *Vietnam: Nation in Revolution*. Westview Profiles, Nations of Contemporary Asia. Boulder: Westview Press, 1983.

Duiker, William J. *Vietnam Since the Fall of Saigon*. Monograph in International Series, Southeast Asia Series no. 56A. Athens: Ohio University Press, 1989.

Dumbrell, John. *American Foreign Policy: Carter to Clinton*. Basingstoke: Macmillan Press Ltd., 1997.

Dumbrell, John. *The Carter Presidency: A Re-evaluation*. 2nd ed. Manchester: Manchester University Press, 1995.

Ehrman, John. *The Rise of Neoconservatism: Intellectual and Foreign Affairs, 1945–1994*. New Haven: Yale University Press, 1995.

Elliott, David W.P., ed. *The Third Indochina Conflict*. Epping: Bowker, 1982.

Engelbert, Thomas, and Christopher Goscha. *Falling Out of Touch: A Study on Vietnamese Communist Policy Towards an Emerging Cambodian Communist Movement, 1930–1975*. Warrnambool: Amazon Press, 1995.

Evans, Grant, and Kelvin Rowley. *Red Brotherhood at War: Vietnam, Cambodia and Laos Since 1975*. 2nd ed. London: Verso, 1990.

Férier, Gilles. *Les Trois Guerres d'Indochine*. Lyon: Presses Universitaires de Lyon, 1993.

Fishlock, Trevor. *The State of America*. London: John Murray Publishers, 1986.

Franklin, Bruce H. *MIA or Mythmaking in America: How and Why Belief in Live POWs Has Possessed a Nation*. New York: Lawrence Hill Books, 1992.

Frey-Wouters, Ellen, and Robert S. Laufer. *Legacy of a War: The American Soldier in Vietnam*. London: M.E. Scharpe, 1986.

Gaiduk, Ilya V. *The Soviet Union and the Vietnam War*. Chicago: Ivan R. Dee, 1996.

Garthoff, Raymond L. *Détente and Confrontation: American-Soviet Relations from Nixon to Reagan*. 2nd ed. Washington D.C.: The Brookings Institution, 1994.

Garthoff, Raymond L. *The Great Transition: American-Soviet Relations and the End of the Cold War*. Washington D.C.: The Brookings Institution, 1994.

Garver, John W. *The Sino-American Alliance: Nationalist China and American Cold War Strategy in Asia*. London: M.E. Scharpe, 1997.

Gelb, Leslie H., and Richard K. Betts. *The Irony of Vietnam: The System Worked*. Washington D.C.: The Brookings Institution, 1979.

Gilks, Ann. *The Breakdown of the Sino-Vietnamese Alliance, 1970–1979*. China Research Monograph no. 39. Berkeley: Center for Chinese Studies, Institute of East Asian Studies, University of California, 1992.

Greene, Bob. *Homecoming: When the Soldiers Returned from Vietnam*. New York: Putnam's, 1989.

Guiloineau, Jean. *La Chine, l'U.R.S.S et les autres: l'Asie du Sud-Est et le conflit sino-soviétique*. Paris: Plon, 1980.

Hartmann, Robert T. *Palace Politics: An Inside Account of the Ford Years*. New York: McGraw-Hill Book Company, 1980.

Hass, Kristin A. *Carried to the Wall: American Memory and the Vietnam Veterans Memorial*. Berkeley: University of California Press, 1998.

Hellmann, John. *American Myth and the Legacy of Vietnam*. New York: Columbia University Press, 1986.

Herring, George C. *America's Longest War: The United States and Vietnam, 1950–1975*. 2nd ed. Philadelphia: Temple University Press, 1986.

Herring, George C. *The Secret Diplomacy of the Vietnam War: The Negotiating Volumes of the Pentagon Papers*. Austin: University of Texas Press, 1983.

Hess, Gary R. *Vietnam and the United States: Origins and Legacy of War*. Twayne's International History Series no. 7. Boston: Twayne Publishers, 1990.

Hinckley, Barbara. *Less Than Meets the Eye: Foreign Policy Making and the Myth of the Assertive Congress*. Chicago: University of Chicago Press, A Twentieth Century Fund Book, 1994.

Honey, P.J. *Communism in North Vietnam: Its Role in the Sino-Soviet Dispute*. 2nd ed. Cambridge: The MIT Press, 1966.

Hood, Steven J. *Dragons Entangled: Indo-China and the China-Vietnam War*. London: M.E. Scharpe, 1992.

Hopf, Ted. *Peripheral Visions: Deterrence Theory and American Foreign Policy in the Third World: 1965–1990*. Ann Arbor: University of Michigan Press, 1994.

Hsiung, James C. *U.S.-Asian Relations: The National Security Paradox*. Praeger Special Studies. New York: Praeger, 1983.

Hsiung, James C., and Winberg Chai. *Asia and US Foreign Policy*. New York: Praeger, 1981.

Hunt, Michael H. *Ideology and U.S. Foreign Policy*. London: Yale University Press, 1987.

Hurst, Steven. *The Carter Administration and Vietnam*. Basingstoke: Macmillan, 1996.

Isaacs, Arnold R. *Vietnam Shadows: The War, Its Ghosts, and Its Legacy*. London: The Johns Hopkins University Press, 1997.

Isaacs, Arnold R. *Without Honor: Defeat in Vietnam and Cambodia*. Baltimore: The Johns Hopkins University Press, 1983.

Joyaux, François. *La nouvelle question d'Extrême-Orient /2: L'ère du conflit sino-soviétique: 1959–1978*. Bibliothèque historique Payot. Paris: Payot, 1988.

Kamm, Henry. *Cambodia: Report From a Striken Land*. New York: Arcade Publishing, 1998.

Kaonh, Vandy. *Cambodge 1975–1995: la nuit sera longue*. Paris: Association Fonds d'Aides au Cambodge, 1996.

Karp, Walter. *Liberty Under Siege: American Politics: 1976–1988*. New York: Henry Holt and Company, 1988.

Katsiaficas, George, ed. *Vietnam Documents: American and Vietnamese Views of the War*. London: M.E. Scharpe, 1992.

Kattenburg, Paul M. *The Vietnam Trauma in American Foreign Policy: 1945–1975*. New Brunswick: Transaction Books, 1980.

Kaufman, Burton I. *The Presidency of James Earl Carter, Jr.* Lawrence: University Press of Kansas, 1993.

Kiernan, Ben. *The Pol Pot Regime: Race, Power, and Genocide in Cambodia Under the Khmer Rouge, 1975–1979*. New Haven: Yale University Press, 1996.

Kusnitz, Leonard A. *Public Opinion and Foreign Policy: America's China Policy 1949–1979*. Contributions in Political Science no. 114. London: Greenwood Press, 1984.

Langlet, Philippe, and Quach Thanh Tâm. *Introduction à l'histoire contemporaine du Viêt Nam de la réunification au néocommunisme (1975–2001)*. Paris: Les Indes Savantes, 2001.

Lawson, Eugene K. *The Sino-Vietnamese Conflict*. New York: Praeger, 1984.

Le Boutillier, John. *Vietnam Now: A Case for Normalizing Relations with Hanoi*. New York: Praeger, 1989.

Lee, Chin Chuan, ed. *Voices of China: The Interplay of Politics and Journalism*, The Guilford Communication Series. New York: The Guilford Press, 1990.

Leffler, Melvyn P. and David S. Painter. *Origins of the Cold War: An International History*. London: Routledge, 1994.

Light, Margot, ed. *Troubled Friendships: Moscow's Third World Ventures*. London: British Academy Press, 1993.

Lodha, Sanjay. *The Communist Tug-of-War in Indochina*. Jaipur: Printwell, 1997.

Louvre, Alfred, and Jeffrey Walsh. *Tell Me Lies About Vietnam: Cultural Battles for the Meaning of the War*. Milton Keynes: Open University Press, 1988.

Luu Van Loi. *Fifty Years of Vietnamese Diplomacy, 1945–1995*. Volume II: 1975–1995. Hanoi: Thê Gioi Publishers, 2002.

Madsen, Richard. *China and the American Dream: A Moral Inquiry*. Berkeley: University of California Press, 1995.

Mann, James. *About Face: A History of America's Curious Relationship with China, from Nixon to Clinton*. New York: Alfred A. Knopf, 1999.

Maze Carter, Holly K. *The Asian Dilemma in U.S. Foreign Policy: National Interests Versus Strategic Planning*. London: M.E. Sharpe, 1989.

McNamara, Robert S., James G. Blight, and Robert K. Brigham. *Argument Without End: In Search of Answers to the Vietnam Tragedy*. New York: Public Affairs, 1999.

Melanson, Richard A. *American Foreign Policy Since the Vietnam War: The Search for Consensus from Nixon to Clinton*. 2nd ed. London: M.E. Sharpe, 1996.

Melling, Phil, and Jon Roper. *America, France and Vietnam: Cultural History and Ideas of Conflict*. Aldershot: Avebury, 1991.

Min Chen. *The Strategic Triangle and Regional Conflicts: Lessons from the Indochina Wars*. Boulder: Lynne Rienner Publishers, 1992.

Morris, Stephen J. *Why Vietnam Invaded Cambodia: Political Culture and the Causes of War*. Stanford: Stanford University Press, 1999.

Neuringer, Sheldon M. *The Carter Administration, Human Rights and the Agony of Cambodia*. Lewiston: The Edwin Mellen Press, 1993.

Nguyen Van Canh, and Earle Cooper. *Vietnam Under Communism, 1975–1982*. Stanford: Hoover Institution Press, 1983.

Nixon, Richard. *No More Vietnams*. London: W.H. Allen, 1986.

Olson, James S., and Randy Roberts. *Where the Domino Fell: America and Vietnam, 1945 to 1990*. New York: St. Martin's Press, 1991.

Osborne, John. *White House Watch: The Ford Year*. Washington D.C.: New Republic Books, 1977.

Oye, Kenneth A., Donald Rothchild, and Robert J. Lieber, ed. *Eagle Entangled: U.S. Foreign Policy in a Complex World*. New York: Longman, 1979.

Palmujoki, Eero. *Vietnam and the World: Marxist-Leninist Doctrine and the Changes in International Relations, 1975–1993*. Basingstoke: Macmillan Press Ltd., 1997.

Patterson, James T. *Grand Expectations, The United States 1945–1974*. Oxford: Oxford University Press, 1996.

Payne, Richard J. *The Clash with Distant Cultures: Values, Interests, and Force in American Foreign Policy*. Albany: State University of New York Press, 1995.

Peterson, Paul E. *The President, The Congress and the Making of Foreign Policy*. Norman: University of Oklahoma Press, 1994.

Pike, Douglas. *Vietnam and the Soviet Union: Anatomy of an Alliance*. Boulder: Westview Press, 1987.

Porter, Bruce D. *The USSR in Third World Conflicts: Soviet Arms and Diplomacy in Local Wars: 1945–1980*. Cambridge: Cambridge University Press, 1984.

Porter, Gareth. *A Peace Denied: The United States, Vietnam, and the Paris Agreement*. Bloomington: Indiana University Press, 1975.

Portes, Jacques. *Les Américains et la Guerre du Vietnam*. Brussels: Editions Complexes, 1993.

Regaud, Nicolas. *Le Cambodge dans la tourmente: Le troisième conflit indochinois, 1978–1991*. Paris: L'Harmattan, 1992.

Rigal-Cellard, Bernadette. *La Guerre du Vietnam et la Société Américaine*. Bordeaux: Presses Universitaires de Bordeaux, 1991.

Rosati, Jerel A. *The Carter Administration's Quest for Global Community: Beliefs and Their Impact on Behavior*. Columbia: University of South Carolina Press, 1987.

Ross, Robert S. *The Indochina Tangle: China's Vietnam Policy, 1975–1979*. Studies of East Asian Institute. New York: Columbia University Press, 1988.

Schaller, Michael. *The United States and China in the Twentieth Century*. 2nd ed. Oxford: Oxford University Press, 1990.

Schulzinger, Robert D. *American Diplomacy in the Twentieth Century*. 2nd ed. Oxford: Oxford University Press, 1990.

Schulzinger, Robert D. *U.S. Diplomacy Since 1900*. 4th ed. Oxford: Oxford University Press, 1998.

Scruggs, Jan C. *The Wall That Heals*. Washington D.C.: The Vietnam Veterans Memorial Fund, 1992.

Scruggs, Jan C., and Joel L. Swerdlow. *To Heal a Nation: The Vietnam Veterans Memorial*. New York: Harper Perennial, 1992. 1st edition: 1985.

Smith, Gaddis. *Morality, Reason and Power*. New York: Hill and Wang, 1986.

Smith, Tony. *America's Mission: The United States and the Worldwide Struggle for Democracy in the Twentieth Century*. A Twentieth Century Book Fund. Princeton: Princeton University Press, 1994.

Solomon, Richard H. *Exiting Indochina: U.S. Leadership of the Cambodia Settlement & Normalization with Vietnam*. Washington D.C.: United States Institute for Peace Press, 2000.

Stearns, Monteagle. *Talking to Strangers: Improving American Diplomacy at Home and Abroad*. A Twentieth Century Fund Book. Princeton: Princeton University Press, 1996.

Steinmetz, Sara. *Democratic Transition and Human Rights: Perspectives on U.S. Foreign Policy*. Albany: State University of New York Press, 1994.

Stern, Lewis M. *Imprisoned or Missing in Vietnam: Policies of the Vietnamese Government Concerning Captured or Unaccounted for United States Soldiers, 1969–1994*. London: McFarland, 1995.

Sutter, Robert G. *The Cambodian Crisis and U.S. Policy Dilemmas*. Westview Special Studies on South and Southeast Asia. Boulder: Westview Press, 1991.

Tan Qingshan. *The Making of U.S. China Policy: From Normalization to the Post-Cold War Era*. Boulder: Lynne Rienner Publishers, 1992.

Tauriac, Michel. *Viêt Nam: Le dossier noir du communisme*. Paris: Plon, 2001.

Ton That Thien. *The Foreign Politics of the Communist Party of Vietnam: A Study of Communist Tactics*. London: Crane Russak, 1989.

Tow, William T. *Encountering the Dominant Player: United States Extended Deterrence Strategy in the Asia-Pacific*. New York: Columbia University Press, 1991.

Valone, Stephen J. *Two Centuries of United States Foreign Policy: The Documentary Record*. London: Praeger, 1995.

Van Wie Davis, Elizabeth. *Chinese Perspectives on Sino-American Relations, 1950–2000*. Chinese Studies Vol. 12. Lewiston: The Edwin Mellen Press, 2000.

Westad, Odd A., ed. *The Fall of Détente: Soviet-American Relations During the Carter Years*. Oslo: Scandinavian University Press, 1997.

Whitcomb, Roger S. *The American Approach to Foreign Affairs: An Uncertain Tradition*. London: Praeger, 1998.

White, Donald W. *The American Century: The Rise and Decline of the United States as a World Power*. London: Yale University Press, 1996.

Yoder, Amos. *The Conduct of American Foreign Policy Since World War II*. Pergamon Government and Politics Series. Oxford: Pergamon Press, 1986.

Young Jin Choi. *L'Asie de l'Est et le Rapprochement Sino-Américain*. Mondes en devenir: Documents et Essais. Paris: Berger-Levrault, 1987.

Young, Marilyn B. *The Vietnam Wars, 1945–1990*. New York: Harper Perennial, 1991.

Zhai, Qiang. *China and the Vietnam Wars, 1950–1975*. Chapel Hill: The University of North Carolina Press, 2000.

INDEX

Aaron, David 7, 15
Abramowitz, Morton 171
Abzug, Bella 75
accords *see* Paris Peace Accords
Afghanistan 37, 162
Agent Orange 22
aid to Vietnam: Chinese 38, 40, 41–42, 151, 157, 160, 163, 178; EEC 219; linked to MIAs 30, 31, 32, 44, 67, 75, 76, 88, 94, 101, 110, 114, 121, 124, 143, 195, 196–197, 235; reconstruction (U.S.), sometimes referred to as "humanitarian" or "economic" 2, 13, 16, 18, 24, 25, 27–32 *passim*, 36, 42, 43, 44, 45, 49, 50, 51, 57, 58, 59, 60, 61, 62, 63, 65, 69, 73, 75, 76, 81, 82, 83, 91, 94, 95, 96, 97, 99, 100, 101, 102, 103, 104, 108–29 *passim*, 131–37 *passim*, 139, 141, 142, 143, 146, 154, 159, 161, 162, 163, 164, 177, 179, 180, 181, 183, 184, 187, 188, 191, 194, 195, 196, 198, 199, 206, 207, 209, 210, 215, 219, 235, 236, 237, 241; Soviet 36, 40, 41–42, 115, 154, 177, 218; U.S. humanitarian organizations 18, 26, 65, 69, 138, 143, 164, 188; U.S. humanitarian shipments 25–26, 27, 39, 42–43, 46, 49, 56, 65, 69, 88, 90, 92, 96, 99, 100, 101, 104, 113, 114, 118, 124, 143, 188, 199, 237; World Bank 219; *see also* Nixon's secret letter; Paris Peace Accords, Article 21
Algeria 24, 32, 38
American Academy Awards 23
American Civil Liberties Union 93
American Conservative Union 116; Education and Research Institute 184
American Friends Service Committee 25–26, 27, 39, 43, 91, 92, 95, 97
Amnesty International 22
Anderson, Robert 29, 34
Angola 169, 173,
anti-war movement 23, 25, 26–27, 91, 93, 130, 143, 192
archives 13–14, 79, 112, 239, 240, 241
ASEAN 47, 54, 65, 115, 135, 148, 149, 152, 161, 177, 185, 189, 191, 193–94, 195, 202, 205, 207, 217, 219, 233
Ashbrook, William 14, 115–116, 117–118
Asian Development Bank 71
Australia 179, 180, 183, 209

Bach Mai Hospital Relief Fund 39, 43, 65
Bangkok Radio 29
Bank of America 31
Barber, Stephen 86, 181
Barre, Raymond 151
Becker, Elizabeth 17, 140, 208, 237, 238
Begin, Menachem 196, 212
Beijing Review see *Peking Review*
Beilenson, Anthony 195
Belgium 12, 110, 118
Bergland, Bob 181
Berman, Larry 129
Bingham, Jonathan 1, 24, 26, 31, 43, 46, 104, 195
Blumenthal, Michael 231–232
Borneo 144
Boumediene, Houari 32
Brezhnev, Leonid 153, 177, 204, 212, 213, 214, 215, 222, 230, 233
Brown, Frederick Z. 90, 92, 180, 181
Brown, Harold 222
Brzezinski, Zbigniew 2, 14, 17, 86, 87, 90, 91, 118, 131, 139, 163, 166, 167–175 *passim*, 179, 181, 183, 185, 186, 189, 191, 194, 195, 197, 199, 200, 201, 207, 208, 210–216 *passim*, 223, 224, 225, 226, 227, 229, 230, 232, 233, 238, 239; anti-Soviet views 87, 90, 118, 167–175 *passim*, 190, 201, 212, 213, 214, 215, 222, 225, 233; and Deng Xiaoping's visit to the U.S. 211, 222, 223, 224, 225, 226, 230; globalist approach of 2, 85, 118, 166–167, 169, 172, 174, 214, 222; influence on Carter 85, 87, 131, 168–169, 170, 173, 175, 181, 182, 199–200, 208, 212, 214, 222, 223, 224, 225, 229, 238, 239; and Kissinger 85, 86, 166–167, 170–171; rivalry with Vance 86–87, 168–173 *passim*, 175, 182, 188, 194, 199–200, 201, 207, 208, 213, 214, 225, 233, 238, 239, 241; 163, 165–175, 189, 201, 211, 222, 230, 238 and Vietnam 86, 89, 118, 131, 143, 173–175, 197; visit to Peking 17–18, 159, 160
Bui Tin 14, 19, 77–78, 79, 161, 218
Burchett, Wilfred 150
Bush, George H.W. 42
Byrd, Robert C. 126–127

Caldwell, Lawrence 174
Cam Ranh Bay 81, 136, 183, 187, 203, 204, 207

301

Cambodia 19, 24, 25, 26, 28, 30, 38, 50, 96, 97, 111, 119, 133, 134; "Angkar" government 111; embassies 140; human rights violations 133, 134, 191, 192, 193, 202, 220; Ministry of Foreign Affairs 157; 1975 fall of Phnom Penh 12, 111, 150, 218–219; "reconstruction campaign" 111; relations with China 36, 40, 80, 111–112, 136, 140–142, 148–152 *passim*, 154, 155, 157, 159, 160, 161, 189, 192, 193, 195, 205–206, 210, 218, 219, 233, 238, 239; relations with Laos 219; relations with U.S. 30; relations with Vietnam 2, 11, 17–19 *passim*, 49, 50, 53, 77, 78, 85, 110–112 *passim*, 135, 136, 140–142, 143, 148–155 *passim*, 157–159 *passim*, 161–162, 165, 174, 176–177, 182, 183, 185, 187–194 *passim*, 196, 199, 202–205 *passim*, 207, 210, 211, 216–221 *passim*, 222, 223, 227–229 *passim*, 231–233 passim, 236–241 *passim*; Vietnamese presence during Vietnam War 123–127 *passim*; *see also* Democratic Kampuchea; Pol Pot

Cambodian Communist Party 140, 153, 218; *see also* KCP

Carlson, John 69

Carter, Chip 168

Carter, Hodding 220, 230

Carter, Jimmy 1, 2, 15, 16, 17, 61, 74, 83–86 *passim*, 89, 90, 91, 102, 103, 132, 134, 139, 161, 168–172 *passim*, 175, 181, 182, 214, 215, 220, 236, 238, 239; election campaign (1976) 61, 68, 71, 72, 73, 94, 97; inexperience with foreign nations 2, 17, 85, 93, 103

Carter administration 1, 2, 13, 15–18 *passim*, 26, 28, 31, 36, 51, 77, 84, 116, 117, 141, 162, 165, 168, 233, 236, 240; amnesty 84; China card 2, 167, 168, 190, 191, 210, 213, 233, 240; and human rights 92, 93, 134, 161, 165, 173, 179, 192; and MIAs 1–2, 28, 35, 36, 64, 65, 68, 71, 72, 75, 88, 89, 92, 95, 96, 98, 101, 103, 104, 105, 106, 108, 121, 134, 186; and negotiations with China 90, 165–175, 192, 195–196, 198–201, 207, 209, 210–216, 221, 222–226, 231, 232; and negotiations with Vietnam 76, 77, 78, 85, 88, 91–121, 122, 130–144, 146, 150, 161–165, 176–203, 206–210, 236, 237; political shift from regionalist to globalist approach 2, 3, 13, 16, 17, 20, 84, 85–86, 89, 166, 169, 209, 212, 214, 222, 234, 237, 238, 239, 241; reaction to Third Indochina conflict 222–225, 226, 229, 230, 231, 232, 252–253

Chai Zemin 233

Chanda, Nayan 15, 17, 21, 36, 102, 180, 200, 237

Chau Doc 111

Chen Chih-fang 38

Chiao Kuan-hua 40

Children's Defense Fund 94

China 2, 19, 32, 33, 34, 38, 51, 63, 78, 80, 81, 89, 92, 106, 111, 115, 118, 131, 135–136, 139, 152; "American card"190, 191, 210, 233, 240; Chinese National People's Congress 206; dispute over Paracel islands and Spratly islands 53–54, 190; embassies 151, 157, 178, 179, 221, 225; fear of Vietnamese expansionism 30, 36–37; islands dispute 53–54; Kwangsi province 228; Lai Chau province 225; media 36, 40, 78, 81, 102, 136, 140, 149, 150, 155, 156, 160, 163, 173, 182, 190, 216, 221, 225, 228; Ministry of Foreign Affairs 159, 221, 228; Overseas Chinese Affairs Office 156; relations with Cambodia 36, 38, 40, 80, 111–112, 136, 140–142, 148–152 *passim*, 154, 155, 157, 159, 160, 161, 189, 192, 193, 195, 205–206, 210, 218, 219, 233, 238, 239; relations with U.S. 2, 3, 11, 17, 18, 20, 36, 41, 47–48, 90–91, 106, 107, 131, 136, 142, 146, 150, 159, 161–175 *passim*, 177, 181, 182, 183, 189–198 *passim*, 200, 201, 202, 204, 207, 209, 210–216, 220, 221–234 *passim*, 237–240 *passim*; relations with the USSR 17, 18, 36–42 *passim*, 47, 48, 81, 82, 83, 91, 110, 148, 151, 152, 167–175 *passim*, 177, 178, 182, 189, 190, 194, 199, 203, 209–214 *passim*, 220–226 *passim*, 230–234 *passim*, 239–240; relations with Vietnam 1, 2, 3, 17, 18, 19, 30, 36–42 *passim*, 48–49, 52–54 *passim*, 71, 77, 78, 80–82 *passim*, 85, 89, 92, 110, 111–112, 115, 135–136, 139–144 *passim*, 148–152 *passim*, 154, 163, 164, 165, 173–179 *passim*, 182, 183, 188–195 *passim*, 199–205 *passim*, 208, 210, 211, 213, 216, 217, 219–234 *passim*, 236, 238–240 *passim see also* Hoa crisis; treaty with Japan 172, 189, 204; Vietnamese "lesson" 2, 13, 18, 37, 189, 222, 223, 224, 226, 227–234, 239; Vietnamese "ungratefulness" 38, 39, 112, 178; Yunnan Province 179, 228; *see also* aid to Vietnam

Chinese Communist Party (CCP) 189, 205, 206, 226, 227; Central Committee 216; leadership 36, 53, 149, 150, 168, 171, 172, 189, 190, 204, 211, 216, 229, 238; Military Commission 226

Chirac, Jacques 109

Cholon 154, 155, 156

Chung Hsi-tung 193

Church, Frank 127, 169

Church World Service 26, 39, 65, 164

CIA 41, 42, 122, 183, 199, 207, 211

Clinton, Bill 11, 241

Colby, William 42

Cold War 3, 17, 20, 83, 84–85, 87, 146, 148, 152, 167, 191, 210, 214, 234, 236, 240

Collet, Wallace 92

COMECON 41, 81, 112, 152, 153, 177, 178, 204

communist ideologies 78, 80, 82, 83, 153, 154, 162, 165, 182

Communist International 41

communist parties *see under* country name

Congress *see* U.S. Congress

Congressional Quarterly 233

Crowley, Monica 128, 165

Cuba 25, 91, 97, 117, 118, 142, 143, 146, 172, 178, 218, 226; involvement in Africa 146, 167, 169, 172, 173, 238; Vietnam as an "Asian Cuba" 173, 203, 224, 238

Dallin, Alexander 174

Da Nang 207, 227

Danielson, George 187

Democratic Kampuchea 53, 111, 140, 151, 152, 153, 182, 208, 217, 219, 220 221, 226; *see also* Cambodia

Democratic Party 2, 25, 61, 62, 71, 119, 184, 185–86, 192, 194

Democratic Patriotic Front for National Salvation 219

Democratic Republic of Vietnam (DRV or DRVN) 12, 13, 28, 29, 35, 36, 40, 46, 53, 59, 127; *see also* North Vietnam

Deng Xiaoping 37, 38, 39, 151, 168, 171–172, 173, 178, 189, 194, 203, 205, 207, 211, 212, 215, 216, 228–233 *passim*; letter from Carter 223–224; visit to the U.S.221–227

Denmark 98

détente 17, 41, 61, 86, 87, 90, 166, 167, 173, 213

Detroit Economic Club 45

Dinh Ba Thi 34, 35, 39, 41, 66, 67, 74, 137, 138, 139, 145

Diplomatic notes (U.S.-Vietnam) 58–66 *passim*; 247–251 *passim*; *see also* New York talks; Paris talks

Do Thanh 60, 61, 63, 66, 67, 70, 73, 76

Dobrynin, Anatoly 213, 214, 225

Dole, Robert 133, 137

Index

Domenici, Peter 69
domino theory 158, 165
Dong, Pham Van *see* Pham Van Dong
Donovan, Hedley 223
Duiker, William 82, 238
Dumbrell, John 17, 87, 213, 238, 239

East-West conflict 2, 3, 36, 85, 174, 214, 240
economic aid *see* aid to Vietnam
Edelman, Marian Wright 94
EEC Council of Ministers 219
Egypt 150, 196, 212
elections: Carter elected as president 83, 84, 85, 88, 90; Carter's presidential campaign 71–73, 88, 90, 91, 93, 97; Ford's relection campaign and Vietnam 31, 36, 47, 51, 56, 58, 59, 60, 65, 66, 68, 69, 70, 72, 73, 74, 104; and MIAs 28, 31, 36, 56, 62, 65, 66, 68, 69, 72, 73, 76, 88; Nixon election (1968) 235; Nixon's reelection (1972) 121, 122, 128; U.S. congressional 2, 25, 69, 181, 184, 185, 188, 194, 198, 199, 201, 207; U.S. presidential of 1976 1, 28, 29, 36, 42, 46, 47, 55, 56, 58, 60, 61, 62, 69, 71, 72, 73, 76, 116; U.S. presidential election of 1980 91; Vietnamese 52, 60, 79, 108, 155
Elliot, David W.P. 238
Ethiopia 110, 169, 172
Evans, Grant 18, 238
executive branch *see* U.S. government

Far Eastern Economic Review 155, 181, 185, 204
FBI 131, 144
Ferguson, Clarence C. 25
Fitzgerald, Frances 23
Ford, Gerald 2, 15, 16, 26, 27, 28, 33–36 *passim*, 42, 45, 47–51 *passim*, 57, 59–77 *passim*, 84, 89, 91, 92, 95, 97, 100–104 *passim*, 109, 146, 166, 186, 212, 215, 220, 235–37 *passim*, 241; amnesty of draft dodgers 84; candidacy for reelection 1, 15, 31, 36, 42, 50–76 *passim*, 104; in China 47–48, 90, 166; Pacific Doctrine 47, 49; pardon of Nixon 72; Tulane speech 33
Ford administration 1, 13, 15–16, 26, 28, 31, 42, 50, 58, 59, 70, 72, 73, 75, 76, 77, 84, 89, 93, 97, 99, 101, 103, 106; reshuffling of 42; Vietnamese policy 2, 25, 35, 50, 51, 56, 76, 84, 88, 95, 104, 109, 220, 235–37 *passim*
Formosa 27
Forty Committee 42
France 2, 12, 14, 16, 21, 28, 45, 46, 48, 49, 55, 56, 58, 59, 60, 63–76 *passim*, 92, 93, 102, 103, 108, 109, 112–116 *passim*, 118, 120, 123, 125, 127, 129, 130, 131, 132, 141, 142, 144, 145, 148, 151, 158, 159, 161, 162, 168, 180, 181, 182, 185, 187, 188, 198, 204, 215, 240, 241; embassies 109, 127; media 110, 133
Friendshipment 39
Frost, David 117, 119
Funnell, Victor 238
Funseth, Robert 30, 74

Gammon, Samuel Rhee 73
Garthoff, Raymond 17, 167, 238
Geneva Accords (1954) 14, 66, 159
Germany 27, 126, 179, 205
Giai-Phong 22, 35
Giap, Vo Nguyen *see* Vo Nguyen Giap
Gilman, Benjamin 48, 104, 105, 120
Giscard D'estaing, Valéry 69
Glenn, John 133
Gonzalez, Henry 44–45, 49, 139
Gorski, Dennis T. 133
Grechko, Andrei 42
Griffith, Ann Mills 28
Gromyko, Andrei 40, 215
Guam 138

Ha Van Lau 146, 174, 229
Habib, Philip 15, 57, 62, 64, 74
Haiphong 161, 218, 227
Hannan, Philip 184
Hanoi Radio 29, 47, 51, 59, 60, 81, 101, 110, 151, 217
Harkin, Tom 134
Harriman, Averell 93
Hatfield, Mark 75
Hearts and Minds 23
Heder, Stephen P. 238
Helsinki Conference on European Security 41
Heng Samrin 217, 218, 219
Hersh, Seymour 209
Hiebert, Murray 63, 175
Ho Chi Minh 12, 22, 37, 67, 77, 78, 79
Ho Chi Minh City 144, 152, 186, 198 *see also* Saigon
Hoa crisis 80–81, 154–161, 163, 164, 178, 179, 192, 193, 208, 209 *see also* Indochina, refugees
Hoang Bich Son 146
Hoang Dinh Cau 55
Hoang Tung 23, 111, 150
Hoang Van Hoan 19, 78, 154, 158
Holbrooke, Richard 15, 51, 89, 94, 97, 99, 103, 106, 108, 109, 110, 113, 114, 115, 117, 130–133 *passim*, 136, 137, 139, 141–144 *passim*, 146, 162, 163, 165, 168, 171, 172, 174, 175, 180–183 *passim*, 185, 188, 196–201 *passim*, 207–210 *passim*, 220, 222, 231, 238, 239
Hong Kong 42, 144, 155, 161, 173, 193, 204, 209, 211

Hop Tac 81
Horn of Africa 2, 17, 146, 162, 173, 238
Hua Guofeng 150, 168, 172, 203, 211, 214
Huang Hua 200
Huberman, Benjamin 171
Hughes, Richard 65
Humphrey, Hubert 71
Humphrey, Ronald 144–145
Huntington, Samuel 171
Hurst, Steven 15, 16, 17, 29, 82, 208, 237, 239
Huynh Tan Phat 155
Huynh Thanh 46

Ieng Sary 202
India 12, 83, 92, 144, 163, 181, 204
Indochina 1, 12, 13, 14, 16, 18, 19, 21, 22, 24, 25, 26, 30, 31, 37, 39, 41, 42, 44, 47, 50, 53, 57, 60, 61, 62, 63, 66, 71, 76, 85, 88, 92, 95, 100, 105, 106, 109, 111, 112, 118, 119, 123, 125, 127, 128, 129, 135, 149–154 *passim*, 156–159 *passim*, 165, 166, 175, 183, 188, 191, 192, 195, 210, 218, 219, 220, 229, 233, 237, 239, 241; first conflict (France) 28; refugees 2, 18, 21–25 *passim*, 45, 55, 62, 138, 152, 153, 161, 164, 165, 179, 184, 185, 192–93, 202, 203, 207, 208, 209–10; second conflict (U.S.) 12, 15, 16, 23, 40, 43, 45, 63, 66, 71, 93, 103, 106, 108, 109, 128–129, 158, 165, 166, 192, 229 *see also* Vietnam War; "special relationship" 135; tensions 1, 111–112, 136, 139, 149, 237; third conflict (Cambodia and China) 1, 11, 15, 19, 37, 49, 164–165, 175, 190, 191 *see also* Cambodia; Laos; Vietnam
"Indochina Federation" 149, 157, 158, 159, 182, 192, 234, 236
Indochina Resource Centre 47
Indochinese Communist Party 153, 158
Indonesia 47, 54, 157, 195
Inter-American Development Bank 134
International Bank for Economic Cooperation (IBEC) 112
International Court of Justice 34
International Monetary Fund (IMF) 71, 133, 195
Israel 150, 196, 212

Jackson, Donna 17, 238
Japan 12, 14, 21, 45, 49, 53, 111, 129, 168, 172, 179, 180, 181, 189, 194, 206, 211, 212, 215, 223, 226, 231; Japan formula 168; Japanese Society 30; media 215; reparations to Vietnam 27; treaty with China 172, 189, 204; as a U.S. ally 47, 86, 162, 163, 172, 189, 223, 231; and World War II 21, 125, 126, 129

Index

Jean Sainteny papers 14
Johnson, Lyndon B. 49, 71, 87, 123, 124
Joint Casualty Resolution Center 27, 101, 106, 114, 137, 144
Joint Economic Commission 49, 50, 56, 57, 92, 116, 125
Jordan, Hamilton 87, 171, 186, 212

Kampong Son 151
Kampuchean National United Front for National Salvation (KNUFNS) 217, 218
Kaysone Phomvihane 135
KCP 140, 157, 189; *see also* Cambodian Communist Party
Kennedy, Edward 1, 25, 35, 46, 48, 55, 62, 65, 164, 225; trip to Vietnam 183–186 *passim*
Kennedy administration 86, 93
Khieu Samphan 111, 127, 154, 157, 206
Khmer Rouge 111, 112, 141, 150, 153, 155, 157, 161, 165, 176, 179, 190, 193, 194, 205, 207, 217–220 *passim*, 241
KIAs (killed in action) 27, 28, 94, 95, 105, 113, 236
Kissinger, Henry 12, 15, 23, 24, 26, 30, 31, 33, 34, 37, 42–46 *passim*, 48–49, 56–63 *passim*, 66, 67–68, 69, 72, 73, 75, 76, 79, 84, 86–87, 90, 97, 109, 114, 116, 117, 120–131 *passim*, 149–150, 158, 159, 166, 167, 169–172 *passim*, 175, 212, 213; and Nixon 90, 117, 122, 129, 170, 175, 240
Korea, South 33, 34, 35, 38–41 *passim*, 67, 101, 227; North 34, 97, 110, 219
Korean War 28, 105, 216
Kosygin, Alexsey 226
Kukrit Pramoj 172

Lang Son 229
Laos 37, 50, 71, 74, 93, 96, 123, 127, 133, 134, 135, 151, 158, 219; Cambodian pact 219; communist victory in 12; Lao People's Revolutionary Party (LPRP) 135; Lao-Vietnamese friendship treaty 135, 136, 149; POWs/MIAs in 123, 124, 187; relations with Vietnam 38, 135, 136, 154; 159, 219; U.S. prisoners in 123, 124; Vietnamese presence in 125, 126; Vietnamese withdrawal from 123, 127
Le Duan 14, 19, 39, 40, 41, 42, 52–53, 71, 78–80, 82, 111, 135, 140, 141, 152, 153–154, 158, 177, 189, 196, 203, 206, 228, 236
Le Duc Tho 12, 15, 19, 78–79, 81, 111, 112, 123, 124, 130, 136, 141, 152–154 *passim*, 159, 176, 196, 205, 218, 236

Le Quoc Than 81
Le Thanh Nghi 36, 39, 79
Leffler, Melvyn 240
legislature *see* U.S. Congress
Lenin, Vladimir 168
Leninism *see* communist ideologies
Li Hsien-nien 36, 228
Libya 69, 110
Lien Kuan 160
Long, Clarence 134
Luu Van Loi 19, 101, 149, 206, 209, 218, 224

Mackellar, Michael 209
Malaysia 54, 110, 145, 193, 202, 209
Mann, James 166, 214, 233
Mansfield, Mike 15, 66, 93, 102
Mao Zedong 40, 71, 154, 156, 157, 176
Maoism *see* communist ideologies
Marshall Plan 65
Martin, Graham 109
Marx, Karl 80
Marxism *see* communist ideologies
Mather, Paul 101
Mayaguez incident 30, 72
McAuliff, John 95, 235
McCloskey, Paul 48, 62, 195
McGovern, George 1, 44, 55, 56, 59, 60, 65, 75, 191–192; 1976 congressional trip to Hanoi 55–56, 58
McHenry, Donald 137
McNamara, Robert 50, 100, 134, 182, 239
media 22, 74, 88, 113, 171, 196, 212; Asian 166; Cambodian 153, 219; Chinese 36, 40, 78, 81, 102, 136, 140, 149, 150, 155, 156, 160, 163, 168, 173, 182, 189, 190, 216, 219, 221, 225, 228; Danish 98; French 110, 133; Hong Kong 173; Indian 83; Italian 72; Japanese 215; press conferences 24, 29, 32, 35, 39, 45, 52, 59, 61, 67, 69, 86, 90, 102, 103–4, 116, 126, 134, 167, 179, 209, 213, 214, 223, 226, 230; press releases 93, 96, 131, 149, 213; U.S. 30, 32, 34, 45, 49, 50, 55, 60, 69, 74, 83–84, 86, 87, 91, 96, 97, 98, 102, 104, 115, 116, 119, 120, 126, 133, 140, 144, 159, 164, 167, 168, 169, 173, 179, 184, 201–202, 204, 207, 208, 212, 220, 221, 222, 223, 225, 228, 229, 233; Soviet 38, 145, 164, 167, 174, 189, 205, 225, 230, 232; Thailand 29, 178; Vietnamese 14, 22, 23, 24, 29, 30, 31, 36, 45, 47, 51, 52, 55, 56, 59, 60, 68, 70, 72, 75, 77, 81, 84, 87, 92, 96, 101, 106, 110, 111, 116, 117, 118, 119–120, 132, 133, 145, 149, 150, 151, 153, 155,

156, 160, 161, 166, 176, 178, 182, 204, 205, 217, 218, 226, 228, 229, 231, 232; Western 22, 49, 112, 202, 229
Mennonites 27; Mennonite Central Committee 25–26, 43, 65
MIAs (missing in action) 1–2, 15, 16, 18, 124, 125, 235; accounting linked to aid *see* aid to Vietnam; humanitarian issue 13, 44, 61–62, 63, 68, 69, 73, 74, 75, 95, 99, 100, 101, 114, 183, 195; National POW-MIA Day 186; 1973 Agreement 13, 29, 30, 44, 63, 73, 75, 99, 101, 113, 114, 235 *see also* Paris Peace Accords, Article 8b; and Nixon 1, 28, 62, 64–65, 95, 104, 118, 120, 123, 124, 125, 235; reclassification as KIA 94–96, 105, 113, 187, 236; release of information or remains 35, 42, 43, 46, 48, 55, 58, 62, 66, 68, 74, 75, 92, 95, 99–103 *passim*, 108, 109, 110, 111, 114, 123, 131, 137, 138, 178, 187; as statistics 27–28, 105–106; under Carter 16, 65, 68, 71–72, 88–106 *passim*, 108–111 *passim*, 113–115 *passim*, 118, 120, 121, 131, 132, 134, 137, 138, 143, 178, 179, 183, 185, 186, 187, 195, 196, 197, 198, 236, 237; under Ford 25, 27–36 *passim*, 42–50 *passim*, 55–58 *passim*, 61–76 *passim*, 95, 186, 235; and U.S. elections 28, 31, 36, 42, 56, 61–69 *passim*, 72, 73, 76, 88; and Vietnamese membership for the UN 36, 67–76 *passim*, 88, 92, 95, 109, 235–236; *see also* House of Representatives Select Committee on Missing Persons in Southeast Asia
Middle East 192, 210
Miller, Robert 25
Minh, Ho Chi *see* Ho Chi Minh
Mondale, Walter 163, 222, 225
Mongolia 37, 178, 203
Montgomery, Gillespie "Sonny" 1, 14, 42–50 *passim*, 56, 57, 61, 64, 93, 94, 95, 96, 105, 106, 116, 164, 184, 186, 187, 188, 190, 192; 1975 congressional trip to Paris 46–48 *passim*, 241; 1978 congressional trip to South Vietnam 186, 187, 188, 190
Montgomery Committee *see* U.S. House of Representatives, Select Committee on Missing Persons in Southeast Asia
Moore, Henson W. 186, 187
Morris, Stephen 19, 205, 238, 239
Moscow Radio 38
Moynihan, Patrick 32–33, 34, 35, 39, 40
Murtha, John P. 188

Mutual Defense Assistance Control Act (1951) 26

National Association for the Advancement of Colored Peoples (NAACP) 93
National League of Families of Prisoners and Missing In Southeast Asia 28, 61, 64, 65, 71, 89, 92, 93, 94, 95, 96, 97, 104–105, 115, 120, 198
National Liberation Front (NLF) 21, 23
National Review 204
National Security Council (NSC) 2, 15, 18, 28, 42, 57, 86, 87, 110, 118, 141, 162, 163, 167, 168, 169, 170, 171, 173, 174, 175, 181, 184, 185, 186, 188, 191, 194, 199, 200, 201207, 208, 213, 214, 232, 239; *see also* Brzezinski; Kissinger
Nessen, Ron 29
New China News Agency 221
New Economic Zones (NEZ) 22, 82
New Times 189
New York talks 18, 139–140, 182, 185, 192–204 *passim*, 209, 239; "Jerusalem formula" 198
New York Times 91, 97, 133, 144, 202
Newsweek 87, 169
Ngo Ba Thanh 187
Ngo Dien 99, 185
Ngo Nguyen Phuong 58
Nguyen Co Thach 15, 78, 84, 141, 150, 161, 163, 178, heads delegation to New York (1978) 192–203, 204, 209
Nguyen Duy Trinh 27, 28–29, 46, 54, 55, 58, 61, 79, 93, 138, 139, 141, 145, 148, 161, 198, 203, 209, 215, 228
Nguyen Thi Binh 45, 52, 55
Nguyen Trong Vinh 159
Nguyen Van Cau 32
Nguyen Van Luu 32, 34, 35, 39, 41
Nguyen Van Thieu 21, 30, 38, 121, 122, 128, 163
Nhan Dan 14, 23, 29, 31, 55, 59, 60, 72, 75, 84, 87, 110, 111, 116, 117, 119, 120, 145, 150, 153, 166, 176, 178, 182, 205, 226
Nixon, Richard 12, 29, 47, 50, 56, 57–58, 60, 64–65, 71, 83, 84, 87, 90, 97, 99, 102, 113, 115–121 *passim*, 121–130 *passim*, 131, 141, 165, 170, 188, 191, 210, 212, 237; and China 90, 166, 167; Ford's pardon of 72; "go public" campaign 28, 235; and Kissinger 90, 117, 122, 129, 170, 175, 240; and MIAs 28, 62, 64–65, 95, 104, 118, 120; "Nixon doctrine" 127; reelection of 2, 122, 192; Vietnam ceasefire 29
Nixon administration 12, 57, 72, 95, 116, 129, 130

Nixon's secret letter 2, 13, 16, 44–45, 49, 50, 56, 57–58, 60, 83, 90, 97, 99, 113, 115–130 *passim*, 131, 141, 188, 191, 198, 210, 236, 237, 240; full text of 243–244; Pham Van Dong's reply to 116, 245–246
Nobel Peace Prize 12, 62, 79, 129
Non-Aligned Movement 65, 74; Vietnamese membership of 32
normalization, U.S.-China 2, 3, 17, 18, 87, 90–91, 107, 131, 162–163, 166–172, 175, 181, 189, 190, 192–196 *passim*, 200, 201, 206, 207, 209–216 *passim*, 221, 222, 223, 231, 237, 238, 239, 241; Soviet-Vietnamese 145; U.S.-Soviet 143; U.S. and Third World powers 214; U.S.-Vietnam 1, 2, 11, 12, 16–19 *passim*, 23, 25, 27, 28, 31–36 *passim*, 38, 43–46 *passim*, 48, 50, 52, 54–56 *passim*, 58, 59, 61–63 *passim*, 65, 67–69, 71–73, 75, 83, 85–95 *passim*, 97–104 *passim*, 107, 108–119 *passim*, 125, 127, 130–133, 135, 137, 138, 140–143, 145, 146, 151, 162–164, 174, 175, 177, 179–188 *passim*, 191, 194–210 *passim*, 214, 215, 220, 234, 236–241 *passim*; Vietnam-FDR Germany 27; Vietnam-Formosa 27; Vietnam-Japan 27; Vietnam-Philippines 54; Vietnam-Thailand 54
North Vietnam 2, 12, 13, 19, 21, 22, 24–30 *passim*, 57, 58, 61, 62, 64, 69, 77, 82, 109, 114, 117, 119, 121–130 *passim*, 142, 155, 156, 157, 160, 235; application to UN 32–51 *passim*; bombing raids against 21, 122, 125, 138; Council of Ministers 53; Ministry of Foreign Affairs 127; reunification with South Vietnam 23, 51–54 *passim*, 65, 78, 79, 82, 108, 135, 156, 236 *see also* Democratic Republic of Vietnam; Nixon's secret letter

Oakley, Robert 113, 198, 202, 203, 207, 208, 220
Obey, David 134
Odom, William 15, 232
Oksenberg, Michael 15, 118, 139, 141, 142, 146, 169, 170, 173, 174, 175, 181, 184, 186, 194, 197–201 *passim*, 207, 208, 211, 212, 222, 227, 232
Ottinger, Richard 31, 48

Painter, David 240
Pakistan 110
Palestine Liberation Organization 90
Panama 91; *see also* treaties
Panama Canal Treaties *see* treaties

Pao-Min Chang 149, 209
Paracel islands *see* China
Paris negotiations: Holbrooke-Phan Hien talks (1977) 2, 16, 102, 103, 108–116 *passim*, 118, 120, 123, 125, 127, 130–145 *passim*, 148, 159, 161, 162, 168, 180, 181, 182, 185, 194, 196, 198, 210, 236, 237
Paris Peace Accords (1973) 12, 13, 14, 23, 24, 27–32 *passim*, 34, 35, 36, 43, 44, 45, 49, 50, 55, 56, 57, 58, 61, 62, 63, 72, 73, 75, 92, 97, 99, 100, 101, 113–129 *passim*, 132, 142, 159, 235, 237, 241; Article 8b (MIAs) 13, 30, 44, 62, 73, 75, 92, 100, 101, 235; Article 20 (North Vietnamese withdrawal from Cambodia and Laos) 123; Article 21 (reconstruction aid) 13, 28, 30, 44, 49, 55, 57, 61, 75, 92, 97, 100, 113, 122, 183, 235; Article 22 (bilateral relationship) 12 *see also* aid to Vietnam; MIAs
Paris Peace Agreement *see* Paris Peace Accords
Pathet Lao 12, 135
"Peace with Honor" 12, 127, 129
Peacock, Andrew 180
Peking Review 78, 136, 160, 225
Pentagon *see* U.S. government, Department of Defense
Pentagon papers 109
People's Daily 168, 182, 189, 216, 219
Peru 110
Peterson, Peter 11
Pham Duong 32
Pham Hung 52, 133
Pham Ngac 32
Pham Van Dong 2, 13, 15, 27, 28, 29, 31, 32, 38, 45, 48, 49, 50, 51, 52, 55, 56, 61, 65, 66, 72, 78, 79, 98, 99, 100, 101, 102, 108, 110, 116, 119, 122, 123, 125, 129, 130, 131, 135, 136, 159, 183, 187, 189, 193, 194, 196, 202, 203, 205, 206, 219, 228
Phan Hien 49, 54, 63, 65, 91, 92, 98, 99, 101, 102, 109, 110, 112, 113, 140, 141, 142, 143, 145, 146, 158, 168, 179, 186, 187, 193, 215
Phan Huy Thong 58
Philippines 47, 53, 54, 55, 63, 65, 110, 157, 207
Pike, Douglas 13–14, 15, 33, 37, 46, 56, 61, 63, 67, 177
Pol Pot 17, 18, 111, 112, 135, 136, 140, 148–153 *passim*, 157, 161, 165, 176, 177, 182, 189, 196, 202, 205, 216–220 *passim*, 223, 228, 230, 238; death of 11
Poland 86
Porter, Gareth 47, 122, 128, 183, 238
Powell, Jody 134, 213
POWs (prisoners of war) 28, 46, 55, 62, 65, 71, 94, 95, 104, 105,

106, 123, 124, 134, 184, 186, 235, 241
Pravda 205, 230, 231
presidential libraries 13, 241
Press, Frank 181, 226
Prince Norodom Sihanouk 150
PRM-10 171
PRM-24 131, 167, 168, 182, 237, 241
Provisional Revolutionary Government (PRG) 21, 22, 32, 36, 38, 46

Quakers 27
Quan Doi Nhan Dan 24, 30, 47, 59, 60, 77, 120

Reagan, Ronald 28, 48, 60, 61, 62, 63, 241
reconstruction 13, 21, 22–23, 24, 27, 31, 36, 39, 49, 50, 53, 55, 58, 63, 65, 73, 82, 91, 100, 101, 103, 111, 113, 121, 124, 129, 135, 139, 152
Red Cross 183
reeducation camps 21–22
refugees *see* Indochina
reparations *see* aid to Vietnam
Republic of South Vietnam (RSVN) 35, 40, 52, 94, 198; *see also* South Vietnam
Republican Party 48, 61, 63, 83, 185, 186, 188
Reynolds, David 240
Rogers, William 87, 117, 120, 126, 170
Romulo, Carlos 192
Rosati, Jerel A. 17, 238
Ross, Robert S. 190
Rowley, Kelvin 18, 238
Rumsfeld, Donald 42, 75

Sadat, Anwar 196, 212
Saigon 1, 12, 14, 21, 22, 23, 24, 27, 29, 32, 34, 38, 40, 42, 43, 45, 47, 51, 52, 60, 63, 66, 97, 109, 110, 112, 122, 127, 128, 129, 137, 152, 154, 155, 156, 161, 166, 178, 187, 209, 218; fall of 1, 12–13, 15, 23, 24, 28, 32, 37, 42, 65, 76, 78, 89, 91, 104, 110, 111, 112, 125, 144, 152, 155, 166, 235, 242; *see also* South Vietnam
Saigon Giai Phong 22, 35
Saigon papers 23
Saigon Radio 22
Sanjay Lodha 211
Sar, Saloth *see* Pol Pot
Saturday Review 229
Schlesinger, James 42, 181, 182, 207
Scowcroft, Brent 117
Scranton, William 68–70 *passim*, 74
Scruggs, Jan 241
secret letter *see* Nixon's secret letter
Shanghai Communiqué 166, 170, 213

Shields, Roger 62
Sieverts, Frank 75, 114, 131, 138, 180, 184
Sihanouk, Norodom *see* Prince Norodom Sihanouk
Singapore 53, 54, 157, 193
Sino-Soviet rivalry 2, 17, 36, 37, 41–42, 82, 90, 110, 148, 149, 158, 167, 171, 182, 194, 211, 221, 227, 233
Smith, Gaddis 15, 18, 225, 238
Smith, Morton 114
Snepp, Frank 122, 123
So Phim 153, 176, 186
Solarz, Stephen 191, 230
Solomentsev, Mikhail 39
Somalia 169
Son Sen 189
Sonoda, Sunao *see* Sunao Sonoda
South China Sea 53–54, 190, 227
South Vietnam 21–27 *passim*, 29, 30, 51–53 *passim*, 69, 71, 78, 80, 82, 114, 125, 126, 127, 144, 154, 155, 157, 186, 193, 198; application to UN 32–51 *passim*; economy 23; Ministry of Foreign Affairs 35, 36; and Nixon 121–123, 128–129, 235; People's Revolutionary Party (PRP) 78; reunification with North Vietnam 23, 51–54 *passim*, 65, 78, 79, 82, 108, 135, 156, 236; stranded U.S. nationals in 59, 64, 65, 164, 177, 184; U.S. assets in 24, 198; *see also* Provisional Revolutionary Government
Soviet Union *see* USSR
Spratly islands *see* China
spying affair 2, 16, 131, 142–143, 144–147, 162, 163, 178, 237
Sri Lanka 65, 74
Stalinism *see* communist ideologies
State Department *see* U.S. government
Stowe, Judith 14, 79
Strategic Arms Limitation Treaties (SALT) 86, 87, 118, 141, 146, 167, 168, 171, 173, 196, 212, 213, 215, 230, 232, 237
Sunao Sonoda 194, 206
Suslov, Mitchail 81
Sweden 27
Switzerland 12, 32, 209, 215

Taiwan 14, 53, 154, 166, 168, 200, 201, 228; U.S.-Taiwanese Mutual Defense Treaty 168
Takeo Fakuda 226
talks *see* New York talks; Paris negotiations; U.S.-Vietnamese negotiations
Tass 225
Taylor, Patrick 86
Teng Ying-Chao 151
Thach, Nguyen Co *see* Nguyen Co Thach
Thailand 54, 65, 66, 110, 115, 144,
157, 172, 178, 196, 202, 207, 209, 219, 220; U.S. bases in 47, 66, 135, 207, 220; U.S. embassy in 110, 144, 164, 220; U.S. relations with 48, 110, 115; Vietnamese broadcasts in 29, 67; Vietnamese normalization with 54; Vietnamese relations with 157, 194, 196, 207
Thieu, Nguyen Van *see* Nguyen Van Thieu
Tho, Le Duc *see* Le Duc Tho
Tigar, Michael 144–145
Time 167, 215, 225
Tin Sang 52
Tonkin Gulf 161
Tonneson, Stein 79
Trading with the Enemy Act 24, 26
Tran Hoan 66, 73
Tran Quang Co 187, 203
Tran Van Lam 123
Tran Van Tra 153
Tran Van Van 32
treaties: Panama Canal Treaties 91, 137, 141, 142, 146, 168, 169, 170, 237; Sino-Japanese 172, 189, 204; Soviet-Vietnamese 18, 37, 177, 203–209 *passim*, 212, 218, 232, 233, 238; U.S.-Taiwanese Mutual Defense Treaty 168; Vietnamese-Cambodian 219, 228; Vietnamese-Lao 135, 136, 149
Treaties in Force 50
Trilateral Commission 86, 118
Trinh, Nguyen Duy *see* Nguyen Duy Trinh
Truong, David 144–145
Truong Chinh 52, 88, 153
Turkey 110
Tyler, Patrick 212

Uganda 134
United Nations 15, 16, 25, 32–35 *passim*, 38, 39, 41, 65–70 *passim*, 87–90 *passim*, 93, 106, 139, 145, 146, 162, 165, 180, 192, 194, 196, 197, 202, 208, 209, 210, 220, 222, 223, 228, 229, 237, 241; General Assembly 32, 35, 38, 39, 40, 41, 74–75, 124, 137–38, 139, 141, 182, 185, 194; Indochina Assistance Program 25; Security Council 34, 35, 36, 38, 40, 41, 68, 69, 73, 74, 75, 118, 137, 228, 231; South Korean membership 33–34, 35, 41; UN Charter 34, 69, 145; U.S. veto on Vietnamese membership 31, 33, 34, 35, 36, 38, 39, 40, 41, 51, 65–71 *passim*, 73–76 *passim*, 88, 101, 139, 235–36; USSR veto on South Korean membership 33; Vietnamese membership 31, 32–51 *passim*, 62, 67–68, 69, 71, 73, 74, 75–76, 89, 92, 93, 96, 102, 109, 113, 137, 138, 139, 196, 235–36

United Nations Development Program 92
United Nations Disaster Relief Organization 152
United Nations High Commission for Refugees 22, 165, 191, 192, 209
United Nations World Meteorological Association, Vietnamese membership of 32
United States of America: aid to South Vietnam during the war assets in South Vietnam 24, 198; 12, 23, 30, 82; Camp David 196, 210; Chamber of Commerce 114; embassies 12, 23, 24, 56, 58, 60, 63, 66–70 *passim*, 73, 85, 93, 102, 109, 130, 144, 145, 163, 164, 179, 181, 188, 198, 220, 232; lobby groups 26, 27, 28, 44, 76, 115, 117, 164, 192; media 30, 32, 34, 45, 49, 50, 55, 60, 69, 74, 83–84, 86, 87, 91, 96, 97, 98, 102, 104, 115, 116, 119, 120, 126, 133, 140, 144, 159, 164, 167, 168, 169, military laboratories 48, 180; polls 60, 72, 126, 137, 194, 196, 209; public opinion 11, 13, 15, 16, 23, 26, 36, 43, 60, 61, 62, 63, 70, 75, 83, 84, 91, 96, 98, 104, 115, 119, 120, 126, 127, 129, 137, 141, 143, 161, 164, 166, 169, 172, 177, 184, 186, 192, 202, 209, 223, 224, 231, 232, 235, 239; relations with developing countries 2, 17, 85, 214; Vietnamese assets in 24, 198; *see also* U.S. government

U.S. Congress 1, 2, 13, 15, 16, 18, 24, 25, 26, 28, 29, 31, 42, 43, 45–46, 48, 50, 55–60 *passim*, 64, 75, 76, 83, 88, 90–96 *passim*, 99, 104, 108, 113, 115, 116–121 *passim*, 122–139 *passim*, 142, 143, 146, 162, 163, 165, 168, 174, 179, 181–187 *passim*, 191, 192, 195, 198, 199, 207, 212, 220, 224, 225, 230, 231, 232, 233, 237, 239; amendments to bills 26, 29, 39, 115, 117, 118, 126, 133, 134; Congress for Peace Through Law 191, 195; congressional elections 2, 25, 69, 181, 184, 185, 188, 194, 198, 199, 201, 207; congressional trips *see* Kennedy (George), McGovern, Montgomery; legislative prohibitions 2, 115, 117, 118, 119, 123, 133–135, 139, 141, 199, 237; liberal Democrats in 2, 25, 76, 94, 119, 165, 238; *see also* U.S. House of Representatives; U.S. Senate

U.S. embargoes on Indochina, trade 24, 25, 26, 36, 46, 48, 55, 56, 91, 97, 104, 113, 117, 141, 142, 143, 163, 183, 184, 185, 188, 196, 197, 209, 241; private shipments 25–26; 27; 39; telecommunications 241

U.S. government, Department of Commerce 26, 196, 199; Department of Defense 14, 27, 28, 43, 75, 95, 105, 144, 168, 171, 182, 199, 222; doves 26, 165; executive branch 24, 25, 26, 28, 31, 33, 36, 39, 43, 45, 46, 50, 56, 57, 58, 59 61, 64, 66, 67, 76, 83, 87, 89, 93, 106, 108, 116–119, 132, 135, 163, 185, 186, 192, 195, 225, 235, 239; foreign policy 1, 2, 3, 16, 17, 24, 59, 61, 63, 72, 84, 85, 86, 87, 89, 90, 91, 93, 127, 128, 143, 166, 168, 169, 170, 171, 173, 175, 181, 184, 212, 214, 226, 237, 241; General Accounting Office 72; globalist policies 2, 3, 14, 16, 17, 20, 85, 86, 148, 166, 169, 174, 212, 214, 222, 230, 233, 234, 238, 239 *see also* Brzezinski; Justice Department 145; hawks 89; 94, 95, 165; political shift under Carter 2, 3, 13, 16, 17, 20, 85, 166, 209, 212, 214, 222, 234, 237, 238, 239, 241; State Department 2, 13, 15, 18, 24, 26, 27, 28, 29, 30, 34, 35, 42, 43, 45, 50, 56, 57, 61, 65, 69, 73, 74, 75, 85, 86, 87, 88, 90, 92, 97, 103, 107, 110, 113–120 *passim*, 131, 132, 139, 142, 144–146, 152, 162, 163, 164, 167, 169–175, 179–186 *passim*, 188, 191, 194, 198–201 *passim*, 206–210 *passim*, 213–15 *passim*, 220, 229–31 *passim*, 234, 238–41 *passim*; Treasury Department 24, 25, 26, 199, 231, 232; White House Congressional Liaison office 96; *see also* U.S. Congress

U.S. House of Representatives 1, 24, 27, 31, 42, 43, 47, 48, 57, 58, 64, 74, 96, 101, 115, 117, 120, 124, 125, 126, 132, 133, 134, 137, 139, 170, 188, 191, 195; Committee on International Relations 132; Foreign Operations Subcommittee 134; International Relations Subcommittee 120, 125; Select Committee on Missing Persons in Southeast Asia 1, 42–50 *passim*, 56–64 *passim*, 74, 88, 92, 93, 95, 96, 104, 186, 188, 241; report 88, 92–96 *passim*, 103–106 *passim*; Subcommittee on Asian and Pacific Affairs 101, 117, 137, 188; Subcommittee on International Development 139; Subcommittee on International Trade and Commerce 24, 25, 26, 39, 43, 48, 104, 139

U.S. News & World Report 69

U.S. Senate 62, 83, 92, 124, 126, 133, 134, 141, 142, 146, 168, 169, 191, 195, 220; Foreign Relations Committee 117, 169; Judiciary Committee 184; Near Eastern and South Asian Subcommittee 55; Subcommittee on Refugees 21, 164

USSR 2, 19, 20, 32–34 *passim*, 38, 47, 89, 112, 115, 135–136, 139, 140, 141, 145, 152, 167, 168, 169, 196, 231; expansionism 3, 158, 173, 174, 210, 224, 238; involvement in Africa 2, 17, 146, 162, 173, 238; media 38, 145, 164, 167, 174, 189, 205, 225, 230, 232; relations with Asia 37; relations with China 17, 18, 36, 37, 38, 39, 40, 41, 42, 47, 48, 81, 82, 83, 91, 110, 148, 151, 152, 167–175 *passim*, 177, 178, 182, 1189, 190, 194, 199, 203, 209–214 *passim*, 220–226 *passim*, 230–234 *passim*, 239–240; relations with U.S. 17, 30, 42, 83, 85, 167, 168, 170–175 *passim*, 209, 212–215 *passim*, 221–223 *passim*, 225, 227, 230–234 *passim*, 238, 240; relations with Vietnam 1, 2, 3, 18, 19, 22, 32, 36–42 *passim*, 48–49, 52, 55, 63, 71, 80–83 *passim*, 86, 87, 110, 112, 115, 135–136, 139–141 *passim*, 145, 148, 151–154 *passim*, 156, 157, 160, 162, 163, 164, 177, 181, 183, 184, 190, 191, 194, 195, 199, 202, 203–210, 212, 218, 222–223, 224, 226–234 *passim*, 236, 238–240 *passim*; treaty of friendship and cooperation with Vietnam 18, 37, 177, 203–209 *passim*, 212, 218, 232, 233, 238 *see also* aid to Vietnam; Strategic Arms Limitation Treaties

Ustinov, Dmitri 153, 205

Van Tieng Dung 15, 177, 205, 218

Vance, Cyrus 2, 15, 17, 51, 85, 86, 87, 88, 89, 90, 93, 94, 96, 97, 109, 110, 116, 132, 142–43, 145, 170, 174, 175, 182, 185, 186, 194, 196, 199, 200, 201, 206, 207, 221, 222, 223, 225, 231, 239; appointment 86; confirmation hearing 95–96; regionalist approach 2, 86–7; resignation 173; visit to China 136, 142, 146, 168; and SALT 146, 167, 173, 212, 215; and U.S.-Chinese normalization 212, 213, 214; Vance-Brzezinski quarrel 17, 86–7, 169–173, 175, 181, 199–200, 201, 212–215 *passim*, 222, 223, 225, 233, 238–39, 241

Vientiane 25, 50, 144, 187, 219; fall of 135

Vietcong 12, 23, 29, 38, 122, 123, 217, 235

Việtnam 204
Vietnam, Socialist Republic of (SRV): "American card" 162, 191, 176–192, 210, 240; assets in U.S. 24, 198; Chinese "lesson" on 2, 13, 18, 37, 189, 222, 224, 226, 227–234, 239; Confucian tradition 154; declaration of independence 38, 52, 67; discussions on opening of U.S. embassy in Hanoi 113, 141, 180, 198, 201; economy 22, 23, 27, 53, 80, 82, 139, 155, 157; embassies 56, 58, 59, 66, 67, 93, 113, 144, 145, 193, 198, 215, 228; independence from China and USSR 22, 32, 37, 38, 40, 42, 44, 70, 80, 81, 88, 89, 110, 136, 184, 187, 193, 206, 208, 234, 238; invasion of Cambodia 2, 18, 19, 217–221; media 14, 22, 23, 24, 29, 30, 31, 36, 45, 47, 51, 52, 55, 56, 59, 60, 68, 70, 72, 75, 77, 81, 84, 87, 92, 96, 101, 106, 110, 111, 116, 117, 118, 119–120, 132, 133, 145, 149, 150, 151, 153, 155, 156, 160, 161, 166, 176, 178, 182, 203, 204, 205, 217, 218, 226, 228, 229, 231, 232; policies towards U.S. 24; postwar expansionism 30, 48, 111, 136, 156, 158, 159, 193, 201, 219, 220, 223, 224; reconstruction 22–23, 53, 152; reunification 23, 51–54 *passim*, 65, 78, 79, 82, 108, 135, 156, 236; and UN membership 31, 32–51 *passim*, 62, 67–68, 69, 71, 73–76 *passim*, 89, 92, 93, 96, 102, 109, 113, 137, 138, 139, 196, 235–36; withdrawal from Cambodia 11; *see also* aid to Vietnam, North Vietnam, South Vietnam, Vietnamese Communist Party
Vietnam News Agency 45, 96, 149, 156
Vietnam War 11, 12, 13, 15, 17, 18, 22–29 *passim*, 31, 33, 35–38 *passim*, 41, 43, 45, 46, 49, 50, 53, 54, 55, 58, 60, 61, 62, 66, 69, 70, 71, 73, 75, 76, 80, 82–87 *passim*, 91, 93, 94, 95, 97, 99–102 *passim*, 104, 105, 106, 108, 109, 110, 119, 121, 123–130 *passim*, 132–139 *passim*, 141, 145, 154, 155, 157, 158, 159, 161, 163, 165, 167, 175, 183, 184, 187, 190, 192, 194, 202, 216, 218, 229, 233, 235, 239, 242; bombing 21; casualties 21, 22, 38; Chinese aid to Indochina during 36, 37, 38, 112, 116, 166, 178; collapse of Saigon regime 45; end of 13, 21, 24–28 *passim*, 38, 42, 48, 51, 53, 65, 73, 78, 82, 111, 112, 116, 119, 128, 129, 130, 154, 159, 187, 218; fall of Phnom Penh 12, 111, 150; peace negotiations 37; Soviet aid to Indochina during 37, 40, 116; Tet Offensive 205; U.S. evacuation (1975) 23, 29, 42; U.S. military withdrawal (1973) 26; veterans 91, 93, 241
Vietnamese-Cambodian relations *see* Cambodia
Vietnamese-Chinese relations *see* China; Vietnam
Vietnamese Communist Party (VCP) 14, 16, 52–3, 111, 116, 135, 136, 142, 152–156 *passim*, 158, 159, 161, 176, 183, 186, 196, 205, 218, 236, 239; Central Committee 78, 79, 81, 111, 135, 152, 154, 155; Fifth Party Congress 218; Fifth Plenum 176, 177, 182; Fourth Party Congress 77–83, 84, 130, 155, 158, 169, 236, 239; Party Committee for the Eastern Zone 136; Politburo (leadership) 19, 51, 52, 53, 77–78, 79, 80, 82–83, 101, 102, 104, 110, 111, 119, 130, 133, 146, 149, 152, 153, 154, 158, 159, 161, 176, 196, 197, 205, 218, 236 *see also* Le Duc Tho *and* Le Duan; rivalries and factions 2, 14, 18–19, 52–53, 77–79, 81–83, 111, 130, 142, 146, 153, 176, 196, 236, 240; *White Book* (1974) 127
Vietnamese government: Ministry of Culture 66; Ministry of Foreign Affairs 70, 75, 96, 97, 103, 114, 116, 119, 145, 159, 180, 183, 187, 200, 203, 225; *see also* North Vietnam *and* South Vietnam (for pre-1976); *and* Vietnamese Communist Party (for post-1976)
Vietnamese-Lao relations *see* Laos
Vietnamese National Assembly 27, 28, 51, 52, 132, 176, 187
Vietnamese-Soviet relations *see* USSR
Vietnamese Workers' Party (VWP) 23, 29, 39, 52, 77, 78, 81; *see also* Vietnamese Communist Party (VCP)
Vithaya Sourinho 74
Vo Dong Giang 193
Vo Nguyen Giap 53, 78, 136, 177, 205, 215
Vo Van Sung 46, 48, 64, 65, 92
Voice of Democratic Kampuchea 219
Voice of Vietnam 203
Vu Hoang 103, 114, 131, 180, 183, 184, 187

Waldheim, Kurt 32, 33, 66, 146, 202, 210, 228
Wang Dongxing 205
War Powers Act 119
Washington *see* U.S. government
Washington Star 223
Watergate scandal 83, 91, 119, 120, 125, 128
Weinstein, Jack B. 105
Weiss, Cora 164
Wen Wei Pao 160
Westad, Odd Arne 17, 84, 238
White House *see* U.S. government
Williams, Maurice 116, 119
Wilson, Woodrow 84
Wolff, Lester L. 117–121 *passim*, 125, 134, 220, 231
Woodcock, Leonard 15, 93, 94, 95, 97–107 *passim*, 109, 111, 113, 134, 137, 138, 145, 171, 172, 175, 181, 236; as head of U.S. liaison office in China 106, 200–201, 206, 211, 212, 213, 216, 222; mission to Vietnam 2, 16, 91–107, 108, 109, 111, 113, 114, 115, 117, 120, 133, 134, 137, 138, 144–145, 187, 188, 236; report 100, 102, 103, 104, 105, 106, 120, 145
World Bank 71, 90, 133, 134, 195, 219
World Conference on Women 32
World Health Organization 55
World War II 21, 28, 33, 105, 125, 126, 199, 228

Xinhua 92
Xu Shiyou 227
Xuan Thuy 156, 183

Yeh Chien-ying 203, 206
Yemen 162
Yost, Charles 93
Young, Andrew 88–90, 93, 96, 139, 231
Young, Bill 133, 134
Yugoslavia 89, 144, 196

Zaire 169
Zhou Enlai 40, 151, 166, 178
Ziegler, Ron 126

www.ingramcontent.com/pod-product-compliance
Lightning Source LLC
Chambersburg PA
CBHW081539300426
44116CB00015B/2693